Political Values
and Health Care:
The German Experience

MIT Press Series on the Humanistic and Social Dimensions of Medicine

Stanley Reiser, general editor

# Political Values and Health Care: The German Experience

edited by
Donald W. Light
and
Alexander Schuller

The MIT Press
Cambridge, Massachusetts
London, England

This book was set in Palatino by The MIT Press Computergraphics Department from computer disks prepared by the volume editors, and was printed and bound by The Murray Printing Co. in the United States of America.

The preparation of this volume was made possible by a grant from the Translations Program of the National Endowment for the Humanities, an independent Federal agency.

**Library of Congress Cataloging in Publication Data**

Main entry under title:
Political values and health care.

(MIT Press series on the humanistic and social dimensions of medicine; 4)
Includes bibliographies and index.
1. Medical care—Germany—History. 2. Medical policy—Germany—History. 3. Insurance, Health—Government policy—Germany. 4. Public health—Germany—History. 5. Medicine—Germany—History. I. Light, Donald, 1942-. II. Schuller, Alexander. III. Series. [DNLM: 1. Delivery of Health Care—Germany. 2. Political Systems. W1 MI938M v.4 / W 84 GG4 p7]
RA501.P65 1985   362.1'0943   85-9697
ISBN 0–262–12109–3

To Susan Mango and Peter Ruof, foundation officers whose patience, understanding, and good judgment made this book possible.

# Contents

# Foreword

Around the world, many a nation is devoting increasing time to analyzing the development of its health-care system, in order to rethink its organization and priorities. This examination has been caused mainly by the possibilities of making greater inroads in preventing and treating illness—the results of a diverse, powerful, and enlarging medical technology—and by the social and personal costs of such care.

Questions continue to be asked about the advantages of one form of health-care organization over another. Is a state-supported system of government-run clinics and hospitals with the medical staff employed full-time by government the most effective agent of health-services delivery? Does the model based on the professional freedom of physicians and the freedom of patients to choose their doctors and their care best suit the technological and humanitarian possibilities of medicine? Does a health-care system bound to the goals and cost-effectiveness criteria of modern industrial corporations and organized as a business offer the best hope of harnessing medical costs and maximizing the efficient use of medical technology?

Although much has been written in efforts to answer such questions, no work before this one has explored the functioning of two different systems of health care having a common cultural heritage. The setting for such a study came into being when Germany was divided at the conclusion of World War II. Here are two systems, side-by-side, representing alternative ideological and organizational views of health care—two systems embracing different views of the place of health professionals in medical care, the proper organization of health-care resources, the role and responsibility of individuals with regard to their own health, and the scope of the entitlement of citizens to receive health-care benefits, to enumerate just some of the differences.

In bringing together a comprehensive comparative analysis of the health systems of the two Germanies, Donald Light and Alexander Schuller provide us with unique insights into some basic and perplexing questions of modern health care.

Stanley J. Reiser, M.D., Ph.D.
Program on Humanities and
Technology in Health Care
University of Texas Health Science Center
Houston

# Acknowledgments

This large and complex project was made possible by a generous grant from the Ford Foundation and would not have been completed without the good faith and understanding of Peter Ruof, the Program Officer at the Foundation responsible for the project. Seeing that we were sincere in pursuing the project and were spending the Foundation's money carefully, he permitted several extensions that allowed the work to be completed. By the end of the grant period almost all the chapters were in; however, they needed to be translated and edited for English-speaking audiences. For this we applied to the Commonwealth Fund and the National Endowment for the Humanities, both of which have programs for the preparation of manuscripts. The grants awarded by these two agencies allowed us to ready the manuscript for publication. We are particularly grateful to Susan Mango, Program Officer at the National Endowment for the Humanities, for her interest in this project, her excellent management of the grant, and her understanding of the complexities the project faced.

The process of translation forced us to ask many of the authors to explain passages and to clarify lines of argument. Dr. Schuller, whose mother tongue is English, played the key role of translator, while I served as editor and project director.

We would like to thank Dieter Koch-Weser, Deborah Stone, and Christine Altenstetter for their careful review of the manuscript and their constructive criticism. In these and other ways they helped improve the manuscript. We also wish to thank Benjamin L. Cohen, Richard F. Leedy, and William F. Ranieri for the vital support they provided by giving us time to complete this project. Our research assistants, Mindy Brown, Gisela Schonrock, James Morgan, Gail Donner, and Mindy Widman, did vital work on various aspects of this project, and we feel fortunate to have had the use of their talents. Our editor at The MIT Press improved the manuscript with his astute judgment, and Pat Giosia was a great help in preparing the final changes. Finally, behind any project of this size one finds a secretary and coordinator whose many skills, good judgment, and moral support carries the project forward, week in and week out, to its completion. That person for all seasons is Nancy Villafane-Velez.

Donald W. Light

Political Values
and Health Care:
The German Experience

# Introduction

## State, Profession, and Political Values

## Donald W. Light

Q: What is the difference between capitalism and socialism?

A: Under capitalism man exploits man—under socialism it's the other way around.

Soviet joke

Comparing the health-care system of one nation with another confronts one with the intransigent differences of language, culture, history, and institutional arrangements between societies that makes their comparison a questionable enterprise. Various attempts have produced laundry lists of characteristics from which the author chooses different items when examining one country or another, vignettes of different countries that suggest their essential noncomparability, and schemata so broad that the rich texture of the systems being compared is lost. Germany offers a unique opportunity to surmount these problems, for its division after World War II constitutes a natural experiment in history. One nation, albeit young, with a common culture, a common language, the same economy, and the same institutions delivering health, education, and welfare, was arbitrarily divided by an accident of war so that one-third of it fell under communist rule. Thus, the comparative study of East Germany (the German Democratic Republic; the GDR) and West Germany (the Federal Republic of Germany; the FRG) allows one to analyze the impact of political-social values while controlling for institutional traditions, culture, history, and other relevant dimensions of society.

The study of Germany and its division offers a second advantage. To date, all other studies comparing pre-communist society with life after a communist takeover—as in Russia, China, or Cuba—inevitably find that their political and sociological analysis is contaminated with the problem that the pre-communist society existed in a previous era. These studies essentially compare the fabric of life in one historical period with life in another period after a major upheaval. One does not know how the social institutions before the upheaval would have developed had they not been disrupted. Germany, by contrast, provides a natural experiment in history in which a third of a modern industrial society experienced a major political and social transformation while the rest of the society continued more or less as it had before.

Attempting the first overview of how health-care services in Germany evolved from Bismarck to the present has yielded a third and unexpected advantage. The struggles to produce the world's first and most sophisticated health-care delivery system, and the subsequent ideological division of that system, illuminate the fundamental questions of our time about health care: To what extent should the medical profession's emphasis on providing the very best care once a person is sick determine the organization and financing of care? How shall that emphasis be balanced against the priorities of any state to prevent citizens from getting ill and to provide cost-effective care when they do become ill? In addition, how do the interests of profession and state fit with the wishes of citizens, and what kind of health-care system would evolve were their values to prevail? The German health-care system addressed these questions as it evolved during the nineteenth and twentieth centuries, and it produced some interesting policies in answering them.

To carry out this study, we selected a score of West German social scientists with expertise on different aspects of health care in the two Germanies. Previously, almost three years were spent attempting to recruit authors from East Germany. While their participation was formally arranged, no essays were sent, and we finally had to give up on their contribution to the project. Although East German authorities failed to cooperate in the publication of the book, we were fortunate that some of the West German authors were knowledgeable of and sympathetic toward the East German health-care system. German contributors worked together on the book and completed their chapters between 1979 and 1984 using the best data available to them. The results illuminate many aspects of health care in East and West Germany that will give readers in other nations a new perspective on their own health care.

The collection and analysis of data on health care is not so advanced in the two Germanies as it is in the United States or Great Britain, and therefore the reader will not find as many tables as might be expected. More important, health-care data are collected and assembled differently in the two Germanies, so that the more one knows about the resulting health-care statistics, the less sure one is of their comparability. For example, infant mortality figures in the FRG include all stillborn infants and premature infants who die after birth. In the GDR, the same births are considered premature, as are miscarriages, and therefore are not registered. The focus of this volume is therefore more on an interpretative history of the German health-care system and its division. As Fry (1970, pp. 5–6) observed: "Comparison of published national statistics only begins to show some of the differences between nations. Examination and analysis are necessary of the ways in which systems are organized and administered and the services provided in order that something more meaningful may emerge." Interpretation raises the question of bias, and indeed some of our authors favor one system over the other. However, they make their preferences clear so that the reader can adjust for them, and overall the biases counterbalance each other. They also help to accentuate the rival systems that have emerged under the two great political-economic ideologies of our time.

The following pages of this essay provide an overview of our subject by identifying competing models of health delivery which shaped the ways in which German health care was organized. These models serve as a framework for understanding the countervailing values of forces that struggled for ascendancy during different periods of the German health-care system and its ultimate division.

## The Foundations: 1883–1945

In 1883 the Germans put into law the world's first national health insurance program. It was part of a series of social insurance programs initiated by Bismarck to quell socialist sentiments among the workers pouring into the factories as the Industrial Revolution came to Germany. Away from their homes and their villages, where relatives and neighbors had helped them in times of sickness, these workers were unprotected by their corporate employers when accident and illness struck. Bismarck's goal was to establish a health-care system run by the government so that workers would depend on and appreciate the state for their welfare and thus be less attached to trade unions. Although Germany had only become a nation-state as recently as 1870, Bismarck's initiative built on a Prussian tradition of state responsibility for citizens' health. Compulsory health insurance began in the eighteenth century for civil servants. By the early nineteenth century, Prussia had laws regulating health care for miners and domestic servants as well. After

1848, the state passed laws allowing municipalities to require that workers join mutual welfare funds and that employers contribute to them. In this way, "the feudal obligation of the employer to his work-people was given legislative force in a society developing national markets where the employer without an obligation to pay to a sick fund might undercut the employer who has such an obligation" (Abel-Smith 1976, p. 14). These actions built on the tradition of Medizin-alpolizei, or medical police, in which an authoritarian and paternalistic government designed a comprehensive plan of hygiene, public health, and social medicine to protect its citizens from the ravages of disease (Rosen 1979).

For a long time, Germans have valued a strong state. Hegel took the state model to its logical endpoint by arguing that individual identity and reality come only through the state. "The state is the true embodiment of mind and spirit, and only as its member does the individual share in truth, real existence and ethical status." (in Kohn 1946, p. 11) This view is echoed by many German writers and philosophers, and so one is not surprised to learn that Bismarck was regarded as the personification of the state (Craig 1978, chapter 5). He seems to have assented to this opinion, which meant that serious opposition was not to be tolerated. In 1878, Bismarck passed the Socialism Law, which "gave local police authorities the right to forbid the existence of clubs and organizations of any kind, including co-operative funds and publications that supported social democratic, socialist, or communist activities designed to subvert the existing political and social order" (Craig 1978, pp. 145–146). The results were devastating. Of the 47 party newspapers, 45 were suppressed immediately, and all trade unions were crushed. Berlin, the center of socialism and the home of the largest concentration of Jews in Europe, was put into a minor state of siege. Hatred of socialism and Jews fused in the minds of many, as they would again 50 years later.

Bismarck did not entirely get his way in wanting a national health-care system run by state administrators and financed by taxes. In the political debates, an even older tradition of workers' banding together and providing protection when a member was struck down by illness or accident asserted itself. Workers' sickness funds had begun among coal miners in the thirteenth century and spread to the guilds over the next 250 years. By the eighteenth century, such funds were well established among a number of labor groups (Abel-Smith 1976, chapter 1). As Germany and other nations industrialized, this guildlike tradition was adapted by unions and sometimes by employers of factory workers to suit their circumstances. Thus, in the debates over Bismarck's program for a state-run system, the distaste of both workers and employers for governmental administration combined with the vested interest of existing sickness funds to produce a national plan for health care run by the sickness funds. Employers and employees would manage the funds and negotiate with physicians for services. The existing funds were joined by new ones organized by locality and by occupation. Financing came from premiums. The funds neither then nor later received government subsidies, an approach to national health insurance that American policymakers have not considered. Thus, Bismarck succeeded in tying workers to employers and preventing unions from taking over health care, but he failed to get a system run and financed by the state.

The sickness-funds compromise represents Germany's unique contribution to the organization of health care: corporatism. As Deborah Stone (1980) explains, corporatism has two distinct characteristics. First, it is a set of institutions intermediary between citizens and the government with compulsory membership for designated groups. In the case of Germany, these were primarily occupational groups. Second, these institutions are given statutory authority over relevant behavior of their members and over the administration of relevant government programs. Corporatism, therefore, is a quasi-public form of representative government over a specific program area in which the role of the state is to oversee and coordinate the activities of the corporatist institutions and to ensure that they act in the national interest. The state serves as rule-setter and umpire. Corporatism is also a way of bringing different parties together to run services such as a health-care system. It is a form of managed conflict. When the state sees that the balance of power is becoming skewed or that the system is moving too far in one direction, it can step in and change the rules through legislation. There is nothing comparable to corporatist institutions in the United States.

After 1883, the national health insurance program grew slowly. Membership was compulsory only for manual laborers. But over the years, new legislation enlarged the circle of workers to which it applied. More important, employees paid two-thirds of the premiums and held two-thirds of the seats on the boards of the sickness funds. Since employers showed little interest in these funds, they became worker-managed. With the help of sympathetic physicians interested in workers' health and social medicine, worker-managed sickness funds pioneered a number of efficient delivery systems, including a prototype of ambulatory health maintenance organizations (HMOs) in which physicians would be hired to provide services for established salaries or fees. They also created a type of preferred provider organization (PPO) in which funds would contract with a closed panel of community physicians for services. Some of the larger funds contracted with hospitals for inpatient care and even published pamphlets about health care for their members. They also used nonphysicians to hold costs down. Thus, many of the contemporary American programs designed to hold down health-care costs were pioneered by worker-run insurance funds in Germany before the turn of the century.

As these funds matured and expanded, the German medical profession became increasingly concerned. First, the widening circle of eligible workers was beginning to cut into the patient panels of private practitioners. Second, the funds drove a hard bargain for contracted services, so that physicians who worked for them received less money per case in return for guaranteed business. Third, some physicians found it unprofessional to have worker-managers administer their services and review the quality of care. More deeply, it offended physicians' social sensibilities to have people of low breeding and little education overseeing their work (Stone 1980, chapter 3).

During the nineteenth century physicians in Germany were not legally recognized as a profession and did not have strong organizations. They had tried many times to attain legal recognition as a profession, which under German law would guarantee them a monopoly over health care, but they had failed and were legally considered a business. Thus, the medical profession had not even been mentioned in the health insurance law, and sickness funds could hire any kind of providers they wished. Indeed, they retained a variety of nurses and other nonphysician providers. Gradually, over the period 1887–1926, one German state after another changed physicians' status from a business to a profession, but the national government did not (Stone 1980, chapter 3). Thus, physicians found themselves the weakest party to the new sickness funds.

By 1898, a certain number of German physicians were ready to take militant action in light of a number of circumstances that have a contemporary ring to American ears. The sickness funds were pitting one doctor against another in bids for contracts to treat their patients. As the funds expanded, they made further inroads into the local markets of private physicians. To make matters worse, a surplus of physicians had developed, and physician income was declining. Politically, the Social Democrats were active again and were calling for the nationalization of physicians into a system of free medical care. Moreover, some of the workers' funds became interested in a new system of care that would reduce the number of referrals, hospitalizations, and prescriptions by limiting them to average rates for the previous three years. Other features of the system included on-call service outside of regular clinic hours and a rotation system for handling weekend emergencies.

Trying out this system led to the first doctors' strike, in 1898, which ended with the government intervening on the physicians' behalf (Stone 1980). Soon thereafter, a militant doctors' union, the Leipziger Verband, was formed and began to use trade union tactics. Combining doctors' strikes with boycotts to prevent workers' funds from bringing in "scabs," the LV won 90 percent of its conflicts, which numbered about 200 a year. By 1904, half of all German physicians had joined the LV, and by 1908, 70 percent were members. The LV also created strike funds, a job placement agency, a credit union, a widows' fund, a pension fund, and a burial fund for physician-members.

Within a few years the balance of power had shifted. Indeed, one could say that physicians finally coalesced as a profession around their opposition to self-managed workers' sickness funds. Their relations with the funds remained strained, and the government finally intervened in 1913 to create committees with equal representation of physicians and sickness funds responsible for admitting physicians to funds, writing contracts, and arbitrating conflicts. Subsequent conflicts and strikes led to a series of decrees in the 1920s and the early 1930s that further strengthened the medical profession by creating regional associations of insurance doctors and giving them statutory power to bargain for medical services and a virtual monopoly over ambulatory care. This also meant that sickness funds could no longer bargain with individual providers, and thus a major source of competition and flexibility was eliminated. In essence, the LV had become part of the government, invested with public authority to represent all physicians treating sickness-fund patients under national health insurance. This central economic and political authority remains intact to this day (Stone 1980, chapter 3).

Despite growing concessions to their demands, German physicians remained discontented. The government decrees of the 1920s and the early 1930s, which had given the doctors statutory powers, had also strengthened the sickness funds by giving them new authority to monitor physicians' performance and by creating a capitation system. This meant that physicians were paid a fixed sum per year for all care for each patient. It put physicians at risk if they exceeded the year's budget. Moreover, some sickness funds continued to run clinics, HMOs, PPOs, and other systems that weakened the profession's control over ambulatory care. Medical associations took the funds to court, but the courts generally ruled in favor of the funds. It was not until Hitler's National Socialists came to power in 1933 that the medical profession was finally able to crush worker-run sickness funds. The Nazis' stand against unions, Jews, and socialists attracted physicians to join the Party in greater numbers than any other profession. Hitler's 1933 emergency decrees against communists and socialists remind one of Bismarck's Socialism Law of 1878 and had an even more devastating effect. Physicians in local medical societies prosecuted sickness-fund physicians with such reckless zeal that many of those charged as socialist or Jewish had their cases reversed by Hitler's Minister of Labor for lack of evidence. It was a witch hunt, a moment of revenge by the majority of private physicians against the worker-run sickness funds and physicians sympathetic to them. By 1936, workers' programs in health care had been destroyed, the physicians involved had been forbidden from practicing, and the self-management of sickness funds had been replaced by appointed administrators as part of Hitler's effort to enhance loyalty to the state through health and welfare programs (deWitt 1978). New laws further strengthened the power of physicians, first by finally recognizing them nationally as a profession and outlawing other clinicians from practicing medicine and second by strengthening their hand as a national bargaining unit against the regional sickness funds. In four decades, the medical profession had risen from the weakest to the strongest party shaping the sickness funds and the German health-care delivery system. As Stone concludes, "It seems clear from this history that the idea that the medical profession's political strength derives entirely from its special status as a profession or from its monopoly on technical expertise must be dismissed" (1980, p. 53).

## Comparative Models of Health Care

In this overview of how the German health-care system developed before it divided after World War II can be found four models of delivery systems. The models do not attempt to describe actual systems, but rather highlight the basic dimensions and outline the underlying logic of the alternatives that the actual systems approximate.

The construction of models or ideal types has been the subject of much discussion since Max Weber first developed them as a sociological tool. In the most important contribution in recent years, Stark and Bainbridge (1979) showed that, contrary to Weber's instructions, it is not best to list as many characteristics of different types as one can, because then it becomes impossible to think clearly about various mixed cases having, say, five characteristics of one type and three of another. Rather, they concluded, there should be a single dimension or characteristic on which each ideal type turns. In the case of the German health-care system, it would appear that political values are the key dimension. Most writers emphasize the economic or organizational aspects of health-care systems, but they overlook the fundamental role which political values have played in determining the economics and organization of health care.

It is important to emphasize that medical care and health services are acts of political philosophy. Political and social values inform the choices made, the institutions formed, and the funds provided or withheld. The technological thrust of modern medicine is itself highly political in its definition of which problems are important to address and how they are to be defined. Banning nuclear power or altering polluting industries, for example, would require national policy and programs and cannot be accomplished through individual action. In West Germany today there is a vocal group arguing that societal causes of disease require societal solutions (Schuller 1981; Schaefer, Standfest, and Neuhaus 1979; Goeckenjan 1980). Thus, seemingly nonpolitical decisions about how to treat a cancer or a case of hypertension are freighted with political values about cause and responsibility.

The term *values* means something broader than ideology yet narrower than political culture. Ideology connotes a logical consistency and coherence that may not be present, or that if present (as in some communist countries) is not sufficient to account for the shape of social welfare institutions such as the health-care system. Political culture, on the other hand, has such breadth and contains so many elements that it is not useful for analysis. Thus, the four models that follow show how the organization, financing, and power of different health-care systems are united by political values that define their character. Like all models and ideal types, these lose the rich complexity of actual events as they elucidate the basic forces at play. However, they allow one to think comparatively about health-care systems.

The Mutual-Aid Model

As its name implies, the mutual-aid model consists of people organizing themselves to help each other and make provisions for their needs (table 1). It is found wherever people are discontented with current services (as in the case of the women's health movement) or have no services to meet their needs. As applied to health, the mutual-aid model has a core value of improving the health of fellow members. From this core derives a sense of individual and mutual responsibility. This leads to an epidemiological rather than clinical way of thinking about group patterns of illness and collective needs. Social control and behavioral education can result, but it is among colleagues of many years rather than by an outside bureaucracy. The mutual-aid perspective also leads to the planning and coordination of services. Generally, all members contribute to a sickness fund, which then contracts for professional services and organizes educational activities. This makes mutual-aid groups independent of both the state and the professions.

Mutual-aid groups often are small and informal. They assume that their members are active and informed. In these ways they exemplify the model of collectivist organizations described by Rothchild-Witt (1979). Authority rests in the group as a whole. Social control comes from peer pressure and belief in the organization's goals. Social relations are informal and collegial. Specialization is kept to a minimum, as is hierarchy. Nevertheless, there is the danger that leaders will take over the organization. One must not forget that it was from observing socialist labor parties that Robert Michel developed his Iron Law of Oligarchy that those in power will become increasingly preoccupied with maintaining their power.

Although mutual-aid groups date back at least as far as the thirteenth century and were found in most Western societies, their demise in the twentieth century has obscured their theoretical importance as a grassroots alternative to more bureaucratic, professionalized care. We have seen the significant role they played in the formation of the German system and in the development of client-controlled, cost-effective services that emphasized active, informed members working to minimize illness.

**Table 1**
The mutual-aid model.

---

### Inherent values and goals

To improve the health of fellow members.

To promote ties and mutual support among members.

To promote democratic decision making and shared responsibility.

To educate, to prevent disease, to make each member a provider of care for self and others.

To minimize health-care costs.

To be sure no major outside force (state, profession) controls the health system.

### Organization

A loose federation of member groups.

Administratively collegial.

Egalitarian services.

Emphasis on low-technology primary care and preventive programs.

Strong ties to community programs (educational, occupational, social service).

Organized around epidemiological patterns of illness.

### Key institutions

Mutual Benefit associations.

### Power

Local control within common rules.

State and profession relatively weak; facilitative role.

### Finance and cost

Members contribute to an insurance fund which contracts with physicians and facilities for service.

Doctors' share of all costs relatively low.

### Image of the individual

Active, self-responsible, informed member of the group.

### Division of labor

Egalitarian. More teams and delegation. Fewer physicians and specialists.

### Medical education

Cooperative, egalitarian training of health-care teams is favored.

---

The State Model

Equally strong in the German-Prussian tradition was the state model of health care and welfare (table 2). Its core goal is to strengthen the state by fostering a healthy, vigorous population. In one sense, this parallels the core goal of mutual-aid groups at a more impersonal, macro level. As a consequence, both take an epidemiological approach to health care, and both want to minimize costs. Both lead to an emphasis on primary care, prevention, and health promotion. The fundamental differences center around power and the image of the individual in the system. The state takes a more paternalistic and controlling role, leading perhaps to compulsory programs and forms of indoctrination. Planning and coordination of services is done centrally. From this centralization follow decisions about manpower, the nature of professional education, the proportional distribution of specialists, and the proportion of nonphysicians. The state model regards health as a source of power and freedom. Maintaining health and restoring the ill make the citizenry more productive (King 1973; Heidenheimer 1973; Lockhart 1981). The state emphasizes that health care is a cooperative venture between the state and individual citizens; without active participation, success will be limited.

There are two variants of the state model: the democratic and the autocratic approach. Under the democratic approach, as in Great Britain, power is decentralized to regional and district councils. Under the autocratic approach, as in the Soviet Union and East Germany, power is concentrated in a Ministry of Health and in the central party. Professional societies play a smaller role or no role at all, and the system is used to pursue larger political goals of indoctrination and loyalty.

Under the state model, physicians and other providers are likely to be on salary or on a capitation payment system. The state usually runs hospitals and clinics by means of an elaborate bureaucracy. Typically the patient is assigned to or chooses a primary-care physician, with whom he or she normally stays. This physician manages the patient's care and calls in specialists when necessary. The medical profession is weak, and in the pure case the medical association is abolished. Matters of licensure, regulation, and quality assurance are usually carried out by state officials. On the other hand, the physicians fortunate enough to run the system have a degree of power unknown in any other model. By the same token, they and other high officials of the state or the party are likely to receive a special class of care. Despite these secondary

**Table 2**
The autocratic state model.

---

**Inherent values and goals**

To strengthen the state via a healthy, vigorous population.
To minimize illness via preventive medicine, public health, and patient education.
To indoctrinate through health care; to enhance loyalty to the state.
To increase the power of the state by controlling the health-care system.
To minimize the cost of health care to the state.
To provide good, accessible care to all sectors of the population.

**Organization**

A national, integrated system.
Administratively hierarchical.
Egalitarian services and recruitment patterns.
Organized around primary care units.
Strong ties to other social institutions, such as schools and the workplace.
Organized around epidemiological patterns of illness.

**Key institutions**

Ministry of Health.
Regional/district councils (or regional/district health officers).

**Power**

State the sole power.
Professional associations prohibited.

**Finance and cost**

All care free; tax-supported.
Doctors' share of costs relatively low.

**Image of the individual**

A member of society; thus the responsibility of the state, but also responsible to stay healthy.

**Division of labor**

Proportionately fewer physicians; more nurses and auxiliary health-care workers.
Fewer specialists.
More middle-level providers (nurse-clinicians); more delegation; more teamwork.

**Medical education**

A state system for all providers, including a system of continuing education.

---

effects, the system tends to be relatively inexpensive and succeeds in keeping the health of its people at a high level. All these characteristics are correlates but not necessary features of the state model that reflect its underlying values.

The autocratic state approach to health care was clearly manifested in Bismarck's proposal for a state-run national system. Having outlawed the Social Democrats, and seeking to undermine mutual-aid groups among workers, Bismarck wanted the state to take responsibility for workers' health problems and thereby strengthen political ties to them. His design called for a national system of primary-care units. Relatively little attention was paid to the medical profession. The focus was on fostering political loyalty and ensuring a vigorous labor force.

The Professional Model

A coherent profession attempting to run a health-care system is a twentieth-century phenomenon and in Europe came about in part as a response to mutual-aid societies. Mutual-aid societies proliferated with industrialization throughout Austria, Switzerland, Scandinavia, and Great Britain, and more sporadically elsewhere. In Great Britain by 1900 there were 7 million members of "friendly societies," who received cash benefits, the services of a physician, and prescribed drugs. "Thus in these countries the consumers of medical care came to be organized before the doctors were effectively organized, and they were in a position to dictate the terms of services of the doctors whom they engaged to provide services. From being masters, doctors found themselves servants of the funds." (Abel-Smith 1976, p. 9) The societies selected some doctors, thereby excluding others. Lay committees often handled disciplinary matters, and the societies determined remuneration. Physicians found these terms intolerable, and an international movement arose for a "free profession." A similar series of events occurred in many Latin American and European countries. As Abel-Smith notes, the medical profession in many other countries besides Germany coalesced under the pressure of health care being organized by workers and their unions as industrialization brought larger numbers of workers together.

The core value of the professional model (table 3) is to provide the best possible care to every sick patient. From this value stems an emphasis on high quality and control by physicians. Economically, the professional model emphasizes fees for service and professional autonomy. Unlike the other two models, the professional approach focuses on the individual patient and organizes itself to be as effective and powerful as it can in responding to individual cases.

Under the professional model, health is an individual responsibility and medical care is a professional responsibility. State intervention into either is considered a pernicious form of "creeping socialism." This leads to clinical thinking and case-by-case planning to address the individual treatment needs of patients. Using medicine for social control or introducing "Big Brother" health indoctrination is repugnant to the medical profession, since the highest value is placed on the special relationship that arises when an individual patient chooses an individual physician and pays him individually. This means that health services appear in a relatively unplanned way in response to demand.

The professional model holds that only the medical profession is qualified to educate, license, and monitor medical practice. State laws merely facilitate and enforce this principle. Health care is not to get entangled in other matters, such as housing, food, welfare, or employment, and ideally it should not depend on any state financing, for the hand that feeds soon controls. Thus, physicians should remain free agents, taking neither salaries nor capitation payments because both of these weaken the doctors' control over the patient relationship.

Like other professions, the medical profession values expertise. It bestows prestige and often wealth on the specialist and the subspecialist. Thus, an entire system of institutions, financing, and politics arises to promote professional expertise. At the heart of this system are medical schools and their medical centers. Since expertise is a matter of technique and knowledge, the professional model is driven by a heavy focus on technical breakthroughs and research. These usually have a negligible or marginal effect on the health of a population, because they focus on esoteric problems or advanced stages of disease. Consequently, the professional model leads to expensive, hospital-based care of high quality. This focus on specialized clinical skills also means that the professional model gives public health little support. The budgets of public health departments are usually the poor stepchild of budgets for hospitals, where the victims of poor health are later treated at great expense. Under this model, medical schools and the physicians they produce give little attention to nutrition, pollution, preventive medicine, or occupational health.

A closer examination of the special doctor-patient relationship reveals the high value placed on the physician's individual freedom at the

**Table 3**
The professional model.

**Inherent values and goals**
To provide the best possible clinical care to every sick patient.
To develop scientific medicine to its highest level.
To protect the autonomy of physicians and keep the state or others from controlling the health-care system.
To increase the power and wealth of the profession.
To generate enthusiasm and admiration for the profession.

**Organization**
A loose federation.
Administratively collegial and decentralized.
Services and recruitment follow the stratification of the society.
Emphasis on acute, high-technology intervention and specialty care.
Organized around hospitals and private offices.
Weak ties with other social institutions.
Organized around clinical cases and doctors' preferences.

**Key institutions**
Physicians' associations.
Autonomous physicians and hospitals.

**Power**
Profession the sole power.
Uses state powers to enhance its own.
Protests state interference.
Protests and boycotts all competing models of care.

**Finance and cost**
Private payments, by individual or through private insurance plans.
Doctors' share of costs relatively high.

**Image of the individual**
A private individual. Chooses how to live and when to use the medical system.

**Division of labor**
Proportionately more physicians.
More specialists.
More individual clinical work by the physician; less delegation.

**Medical education**
A private and/or autonomous system of schools with tuition.
Disparate, loosely coupled continuing education.

expense of the patient's autonomy. The professional model does not favor sharing information with patients, so the relationship is highly asymmetrical and makes the patient dependent on the doctor's decisions. These decisions, in turn, produce income, so the fee system contains an inherent conflict of interest between the patient's health and the physician's income. Abel-Smith (1976) identifies the systemic effects of the fee for service, especially when it is accompanied by coverage from health insurance. First, if physicians can charge a fee for any service, true specialization gets watered down as various specialists take on general patients and cases outside their area as a source of income. This pattern is typical in the United States and spreading rapidly (Aiken 1979). Second, the quality of care declines, insofar as physicians treat patients beyond or beneath their specialty training, for the best care is given by those working on problems near the peak of their abilities. In general ambulatory care, this peak is rather low because most cases are not technically complex. Third, the fee system tends to focus on specific tests and procedures, because they are easily identified for reimbursement, and it discourages listening, talking, counseling, and the coordination of care. Finally, the fee system encourages costs to be run up at every point in the system.

Opinions have differed on the source of power in the medical profession, though in effect much of this debate concerns the sources of power in the professional model. Some hold that medicine gains a unique degree of power from the vital and technical nature of its service (Marmor and Thomas 1971, 1972); others believe that the political values and structure of government lie behind the power of the medical profession (Eckstein 1960). Both camps are correct; the first develops its perspective from looking at professional systems (such as that of the United States), while the second draws conclusions from state systems (such as those of Great Britain and the Soviet Union). The vital and symbolic nature of medical work is present in both models, as are political values and the structure of government. In professional systems, political values and governmental structure promote professional power, whereas in the state systems they constrain it.

## The Corporatist Model

The genius of the German solution to the conflicting values and concerns of citizens, state, and the profession was to bind these forces together and give them each significant legal powers to negotiate their differences in order to arrive at binding contracts for medical services. The corporatist model is outlined in table 4, and one can see that each party was formally organized and then brought together with the others in a structure of countervailing powers.

Because of its amalgamated character, the direction and the priorities of the corporatist model are not clear but are subject to negotiation. Are preventive medicine and cost-effective care most important? This was so initially, when the mutual-aid model of sickness funds prevailed. Are high-quality clinical medicine and the latest techniques most important? This became so as organized medicine grew to be the strongest horse in the troika. Thus, the corporatist model differs from the other three in being more an arena for managed conflict than a program for policy or a vision of what health care should be.

## The Division of Germany after 1945

What makes Germany particularly interesting for comparative analysis is that it embraced strong traditions of mutual aid, autocratic state rule, professionalism, and corporatism. The two halves of Germany following World War II built on combinations of these models. Moreover, the line for dividing Germany was decided before 1945 and echoed old geographic and cultural differences between eastern, Prussian regions and western, democratic areas. (See Appendix.)

The Creation of the East German System

After 1945 in the Soviet-occupied zone, both East German communists and Russian advisors saw the opportunity to create a comprehensive system of social medicine that would build on the work of Johann Peter Frank, Alfred Grotjahn, and other German socialists who had had a wide influence on the development of social medicine in other countries, notably in central and eastern Europe (Rosen 1979, p. 36). The emphasis of these German pioneers on public health and preventive medicine through an integrated system of care had influenced Lenin when he created the Soviet health-care system (Rosen 1979; Kohn 1946; Durant and Durant 1965, 1967; Riasanovsky 1967). In Russia, the Soviets inherited a centralized state system that had controlled medical education, the medical profession, and most hospitals for a long time but lacked an emphasis on public health. Faced with mass starvation and epidemics, Lenin kept central control but redirected the system toward prevention

**Table 4**
The corporatist model.

---

**Inherent values and goals**

To join employees, employers, and physicians in administering the health-care system.

To minimize conflict between those served, those who provide, and those who pay.

To balance costs against provider demands.

**Organization**

Numerous funds by occupation and geography with administrative and negotiating boards of employees' and employers' representatives.

Citizens must join a fund.

Physicians and health facilities are autonomous and bargained with for services. (See professional model.)

(Other original features subject to negotiation.)

**Key institutions**

Sickness-fund boards, sickness-fund physicians' associations.

State as setter of rules and referee.

**Power**

Countervailing power structure subject to imbalance by one party or another.

Statutory power to determine financing, mix, and range of services.

State as setter of rules and referee.

**Finance and cost**

Employers and employees contribute premiums.

Costs depend on balance of interests in negotiations. Have tended to be high due to professional dominance.

Doctors' share has tended to be high because they run services and dominate negotiations, but not inherent in model.

**Image of the individual**

A private individual. Chooses how to live and when to use the medical system.

**Division of labor**

Physicians dominate, because they run services.

**Medical education**

Has not been a point of focus, though model allows for it to be.

---

and primary care. Speaking of the typhus epidemic, Lenin said: "Comrades, all attention to this problem! Either socialism conquers the lice, or the lice will conquer socialism." The Soviets set out to establish local health stations throughout the country and then to coordinate them through a central health organization. At the same time, they dissolved the two leading medical associations because of their resistance to socialist medicine. At the Fifth All-Russian Congress of Soviets in 1918, six principles of health-care policy were laid down (Leichter 1979, p. 211):

1. Health care is a responsibility of the state.

2. Health care should be available to all citizens at no direct cost to the user.

3. The proletariat occupies a preferential position in Soviet society, including its health-care delivery system.

4. There should be centralized and unified administration of health-care policy.

5. "Public" health depends upon active citizen involvement.

6. The primary substantive emphasis in Soviet health care is on prophylactic or preventive medicine.

The Soviets moved rapidly to create a network of territorial and occupational polyclinics that provided preventive, public-health, curative, and rehabilitative services. These were financed by a social insurance scheme based on the German model that initially covered workers and the poor but not peasants or the self-employed. This preference for the proletariat was also reflected in medical school admissions as part of a design to create a Marxist-oriented medical profession.

Thus, the Soviets arrived in Germany fresh from the experience of developing their own health-care system based to a considerable degree on German ideas. They and prominent German socialist physicians significantly altered the German health-care system by integrating ambulatory and hospital care, providing free care to all, establishing regional systems of care under a central administration, developing a network of rural and urban clinics, instituting a comprehensive system of preventive care, and creating a government-run system of occupational medicine. More than the East Germans would like to admit, their health-care system echoes the state model Bismarck and even Hitler tried to manifest. It is a direct descendant of the German political tradition that valued a strong, paternalistic state looking after the welfare of its citizens and using welfare services to bind citizens to itself.

## Health Care in West Germany

It is commonly observed that in the postwar period the West German system continued the corporatist model that had developed before. Although this is true, it overlooks the changing balance of countervailing powers in the corporatist model. The Allied forces were reluctant to impose any particular system on West Germany during reconstruction, but the German medical profession was not so reticent. Though the West Germans were generally intent on de-Nazifying their society, the medical profession quickly mobilized to secure the gains it had won during the Nazi period and to secure laws that discouraged or prevented workers' sickness funds from governing themselves or running medical services for their members. They succeeded in prohibiting industrial or public-health physicians from treating patients and in securing a monopoly over ambulatory care by office-based physicians. Other rules discouraged physicians from using physician assistants, forming group practices, or creating clinics. By the 1960s, capitation had been replaced by a fee-for-service system, and costs escalated for years, until the state intervened during the late 1970s to put caps on health budgets. In other ways as well, the medical profession took over the corporatist model. For example, specialization among physicians grew rapidly, fees focused and reinforced technical procedures, and hospitals gained an increasing proportion of the health budget.

What distinguishes the West German system from more classic cases of the professional model, such as in the United States, is that all this happened within a powerful legal framework that allows imbalances to be checked. The budget caps are only one sign that the West German medical profession is being brought under control in the 1980s. In addition, there are indications that the mutual-aid model is being revived, not only in Germany but also in other countries. It is part of a general cluster of trends in modern society toward decentralization, self-help, participatory democracy, and networking (Light 1982; Naisbett 1982; Herder-Dornereich and Schuller 1981). Thus, the balance of power between workers, the medical profession and the state within the corporatist model continues to realign itself.

# References

Abel-Smith, B. 1976. Value for Money in Health Services: A Comparative Study. New York: St. Martin's.

Aiken, L. 1979. "The contributions of specialists to the delivery of primary care: A new perspective." New England Journal of Medicine 300(24):1363–1370.

Craig, G. 1978. Germany: 1860–1945. New York: Oxford University Press.

deWitt, T. E. J. 1978. "The economics and politics of welfare in the Third Reich." Central European History 11(3):256–278.

Durant, W., and A. Durant. 1965. The Age of Voltaire. New York: Simon & Schuster.

Durant, W., and A. Durant. 1967. Rousseau and Revolution. New York: Simon & Schuster.

Eckstein, H. 1960. Pressure Group Politics: The Case of the British Medical Association. Stanford, Calif.: Stanford University Press.

Fry, J. 1970. Medicine in Three Societies. New York: American Elsevier.

Goeckenjan, G. 1980. "Politik und Verwaltung präventiver Gesundheitssicherung." Soziale Welt 30:156–175.

Heidenheimer, A. J. 1973. "The politics of public education, health, and welfare in the U.S.A. and Western Europe: How growth and reform potentials have differed." British Journal of Political Science 3:315–340.

Herder-Dornereich, P., and A. Schuller. 1982. Spontanität oder Ordnung: Laienmedizin gegen professionelle Systeme. Stuttgart: Kohlhammer.

King, A. 1973. "Ideas, institutions, and the policies of governments: A comparative analysis." Parts I and II. British Journal of Political Science 3:291–313.

Kohn, H. 1946. Profits and Peoples. New York: Collier.

Leichter, H. M. 1979. The Comparative Study of Public Policy. Cambridge University Press.

Light, D. W. 1982. "Lay medicine and the medical profession: An international perspective." In Herder-Dornereich and Schuller 1982.

Lockhart, C. 1981. "Values and policy conceptions of health policy elites in the United States, the United Kingdom, and the Federal Republic of Germany." Journal of Health Politics, Policy, and Law 6(1):96–119.

Marmor, T., and D. Thomas. 1971. "The politics of paying physicians: The determinants of government payment methods in England, Sweden, and the United States." International Journal of Health Services 1:71–78.

Marmor, T., and D. Thomas. 1972. "Doctors, politics, and pay disputes: 'Pressure Group Politics' revisited." British Journal of Political Science 2:412–442.

Naisbett, J. 1982. Megatrends: Ten New Directions Transforming Our Lives. New York: Warner.

Riasanovsky, N. 1967. Nicholas I and Official Nationality in Russia, 1825–1855. Berkeley: University of California Press.

Rosen, G. 1979. "The evolution of social medicine." In Handbook of Medical Sociology, ed. H. E. Freeman, S. Lavine, and L. G. Reeder. Englewood Cliffs, N.J.: Prentice-Hall.

Rothchild-Witt, J. 1979. "The collectivist organization: An alternative to rational-bureaucratic models." American Sociological Review 44:509–527.

Schaefer, H., R. Standfest, and B. Neuhaus. 1979. Plädoyer für eine neue Medizin. Munich: Piper.

Schuller, A. 1981. Medical Prevention, Health Policy, and Society. Unpublished manuscript.

Stark, R., and W. S. Bainbridge. 1979. "Of churches, sects, and cults: Preliminary concepts for a theory of religious movements." Journal for the Scientific Study of Religion 18:117–133.

Stone, D. A. 1980. The Limits of Professional Power: National Health Care and the Federal Republic of Germany. University of Chicago Press.

# I       State and Society

# 1

## Structure and Values of State and Society

### Ulrich Lohmann

*In this suggestive essay, Ulrich Lohmann outlines twelve points of contrast between the two German societies in terms of their structure and values. Although somewhat overdrawn, these contrasts suggest ways in which the health-care systems in the two countries may differ in analogous fashion. Thus, the essay needs to be read at two levels.*

*One force underestimated in the author's enthusiasm for the West German principles of individualism and pluralism is corporate power. The corporate power of sickness funds, of unions, of the medical profession, of the pharmaceutical industry, and of other corporations in the medical field means that the pluralism in West Germany has acquired highly organized forms. When such corporate forms are compared with the power of the East German state, which attempts to speak for the interests of all groups and institutions in matters of health, interesting implications for the delivery of health-care services suggest themselves.*

## State and Society

### Conceptions of the State[1]

In the Federal Republic of Germany (FRG; West Germany), the state is thought of as a subsystem of the society. This concept of the state falls within the tradition of the liberal political and social theories whose formulation paralleled the struggle of the rising bourgeoisie against the feudal organization of society.[2] The bourgeoisie replaced the all-embracing, hierarchical feudal order, characterized by estates and guilds, and made the pursuit of particular interests legitimate. The move away from the feudal organization of society, in which the political position and the socio-economic function of the individual were clearly prescribed, corresponded to the growing possibilities of more effective production through industrialization and the emphasis on the legitimacy of individual claims as an expression of the primacy of individual societal forces over the sovereignty of the whole. Afterward, it became the task of the constitutional state, as an institutional framework, to secure the material, organizational, and normative bases of social, economic, and cultural life.

The priority of individual and social forces is expressed in article 1 of the Basic Law in the constitution of the FRG.[3] That article assumes that the existence, the value, and the dignity of the individual take precedence over the state and obligate the state to respect and protect these as fundamental. The priority of the individual is legally ensured by article 2 of the constitution.[4] This freedom is, on the side of the state, not limited by any material purpose. However, article 2 requires that the rights of others not be violated. More generally, the preservation of the "constitutional order" and "moral code" also serve to limit individual freedom (Grundgesetz, article 2, paragraph 1).

The dominant interpretation of the state in the FRG has retained the separation of state and society and maintains the primacy of the latter (Bockenforde 1976; Forsthoff 1971). In the face of growing interdependence and complexity in economic and social life, however, the state has been forced more and more to intervene in the processes of production, reproduction, and consumption and to integrate them in order to guarantee the functioning of society (Offe 1972). This qualitative extension of the state's activity is expressed both in its broader and increasingly interdepartmental administration and in long-range planning. The goals of these encompassing "economic and financial measures" (Gesetz zur Förderung der Stabilität und des Wachstums der Wirtschaft, paragraph 1, June 8, 1967) and of "long-term financial planning" (Grundgesetz, article 109, paragraph 3) are as much as possible legally secured, and they constitute the "magic square" of price stability, a high rate of employment, a balanced foreign-trade budget, and economic growth. They are specific characteristics of the construction of the liberal state.

In opposition to the fundamental liberal principle of the separation of state and society, the concept of the state in the German Democratic Republic (GDR; East Germany), as a part of the Marxist-Leninist world view, assumes that economic and social processes have become so highly interdependent that the division between state and society has largely disappeared. The state, as the sovereign public organization of workers and farmers (i.e., of the great majority of the population), organizes and guides from the outset all societal processes of production and consumption (Institut für Theorie des Staates und des Rechts der Akademie der Wissenschaften der DDR, 1975, chapter 10). It aims to realize the interests of the workers and farmers, or, more exactly, the interests ascribed to them. These interests, deduced from theories of historical and dialectical materialism, are said to be objective interests and are finally synonymous with the establishment of socialism/communism (Fiedler et al. 1974). In the GDR, the state is seen as an instrument for the achievement of this goal—indeed as the "main instrument in the formation of the developed socialist society and on the path toward communism" (minutes of Ninth Congress of Sozialistische Einheitspartei Deutschlands, 1976, p. 237). In the GDR the state is also conceived of as institutional and neutral in its relation to social, political, and ideological groups and movements, whereas in the FRG the state is instrumental and characterized by its nature as a class state.

## Conceptions of Democracy

The views on democracy in the FRG and the GDR diverge with the concepts of the state and how political decisions are generated and implemented. In the GDR, it is constitutionally established (and sovereignly enforced) that democracy is "the political organization . . . under the leadership of the proletariat and its Marxist-Leninist party" (constitution, article 1). The confusing duality of the leading subjects is dissolved by Lenin's position (Lenin 1961, p. 355), which Soviet socialism supports. According to this position, the "proletariat" has not yet developed an adequate political consciousness, so that politically the "party of the proletariat" must act as an "avant-garde" for the working class. Hence, the proletariat can only realize its function of leadership through its party. The Sozialistische Einheitspartei Deutschlands (SED), or Socialist Union Party, as the communist party in the GDR, claims a priori leadership. The SED exercises its influence through "directives," which are obligatory for all governmental organs, through the "cadre monopoly," which ensures that no position of importance is filled against the will of the party, and through the legislative stipulation that all governmental organs—above all, the Ministerrat (Council of Ministers)—will act "under the leadership" and "in realization of the decisions of the party of the proletariat" (Gesetz über den Ministerrat der DDR, October 16, 1972, paragraphs 1 and 2). This definition of the SED is defended with the quantitative argument that the proletariat makes up the majority of the population in an industrial society and that the "party of the proletariat" must therefore exert leadership. The qualitative argument maintains that the proletariat is the class most closely involved in modern mass production, and that it is the most highly organized and progressive class; therefore its party, also the most progressive, should have leadership. Finally, the role of the party is justified with the epistemological argument that the SED, through Marxism-Leninism, "is equipped with the only scientific world view" (Hager 1971, p. 16). This Leninist theory of democracy and the self-legitimation of the party is based on these given or claimed facts; the endorsement of even the proletariat does not represent a constitutive element of the political process.

The Western understanding of democracy is also based on the claim that it represents the majority while the most capable are in the positions of leadership and form the government. However, the concrete realization of these criteria is left to the judgment of those affected through elections. This process is based not on the claim that the decision of the people is always correct but on the argument that, in the long run, the people are the best judge of their own interests; in the words of Churchill, "democracy is the worst form of government, except for all other forms that have been tried from time to time."

The Marxist-Leninist concept of democracy can be characterized as objective, being based on given or claimed facts; the Western concept can be considered subjective. *Objective* here refers to factors claimed to lie outside the individual consciousness, whereas *subjective* refers to factors within the individual consciousness.

Parties and Elections

In the GDR there are four political parties in addition to the SED (the party of the proletariat). However, they do not question the SED's claim to general political leadership, but in fact emphatically support it on every occasion. These parties view themselves as political representatives of minority groups allied with the proletariat. The German Democratic Farmers' Party (DBD) is supposed to represent the cooperative farmers. The Liberal Democratic Party of Germany (LDPD) represents the element of private enterprise, though today it barely exists. In addition, there are two other parties which define themselves according to characteristics of consciousness rather than socio-economically: the German Christian Democratic Union (CDUD), which represents Christians regardless of their social position, and the National Democratic Party of Germany (NDPD). In the earlier days of the GDR, the NDPD was meant to integrate nonfascist nationalist groups (particularly members of the former German armed forces) into the political system. The smaller parties (the DBD and the CDUD) are, on the one hand, supposed to advocate the views and interests of their specific population groups, even though the final power of decision remains undiminished in the hands of the SED. On the other hand, they also have the task of conveying centrally formulated policies back to the population.

In the FRG, the constitution charges the parties to "participate in the formation of the political will of the people," to organize and channel existing political opinion and interests, and to contribute to the formation of a majority. The parties of the center, which are based on this principle, are the conservative Christian Democratic Union/Christian Social Union (CDU/CSU), the Social Democratic Party (SPD), and the liberal Free Democratic Party (FDP). There are also several other parties, such as the ecologically oriented Grünen (Greens), the National Democratic Party (NPD), and the Moscow-oriented German Communist Party (DKP); however, most fall short of the 5 percent quorum required to enter the parliament. Parties may be freely established, but can be forbidden by the federal constitution court upon application of the federal government, the parliament, or the federal council if they are unconstitutional.[5]

The function of elections differs in the GDR and the FRG, corresponding to the differing conceptions of democracy and party structure depicted here. In the FRG, elections are the means for selection among competing political directions. Because people vote for candidates on both a party basis and a personal basis, and because the nomination of candidates is internal to the parties, the voters have little influence on the personal composition of the parliament. In the GDR, where the "leading role" of the SED is plainly established and no other parties compete, the elections that do take place do not select among different political directions. Instead, selection is limited to the personal composition of the bodies of popular representation—a possibility given in electoral law but never yet realized in practice. According to this provision, the candidate on the single ballot, made up jointly by all parties and other popular organizations, is considered to have not been elected if more than half of the voters have deleted his name. His place is then taken by a succeeding candidate of the same political affiliation. In more than 99 percent of the aggregated normal cases, the voter drops the ballot into the ballot box with no changes; this is then taken to be a vote in support of the proposed candidate. The early and open delivery of the unchanged ballot is promoted as a particular civic virtue, even though it is not legally required. In general, elections serve to legitimate the ruling group both at home and abroad. They are orchestrated as "high points of public life" and to mobilize the population (preamble to Electoral Law of the GDR, July 31, 1963). They are meant to offer the citizens an opportunity to discuss minor problems at election meetings.

## The Organization of the State

The differing conceptions of the state and of democracy are also reflected in the organizational principles that structure state and society. The institutional character of the state in the FRG results in the horizontal separation of power and in vertical federalism, because these organizational forms best guarantee the freedom of action of political groups and movements. The principle of the separation of power molds the three major functions of the state—legislation, administration, and jurisdiction—into separate powers with equal rights, namely the parliament (Bundestag), the federal government (Bundesregierung), and the federal court (Bundegericht). The principle of the separation of power is, however, not strictly realized in the FRG, since the Bundestag elects the Bundesregierung and can remove it from office. The politically more relevant dynamic in the FRG is that between the Bundesregierung and the parliamentary majority, on the one hand, and the opposition on the other. The vertical federal structure in the FRG is visible in the relative independence of the Länder (states), with their exclusive areas of authority, and in the degree of self-administration vested in local communities.

In contrast, "democratic centralism," the organizing principle of the GDR, stems from the subordination of all social and political organizations to the socio-political goals of socialism/communism as carried out by the state. Democratic centralism implies the basic democratic criterion of eligibility from bottom to top, but also the centralist elements of the unconditional subordination of lower organs to higher ones, the unconditional subordination of the minority to the majority, and the subordination of peripheral organs to those that are more central. In terms of the construction of the state, the specifications of these principles of organization lead to a horizontal concentration of power and to vertical centralism, for the autonomy of functional or regional units could only hinder the achievement of the goals of socialism/communism, established by the SED. According to the principle of unity of power, the highest power of the state is to be concentrated, undivided, in the Volkskammer (People's Chamber), the highest organ of popular representation. The other organs of the state, namely the Council of Ministers and the Supreme Court, are responsible and accountable to the Volkskammer. Unity of power does not, however, mean the negation of the separation of functions. The Volkskammer does not have authority to take on individual administrative or jurisdictional matters; instead, it serves to determine the "fundamental principles of the activities" of the other (central) organs of the state (constitution, article 49, paragraph 3). That no controversial discussions take place in the Volkskammer and that all resolutions are passed unanimously indicates that no real decisions are reached.[6] Instead, decisions that have been reached in the Politburo or in the Central Committee of the SED are merely transformed into universally binding norms and laws of the state. In the vertical organization of the state, "democratic centralism" means the hierarchical subordination of the administration. Communities, districts, and regions possess therefore no unconditional autonomy or exclusive decision-making authority; on the other hand, the centralist organization does not mean that the higher administrative organs make all decisions themselves, although they can repeal and replace any decision made by a lower organ—and this not only in regard to legality, but also in regard to expediency.

## The Organization of Society

The same principles by which the two states are organized penetrate the structure of the societies generally.

In the FRG, the society is characterized by competitive associations and labor unions, which may be freely established. The formation of their political will is autonomous so long as it is not directed against the pluralistic order itself. Examples of active groups within this framework are the labor unions, the German Federation of Trade Unions, the German Employee's Federation, the Christian Federation of Unions, various denominational groups, women's and youth associations, and assorted conservative and progressive artists' associations.

Within the hierarchical structure of the GDR, with the SED at its summit, there is one and only one "mass organization" for all the varying sectors of social life. This is meant to achieve, within its designated areas and under the general political leadership of the SED, the established goals of socialism/communism. There are many groups that function on this basis, for example the Free German Federation of Unions, the German Democratic Association of Women, the Free German Youth, the Cultural Association of the GDR, and the Society for German-Soviet Friendship. Besides these departmentally oriented organizations, the National Front takes on tasks of mobilization and social control. The National Front is organized according to the citizens' places of residence and functions through local committees and communal housing groups. Hence, a citizen is generally bound in a matrix of several large organizational units.

In the GDR, besides the hierarchical organization of the relations between party and state and between party and society, the principle of democratic centralism determines the internal organization of party and mass organizations. This guarantees more concretely that, in the case of the formal election of functionaries (from below to above) and of accountability (from above to below), the minority submits to the majority and the lower level subordinates itself to the higher. This signals the concentration of power in one group: the majority in the highest authoritative body. The democratic components of eligibility and accountability are undermined as a consequence of the undivided concentration of power at the top; candidates up for election must be confirmed by the next highest organ. Thus, officers have themselves represented in all the organs of the party, and the highest organs replenish themselves through cooptation of the mass organizations below.

## Civil and Legal Rights

In the FRG an inviolable sphere of the individual, free of the state and independent of the community, is assumed. This is a result of the original liberal assumption of the existence and value of the individual prior to the state or even prior to society, and of the constitution of the state by limited agreements (the "social contract"). With the purpose of protecting this freedom of the individual, the Basic Rights established in the Basic Law check the state's intervention in the autonomous development of the personality (within the framework of the state's socio-economic possibilities). In addition to their classic function of protecting rights, the Basic Rights are increasingly taken as an "objective set of values." Owing to their general clauses and indefinite legal concepts, the Basic Rights now enter into other spheres of the law and of social life, such as the economy, the family, and the workplace.[7]

The basic rights listed in the constitution of the GDR must be seen against the background of the individual's involvement in and duty toward society. Their purpose is not to draw the boundaries between the individual and the community but rather to define the individual's place in the community; the basic rights are integrational and not protective. This has the result that the socialist basic rights are not limited to the relationship of the state to the individual (i.e., to the political sphere in the narrowest sense) but are equally applicable to other spheres of human life, such as the economic, social, and cultural dimensions. Accordingly, rights to work, housing, health care, education, and cultural activities are constitutionally guaranteed.

In both Germanies, the basic rights are not granted boundlessly but are subject to specific limitations. In the FRG, political freedom ends where the freedom of others begins; likewise, the exercise of the basic rights may not be directed against the pluralistic formation of opinion and decisions. In such a case, the Federal Constitutional Court can forfeit the exercise of basic rights (Grundgesetz, article 18). In the GDR, the basic rights are subject to the priority of the community, which restricts the basic political right to an "agreement with the basic principles and goals of the constitution" (constitution, article 29). The constitution normatively establishes a substantive and specific political goal—the achievement of socialism/communism—as well as the status of the SED as the sole legitimate interpreter of this goal. Hence, the stipulation of conformity to the constitution demands, in the final result, the concordance of all political activities with the given policy of the SED. Economic, social, and cultural rights are equally subject to the proviso of "societal requirements" (constitution, article 24, paragraph 1) or "possibilities" (article 37, paragraph 1), which, once again, only the party may interpret and implement.

The respective structures of jurisdiction in the two German states reflect the different relationship of the individual to the community and the different functions of the basic rights that follow from this relation as well as from the legal position of the individual in other spheres. In the area of civil and labor legislation, the courts in the FRG settle cases involving contested subjective rights without forcible means. The involved parties steer the course of such a trial with motions and proposals; the judge reaches his decision on the basis of the facts presented in court. In the cases of family and criminal law, considered to be more important for the public's welfare, the court is required to research the facts independently and base its decision upon them. Finally, there is administrative and constitutional jurisdiction, an essential organizational feature of the liberal state. Here, the citizen can demand that the legality of provisions of the state be reviewed.[8] This type of administrative and constitutional jurisdiction is unknown in the GDR. The citizen can only lodge a complaint about an allegedly illegal act of the state with the superior administrative organ. Should this organ, out of considerations of legality or expediency, agree with the first, then no further legal channels are available to the citizen. The primary task of jurisdiction in the areas of civil, family, labor, and criminal law in the GDR is not to preserve and enforce the subjective rights of the citizen but to serve the realization of the objective law. Therefore, the courts must always, in all types of cases, research the facts themselves, and the public prosecutor can participate in all trials.

## Economy and Labor

### Property Rights

The first structural characteristic that differentiates the two economic systems (in addition to the procedural peculiarities, which will be discussed later) is property ownership, that is, who has the right to dispose of and utilize the means of production. In the FRG, the property of business enterprises lies largely in the hands of private owners. This includes not only personal ownership, but also partnerships or corporations, the shares of which belong to private persons who take part in shareholders' or stockholders' meetings and determine a business's policies. This form of property implies the economic goal of profit and the increase of capital, generally achieved by supplying goods that are in demand.

In contrast, there is no private ownership in the GDR of the means of production within industry, the most important economic sphere. Instead, there is "popular" or nationalized property. The GDR itself, by using the term "popular property," does not mean that the people exercise their function as owners through an assembly of representatives of the citizens in a community in which an industrial enterprise is located, nor does the labor force of a particular enterprise possess this competence. The people's ownership function is exercised only by the state. Specifically, the relevant economic administrative organs, at the highest level the Ministries of Industry or the Council of Ministers, have jurisdiction over disposal and utilization. This circumstance seems to correspond more closely to a concept of state property, as the state does not legitimate its actions through the consensus of the population but through alleged "historically objective necessities." According to this principle of property, the goal of the economy is the direct satisfaction of needs; this implies the need for the accumulation of capital.

The primary form of "property" in socialist countries among agriculture and skilled trades is not state property but cooperative property. In the GDR, however, this does not mean that a farmer or a tradesman can enter or leave a cooperative at will, or that the cooperative organs can determine their policy autonomously. Like industrial enterprises, the cooperatives are incorporated into the central planning and management of the state. The difference between these two forms of property concerns how workers are paid. Those employed within industry are generally paid tariff wages according to the amount of work done, and the profit of the enterprise affects only the yearly bonus. In contrast, the income of the members of a cooperative is determined by the total profit that the cooperative attains; this profit is divided among the members according to their specific contribution during the course of the year. By pursuing their own financial interests, the cooperative's members, whose work is not as standardized or as controllable as in industry, are rewarded for higher productivity in their own and their cooperative interests. The reason for this difference in the forms of remuneration and of property disappears to the degree that "industrial methods of production" are introduced into agriculture. In the long run, the GDR is striving for the establishment of "popular" or state property in agriculture as in industry.

## Management and Control

The second basic difference between the two German economic systems is in the methods of planning and management aimed at combining the factors of production (e.g., raw materials, labor, capital, and energy). In the FRG, this remains the task of economic markets. Antitrust laws and legislation against unfair competition are meant to eliminate distortions of competition; distribution and allocation are regulated through the market price which reflects changes in supply and demand. This supposes that the seller who produces most effectively and at the lowest price will sell his products most successfully, and that the buyer who can most effectively make use of a product, and is therefore prepared to pay the highest price, acquires the product. In this system of distribution, which is, in principle, oriented toward particular economic effectiveness and demand, interests above the individual level (such as environmental protection and the needs of weaker economic and social sectors of the population) are not sufficiently taken into consideration.

In the GDR, a state plan replaces the market in its function of guiding the economy as a whole. The plan establishes the type, quantity, and manufacturer of all the goods to be produced. The goal of a planned economy is the direct satisfaction of politically weighed and defined demand (Hamel 1977, p. 56). The clear-cut, planned coordination of defined demand and available capacities strives to obviate the danger inherent in the market model that different producers, unaware of each other's activities, invest to fulfill a certain accepted demand, only to discover that they have invested and produced too much; developed production capacity is liquidated through this excess expenditure of resources. In addition, the specific and planned coordination of demand and economic capacity ought to circumvent the duplication that is inherent in the market model. This applies, for example, to research and development. Through planning, all economic efforts supposedly unite to contribute to a high level of production. The theory of a market economy does not deny the possibility of economic losses, but they are tolerated for the highly valued advantages of the competitive market.

One disadvantage of a centrally planned economy is the greatly reduced capacity to respond to changed conditions of production because all important economic decisions must filter through the centers of information and authority. Furthermore, local production difficulties can set off a chain reaction, quickly leading to general economic disturbances. Since production capacity is planned as much as possible, inevitably it is also to some extent misplanned.

In the GDR, five-year plans are passed at the party congresses of the SED. As "directives" of the party, they are then transferred to the Volkskammer, which without substantial discussion transforms them into universally binding state law. The approved five-year plans demarcate the legally binding framework for management and planning in all spheres of the state and society. In the spring of each year the State Planning Commission in the Council of Ministers designs a political-economic "draft plan" for the coming year. This draft is based upon the scheme of the five-year plan, actual developments of domestic and foreign trade, and the requirements of economic policy. The annual plan, providing concrete and operative guidance, determines the production and cooperation of individual enterprises and other economic base units. The draft plan established by the Planning Commission is further differentiated according to periods and territories. Through the various managerial levels, it is handed down to the enterprises themselves and to other institutions, which then engage in "planning discussions," during which hidden reserves and the possibility of superseding the centrally set goals of production are debated. The "counter plans" formulated by the enterprises are then reconsolidated at the next higher managerial level and once more converted by the Volkskammer into universally binding law. In this binding form, the plan is again broken down according to branches and levels, from the coalitions of state enterprises, production associations, and other enterprises to the individual workplaces. At the level of citizens, the plan does not prescribe any particular conduct for them; it eliminates undesirable activities, however, by limiting the choices to alternatives offered by the plan.

Elements of planning are not foreign to the economic system of the FRG. There, in contrast to the GDR, individual businesses do the planning independent of each other and according to their particular interests and criteria. In the FRG, national economic policy supplies no operative planning or management. Limiting itself to purely economic means, it attempts to achieve through overall guidance the goals of the "magic square": price stability, a high rate of employment, balanced foreign trade, and growth.

## Work

In the FRG, employees pursue gainful employment in order to earn their subsistence. Work is not considered to have meaning and purpose in itself but is a means to support and develop personal, familial, and social life. At the same time, employment is increasingly expected to be diverse, interesting, and generally satisfying.[9]

In the GDR, the planning of production and the elimination of privately owned means of production are supposed to have transformed work into a conscious, creative activity that develops the "socialist personality." The claim that reification and alienation have been overcome, however, has doubt cast upon it by the steadily advancing standardization and division of labor, the strict authority and performance standards that permeate the sphere of work, the "central management and planning" (constitution, article 9, paragraph 3) that descend from above the producing concerns, and the circumstance that the working people receive wages for their labor.

Independent of these differing characterizations of work in the FRG and the GDR, the motivation of most people in both states is increased by the achievement principle. In addition to financial incentives to work, "ideal" or "moral" stimuli, such as public recognition in the form of decorations and medals, are systematically applied in the GDR as manifestations of this principle.

In both German states, work relations are grounded in an employment contract, i.e., a mutual agreement between a business enterprise and the person seeking work. But the forms of the contract differ in East and West. In the FRG, work relations are regulated (in principle) by the labor market. Employers offer positions according to their own economic perspectives, and people choose their place of work on the basis of their qualifications and interests. The state may not take any binding actions to manage or control the labor force (Grundgesetz, article 12), although the state contributes to the market mechanism through the free service of its employment offices (Arbeitsamte). Performance and compensation are established in the employment contract. The state sets certain conditions to protect the employee, such as the period of notice, the maximum number of working hours, and the minimum vacation requirements. The determination of working conditions and wages above these minimum standards is handled, as a rule, not between the employer and the individual employee but through collective contracts negotiated between unions and employers. An extreme market situation or an individual's unusual knowledge and ability can constitute an exception to this rule as agreed upon in the contract.

In the GDR, the state, as the owner of all business enterprises and the subject of economic planning and management, participates in the organization of work contracts. Although the factor "work" is included in central planning and management, work relations are still grounded in a contract between the enterprise and the worker; they are not determined by administrative assignment. The requirements of planning and management are followed. Economic and regional administrative organs can give a business concern binding instructions. These can be either general or specific. For example, the instruction can be given not to employ certain groups of people or particular individuals. In addition, the economic administration has indirect means of managing the working population, such as bonuses for work in certain branches, regions, or projects. Although businesses remain bound to the political decisions about personnel planning and management, workers can choose according to their interests among the positions this planning makes available. The mutual agreement between business enterprise and worker does not determine working conditions (such as working time and vacation) in the GDR. These conditions are determined by legally binding prescriptions of labor legislation, the goal of which is to substantially shape work relations. The wages to be paid for a particular activity are equally binding and are established in the tariff contract between the union and the appropriate central organ of economic administration (generally the Ministry). Divergences from these binding prescriptions are permitted only in cases of "individual contracts"; these contracts can be made, with the agreement of the Ministry, in cases of "consistently superior performance" (for example, of a scientific or artistic nature) (Arbeitsgesetzbuch, June 16, 1977, paragraph 46).

## The Structure of Business

The particular structure of a business is a second major element in the sphere of work, determined by the reigning form of property and the general organizational principle of a state.

In the GDR, where the organizational principle is democratic centralism, a business is run according to the principle of individual management by a director who is appointed and can be removed by a national organ of economic administration and is considered a "representative of the socialist state authority." It is the director's task to evaluate the opinions and suggestions of the workers or of the union representing them about matters of production (Arbeitsgesetzbuch, June 16, 1977, paragraph 20). These suggestions are not binding, but the director must give reasons if he disregards them. In certain social matters or in personnel matters, the management and the union must reach a common decision or the director's decisions must be approved by the union leadership.

In the FRG, either an enterprise is managed directly by the capital owners or they appoint a board of directors, which is complemented by graduated degrees of participation of the Workers' Council (Betriebsrat). In the economic sphere, the Betriebsrat has the right to information concerning "the economic affairs of the enterprise . . . as well as the effects of these plans on personnel" (Betriebsverfassungsgesetz, November 10, 1971, section 106, paragraph 2). The managerial staff must consult with the Betriebsrat or procure its agreement on issues regarding the place of work, the work process and environment, general affairs of personnel, vocational training, and certain specific actions affecting personnel.

The unions in the GDR, as part of their right to co-management and co-determination, must not only represent the interests of the workers but also consider "the universal strengthening of the socialist societal order and the stable development of the socialist economy" (Arbeitsgesetzbuch, June 16, 1977, section 6, paragraph 3). Extreme measures in labor disputes, such as strikes, are therefore foreign to the legal conception of labor in the GDR. In the FRG, the Betriebsrat and the management of an enterprise must "cooperate in good faith with the unions represented in the enterprise and with the associations of employers, to the benefit of the employee and of the enterprise" (Betriebsverfassungsgesetz, November 10, 1971, section 2, paragraph 1). Beyond the sphere of the individual enterprise, the unions represent only the interests of the employees, especially in agreements on wages and working hours. In the face of resistance from employers, unions in the FRG make use of various means of labor disputes, including strikes.

The employment contract requires the employee or the worker in West and East respectively to complete the tasks that have been agreed upon and to behave in accordance with the order of the work or business. Every worker in the GDR is also subject to the disciplinary authority of the management of the concern or the public agency involved. Disciplinary offenses are punished, including behavior within and beyond the sphere of official duties; lack of consideration of the "duties of a citizen" is one such offense (Arbeitsgesetzbuch, June 16, 1977, section 56, paragraph 1).

The law protecting workers against dismissal is an important aspect of the social security system that protects the employee in the FRG from arbitrary or socially unjustifiable dismissal. However, termination of employment due to "urgent business conditions that preclude the continuation of the employee's occupation in this enterprise" (Kundigungsschutzgesetz, August 25, 1969, section 1, paragraph 2) is permitted. In the GDR, the protection against unjustified dismissal goes a step further: As a consequence of the constitutionally guaranteed right to work, a worker can be given notice only if he has refused a "transitional contract" for another place of employment. Hence, in the GDR a worker cannot be deprived of a job if business conditions change.

Besides the individual exchange of services rendered and compensation, especially large enterprises in the GDR (and also in the FRG) provide facilities for social activities and leisure. Many enterprises provide company housing or support members of their labor force who wish to build their own homes. The organization of athletic teams and hobby circles is also widespread. In the more strictly cultural sphere, libraries are maintained and musical groups are organized. Enterprises in the GDR also provide a great deal of social care through the establishment and maintenance of company nurseries, kindergartens, rest homes, and clinics. Varying with regional factors, enterprises in the GDR are also obligated to ensure that their workers are able to purchase goods for their daily needs and that commuter traffic circulates efficiently.

## Politics and Everyday Life

Goals of State and Society

In the GDR, the total societal goal is the continuous development of socialism and its transition into communism. This goal, clearly set in the preamble of the constitution and in the party program of the SED ("Der Kommunismus unser Ziel," chapter 5) is the basis of the organization of the state and the structure of political and economic life described here. In the theoretical and ideological reversal of 1971, Walter Ulbricht was replaced by Erich Honecker and Soviet doctrines were once more completely adopted. Before, socialism was described as a "relatively autonomous socio-economic formation" (Ulbricht 1969, p. 38) that develops according to its own fundamental principles and in conformity with its own laws; however, since 1971 the transitory nature of socialism has been stressed and it is now considered "a phase in the united transformation of society to communism" (Hager 1971, p. 30). Within the sphere of constitutional law, this reversal was consummated in 1974, when the goal of communism became firmly anchored in the constitution. Honecker commented that "the gradual transition to communism" is "a present task for us, not a job that can first be tackled in the year 2000" (Neue Deutschland, February 16, 1976).

In addition, in 1971 the universally proclaimed systemic nature of socialism was revoked and concepts that tended toward societal self-regulation, such as "the socialist people's community" (constitution, 1968, article 18) and the "political and moral unity of the people"[10] were also retracted for the benefit of a greater emphasis on the "class nature of socialism" (Hager 1971, p. 27) and on the political guidance of the party.

The first important aspect of the further (re-) formation of East German society that has been pursued is the tendency towards greater social, economic, and cultural homogeneity. After the elimination of private ownership in industry and its reduction in the skilled trades and commerce, the next step is the introduction of industrial production methods into agriculture. This is meant to do away with the difference of lifestyle between the peasants and the proletariat. In the long run, the differences between those directly involved in production and those in organization and administration are supposed to decrease and disappear as a result of the increase in intellectual work that will be required for the programming, operation, and maintenance of more automated and complex production plants. A second goal on the pathway to socialism/communism is the development of the consciousness of the people, aiming for the adoption and internationalization of the Marxist-Leninist world view and "communist" morality. The realization of this goal is the duty of all state and societal institutions; besides the schools and other educational institutions, the entire public administration, industry, all cultural establishments, and the mass media must consider the political education of the citizen to be a major part of their activities. As a third important goal, the improvement of the standard of living and of production is emphasized. This is expressed in the "major task," formulated in 1971, of "the continuing rise of the people's material and cultural standard of living on the basis of a high rate of development of socialist production, increased effectivity, scientific and technical progress, and the growth of the productivity of labor."[11]

The FRG has no such overall societal goals, since it assumes the priority of the social, economic, and cultural spheres—social forces whose goals differ. The societal and governmental foundations that give shape to public life are, in principle, the formal goals of the democratic state (Grundgesetz, article 20, paragraph 1, and article 28, paragraph 1), which essentially maintain the following: the pluralistic formation of opinion and political power; the principle of legality of the constitutional state, according to which the autonomous position of the individual within a legal framework cannot be affected by interests of expediency; the aims of the social state, i.e., the consideration of the social dimension of human life in all governmental activities (especially legislation); and, last but not least, federalism, which grants regional subdivisions autonomy and decision-making authority. The legislative goals of governmental economic policy are the generalized elements of the "magic square": monetary stability, a high rate of employment, balanced foreign trade, and growth.

On another level, the socio-political values in the FRG can be considered in addition to the universally binding formal goals of the state. The two major parties both consider these values to be the basis of their national and regional policy. The values are (concurrently) freedom, justice, and solidarity (SPD) and freedom, solidarity, and justice (CDU). Both slogans give first rank to freedom, that is, the absence of external determination, a nondirective value that promotes individual autonomy and therefore a plurality of goals with differing specific life perspectives. The broader value of solidarity is, as a concept, similarly advocated by both parties, but there are characteristic differences in its concrete realization. According to the CDU reading, solidarity through subsidiarity (Subsidiarität) means assisting individuals, families, or social groups who are unable to master conditions they normally would be able to handle on their own.[12] In contrast, the SPD version points more toward a lasting, collective solidarity. The Social Democrats conceive of a system oriented from the very start toward the assistance of all people involved, in the sense of a shared risk borne by the community so that not only unexpected burdens but also predictable ones will be equally distributed on as many shoulders as possible. The CDU and SPD conceptions of justice diverge as well. Social Democrats understand *suum cuique* concretely as equal opportunity for all, while the Christian Democrats postulate a just opportunity according to which possibilities of participation and proprietorship remain bound to the differing social positions already attained in the course of life.

## Concepts of Equality

The concepts of justice, like all the conceptions of goals and values in East and West Germany, are reflected in constitutional articles regarding equality as well as in the political conception of equality.

In the FRG, the Basic Law proclaims the equality of all before the law in the classic liberal style and forbids discrimination for reasons of sex, race, language, or descent, or for ideological or political reasons (Grundgesetz, article 50). This conception of the rule of equality renounces the class privileges and discrimination of feudalism and places all individuals under the same conditions. Correspondingly, the fact that unequal results follow from the same efforts is not only tolerated but fully accepted, since it is viewed as an expression of the "natural" inequality of individuals. In the socio-political spectrum of the FRG, the Christian Democrats share this conception of equality, which is a consequence of the unconditional priority of free and individual development over collective solidarity.[13] The Social Democrats, however, do not wish to place all unequally developed individuals under the same law. Instead, they hope to create and maintain an equal social basis of departure for individual endeavors so that only unequal abilities and especially unequal efforts will result in unequal performance. In opposition to the formal, original equality that the Christian Democrats attribute to all individuals, the Social Democrats advocate a material and permanent continuous equality.

The different West German concepts of equality become particularly visible in educational policy. The CDU adheres to a threefold division of the school system, with a differentiation of students after the fifth grade into different courses of study. This selection, meant to promote the more capable students, also affects probable social status and income in later life. The SPD's school model integrates the different performance groups (courses of study) in one school where students can easily change tracks throughout their school years. This is to ensure that the educational group (and later the income group) to which a student belongs will be as accurate a reflection as possible of his real abilities and achievements.

The conception of equality in the GDR is apparent in its school system in two ways. First, students in the general educational school (up to the tenth grade) all learn the same material.[14] The opportunity to continue in secondary school and later in university studies (contingent upon planned professional needs) is affected by the policy that the majority of continuing students, and therefore the majority of those who will complete university degrees, must come from worker or peasant families. Were selection based purely on criteria of achievement, the majority would come from academic families.

The strategies to overcome the conventional inequality of the sexes are also characteristically different. In the FRG, emancipation aims at the autonomous and independent development of women.[15] The GDR aims at equal rights, including the equal participation of women in economic, social, and cultural life. In this area as well, the GDR strives towards final equality, whereas in the FRG the realization of individuality is stressed. The GDR does not aspire toward an original equality or a continuous equality of process; rather, in a reversal of the classic liberal declaration of equality, disadvantaged groups are given compensatory advantages to achieve equality of result. In article 20 of the constitution of the GDR, which sets the standard of equality, women (disadvantaged by traditional views) and youth (disadvantaged by their age) are given particular assistance by the state.

## Modes of Social Change

The different systems of control and management in the two Germanies correspond to different goals and values.

"The principle of management and planning of the economy and of all other social spheres" corresponds to the major goal of the GDR, which is centrally established from the start (constitution, article 9, paragraph 3). The system of management and planning, in conformity with democratic centralism, is structured in a strictly hierarchical and centralized fashion. There are no legal channels through which ideological, theoretical, or regional minorities can articulate opposition or exert any influence. Under Ulbricht, the "driving force of the socialist society" was seen to be the "conformity of the . . . interests of the workers and collectives with the needs of society" (constitution, 1968, article 2, paragraph 4). This is theoretically consistent for a society in which harmony is claimed between system and subsystem. This declaration of an inherent societal motor was abandoned in 1971, as were the concepts of the "socialist people's community" (constitution, 1968, article 18) and the "political and moral unity of the people."[16] All these concepts, which imply the self-regulation of society and a tendency to oppose political repression and bureaucracy, were replaced by externally applied factors in the form of the "main task" and the "noble goal" of communism.[17] The secondary motivation of the achievement orientation on the micro level corresponds to this exogenous mobilization on the macro level. The achievement principle should be "consequentially applied" and is intended to "liberate new forces for economic and social progress" (SED Party Program, chapter IIA). The GDR sees itself as differing from the FRG in that it has implemented a pure achievement principle, since all persons are evaluated in terms of the single standard of work and none can gain income by the investment of capital accumulated through the work of others. Yet it does seem that exceptional political loyalty in the GDR can make "income without work" possible.

In the economy of the FRG, the individual desire for gain is the motor of economic development. In the system of the competitive market, this should lead to the greatest success—in the long run, the satisfaction of individual interests should result in the best for the whole. To ensure this mechanism of incentive, there is anti-trust legislation, legislation governing unfair competition (meant to keep competition functioning), and ideological stimulation of the desire for possessions. The same incentive principle functions in the political and ideological sphere, where it is called pluralism, as social movements compete for influence and effective power.

## Moral Standards

Finally, standards of individual morality and personal behavior differ in East and West Germany.

Although the decalogue[18] contained in the SED party program of 1963 is officially no longer valid since the program has been changed, the essentials of propagated communist morality have not changed. Values and standards with essentially the same content can be found in the "Socialist Way of Life" section of the party program of 1976: active participation in the direction and solution of all societal matters; active participation in the development of socialism; conscious acceptance of obligations to society; struggle for the revolutionary cause of the proletariat, loyalty to socialism, and the preparedness to protect and defend its achievements; mutual respect and support, comradely assistance and consideration; conscientious, honest, socially useful work; criticism and self-criticism; active responsibility for tasks accepted; creative participation in work, planning, and governing; and a healthy life, physical fitness, and sports. A distinguishing feature of this morality is that it does not require or forbid any particular act (as does, for instance, the Judeo-Christian decalogue), but merely provides a general structure. Nevertheless, the Marxist-Leninist ethic does not call upon the individual to spell out these guidelines as an autonomous moral subject. As in the model of the formation of political opinion and will, the party retains the exclusive authority of interpretation. By its mere structure, but especially through the specific interpretations of the SED, the propagated morality of the GDR appears as one in which the collective dominates and as one that in cases of conflict calls for altruistic behavior. This sort of morality may be seen as the expression of a society that is pervaded by conflicting interests—a fact that, in order to retain credibility, it attempts to veil. Nevertheless, this moral code does seem to have an impact upon the way people behave.

As in all other questions of substance, there is no uniformity of morality in the FRG. Ethical concepts there are manifold, partly competing and partly overlapping; moreover, they do not appear in an organized and quantifiable form. If one were to try to establish common or widespread norms and values in the FRG, one could name the traditional virtues of industriousness, thrift, and frugality as well as more recent values and norms such as creativity, responsibility, and tolerance (Bollnow 1958). For the postwar period observers have claimed a "weakening of middle-class standards," a "disintegration of traditional value systems" (Kmieciak 1976, p. 461). The question is raised whether "we are becoming part of the proletariat" (Noelle-Neumann 1977, p. ix), although these emerging values and norms can also be viewed as an increase of autonomy and self-realization.

The societal and collective tendency of public morality in the GDR and the individualistic and particularistic tendency of Western ethics are also reflected in the specific structure of deviant behavior. In the GDR, the release of built-up frustrations and aggressions generally is not directed against others but takes the form of alcoholism, drug abuse, and suicide. In the FRG, deviant behavior is often directed against others in the form of violent crimes and crimes involving property.

## Conclusion

The GDR is—formally—oriented toward social needs and the harmonious development of a social totality. The FRG is oriented toward pluralism and individualism as well as profit. In the developmental dimension of goals for the future, the GDR can thus be designated as social, the FRG as individual. Regarding the methods with which these goals and criteria of development are to be realized, the GDR can be characterized as hierarchical and centralistic, or authoritarian, the FRG as participatory. When these two dimensions are combined, it becomes apparent that each of the two Germanies has its particular advantages and deficiencies.

## Notes

1. The underlying theory of knowledge and the method of this article attempt to supersede the limits of the empirical, analytical concept of truth by integrating elements of heuristic sociology and dialectic theory of society. See various views within this controversey in Adorno 1969 and Hondrich and Matthes 1978.

2. See works of the early classical theorists, such as Hobbes, Montesquieu, Rousseau, Ricardo, and Smith.

3. "The dignity of man is inviolable. It is the duty of all state power to respect and protect this dignity. . . ."

4. "Everyone has the right to the free development of his/her personality. . . ."

5. This occurred in the cases of the Sozialistische Reichspartei in 1952 and the Communist Party of Germany in 1956.

6. The only exception to this was the case of the "Gesetz über die Unterbrechung der Schwangerschaft" (March 9, 1972), in which some delegates of the CDU abstained from voting.

7. There may also be a tendency to win basic rights as participatory rights; this is implied, for example, in the judgment of the Federal Constitutional Court concerning the constitutionality of abortion, in which the duty of the state to protect the unborn child is denied.

8. An exception is the suspension of the confidentiality of postal and telephone connections for the protection of the "free, democratic order" or of the existence or security of the federal government or of a Land. In this case, state actions are investigated by organs chosen by the Bundesrat rather than through regular courts. See article 10, paragraph 2 of the Grundgesetz. This suspends the right of the citizen to invoke the courts against the state; however, in contrast with the GDR, a third party is involved.

9. Other reflections in the Western theory of economics and work—going beyond Taylor and Ford—are the concepts of job enlargement, job enrichment, and partially autonomous work teams.

10. See the term in *Kleines Politisches Wörterbuch* (East Berlin: Dietz, 1967), p. 502.

11. This is identical in article 2 of the constitution of the GDR, the party program of the SED (chapter II), and other programmatic documents.

12. See part 24 of the basic program of the CDU.

13. See the much-discussed work by J. Rawls (1975).

14. Exceptions, meant to stimulate performance, are the differentiation of academic subjects in special schools and the differentiation according to performance in classes preparing for higher schools.

15. The title of the most widely distributed relevant magazine in the FRG is *Emma*, suggesting emancipation.

16. This concept, used often before 1971, did not appear in the new party program.

17. Quoted from last sentence of SED party program.

18. a. You must always strive for the international solidarity of the proletariat and all working people, and for the inviolable bonds between all socialist nations.
b. You must love your fatherland and always be prepared to apply all your energies and abilities to defend the workers and peasant state.
c. You must help do away with the exploitation of man by man.
d. You must do good deeds for socialism because socialism leads to a better life for all working people.
e. You must struggle for the development of socialism in the spirit of mutual assistance and comradely cooperation; you must respect the collectivity and bear its criticism in mind.
f. You must protect and increase collective property.
g. You must always strive to improve your performance to be thrifty, and to strengthen the socialist work discipline.
h. You must raise your children in the spirit of peace and socialism to be all-round educated people with sound character and bodies of steel.
i. You must live cleanly and decently and respect your family.
j. You must practice solidarity with all peoples fighting for or defending their national independence.

## References

Adorno, T., et al. 1969. Der Positivismusstreit in der Deutschen Soziologie. Darmstadt and Neuwied: Luchterhand.

Bockenforde, E. W. 1976. Staat, Gesellschaft, Freiheit: Studien zur Staatstheorie und zum Verfassungsrecht. Frankfurt: Suhrkamp.

Bollnow, O. F. 1978. Wesen und Wandel der Tugenden. Frankfurt: Ullstein.

CDU-Bundesgeschaftsstelle, ed. 1958. Grundsatzprogram der Christlich-Demokratischen Union Deutschlands. Bonn.

Fiedler, F., et al., eds. 1974. Dialektischer und historischer Materialismus: Lehrbuch für das marxistisch-leninistische Grundlagenstudium. East Berlin: Dietz.

Forsthoff, E. 1971. Der Staat der Industrie-gesellschaft. Dargestellt am Beispiel der Bundesrepublik Deutschland. Munich: C. H. Beck.

Hager, K. 1971. Die entwickelte sozialistische Gesellschaft. Aufgaben der Gesellschaftswissenschaften nach dem VIII Parteitag der SED. East Berlin: Dietz.

Hamel, M., ed. 1977. BRD-DDR: Die Wirtschaftssysteme: Soziale Marktwirtschaft und sozialistische Planwirtschaft im Systemvergleich. Munich: C. H. Beck.

Hondrich, K. O., and J. Matthes. 1978. Theorievergleich in der Sozialwissenschaften. Darmstadt and Neuweid: Luchterhand.

Kmieciak, P. 1976. Wertstrukturen und Wertwandel in der Bundesrepublik Deutschland. Grundlangen einer interdisziplinaren empirischen Wertforschung mit einer Sekundaranalyse von Umfragedaten. Göttingen: Otto Schwartz.

Lenin, V. I. 1927–45. Collected Works of V. I. Lenin. New York: International Publishers.

Noelle-Neumann, E. 1977. Allensbacher Jahrbuch der Demoskopie, vol. 8. Vienna: Molden.

Offe, C. 1972. Strukturprobleme des kapitalistischen Staates. Frankfurt: Suhrkamp.

Rawls, J. 1975. Eine Theorie der Gerechtigkeit. Frankfurt: Suhrkamp.

Ulbricht, W. 1969. Die Bedeutung des Werkes "Das Kapital" von Karl Marx für die Schaffung des entwickelten gesellschaftlichen Systems des Sozialismus in der DDR und den Kampf gegen das staatsmonopolistische Herrschaftssystem in West Deutschland. East Berlin: Dietz.

## Legal References

Arbeitsgesetzbuch der DDR, June 16, 1977.

Betriebsverfassungsgesetz, November 10, 1971.

Gesetz über die Unterbrechung der Schwangerschaft, March 9, 1972.

Gesetz zur Förderung der Stabilität des Wachstums der Wirtschaft, June 8, 1967.

Grundgesetz.

Kundigungsschutzgesetz, August 25, 1969.

Verfassung der DDR.

Wahlgesetz der DDR, July 31, 1963.

# 2 The Medical-Industrial Complex

## Erich Klinkmüller

*In this chapter, Erich Klinkmüller attempts to give the term* medical-industrial complex *specific shape. His discussions about how this complex differs in the two German states provide some of the answers to the question of how the contrasts in structural values outlined by Lohmann in chapter 1 take specific form in the health-care delivery system. Along the way he makes some remarks that are interesting from an American point of view. For example, he claims that West Germans demand more and more medical services partly because they want to get all they can for the compulsory contributions that come out of their wages and salaries. This reason goes beyond the American concern that the demand for services will increase because they are free, and it adds another dimension to how people may think about high insurance payments that are not counterbalanced by co-payments. Klinkmüller also concludes that financing health care through specific taxes rather than out of a general budget increases the demand for services. Another point to emerge from this chapter is that the East German health-care system is considerably more efficient, producing similar figures of morbidity and life expectancy with about half as much of the GNP as the West German system uses.*

If people were to be asked what the term *medical-industrial complex* (MIC) makes them think of, most would probably answer "the military-industrial complex." This association is intended, and so are the negative emotions the phrase so frequently evokes. However, widespread use of this term has not diminished the wealth and power of those whom it labels.

This chapter is based on the assumption that an MIC exists in every industrial society. Based on this assumption, it attempts to answer the question: What are the most important macroeconomic differences between the MICs in the Federal Republic of Germany (FRG; West Germany) and the German Democratic Republic (GDR; East Germany)? I begin by describing the institutions that make up the MIC; then I deal with the differences that exist between the MICs to be found in the FRG and the GDR with respect to organization, income distribution, financing, marketing, and public relations.

To my knowledge, this subject has never been examined from an economic point of view.[1] At best, the available studies (for example, Pritzel 1978) devote only a few brief remarks to a macroeconomic comparison of the MICs in the two German states. This being the case, three main sources of information on the subject are available: general monographs and essays on health economics that can be helpful in determining which issues should be examined (Feldstein 1967; Klarman 1965; Perlman 1974), institutional descriptions of the MICs in both German states (Mitzscherling et al. 1974), and critical discussions of the burden the MICs place on the socio-economic environment (Illich 1976). In addition, I can make use of my own experiences with MICs in the FRG, the GDR, and the United States. Of course, such experiences are not necessarily typical and are limited to my individual observations of the three systems, but they do provide a point of reference.

The term *medical-industrial complex* designates the entire system of organizations whose members derive their incomes, social status, or political influence from maintaining or restoring human health.

First of all, the MIC is composed of those enterprises that are directly concerned with treating illness: inpatient institutions (hospitals, hospitals for incurables, and sanatoriums) and outpatient clinics (dispensaries, doctors' and dentists' offices, physical therapy institutions, pharmacies, etc.). In addition, the MIC includes public and private health-insurance organizations and those industries that manufacture or provide primarily health-related products or services; some examples of the latter are the pharmaceutical industry, the medical apparatus industry, manufacturers of artificial limbs, enterprises thatprovide ambulance service, diagnostic laboratories, and funeral parlors. Furthermore, the MIC includes a number of associations representing the interests of the organizations and groups active in the MIC, both within the MIC and with respect to the rest of society. Physicians' associations are a prime example, but there are also associations of insurers, industrialists, and public administrators, and there are the unions. The universities, the research institutes, the technical schools, the conventions, and the technical publishing houses, serve the purpose of training new personnel and providing channels of communication within the MIC.

Other MIC members are the various health administrations, from the local public-health offices to the federal health and drug administration and the parliamentary committees that deal with health issues. Public opinion tends to view this hierarchy of health agencies as the guardian of society's interest in the area of health care. As far as the local and regional public-health authorities are concerned, this view is essentially correct. However, as one moves toward the upper levels of the hierarchy the interests of the MIC itself begin to outweigh society's interests. In contrast with other industries that produce goods and provide services, the MIC's interests are represented by a cabinet-level minister and by a special parliamentary committee. It is precisely the fact that the MIC's interests are represented within the government administration that makes this complex different from mere branches of industry. The West German MIC shares this form of inside influence with agriculture, education, and transportation; industries such as textiles and retail trade are not represented at the cabinet or the parliamentary level.

Both inpatients and outpatients have been included in the MIC. Their role in the MIC differs from that of the institutions described above mainly in that they lack an organization to represent their interests (despite the Vertreterversammlungen, which are supposed to represent their interests in health-care negotiations). They experience the MIC primarily as "suffering masses" (in the Marxist sense as well as the medical sense), and they serve more as the MIC's objects than as its subjects. Their independent contribution to the system is mostly limited to their being willing to play the socio-economic role of patients.

The MIC's macroeconomic relations with the rest of society are apparent in: the influx and efflux of patients, the inflow and outflow of money, the inflow and outflow of goods and services, the integration of the MIC into the socio-philosophical concept of man by means of health legislation and public relations, and the way the MIC uses health marketing and health propaganda in the mass media in order to manipulate public opinion.

## Organization

The best way to determine what organizational differences exist between the MICs in the FRG and the GDR is by examining the constitutional provisions governing freedom of association in the two states. In the FRG, article 9 of the constitution guarantees freedom of association. Paragraph III refers specifically to the right to form associations for economic purposes:

The right to form associations for the purpose of protecting and improving labor and economic conditions is guaranteed to everyone and for all occupations. Agreements that restrict this right or attempt to interfere with it are void; measures aimed at restricting or interfering with these rights are illegal.

In contrast, the constitution of the GDR (article 29) permits associations only insofar as they serve the interests of the general public:

The citizens of the German Democratic Republic have the right to associate in political parties, social organizations, associations, and collectives in order to realize their interests in accordance with the principles and objectives of the constitution. (Mampel 1972, p. 662)

In the GDR, associations for the purpose of exercising economic control are expressly prohibited by article 14(3):

Private economic associations to establish economic control are not permitted. (Mampel 1972, p. 370)

Because of its constitutional provisions, the FRG has a large number of autonomous associations that represent the private interests of the natural and juristic persons working in the MIC. This contrasts sharply with the organizational monopoly of the dominant political party, the SED, in the GDR. In the GDR, government agencies carry out many of the functions that autonomous associations perform in the FRG. Therefore, in the GDR there is no sharing of power between public-health authorities and interest groups; rather, public-health authorities exercise sole authority in the health area. One important consequence of this is that the economic, social, and professional interests of doctors are not represented by autonomous groups such as the Hartmannbund or the American Medical Association. Another is that no lobbies represent the pharmaceutical industry, the manufacturers of medical apparatus, the health insurers, or the "funeral industry."

In the FRG, the industries that belong to the MIC are mostly organized as private corporations. In the GDR they exist exclusively as nationally owned enterprises subject to directives from higher government agencies. This difference is also a consequence of the right to freedom of association in the FRG as opposed to the government organizational monopoly in the GDR. In addition, article 12 of the GDR's constitution expressly states that private ownership in larger industrial enterprises and insurance institutions is unlawful:

Mineral resources, mines, power stations, dams and large bodies of water, natural resources on the continental shelf, larger industrial enterprises, banks and insurance institutions, nationally owned farms, highways, the means of transport such as railroads, ocean shipping and aerial navigation, and postal and telecommunications equipment are national property. Private ownership of any of these is unlawful. (Mampel 1972, p. 344)

The differences in the organization of enterprises lead to particularly significant differences in management goals. A private corporation is primarily interested in retaining and increasing its market share and its profits by means of marketing, research, and advertising. The goals of a nationally owned enterprise are to retain and increase organizational slack and individual career chances, using plan fulfillment, established procedures, and political propaganda to achieve these ends. Furthermore, the government's foreign-trade monopoly insulates the nationally owned enterprise from international market pressures. In the GDR this monopoly is based on article 9(5) of the constitution,[2] which frees the nationally owned enterprises that manufacture pharmaceutical products and medical apparatus from the need to compete on the world market (Mampel 1972, p. 258) and, at the same time, guarantees almost effortless domestic sales. The negative influence exerted by the foreign-trade monopoly is one reason why nationally owned enterprises in the GDR function less efficiently than private corporations in the FRG (Brown 1961; Kindleberger 1968, pp. 202–218; Klinkmüller 1965, pp. 484–514; Wilczynski 1965; Wiles 1968; Bryson and Klinkmüller 1975).

Turning from enterprises and the organization of business to the health-insurance system, one notes that the FRG has a mixed system of government authorities, public institutions, and private corporations. In the GDR there are no private corporations, but otherwise both German states have systems of health insurance that are founded on their common tradition prior to World War II. Due to this common social tradition, institutions providing outpatient and inpatient care are also structured in a similar manner. Deviations from these traditions, however, include East German policies to discourage independent practitioners and to replace them with a network of polyclinics and dispensaries (Pritzel 1978, p. 100). This has led to a drastic reduction in the number of self-employed doctors and dentists and their partial replacement by polyclinics (Pritzel 1978, p. 78). East German regulations have also caused almost all nongovernment pharmacies to vanish (Pritzel 1978, p. 100). Thus, not only do physicians, dentists, and other professionals lack an autonomous organization to represent their economic, social, and professional interests; they also have no independent financial resources to employ in defending these interests.

## Income Distribution

The part of national income that is distributed throughout the MIC can be subclassified into the net earned income of those who work in the MIC, the net profits of the enterprises that belong to the MIC, the tax receipts that flow into public funds, and the transfer income of the patients. This classification applies to industrial societies in general and to the FRG and the GDR in particular. The two German states differ in the share of the gross national product that is claimed by the MIC and in the proportional relationships among the types of revenue collected by the subgroups within the MIC.

In tables 1–4 an attempt has been made to describe the structure of income distribution within the MIC in the two German states. Some time-consuming calculations were necessary to arrive at these statistics, because the statistical information available has not been compiled with a view to providing material for an economic study. Rather, each institution publishing such information does so primarily to report on its own performance. (These tables are meant to illustrate the economic structure of the medical-industrial complex in West and East Germany, and therefore their datedness is of secondary importance.)

Because of the sources, it was necessary to bridge information gaps, clarify overlaps, and make sure each set of statistics was included only once. In order to do this, I constructed an input-output table showing the flow of payments between the various institutions in the MIC. This procedure makes it possible to determine with some accuracy to what extent the data are mutually compatible. Nevertheless, it would be unrealistic to overestimate the reliability of the values in the tables. The fact that the aggregates of MIC turnover cited in tables 1 and 2 happen to be identical is a formal necessity. Actual figures of this nature rarely coincide exactly. In the present case, the fact that there is no discrepancy in turnover figures merely reveals that the technique of using input-output tables has made it possible to bridge over some informational gaps.

**Table 1**

Income distribution of medical-industrial complexes of FRG and GDR at current prices.[a]

| | FRG (billions of 1975 marks)[b] | GDR (billions of 1976 marks)[c] |
|---|---|---|
| Gross national product | 1,030.3 | 163.7 |
| Turnover of MIC | 142.4 | 13.4 |
| Net purchases of goods and services[d] | 18.7 | 1.7 |
| Imports[d] | 1.9 | — |
| Net wages, salaries, and compensations of work force in MIC | 41.5 | 4.2 |
| physicians, dentists, pharmacists[e] | 14.0 | 0.8 |
| all other members of MIC work force | 27.5 | 3.4 |
| Net profits of enterprises[f] | 6.5 | } 1.7 |
| Revenues collected by fiscal authorities | 20.6 | |
| taxes on wages and other income | 9.3 | 0.4 |
| social security taxes | 9.1 | 0.3 |
| Transfer income of patients | 55.0 | 5.8 |
| continued wage and salary payments during sick leave[h] | 33.4 | 3.0 |

a. Calculations by Department of Economics, Osteuropa-Institut, Freie Universität Berlin. All are net values.
b. One billion 1975 marks, converted at the average market rate in Zurich, represented an international purchasing power of 2,260,000 Krugerrands (each equivalent to one ounce of coined 24-karat gold). This information can be used to get an idea of what the amounts of money cited are worth in other national currencies and at various times. To convert, it is necessary to multiply the data in the table by $226 \times 10^4 \times$ the market price of the Krugerrand expressed in the national currency. Thus, the international purchasing power of 100 1975 marks was equal to 36.41 1975 U.S. dollars.
c. One billion 1976 marks, converted at the average Zurich market rates, represented 830,000 Krugerrands in international purchasing power. The method of computation described in note b can also be used here. Thus, the international purchasing power of 100 1976 marks was equal to 10.36 1976 U.S. dollars.
d. Net purchases of goods and services include purchases of institutions and enterprises within the MIC from enterprises and institutions outside the MIC only. Transactions within the MIC are excluded. Also excluded are sales taxes and customs. Sales taxes and customs paid by the MIC are shown under "revenues collected by fiscal authorities."
e. Net wages, salaries, and compensations are the aggregate net income of the work force (see table 3) in the MIC. Net income is gross income minus taxes on wages and income, minus compulsory contributions to public old-age, health, and salary payments during sick leave. Income taxes and compulsory contributions are shown under "revenues collected by fiscal authorities." Continued wage and salary payments during sick leave are given under "transfer income of patients."
f. Gross profits minus taxes on profits.
g. Total of revenues collected by the fiscal authorities from the MIC. Aside from taxes on wages, other income, and profits and compulsory contributions to public old-age, health, and accident insurance, this position includes sales taxes on transactions within the MIC and for purchases of goods and services from outside the MIC, and customs on the importing of such goods and services.
h. The "continued wage and salary payments during sick leave" in table 1 are 19 billion marks (FRG) and 2 billion marks (GDR) larger than the respective values in table 2. This difference is equal to the sick-leave payments of the MIC to its own work force. As indicated in note e, the sick-leave payments of the MIC have been subtracted from the gross income of the MIC work force.

**Table 2**
Financing of medical-industrial complexes of the FRG and the GDR at current prices.[a]

| | FRG (billions of 1975 marks)[b] | GDR (billions of 1976 marks)[c] |
|---|---|---|
| Gross national product | 1,030.3 | 163.7 |
| Turnover of MIC | 142.4 | 13.4 |
| Budgetary expenditures | 23.1 | 9.9 |
| expenditures for health care | 21.4 | 2.1 |
| grants-in-aid for civil servants | 1.7 | — |
| Subsidies from social security pension fund | 19.4 | |
| Compulsory contributions for specific purposes | 81.6 | 7.8 |
| health-insurance tax | 42.9 | |
| accident-insurance tax | 7.2 | 0.2 |
| continued wage and salary payments during sick leave[d] | 31.5 | 2.8 |
| Sales of goods and services | 10.5 | 0.5 |
| exports | 4.0 | — |
| Voluntary private insurance payments | 7.8 | — |
| health insurance | 6.5 | — |
| accident insurance | 1.3 | — |
| liability insurance of physicians | — | — |

a. Calculations by Department of Economics, Osteuropa-Institut, Freie Universität Berlin. All are net values.
b. See table 1, note b.
c. See table 1, note c.
d. The positions "continued wage and salary payments during sick leave" in table 1 are 19 billion marks (FRG) and 2 billion marks (GDR) larger than the respective positions in table 2. This difference is equal to the sick-leave payments of the MIC to its own work force. The sick-leave payments of the MIC have been subtracted from the gross income of the MIC work force.

**Table 3**
Work forces of the medical-industrial complexes of the FRG and the GDR (thousands).

| | FRG, 1975 | GDR, 1976 |
|---|---|---|
| Physicians | 119 | 32 |
| self-employed | 56 | 1 |
| Dentists | 32 | 8 |
| Pharmacists | 26 | 4 |
| Others | 1,260 | 360 |
| hospital employees | 660 | 140 |
| Total | 1,437 | 404 |

Note: Total work forces were 25,960,000 (FRG) and 8,483,000 (GDR).

**Table 4**
Income distribution and financing per member of work force in FRG and GDR at current market prices (marks).[a]

| | FRG, 1975 | GDR, 1976 |
|---|---|---|
| Gross national product[b] | 39,688 | 19,297 |
| Turnover of MIC[c] | 99,095 | 33,168 |
| Payments out of all public budgets from the state budgets[b] | 1,637 | 1,167 |
| Budgetary expenditures for health care[b] | 824 | 248 |
| Subsidies from social security pension fund[b] | 747 | |
| Compulsory contributions for specific purposes[b] | 3,143 | 919 |
| health-insurance tax[b] | 1,653 | |
| accident-insurance tax[b] | 277 | 24 |
| Sales of goods and services[c] | 7,307 | 1,238 |
| Purchases for goods and services | 13,013 | 4,208 |
| Net per capita income of total work force in MIC[c] | 28,880 | 10,396 |
| physicians, dentists, pharmacists[d] | 79,096 | 18,182 |
| remaining work force in MIC[e] | 21,825 | 9,444 |
| Net profits of enterprises[c] | 4,523 | 4,208 |
| Revenues collected by fiscal authorities | 14,466 | |
| taxes on wages and other income[c] | 6,472 | 990 |
| social security taxes[c] | 6,333 | 743 |
| Transfer income of patients[b] | 2,118 | 684 |
| continued wage and salary payments during sick leave[b] | 1,287 | 354 |

a. Calculated by dividing values from tables 1 and 2 into values from table 3.
b. GNP etc. divided into total national work force.
c. Turnover of MIC etc. divided into total work force of MIC.
d. Aggregate net earnings of physicians, dentists, and pharmacists working in MIC divided into number of physicians etc. given in table 3.
e. Work force of MIC excluding group cited in note d.

The share of the GNP claimed by the MIC is considerably larger in the FRG than in the GDR. There is first the number of employees. In the FRG, 5.5 percent of all employed persons receive their income directly from the MIC;[3] in the GDR the comparable figure is 4.8 percent. The main reason for this difference is the greater economic role played by the pharmaceutical industry and the medical-instrument manufacturers in the FRG. Private health-insurance companies, which have no equivalent in the GDR, also provide additional employment in the FRG.

The greater significance of the MIC in the FRG is dramatically illustrated by the size of its turnover as a percentage of the GNP in tables 1 and 2: 13.82 percent (almost twice the 8.19 percent of GNP distributed by the MIC in the GDR). The best statistical explanation for this is that West German doctors, dentists, and pharmacists have much higher net earnings than their East German colleagues: In the FRG the earnings of these professionals amount to 1.4 percent of the GNP, while in the GDR the corresponding figure is only 0.5 percent. Moreover, in the FRG the net profits of industries and insurance companies in the MIC amount to 0.6 percent of GNP.

The greater affluence of the FRG provides the best economic explanation for the higher proportion of the GNP devoted to the MIC there. Since the FRG is more prosperous, individuals and groups there spend a greater part of their income on health care. This trend is intensified by the tendency of individuals in both states to be more concerned about their health as their income rises, an inclination that is strongly reinforced by the much more intensive health-care propaganda of government agencies and private industries in the FRG. The influence exercised by special-interest groups on public opinion and health care is also a contributing factor.

Another striking difference between the two German states is in the size of the transfer income distributed by the MIC (table 1). In the FRG, 55 billion (i.e., $55 \times 10^9$) marks were transferred to the private households of patients as income-substituting subsidies, a figure amounting to 5.3 percent of the GNP. In the GDR, the corresponding figure was 5.8 billion marks, equivalent to 3.5 percent of the GNP. These statistics might lead one to suspect that it is easier to obtain sick leave in the FRG than in the GDR. However, it is much more likely that these figures reflect the much lower incomes earned in the GDR. This proposition is supported by the fact that in the GDR transfer payments made because of illness amount to 76.3 percent of all other payments made by the MIC, whereas the percentage was only 62.9 in the FRG.

## Financing

Like any other economic complex, the medical-industrial complex must finance the incomes it distributes. Table 2 cites four sources of financing the turnover within the MIC: general budget subsidies, compulsory contributions for specific purposes, voluntary insurance contributions, and product sales. All four types of financing exist not only in the two German states but in other countries as well. Furthermore, they represent sources of funding not only for the medical-industrial complex but also for other complexes within industrial societies, such as the transportation complex and the educational complex.

If one examines these sources of financing in terms of the MIC's employment and income interests, it becomes apparent that compulsory contribution for specific purposes is the optimal form of financing.[4] The volume of employment and level of income in the MIC as functions of the health-insurance contributions are primarily dependent on the influence of the MIC on tax rates, the number of persons subject to health-care taxation, and the range of services provided by the compulsory health-insurance program. All three factors vary according to how effectively the public authorities and private associations active in the MIC exert their influences. Any time one of these factors increases, so do employment opportunities and incomes within the MIC. These three factors are mutually supportive of each other. An expansion of the extent of required services can be used as an instrument for extending the personal tax basis as well as raising tax turnover. In particular, expanding the coverage offered by compulsory health insurance can be used as an argument for increasing the tax base for individual incomes and also the tax rate.

Market expansion due to compulsory health-insurance contributions is limited mainly by the percentage of net income the insured are willing to pay as compulsory contributions and the reduced ability of these taxpayers to pay other kinds of taxes. In practice, it is difficult to determine where these limits are. Therefore it is not clear to what extent they are likely to restrict growth in the MIC's turnover.

Financing by means of general budget subsidies represents a completely different situation. In this case, such subsidies must compete with other budget-financed public expenditures. The claims of MIC authorities and associations conflict directly with the employment and income interests of equally well-organized competitors, such as public authorities (and private associations) in the agricultural complex, the transportation complex, and the military-industrial complex.

In general, market sales play only a subsidiary role as a source of financing for the MIC in most industrial societies except, to a limited degree, the United States. This is clearly true of both German states. According to table 2, market sales finance only 7.4 percent of total turnover in the FRG and only 3.7 percent in the GDR. The direct sale of MIC goods and services to their ultimate consumers appeals mostly to the willingness of private households to spend money to enhance their social status. Also included in this figure are sales resulting from the mania for medications.[5]

The remaining source of financing is the premiums paid for private health insurance. Such premiums exist only in the FRG, where they represent 5.5 percent of turnover. The fact that they do not exist in the GDR has two consequences: The desire to defend one's social status that lies behind this form of health care has no opportunity to express itself as demand in the health-care market, and a supply of qualitatively superior health-care services to meet this demand is not available.

On the whole, a comparison of the financial structure of turnover in the MICs in the two German states (table 2) reveals the following: The relative proportion of overall budgetary appropriations that goes to the MIC is about the same (in the FRG 21.4 billion marks out of 142.4 billion; in the GDR 2.1 billion out of 13.4 billion). This also applies to the burden placed on the economy by wage-substituting payments in case of illness. These two sources of financing account for about a third of MIC turnover (in the FRG 31.5 billion marks out of 142.4 billion; in the GDR 2.8 billion out of 13.4 billion). The amount of funding provided by compulsory health-insurance contributions is considerably higher in the GDR (58.2 percent)[6] than in the FRG (48.8 percent).[7] Private health-insurance premiums and the larger sales of health-care goods and services in the FRG make up for most of this difference.

The FRG's financing structure stimulates demand much more effectively. This means that, compared with the GDR, the MIC costs the West German economy more and offers a wider variety of goods and services.

## Marketing

A prejudice, which is equally strong in both German states, makes it unusual to associate the concept of marketing with health. West Germany's pharmaceutical industry and private health-insurance companies certainly wage advertising campaigns, but open advertising of physicians' services is a thing of the past. Yet advertising takes place in other guises. When politicians, journalists, scientists, and even presidents' wives make public statements about health care, economic advertising masquerades as concern for social progress and general well-being. The political, journalistic, and scientific comments on health issues published in the East and West German mass media work much like paid advertising as far as retaining, expanding, and creating markets is concerned. The positive effect such hidden advertising has on turnover, employment, and income in the MIC is little different from that of conventional advertising. The differences lie in the kind of people who are doing the advertising and are due to the fact that such hidden advertising is free of charge. In addition, one could note that health advertising hidden in the editorial sections of the mass media is not easily identifiable as propaganda. While even school children are aware of the socio-psychological approaches used in commercial advertising for cigarettes and detergents, the general public views health propaganda with astonishing naiveté. As a consequence, it fails to view such propaganda with sufficient skepticism, in contrast with its reaction to conventional advertising.

Of course, this should not be taken as meaning that, if the MIC did not advertise, it would lack enough patients to treat. The most important causes of health-care demand by private households[8] must be seen in turn as part of a basic economic framework that determines the overall structure of demand for health care in industrial societies. Health care cannot be promoted effectively without taking into account these microeconomic reasons for demand, as well as the overall macroeconomic framework. On the contrary, if health propaganda is to be successful, it is essential for the promoters to be well informed about both these factors and to apply this knowledge. Simple advertising does not become effective marketing unless a conscious attempt is made to determine what opportunities exist and what limitations are imposed by the material, social, economic and intellectual conditions that prevail in the society.[9]

The central marketing concept of the MIC is "health." According to a standard World Health Organization definition, health is a "state of complete physical, mental, and social well-being." If one takes this definition seriously, almost everyone needs medical treatment of some kind. Thus, the WHO's definition serves as an excellent marketing concept. However, this formulation also represents an impossible claim on the public health-care system, and it is meaningless as a medical concept in that it fails to define clearly the emotional and even more the social components of "health."

Let it be said in passing that the use of the concept of "health" to promote sales is not necessarily any more beneficial to consumers than the advertedly high-pressure sales techniques of commercial advertisers are harmful. In fact, just the opposite is true: Private households can refuse to purchase goods offered in the marketplace, but they usually cannot refuse to pay taxes or to make compulsory health-insurance contributions. About the only way to react to this situation is to try to obtain as many services as possible from the MIC in return for the money that must be paid. This means that the demand for the MIC's goods and services increases even more than it would if the services it provided were free.

As far as the patient is concerned, there are three main factors that limit the demand for health care under the above conditions: the time expenditure necessary to take advantage of the goods and services offered by the MIC, the fear of medical treatment, and the necessity of justifying to one's family and employer the time lost at work because of medical treatment.

A patient naturally has other claims on his time. The more time one spends as an outpatient or an inpatient, buying and using medications, the less time is available for other types of production and consumption. Stated as a formal proposition, time expenditure for health care can be increased only to the extent that the marginal utility the patient derives from the MIC's goods and services is greater than the marginal utility he gains from alternative modes of time expenditure. In reality, this formal statement gains in significance to the extent that no attempt is made to regulate demand by means of price.[10] The results can be seen in overcrowded waiting rooms, long waits for appointments, a reduction in time taken to consult with each patient, and an increased number of patient visits per case of illness.

Now that we have examined the many similar aspects of health marketing in the two German states, the differences that exist seem rather insignificant. We can begin by postulating that the GDR has a much less developed system of health marketing. The naive assumption apparently still prevails there that propaganda can manipulate ideas and actions at will, without taking existing structures into account. Other reasons for the less intensive pursuit of health marketing in the GDR are that it is not as necessary for the political leadership to justify being in power by advertising achievements in the area of health care, that strong reservations exist about extending the concept of health to include not only physical health, but also psychological and social factors, and that preventive medicine and medical treatment are not goals in themselves but are intended to increase labor productivity.

In the FRG, publicity about health-care services that are planned or already provided serves as an important instrument in the political parties' competitive struggle to gain support from associations and voters and to gain public jobs and political power. Since the GDR's political elite is not subject to comparable pressures, it can afford to be less concerned about such matters. According to the prevailing ideology, concern for human beings is by definition much greater under socialism than under the conditions of capitalist exploitation. Therefore, it is hardly necessary to prove this premise with regard to health. Since this is the case, in the GDR it also seems unnecessary to include psychosomatic and socio-psychological disorders in a definition of illness. Doing so would make it necessary to admit that these types of disorders are less a product of the capitalist mode of production than a characteristic common to all industrial societies. Furthermore, expanding the concept of health would increase the influx of patients. In the FRG it might be desirable to do this and thus improve employment and earning opportunities within the MIC. However, in the GDR similar arguments would be outweighed by the consideration that an increase in spending for health care means a decrease in alternative expenditures of national income. Furthermore, it is important to emphasize the subsidiary role played by preventive health care and medical therapy in the GDR. The main purpose of both is to get the patient back to work. In socio-philosophical terms, East German health propaganda views man in a Hegelian sense as achieving self-realization in his work. It is true that similar ideas prevail in West German literature on health economics; however, West German health propaganda is pervaded by the idea of health as something to be sought for its own sake.[11]

**Public Relations**

In socio-economic practice, it is often difficult to distinguish between public relations and marketing as forms of health propaganda, since the two are closely related. In the preceding section, marketing was discussed with reference to efforts to maintain and increase the influx of patients into the MIC. By contrast, public-relations efforts are aimed at influencing legislation that affects the MIC, defending the MIC's tax-collection privileges and budget appropriations, and protecting its relatively high incomes and social status. It would be impossible to discuss in sufficient detail all the issues raised here. Instead, three particularly important topics will be mentioned: quality control by lawyers and courts of the goods and services the MIC offers, the lack of a free press in the GDR, and the influence the FRG exerts by serving as an example for the GDR.

Legal review of medical services has played only a minor role in both German states up to now. Nevertheless, it can be assumed that the professional behavior of physicians in the FRG has been influenced noticeably by the mere possibility of such a review. Thus, examinations and treatments are undertaken as a precaution against possible legal charges, even though overall circumstances and statistical possibilities do not warrant such measures. To my knowledge, there is no similar tendency in the GDR.

The economic consequence of defensive medicine is an increase in the cost of health care. West German doctors perform diagnostic investigations and therapies in order to protect themselves against legal prosecution rather than because they are necessary from a medical point of view. In addition, West German doctors have to pay premiums for liability insurance. Both types of expenditure do not exist in the GDR.

The lack of an independent press in the GDR means that public discussion of medical issues is much less common there than in the FRG. East German magazines and newspapers do not have to attract readers by publishing reports about new methods of treatment and medications, miracle doctors, and grateful patients.

The shadow that the West German MIC casts on public relations in the GDR is a constant source of irritation for the official East German socio-philosophical self-understanding. The problem is insoluble because the more prosperous West German society can simply afford a more expensive health-care system. In addition, the GDR's health propaganda cannot stand up to the influence the West German example exerts on the population of the GDR. Very few West German magazines and newspapers circulate in the GDR, and the health propaganda broadcast to East Germany by West German television and radio is not all that intensive. Nevertheless, the millions of West Germans who visit the GDR every year bring with them not only delicacies and the latest fashions but also a great deal of information about health care in the FRG. All this is communicated mostly from the patient's point of view, but it also becomes clear that health workers in the West German MIC (especially physicians) are much better off economically than their East German colleagues. The fact that morbidity figures and life expectancy for all age groups are practically the same in the GDR as in the FRG does not mollify the East Germans' envy of the West German system.

## Acknowledgments

I would like to thank Mary Hess of the Osteuropa-Institut for translating this paper.

## Notes

1. Such assertions always contain the danger of chiefly informing the reader of the author's deficient knowledge of the literature. In spite of this, this statement appears to me to be unavoidable in the present text.

2. Article 9(5) of the GDR's constitution says that "foreign business, including foreign trade and currency exchange, is a state monopoly."

3. The domestic commodity purchases of the MIC furthermore lead to the induced employment of manpower in other areas of the economy through the demand for health supplies and services.

4. Good examples of such special taxes, in addition to mandatory health and retirement insurance, are the radio and television fees typical in West Germany.

5. For the sake of completeness, illegal trade in medications—which cannot be recorded statistically—should be mentioned at this point. However, it is unlikely that taking this trade into account would result in any substantial changes in the statements made here. In fact, the volume of such trade turnover is probably low enough to be statistically insignificant in terms of the cutoff criterion of 50 million marks.

6. Payments from the "social security budget": 7.8 billion marks; accident-insurance tax: 0.2 billion marks.

7. Health-insurance tax: 42.9 billion marks; accident-insurance tax: 7.2 billion marks.

8. In Klinkmüller 1979, persons demanding health care are listed as follows: the dying; the senile; hypochondriacs and the bored; psychosomatics and the stressed; victims of acute physiological illness; victims of work and household accidents; victims of traffic accidents; abusers of alcohol, tobacco, drugs, and food; those referred by third parties (relatives, employers, doctors); checkup clients; pregnant women; avoiders of risk and/or responsibility; and spongers and malingerers.

9. It cannot be proved, but seems plausible, that there is less awareness of these factors in reference to health propaganda than in the case of advertising in other branches of industry (for example, in the automobile industry).

10. According to Gustav Cassell's classic formulation, price has the function of reducing demand to the extent that it can be met by available supplies. Regulating health-care demand solely by means of price was already questioned long ago, out of socio-political considerations. Extending this criticism of regulation by price to include more and more areas has created a situation in which the market price now plays only a minor role in limiting demand for health care in both German states. In fact, the role of price can almost be disregarded from a macroeconomic point of view.

11. Incidentally, this applies to the social philosophy behind actual health-care expenditures. The extreme increase in expenditures for old-age pensioners cannot serve the purpose of getting them back into the work force. Such pensioners can be economically useful to the rest of society only as consumers, for example, of the goods and services offered by the MIC. Another aspect is the role of old-age pensioners as voters who can be influenced by health propaganda.

## References

Brown, A. A. 1961. "Centrally planned foreign trade and economic efficiency." American Economist 5:11–28.

Bryson, P. J., and E. Klinkmüller. 1975. "Eastern European integration: Constraints and prospects." Survey, No. 1/2 (94/95), pp. 101–127.

Feldstein, M. S. 1967. Econometric Analysis for Health Service Efficiency. Econometric Studies of the British National Health Service.

Illich, I. 1976. Limits to Medicine. London: Marion Boyars.

Kindleberger, C. P. 1968. International Economics, fourth edition. Homewood, IL: Irwin.

Klarman, H. E. 1965. The Economics of Health. New York: Columbia University Press.

Klarman, H. E., ed. 1974. Empirical Studies in Health Economics. Baltimore: Johns Hopkins University Press.

Klinkmüller, E. 1965. "Organisation und Planung der Aussenwirtschaft." In Sowjetunion: Das Wirtschaftssystem, ed. W. Markert. Cologne: Bohlau.

Klinkmüller, E. 1979. "Die Nachfrage nach Krankenversorgungsgutern." In Gleichgewicht, Entwicklung und soziale Bedingungen der Wirtschaft, ed. G. Ollenburg and W. Wedig. Berlin: Iuncker and Humblot.

Mampel, S. 1972. Die sozialistische Verfassung der Deutschen Demokratischen Republik. Frankfurt am Main: Metzner.

Mitzscherling, P., et al. 1974. DDR-Wirtschaft. Eine Bestandsaufnahme. Frankfurt: Fischer.

Perlman, M. 1974. The Economics of Health and Medical Care. Proceedings of a conference held by the International Economic Association.

Pritzel, K. 1978. Gesundheitswesen und Gesundheitspolitik der Deutschen Demokratischen Republic. Reports of Osteuropa-Institut, Freie Universität Berlin.

Wilczynski, J. 1965. "The theory of comparative costs and centrally planned economies." Economic Journal 75:63–80.

Wiles, P. J. D. 1968. Communist International Economics. Oxford: Blackwell.

# 3     Sociological Portraits of
       the Two Germanies

## Ulrich Lohmann

*In this chapter Ulrich Lohmann again provides important background material with many implications for health-care delivery in the two German states: the much lower population density in the GDR, the significant population of non-Germans in the FRG, the disparities in personal affluence, the claimed superior system of child care in the GDR, and the markedly greater amount of crime in the FRG, to mention a few of the contrasts. Most interesting are his conclusions about the ironic discrepancy between the philosophical values of each country and the criteria by which they measure progress. His conclusion—that neither German society has created conditions in which humans can live harmoniously—takes us to the heart of what an enlightened health-care system is concerned with. Although the GDR is somewhat ahead on this matter, it would appear that neither health-care system has organized itself to address the effects of stress and alienation on mind and body.*

## Population

The Federal Republic of Germany (FRG; West Germany) has a population of 61.3 million, of whom 6.5 percent are foreigners.[1] Most of the foreigners came to the FRG as "guest workers" in the period from the beginning of the 1960s to 1974. Starting with the largest group, the foreign population is made up primarily of Turks, Yugoslavians, Italians, Greeks, and Spaniards. The population of the German Democratic Republic (GDR; East Germany) is 16.8 million, including the Slavic Serbians in the area of Cottbus and Dresden, who make up 0.7 percent of the population (*DDR Handbuch* 1979, p. 60).

In both Germanies the age distribution of the population deviates from the normal pyramid in the cases of adults in the age groups of

63, 47, and 33 years. This is due to the lack of births resulting from World War I, the world economic depression, and World War II. However, the fact that more than 2 million Germans left the GDR to take refuge in the FRG from 1945 to 1961[2] has resulted in differences in age distribution, since more than half of these refugees were under 25 years of age (*DDR Handbuch* 1979, p. 401). When the population is divided into age-group decades persons between 30 and 70 make up a larger portion of the total population in the FRG, whereas in the GDR persons aged 70 and older are more highly represented (table 1).

In both the FRG and the GDR there are more women than men aged 52 years and up. This is a consequence of the two world wars. The percentage of women increases with age as well, as women have a longer average life span in both countries. The surplus of women between 30 and 80 years (greatest in the group between 50 and 60) is larger in the GDR than in the FRG; this can also be interpreted as a consequence of the population movement until 1961, since more men than women left the GDR (table 2).

In the FRG the average population density is 247 persons per square kilometer, with a minimum of 152 per km[2] in Lower Saxony and (calculated in terms of the area of the "Länder" which are not cities, i.e. Berlin, Bremen, and Hamburg) a maximum of 499 per km[2] in North Rhine-Westphalia. The average density in the GDR is considerably lower than that in the FRG; it is 155 per km[2] with a minimum of 58 per km[2] in the district Neubrandenburg and (once more in terms of districts only) a maximum of 324 per km[2] in the district Karl-Marx-Stadt. The lower population density in the GDR can partly be explained historically; before the war, fewer people lived there than in the area of the present-day FRG. The movement of refugees from the East to the West, the originally higher birth rate in the FRG, and the flow of foreign laborers into the FRG are additional factors affecting population density. Corresponding to population density, in the FRG there is also a higher degree of urbanization. Whereas 26 percent of West Germans live in communities with populations of less than 10,000, this figure is 44 percent for the GDR. Forty percent in the FRG and 31 percent in the GDR live in communities with a population range of 10,000–100,000, whereas cities with more than 100,000 inhabitants are home to 34 percent of West Germans and only 25 percent of East Germans (table 3). Areas of particular concentration of population and industry are (in the FRG) Hamburg and its vicinity, the Ruhr area, and the Frankfurt area and (in the GDR) the areas of Berlin and Karl-Marx-

**Table 1**
Population according to age (percentage by ten-year age groups).

|  | 0–10 | 10–20 | 20–30 | 30–40 | 40–50 | 50–60 | 60–70 | 70–80 | 80+ |
|---|---|---|---|---|---|---|---|---|---|
| GDR | 12 | 16 | 15 | 13 | 13 | 10 | 9 | 8 | 3 |
| FRG | 11 | 16 | 14 | 14 | 13 | 11 | 10 | 7 | 2 |

Sources: The sources for this and the following tables are the statistical yearbooks and volumes on social statistics for the FRG and the GDR, 1976–1979, unless noted otherwise.

**Table 2**
Population according to sex (number of men per 100 women in the given age group).

|  | 0–10 | 10–20 | 20–30 | 30–40 | 40–50 | 50–60 | 60–70 | 70–80 | 80+ |
|---|---|---|---|---|---|---|---|---|---|
| GDR | 105 | 105 | 105 | 101 | 99 | 64 | 58 | 59 | 43 |
| FRG | 105 | 105 | 104 | 107 | 105 | 75 | 65 | 60 | 41 |

**Table 3**
Percent population according to size of community.

|       | 1–10,000 | 10,000–100,000 | 100,000+ |
|-------|----------|----------------|----------|
| GDR   | 44       | 31             | 25       |
| FRG   | 26       | 40             | 34       |

**Table 4**
Percent population according to size of household (1971).

|       | 1  | 2  | 3  | 4  | 5+ |
|-------|----|----|----|----|----|
| GDR   | 10 | 22 | 23 | 23 | 21 |
| FRG   | 10 | 21 | 22 | 23 | 23 |

Stadt. Regional mobility, expressed in moves across municipal borders, is about twice as great in the FRG as in the GDR. Respectively, there are 49 and 24 such moves per 1,000 inhabitants. The probable reasons for this difference are the fact that the GDR is more agrarian, the greater job security in the GDR, and the greater difficulty in procuring living quarters in the GDR.

One element of community life—the structure of private households—is very similar in the FRG and the GDR. Tables 4 and 5 show that the distribution of persons by household size and the distribution of households by size are nearly the same for the two Germanies. In 1971, the average number of members of a household was 2.7 in the FRG and 2.6 in the GDR (Ballerstedt et al. 1979, p. 35). In both German states, households of one or two persons are dominant; however, the similar percentages of one-person households conceal the different biographical and social reasons for living alone. In the GDR, one-person households are, for the most part, those of women (82 percent), widowed persons (65 percent), and persons over 65 (57 percent). In the FRG, those who live alone are more often men (27 percent), single, married, or divorced persons (together, 45 percent), and persons under 65 years (52 percent). This could express being single as a chosen form of life.

In terms of marital status, a second element of micro-social community life, married persons are by far the largest sector of the population (viewed within age groups) in both German states (tables 6 and 7). Apart from this general finding, there are discernible differences; marriages in the GDR take place more frequently and at a younger age. For every 1,000 inhabitants, there are 5.8 marriages in the FRG and

**Table 5**
Percentage of households by number of members.

|       | 1  | 2  | 3  | 4  | 5+ |
|-------|----|----|----|----|----|
| GDR   | 26 | 28 | 20 | 15 | 11 |
| FRG   | 27 | 27 | 19 | 15 | 12 |

**Table 6**
Percent population according to marital status.

|       | Single | Married | Divorced | Widowed |
|-------|--------|---------|----------|---------|
| GDR   | 37     | 50      | 4        | 9       |
| FRG   | 39     | 49      | 3        | 9       |

8.4 in the GDR. The marriage partners are similarly divided into those who have never been married (81 percent in the FRG, 79 percent in the GDR), those who have been divorced (15 percent in the FRG, 18 percent in the GDR); and those who have been widowed (3 percent in both states). The average age of marriage is, for the FRG and the GDR respectively, for men 28.8 and 26.5 years and for women 25.5 and 23.9 years. The average age for first marriages is 25.7 (men) and 22.9 (women) in the FRG and 23.3 (men) and 21.4 (women) in the GDR. The housing situation could partially explain the numerous and early marriages in the GDR. Young persons who wish to leave home on their own or unmarried couples who wish to live together have great difficulties in procuring living quarters from the public housing administration. On the other hand, and in contrast with the situation in some areas of the FRG, pregnancy is no longer often considered a reason for marriage in the GDR. The frequency of divorce is also higher in the GDR—2.8 as opposed to 1.7 legal divorces per 1,000 inhabitants in 1976.[3] Reflecting a less strict Protestant concept of morality, legislation that has been more conducive to divorce since 1965 (allowing irreconcilability as grounds), and the greater economic and social independence of women (due to their widespread employment) may all be relevant to the frequency of divorce.

The natural movement of the population in the FRG is slightly on the decrease, with a birth rate of 9.4 and a death rate of 11.8 per 1000 inhabitants; in the GDR it is now stable, with 13.9 live births and the same number of deaths. In correlation, the fertility rate[4] is 45.5 in the FRG and 63.1 in the GDR (table 8). If only the German population is

**Table 7**
Population according to age group and marital status (percentage of the total population with marital status in the given age group).

|          |     | 0–15 | 15–30 | 30–45 | 45–60 | 60–75 | 75+ |
|----------|-----|------|-------|-------|-------|-------|-----|
| Single   | GDR | 100  | 57    | 6     | 5     | 5     | 7   |
|          | FRG | 100  | 66    | 10    | 7     | 7     | 9   |
| Married  | GDR | 0    | 41    | 86    | 82    | 59    | 32  |
|          | FRG | 0    | 33    | 84    | 82    | 60    | 31  |
| Divorced | GDR | 0    | 2     | 7     | 6     | 5     | 1   |
|          | FRG | 0    | 1     | 5     | 4     | 3     | 2   |
| Widowed  | GDR | 0    | 0     | 1     | 7     | 31    | 60  |
|          | FRG | 0    | 0     | 1     | 7     | 30    | 58  |

**Table 8**
Natural movement of the population (number per 1,000 inhabitants).

|     | Marriages | Divorces   | Live births | Deaths |
|-----|-----------|------------|-------------|--------|
| GDR | 8.4       | 2.8        | 13.9        | 13.9   |
| FRG | 5.8       | 1.7 (1976) | 9.4         | 11.8   |

considered, the general picture for the FRG is even more disadvantageous, as the percentage of births to foreigners is twice as great as their percentage of the population. The GDR acclaims this high birth rate as an expression of the people's faith in a safe, positive future under "real socialism"; yet the escape from an unfriendly society into the sphere of private family life could explain the greater desire to have children equally well. Independent of any consideration of motivation, childbirth has been made much easier for working women in the GDR (Vortmann 1978, p. 210). Since 1974, a woman who already has at least one child is released from work until the end of the new child's first year. In the FRG a half-year maternity leave was introduced in 1979, beginning with the first child; the effects of this remain to be seen.

## Gainful Employment and Occupational Activity[5]

In both the FRG and the GDR, 62 percent of the population are of working age (for men, 15–65 years; for women, 15–60 years[6]), 20 percent are children, and 18 percent have reached the age of retirement (table 9). Despite an equal work potential, the percentage of the population

**Table 9**
Work potential (percentage of the population in different age groups).

|       | Children | Working age | Retirement age |
| ----- | -------- | ----------- | -------------- |
| GDR   | 20       | 62          | 18             |
| FRG   | 20       | 62          | 18             |

**Table 10**
Employment rates (percent).

|       | Total population | Men | Women |
| ----- | ---------------- | --- | ----- |
| GDR   | 51               | 56  | 48    |
| FRG   | 44               | 57  | 32    |

who are gainfully employed in the FRG is 44 percent, notably different from the 51 percent of the population of the GDR who work (table 10). The proportion of men who work is virtually the same (57 percent in the FRG, 56 percent in the GDR); the difference can be located in the percentage of women who work—48 percent in the GDR and 32 percent in the FRG. In the GDR the integration of women of working age into the work process is almost complete—87 percent by 1977, as opposed to 52 percent in the FRG, where a considerable number of women are exclusively concerned with home and family (Kuhrig 1978, p. 52). Possible reasons for the high proportion of working women in the GDR are the permanent lack of labor power associated with the low level of productivity, a historical habit arising from the depletion of manpower after World War II, and the SED's advocacy of "the equal rights and equal duties of women to participate in societal production." In West and East, preference is given to one or the other of these explanations.

In the FRG there are more than 1 million unemployed; when these are subtracted from the potential labor force, the proportion of the total population that is gainfully employed is reduced to 42 percent. This is not the case in the GDR, where there is no (accounted) unemployment.

The distribution of persons actually engaged in the work process shows charactertistic divergences between the two German states. For example, while 6 percent of those gainfully employed in the FRG are engaged in agriculture (including forestry and fishing), this figure is 11 percent in the GDR.

**Table 11**
Percent employed by economic sphere (sector).

|      | Others | Agriculture | Industry, construction, skilled trades | Transportation, media | Trade | Services |
|------|--------|-------------|----------------------------------------|-----------------------|-------|----------|
| GDR  | 11     | 48          | 8                                      | 10                    | 20    | 3        |
| FRG  | 6      | 45          | 6                                      | 12                    | 29    | 2        |

Approximately equal proportions of the work force in East and West are occupied in the remaining spheres of material production (industry, construction, skilled trades), with 45 percent (FRG) and 48 percent (GDR) and in transportation and media, with 6 percent (FRG) and 8 percent (GDR). The FRG has somewhat higher proportions of the population occupied in commerce (12 percent, versus 10 percent in the GDR) and in services (29 percent, versus 20 percent in the GDR) (table 11). If these structural differences are ordered dynamically in a developmental and historical transition of the labor force from agriculture, through various intermediate stages, up to the "tertiary sector," the economy of the FRG must be considered more advanced than that of the GDR.

The question of the ratio of blue-collar and white-collar workers cannot be directly answered for the GDR, since the central (published) statistics of the GDR always indicate the groups in aggregate. The reason for this may be that any even relative depletion of the "proletariat" would be viewed as detrimental. According to the political and economic doctrine of the GDR, those involved directly in material production are the core of the proletariat and the most progressive sector of society; this group is also the legitimation of the "party of the proletariat" and of the "socialist state." The aggregation of the two groups may also be intended to hide the probable socio-economic differences between them and to emphasize their unity. For the year 1971, there is one remark in the literature that of all those "active in the economy," 65 percent are occupied in "predominantly physical" work and 35 percent in "predominantly mental" work (Grundmann et al. 1975, p. 175). If one compares these figures with those for blue-collar and white-collar workers in the FRG from that time, it appears that the proportion of blue-collar workers was eight points higher in the GDR than in the FRG (55 percent versus 47 percent). Since then, the

**Table 12**

Working people according to socio-economic position (percentage of working people with the position).

|       | Blue-collar workers | White-collar workers[a] | Members of collectives | Independent[b] | Cooperating family members |
|-------|---------------------|--------------------------|-------------------------|-----------------|-----------------------------|
| GDR   | (55)[c]             | 89                       | (30)                    | 9               | 2                           |
| FRG   | 42 (47)             | 87                       | 45 (37)                 | 9               | 4                           |

a. For GDR, civil servants are included.
b. For GDR, general partners and commissioned tradesmen are included.
c. Figures for 1971 are given in parentheses.

proportions of blue-collar and white-collar workers in the FRG have about evened out, to 45 percent and 42 percent respectively. Despite the same general tendency in the GDR, this point of balance has most likely not yet been reached there. It is probably accurate to estimate that blue-collar workers no longer make up the majority of working people in the GDR but still are the larger group (table 12).

Because of the differing forms of property in the FRG and the GDR, it is difficult to compare the labor forces; some economic categories are irreconcilably different. The members of collectives in agriculture and skilled trades, members of the legal boards, general partners (Komplementäre), and commissioned tradesmen in the GDR have no equivalents in the FRG. Likewise, autonomous business as it exists in the FRG has completely disappeared in industry and to a very large extent in agriculture and skilled trades in the GDR. However, despite the great incompatibility of the legal structures of the economy, the 11 percent in the GDR who belong to cooperatives or are engaged in private or self-employed activities can be roughly compared to the 13 percent in the FRG engaged in independent business (including participating family members). This comparison is legitimate, since the large majority of those independently employed in both the FRG and the GDR are similarly engaged in agriculture, commerce, or skilled trades, while the proportion of autonomous businessmen within industry in the FRG is socio-economically (but not necessarily politically) negligible.

The occupational and professional structure of the economically active population is a third dimension of economic life (table 13). The proportions of the population with university degrees are comparable (5 percent in the FRG and 6 percent in the GDR), especially if one adds

**Table 13**
Percent working people by educational qualification.

|  | University degree | Technical/ specialized university degree | Vocational school | Skilled training[a] |
|---|---|---|---|---|
| GDR | 6 | — | 11 | 60 |
| FRG | 5 | 2 | 6 | 53 |

a. For FRG, apprenticeships are included.

to this the 2 percent in the FRG with degrees from technical colleges (Fachhochschulen, for which there is no equivalent in the GDR). The figure for persons with vocational training is 11 percent in the GDR, and 6 percent in the FRG. This can be viewed as a result of the planning and management of education in the GDR, corresponding to general economic and technological needs and goals. There is also a larger proportion of skilled labor in the GDR, where the constitution (article 25, paragraph 4) says that "all young people have the right and the duty to learn an occupation." This proportion will increase further as older generations leave the labor force and are replaced by younger ones who have passed through the educational system of the GDR; eventually, almost 100 percent of working people will have had some vocational or professional training.

In the FRG the temporal framework of employment varies (table 14). The 5-day, 40-hour week has been generally agreed upon through labor contracts. Statistically, the large majority (2/3) of employed people work 40–41 hours per week; 1/5 work 42 hours or more, and the rest work fewer than 40 hours (including part-time employment). Average annual leave can be estimated at about 30 work days, in addition to 9–13 holidays (varying regionally). For both men and women, the maximum working age is 65, although retirement is possible 2–5 years earlier. Statistics suggest that early retirement is often preferred; the employment rate for the 60–65 age group is only 22 percent whereas that for the 55–60 age group is 64 percent. About 5 percent continue to work after reaching retirement age (Ballerstedt et al. 1979, p. 352). In the GDR the normal work week (centrally established by the state) is 43 3/4 hours over 5 days. For persons employed in a two-shift system, working hours are reduced to 42 hours; those in a three-shift system and other quantitatively insignificant groups work 40 hours per week.

**Table 14**
Working time, sick days, and labor disputes.

|     | Average no. of weekly working hrs. | Average no. of working weeks per year | Sick days per blue- and white-collar worker | Labor-dispute cases per blue- and white-collar worker |
| --- | --- | --- | --- | --- |
| GDR | 42 | 46 | 17 | 0.5 |
| FRG | 40–41 | 42 | 11 | 1.5 |

The percentage of people who work on a part-time basis in the GDR has not been published, but this figure probably does not differ greatly from that in the FRG. Annual leave in the GDR is normally 21 work days of base vacation, plus 1–5 extra days in case of strenuous working conditions or other social burdens. In addition, there are 7 paid holidays per year. The retirement age is set uniformly at 65 for men and 60 for women, but one out of every five persons continues to work after this age (Erbe et al. 1978, p. 390). Although some data are lacking or cannot be directly compared, it is safe to assume that the volume of work per working person in the GDR is about 1/10 higher than that in the FRG, and 3/10 higher per inhabitant. This follows from the greater number of working hours, days, and years in the GDR.

According to estimates from 1975, 19 percent of working people in the FRG are engaged in shift work (including night work), 22 percent of whom are dependent workers within production (i.e., industry, construction, and skilled trades) (Ballerstedt et al. 1979, p. 210). In the GDR in 1978, 43 percent of factory workers in centrally managed industry (about 0.9 million people) worked in shifts; these people made up 29 percent of blue-collar and white-collar workers within industry. Because there is comparatively little shift work in construction and skilled trades, the figures for the FRG and the GDR seem quite close.

From the available indicators of working conditions it can be established that there are 6.8 work accidents per 100 members of legally regulated accident insurance programs in the FRG, 3.1 per 100 in the GDR. Since the levels of technical safety installations may well be the same, the higher rate of accidents in the FRG may be due to a higher intensity of work, leading to a more rapid decrease of concentration and greater negligence. In the FRG 11 work days per year are lost because of sickness per member of legally regulated health insurance programs; in the GDR the figure is 17 work days per worker. As the general level of health is the same and working conditions appear to be safer in the GDR, this may be an expression of a lower motivation to work in the GDR. In the FRG, 20 work days are lost per year per 100 workers because of strikes and lockouts, which have no equivalent in the GDR. Legal disputes in the FRG lead to 1.5 complaints to the labor courts per year per 100 blue-collar and white-collar workers; for the same group in the GDR there are 0.5 such cases submitted to the Konfliktkommissionen, which govern labor disputes. It must remain open whether the lower frequency in the GDR is indicative of an absence of conflict or of a greater reluctance to contradict actions taken by the management. Empirical comparative investigations, which might provide information about work motivation and contentment, are normally impossible under existing political conditions. However, one point-by-point comparative study of construction and assembly workers in the two Germanies has (somewhat adventurously) been undertaken.[7] This study shows that 50 percent of those interviewed in the FRG like their work "well" or "very well," as opposed to 28 percent in the GDR; 5 percent (FRG) and 17 percent (GDR) do not like their work at all (Messing 1978, p. 125).

Comparison does not become any less difficult when one proceeds from this type of singular economic datum to macroeconomic quantities. On the basis of different concepts of society in East and West as well as on the basis of differing economic theories and different theories of work, different data and different relations between these data are generated. For example, Western economic statistics present the "gross national product" (GNP), an all-encompassing quantity, as the sum of the value of all goods produced and all services rendered in a given period of time. In contrast, the GDR calculates the "produced national income," which is "exclusively created by the productive labor of workers in industry, agriculture, construction, transportation, and the media, insofar as they contribute to material production, and to some extent by commerce" (Joswig 1979, p. 628). Besides the difficulties of all international comparisons, such as the differing forms of price setting and the distorted currency relations,[8] there is the additional difficulty in the East-West comparison that in the FRG all goods and services enter the accounts at their market value whereas the GDR is solely oriented toward material quantities supposedly determined by use value.[9] Other services, such as health and education, are considered as subsidiary functions assisting and supporting material production. To make any comparisons at all, it is necessary to recalculate the available East Ger-

**Table 15**
Estimates of GNP for the GDR.

| | Year of publication | Year of comparison | Index of artificially constructed "gross national product" of GDR (FRG = 100) |
|---|---|---|---|
| International Institute for Strategic Studies | 1974 | 1971 | 56 |
| Alton | 1974 | 1972 | 58 |
| U.S. Dept. of State | 1973 | 1972 | 62 |
| World Bank | 1977 | 1976 | 57 |
| Wilkens | 1978 | 1976 | 81 |

**Table 16**
Contributions of economic areas to 1976 GNP (in FRG prices).

| | GDR (percentage) | FRG (percentage) |
|---|---|---|
| Agriculture and forestry | 4 | 3 |
| Enterprises producing goods | 54 | 51 |
| Commerce and transportation | 17 | 15 |
| Services | 25 | 31 |

Source: Wilkens 1978.

man data according to Western patterns and estimates. The estimates made by Western authors appear in table 15.

According to Wilkens (1978, p. 52), the "Gross National Product" of the two German states is composed of the four economic areas outlined in table 16.

The per capita GNP of the GDR is about 4/5 that of the FRG; work productivity (taking into consideration the higher proportion of people who work in the GDR) is lower, about 2/3 that of the FRG. Reasons for this could be the narrower basis of raw materials in the GDR, the GDR's reparational services to the USSR after the war while the United States contributed to reconstruction in the FRG, the more modern machinery in the FRG, and the lower intensity of work in the GDR (due partly to the impossibility of giving notice and partly to a deficient work motivation resulting from overcentralized and external administrative control).

**Table 17**
Percent expenditure of gross national product, 1976.

|       | Investment | Private consumption | State expenses |
|-------|------------|---------------------|----------------|
| GDR   | 25         | 45                  | 29             |
| FRG   | 22         | 55                  | 23             |

Income, Consumption, and Style of Living

The 1976 figures concerning the use of funds indicate similar proportional expenditures for investment purposes (22 percent for the
FRG, 25 percent for the GDR) but a 10-percentage-point-higher figure
for private consumption in the FRG (55 percent, as opposed to 45
percent in the GDR) (Wilkens 1978, p. 52) (table 17). The proportion
of the GNP used for governmental expenditures in the GDR was 29
percent, 6 percentage points higher than the 23 percent in the FRG.
This is undoubtedly related to the greater expenditures for administration, defense, and national security in the GDR.

In 1977 the average monthly income of persons gainfully employed,[10]
the most important source of funds for private consumption, was 1,976
Deutsche Marks in the FRG and 830 East Marks in the GDR (DDR
Handbuch 1979, p. 54). Of these amounts, 598 DM in the FRG and
113 M in the GDR were paid in taxes and social security. With social
benefits (such as child support) and other kinds of income added, net
income was 1,632 DM (FRG) and 839 M (GDR). Differing rates of
employment (especially among married women) skew these figures
slightly to the benefit of the GDR; if family income is considered rather
than individual income, the averages are 2,489 DM in the FRG and
1,343 M in the DDR. Table 18 shows the stratification of net income
for blue-collar and white-collar workers and how much they differ in
the two Germanies. The average monthly retirement pension in 1977
paid 865 DM in the FRG and 292 M in the GDR, equivalent to 44
percent and 35 percent (respectively) of the average working income.
This difference helps explain the greater motivation in the GDR to
continue working past the retirement age. Pensions for widowed people
averaged 614 DM (FRG) and 240 M (GDR), and those for the disabled
495 DM (FRG) and 306 M (GDR).

In both the FRG and the GDR, the consumer benefits from the fact
that public funds largely pay for education, cultural institutions, health
care, and other social services. In the GDR, it must also be taken into

**Table 18**
Percent of blue-collar and white-collar households by net income, 1976. (Current figures for GDR follow in parentheses.)

|       | 1,000 marks | 1,000–2,000 marks | 2,000 marks |
|-------|-------------|-------------------|-------------|
| GDR   | 25 (20)     | 66 (68)           | 9 (12)      |
| FRG   | 4           | 39                | 57          |

**Table 19**
Income and assets (average amounts in East Marks or Deutsche Marks).

|       | Work income | Retirement pension | Saved assets |
|-------|-------------|--------------------|--------------|
| GDR   | 984         | 437                | 5,495        |
| FRG   | 1,632       | 865                | 7,717        |

consideration that "rent, tariffs, and consumer prices of food, industrial products used by the population, transportation, repairs and other services" (*Statistisches Jahrbuch* 1979 DDR, p. 248) are subsidized by the government with 145 M per month per working and retired person; this sum must be added to the GDR average income when comparing the figures (table 19).[11] Parallel to the income slope, personal assets are also higher in the FRG; the average saved capital is 7,717 DM per capita versus 5,495 M in the GDR.

The consumer expenditures of four-member households differ typically (table 20). In the GDR (the less developed economy) a larger proportion is spent on food and semi-luxury items, whereas the proportion spent on rent and related maintenance in the FRG is very high in comparison with the GDR. Although there may be a difference in the actual cost of living quarters, this may be balanced by the fact that in the GDR construction and maintenance are directly subsidized by the state, whereas in the FRG persons in lower income groups receive a portion of their rent in the form of welfare payments (Wohngeld). Also, the higher proportion of private expenditures in the FRG for education, entertainment, and recreation suggests a transition to a "postindustrial" style of living.

The pattern of consumption of food and semi-luxury items is more traditional in the GDR than in the FRG (table 21). Whereas in the GDR, 1.7 times as many potatoes and 1.4 times as much bread is eaten, the consumption of meat and fats is about equal. The West Germans eat

**Table 20**
Percent of consumer expenditures in a four-person household.

| | Food | Semi-luxury items | Clothing, shoes | Furnishing, household appliances | Education, entertainment, recreation | Rent and related expenses | Public transportation | Other goods and services |
|---|---|---|---|---|---|---|---|---|
| GDR | 31 | 10 | 15 | 8 | 4 | 5 | 1 | 26[a] |
| FRG | 25 | 4 | 9 | 7 | 10 | 21 | 1 | 23[a] |

a. Including 20 percent other industrial goods.
b. Including 12 percent expenditures for motor vehicles.

**Table 21**
Consumption of specified foods and semi-luxury items (per capita, in kilograms).

|  | Potatoes | Breads and cereals | Fats | Meat | Fresh and tropical fruits | Fresh vegetables |
|---|---|---|---|---|---|---|
| GDR | 139 | 88 | 26 | 86 | 48 | 65 |
| FRG | 83 | 64 | 26 | 87 | 101 | 72 |

**Table 22**
Percent of households with long-term consumer goods.

|  | Passenger vehicle | Television | Refrigerator | Washing machine |
|---|---|---|---|---|
| GDR | 34 | 87 | 99 | 79 |
| FRG | 62 | 93 | 96 | 81 |

10 percent more vegetables and more than twice as much fresh and tropical fruit.

East and West German households are equipped with electrical appliances, such as refrigerators and washing machines, to about the same degree, although the Western German appliances may well be technically more advanced (table 22). The FRG has slightly more television sets and a clearly greater number of automobiles. The West German lead in these areas increases if technological modernity is considered.

Living quarters in the GDR are older, smaller, and less well equipped, as indicated in table 23. In 1977, 60 percent of housing in the FRG but only 30 percent in the GDR had been built after 1945. The average size of a residence was approximately 77 square meters in the FRG and approximately 58 square meters in the GDR. The older housing in the GDR is equipped with less modern facilities, too. In the FRG 50 percent of all residences have central heat and 85 percent a bath, while in the GDR only 20 percent have central heat and 48 percent have a bath.

In the FRG, only 1 percent of children aged 0–3 years and 72 percent of children aged 3–6 years attend nursery schools or day-care centers; in the GDR 41 percent of children 0–3 and 90 percent of children 3–6 are cared for in similar institutions (table 24). This reflects the differing rates of employment of women. In schools, attended by all children aged 6 and older in both Germanies, there was a considerable difference in class size according to the data from 1976. The average class size

**Table 23**
Percent of living quarters, by age, size, and features, 1977. Source: *Zahlenspiegel* 1978.

|      | Built before 1919 | Built 1919–1945 | Built after 1945 | Size (m²) | With bath | With central heat |
|------|-------------------|-----------------|------------------|-----------|-----------|-------------------|
| GDR  | 50                | 20              | 30               | 58        | 48        | 20                |
| FRG  | 25                | 15              | 60               | 77        | 85        | 59                |

**Table 24**

|      | Percentage in day-care centers | Percentage in nursery schools | Students per class | Students per teacher |
|------|--------------------------------|-------------------------------|--------------------|----------------------|
| GDR  | 41                             | 90                            | 24.7 (23.5[a])     | 51.1                 |
| FRG  | 1                              | 72                            | 28.4               | 21.6                 |

a. 1976.

**Table 25**
Health-care resources per 10,000 inhabitants.

|      | Hospital beds | Physicians | Dentists | Pharmacists |
|------|---------------|------------|----------|-------------|
| GDR  | 106           | 19.3       | 5.3      | 2.1         |
| FRG  | 118           | 20.4       | 5.2      | 2.3         |

was 28.4 students in the FRG and 24.7 in the GDR (*Zahlenspiegel* 1978, p. 68). The superiority of the facilities in the GDR becomes even more evident in light of the student-teacher ratios of 21.6 in the FRG and 15.1 in the GDR.

The per capita availability of medical personnel and facilities seems to be about equal (table 25). Per 10,000 inhabitants, there are, in the FRG and GDR respectively, 118 and 106 hospital beds, 20.4 and 19.3 physicians, 5.2 and 5.3 dentists, and 2.3 and 2.1 pharmacists.

Statistics for the organization of time are approximately the same (table 26), showing 10.3 hours (FRG) and 9.4 hours (GDR) per day spent on the satisfaction of physiological needs, such as eating and sleeping.[12] The figures for time spent on housework are less similar: 2.6 hours (FRG) and 4.3 hours (GDR). In this case, more time was spent by the East Germans because of the greater rarity of electrical appliances, prepared (e.g., frozen) foods, and services (e.g., dry cleaning). The greater difference in the amount of per capita time at or related

**Table 26**
Time budget (1974), by percent.

|  | Professional activity[a] | Housework[b] | Satisfaction of physiological needs | Free time |
|---|---|---|---|---|
| GDR | 26 | 18 | 39 | 17 |
| FRG | 16 | 11 | 43 | 30 |

a. Including travel to and from work.
b. Including shopping and child care.

to work (3.9 hours per day in the FRG, 6.2 hours in the GDR) is due only partially to an actual difference in working hours; it reflects more the differing rates of employment, yielding data that should be taken as total societal averages and not primarily as individually applicable values. When the similar time expenditures for the satisfaction of physiological needs and the greater amount of time spent in the GDR on housework and professional work are considered, the average amount of free time in the FRG (7.2 hours) is almost twice that in the GDR (4.1 hours).

## Leisure Activities, Political Activities, and Communications

The most popular form of entertainment in both German states is television, and a large portion of the population of the GDR watches broadcasts from the FRG (table 27). The next most popular leisure activity in the GDR is work in the home and the garden; this reflects the lower degree of urbanization there. Third place in the GDR is held by taking walks and the like, which has second place in the FRG. Reading and socializing with relations and friends also rank high.

In 1977, 3.2 percent of West Germans were members of political parties (table 28). One million belonged to the SPD, 806,000 to the CDU/CSU, 78,000 to the FDP, 49,500 to the DKP/SEW, and 15,000 to the NPD. In the GDR, the SED had 2,044,000 members, the CDUD 115,000, the DBD 92,000, the NDPD 85,000, and the LDPD 75,000 members.[13] All told, 14.3 percent of East Germans belong to political parties. This enormously high rate of party affiliation need not imply an equally greater interest in politics in the GDR; because of the close connection between politics, the economy, culture, and science, membership in a party can be particularly useful for professional advancement. In the FRG, 9,092,103 or 42 percent of working people are

**Table 27**
Preferred leisure activities in FRG and GDR (percentage of those questioned who participate in activity named).

**FRG[a]**

| | |
|---|---|
| Watching television | 69 |
| Walks | 50 |
| Visiting friends, relatives | 45 |
| Reading newspapers | 43 |
| Listening to radio | 33 |
| Entertaining at home | 32 |
| Making repairs | 30 |
| Reading magazines | 29 |
| Reading books | 29 |
| Taking a drive | 29 |
| Playing or spending time with children | 27 |
| Working on garden or property | 26 |
| Handicrafts | 25 |
| Going to restaurants, bars | 21 |
| Going to sport events | 17 |
| Dancing | 17 |
| Cards, chess | 16 |
| Hiking | 16 |
| Sports | 14 |
| Cinema | 11 |
| Theater | 9 |
| Playing music, singing | 9 |
| Continued professional training | 8 |
| Concerts | 7 |
| Collections | 7 |
| Photography, painting | 6 |
| Visiting exhibits, museums | 5 |
| Going to lectures, meetings | 4 |

**GDR[b]**

| | |
|---|---|
| Watching television | 64 |
| Working on home and garden | 59 |
| Hiking, walking, excursions | 56 |
| Spending free time with children | 51 |
| Reading books, listening to radio or records | 49 |
| Working on automobile | 34 |
| Going to organized entertainment events (dances, etc.) | 31 |
| Going to sport events | 26 |
| Cards, chess, etc. | 25 |
| Theater, concerts, performances | 24 |
| Spending time with friends | 23 |
| Handiwork | 23 |
| Cinema | 23 |

**Table 27** (continued)

| | |
|---|---:|
| **GDR**[b] (continued) | |
| Going out for a beer | 22 |
| Crafts | 14 |
| Active involvement in sports | 13 |
| Lectures and other generally educational events | 11 |
| Collecting stamps, coins | 8 |
| Other hobbies | 4 |
| Artistic activity | 3 |
| **GDR**[c] | |
| Watching television | 73 |
| Working in garden or yard | 55 |
| Sports, hiking, walks | 51 |
| Reading | 47 |
| Spending time with friends and acquaintances | 44 |
| Socializing or dancing | 38 |
| Hobbies (collecting, gardening or breeding, crafts) | 26 |
| Concerts and theater | 22 |
| Cinema | 19 |
| Card games, board games, etc. | 19 |
| Studying | 10 |
| Artistic activity | 7 |
| Scientific, technical hobbies | 6 |

a. Source: Noelle-Neumann 1977, pp. 44 ff.
b. Source: Steitz 1979, pp. 96 ff.
c. Source: Hanke 1979, p. 75.

organized in unions. The union in the GDR has 8,557,500 members; this number is greater than the sum of all blue-collar and white-collar workers taken together, so numerically union membership exceeds 100 percent. Sports-club members number 1.2 million people in the FRG (18 percent of the population); in the GDR, the government-controlled Turn- und Sportbund (Exercise and Sport Association) has 2.9 million members, or 17 percent of the population. The Protestant and Catholic churches in the FRG each have about 26.7 million members; together, Christians make up 88 percent of the population. In the GDR, 9.6 million people are members of a Protestant church and 1.3 million belong to the Catholic church; thus, Christians constitute 65 percent of the population in the GDR. These figures cannot be directly equated with the degree of religious belief and practice. In the FRG, for instance, church taxes are automatically collected by governmental financial authorities; a specific explanation before a court is required for withdrawal from the church and abolition of the duty to pay these taxes.[14]

**Table 28**

Rates of organization (percentage of population).

|     | Political parties | Unions (working people only) | Associations | Churches |
| --- | --- | --- | --- | --- |
| GDR | 14 | 100 | 17 | 65 |
| FRG | 3 | 42 | 18 | 88 |

**Table 29**

|     | Volkshochschule[a] | Company-sponsored adult education[b] | Theater[a] | Cinema[a] |
| --- | --- | --- | --- | --- |
| GDR | 3 | 14 | 65 | 500 |
| FRG | 6 | 6 | 35 | 200 |

a. Per 100 inhabitants.
b. Per 100 workers.

In the FRG, 6 percent of the population participate in adult educational courses (general and professional) at Volkshochschulen (public institutions of adult education) and 5.6 percent of working people further their education through opportunities provided by employers (table 29). In the GDR there is a greater emphasis on continuation of professional training, in which 14.1 percent of working people participate within the framework of their place of work; only 3.4 percent of the population is enrolled in courses of the Volkshochschulen.

About 1/3 of the West Germans have attended the theater, whereas almost 2/3 of the East Germans have done so. This is due partly to collectively organized (and perhaps enforced) visits to ideologically desirable plays in the GDR. Films are also much more popular in the GDR; the average is about 5 visits to the cinema per capita per year versus less than 2 in the FRG.

In 1977, 48,736 book titles were published in the FRG (table 30). The 1978 figure for the GDR, 5,096, is barely 1/8 of the West German figure. This is an expression of the economic, political, and cultural control in the GDR. The quantitative ranking of fields represented by this figure is identical, which indicates an identical structure of the need for information. In both Germanies, the largest proportion is political literature[15] (28 percent in the FRG and 21 percent in the GDR). Next come literary texts (19 percent in the FRG and 20 percent in the GDR). Third place is taken by literature in the fields of mathematics,

**Table 30**
Data on publications (1977).

|      | Book titles[a] | Magazines[b] | Newspapers[c] |
|------|----------------|--------------|---------------|
| GDR  | 5,906          | 1            | 181           |
| FRG  | 48,736         | 2            | 114           |

a. Number.
b. Copies per capita per issue.
c. Copies per capita per year.

**Table 31**
Communications (number per capita per year).

|      | Letters | Packages | Local telephone calls | Long-distance telephone calls |
|------|---------|----------|-----------------------|-------------------------------|
| GDR  | 74      | 3        | 75                    | 37                            |
| FRG  | 188     | 8        | 171                   | 96                            |

natural sciences, and technology (10 percent in the FRG and 16 percent in the GDR). The FRG has a quantitative lead in the production of magazines, with a 1976 average of 2 copies per date of publication per capita, twice as high as the 1978 average for the GDR. The GDR leads in the publication of newspapers, with 181 copies per capita per year versus 114 in the FRG (1976). The newspapers with the largest distribution are, in the FRG, *Bild* (a tabloid) and, in the GDR, *New Germany: Organ of the Central Committee of the SED.*

In the FRG, there is more than twice as much technically mediated individual communication as in the GDR (table 31). Per capita per year, there are 188 letters conveyed in the FRG and 74 in the GDR, 8 and 3 packages, and 171 and 75 local and 96 and 37 long-distance telephone calls, respectively.

The West German uses local public transportation 106 times a year, the East German 117 times a year (table 32). In view of the greater density of passenger vehicles in the FRG and the greater individual traffic this implies, greater local mobility in the FRG is indicated. The same picture appears in the case of long-distance transportation. Public buses and trains are used 121 times per year in both the FRG and the GDR, but the West Germans are probably more mobile when personal vehicles are also taken into account. Every other West German travels by air, versus barely every tenth East German.

**Table 32**
Traffic movements (number per capita per year).

|       | Local public transportation | Public motor and railway transportation | Air travel | Vacation trips |
|-------|----------------------------|----------------------------------------|-----------|----------------|
| GDR   | 117                        | 121                                    | 0.1       | 50             |
| FRG   | 106                        | 121                                    | 0.5       | 50             |

In both the FRG and the GDR every second resident travels on vacation; in the FRG roughly every third person, and in the GDR every eighth person, travels abroad (East Germans to communist-controlled countries only).

Corresponding to the greater amount of general traffic, there are twice as many personal injuries through traffic accidents in the FRG as in the GDR (62 versus 34 per 10,000 inhabitants). (The GDR figure includes material damages over the value of 300 East Marks.) When related to the density of motor vehicles, the frequency of accidents is about the same: 1.5 accidents per 100 vehicles in the FRG and 1.3 in the GDR.

## Deviant Behavior and Special Problem Groups

Crime is significantly higher in the FRG than in the GDR (table 33). Even when the differing ranges of activities defined as criminal, the proportions of unreported incidences, and statistical inaccuracies are taken into account, the difference is clear: 4,131 crimes per 100,000 inhabitants in the FRG versus 559 in the GDR. The reasons for this given in the literature are the permissiveness of West German society, the social networks and controls in the GDR, and the higher standard of living in the FRG. It is also conceivable that the greater technical, ecological, and psycho-social stress of the more developed West German industrial society leads to more normatively deviant behavior. The incidences of various kinds of criminal acts are comparable. In both German states crimes against property are the most common—74 percent in the FRG and 50 percent in the GDR.

Alcoholism is more difficult to grasp and compare quantitatively (table 34), as the definition and the application of the term are more ambiguous and certain conscious or unconscious intentions can enter into the data. The numbers of alcoholics given are approximately 1

**Table 33**
Crimes committed per 100,000 inhabitants.

|      | Premeditated murder | Premeditated bodily injury[a] | Crimes against property | Sex-related crimes |
|------|------|------|------|------|
| GDR  | 1 | 70 | 472 | 16 |
| FRG  | 4 | 86 | 3,971 | 70 |

a. For FRG, grievous only.

**Table 34**
Deviant and problem groups (number per 1,000 inhabitants).

|      | Criminal actions | Alcoholism | Suicides (1970) | Recipients of social-welfare payments or services |
|------|------|------|------|------|
| GDR  | 8 | (8) | 0.3 | 1 |
| FRG  | 54 | 16 | 0.2 | 22 |

million (1.6 percent of the population) for the FRG and 140,000 (0.8 percent) in the GDR (Ballerstedt et al. 1979, p. 365; *Gesellschaftliche Daten* 1977, p. 288; Herber 1978, p. 35). However, this relation seems dubious when the consumption of alcohol is compared. The per capita consumption is 146 liters (FRG) and 130 liters (GDR) of beer, 3.0 liters (FRG) and 3.9 liters (GDR) of pure alcohol in the form of hard liquor, and 23.8 liters (FRG) and 8.9 liters (GDR) of wine, including champagne. While the consumption of beer is about the same, the 1.3 times greater consumption of hard liquor does not indicate a lower rate of alcoholism in the GDR, since spirits are often consumed in order to induce intoxication whereas wine and champagne are generally more social drinks.[16]

Data on suicide are not made public in the GDR. The last figure, disclosed in a Polish publication, was 30.5 suicides per 100,000 inhabitants for the year 1970 (Jarosz 1978). For the same year, the figure for the FRG was 21.5. However, it would be premature to relate the higher rate of suicide in the GDR directly to the political system, since in the part of Germany that constitutes the GDR today the suicide rate has always been higher by the same percentage (Oschlies 1976).

In the FRG 1.4 million people (2.2 percent of the population) receive social welfare payments or services, and in the GDR 0.2 million (0.1 percent). The difference here is a result of the socio-economic integration in the GDR; or on the other hand, of the greater possibility of individual autonomy, and hence of personal failure, in the FRG.

## Conclusion

Any attempt at comparing the preceding data about the two societies and their various institutional spheres entails the problem of finding an appropriate scale, a common unit, with which to measure the relative position of each society. A dynamic developmental perspective might then produce some answers, whether one assumes a more or less uniform pattern of development for all societies or a model of separation and convergence.

It is clear that such a scale—by necessity highly abstract—would be subject to the same inexactness and vulnerability to criticism that generally attaches to high-level theoretical and ideological concepts. What would be the important elements and criteria that would constitute such a scale: the economy, with its system of production and distribution, the polity, with its concern for participation and preservation of individual rights and interests, or the cultural domain, including science and morality? A look at history is not particularly enlightening. Is history the realization of a divine plan, or of the Hegelian absolute spirit? Is it the evolution of human reason and rationality, a consequence of recurring class struggles, or an evolutionary accident?

The most widely accepted Western theory employs the concept of the "industrial society" which is in the process of being replaced by the "post-industrial society" (Aron 1964; Friedmann 1964; Rostow 1960; Bell 1973). According to this theory, the chief criteria of social change are the following:

planned production based on systematic division of labor and automation,

a shift from the manufacturing to the tertiary service sector,

increasing urbanization connected with the two preceding developments,

a general trend toward intellectualization of organization, production, and reproduction,

a high degree of material consumption, and

increased and enriched time for leisure and self-education.

By these standards, the FRG is clearly ahead except in the area of formal education (where the gap is expected to close in the future).

The GDR, on the other hand, views these developments from the perspective of historical materialism and applies the standards connected with changing modes of production, but with the emphasis on social rather than technological determinants (*Grundlagen des historischen Materialismus* 1976). A comparison between the FRG and the GDR in these terms would stress such factors as the private ownership of the means of production and the exploitation of labor as well as the political and cultural oppression of the proletariat. By these standards the FRG could be said to be at an earlier historical stage, as the GDR has not only largely abolished private property but also instituted the domination of the working class.

Looking at these conclusions, one is initially surprised that the West, which normally assigns priority to the human spirit, should be employing technological and economic concepts such as "industrial society," while the East, generally credited with a materialistic world view, should use political and social criteria. This contradiction is resolved when one considers Lenin's modifications of Marxist theory. According to Marx, there is a close connection between the forces and means of production on the one hand and the relations of production and property on the other. The technologically less developed East German and East European societies are therefore not yet ready for socialism, and the so-called "socialist" political, legal, and cultural constitutions of these countries must be seen as futile attempts to impose and graft an unnatural social order on them. Thus, this original version of Marxism—like the Western bourgeois theory—assigns primacy to the economic sector as a criterion for social development, thereby giving the FRG the advantage once again.

One might ask, however, whether both these conceptions, being products of the nineteenth century, are not too short-sighted and one-dimensional. It seems that social-psychological and cultural dimensions need to be given at least equal attention in an adequate evaluation of society, as, for example, the "Frankfurt School" with its psychoanalytic approach, has tried to do. Is a society really more developed and "progressive" if the actual amount of human labor is reduced but the tensions produced by work and leisure increase disproportionately, when man becomes one-dimensional (Marcuse 1967) under the impact of coerced production and when reproduction and material possessions must compensate for a loss of being (Fromm 1976)? Medical science takes cognizance of these facts with the concept of psychosomatic illness, and it seems that the social sciences too must learn to employ a multidimensional perspective.

From a multidimensional perspective it is difficult to ignore that such indicators of stress and tension as crime, alcoholism, and drug abuse are increasing in East and West Germany. This shows that both states are apparently unable to create the conditions that will allow man to live in harmony with himself. In both, man does not exist for himself, in the center of the social order, but is merely an instrument, either for the realization of "objective laws" defined by the party, as in the GDR, or for competition and the maximization of profit and property, as in the FRG.

## Notes

1. Unless otherwise noted, all data have been taken or calculated from the 1979 *Statistischen Jahrbücher* for the FRG and the GDR. All data include West and East Berlin, respectively.

2. The Berlin Wall was built in the summer of 1961. For the FRG, emigration beyond national borders was rated at 8.3 moves per 1,000 inhabitants in 1977. Such moves are not allowed for people under retirement age in the GDR.

3. In 1977 a change in divorce legislation in the FRG became effective, the immediate result of which was a delay in the procedure; consequently, the figures for 1977 to the present cannot yet be considered typical.

4. Live births per 1,000 women aged 15–45.

5. These two differing concepts reflect the fact that in the GDR income cannot be gained through the investment of capital, and also that the meaning of work in the pluralistic public consciousness of the FRG cannot be defined as to content but only as to its purpose of acquiring income.

6. In the FRG the age limit is the same for men and women, but flexible; in the GDR it is fixed but it differs for men and women.

7. A labor psychologist who had fled the GDR established himself in the FRG with an empirical study (not intended for publication) he had conducted; a "methodically comparable" study was to be undertaken in the FRG. See Messing 1978, p. 9.

8. These difficulties are particularly great in the case of East–West comparisons, because of the difference between market and planned prices and because the currency standards of socialist countries are purely internal standards for which the exchange rate is established administratively and (for the most part) independent of buying power.

9. As the tertiary sector expands, the basis of calculation deviates increasingly from that in the FRG.

10. This is according to Wilkens (1978, p. 47). He stresses that the tendential increase of the index number indicates not a real closing of the gap between the GDR and the FRG but a difference in the methods of calculation.

11. Through this "price distortion" it can be determined more exactly which population groups can afford which goods and services.

12. Calculated and partially estimated according to *Gesellschaftlichen Daten 1977*, p. 155, and Schmunk 1975, p. 271.

13. For an explanation of the names and features of the parties, see the beginning of chapter 2 in this volume.

14. The levy of a church tax by the state originated in the Roman Catholic western and southwestern parts of Germany as a result of the large-scale expropriation of church property by Napoleon I, which was compensated for by state financial and administrative support for cultural activities. In predominantly Protestant Prussia, the close alliance of church and state led to a similar outcome (as in Great Britain). The Weimar Republic continued this practice but, in accordance with the principle of religious neutrality, extended its support to religious communities of all persuasions. Under National Socialism, church and state were separated for political reasons and there were some attempts to weaken the church. The FRG restored the old system, but the GDR maintained the separation for ideological reasons.

15. For the FRG, political literature includes: philosophy and psychology; law and administration; economics, sociology, and statistics; politics and defense; education, pedagogics, and child care; and history, cultural history, and ethnology.

16. Twice as many people died of liver cirrhosis in the FRG; the figures are 28 in the FRG and 13 in the GDR per 100,000 inhabitants.

17. This confuses even Marxist-Leninist theoreticians. Berger and Mocek (1976) state: "This is the astonishing fact: Bell's criteria for the post-industrial society are taken directly from Marx."

## References

Aron, R. 1964. Die industrielle Gesellschaft. Frankfurt am Main and Hamburg: Fischer.

Ballerstedt, E., et al. 1979. Sozialogische Almanach: Handbuch gesellschaftlicher Daten und Indikatoren. Third edition. Frankfurt am Main and New York: Campus.

Bell, D. 1973. The Coming of the Post-Industrial Society. New York: Basic.

Berger, D., and R. Mocek. 1976. Bürgerliche Gesellschaftstheorien: Studien zu den Weltanschaulichen Grundlagen und ideologischen Funktionen bürgerlicher Gesellschaftsauffassungen. East Berlin: VEB.

DDR Handbuch. 1979. Second edition. Cologne: Wissenschaft und Politik.

Erbe, G., et al. 1978. Politik, Wirtschaft und Gesellschaft in der DDR. Opladen: Westdeutscher Verlag.

Friedmann, G. 1964. Industrial Society. Glencoe, Ill.: Free Press.

Fromm, E. 1976. Haben oder Sein: Die seelischen Grundlagen einer neuen Gesellschaft. Stuttgart: Deutsche Verlagsanstalt.

Gesellschaftlichen Daten 1977. Bonn: Eigenverlag.

Grundlagen des historischen Materialismus. 1976. East Berlin: Dietz

Grundmann, S., M. Lötsch, and R. Weiding. 1975. Zur Entwicklung der Arbeiterklasse und ihrer Struktur in der DDR. East Berlin: Dietz.

Hanke, M. 1979. Freizeit in der DDR. East Berlin: Dietz.

Herber, F. 1978. Alkohol. East Berlin: Volk und Gesundheit.

Jarosz, M. 1978. "Suicides in Poland." Polish Sociological Bulletin 2:87-100.

Joswig, W., ed. 1979. Wörterbuch der Okonomie: Sozialismus. Fourth edition. East Berlin: Dietz.

Kuhrig, H., ed. 1978. Zur gesellschaftlichen Stellung der Frau in der DDR: Sammelband. Leipzig: Verlag für die Frau.

Marcuse, H. 1967. Der eindimensionale Mensch. Neuwied and Berlin: Luchterhand.

Messing, M. 1978. Arbeitszufriedenheit im Systemvergleich: Eine empirische Studie an Bau- und Montagearbeitern in beiden Teilen Deutschlands. Stuttgart: Kohlhammer.

Noelle-Neumann, E., ed. 1977. Allensbacher Jahrbuch der Demoskopie, volume 7. Vienna: Molden.

Oschlies, W. 1976. "Selbstmorde in der DDR und in Osteuropa." Deutschland Archiv, Köln: Wissenschaft und Politik 1:38-55.

Rostow, W. W. 1960. The Stages of Economic Growth. Cambridge University Press.

Schmunk, G. 1975. Marxistisch-leninistische Sozialpolitik. East Berlin: Tribune.

Statistisches Jahrbuch 1979 der Deutschen Demokratischen Republik. East Berlin: Staatsverlag.

Steitz, L. 1979. Freizeit—Freie Zeit. East Berlin: VEB.

Vortmann, M. 1978. "Geburtenzunahme in der DDR - Folge des 'Babyjahres.' " Vierteljahreshefte zur Wirtschaftsforschung 3:210-232.

Wilkens, M. 1978. Sozialproduktvergleich zwischen der Bundesrepublik Deutschland und der DDR. Cologne: Bundesinstitut für ostwissenschaftliche und internationale Studien.

Zahlenspiegel: Bundesrepublik Deutschland/Deutsche Demokratische Republik—Ein Vergleich. 1978. Bonn: Gesamtdeutsches Institut.

# II

# The Social History of German Health Care

# 4 The Origin and the Development of Compulsory Health Insurance in Germany

## Peter Rosenberg

*Peter Rosenberg describes the social, economic, and political forces that have shaped the German health insurance system. Rosenberg outlines the sociological changes in working conditions, family life, and community ties that accompanied the rise of a new class of industrial workers. Bismarck's national health insurance plan was designed to address these problems in a way that would tie the workers to the state and wean them away from the Social Democrats. However, the principles of self-government and worker community prevailed, thereby providing a new political vehicle for working-class politics.*

*In time, physicians protested against workers' sickness funds managing medical services and fostering competition for service contracts between doctors. Their protest led to the organization of the medical profession as a political force. With the help of employers and the National Socialist Party, the medical profession succeeded in eliminating the democratic structure of the sickness funds, the majority rule of workers, and the existence of direct elections to boards of directors. Little of this democratic tradition was restored after World War II in the FRG, and in the GDR the state took over in the name of all workers.*

*In his conclusion, Rosenberg raises the same issue as Lohmann: that the current health-care system in the FRG pays little attention to the social and psychological factors affecting health and is weak on preventive medicine. He also notes the artificial separation of social policy from health policy, which renders the latter relatively powerless. Rosenberg shows once again in another place and time how political and social values influence the organization of health-care services.*

The system of legal health insurance in the Federal Republic of Germany (FRG; West Germany) covers 90 percent of the population today.[1]

In 1978 it financed medical services and income transfers for patients who were unemployed to the amount of approximately 86 billion marks, which corresponds to 6.3 percent of the gross national product. In 1978 approximately 1,300 sickness funds existed, structured according to regional, professional, and industrial criteria. The large number of sickness funds, their institutional structure, and numerous parts of the Leistungsrecht (the law governing the distribution and kinds of medical services offered in the sickness funds) are intelligible only on the basis of their history.

Since the passing of the first Reichsgesetzes über Krankenversicherung (National Law for Health Insurance) in 1883, an empire has disappeared, the first democratic German state and the National Socialist dictatorship have come and gone, two world wars have caused far-reaching political, economic, and social changes, and Germany has been divided.

In spite of Germany's eventful history, a few important institutional and functional principles established by Bismarck have stood unchanged in the FRG. Although not all historical traces of these principles have been erased in the German Democratic Republic (GDR; East Germany), political developments there have caused some major changes in the health insurance system.

## The Development of Germany from an Agrarian to an Industrial Society

A historical analysis of social security and particularly of health insurance must go back to the beginning of the nineteenth century. Not only did decisive economic and social changes take place then, but the policy debate and the formation of political forces that have been influential until today started during that period.

### Economic and Social Conditions

Until the end of the nineteenth century, half of the population was engaged in agriculture, the rest primarily in trade and commerce. At the beginning of the nineteenth century there were approximately 300,000 factory workers in the area of the future German Reich. Their numbers grew to 2,000,000 by 1867 and then rapidly to 12,000,000 by 1900. Thus a new social class developed which included almost half the population by the turn of the century (Rosenberg 1969).

Such a rapid economic and occupational restructuring was bound to cause difficulties in an agricultural, feudal, caste society. Politically the situation became particularly difficult because the new class of industrial workers lived under conditions of economic uncertainty and social alienation. In agriculture and trade there were ties between worker and employer that encompassed more than the economic relationship (such as providing housing and food in case of sickness), in the factory work contracts obligated the employer to pay only for the actual labor performed. In case of accident, illness, or inability to work, the worker was immediately left without income. Only if he was completely destitute did he receive communal assistance for the poor. The use of this assistance was connected with demeaning conditions (for instance, loss of the right to vote). The loss of income was all the more consequential because the factory worker did not board with the employer and had to rent his own housing (Schmoller 1918).

The lack of social ties was enhanced by the fact that industry did not develop in all regions but became concentrated in specific locations. The workers leaving their rural setting and their social network had to move to metropolitan areas. Whereas at the beginning of the nineteenth century 90 percent of the population lived in rural areas, at the end of the century 50 percent lived in cities. The move to the cities not only destroyed neighborhood networks but also weakened the family as wives and children had to seek work to compensate for the man's low wages—a move that drove wages down still further. The following characteristics describe the economic and social situation of the new class (Rosenberg 1969, p. 49):

a. loss or devaluation of traditional risk-sharing networks, such as neighborhood and family,

b. dependence upon continuous income, which could be severed,

c. growing expenses for life-sustaining needs,

d. greater risk of illness, due to long working hours and poor working conditions,

e. insufficient coverage of living expenses and provisions for the future (old age, illness, unemployment).

The Intellectual and Political Debate

The early nineteenth century was largely influenced by the French ideas of Rationalism. The concept of man as a rational being able to determine his own fate rationally and responsibly and without divine guidance was welcomed by all who felt restricted by moral, religious, and traditional norms. The elevation of reasoning as the sole standard of human behavior meant that the ethical categories of good and bad, just and unjust were transformed into "rational" and "irrational" behavior.

Whether this greatly reduced image of man was really accepted or whether it was just supported for tactical reasons, in the final analysis it influenced the two diametrically opposed philosophies of individualism and collectivism. In the economic and political debate these two directions found their clearest expression in liberalism and communism, respectively (Hofmann 1962; Knies 1883; Smith 1864).

Beyond their common basis of Rationalism, both "schools" rejected any system of social security but for very different interests. The ideas of liberalism were primarily supported by industrialists and academic theorists. The theory of Adam Smith and his successors that individual economic freedom and unfettered competition would automatically result in a fair distribution of income seemed compelling. The national insurance system was not appropriate for this concept because the responsibility of each single person, and with it his economic freedom of action, would be paralyzed. Moreover, liberals argued that the additional costs would endanger the ability to compete in the international market. On the other hand, the representatives of radical socialism or communism believed that only revolutionary action could establish a just income and a just society. To them, reducing social conflict through a national insurance system did not seem to be a solution because they feared that, at least temporarily, this would weaken the revolutionary potential of the working class.

Economic development in the area of the future German Reich seemed to support the representatives of economic liberalism. Trade between the German states flourished, industry created new jobs, and only in a few regions were there problems with the laborers. No unions had as yet been established that would safeguard the interests of the labor force. At the beginning of the nineteenth century, therefore, criticisms of liberalism were rare in the academic and the political arenas.

During the middle of the nineteenth century, however, an intellectual tendency called Realism arose to criticize absolutistic claims, as well as liberal and radical socialist teachings, and gained political importance (Rosenberg 1969, pp. 54 ff; Roscher 1924). Its representatives not only prepared the intellectual basis for political order but also contributed to the political debate on the legal organization of social security for the population (especially the working class). The representatives of this realism held the following general opinions:

- The social situation of the working classes was very bad, and their integration into the national community could be achieved only through a concept of national social policy.

- It was necessary to set up a legally regulated compulsory insurance because large groups of workers were unable to provide for themselves materially as well as morally.

- Certain forms of welfare were rejected as general solutions for social security of the working class because they reduced the dignity of man. For example, those who received welfare in Prussia lost their right to vote.

- Compulsory insurance should be limited to covering a minimum number of services.

- The insured should have a considerable share in the administration of the insurance system in order to create a sense of responsibility.

Although high-ranking representatives of the Protestant and Roman Catholic churches criticized the social conditions and therefore stirred interest in social reforms among their followers, the attitudes of both toward social policy were ambivalent. The Protestant national church of Prussia refrained from criticizing the king of Prussia, who was at the same time the bishop. The Catholic Church rejected mandatory insurance with the argument that it contradicted the subsidiary principle of natural law as taught by the Church. According to this concept, each person is primarily responsible for himself. Only if he and his closest community (family, church) could not offer sufficient protection would the state, as the largest community, be responsible. In various publications, however, it became apparent that it was not only the subsidiary principle that prevented the Catholic Church from agreeing to the concept of compulsory insurance but also the consideration that the influence the Church exerted through social institutions of its own might diminish if public institutions were to be established.

This study is limited to a brief presentation of the intellectual and political discussion between 1800 and approximately 1870. However, it should be clear that, though no social consensus existed when the German Reich was founded in 1871, the situation of the working class desperately required political action.

## Protection in Case of Sickness before 1883

Before the uniform national compulsory insurance system came into effect under Bismarck in 1883, certain groups of the population were protected in case of illness (Peters 1959). Property owners and people with high income could insure themselves privately if they did not wish to risk having to cover an illness directly. Agricultural laborers usually received most of their yearly salary in benefits such as room and board. In case of illness they at least did not suffer from loss of income; however, they could not pay for medication and physicians' fees.

Since the sixteenth century the miners had had institutions of self-help. In the beginning the miners were shareholders of the mines, so it was not originally a workers' insurance system. It became one only after the separation of capital and labor necessitated by the larger amounts of funds necessary to run the mines. During that period the miners' various organizations were generally threatened. As far back as 1784 the existing sickness funds were legally protected in Prussia, and in 1854 all enterprises of mines, foundries, and salt mines in Prussia were legally obligated to join. The body of miners' sickness funds therefore represented the first regulated compulsory insurance in the area of the future German Reich. Their services included sick pay, medication, and rehabilitation.

Artisans too were partially protected through their employers, directly or else through their own sickness funds, against illness, accident, and old age. As a rule, two-thirds of the premiums were paid by the employee and one-third by the employer. Employees managed the sickness funds with the assistance of a master tradesman representing the employer. In 1845, social legislation began with a Prussian law authorizing communities to require (if they chose) both the employer and the employees in an artisan shop to join the sickness funds (Hilfskassen) of their guild. For the factory workers no insurance existed until 1845. Because of political pressure from the industrial employers, however, this law was rarely enforced. In 1876, nationally uniform legal regulations concerning minimum contributions, state supervision, and the management of these sickness funds were enacted. Not everybody, however, was obligated to join. Since the employers did not have to contribute to the financing and since the benefits were often insufficient, the workers did not always utilize the sickness funds; they preferred to depend upon charity in case of illness.

## Health Insurance Legislation under Bismarck and Its Development to 1914

Only in the last third of the nineteenth century did laborers begin to organize politically on a larger scale. Domestic political pressure increased so rapidly that by 1878 Bismarck could have passed the Sozialistengesetz (laws against the Social Democratic party), which prohibited many of the activities of the labor organizations. However, Bismarck realized that these laws neither solved the social problems at hand nor furthered the identification of the laborer with the state. At this time, Bismarck was himself forced to initiate political measures if he wanted to maintain the state. It is generally accepted that Bismarck promoted social insurance more for political reasons than to further social welfare. The opening sentence of the imperial message from 1881 introducing the social enactment reads: "The healing of the social damages cannot be found merely through repression of Social Democratic transgressions." This, however, does not limit the value of the far-sighted conceptions Bismarck held with reference to health insurance laws. From the many fruitless efforts to establish a general health insurance program on a voluntary basis or through the authorization of regional bodies (communities, districts), he drew the conclusions that every endangered person should be required to join, and that the insurance should be established on a cooperative basis, thereby making its members part of the management of the sickness fund. The insurance was thus not to be put in the hands of anonymous capital-holding corporations. Bismarck also concluded that a government grant should be established to show the workers the good will of the state.

Bismarck did not succeed fully in having this concept passed in the Reichstag. The act did not include the agricultural workers or the majority of the employees, and a government grant was not approved. Only two parties of the Reichstag rejected the law completely: the (middle-class) Liberals and the Social Democrats. Compulsory insurance meant interference with social freedom as far as the Liberals were concerned. The Social Democrats opposed the law not only because of their fundamental opposition to the government, which reduced their rights under the Sozialistengesetz, but also because they thought the proposed provisions were insufficient.

The National Law on Health Insurance of the Worker

The National Law on Health Insurance of the Worker (KVA) became effective at the end of 1883. Its title is not entirely precise; not all workers (for instance in agriculture) and not all salaried employees were included. Nevertheless, the KVA showed most of the essential features that are effective in the FRG today.

Workers on wages were to have compulsory health insurance, regardless of their income. For salaried employees, an income limit was established. Health insurance was financed by contributions from both the employer and the employee (1883: two to one; today: one to one). The contributions were determined independent of health risk, in proportion to income. Health insurance was administered by several different types of sickness funds: Ortskrankenkassen (local sickness funds) were responsible for workers in a specific region; Betriebskrankenkassen were industrial sickness funds, which could be established by a company for its employees; Innungskassen were guild sickness funds, which could be established by a specific trade for its members; and Knappschaftskassen were miners' sickness funds.

The reason for the multiplicity of sickness funds lies in the historic fact that the KVA represented the continuation of previously existing organizations. Moreover, the establishment of a completely new organization would have taken considerable time. In 1885 approximately 20,000 sickness funds existed, averaging 215 compulsory members (not counting family members). The reason for the large number of small sickness funds was that most were founded at the community level. In addition to the above-mentioned sickness funds, several Hilfskassen (auxiliary funds) continued to exist, mostly for those employees who were not included in the KVA. Sickness funds of this type still exist today, although in a changed form, as the Ersatzkassen. Today there are seven Ersatzkassen (substitute funds for salaried employees), with more than 10 million members (not counting family members). These make up about 30 percent of the members of all sickness funds. Salaried employees can choose to join an Ersatzkasse instead of being insured by law in an Ortskrankenkasse or a Betriebskrankenkasse.[2]

The sickness funds were managed by the members together with the employers. At the Vertreterversammlung (assembly of delegates) and in the Vorstand (board of directors) the members had, according to their respective financial contribution, two-thirds of the votes and the employer one-third (today, half and half).

The benefits of the KVA consisted of wages during sickness and medical services. The sickness-fund member thus acquired the right to ambulatory and hospital treatment and medication. Payment was made directly through the sickness fund to the physician, the hospital, and the pharmacy. This principle of direct payment to the provider rather than reimbursement is a decisive structural principle of the German health insurance system, and it persists today.

Co-insurance for the nonworking family members was not established by law, as it is today. Although the KVA provided for this option, it entrusted the decision to the self-governing sickness funds. Loss of income during pregnancy and after birth was also taken into consideration by the KVA.

Evaluation of the KVA

Without any doubt the KVA brought about a considerable improvement for the workers in case of sickness, even though the benefits were initially limited and cases of destitution still occurred. More important, it was the beginning of a national social policy in Germany. Although there were individual initiatives before 1883, passing the KVA and the law for workers' accident insurance at the same time opened a new realm of domestic policy. The idea of this policy started by Bismarck was that the welfare of people does not result automatically out of economic growth in a free-market economy; the distribution has to be regulated, and the state should not limit itself to providing economic freedom in the sense of "laissez faire laissez aller." Since World War II, this idea has been elaborated in the FRG under the title Soziale Marktwirtschaft (social market economy). This means that social and economic policy should be one unit to avoid an unjust distribution of income and property and to avoid poverty due to sickness, age, and unemployment. Social policy has to minimize the negative distributive effects of a liberal market economy, but it also has to respect the necessity of economic growth and accept, insofar as possible, the market economy. During the nineteenth century the preeminent question was whether the state should influence social conditions at all, but the discussion since then has centered around the extent of state intervention. By the turn of the century, those who opposed a public social policy except for aid to the poor were reduced to a few insignificant groups.

Despite this highly positive appraisal from a historical context, the health insurance law did not arise because of predominantly progressive motives. The KVA was primarily a means to preserve the existing social order, to minimize social conflicts, and to preserve the state from a radical overthrow. Questions of national budget also played an important role: The uninsured worker who felt sick sooner or later became a burden to the Armenhilfe (Aid for the Poor), which had to be paid for with taxes. Since the Armenhilfe was organized on a communal level, this imposed a considerable burden on certain communities. Therefore the representatives of the communities had a major interest in turning over the financial burden to employers and workers as payers of insurance premiums. Not only are these motives indicated in various contemporary documents; provisions in the KVA itself stress this point. It is characteristic that the law applies primarily to industrial workers, although there were many groups in the population whose conditions were not any better than those of the workers. However, a distinct process of solidarity between political parties and labor unions had started among the workers in the second half of the nineteenth century, and the social problem became a political one.

It is also politically important to understand that the KVA as welfare law introduced, from the start, class differences that have been reduced only in the last few years. Basically, it differentiated among three status groups—wage earners, salaried employees, and civil servants—and allowed salaried employees to choose between Ersatzkassen and the regular sickness funds. This weakness in German social legislation has led each group to pursue its own interests, thereby often preventing or at least hindering the realization of workers' common interests, such as protection against dismissal, sick pay provided by the employer, common rather than separate pension funds for workers on wages and salaries, and common rather than separate election procedures. Ersatzkassen compete for members against regular sickness funds for wage earners, and they try to give their members the status of private patients. Since this means that they offer more benefits and pay their physicians better, this strategy hinders cost containment, because all other sickness funds have to follow the lead of the Ersatzkassen's higher fees and more generous benefits.

The KVA set the premiums according to the income of the sickness-fund member and not according to the health risks. This principle now constitutes the decisive characteristic of the health insurance system, clearly setting it apart from private insurance. The abandonment of the equivalence principle (equivalence of insurance risks and cost of premium) used in private insurance was surely a technical necessity, since few laborers earned enough to pay high premiums, especially when family members had to be insured as well. The equivalence principle therefore was replaced by the principle of Solidargemeinschaft, in which an association of individuals supports and aids a disabled member according to their financial abilities. The legal system of health insurance thereby continues principles of older organizations that had been in existence predominantly in the trades. The principle of self-government too is derived from the concept of Solidargemeinschaft. Within a specific legally defined framework, the insured should determine both benefits and premiums. The insured should see the sickness fund not as an anonymous public administration, but as his own organization through which he would determine his own social security.

## Discussion and Development of the KVA until 1914

The law introducing the sickness funds had a predominantly positive reception in the public, except for criticism that certain branches of the economy and the majority of salaried employees had been left out. These flaws were mostly corrected by the turn of the century, but the principle of an income limit for compulsory health insurance for white-collar workers remained intact. More and more, the Social Democrats also accepted the social insurance scheme, and particularly legal health insurance. This change of opinion was caused primarily by two factors. First and foremost, the social condition of the workers was undeniably improved. This the Social Democrats could not deny if they did not want to lose credibility. Second, the sickness funds, by providing institutions of self-government, offered important power positions for political struggle. These positions, however, could be occupied only by those who accepted the principles of the legal sickness funds.

The debate concerning the advantages and disadvantages of the compulsory sickness funds within the Social Democratic party was identical to the debate concerning the political strategy of the party generally: revolution versus democratic reform. This debate within the Social Democratic party was not settled until during World War I, when the representatives favoring a revolutionary strategy formed a separate party organization.

Bismarck's goal of tying the workers closer to the state had obviously been achieved. However, his goal of alienating the workers from the Social Democratic party had not. The activities of the Social Democrats in the institutions of self-government were not without consequences.

At first the Reich's government and Prussia tried to keep Social Democrats out of important positions in the organization of self-government and to strengthen the influence of the state on the institutions of self-government. As the 1911 uniform codification of the Social Insurance Law (the Reichsversicherungsordnung) was being prepared, the Reich's government advocated equal representation of employers and workers in the self-governing bodies, with the express intent to "counteract the influence of the Social Democrat party in the regional sickness funds." The Zentrum party was mainly responsible for the fact that this restriction of self-government was not passed. The Zentrum was a Catholic conservative party that had been established in 1870. In spite of the fact that early on its representatives had recognized the importance of social problems, the Zentrum's focus was limited to the support of church interests. This Party resisted all attempts of the state to gain greater control of public affairs. Zentrum members supported Bismarck's social legislation, mainly because they expected it to reduce the influence of the Social Democrats. A noticeable change did not occur until 1891 when Pope Leo XXIII published the social encyclical "Rerum Novarum."

As a global ecclesiastical circular letter, "Rerum Novarum" could not enter concrete questions of the social order. It did, however, stimulate the discussion of seminal issues that marked a new beginning of Catholic Soziallehre (social teaching). The encyclical was equally opposed to liberalism and to socialism, and it relinquished the position hitherto held that the Church alone could solve the social problems of an industrial society by asking the state to provide appropriate laws and institutions.

The Zentrum party, which had constituted the strongest faction in the Reichstag from 1884 to 1912, quickly took over the guidelines "Rerum Novarum" had set forth. In spite of its heterogeneous constituency (aristocracy, middle class, working class), the party's connection to the Christian labor movement enabled it to become a strong political factor. The building of a social insurance system, which basically had been accomplished with the codification of the Reichsversicherungsordnung (National Insurance Order) in 1911, was due primarily to the Zentrum party. The Reichsversicherungsordnung, despite frequent amendments, remains the legal framework for social insurance in the FRG.

While health insurance legislation received more and more support from labor unions, political parties, and even by employers, the physicians rejected it because of the manner in which they were being paid for their services. Because up to 1911 the legislation regulated neither the qualifications of physicians working for the sickness funds nor the relationship between the physician and the sickness funds, the sickness funds contracted with physicians individually. These physicians received exclusive rights for treatment of sickness-fund members within a certain region at guaranteed per capita fees. Because competition between physicians for such contracts was very heavy and became stronger as the membership of the insurance program grew, the sickness funds could negotiate extremely low fees, especially in contracts with physicians who had not passed their board exams. The physicians could thus choose between two options: Either they relinquished the treatment of members of the sickness funds, so that the number of their patients decreased with every increase in the membership of the sickness funds, or they entered into a contractual relationship with a sickness fund and tried to treat as many insured patients as possible (or deliver as many services) in order to obtain an adequate income in spite of the low fees. This strategy led in many cases to superficial treatment. The physicians raised three basic demands:

• that only board-certified physicians be allowed to treat sickness-fund patients,

• that the insured patient has the right to choose a physician,[3] and

• that the membership of the insurance not be expanded any further, especially if the possibility of private insurance was to be limited, for fear that the better-paid and more desirable salaried employees would join the funds and not private insurance.

The growing conflicts between sickness funds and physicians, which also burdened their relationship with the insured, led to the acceptance of the demands of the physicians under the Reichsversicherungsord-nung. Although the free choice of physicians was not introduced, the sickness funds granted their members the choice between at least two physicians and the method of payment shifted from per capita to fee for service.

## Health Insurance during World War I and the Weimar Republic

Within 30 years, from 1884 to 1914, the compulsory health insurance system expanded tremendously. The number of members (aside from co-insured family members) rose from about 4 million to 15 million. The number of actually insured persons grew even more, because the eligibility of family members had constantly been widened. With the introduction of the Reichsversicherungsordnung, approximately 55 percent of all working people were members of the legal sickness funds. This growth took place during a steady economic upswing—industrial production increased by 200 percent, with relatively little unemployment. In the next two decades these favorable conditions were reversed. War, inflation, and unemployment endangered the system, which was based on equitable risk sharing and a steady income from premiums.

It was, therefore, not the expansion of the system that characterized the period 1914–1934, but the attempt to save the system in its basic structures despite almost insurmountable financial difficulties. After World War I, industrial production was one-third of the prewar level. At the height of the economic crisis in 1932, 30 percent of workers were unemployed. Inflationary price increases and corresponding pay raises made it necessary to increase the income limits for mandatory members. At the same time benefits were being reduced, members were required to pay for various services individually, and the administrative control of the physicians as well as of the members was intensified.

The first result of the increase in the number of sickness-fund members and the tense financial situation was a growing opposition among the physicians, which led in 1920 to extensive strikes. While a radical minority demanded complete opposition to sickness funds, the more moderate representatives again demanded the free choice of physicians and a reduction in the number of sickness-fund members.

In addition, criticism developed in business circles against the financial burden caused by social legislation. In view of the economic development of the postwar days and the burden of reparations imposed upon Germany in the Treaty of Versailles, the rising cost of social insurance became threatening. Business circles therefore urged limiting social insurance.

Politically, it was primarily the Social Democratic party that was attacked. It had held the responsibility of government after the war until 1932, had subsequently supported the social policies of the Zentrum politician Braun, and had played an important role in the self-government of the sickness funds.

Critics in the medical profession and the business community accused the insured of tremendous abuse and mismanagement caused by Social Democrats in government and in the self-governing bodies of the sickness funds. Both problems were attributed to the majority within the self-governing bodies of the sickness funds (two-thirds insured, one-third employer). Although these critics overlooked the real problems of health insurance, they created in the public's mind the psychological conditions for the major interventions in the health insurance system during the time of National Socialism.

## Health Insurance in the Third Reich, 1933–1944

The political and economic instability of the Weimar Republic, which led to frequent changes in social security legislation and thus to insecurity in social policy, was a welcome reason for the representatives of National Socialism to restructure social policy. The realization that improving social security for the people would lead to their political abstinence, a favorable public opinion, and uncritical approval of the regime made social policy a major instrument of domestic consolidation and thus provided the basis for a strong stand in international politics. This fact as well as the suppression of any opposition to National Socialist objectives make it possible to consider the development of health insurance legislation in the Third Reich in the context of power interests only.

Bismarck saw social policy as a way to minimize class antagonism. The establishment of social insurance was to curtail the revolutionary socialist impact and strengthen the existing social order. The individual was to develop civic spirit without losing his individuality. However, the societal vision of National Socialism entailed a more encompassing role for social policy: the establishment of a Deutsche Volksgemeinschaft (German People's Community). Seldte, the Minister of Labor, elucidated the meaning of this strategy in 1939: "The whole social security system serves only one aim today: the healthy, enthusiastic, productive, militarily fit, racially valuable German man of the future. . . ."

The aims of social policy, the National Socialists argued, should no longer be to secure the basic needs, the right to life, individual autonomy, or human dignity of all individuals, but only to protect those who were "racially valuable" and physically fit and to breed—to use a morbid slogan of those days—"perfect human material." No aspect of social policy could have been more suitable for racial aims than health insurance. It offered the possibility of distributing health services according to racial and eugenic criteria. Seldte charged the German medical profession and the health insurance system not only with the "maintenance and improvement of health" but also with the "biological quality and race of the German people."

The attitude of the Völkische Ärzte (people's physicians) shows the ethical perversion this policy implied. They rejected health insurance because it supposedly helped the weak to survive. Thus, the Minister of Labor, Seldte, pointed to the possibility of making eugenic excellence the prerequisite for membership in the health insurance system.

The new aim of raising a racially and militarily fit elite could not easily be realized with the insurance system that existed in 1933. That system was the product of a democratic process of legislation that respected the individual and represented the interests of the insured through self-government. To realize the new aim, in contradiction to the interests of a good part of the people, it was necessary to reorganize the system in such a way that arbitrary authoritarian measures would at all times be possible. Parliamentary legislation was eliminated in favor of emergency decrees. As early as March 1, 1933, the Reichspräsident decreed that the government was authorized to issue guidelines for the safeguarding of the economy, including sickess funds. In addition, self-government of the sickness funds was eliminated. On March 17, 1933, the first ordinance for the reorganization of health insurance went into effect. The Minister of Labor was thereby entitled to transfer the supervision of individual sickness funds to commissioners under his jurisdiction. On May 18, 1933, the Minister of Labor was empowered to dismiss representatives of the institutions of self-government. Self-government was finally eliminated entirely in July 1934. For each sickness fund, a director was appointed by the Minister of Labor. The decision-making power of the self-governing boards was replaced by advisory boards with equal representation of insured and employers. The insured and the employers now contributed equally to the finances. The last two provisions are important inasmuch as this principle of parity was maintained in the FRG after the war. Self-government is an important instrument for sheltering the interests of the insured, enabling them to control the management of their fund, and providing a pressure group when the government proposes new laws. Thus, its elimination was a serious loss. In yet another change wrought by the National Socialists, "non-Aryan" physicians were excluded from treating sickness-fund patients. To be allowed to treat sickness-fund patients, the "Aryan" physician had to show not only competence but also a knowledge of eugenic race theory and political reliability.

Apparently, a few changes sufficed to convert the liberal social health insurance system, with its self-governing, local character, into a national "health insurance agency." The exterior form of the organization did not have to be changed greatly. The criteria for membership and benefits and the structure of different insurance organizations remained, but the ethical basis had given way to nationalistic objectives. The lively interest of National Socialism in eliminating self-government demonstrates the importance of this form of administration to the interests of the insured. This reform could take place all the more easily because all other forms of opposition were eliminated, and the measures could be put into force using anti-communist and anti-Semitic propaganda. Without expressly referring to the circumstances, one scholar in 1934 commented thus on the elimination of self-government: "The reform [of the social insurance system] started with the sickness funds, which because of their administrative structure were largely power centers of Marxism and in which large-scale personal and financial mismanagement had arisen. The most important thing was to strengthen the control function of the state and to clean up administrations by putting commissars in charge."

In addition to transforming of the sickness funds from self-government by the insured to more or less public institutions, the Third Reich increased the eligibility and the number of sickness-fund members. An independent health insurance agency was established for the recipients of retirement funds and was administered by the Ortskrankenkassen (local sickness funds). The Ersatzkassen were given the choice to insure only salaried employees or only workers on wages. This measure was not important, as the members of the Ersatzkassen were already predominantly salaried employees. More decisive was a further adjustment of the fees and benefits through the Reichsversicherungsordnung. Although intermittently a plan had arisen to institutionally integrate and regionally reorganize the entire health insurance system, this never became reality.

## The Development of a Compulsory Health Insurance System in the FRG

After the collapse of the Third Reich in 1945, health insurance in the three Western occupation zones was reconstructed uniformly according to the Reichversicherungsordnung. A special case was Berlin, where sickness, accident, disability, and old age insurance were institutionally integrated by the Versicherungsanstalt Berlin (Berlin Insurance Company). Between 1950 and 1965 this provision was gradually eliminated. Today a uniform legal status for all of the FRG, including Berlin, has been established.

The first fundamental debate concerning the revival of self-government began before the establishment of the FRG. The trade unions and the Social Democratic party demanded self-government exclusively through the insured or at least through the proportions that had existed before 1933 (two-thirds insured, one-third employer). Contrary to this, the CDU (Christian Democratic Union), the FDP (Free Democratic Party), and the employers endorsed equal representation in the administrative bodies. In 1951 the government constituted by the CDU and the FDP established the principle of parity, by which, in the case of the Orts-, Betriebs-, and Innungskassen, the board of directors and the assembly of delegates were elected or appointed in equal parts by the insured and by the employers. Ersatzkassen are administered by the insured exclusively.

However, the democratic principle that constitutes self-government became progressively less important and less effective. Two main reasons account for this development. First, self-government had initially played a relatively important role in the interpretation and implementation of the law governing benefits and services. Legislation and jurisdiction, however, had to prevent excessive differences in the system of benefits. As a consequence, self-government lost much of its power as the system of benefits became increasingly regimented. Today, the services decided upon by the institutions of self-government are estimated to range from 3 to 5 percent of the total expenditures. Second, although the representative bodies of the organizations of self-government are elected every 6 years, the mechanism is not always a vote of the insured. At the time of "voting," the respective associations (usually unions and employers' associations) submit lists of the proposed candidates. Voting takes place only if there are two lists of candidates, one for the insured and one for the representatives of the employer. The candidates then automatically become representatives in the institutions of self-government. This procedure produces an almost total lack of interest of the insured in self-government. Democratic control by the insured can therefore only be achieved indirectly through unions—if at all.

In 1957 a decisive change of the benefits system of compulsory health insurance took place. Until then, fundamental regulatory differences existed between wage earners and salaried employees in case of disability. Salaried employees continued to receive their pay from the employer during the first 6 weeks of disability and only after this time did the sickness funds start to pay sick pay. Workers, however, received their sick pay from the very start through the sickness fund, though the amount paid was considerably less than their net income before the disability. In 1957 a subsidy was granted to workers to be paid by the employer during the first 6 weeks and to raise the amount to 90 percent of the last net income. In 1961 the subsidy was raised to 100 percent of the net income.

Only in 1970 was complete equality between workers on a wage and salaried employees realized; now workers as well continue to receive their pay during the first 6 weeks of disability. This development greatly reduced the expenditures the sickness funds had to provide for sick pay. Since then, medical payments have been vastly more important. Health insurance grants the right to ambulatory, medical, and dental care, hospital care, medication, orthodontry (including dentures), rehabilitation measures, checkups for specific diseases, and ambulatory and stationary care in case of pregnancy and delivery. A minor contribution by the patient is demanded for medication or for dentures. On the whole, however, the benefits are covered by the premiums. The sickness funds normally settle directly with physicians, hospitals, pharmacists, and other suppliers of medical goods and services, that is, with their respective representative organizations. For ambulatory medical services, the sickness funds contract with the Kassenärztliche Vereinigungen (organizations of the sickness-fund physicians) for treatment of sickness-fund patients. In these contracts the fees for specific medical services are set. Hospital costs are contracted on the basis of the average cost per day and bed per hospital and run as a rule for one year. Average costs include only the operating expenses. Since 1973, investments have been financed by federal, state, and local governments if the hospital is included in the Krankenhausbedarfsplan (hospital demand plan) of the respective state. The prices for medication are basically determined by the manufacturer.

The expenditures for compulsory health insurance increased tremendously in the first half of the 1970s. In this context it is not possible to go into a detailed explanation of the reasons for this development. The political debate concerning the options for keeping expenditures within economically acceptable limits now involves many other areas of social policy, ranging from specific changes of the Leistungsrecht to all-encompassing and radical concepts for the reform of the health system.

## Conclusion

To conclude, I should like to outline some tendencies of the present debate over health and social policy.

The medical system of the FRG stresses natural science as well as somatic and curative aspects. Psychic and social factors are greatly neglected in diagnosis and care as far as the critics are concerned. Concepts for preventive medicine are not developed and can therefore be used neither in training nor in practice.

Health policy (the guidelines for the health system) and social policy (the system of protection from consequences of illness) have in the past developed separately and independently. Health policy was and still is considered by physicians as their territory, for which only they have professional competence. If this view is accepted, as in the past, although medical considerations are obviously closely linked to vested interests, then social policy is reduced to being a corrective factor without changing the basic structure. Many reasons have led to this situation. The political responsibilities are partly on the federal, partly on the state level. The main factor, however, seems to be that the pressure groups working for the suppliers of health services (physicians, hospitals, pharmaceutical industries) are better organized than those working for the insured. Up to the present, the sickness funds have not succeeded in correcting and using information relevant for policy decisions and negotiating with the proprietors of health services on the basis of these data.

To control expenses for compulsory health insurance, four approaches are being discussed:

- Improving the efficiency of the health system through a better integration of various services for health care (practices of medical specialists, hospitals, and rehabilitation facilities).

- Reducing the services offered (technical services, medical prescriptions) that are not necessary for the attainment of health. This presupposes quality control, for which so far all preconditions are missing.

- Reducing prices and fees, or at least reducing the increase of goods and services. These are generally too expensive because of a high profit margin or because of inefficient production. This presupposes a well-informed and well-organized organization on the part of the sickness funds.

• Requiring the insured to share in the costs in case of illness. This would certainly reduce expenses for the sickness funds even if the expected reduction in the utilization of services could not be reached.

All relevant political groups are agreed that the principle of health insurance should be preserved and not replaced by a nationalized health service.

For the next several years one may venture to predict that no fundamental structural change in the health system will be achieved. The development will be limited to marginal changes such as in how the sickness funds use control and management techniques to limit the costs of medical goods and services. Several laws that have been passed envisage a greater role for planning in the health system. These offer the sickness funds the so-far-neglected possibility of influencing the structural conditions of the health system. However, if the sickness funds start to take over the role of active representatives of the interests of the insured, the question of democratic legitimation will arise more strongly than ever before and the question of self-governance will be revived once again.

## Notes

1. Another 9 percent are covered by private insurance companies.

2. Workers on wages generally do not have this choice and are obliged to join a certain sickness fund. The special status of Ersatzkassen and of salaried employees produces a certain competition among the different sorts of sickness funds, not for lower costs and contributions but for higher fees for physicians and for more benefits such as "cures" at German baths.

3. This demand was raised by the physicians as early as 1883 (though the insured could have been expected to raise it themselves) because it was extraordinarily important for setting fees and services. If the insured had a free choice of physicians, then they could set their own fees, or the sickness funds would have to enter into a contract with the totality of the physicians. In both cases the physicians' position to negotiate would be considerably strengthened.

## References

Hofmann, W. 1962. Ideengeschichte der sozialen Bewegung des 10. und 20. Jahrhunderts. Berlin.

Knies, K. 1883. Die Politische Ökonomie vom geschichtlichen Standpunkt. Braunschweig.

Peters, H. 1959. Geschichte der Sozialversicherung. Bad Godesberg.

Roscher, A. W. 1924. Geschichte der National-Ökonomie in Deutschland. Munich and Berlin.

Rosenberg, P. 1969. Die soziale Krankenversicherung—Pflichtversicherung oder freiwillige Vorsorge. Cologne.

Schmoller, G. 1918. Die soziale frage: Klassenbildung Arbeiterfrage, Klassenkampf. Munich and Leipzig.

Smith, P. 1864. "Die sogenannte Arbeiterfrage." Vierteljahresschrift für Volkswirtschaft, Politik und Kulturgeschichte 2.

# 5 Health-Insurance Policy and Berufsverbote in the Nazi Takeover

## Stephan Leibfried and Florian Tennstedt

*Drawing upon new archives and documents, Leibfried and Tennstedt take us deeper into the Nazi period. We would expect the purges of Jewish physicians and the use of health care to build a master race, but the transformation of sickness funds from local organizations run by workers that provided the spawning ground for important experiments in social medicine to a rather uniform national structure is not commonly known or admitted. Nor might we expect the zeal with which leaders of medical societies persecuted their colleagues who ran clinics and other facilities for workers. The authors claim that after World War II the democratic tradition of sickness funds was not restored as the hegemony of the medical profession built up during the Nazi period continued in West Germany. Equally disappointing to them as Marxists was the East German response of totally centralizing workers' health care in a government bureaucracy.*

The standard literature on medical history[1] and the history of social policy and related areas does not confront at all the empirical developments addressed in this essay: the relationship between social policy and the Nazi use of Berufsverbote. These purges of professionals in Germany are barely alluded to in writings on social policy, since the focus of description is usually on administrative and legal changes per se (see Leichter 1979, pp. 133 ff.). When they are discussed, the implicit explanation is that there was some mishandling of ethnic minorities, a matter of pure justice quite independent of any major politics or social policy. What literature there is (see Mitscherlich and Mielke 1978) usually focuses on the medical experiments and racial policies of the Nazis. Structural issues of social policy are overlooked, and personification prevails. The formative processes of the "political power of physicians" (Stone 1980, p. 18) and their role in the "health market" thus tends to be ignored. The standard German literature (Hentschel 1983, pp. 137 ff.) holds that social policy was an island that withstood the Nazi floods, and that the Nazis were aberrant individuals of no relevance to social policy over the long run but only of relevance for the minority issue. This focus tends to dissolve structural issues into total bedeviling and pure moral outrage about all sorts of medical malpractice of a wide assortment of individual doctors (Mausbach and Bromberger 1979; Roth 1980, pp. 152 ff.). This chapter attempts to overcome these weaknesses by combining biographical detail with a structural analysis of policy, for key individuals helped create and institutionalize new health policies. Administrators and doctors from 1890 on formed "health policy reform clusters," which gave rise to many major innovations in health-service delivery until 1933, when they were destroyed.

The democratic character and sensitivity of both the local sickness funds and the professional delivery of service were seriously undermined by the Third Reich and were not restored in the Federal Republic (FRG; West Germany) after World War II. It might well be that these shifts, which have occurred in living memory, are still of such emotional significance that detachment and embarrassment may not be disentangled from reality. At first glance an outsider might find that in the FRG, through the Law of Self-Government and Changes in the Area of Social Insurance of February 22, 1951, "the social insurance system was 'essentially restored' to its pre-1933 status" (Leichter 1979, p. 139). This is not so, even on the legal-administrative level. The self-government of the local sickness funds had been based, from 1883 until 1934, on a two-thirds majority of the representatives of the insured on the fund's board. These representatives, who were mostly connected with the major labor unions, faced a one-third representation of the employers. This structure of some 50 years' standing came to be the dominant view of German classical self-government in this area. Its destruction was in a sense perpetuated when two-thirds parity was not reestablished after World War II; in 1951 the structure was changed to one of parity, and "self-government" was thus paralyzed by any dissent among the representatives of the insured (Dobbernack 1951). During the first national mobilization of conservatives against the local funds, a similar change was attempted, unsuccessfully, in 1911, when all major social insurance legislation was codified in the National Insurance Code (Reichsversicherungsordnung). The undoing of the classical structure of self-government in 1951 did not come about without a broad, vigorous battle by the unions and the Social Democrats, and this was also the case with the general co-determination issue of 1952, which took a similarly abortive course (Tennstedt 1976, pp. 146 ff.). Furthermore, restoration in any practical sense would have meant recruiting personnel displaced in 1933 and/or equivalent progressive activists in social policy for leading positions. Neither of these options was taken. Rather, the tendency was to continue employment of people hired in the 1930s, who subsequently rose to leading positions at the local and national levels of the sickness funds. Stone (1980, p. 83) correctly observes that today "self-administration in practice is quite weak," but does not explain why.

Besides the undermining of self-government, there is another reason. Incrementally since the turn of the century, as the physicians organized nationally, but in giant steps in 1931–32 and after 1933, the "freedom" of managing medical-service delivery at the pleasure of the local sickness funds was limited; the ambulatory clinics, to be analyzed below, are a case in point. The original 1883 sickness insurance legislation, 87 paragraphs short, was completely focused on the structure of the funds and on the relationship of the insured to the funds as overseen by the state. It left the ways and means of service delivery completely up to the fund and thus to the local social power relationships between funds and physicians. Today's overwhelming and expansive body of regulation shapes medical services, standardizes delivery options, and creates a "self-government" of the physicians, to which much of the remaining authority in that area is delegated. Thus, the disappropriation of fund powers and subsequent regulations has preempted much of the traditional territory relevant to a self-government of the insured. Here also, the Third Reich was a major step in effecting this tilting of the Weimar balance of powers toward the organized medical profession. It did so, again, by dismantling organized union opposition, increasing the extent of regulated service delivery, and pioneering much of the professional self-regulation of the physicians in the delivery of services to the insured (Tennstedt 1976, pp. 137–142).

In contrast to such developments in the FRG after World War II, in the GDR several of the leading sickness-fund officials or social-reform activists of Weimar vintage—among them Helmut Lehmann, Fritz Bohlmann, Carl Litke, Erwin Fischer, Walter Axel Friedeberger—were attracted to the reorganization of social insurance in the GDR. These people had been either Social Democrats or functionaries of the non-denominational trade unions in the Weimar period, but had not been communists. They were thus attracted to state service as experts in social insurance, but not to the Communist Party, which on the political level had its own set of social politicians. Unifying sickness insurance (that is, doing away with the division of factory, professional, and local funds) and restructuring the delivery of medical services by the use of ambulatory clinics and general measures against infectuous diseases, became prominent objectives of health policy. Thus, initially, more of the Weimar social-hygiene tradition was taken up in the GDR than in the FRG—this also shows up statistically, since infant mortality, tuberculosis, and infectious diseases in general have had and still have a much lower incidence in the GDR than in the FRG. Nevertheless, the GDR and the FRG are equally unsuccessful in dealing with today's prominent chronic sicknesses, especially heart, circulatory, and degenerative diseases.

Though many of the reforms in the GDR after 1945 partook of the Weimar reform spirit (and its personnel), especially in the perfection and systematization of the ambulatory clinic or polyclinic (i.e., ambulatory care in hospitals) approach, they nevertheless had lost much of the Weimar pioneer spirit and regulatory functions, since the circumstances of the development of these clinics after 1945 in the GDR were completely changed. In Weimar these clinics and such reforms were "nonconformist," since they were structurally at odds with a generally private market in health delivery, drugs, etc. (with respect to which they fulfilled a regulatory function). After 1945 in the GDR these clinics were just the extension of the general "socialization of the means of production" to most elements of the health sphere, leaving no room for a special regulatory scope with respect to a differently structured health market.

Six major points stand out as to why this essay is central to an analysis of the development of German social policy:

• For the first time, original archival material—the files of the former National Labor Ministry (now in Potsdam)—has been used to analyze the effects of the National Socialist takeover of health policy in Prussia, specifically on the sickness-insurance scheme. (Historical Prussia coincides roughly with the northern half of today's Federal Republic of Germany.)

• This detailed study highlights that in certain respects the Nazi regime focused on destroying the role of the German labor movement in the formation and implementation of social policy, as well as on destroying the medical programs of social and socialist activists. Jewish physicians were frequent spokesmen for these groups. In health policy, the unions and these professionals, backed here and there by a ministerial bureaucracy with reformist inclinations, were firmly linked to each other, be it as a lobby for reforms (as in the area of venereal-disease prevention, public infant care, and public-health expansion at the communal level) or through day-to-day cooperation in sickness funds, ambulatory clinics, panel practice, or screening clinics. Jewish doctors in the main industrial cities, especially Berlin, had consistently supported health reform initiatives of diverse sorts. As providers of social services, they opposed or at least transcended the private-practice outlook of the medical profession's association, and they believed that the self-government of the sickness funds, with their strong union base, made progress in social service delivery possible.

• Berufsverbote—in scale and substance only vaguely reminiscent of an old guild practice of excluding unqualified craftsmen—was used after 1933 to destroy social reformers in medicine and not simply to quell individual "disloyalty" or regulate the medical market by removing surplus professionals. Thus, Berufsverbote was a means of changing the democratic structure of social-policy steering and delivery. The whole national framework of health policy was altered. At the individual level, "delivery" may not have seemed to change much; "a doctor is a doctor." But if one takes seriously research showing that trust is a significant aspect of the healing process, then destroying the sensitivity of these physicians and their delivery institutions to the working class they served made a great difference, even though it does not lend itself to easy measurement by prevailing health statistics.

• This research aims at reestablishing the tradition of analyzing social policy in its historical context, which has all but disappeared since 1933. This "critical" empirical tradition arose before and around the turn of the century, became partly submerged during the Weimar period, was suppressed politically after 1933, and remained dormant as a legacy of the Nazi period after 1945, often lost in the pure disciplinary divisions of labor in the social sciences. Social-policy debate thus is dominated by legal, administrative-science, economic, sociological, or socio-psychological paradigms per se and has after 1945 also been bound to present-day events, crowding out its historical roots. Continuities between the Nazi period and contemporary policies are still too painful to contemplate. What little historical perspective there is entails jumping safely back to the nineteenth century or perhaps to the Weimar Republic.

- This essay indirectly contributes to the debate on the political theory of the state (Miliband, O'Connor, Offe, Poulantzas, et al.), especially with respect to the Nazi state. For example, many have the impression that the political force behind the policy of "purification" (Säuberung) and destruction was the state and its bureaucracy, especially the National Ministry of Labor. One might also think that the ministry was blocked or neutralized in its efforts by a private profession—the doctors—oriented toward an "ethics of helping" and socialized in the professional spirit of collegiality. But in fact the process of destruction developed in exactly the opposite way, especially insofar as the practice of Berufsverbote among the organized physicians themselves is concerned. Aided by the Nazi Physicians Association, the "gleichgeschaltete"[2] major medical associations pressed for purges within their own ranks, and their local branches were zealous in their implementation. It was the state bureaucracy, the National Ministry of Labor, that controlled and contained the overzealous professional bodies and reinstated quite a few "communist" and "non-Aryan" (Jewish) doctors to their insurance practice. Thus, social policy reflected a pluralistic structure of political power in the Nazi state, as Neumann (1942) first analyzed. This study thus illustrates the pervasive importance of private interests—here, the medical profession—in mobilizing political power for the Nazi state.

- Finally, these points are illustrated by material from Prussia, especially Berlin, with an excursion into the fate of sickness-fund innovation in the countryside of the Lower Weser region. Berlin was a special case of general significance for health-policy development. As the capital of Prussia, the Reich's leading state, and the capital of the Reich, it contained the most important state and national bureaucracies in the health field. Naturally, unions, political parties, and other national organizations in the health field had their head office or an important branch office in Berlin. Also, Berlin was the largest city and had been a trend setter or laboratory for health reforms since the nineteenth century; thus, it was attractive to physicians with an intellectual and literary bent. If important successes occurred in the countryside or in other larger cities or states, one would often find that the people involved there had strong links to the Berlin "reform cluster." From the standpoint of normalcy, health care in Berlin would seem atypical. From the standpoint of health reforms and health policy, Berlin was the place to look at and from the Nazi perspective the place to bring under control to achieve unchallenged ideological and practical hegemony in the health-policy field. Similar but more minor events of the same nature could be studied in Frankfurt am Main, Munich, Leipzig, and Saxony in general. The Berlin analysis here centers first on the infrastructure of personnel in sickness funds and then later on the parallels among reformist physicians in health policy, rather than on Berlin's service-delivery institutions and their fate. In this way the health reform lobby of Berlin is most readily depicted. The report on the Lower Weser region shows, in the case of ambulatory clinics, one of the most contentious health-policy items in the Weimar Republic: how Berlin developments spread beyond Berlin. This part of the analysis deals with an institution actually delivering health services to the working-class base of the sickness funds. Other institutions (sexual advice centers, communal physicians' practices, etc.) would reveal similar patterns of development and destruction.

## Framing the Issue

The Wiederherstellung des Berufsbeamtentums (reestablishment of a professional civil service) of 1933 gave the Nazi regime a firm grip on the whole government. How this law was developed and framed has been studied in detail (Adam 1972; Mommsen 1966), but not much attention has been paid to its quantitative and qualitative consequences (Scheur 1967). There is good reason to believe that such consequences were most severe in the area of sickness insurance and the delivery of medical services. The sickness funds, which had the status of independent public entities, and their national organizations, especially the local sickness funds (Ortskrankenkassen), had for almost 50 years been close to the general labor movement (Tennstedt 1977). Thus, a law attempting to purge "nationally unreliable" (national unzuverlässige) elements and "non-Aryan" (i.e. Jewish) persons from public service, should have most severely affected this sector and did so. This purge destroyed the self-government of the funds, which rested mostly on unpaid work of union members (honorary officials) on the sickness-fund committees, and led to its long-term eradication. It was undertaken parallel to the purge of all "non-Aryan" and "nationally unreliable" panel doctors, i.e., all doctors holding a (panel) license from sickness funds which assured them of their livelihood by reimbursing for services to the insured. These purges so thoroughly destroyed a reform tradition in German social policy that it is today almost forgotten. It is these destructions in health policy we will focus on, since they were much more incisive than all later measures taken in social insurance by the National Socialist regime (cf. Teppe 1977, pp. 195 ff.; Peters 1973, p. 105; Scheur 1967).

## The Destruction of Union-Oriented Social Policy in the Sickness Funds

### The Dismantling of Self-Government in Sickness Insurance

In 1932 there were 32,026 members of the boards of local sickness funds and there were 49,494 representatives of the insured, serving as members of the basic parliamentary structure in the local sickness funds (*Statistik des deutschen Reiches* 443, p. 11). These people were mostly members of the trade unions. After the German trade unions had been dismantled—their headquarters occupied, their papers prohibited, their leading representatives imprisoned and discharged, their other employed functionaries discharged, their property confiscated—on May 2 and 3 of 1933 (Beier 1975), a law was immediately passed against the self-government structure in social insurance: the Law Pertaining to Honorary Offices in Social Insurance and Reichsversorgung (veterans and similar benefits) of May 18, 1933 (Tennstedt 1977, pp. 184 ff.). According to this statute, honorary officials could be displaced even if they did not satisfy the criteria formulated by the Gesetz zur Wiederherstellung des Berufsbeamtentums (that is, even if they were not "non-Aryan" or "nationally unreliable"). For example, they could be displaced if they had been elected on a ticket of an "economic association" (i.e., a trade union), or if they had achieved such office in other ways on a similar sort of basis and if this association or its "gleichgeschaltete" successor had declared by September 30, 1933, that such officials did not enjoy the organization's support any more. This officious and vague wording was meant to catch all honorary officials in the sickness-fund self-government, whatever their union organization had been.

The Nazi "successor organizations" of the trade unions, which had dominated the self-government election in social insurance of 1927 (Vertretung, 1929), were the German Workers Front (Deutsche Arbeitsfront; DAF) and the National Socialist Organization at Factory Level (Nationalsozialistische Betriebszellenorganisation; NSBO; see Beier 1975 and Schumann 1958). These measures of Gleichschaltung concerned two types of unions: the "free" (i.e., nondenominational, non-Christian) unions, which constituted the overwhelming part of the Weimar trade-union movement, were unified in the ADGB (Allgemeiner Deutscher Gewerkschafts Bund; General German Workmen's Federation), and cooperated loosely with the Social Democrats; and the Christian unions, which were rather small and were affiliated with the Zentrum (Center) Party. Dismantling the major "socialist" unions of the ADGB was important to the Nazis, who perceived them as a major opposing force. One may therefore realistically suppose that these successor organizations withdrew their trust, at least from all those officials who were members of the free unions. If so, about three-quarters of the representatives of the insured in the parliamentary bodies of the sickness-insurance scheme would have been displaced, judging by the results of the 1927 elections. With respect to the boards of the sickness funds, in 45.6 percent of all cases the free trade unions occupied all the seats of the insured on the boards, in 12.5 percent of all cases they had the majority of the seats on the board, and in 7.7 percent of the cases there was no union representation at all. The major part of the sickness funds (especially the local and quite a few factory funds) were dominated by the free trade unions, and correspondingly the displacement effects of the law under discussion were felt here most.

While these measures were being implemented in 1933, the National Ministry of Labor appointed commissary officials to run the boards and the parliamentary bodies of 103 sickness funds and 45 of their associations. The local sickness funds were a special target for commissary takeovers (91 of 103). These takeovers affected 3.16 million members, 27.7 percent of the total membership of all local sickness funds (Knoll 1933; Tennstedt 1977, p. 187). All such measures were then overlaid by the Law on Infrastructure of Social Insurance of July 5, 1934, which superimposed the "Führer" principle on these changes by requiring that "the power of decision rest not with a multi-headed unit but with one responsible man."

## Measures against Officials of the Sickness Funds

In his "Social Theory of Capitalism," Heimann (1928) called attention to a "secondary, but in social reality most important characteristic [of social policy or social insurance] . . . which is the career possibilities for tens of thousands of people from the working classes that exist in the self-government bureaucracy of social insurance. This is what self-government of the insured in the sickness funds is all about. The importance of this fact should never be underestimated, because it provides broad opportunity for the development of administrative talent and business education, thus reinforcing the strength of the working-class social movement." Historical evidence validates this opinion.

If one looks at the development of self-government in sickness insurance between 1848 and 1933 and pays special attention to the elections of insured workers to self-governing local sickness funds, one finds the phenomenon Heimann describes. The development of politically significant working-class self-government in the 1883 national insurance scheme does not date back to the start, but rather to the 1890s, and focuses principally on the local sickness funds, where local officials and pensioned officers of the armed forces were replaced by self-educated blue-collar and white-collar workers on the rise (Tennstedt 1977; Tennstedt 1983, pp. 429 ff.). These workers thus continued a much older tradition of working-class involvement in health politics, dating back to the middle of the nineteenth century (Frevert 1983), in which "private associations" of workers (Unterstützungskassen) were the dominant mode of "self-government" with marginal state regulation.

These workers in the 1890s had been engaged in socialist causes in the free trade unions and/or the Social Democratic Party and had thus been exposed to sanctions, including the loss of jobs and blacklisting. Also, one should remember that people of this political persuasion had no chance for a public job; only in the course of World War I was "the barring of all members of the trade unions from public offices and public jobs discontinued, which had caused so much entrenched embitterment in such a senseless way. Such persons would neither be licensed nor elected nor called to any jobs, from night watchman and postal worker to mayor and leading ministerial official. Suddenly the socialists were not 'elements without a fatherland' anymore; they were not 'enemies of the state' anymore and they could become Prussian civil servants or even officers, at least reserve officers." (Kessler 1929, p. 458; see also Fenske 1973, p. 339; Morsey 1972, p. 101)

There was no special education for the administrative personnel of the sickness funds. The journal of the German sickness funds, *Deutsche Krankenkassenzeitung*, whose first editor had been Paul Kampffmeyer, reported in 1906: "We have rejoiced quite often when, via employment by the sickness funds, a dozen or so bureaucratic entanglements were attacked. An administration and a state in which a man without status or examination counts as a nothing is being contrasted by a branch of government where leading officials, without much ado, can make a civil servant out of a carpenter or a locksmith." The first administrative examinations in this area were introduced by the sickness fund of Dresden in 1897, and in 1906 the Leipzig fund followed suit. It took until 1925–1930 for such examinations to be legally required by state administrative decree (Breithaupt 1925, 1929).

It was against this widely respected tradition that Nazi policies from 1933 on were directed. As Knoll states in his introduction to the major administrative monograph on the process of purging the sickness funds: "The unions dominated the sickness funds almost completely, and their personnel policy in this domain of social insurance, which is so important for the economy and workers, was completely a matter of self-government. Thus they had always tried to restrict the influence of the state in this area. . . . accordingly the civil servants law was to have a rather severe effect on the sickness funds." (Knoll and Keller 1934, p. 2) (See Engel and Eisenberg 1932 as to the nature of the attack.) The leading administrative official of the local sickness fund in Nuremberg, Hans Zimmermann, who had been forced on the local sickness fund as a commissary in 1933, stated in 1938: "After the Machtergreifung [Nazi takeover] the Führer also had to change the sickness funds. The issue was to win back the sickness funds and devote them to the original purpose, that is, to insure all working Germans, and thus to free them from domination by Marxists and Jews." (Zimmermann 1938, p. 388)

There are no general quantitative evaluations of the effects of this legal purge on sickness insurance. To do this post hoc implies some difficult judgments. Some of the administrative personnel of the funds were purged without due process or factual inquiry, since they were thought "unfit" to serve the new regime. Some of the dismissal notices were suspended in 1933 and 1934 or were put on a contractual basis, supposedly relying on the free will of both parties involved. This led either to a legally correct dismissal or to the pensioning off of administrative personnel because of "occupational disability."

We will elucidate this purge by concentrating on the largest sickness fund of the Reich, the local fund of the city of Berlin—probably the fund hardest hit by these purges. According to the available sources (especially an internal report, dated November 4, 1933, by Dr. Alexander

Grünewald, an official in the National Ministry of Labor), 613 dismissals occurred, of which 120 were to be revoked at the time. There exists a comprehensive collection of the personnel files of those to be dismissed; it documents 439 dismissal cases and lists varying legal justifications for dismissal outlined in table 1.

A general overview of the legally effective dismissals, probably compiled at the end of 1934, lists only 255 dismissals for the Berlin local sickness fund. This compilation, which was based on reports of the Prussian Supervisory Agencies in the Insurance Areas (Oberversicherungsämter) and which lists a total of 1,496 dismissals in Prussia (Leibfried and Tennstedt 1979, p. 34), thus is useful in estimating the minimum number of dismissals that took place at the time. There is no accurate way to relate these dismissals to the overall personnel situation. It is nevertheless apparent that two main factors triggered these dismissals: the proportion of personnel of the respective sickness fund thought to be in some trade union or socialist group, and the intensity of local Nazi party efforts, later reinforced through sickness-fund commissaries. If we take into account that the Prussian statistics are estimates, "adjusted" to minimize dismissals (Tennstedt 1977, pp. 189 ff., note 25), our estimate would be that about 2,500–4,000 sickness-fund employees were dismissed in all of the German Reich at this time. In 1932 there were 25,715 persons employed full-time with all sickness funds in the Reich (Statistik des Deutschen Reiches 1934, p. 11). Thus, at least 10 percent of these employees were dismissed, 30 percent of whom were active in the trade unions. Since the purges centered on the local sickness funds, it seems more appropriate to relate the number of dismissals only to their personnel. These funds employed 18,652 persons. Thus, about 15–25 percent of local sickness-fund employees were purged.

These quantitatively significant purges also effected a qualitative break in German social-policy tradition. The sickness funds, especially the local ones, had by themselves and by uniting on the regional and the national level been "missionary agencies in the area of public health" (Kampffmeyer 1903) and had become a social-policy avant garde of the trade unions and of the Social Democratic Party. This had already taken place at a time when, in the words of the non-socialist economist Karl Bücher, the bourgeois parties had "shied away from the social policy waters," since "socialism was for them what the red flag was to the bull in a bullfight and since they would fight against anything, whatever it might be, proposed by the Social Democratic Party" (Bücher

**Table 1**
Reasons for dismissal from Berlin local sickness fund, 1933.

| Section of BBG[a] legitimating dismissal | § 2a | § 3 | §§ 3/4 | § 4 | §§ 4/6 | § 6 | non BGB dismissals |
|---|---|---|---|---|---|---|---|
| Content of section, i.e. reason for dismissal | Not qualified[b] | Not "Aryan"[c] | | Past or present political activity does not give a sure indication of the civil servant's unquestioning loyalty to the national state at any time.[d] | | Economy and efficiency of administration[e] | |
| Number of persons dismissed | 18 | 28 | 3 | 205 | 130 | 52 | 3 |

a. BBG = Professional Civil Service law = Law on Reestablishing the Civil Service.
b. "Lacking the required or customary training for their career or other suitability."
c. "Of non-Aryan descent."
d. "Who, in view of their previous political activity, offer no guarantee that they would always side with the national state without reservation."
e. "For simplification of administration."

1919, p. 244). Only in the last few years do we find culminating evidence that today's trade unions have rediscovered an interest in this destroyed and thus forgotten tradition in health policy and health-service delivery (Standfest 1977; Hansen et al. 1981).

## The Purge of the Berlin Local Sickness Fund

The local sickness fund of the national capital, Berlin, was the largest local sickness fund at the time of the Third Reich, with 433,974 members. It had been especially active in social-policy reform in Imperial Germany and in the Weimar Repubic. The name of Albert Cohen, the leading administrative official of the Berlin fund, almost symbolized a social policy program (Stargardt et al. 1976, pp. 810 ff.). This sickness fund had led the movement toward "integrating" health services at the local level by creating hospitals, ambulatory clinics, x-ray institutes, dental clinics, and health baths owned by the sickness fund. Such institutionalization had always been opposed by professional associations of doctors, dentists, and druggists, among others.

In view of this pioneer tradition and of the National Socialist propaganda against political Bonzen (bonces) (a highly derogatory term used quite outside its original meaning of Japanese priests—an English equivalent might be "mafiosi") and "misuse of funds" in the local sickness funds, it seems appropriate to focus on the example of the personnel changes at the Berlin fund. Ludwig Brucker had dismissed 613 persons in 1933–1934 and replaced them with 560 persons hired permanently and 170 persons hired "provisionally," whom we believe stayed permanently.[3] Here are some reasons for dismissal (Zentrales Staatsarchiv RAM 5569;775, 827, 548, 562, 549, 835, 555, 546):

Circuit rider (official visiting the insured at home to ascertain claims and to advise) K. H.: "H. is known to be very involved in Marxist issues. In addition to being a member of the Social Democratic Party, he was a member of the 'Hammerschaft' [suborganization of the Reichsbanner, a social democrat and free union defense organization of the Weimar Republic; the Hammerschaft operated primarily at the factory level—S.L./F.T.] from its beginning. We have been informed, that H. has always worn a three-arrow button ['Drei-Pfeile-Abzeichen'; these pro-republican symbols stood for unity, activism, and discipline and signified the pro-republican activities of social democrats, free unions, and the Reichsbanner—S.L./F.T.]. He has done so even after the Nazi takeover and the elections of March 5, 1933. H. has ridiculed the swastika flag. Until very recently, he even spat in front of it."

Correspondent W. N.: "He has been extremely derisive. For example he said about the Führer: 'this ape is a foreigner, he should be thrown out.' "

Employee W. K.: "We could not prove that K. was a member of the Communist party, but our investigation has proven that he has had strong Communist leanings."

Cleaning-woman A. J.: "Mrs. J. and her two sons are well known in all of the neighborhood because of their Communist leanings and are thus in ill repute. Her sons are dangerous Communists who do not shy away from anything. They have acquired a reputation as typical red-front-screamers and as heroes with their knives. Their first names are Ali and Franz. Mrs. J. is a rather reserved person but she has the same political inclinations as her sons."

Helper F. S.: "She has been a member of the Social Democratic Party and since 1927 a member of the ZDA [Zentralverband der Angestellten—National Union of White Collar Workers—S.L./F.T.]. We could not prove any political activities of hers. She did, according to evidence presented by some employees, talk ill about the new administration of the fund and the present government."

Helper G. R.: "We could not prove any political activities of R.'s, but we suppose that he has been influenced by his father to be hostile against our state and our movement. His father has been a member of the Communist Party since 1918 and has shown the flag with the sickle on various political occasions. The father was barred from the Communist Party since he had acted against it (parteiwidriges Verhalten), then joined the SPD and flagged 'schwarz-rot-gold' [the colors of the Weimar Republic, which the Nazis despised and ridiculed—S.L./F.T.].

The purge did not lead to a hiring of apolitical bureaucrats; rather, right-wing politicians were brought in. Of the 560 "permanent" new employees, between 235 and 260 were "old fighters" (alte Kämpfer)—that is, they had joined the Nazi party quite some time before 1933 and had membership numbers below 100,000. The wave of dismissals within the Berlin fund thus led to a wave of hirings of untrained persons—quite different, though, from the untrained persons in the founding period of the sickness funds. Then, the funds recruited experienced workers who were union members and who had been trained by the union education program to master white-collar work and to promote service initiatives. Their political orientation, if any, was strongly toward the Social Democratic party; later on, almost no Communist Party members were active in "self-government" structures, except in one town in Saxony during the Weimar Republic.[4] The untrained personnel hired in 1933 consisted mostly of inexperienced or long-unemployed workers who had been estranged from any union movement and had no educational aspirations. Their loyalty was mainly to a political party, and their experience mostly one of political (not economic) struggle in the streets and the beer halls. Since the Nazi party had built up only very small suborganizations for welfare and medical purposes, which were of almost no relevance as training grounds for personnel after the takeover of the sickness funds by the Nazis, these party hacks had few skills and little knowledge. Also, social policy in general was not an area to which the Nazis had paid much attention or in which they had gained much practical expertise before 1933. By contrast, competence, capability, and experience in health policy were an intrinsic characteristic of the working-class struggles in the 1890s, since they built on an old tradition of working-class self-organization in health matters as part of the union movement (Tennstedt 1983, pp. 90 ff., 164 ff., 219 ff., 242 ff., 305 ff., 429 ff.; Frevert 1983). In 1933 the health-policy matters and health problems of the working-class clientele of the funds were quite foreign to the post-putsch personnel. The fact that they were not elected by working-class rank and file, as had been the practice since the 1890s, but had been appointed by party officers, reflected the general policies of the Nazi movement toward autonomous unions (Schumann 1958).

The massive hiring disrupted work at the Berlin sickness fund. Since more people were hired than fired, the office became overstaffed. Only 500 of the earlier employees of the fund remained in their jobs, so that in the fall of 1933 a total of 1,230 employees administered the insurance claims of about 450,000 fund members. The department administering contributions was staffed by 46 old employees and 167 newly hired ones, and the department handling the fund's services was staffed by only 45 old employees and 255 newly hired ones. Since the influx was so massive and took place in a very short time, there was not much chance of on-the-job adaptation, and the work process at the Berlin office came close to breaking down completely. In April 1934 a pile of 200,000 sickness applications sat unprocessed. Visitors to the fund, including members of the Nazi party, complained about the lack of discipline among fund personnel; throughout their office hours they would eat and drink alcohol.

The National Labor Ministry attempted to correct these conditions by nominating a new commissary and new directors to the fund, but these attempts met resistance. On October 27, 1933, the Gestapo occupied the fund's administrative quarters and confiscated six handguns, which were in possession of the "old fighters." A plan to "forcefully remove" the new state commissary for the local sickness fund and the new directors was thus aborted.

Further inquiry into this revolt resulted in an investigation of the training and abilities of the newly hired personnel. Their fear of impending examinations led the "old fighters" to draft a statement saying: " . . . we will resist any examination. We have continuously contributed to building a Third Reich and thus have had no time to prepare for exams in any way. . . . It would take quite a lot of time until we could take such exams, not even to speak of the second exam. Since all jobs providing decent pay have been held up to now by the 'old bonces,' and since we are only employed as helpers, we are obliged as National Socialists to resist any examination whatsoever." These fears and this statement are a consequence of the hiring policies of Ludwig Brucker, the former commissary, who wrote: "Now that we have smashed the walls of the liberal, Marxist, Jewish fortress as a result of a prolonged struggle, we must employ those old fighters who achieved this victory. . . . the major mistake in implementing this policy has been to demand from [these storm troopers] competence, capability, and experience. Such demands cannot possibly be fulfilled. . . . The toughness of these fighters will in a very short time compensate for missing competence and experience. It will even lead to a much higher level of service, which the hitherto trained administrator could never achieve, since they were not prepared by moral principles of obedience to race as the [storm trooper] is. . . ."

Indeed, the National Ministry of Labor felt compelled to pay some respect to this position. According to the Second Decree for Restructuring the Sickness Insurance Scheme of November 4, 1933, the funds were obliged to be especially considerate of front-line fighters in World War I, "approved fighters for the national revolution," and disabled persons. According to the Fourth Decree regulating this matter, such examinations also needed to take into account "general citizens' training" (the National Socialist view of the world) and "racial and hereditary matters."

Whatever the interventions from above, the situation at the local Berlin sickness fund did not change very much. Rumors abounded, and intrigues among personnel increased and impeded work. Instead of dealing with the obvious—the backlog, the qualification problem, and staff morale—some of the new directors, who had obtained their jobs through the Nazi takeover, instigated one bureaucratic innovation after another, such as double bookkeeping, to demonstrate their "competence." In addition, some of the new directors were prosecuted by the state attorney for mishandling of insurance funds. On October 1, 1934, 16 local sickness funds in the geographic area of Berlin and its suburbs that had not belonged to the Berlin fund were united with it. Since these other funds had experienced dismissal rates of only 20–40 percent, it was hoped that the merger would improve the rate of qualified personnel within the Berlin fund. At the same time, the unification led to a surplus of 865 employees. The National Statistical Office had already pointed out in a letter dated June 9, 1934, that the Berlin fund had one administrative employee for every 324 insured, whereas the average in all of the Reich was 1:547. The situation was so messy that an independent and expert report on the fund proclaimed a deadlock, and the state commissary for all of Berlin and the Prussian state, Dr. Julius Lippert, as well as Hitler's personal adviser, Dr. Willi Meerwald, demanded further official investigations.

On January 4, 1935, the National Ministry of Labor found another chance for "changing course" and putting the ship afloat again: Four of the local fund directors were accused of embezzling 5,700 Reichs Mark (RM), dismissed, and imprisoned on remand. The state commissary, who had proved quite helpless in remedying these Nazi activities, was replaced by an expert from the Ministry of Labor, Ministerialrat Dr. Manfred Hoffmeister. Again the "old fighters" resisted the reform, and one of the dismissed directors spoke on their behalf in his appeal: "It is impossible to demand that 'old fighters' cooperate with their old enemies in one office and work together with them. The men feel ridiculed by the National Labor Ministry, which is quite unpopular anyhow." In a letter to the Labor Ministry, the new commissary wrote that the politics of the Nazi party within the Berlin sickness fund had been "arbitrary, immoral, and completely at odds with any professionally correct work in a local sickness fund." After a while these measures by the Labor Ministry brought the Berlin situation under control again and at least established bureaucratic regularity there.

## Measures against the Regional and National Associations of the Sickness Funds

Most historical work on social insurance in Germany does not pay much attention to the role of regional and national associations within sickness insurance, which had developed at the end of the last century on the basis of self-government and had become more and more important as time went on (Tennstedt 1977, pp. 83 ff., 133 ff.). These sickness-fund associations, which were, so to speak, behind and above all the individual funds, remained independent and soon became the backbone of the whole sickness-fund movement.

Several factors contributed to this development. Small sickness funds could only muster a rather small administrative infrastructure. Even if they had a full-time leading administrator, he would usually not be able to deal with all the problems that accumulated over the years. Only the larger local sickness funds could, as a rule, muster a full-time leading administrator and, as the case may be, specialists in certain administrative problem areas. The small local funds and the funds of certain professional groups would probably have broken down had they been required to build up the necessary administrative infrastructure and had they not founded a professional backbone of regional or national associations.

The main purpose of these associations was to simplify and standardize administration and to improve administrative economy. The sickness funds took a lot of pride in their comparatively low administrative costs and in the absence of "bureaucratism." These associations, which in no way dealt directly with the insured, grew more important during the Weimar Republic. They were private associations of the sickness funds, which were themselves public bodies, since this was the only legal option to associate nationally without parliamentary consent.[5] Nevertheless, these private associations by nature fulfilled public tasks. Even so, the state did not grant official public status to them until 1937. To appreciate the importance of the destruction in this area in 1933, one must consider the work of the associations of local sickness funds in more detail.

In 1894 the first national association of sickness funds, the Central Association of Local Sickness Funds in the German Reich (Centralverband von Krankenkassenvereinigungen im Deutschen Reich) was founded (Tennstedt 1977, pp. 84 ff.). In 1903 its administrative headquarters was moved from Leipzig to Dresden, and at the same time this association became more strongly entrenched in the Social Democratic and free-trade-union movement. This development was mainly achieved by the work of Julius Fraesdorf, Eduard Graef, and Albert Cohen. The advisory function of the National Association was expanded. Its board and the leading administrative officials started to lobby for social-policy reforms at the national level and to initiate local reforms in the sickness funds in the area of social hygiene and preventive medicine. Physicians who were close to the working-class movements for different reasons and in different ways played an instrumental role. The physicians active in this respect were Raphael Friedeberg, Dr. Friedrich Landmann, Alfred Blaschko, Alfred Grotjahn, and Ignaz Zadeksen.

In 1914 the "Lehmann era" began. The National Association of German Sickness Funds was chartered, and in 1924 its administrative headquarters was moved to Berlin. Helmut Lehmann, the new leading administrative official (and after 1945 a leading official in the GDR's rebuilding of social policy) had been active in social policy before 1914, and in 1916 he published a "pocket book" on court decisions pertaining to sickness insurance administration. This book, which Lehmann had evolved from his private filing system, later became the basis of one of the first looseleaf commentaries in the legal area. These publishing activities, which were private at first, became part of the association's duties after 1914 when a Publishing Company of German Sickness Funds was founded. The publishing company expanded from 1927 to 1932 by founding the Publisher for Social Medicine Joint Stock Company. After 1916 a further subsidiary organization, the General Pensioners Fund of German Sickness Funds, was activated, and in 1923 a Druggist Services Company (Heilmittel-Versorgungs-A.G.) became active. All these companies were backup organizations for the local funds, providing organizational routines through commentaries, forms, materials on innovative practices in social medicine, pension insurance for fund personnel and standardized and cheaper medical equipment and drugs. This in-kind provision of services by the funds received strong national support. Eventually these associations and their activities formed an infrastructure of support for the funds, run democratically by peers and colleagues.

The associational landscape in Berlin on which the 1933 purges were inflicted differed from the one at the national level. The Association of Sickness Funds in the Area of the Sickness Fund Supervisory Agency of Berlin (Verband der Krankenkassen im Bezirk des Versicherungsamts Berlin), founded in 1919, was an association of a different type, even though it pursued similar goals. It evolved from the Central Commission of the Berlin Sickness Funds (Centralcommission der Krankenkassen Berlins), which was founded in 1896. This regional association, provided for in section 407 of the National Insurance Code, was much more comprehensive than the national association described above, which included only local sickness funds. The Berlin association included not only most Berlin local sickness funds but also some of that city's factory and guild sickness funds, for a total of about 1 million insured. Thus, it was much broader in scope and included health service delivery organizations operating in quite different social-policy climates: union-run local sickness funds, employer-run factory funds, and craft-run guild or "professional" funds. This Berlin association, administered by Max Ebel and Carl Schulz, ran two hospitals and 38 ambulatory clinics. It was the major deliverer of in-kind health services in the Reich, and it operated outside the normal "medical market" controlled by the Hartmannbund (the equivalent of a German Medical Association).

The Berlin association initiated important ventures in regulating the normal medical market. For example, it founded a Drug Commission, which had members from the Berlin Druggists' Association, the professional sickness funds (Ersatzkassen), the physicians' organization, and the central health office of the city of Berlin. They collaborated on "limiting in a rational manner the plethora of drugs and special remedies produced after the war by the chemical industries." The group compiled and published the pathbreaking Greater Berlin Drug Prescription Book, which listed all drugs and special remedies reimbursed by the funds. If other drugs or special remedies were to be prescribed, the doctor would have to apply to this commission. The publication of this Drug Prescription Book led to a restriction of drugs and special remedies used, and also in many cases to lower prices. The producers of the medicines paid the funds a negotiated amount or a percentage of sales. The Drug Commission, at first a provisional body, was put on a continuous footing by contractual agreement in 1925 with the Berlin Druggists' Association, the regional association of sickness funds, and the regional association of factory sickness funds. This so-called Cap Agreement was also later subscribed to by the professional sickness funds. The reimbursements by the producers were used to finance the Drug Prescription Book, a journal (Der Kassenarzt), and other enlightened projects. Dr. Julius Moses, one of the major Social Democratic figures in health policy at the national level (Nadav 1982; Nemitz 1974), edited Der Kassenarzt and made it an important focus of health reform and struggle against the monopolistic actions of the Hartmannbund.

These associations and their own service-delivery institutions were continuously under attack by the organized professionals (physicians, dentists, druggists) and by industry as examples of "socialization," of a "nationalization of health services" in a localized version (Weber 1927; Mahner 1930, 1932). The case study of the ambulatory clinics in the river Weser port region, which follows, sketches the development and the end of one such struggle in detail. Since the Nazi regime (at least initially) pursued policies attractive to the middle classes, it seized on arguments by professional associations against these institutions and smashed the fund-owned service-delivery institutions as well as the boards of those sickness funds that had built up such institutions. By administrative decree the National Ministry of Labor was now empowered to take control of the sickness-fund associations and of their enterprises or the enterprises of their members.

On March 24, 1933, Ludwig Brucker was appointed a Commissary for the National Association of German Sickness Funds. He removed the whole board of this association and dismissed all the employees, with the exception of the registrar. The leading administrative official, Helmut Lehmann, was taken into police custody. Brucker not only replaced the top national functionaries but also took over the authorities of the regional associations. On April 11, 1933, he had it publicly declared in the National Socialist journal *Der Angriff* that a "purification action against the sickness funds" was necessary and that he, "in accord with the National Ministry of Labor and as a commissary leader of the former Marxist National Association of German Sickness Funds," had "radically intervened in the internal affairs of this national association, which comprised about 12 million insured." Brucker also announced to the press that he had taken "a number of economy measures by abandoning all sickness-fund institutions and activities that did not belong to the proper activities of the association. . . . A series of elaborate interconnections between these institutions have been discovered, whose purpose is not easy to identify." This press release was not well received by the National Ministry of Labor. Ministerialdirektor Dr. Hans Engel jotted: "Put the brakes on Mr. B., he just can't go on this way." At first there was no success in stopping Ludwig Brucker. On May 8, 1933, he instigated another publication in the *Deutsche Zeitung* on "the private businesses of Red sickness-fund 'bonces' and the misuse of funds at the National Association by Ahrens and Lehmann."

Brucker's measures against Lehmann as the leading administrative official of the National Association and as a major shareholder of that association's private subsidiaries created substantial conflict for the civil servants at the National Ministry of Labor. Lehmann was one of the few persecuted functionaries who did not shy away from going to court.

These dismissals did not have sufficient legal support in the amended civil service law. Thus, Ministerialrat Dr. Alexander Grünewald noted in his files on December 30, 1933, that the court judge of the Kammergericht (the Prussian Superior Civil Court) presiding in this case, Dr. Karl Hellmut Heyderhoff, had remarked: "How is it that just any minister could issue any administrative decrees? After all, we do have a constitution." He tended to dissallow the dismissals. Grünewald commented that such a likely result "from the viewpoint of the Reich's authority is intolerable." On January 16, 1934, he noted: "It would be desirable if these proceedings could be tabled," and the court was informed that amendments of the law to this effect were being prepared. These amendments were passed on February 16, 1934. Another note by Grünewald in his files indicates that these amendments were a rather dubious legal measure specifically taken against Lehmann: "Should the issue of regulating any contractual arrangements arise in cabinet discussions, we can point out that these amendments are of practical relevance only in the case of L. . . . To issue and publish this law is urgent, since the next session of the Landgericht Berlin in this case is scheduled for February 23, and this law is of importance for the outcome of this case."

Remarkable in this struggle are the actions of Lehmann's attorney, Walther Döhring. In the court proceedings at the Landgericht he talked about the "quacks" (Bönhasen) at the National Ministry of Labor, and on January 4, 1935, he wrote to the ministry:

The "revolutionary" measure of appointing a State Commissary for the new National Association of Local Sickness Funds also needs to be justified in terms of the existing legal order, in part itself promulgated by the revolution, and thus the first appointment of Commissary Brucker has been declared void by a decision of the Kammergericht of November 27, 1933, because it did not conform to any such legal principles. To deal with the consequences of such a null and void measure by dubious amendments indicates strong disrespect for the judgment of a high court. . . . in view of this situation the law of February 16, 1934, especially its article 3 §1, may not be construed as being retroactive. In view of the sloppy drafting and sloppy implementation of the law of March 17, 1933, all persons involved could expect that the measures of the commissary, who in the meantime has been removed for personal causes, would be declared void. These persons will now have to recognize that they should not have conformed to what was then said to be law but rather to what is now retroactively introduced as new law. In this way the national government is trying to compensate for the sloppiness of its first series of measures by a new series of sloppy measures. . . . The English courts, in their self-conscious habits, would know without hesitation and with some precision how to deal with such sloppy work. It is mainly the consequence of our German judicial system and its underdeveloped self-consciousness that it does not educate lawmakers in a clear and precise use of legal language.

Grünewald notified the attorney general on February 14, 1934, of the content of this letter and requested that "everything necessary be undertaken." The files finally reveal that the attorney general initiated disciplinary proceedings against this attorney via the attorney general's office at the Kammergericht.

## The Case of the Lower Weser Region

The service-delivery institutions which the sickness funds ran until they were dismantled by the Nazi regime owed their existence to a legal and administrative principle of social insurance known as the in-kind principle (Sachleistungsprinzip). In the context of health insurance, the in-kind principle placed an obligation on the fund to deliver a service to the insured. It dates back to the 1890s, when it was first used against the traditional, private, working-class funds to raise their costs of existence by obliging them to assure the service itself and not just money for shopping for services in a private market. At the same time, it provided for an expansive, controlling role of the "public" local funds in the developing medical submarkets. This obligation could not be fulfilled by "cashing out" insurance claims and delivering the insured to a private medical marketplace. The principle also was of some significance as a means of regulating the private medical market and as a means of developing preventive health policy.

This sphere of a "social economy" of health delivery was broadly conceived. It included public x-ray institutes, public opticians' services, public massage and bath facilities, public provision of drugs, public provision of dental and all other ambulatory medical services, and public provision of stationary health services. ("Public" in each case denotes sickness funds and not communal or state services, which coexisted in some areas.) In all these cases the "social economy" was not pervasive. It never replaced private delivery in the whole Reich in one sector. Its role was usually either to help regulate the normal and dominating "medical markets" by creating countervailing powers or to provide delivery substituting for a nonexistent local, regional, or national market.

This "social economy" (Eigenwirtschaft)—i.e., the sphere of public enterprises run by the sickness funds—is well symbolized by the ambulatory clinics founded at the time of the Weimar Republic (Tennstedt 1977, pp. 150–180; Hansen et al. 1981, pp. 152–499). The struggle over these institutions was the most visible at the time, because it involved a strongly developing professional organization involving doctors, was conducted at a national level, and involved highly visible action such as a national physicians' strike and a national boycott by the German Medical Association. Nevertheless, such ambulatory sickness-fund clinics existed only in two regions. More clinics existed in the framework of the accident insurance program. Since it was employer-run, the lines of conflict remained much more submerged than in the union-run local sickness funds. These sickness-fund clinics were an attempt to overcome the privatized structure of the medical market, with its individualizing, fragmenting, and organizational consequences. They hired physicians on salary, concentrated them and the necessary equipment in a fund-administered building and made the services available to the insured at their choice.

These ambulatory clinics were important after 1924 in Berlin and Geestemünde, but were destroyed in 1933 under those pressure of the organized providers who allied themselves with Nazi organizations and whose onslaught had built up since the turn of the century as a middle-class "storming of the funds" (Hoffmann 1912). To balance our Berlin-centered argument, the following analysis will focus on the rise and fall of the ambulatory clinics of the funds in Geestemünde, a process extensively researched by Hansen et al. (1981), who also studied the Berlin case.

At the end of 1923 there was a physicians' strike in all of the Reich, as there had been in 1920. The reason for this strike was an Emergency Decree of the National Government of October 30, 1923. The panel doctors, who were mostly organized with the Hartmannbund, opposed the obligations to the sickness funds put upon them by this decree. They especially opposed the supervision of the delivery of medical services by the sickness-fund boards, which they thought to be much too strong. Even though their protests were of some success, that did not head off a strike in December of 1923, which was later justified by demands for higher fees. For the duration of the strike, the insured were treated by the doctors not as panel patients but rather as private patients who had to pay their own way.

The sickness funds in Berlin and in the cities in the Lower Weser region took the offensive and made sure they provided in-kind medical services to their members so that they would not have to pay the especially high fees (Kampfhonorare) demanded by the doctors during this so-called "contractless situation." These funds advertised for and hired doctors, often from out of town, who then took charge of provisional ambulatory clinics which the sickness funds had set up during the strike. The development of such institutions, run and owned by the local funds, occurred in Berlin on a much larger scale than it did in the cities of the Lower Weser region. At certain points the Berlin sickness funds ran more than 40 ambulatory clinics, which were headed by Dr. Felix Koenigsberger until 1925 and then until 1933 by Dr. Kurt Bendix. Dr. Walter Axel Friedeberger (after 1959 to be Deputy Secretary of Health of the GDR) was the deputy head of these clinics as long as they existed.

The local sickness fund of Geestemünde ran one ambulatory clinic in Geestemünde and one in Lehe. In addition, the local funds of Bremerhaven and Lehe supported a common ambulatory clinic of their own, the Medical Department of Bremerhaven. These clinics were opened in 1924 with two doctors apiece, which made them rather small and unspecialized in comparison with those developing in Berlin. Nevertheless, they seem to have been much better integrated with the local working class than were private, fee-for-service physicians.

The ambulatory clinic of Geestemünde was rather popular with the insured. Already in 1924 up to 500 persons daily consulted this institution. The demand was so high that at the end of 1928 the local sickness fund decided to build a special building for the ambulatory clinic. The leading physician of the clinic, Otto Kissel, was very active in designing the new clinic. Otto Okrass, the leading administrative official of the Geestemünde fund, who closely cooperated with Albert Kohn in Berlin, was the other major person behind this plan, because he had been originally responsible for implementing the idea of ambulatory clinics in the area. The new clinic had its own laboratory and was centered around a large x-ray machine of the newest design. It sponsored all sorts of rooms for different kinds of physical therapy. In addition, it had its own health baths, inhalation rooms, and living quarters for the doctors employed in the building. The two doctors were supported by four nurses, a bookkeeper, and a supervisor. Public lectures, courses, and instructional material of all sorts on questions of social hygiene and preventive medicine were provided to the insured as a routine in the clinic's work. With the exception of the baths, the Medical Department of Bremerhaven delivered the same services as did the Geestemünde clinic.

The responsible administrative officials of the sickness funds in the Lower Weser cities left no doubt that these ambulatory clinics were not to be thought of as stop-gap devices in time of strike. Instead, they were thought of as institutions that, by their continuity of services, could prevent future strikes of the local private physicians, and that would also be more effective in delivering medical services to the members and provide more "outreach." The funds made it known publicly that now the poorest of the poor in the region could also obtain the best of medical help. Patients would obtain all help in one place and thus would not have to walk all over the region and lose a lot of time getting different services in different places. The hours of the ambulatory clinics were extended to prevent long waiting periods, and physicians' help could be obtained at any time of day or night. Otto Okrass emphasized that, for economic reasons, the private physicians would be unable to support such comprehensive medical-service delivery.

With the opening of a subsidiary of the Geestemünde ambulatory clinic in the Lehe quarter of Bremerhaven in July 1926, the expansion phase of ambulatory clinics in this region ended. The "social economy" of the sickness funds seems to have been much in demand and rather popular with the insured. The data on the use of these clinics by the insured and their family members show that about one-fourth of all the cases of sickness in the Lower Weser region were taken care of here, and it needs to be underlined that the insured had free choice between visiting these clinics and seeing a private physician at the fund's expense. During much of the time of these institutions' existence, only four physicians in permanent employment were responsible for delivering service. However, the popularity of these institutions meant that these doctors had become major competition for the 45 private physicians practicing in the region.

Thus, conflict accompanied the ambulatory clinics from their birth to their death in 1933. On the physicians' side were the local organization of the Hartmannbund and the Association of the Panel Doctors in the Lower Weser Region; the local sickness funds were on the other side. The local press constantly reported on these emotionally charged struggles. The private physicians thought of the clinics as illegal, since they had discontinued their strike and had offered their services to the funds in accordance with the conditions that had obtained before the strike broke out. The funds, on the other hand, did not want to give up their ambulatory clinics. In addition, they hoped to decrease the number of panel doctors in the region. Thus, the struggle over the ambulatory clinics turned into a struggle over the general shape of the medical market in the region, with the focus on the principle of maximizing the "system of free choice of (private) physicians" in the region. This struggle was carried out on all arbitration levels within the sickness-insurance scheme. The organized panel doctors in the proceedings at the National Insurance Bureau in Berlin stated that "these warehouses of medical treatment must disappear from the earth, which will only be beneficial to the insured in the Lower Weser region" (Stadtarchiv Bremerhaven 020–1712). But even the highest court of arbitration decided in favor of the legality of ambulatory clinics: The sickness funds had only, as was demanded of them in their by-laws, taken the necessary measures to ward off interruptions of medical services to their insured. This did not end the conflict, however.

The local panel doctors still thought of the ambulatory clinics as institutions that were purely a consequence of the "Marxist power lust" of the sickness-fund bureaucrats—a stand that can be taken only if one shares in an uncompromising free-enterprise ideology, to which regulating the medical market is in principle a foreign, "Marxist" idea. The idea of peaceful collaboration with the ambulatory-clinic doctors was denounced. Negotiations between the sickness funds and the local association of panel doctors were abortive. All interim contracts between the two parties were agreed to only after all arbitration procedures had been exhausted. A contract between the local sickness fund at Gees-temünde and the corresponding association of panel doctors, which had been agreed to after drawn-out negotiations, was prolonged year by year, as renegotiation proved impossible. Only after the Nazi takeover and the destruction of the ambulatory clinics could a new contract be negotiated.

After all means had been exhausted to declare the ambulatory clinics illegal, the attacks of the organized physicians were directed against the physicians employed there. The physicians who had offered their services to the Berlin sickness funds during the strike had already received threatening anonymous letters and had been threatened by roughnecks. The physicians' organizations thought of these doctors as strikebreakers and disbarred them from membership in their organization. The Hartmannbund attempted to thus increase the social sanctions against such doctors and also attempted to bar them from membership in medical scientific organizations. Starting in 1925, the local association of panel doctors attempted by "permanent cold war" to bar these ambulatory-clinic doctors from panel practice, and they thus hoped to win back patients who had attended the clinics. In addition, they tried to make any additional hiring of physicians by these clinics impossible, and in 1930 they attempted to seize on loose legal language to have the licenses of these physicians revoked.

These continuous attacks on the ambulatory clinics and their doctors did not succeed until 1933, when the local panel doctors found a powerful ally in the Third Reich. Three doctors who had worked for the ambulatory clinics in the Lower Weser cities were severely persecuted under the Nazi regime. The leading doctor of the Geestemünde clinic, Otto Kissel, was Jewish. Thus, he could not, as some colleagues of his were able to, take up panel practice when the authorities closed down the ambulatory clinic. Shortly before his natural (?) death in July of 1936, Kissel was denounced by a former patient who argued that the "racial belonging" of Dr. Kissel caused the patient's "bodily decay." (This was quite in line with the official propaganda of the party.)

Dr. Paul Marx, who had worked for a shorter period of time in the subsidiary Geestemünde clinic in Lehe in 1926–1927, was Jewish, but since he had fought on the front lines in World War I he was allowed to continue panel practice until 1938. He had to close down his practice then, since not only his panel practice but also his medical license was taken away from him for "racial reasons." Marx went underground to avoid being sent to a concentration camp and stayed in this "illegal" situation until his arrest by the Gestapo in July 1944. He was beaten and sent to the Flossenburg camp, where he survived further beatings. Freed as the war ended, he started a new practice, notwithstanding his eventually fatal disabilities stemming from his concentration-camp experience.

Dr. Walter Jungfermann had been an assistant to Dr. Ernst Rudolf Adam at the Medicine Department of Bremerhaven toward the end of the Weimar Republic. He was arrested repeatedly because of his anti-Nazi orientation, was continuously labled "non-Aryan," and was beaten four times. One beating in October of 1939 led to serious head injuries. He died in 1965 from later complications of this beating. His career is rather typical of the humanistic and social practice that characterized many ambulatory-clinic physicians in Berlin and the Lower Weser region. Usually it was not "the socialization of health care" or some other grand political scheme that led them into practice in ambulatory clinics, but the potential for technically and socially better professional work. The death of Dr. Jungfermann was not atypical of doctors who chose to stay on or could not leave.

Let us now turn to the institutional consequences of the Nazi takeover for the ambulatory clinics in the Lower Weser cities. A closer look at Nazi health policy reveals three main tiers. Above and beyond population and racial policy, the Nazis took the offense against the "Red" and "bonce" institutions created for the working class by union social policy. In addition, the initially middle-class orientation of the Nazis in the health sector linked the party strongly with physicians, dentists, druggists, opticians, and other health professionals. This tipped the balance. Whereas the Social Democrats and the free trade unions had given support during the Weimar Republic to self-government in sickness insurance within the local sickness funds and thus had also provided a place for "social economy" in this area to expand, their influence was now erased. In addition, the Christian Labor orientation of the Weimar Ministry of Labor had provided a crucial protection at the level of the responsible agency of the national government; this protection now became quite fragile and spotty. Thus, the Gleichschaltung of the sickness funds and the destruction of their "social economy" were of special importance in 1933 to the interconnected interests of the Nazis, the professional associations, and the professional markets. This was the case in Bremerhaven, Geestemünde, and Lehe, and not just in Berlin.

With political opponents removed, the Nazi party and the health-care professionals took action. The First Decree for Establishing a New Order in Sickness Insurance of March 1, 1933, established special control powers over the sickness funds and allowed investigations of the "social economy" institutions run by the funds. If found "uneconomical," these institutions were to be closed.

On April 18, 1933 the chief members of the board and the leading administrative official of the Geestemünde and Lehe sickness funds, Otto Okrass, attended a conference at the Insurance Bureau in Wesermünde. They were confronted with the new legal situation, and its consequences for the ambulatory clinics were especially stressed. An immediate economic study of the dental clinics and the ambulatory clinics was recommended (Stadtarchiv Bremerhaven 020–14–4). This meeting was preceded by demands from the Association of Panel Doctors in the Lower Weser Region, i.e. the professional association of insurance physicians, who were allied with the National Socialist Physicians Union, to close the ambulatory clinics immediately. These two doctors' associations sent the same demand to the Ministry of Labor. They argued that the ambulatory clinics were uneconomical because one physician in the ambulatory clinic took away the income of four physicians in private practice. The irony of calling such economy uneconomical seems to have eluded them. The memorandum states:

That these warehouses are enemies of the middle class is already shown by the fact that, proportional to their expansion, the economic space—in this case of physicians in private practice—is being destroyed. Neither the national good nor moral principles legitimate such a development, as deviation from the principle "the common good supersedes individual advantage" shows. . . . These institutions are a product of scheming, brutalized power, and are an expression of the obvious trend to gag a free profession and continuously prepare it for socialism. No profession is less suitable for such socialism than the medical one. This way of discharging a doctor's duties may be compared only to large factories and consumer cooperatives. Quite apart from the fact that such ways of delivering medical services by medical bureaucrats, who can neither rely on a patient's trust nor have any compassion for their patients, are incompatible with the essence of the healing process, not only can we do without such institutions, but in addition they violate sound economic principles according to which the free-enterprise spirit, creativity, individual endeavors, and personal responsibility should find roots with a maximum number of citizens.

The next month saw the measures described earlier to purge the sickness funds of indigenous workers put into practice. From October 9 to October 11 the ambulatory clinic in Geestemünde was audited. Otto Okrass had already informed the auditor that the Geestemünde local sickness fund intended to close down its "social economy" institutions by December 31. This corresponded to the demands of the local and the Nazi physicians' associations. "The costs per case in the ambulatory clinic are substantially higher than with private panel physicians" [this statement is factually false—cf. Hansen et al. 1981, pp. 314 ff.] . . . "therefore," the auditor reasoned, even though he had already agreed with Otto Okrass in advance of the audit on all the specifics of the dismantling, "the closing of the ambulatory clinic is advised" (Niedersächsisches Staatsarchiv Stade OVA: acc. 18–64 F 35a Nr. 7). Thus, the decision to close these clinics and like institutions, which had politically already been taken, found its post hoc expert rationalization in the auditor's report.

With the clinics dismantled, the "free" physicians finally were able to attain their goals in the context of the "national revolution." As the clinics closed, the lump sum per capita fees paid out to the local physicians were raised from 10.95 RM to 13.77 RM. As a final gesture, the former clinics were used as administrative headquarters for the district leadership of the Nazi party and its organizations.

Whether the sickness funds received any compensation for this destruction after World War II could not be discovered, but it is unlikely. Nevertheless, it is remarkable that the Association of Panel Doctors in the Lower Weser Region had its headquarters on the lower floor of the major Geestemünde ambulatory clinic for a short time after World War II. Thus, the former enemies of the ambulatory clinics came to occupy the former "fortress" and were in no way obliged after 1945 to undo the health-policy damage they had completed in 1933. On the contrary, any alternative ideas about health delivery in the region remained displaced.

The destruction of the Medical Department of Bremerhaven took a similar course. Here Christian Brandau, the commissary and SA member, displayed a dashing style. The administrative headquarters of the local sickness fund was occupied by the SA. All personnel were dismissed as a "precaution" effective October 1, 1933, and all medical appliances of the Medical Division were sold dirt-cheap locally. Brandau was later reprimanded by another auditor for his rash dismantling: "If the local sickness fund of Bremerhaven together with the funds of Geestemünde and Lehe, which had their own ambulatory clinics and participated in the common dental clinic, had insisted on negotiations with the associations of the physicians and the different dental professions, the chances for a more favorable way of dismantling would have grown substantially." (Niedersächsisches Staatsarchiv Stade OVA acc. 18–64 F 35a Nr. 7)

It seems proper to finish this section on the consequences of the Nazi takeover for the sickness-fund administration with a short analysis of the effects on the fund personnel in the Lower Weser region. The first Berufsverbot in that region affected Bernhard Vogelsang, a rather active member of the free trade unions and a Social Democrat. He had been elected on January 1, 1933, by the requisite two-thirds majority of the representatives of the insured to the position of leading administrative official of the Bremerhaven local sickness fund. Interestingly, this case of Berufsverbot predates the general Nazi takeover and elucidates the role some employer representatives in the self-government structure of the funds played under these conditions. They used the swelling "national revolution" to get rid of Vogelsang, whom they thought of as an uncomfortable administrator. They appealed to the Insurance Bureau in Bremerhaven, attacking the validity of his election by enclosing a flyer, signed by Vogelsang, in which the nomination of Adolf Hitler as chancellor was criticized harshly and described as "a symbol of the impending attack against all rights of the working-class movement" (Stadtarchiv Bremerhaven F 288–24). The Bremerhaven Insurance Bureau caved in and upheld the appeal.

After the Nazi takeover and parallel to the purges of sickness funds all over the Reich, the Bremerhaven fund was "cleaned out." Of its 16 employees, almost a dozen were fired and replaced by SA men and "old fighters" of the National Socialist movement. Here again Christian Brandau played a decisive role.

The "purification" of the local sickness funds in Geestemünde and Lehe took place in three consecutive and ever more intense phases. At first the changing of the legal infrastructure of hiring had indirect but nevertheless very effective consequences for the employment situation. Of the 26 employees of these funds, three went into early retirement, all of them members of the Social Democratic party (SPD) or the Reichsbanner. Among them was the leading physician of the Geestemünde ambulatory clinic, Otto Kissel. Beyond that, an increased incidence of serious illnesses among the employees is notable, and retirement due to disability increased.

After the union personnel had been purged from the self-government structure of the funds, there was room for a second phase of "purification" through Berufsverbote. The new chairman of the board of the Geestemünde local fund dismissed the deputy administrator of the fund (Heinrich Brinkmann) and the supervisor of the building. Both these dismissals were on grounds of membership in the SPD and the Reichsbanner. In addition, three women employees were dismissed according to paragraph 6 of the Law on Establishment of a Professional Civil Service, which allowed for dismissals to "simplify administration." In contrast to the men, two of these women were in a position to appeal successfully with the proper insurance bureaus; however, their appeals were based more on questions of equal treatment than on political reasons.

At the end of 1933 the situation turned for the worse. The leader of the Nazi party district of Lower Saxony had intervened with the Higher Insurance Bureau to increase the pressure for more dismissals at the local sickness funds. The employees had already been asked to list their political activities and answer questions pertaining to "racial" origin. Twenty-one members of the SPD and the Reichsbanner had to declare themselves, and this stimulated further "clean up" operations. The Higher Insurance Bureau advised the boards of the local sickness funds to dismiss all employees who had been members of the Reichs-

banner or the SPD. Seven further employees were dismissed. This
resulted in a series of appeals, which were not decided upon until late
1934—most unfavorably. In summary, of the 37 persons employed
with the sickness funds of Geestemünde and Lehe and in its "social
economy" institutions (excepting the dental clinics) at the beginning
of 1933, only 10 employees remained in the service of these funds at
the end of 1934. These funds thus were purged more strongly than
the national averages would indicate. This fact is due to the importance
of "social economy" institutions for the sickness funds in this region
and the conspicuous struggle over their institutionalization in a small
town, which made some employees easier targets for recrimination in
1933.

Conclusion

The Nazi destruction of the sickness funds' ability to deliver medical
services is important today because this ability continues to be suppressed (Rohwer-Kahlmann 1982; Hansen et al. 1981; Tennstedt 1981).
In 1955, the parliament of the FRG imposed a legal freeze by passing
the Gesetz über das Kassenarztrecht (Act on Panel Doctors), which
stopped further development of sickness-fund clinics by making it contingent on the agreement of the physicians' organizations (Naschold
1967; Safran 1967). This clause was part of an overall regulation of
the status of panel doctors and their hegemony over treatment. Even
though ambulatory clinics were done away with de facto in the Nazi
period, the National Ministry of Labor had been able to resist efforts
to make them generally illegal. Such efforts met partial success only
in 1955, and have been extended into other realms of health policy by
the national civil court (Rohwer-Kahlmann 1982). Thus a short post-
World War II era of social reform, which aimed at a uniform and
universal coverage and again involved Berlin (Reidegeld 1982) and
Bremerhaven, came to an end (Hockerts 1980, pp. 149 ff.).

As our short sketch of the history of self-government of the sickness
funds has already indicated, we find much continuity in the politics
of service delivery of the 1930s, the 1940s, and the 1950s. The social
policy of the FRG did not return to pre-1933 self-government conditions.
Rather, it consciously or unconsciously perpetuates much of the destruction effected by the Third Reich's social policy. In the case of in-
kind delivery of services it even went much further by giving such

destruction a halo of legality, which it did not even have under the Third Reich (Hansen et al. 1981, pp. 547 ff.).

## Measures Against Jewish and Socialist Physicians, Dentists, and Dental Technicians

The first part of this study dealt with the effects of the Nazi takover of the administration of health insurance, the result of which was that the traditional connection between the labor movement and insurance sickness funds, in which these funds represented the vanguard of social policy for the unions and the Social Democratic party, was destroyed by eliminating honorary union officers and thus eliminating the self-administration of the funds. "National unreliables" and "non-Aryans" in full-time jobs at the funds were removed. These processes must be considered among the decisive actions concerning institutional social policy of the Nazi period, for none of the later changes in health insurance had such a profound impact. Thus was destroyed one of the elements of the "health policy reform cluster" which had formed in Germany since the turn of the century and which was responsible for most of the innovation in the health area.

It will become clear in the following that in respect to health policy National Socialism attacked and destroyed the German labor movement and the Jewish citizens as a functional, homogeneous entity. It was primarily the self-administered worker sickness funds that provided social space for progress in health policy, be it in technical improvement or in service-delivery innovations. It was chiefly Jewish panel doctors who delivered the services and propagated reforms in the insurance context. They had settled in industrial or other boom areas—mainly in big cities, and especially in Berlin, the pace setter of health reform in industrial Germany. Destruction of a labor-oriented health and social policy could not be limited to demolishing the administrative structure, as described in previous sections. It also had to hit the service infra-structure, the physicians, the other decisive elements of the "health policy reform cluster."

Looking for progressive tendencies in health policy only in the sick-ness funds would be a rather incomplete approach. Health reform at the local government level (Loewenstein 1981) became at least as im-portant in dealing with rapid industrialization and large-scale immi-gration of agricultural workers or farmers into the cities. As the membership of the sickness funds expanded, moving in large steps toward universal coverage, and as the output of the funds shifted radically from monetary transfers to delivery of services and as they consequently developed preventive and advisory capacities, the "local government" approach and the insurance approach overlapped and combined. This became evident with the development of local hospitals around the turn of the century (Labisch 1981; Labisch 1981–82) in which the sickness funds played a decisive role as "financiers" of institutional medical care and as the co-founders and co-sponsors of free clinics and advice centers. If prior institutions of a similar nature had existed at all, they were either bound confessionally or tied to old feudal privilege, or they were private polyclinics or polyclinics attached to the universities. These forms of service delivery were not adequate to deal with rapid industrialization and urbanization as it took place primarily in northern Germany. These processes of reinstitutionalizing health policy would not be comprehensible if attention were to focus on the institutional sphere only. Rather, a focus on personnel delivering service and promoting reform will be another key to understanding the social forces involved.

Socialist physicians played an important role in these developments, especially where the industrial working class was socially dominant (as in the larger northern cities and in Munich). In Germany (and Austria), socialist intellectuals and academics of the time were often physicians, most often with a Jewish background. Physicians spearheading the socialist movement could rely on a well-established tradition: the medical reform movement of 1848, during which Virchow had labeled doctors natural spokesmen for the poor; the preventive and hygiene movement that started in the 1860s; and British investigations of the conditions of the working classes, initiated there by physicians and factory inspectors and continuously reported in Germany through Karl Marx, Friedrich Engels, August Bebel, et al. Also, quite a few physicians who strongly identified with the shift to medicine as a natural science were attracted to social-Darwinist undercurrents in German Social Democratic circles.

As the labor movement was able to overcome the restrictions of an election system based on ownership of property at the local level and took over substantial areas of self-government in the health-insurance sickness funds, these physicians helped design and partly implement health-service delivery or local social policy in general. Their politics were also crucial in breaking down cultural barriers and political mistrust against professionalized medical institutions and services. This resistance was well entrenched in the working class of the time and quite visible in the support of quacks and faith healers in working-class quarters. In addition, these doctors gained in their daily medical practice a deep understanding of working-class conditions that informed their social policies.

The cooperation between socialist physicians and the labor movement began in the 1890s with the sickness funds and the health self-help movement in the Labor Health Boards (Arbeitersanitätskommissionen) and the Labor Samaritan Association (Arbeitersamariterbund) (Labisch 1978). These physicians and labor groups organized a strike of working-class patients against scandalous conditions of treatment at the major Berlin charity hospital, which led to the modernization and expansion of the hospital. Through their activities in city government and in city health boards, they shaped the developing local health-service structure of hospitals, sanatoriums, infant and child care facilities, advice centers, etc. They were also quite active in fighting infectious diseases, in research on industrial hygiene, and in the treatment of industrial diseases.

The mediating function of the socialist physicians is especially apparent as the general medical profession prepared for a "general strike" against the sickness funds. The general political conditions in Imperial Germany, though, were not conducive to broad and overall success of such initiatives, because they were mostly private and faced strong political opposition. Only with the start of the Weimar period, with the democratization of the Reich after 1918, did such initiatives have a chance to shift to the public sphere on a large scale, involving all the labor unions, the Social Democratic party, the sickness funds, and the local or state social-policy bureaucracy. In this respect the beginning of the Weimar period is a landmark for such health-policy reforms. They attracted national political attention and broad support in the new constitutional openness of the republic. Economic conditions for such reforms, however, were much worse than they had been before 1914. Yet the long-term economic malaise made the preventive and welfare dimensions of health services all the more critical at both the local and the national level. Thus, statistical-epidemiological research at the fund level or the local government level developed. The analysis of social conditions and social patterns of disease focused on preventive activities. Ambulatory clinics played a key role in this work and also in developing an integrated, social-therapeutical approach to patient care. All in all, in theory and in practice, the social-hygiene component of the health sector became dominant after 1918. Thus, socialist physicians (most of them Jews) and their local and national organizations (whose members had stressed the research and practice of social hygiene for a long time) played a leading role in health policy of the Weimar Republic. This was especially true in Berlin, which had been and still was a laboratory for almost every conceivable reform in health policy. Naturally, the dismantlings starting in 1933 would have special repercussions also for the medical personnel involved in the "health-policy reform cluster."

## The History of the Jewish Contribution to Medicine

The licensing of physicians, dentists, and dental technicians was regulated anew in the context of legislation for the "reestablishment of the professional civil service." It was above all Jewish physicians who were affected. The prominent role of Jewish physicians in the development of medicine as a science in Germany has already been studied (Kaznelson 1962; Oppenheimer et al. 1971; Engelmann 1979), but their role in medical-service delivery and health reform has gone unnoticed. By practicing in the medical profession, Jews could at the same time link up with two very old Jewish religious traditions: idealistic selflessness and helping the poor. This social tradition and the experience of discrimination (Ackerknecht 1979) may have moved Jewish physicians to join or be sympathetic to the German labor movement. From this point of view, the persecution of Jewish physicians was of particular relevance to the end of a worker-oriented and union-oriented social policy.

Silbergleit (1930, p. 116) calculated on the basis of the 1925 census that there were 4,579 Jewish physicians in Prussia in that year, of whom 3,670 were independent and 835 were employed in clinics. These numbers, however, refer only to physicians who identified themselves as belonging to the Jewish religion. Their portion in the total number of physicians in Prussia at that time came to a little more than 15 percent. The National Socialist concept of non-Aryan physician was more broadly conceived. Hadrich (1934) reported that there were 6,488 Jewish physicians when the so-called Aryan legislation was introduced (see also Aron 1935). Thus, out of a total of 50,000 physicians the proportion identified as Jewish was 13 percent. But again the "non-Aryan" physicians who were active as scientists, university teachers, hospital administrators, head physicians, assistant physicians, and civil servants were not taken into account here, which makes the estimate incomplete on its own terms.

The significance of Jewish physicians in the large cities in Germany was considerable. In July 1933, 3,423 out of a total of 6,558 Berlin physicians, or 52.2 percent, were "non-Aryans." The relative proportion of Jews among physicians accredited for insurance practice was surely higher, for in October 1933, after the first "act of elimination," 2,077 out of 3,481 panel doctors in Berlin—that is 59.7 percent—were "non-Aryans." In other large cities, usually between 25 and 30 percent of the physicians were "non-Aryans," a lower percentage than in Berlin, where 37 percent of all Jewish panel doctors may have resided.

The situation in the large cities, and in Berlin in particular, was first of all a reflection of the urbanization of the Jews. Practically a third of the German Jews lived in Berlin. This urban movement, largely to Berlin and Breslau, had been intensified by the loss of the province of Poznan after the First World War (Adler-Rudel 1959; Breslauer 1909). The larger proportion of Jews in the city population opened corresponding possibilities for a Jew in insurance practice. Because of the prevailing discrimination against Jews in the provinces, be it in university careers, civil service, large industry, the chemical industry, or the medical corps and hospitals, Jews concentrated in the cities. The large cities, with their new hygienic and social improvements, demanded medical specialization and medical reforms—a challenge medically, administratively, and politically. Thus, it is no wonder that the proportion of specialists among Jewish physicians was particularly high, and that hygiene, public health, and like issues attracted their attention, integrating them into the "health-policy reform cluster." Jewish physicians took a prominent part in combating infant mortality, tuberculosis (the proletarian disease), and venereal diseases through programs in social hygiene, partly implemented through their own private and insurance practices. Two outstanding doctors who should be mentioned here for their exemplary practice in this respect are Raphael Friedeberg and Alfred Blaschko (Bock and Tennstedt 1978; Tennstedt 1979).

The Implementation of Berufsverbote among Panel Doctors

On April 22, 1933, and June 2, 1933, the National Ministry of Labor put into effect two regulations that basically excluded "non-Aryans" from further activity in local sickness funds or national health insurance. Exceptions were made for those who had fought at the front during the First World War, including those who had worked in military hospitals for infectious diseases, and for those who had established practices before August 1, 1914 (Goldschmidt 1979). Beyond this, the provisions of these laws excluded from insurance practice all previously accredited physicians, dentists, and dental technicians who had engaged in communist activities (Karstedt 1934, pp. 179 ff.).

The associations of panel doctors and dentists were charged with communicating their decision to the person affected and to the executive committee of the German Medical Association. They had to give reasons for their decision. The excluded physician then had the right to appeal first to the German Medical Association and then to the Minister of Labor, who made the final decision. These cases had to be settled by the end of 1933 in accord with the regulations of April 22 and June 2, 1933. They represented only the first phase of proceedings against Jewish physicians. Actions against them went on in other forms, including total exclusion from medical practice by delicensing and massive persecution (Ostrowski 1963).

The statistical records on the purely quantitative effects of these regulations are incomplete. One might take as a point of reference that there were 35,000 physicians and 8,000 dentists accredited for insurance practice on January 1, 1933, in Germany. There were about 12,000 dental technicians. How many of these were active for the sickness funds is unknown. Global data of the respective proportion of "non-Aryans" do not exist.

From the information on the exclusions from medical or dental panel practice that can be established with certainty, and from what one would assume on the basis of experience, about half of the physicians excluded by the local Panel Doctors' Associations appealed. From the data on all appeals against exclusion from panel practice that can be established with certainty, and from the fact that the ratio of appeals to exclusions is roughly 1:2, one would estimate that at least 2,800 physicians, 500 dentists, and 200 dental technicians had been excluded from insurance practice by December 31, 1933 (table 2).

The "proceedings" of the Associations of Panel Doctors against their colleagues varied with the degree of attack on the insurance funds and with the locale (they were particularly ruthless in Berlin). The waiting periods for admission to the panel of insurance doctors varied in length, and for young physicians this made things particularly difficult. After all, admission to insurance practice was limited, and the medical profession in large cities was officially considered overcrowded even after

**Table 2**
Appeals against exclusions by panel doctors' associations from panel national health insurance practice, 1933.

|  | Physicians | Dentists | Dental technicians |
|---|---|---|---|
| Exclusions of the panel doctors' association appealed to Ministry of Labor: |  |  |  |
|    exclusion due to non-Aryan descent | 1,030 | 206 | 79 |
|    exclusion due to communist activity | 338 | 37 | 13 |
|    exclusion for other reasons | 9 | 3 | 3 |
| Total appeals | 1,377 | 246 | 95 |
| Appeals denied by National Ministry of Labor | 827 | 174 | 52 |
|    of these, due to communist activity | 91 | 16 | 3 |

Source: Karstedt 1934, p. 181.

these exclusions had taken place. Young SA or Nazi physicians received preference in filling "vacated" panel-doctor positions. The new leading officials of the Panel Doctors' Association in Berlin were the SA physicians Martin Claus and Erwin Villain. Later, Dr. Heinrich Grote and Dr. Hans Deuschl, two ranking Nazi officials, acquired increasing influence upon the practice of Berufsverbote. In particular, Claus had a prominent part in the spiteful arrests and mistreatment of 40 "Marxist" and "Jewish" physicians and professors in July 1933, which attracted general public attention (Leibfried and Tennstedt 1979, p. 95; Goldschmidt 1979, pp. 24 ff.).

These actions prompted a classic conflict between party enthusiasts, who wanted to execute their policies as quickly as possible, and government bureaucrats, who insisted on rules, evidence, due process, and proper procedures. The National Ministry of Labor attempted to bridle these "old warriors," but was only partially successful. The official ministerial expert, Dr. Schwartz, noted on August 21, 1933, that

Out of 50 appeals entered against decisions of the Panel Doctors' Association of Berlin between August 12 and 21, 1933, 27 have had to be upheld. Only in 23 cases was the decision of the Panel Doctors' Association justified. The Hartmannbund [which was the appeals court of first resort] already recognized the 27 cases as untenable with one or two exceptions. These numbers confirm the observation that the Panel Doctors' Association of Berlin announced the dismissals in many cases with a wantonness that cannot be exceeded. If one bears in mind that physicians affected had been almost altogether excluded from panel practice since July 1, 1933, the result is that an enormous sum of injustice and material damage has been brought about by the proceedings of the Panel Doctors' Association of Berlin. (Zentrales Staatsarchiv RAM 5135:157)

The chief reviewer of the Ministry, Dr. Oskar Karstedt, noted on September 15, 1933, that the method of operation of the Panel Doctors' Association of Berlin was particularly bad, using rumors and gossip from irresponsible persons as valid evidence. While the bureaucrats in the Ministry were trying to maintain due process and civil rights, Hitler's National Physician General, Dr. Gerhard Wagner, complained of "a high degree of irritation against the previous decisions of the National Ministry of Labor among physicians" (Zentrales Staatsarchiv RAM 5135:91). On July 27, 1933, he responded to the answer he received as follows: "It is unfortunately sufficiently known to us that the Ministry of Labor abides by the provisions of federal law. We National Socialists, however, believe that the meaning of the National Socialist revolution cannot be exhausted in these provisions of federal law. In the final analysis the benefit of the German people stands once again above all as the supreme law." (Zentrales Staatsarchiv RAM 5134:99) Nevertheless, the particular personal contacts (already mentioned) which some officials of the Ministry of Labor maintained with leading members of the Nazi party probably then caused Wagner at least to try in some sense to bridle his overenthusiastic and fanatical accomplices in Berlin. This manifested itself chiefly in his dismissing at the end of October 1933 Martin Claus, Medical Standard Bearer of the Horst Wessel Brigade, as his deputy for Berlin. He thus withdrew the person chiefly responsible for the concrete practice of Berufsverbote by suspending panel accreditation. At the same time, however, he called it untenable in the long run that, even after the actions of Claus, over 60 percent of the "non-Aryan" panel doctors in Berlin were still active. The ordinance relevant to this was published in the Deutsches Ärzteblatt, which was distributed to physicians all over Germany. Claus published alongside this ordinance an "explanation" in the Berliner Ärztecorrespondenz (a local physicians' journal) on November 4, 1933, which was supposed to make it clear that his "resignation" was engineered by the Ministry of Labor, with Wagner as its agent. According to him, the Ministry bore responsibility for the "catastrophic development of panel and welfare doctors' care of the population," which had dishonored him as a National Socialist. Claus felt that he and his co-workers had been crudely offended and slandered by officials of the Ministry. Yet Wagner had explained to him shortly before that these disputes with the Ministry did not concern him.

After this "explanation," Wagner excluded Claus even from the Nazi Federation of Physicians, with full knowledge and approval of the party's chief of staff, Martin Bormann. Thereupon, Claus behaved as though he had been personally persecuted. He agitated to such an extent that Wagner had to present himself before the Führer's deputy, Rudolf Hess, and receive authorization to "proceed as severely as possible against further perpetrators of intrigue." On November 11 the Gestapo decreed an end to the *Berliner Ärztecorrespondenz*, the official physicians' journal of Berlin (Leibfried and Tennstedt 1979, p. 93). Interestingly, it was Wagner who later initiated continuing education courses for Jewish physicians in Berlin and entrusted them with the health administration of the Jewish community of Berlin so that only Jews would treat Jews. Highly qualified Jewish instructors from Berlin held continuing education courses until increasingly repressive measures forced emigration and with it the end of this program (Ostrowski 1963). These "small steps" and the contacts, motivations, interests, and rivalries that underlay them have received little notice until now.

Mason (1977) states that these interest and party struggles had "unmistakably the character of transitional phenomena which gradually lost significance with the step-by-step construction of a new form of government." This, however, is probably not quite so, because, as Neumann observed in his classic analysis (in Mason 1977, p. 357): "The party did not succeed in breaking up the power of bureaucracy in the army and navy, justice and administration. The Party controlled only the policy, youth, and propaganda."

Mason is more correct when he writes that the state bureaucracy was concerned with "preserving tried and true organizational structures in the state, the economy, and all areas of public life from the revolutionary intervention of the National Socialist Movement which was leading to chaos." This conclusion is supported by the fact that the Ministry of Labor brought about the overthrow of Claus, a Nazi functionary outside the area of competence proper to the Ministry. Basically, such rivalries between the ministerial bureaucracy and the party did not necessarily have such relatively positive effects, because "the ministerial bureaucracy [was] a closed caste which tolerate[d] no outsiders in its ranks. . . . Its members [were] neither for nor against National Socialism, but for the ministerial bureaucracy." (Neumann, in Mason 1977, p. 433)

In addition to this, the Ministry of Labor maintained its reputation of being "filled with many upright democrats," mostly of the Weimar Centrist (Catholic) party. On the side of the higher party echelons, calculations of power politics were probably decisive in cases of "softness" of this sort. They were dependent upon the specialists of the ministerial bureaucracy in the Ministry of Labor, which alone controlled the complicated apparatus of the social security system. Subsequent history shows that the physicians who remained with Wagner and Leonardo Conti (the chief physician for the SS) were no better in any humanitarian sense.

Arbitrary arrests and conflicts with Labor Ministry officials were not confined to Berlin. Dr. Oskar Karstedt, in the National Ministry of Labor, had to complain about the Düsseldorf Panel Doctors' Association in a manner similar to the way he complained about the Berlin Panel Doctors' Association; the former had made assertions that "already at first glance turned out to be wholly untenable" (Zentrales Staatsarchiv RAM 5135:152). Thus, "the National Minister of Labor for his part had to take the trouble to obtain further clarification in hundreds of cases, chiefly in the sense of elucidation by suitable authorities or by those which otherwise could be of help. This was all the more necessary because a formal hearing of witnesses by the Minister of Labor himself was possible only in exceptional cases. On the other hand, however, everything had to be done in the sense of constitutional procedure to clear up the case as thoroughly as possible." (Karstedt 1934, p. 181) As far as can be seen, decisions in favor of the physicians in question were mostly related to cases of the following types: "soldier at the front," "active at the front as a physician," and "communist activity not proved." The director of the Hartmannbund, Dr. Hermann Lautsch, had examined in a preliminary manner and approved 86, 64, and 110 appeals on these grounds, respectively. The numbers of appeals allowed by the Ministry of Labor were considerably higher: 124, 96, and 231. The relatively high allowance of appeals for charges of communism was due to the fact that numerous Panel Doctors' Associations and the chief director of the Hartmannbund included as grounds for dismissal "any membership in Social Democratic organizations or cooperation with their subsidiaries." However, the Ministry of Labor could not abide by this procedure. Nazi party leaders protested against Karstedt's allowing so many appeals, and they made him discuss all cases in which he wished to deviate from the vote of the Hartmannbund in favor of the complainant with a group of senior party physicians, Drs. Deuschl, Grote, and Haedenkamp.

Dr. Karl Haedenkamp, after World War II a leading official of the West German National Physicians' Organizations, was not, like his two colleagues, an SA or SS doctor with the particular trust of the National Physicians General, but was director of the Berlin office of the Hartmannbund and was also probably considered somewhat trust-worthy as a former DNVP (German National People's Party) member of parliament. In fact he cooperated more with the ministerial bureau-cracy than with the Physicians General.

Suspension from panel practice in effect ended a doctor's secure existence in almost every respect, for most private health insurance groups conformed to decisions of the Panel Doctors' Associations. They sent out or published exclusion lists of physicians and dentists (Leibfried and Tennstedt 1979, pp. 241–269). The Association of Private Health Insurance Companies of Germany, with its headquarters in Leipzig, sent out these exclusion lists with the title List of Physicians Hostile to the State. Karstedt found this "disagreeable and hardly tolerable politically," especially since it affected physicians who had "acquired great merit with the public." He did not, however, see any possibility of taking steps against their "being defamed by a private enterprise in the manner characterized" (Zentrales Staatsarchiv RAM 5147:540). However, in very large cities some doctors of high reknown and spe-cialization could not subsist without some insurance backup, public or private. Thus, for most of the physicians affected there remained only changing careers or leaving. For this reason, 806 Berlin physicians left between 1933 and 1934, as did 150 physicians from Munich (Reichs-medizinal Kalender 1933, 1934). Some 3,000 Jewish physicians fled from Germany at this time, to which purely political exiles, or perse-cutions due to homosexuality would have to be added (Leibfried 1982, pp. 9 ff.). Also added should be the delicensing of women in certain cases (ibid.). The data compiled by the National Office for German Jews on the exact shape of the persecution and flight of Jewish physicians between 1934 and 1938 (table 3) allow some conclusions as to the nature of emigration: Emigration peaked in 1933–34 and in 1936. Exodus from the Reich was always higher than exodus from Berlin. The only

**Table 3**

Exodus of Jewish physicians from Germany as a whole and Berlin in particular, 1933–1938.

| | Germany | | Berlin | |
|---|---|---|---|---|
| | Number Jewish physicians at beginning of time period (% with panel license) | Number Jewish physicians fleeing during time period | Number Jewish physicians at beginning of time period (% with panel license) | Number Jewish physicians fleeing during time period |
| Jan. 1, 1934 to June 30, 1934 | 9,000 (—) | 2,000 | 3,423 (—) | 874 |
| July 1, 1934 to Dec. 31, 1934 | 7,000 (57) | 1,000 | 2,549 (55) | 149 |
| Jan. 1, 1935 to Dec. 31, 1935 | 6,000 (60) | 1,000 | 2,400 (—) | 355 |
| Jan. 1, 1936 to Dec. 31, 1936 | 5,000 (56) | 1,700 | 2,145 (52) | 645 |
| Jan. 1, 1937 to Sept. 30, 1938 | 3,300 (—) | 148 | 1,500 (—) | +123 |
| Total left as of Oct. 1, 1938 | 3,152 | | 1,623 | |

Source: Leibfried 1982, p. 11.

exception is 1933, when Berlin lost 25.5 percent of its Jewish doctors and the Reich 17 percent. Two factors need to be kept in mind here: the special role of Berlin in health policy and the correspondingly excessive efforts of the Nazi doctors to purge Berlin. Also, Berlin was the first place turned to by Jewish and socialist physicians who fled the countryside or the smaller cities, where repression was extreme. Berlin was the largest city, so it guaranteed some anonymity, and it provided easier ways of escape since all the foreign embassies were there. Thus, the emigration from Berlin after 1933 was usually low because of quotas related to intra-German migration into Berlin. From January to September 1938 the number of Jewish doctors in Berlin grew by 8.5 percent while it diminished nationally by 4.5 percent. Also, Berlin was the only town in Germany with a large market for private practice quite independent of any insurance reimbursements, which allowed the chance of subsistence to at least some physicians. As table 3 shows, in 1938 there were still 3,152 Jewish doctors left in the Reich, 1,623 of them in Berlin.

For most of these physicians exodus meant a wholly new beginning. Most were destitute. Their German medical examinations were not recognized, so they had to begin medical studies all over again if they wished to resume practice (Pearle 1981; Leibfried 1982). They turned to a variety of countries—at the beginning, in 1933, mostly to Palestine; later on more often to the United States. Younger physicians were more likely to leave, older ones more likely to stay. This age distribution is quite important, because those doctors left in Germany were the most immobile and most vulnerable to the persecutions still to come. Complete data only exist for 1933, and good estimates of similar precision from the same source exist for 1934.

In 1934, 1,307 physicians left officially (2.4 percent of all German doctors), 572 of whom came from Berlin. Two-thirds were 30–45 years old, over one-tenth were younger and not even a quarter were older. The corresponding age distribution for all German doctors was: 50 percent/10 percent/40 percent. Whereas 6.85 percent of all doctors were women, 16 percent of emigrating physicians were women (Dornedden 1935, p. 515).

Of 67 of the 104 Berlin physicians declared to be "enemies of the state" (Leibfried 1982, pp. 18–19), 5 died under the Nazi regime, 2 died in the USSR under Stalin, 43 stayed abroad (20 in the US, 11 in Palestine), and 6 returned to Germany after World War II. Thus, a whole generation of socialist physicians with the experience and the

political values of health reforms during the Weimar period were eliminated from policy-making after 1945 (Boenheim et al. 1981; Frankenthal
1981, pp. 266 ff.).

These events are touched upon in Schadewaldt et al. 1975 (p. 143):

There are many examples of collegiality triumphing over the thought
of race, and of persecuted Jewish colleagues receiving substantial assistance. On the other hand, the official organizations did not in fact
protest against the Aryanization paragraphs. Rather, the members of
their governing bodies attempted to prevent the strongest infringements
through individual assistance. It remains a scandal, however, that the
"German Federation of Medical Associations" urged the international
board not to comply with the wishes of those physicians or medical
students who wished to emigrate from Germany and who requested
medical positions elsewhere.

The lack of protests, indeed the demand for an international boycott
of Jewish émigrés, can be associated with a particular National Socialist
exposure of the remaining members of this profession. Thus, membership in the National Socialist Physicians' Federation grew rapidly
in this period. Already in 1935, 14,500 physicians belonged to it, almost
a third of the non-Jewish German physicians. In 1940, the state leader
of the National Socialist German Physicians' Federation in Württemberg,
Dr. Eugen Staehle, remarked on the period of the early 1930s with a
certain pride (Staehle 1940, p. 10; see also Kudlien 1979, p. 354): "No
other academic profession found its way to the NSDAP (the Nazi party)
to this extent and as early as the healing professions." This statement
is confirmed by current research. In comparing teachers (who used to
be considered the most Nazified profession) with physicians, Kater
(1979) writes:

After January 30, 1933, there were professions in Germany that were
in no way as exposed to social and political pressures for conformance
with Nazi politics as were the teachers and that nevertheless had quite
a high membership rate in NS organizations. . . . A typical example
are the doctors. All in all, about 45 percent of the Reich's physicians,
seemingly by their own choosing, became members of the NSDAP,
about twice the rate of the teaching profession. About 26 percent of
the male doctors were active in the SA versus 11 percent of the teachers.
The SS had 7.3 percent of all male physicians within its ranks, compared
with 0.4 percent of the teachers. In 1937 physicians were represented
seven times as much in the SS as in the whole labor force, whereas
teachers participated only a little over their proportion. . . .

This legislation was only the beginning of the persecution of Jewish
physicians, but a few constitutional procedures were preserved, as presented above. Thus, Dr. Heinrich Grote wrote retrospectively:

Corresponding to the purge of the professional civil service, steps were taken toward purging the medical profession of Jewish and communist elements. This activity, which required a great deal of work on into 1934, did not in any case lead to the results hoped for. The legal provisions laid down by the Reichspresident at that time provided that proof of communist activity had to be brought against these communist elements in order to be able to exclude them from panel practice. But the Marxists or communists often knew how to camouflage themselves in time or to destroy their material, so that it was not always possible to produce airtight proof of communist activity. Furthermore, those Jewish physicians who had taken part in the war as soldiers at the front or who had already established themselves by 1914 were allowed to continue their panel practice. That even today a third of all accredited panel doctors are Jewish shows how unsatisfactory this solution finally turned out to be. (Grote 1938, p. 11)

The persecutions continued until the "complete elimination of Jewish physicians" took place with the fourth ordinance to the Law on Citizenship of July 25, 1938. Paragraph 1 of this ordinance states: "Licenses (approbations) of Jewish physicians expire on September 30, 1933." The professional designation of physician was basically disallowed for Jews. In a few months, by the end of 1938, only 185 Jewish "treaters of the sick" (Krankenbehandler) were still active in Germany, whereas there had been 709 on October 1, 1938. The journal *Ortskrankenkasse* (Local Sickness Fund), which owed many excellent articles to the Jewish hygienists of the Weimar Republic, reported on this in traitorous "officialese" in a 1938 article headlined No Jewish Doctors Anymore: "As opposed to previous partial solutions, the fourth ordinance of the Imperial Civil Code now brings about the complete elimination of Jews from the health profession. Obviously measures have been taken in advance to guarantee sufficient medical care after the elimination of the Jews." The journal did not provide proof for the last assertion. The conditions in the concentration camps, the mass annihilation of the Jews which was initiated soon thereafter, and the Second World War were soon to make this a minor problem.

Berufsverbote and the Association of Socialist Physicians

The Association of Socialist Physicians played a special role in the exclusion of physicians from insurance practice on account of political activity. Oskar Karstedt (1934, p. 183) records:

The number of persons excluded because of membership in the Communist Party or its associated organizations is comparatively small. Significantly greater is the number of those who, without their having been affiliated with a clearly communist organization, consciously or unconsciously advanced communism through their membership or activity in associations, such as the Association of Socialist Physicians, The Fichte Federation [a sports organization of the labor movement], certain (not all) Worker Samaritan Columns, and similar institutions. Accordingly, their appeals had to be rejected.

To understand the link between Berufsverbote and the Association of Socialist Physicians made in this statement, one needs some background. At the turn of the century, the rapidly intensifying economic conflicts between the insurance funds and physicians led to the founding of the Hartmannbund. The main questions under dispute for these physician-employees were collective vs. individual contracts, free choice of physician vs. limited selection, and physicians' income (Tennstedt 1977, pp. 75 ff., 125 ff.). These disputes led to 873 doctors' strikes and boycotts through 1911. Then the Hartmannbund planned a general strike for 1914, when the reformed and codified national health insurance of 1911 was to take effect. This strike was averted at the last minute by the "Berlin Agreement."

This general situation put those physicians attached to the labor movement in a difficult position. On the one hand, they supported and worked for health insurance, especially with the funds oriented to social democratic principles and to free trade unions. On the other hand, they could accept the humiliating practices of the funds no more than they could the official policies of the medical profession. They believed that physicians and health insurance funds should join hands in promoting the interests of workers and implementing the programs of social hygiene.

Based on an analysis of this situation (Kollwitz 1913, p. 222), Dr. Karl Kollwitz and three prominent socialist physicians founded the Social Democratic Physicians' Association (Tennstedt 1982). This association was supposed to mediate between funds and physicians for the benefit of the sick. Members presented papers before health insurance associations on social hygiene and health policy and in the process educated and recruited more prominent physicians.

As time passed, the Social Democratic Physicians' Association split and recombined in different ways. During the Weimar Republic, the association expanded its political spectrum to embrace left-wing communists, who did not (or did not fully entertain) the pragmatic approach of the Social Democratic Party. Members stood for socialized medicine and demonstration experiments to translate the results of research on social hygiene into medical and political practice. A number of prominent physicians held key posts on the board of the association. However, these mediating institutions (Wickham, 1979, pp. 8–9), which promoted workers' interests above party lines, split in 1924 over disputes about ambulatory clinics (Hansen et al. 1981, pp. 155 ff., 433 ff.). The majority of the old guard founded the Association of Socialist Physicians, in which membership was largely independent of party affiliation. It had members all over Germany and published its own journal, *Der sozialistische Arzt* (The Socialist Physician).

Meanwhile the Social Democratic Physicians' Association amalgamated with the Social Democratic Physicians' Federation in 1926 to form a Study Group, which became part of the Social Democratic party (SPD). All SPD physicians belonged to it, and its tasks were to promote SPD health policy in the party organization, in public health organization, and in the labor unions, and to attract and train physicians with similar attitudes. The leadership and organization of the Study Group corresponded to that of the SPD. Some of the most prominent pioneers in social medicine participated, among them Dr. Julius Moses, a Reichstag member and the SPD health expert at the national level; Dr. Raphael Silberstein; Alfred Grotjahn, a pioneer of social hygiene academically and the first professor for the subject area; Beno Chajes, a leading academic in industrial hygiene; Dr. Franz-Karl Meyer-Brodnitz, a leading industrial hygienist of the labor unions, and Dr. Felix Koenigsberger, the founder of the Berlin ambulatory clinics.

The Association of Socialist Physicians was the only professional association with both Social Democrats and communists as members. Its mixed membership is apparent from its list of major board members after 1925. Whereas Dr. Georg Loewenstein, Dr. Salo Drucker, and to some extent Dr. Ernst Simmel stayed close to the SPD line, Dr. Ewald Fabian, Dr. Franz Rosenthal, Dr. Minna Flake, and Dr. Leo Klauber were either independent socialists or associated with the Communist Party. Loewenstein was responsible for the programmatics of the association (Loewenstein 1981); Fabian was the long-time editor of *Der sozialistische Arzt*. Thus, the association came into repeated conflict with the upper party echelons of the SPD. Simmel was repeatedly summoned before the SPD's governing body, and for years *Vorwärts* (Forward), the official party paper of the SPD, blocked his columns for the association. The Social Democrats had become so attached to the establishment that by 1929 they made sure that no representatives of or sympathizers with the Communist Party had even an indirect voice. The opposition between the two parties made "being above politics" difficult. Some KPD members were also thrown out of the Association of Socialist Physicians in 1929 after publicly demanding "fierce struggle against the traitorous actions of the Social Democrats" in the Berlin Physicians' Chamber. All in all, the members' common interest in improving and studying social hygiene and the idea of neutralizing the rapidly spreading nationalist and National Socialist movement in the professional associations is the most likely uniting bond among the members of this group. (See also Frankenthal 1981, pp. 182 ff.) The activity of the association, beyond publishing the journal, was to conduct public lectures and seminars and public campaigns on certain health issues. Politically these physicians also stood for elections in the Berlin Physicians' Chamber, a professional regulatory body concerned with continuous education, fees, struggle about the shape of health delivery, and professional ethics. Also, it was especially the Berlin association which was most active internationally, at least in stimulating the founding of similar organizations in Czechoslovakia (Loewenstein 1981, pp. 235 ff.) and England (Honigsbaum 1979, p. 260) and sponsoring international meetings of like-minded physicians, as 1931 at Karlsbad.

In other cities, branches of the association were less politicized and focused on discussing technical questions of health insurance, public health, and social hygiene. Outside of Berlin, local centers of activities of the socialist physicians were Chemnitz, Leipzig, Frankfurt am Main, München, and Breslau. In these cities the local associations had almost only Social Democrats as members, the majority of whom were Jewish physicians.

To ruin a man's career in 1933–34 for affiliation with one of these socialist associations seems all out of proportion, unless the goal was to destroy any base for shaping health-care services according to worker-based socialist values (Boenheim et al. 1981). As one senior administrator of the Hartmannbund, Dr. Hermann Lautsch, aptly summarized such destruction, "Our perspective in passing judgment on these appeals is informed by the principle: in dubio non pro re, sed contra rem—when in doubt, [decide] not for but against." (Zentrales Staatsarchiv RAM 5135:169).

## Notes

1. A systematic review can be found on pp. 431 ff. of Labisch 1980.

2. *Gleichschaltung* is a smokescreen term of Nazi origin; technically it means something like "coordination," even though it was actually used for the de-

struction or supplanting of all organizations in the political and social sphere that were at odds with Nazi policy.

3. Except where otherwise noted, data and quoted material in this section and the next are from Zentrales Staatsarchiv RAM 5135, 5136, 5360, 5361, 5382–5384, and 5569.

4. Communists were most likely to be active in private practice or in public health directly; a few were employed in ambulatory clinics.

5. This private combination of public bodies is not specific to social policy but is often found in "state interventionist" domains in Germany.

## References

Ackerknecht, E. H. 1979. "German Jews, English Dissenters and French Protestants as pioneers of modern medicine and science during the 19th century." In Charles Rosenberg, ed., Health and Healing: Essays for George Rosen. New York: Watson.

Adam, U. D. 1972. Judenpolitik im Dritten Reich. Düsseldorf: Droste.

Adler-Rudel, S. 1959. Ostjuden in Deutschland 1880–1940. Zugleich eine Geschichte der Organisationen, die sie betreuten. Tübingen: Mohr.

Aron, F. 1935. "Die nicht-arischen Ärzte in Deutschland." CV-Zeitung, February.

Beier, G. 1975. Das Lehrstück vom 1. und 2. Mai 1933. Frankfurt and Cologne: Europäische Verlagsanstalt.

Bock, H. M., and F. Tennstedt. 1978. "Raphael Friedeberg: Arzt und Anarchist in Ascona." In Harald Szeemann et al., eds., Monte Verita, Berg der Wahrheit. Milano: Electa.

Boenheim, F., K. Frankenthal, and K. Glaser. 1981. "Aufbau eines demokratischen Gesundheitswesens in Deutschland (New York City, NY, USA—Mai 1945)." Forum für Medizin und Gesundheitspolitik 17:77–95.

Breithaupt, H., et al., eds. 1925 and 1929. Die Beamten und Angestellten der Reichsversicherung. Two volumes. Munich: Verlag für Reichsversicherung.

Breslauer, B. 1909. Die Abwanderun der Juden aus der Provinz Posen. Denkschrift im Auftrag des Verbandes der Deutschen Juden. Berlin: Levy.

Brucker, L. 1934. "Die SA als Garant der Zukunft." Der SA-Mann 3 (February 17):1–2.

Bücher, K. 1919. Lebenserinnerungen. Volume 1, 1847–1890. Tübingen: H. Lauppsche.

Dobbernack, W. 1951. Die Selbstverwaltung in der Sozialversicherung. Essen: Essener Verlag für Sozialversicherung.

Dornedden, H. 1934. "Aus Deutschland im Jahre 1933 ausgewanderte Ärzte." Berliner Ärzteblatt 39:28–29.

Dornedden, H. 1935. "Deutschlands Ärzteschaft." Deutsches Ärzteblatt 65 (21):514–515.

Engel, J., and F. Eisenberg. 1932. Millionen Klagen an: Aktenmassige Aufdeckung Marxistischer Misswirtschaft in der Krankenversicherung. Munich: J. F. Lehmanns.

Engelmann, B. 1979. Deutschland ohne Juden: Eine Bilanz. Munich: Goldmann.

Fenske, H. 1973. "Preussische Beamtenpolitik vor 1918." Der Staat 12(3):339–356.

Frankenthal, K. 1981. Der dreifache Fluch: Jüdin, Intellektuelle, Sozialistin: Lebenserinnerung einer Ärztin in Deutschland und im Exil. Frankfurt am Main: Campus.

Frevert, U. 1983. Krankheit als politisches Problem. Die Pathologie sozialer Unterschichten in Preussen zwischen medizinischer Polizei und staatlicher Sozialversicherung. Göttingen: Vandenhoeck & Ruprecht.

Goldschmidt, F. 1979. Meine Arbeit bei der Vertretung der Interessen der jüdischen Ärzte Deutschland seit dem Juli 1933. Bremen: University.

Grote, H. 1938. "Die kassenärztliche Versorgung des deutschen Volkes." Deutsches Ärzteblatt 68, addition to no. 34 (Festgabe für Gerhard Wagner):10–15.

Hadrich, J. 1934. "Die nicht arischen Ärzte in Deutschland." Deutsches Ärzteblatt:1243–1245.

Hansen, E., et al. 1981. Seit über einem Jahrhundert . . . Verschüttete Alternativen in der Sozialpolitik: Sozialer Fortschritt, organisierte Dienstleistermacht und nationalsozialistische Machtergreifung: der Fall der Ambulatorien in den Unterweserstädten und Berlin. 100 Jahre Kaiserliche Botschaft zur Sozialversicherung: Eine Festschrift. Cologne: Bund.

Heimann, E. 1928. Soziale Theorie des Kapitalismus. Tübingen: Mohr. Theorie der Sozialpolitik. Frankfurt am Main: Suhrkamp, 1980.

Hentschel, V. 1978. "Das System der Sozialen sicherung in historischer Sicht 1880 bis 1975." Archiv für Sozialgeschichte 18:307–352.

Hentschel, V. 1983. Geschichte der deutschen Sozialpolitik 1880–1980. Soziale Sicherung und kollektives Arbeitsrecht.

Hockerts, H. G. 1980. Sozialpolitische Entscheidungen im Nachkriegsdeutschland: Alliierte und deutsche Sozialversicherungspolitik 1945 bis 1975. Stuttgart: Klett-Cotta.

Hoffmann, F. 1912. Die Neuordnung der Sozialversicherung in Deutschland. Berlin: Franz Vahlen.

Honigsbaum, F. 1979. The Division in British Medicine: A History of the Separation of General Practice from Hospital Care 1911–1968. London: Routledge & Kegan Paul.

Kampffmeyer, P. 1903. Die Mission der deutschen Krankenkassen auf dem Gebiet der öffentlichen Gesundheitspflege. Programmatische Gedanken zur

Reform der Krankenversicherung. Frankfurt am Main: Verlag der sozialpolitischen Rundschau, Dr. E. Schnapper.

Karstedt, O. 1934. "Die Durchführung der Arier- und Kommunistengesetzgebung bei den Kassen-Ärzten, Zahnärzten usw." Reichsarbeitsblatt 2 (15):179–183.

Kater, M. H. 1979. "Hitlerjugend und Schule im Dritten Reich." Historische Zeitschrift 228 (3):572–623.

Kaznelson, S., ed. 1962. Juden im deutschen Kulturbereich: Ein Sammelwerk. Third edition. Berlin: Jüdischer Verlag.

Kessler, G. 1929. "Die Lage der Arbeiterschaft seit 1914." In B. Harms, ed., Strukturwandlungen der Deutschen Volkswirtschaft, Second edition, volume 1. Berlin: Reimar Hobbing.

Knoll, E. 1933. Die Neuordnung der Kranken- und Knappschaftsversicherung. Stuttgart: Kohlhammer.

Knoll, E., and W. Keller. 1934. Wiederherstellung des Berufsbeamtentums bei den Krankenkassen: Die Durchführung des Gesetzes vom 7. IV. 1933 unter besonderer Berücksichtigung seiner finanziellen Auswirkungen, Hauptwerk und Nachtrag. Two volumes. Berlin: Heymann.

Kollwitz, K. 1913. "Ärzte und Krankenkassen." Sozialistische Monatshefte 222–232.

Kudlien, F. 1979. "In der Schule der Diktatoren. Medizin und Nationalsozialismus." Moderne Medizin 7:354–362.

Labisch, A. 1978. "The workingmen's samaritan federation." Journal of Contemporary History 13:297–322.

Labisch, A. 1980. "Zur Sozialgeschichte der Medizin: Forschungsbericht und methodologische überlegungen." Archiv für Sozialgeschichte 20:431–469.

Labisch, A. 1981. "Das Krankenhaus in der Gesundheitspolitik der deutschen Sozialdemokratie vor dem Ersten Weltkrieg." Medizinsoziologisches Jahrbuch 1:126–151.

Labisch, A. 1981–82. "Das Krankenhaus in der sozialdemokratischen Kommunalpolitik in Berlin um die Jahrhundertwende." Historia Hospitalum 14:337–345.

Leibfried, S. 1982. "Stationen der Abwehr. Berufsverbote für Ärzte im Deutschen Reich 1933–1938 und die Zerstörung des sozialen Asyls durch die organisierten Ärzteschaften des Auslandes." LBI-Bulletin 62:3–39.

Leibfried, S., and F. Tennstedt. 1979. Berufsverbote und Sozialpolitik 1933 Die Auswirkungen der nationalsozialistischen Machtergreifung auf die Krankenkassenverwaltung und die Kassenärzte. Bremen: University.

Leichter, H. M. 1979. A Comparative Approach to Policy Analysis: Health Care Policy in Four Nations. Cambridge University Press.

Loewenstein, G. 1981. Kommunale Gesundheitsfürsorge und sozialistische Ärztepolitik zwischen Kaiserreich und Nationalsozialismus. Autobiographische, biographische und gesundheitspolitische Anmerkungen. Bremen: University.

Mahner, E. (i.e., Kurt Maretzky and Gustav Gassert). 1930–1932. Eigenbetriebe der Ortskrankenkassen. Two volumes. Berlin: Verlag für Wirtschaft und Verwaltung.

Mason, T. W. 1977. Sozialpolitik im Dritten Reich. Arbeiterklasse und Volksgemeinschaft. Opladen: Westdeutscher Verlag.

Mausbach, H., and B. Bromberger, eds. 1979. Feinde des Lebens: NS-Verbrechen an Kindern. Frankfurt: Roederberg.

Mitscherlich, A., and F. Mielke. 1978. Medizin ohne Menschlichkeit: Dokumente des Nürnberger Ärzteprozesses. Frankfurt: Fischer.

Mommsen, H. 1966. Beamtentum im Dritten Reich. Mit ausgewählten. Quellen zur nationalsozialistischen Beamtenpolitik. Stuttgart: Deutsche Verlags-Anstalt.

Morsey, R. 1972. "Zur Beamtenpolitik des Reiches von Bismarck bis Bruening." In Demokratie und Verwaltung. 25 Jahre Hochschule für Verwaltungswissenschaften Speyer. Berlin: Duncker und Humblot.

Nadav, D. 1982. Politics of Social Hygiene—Julius Moses (1868–1942) and Social Hygiene in Imperial Germany and the Weimar Republic. Ph.D. diss., Tel Aviv University. (The original text is in Hebrew.)

Naschold, F. 1967. Kassenärzte und Krankenversicherungsreform. Zu einer Theorie der Statuspolitik. Freiburg im Breisgau: Rombach.

Nemitz, K. 1974. "Julius Moses—Nachlass und Bibliographie." IWK (Internationale Wissenschaftliche Korrespondenz zur Geschichte der deutschen Arbeiterbewegung) 10(2):219–241.

Neumann, F. L. 1942. Behemoth: The Structure and Practice of National Socialism 1933–1944. New York: Oxford University Press.

Oppenheimer, J. F., et al., eds. 1971. Lexikon des Judentums. Guetersloh: Bertelsmann.

Ostrowski, S. 1963. "Vom Schicksal jüdischer Ärzte im Dritten Reich. Ein Augenzeugenbericht aus den Jahren 1933–1939." LBI-Bulletin 313–351.

Pearle, K. M. 1981. Preventive Medicine. The Refugee Physician and the New York Medical Community 1933–1945. Bremen: University.

Peters, H. 1973. Die Geschichte der sozialen Versicherung. Third edition. Bonn: Asgard.

Reichs-medizinal Kalender, Zweiter Teil. 1933 and 1934. Leipzig: Georg Thieme.

Reidegeld, E. 1982. Die Sozialversicherung zwischen Neuordnung und Restauration. Soziale Kräfte, Reformen und Reformpläne unter besonderer Berücksichtigung der Versicherungsanstalt Berlin (BAB). Frankfurt am Main: Haag und Herchen.

Rohwer-Kahlmann, H. 1982. "BGH untersagt RVO Kassen die Selbstabgabe von Brillen." Die Sozialgerichtsbarkeit 29(10):373–383.

Roth, K. 1980. " 'Auslese' und 'Ausmerze.' Familie- und Bevölkerungspolitik unter der Gewalt der nationalsozialistischen Gesundheitsführung." In Baader et al., eds., Medizin und Nationalsozialismus. Berlin: Verlagsgesellschaft Gesundheit.

Safran, W. 1967. Veto-Group Politics: The Case of Health Insurance Reform in West Germany. San Francisco: Chandler.

Schadewaldt, H., P. Grzonka, and C. Lenz. 1975. 75 Jahre Hartmannbund. Ein Kapitel deutscher Sozialpolitik. Bonn: Verband der Ärzte Deutschlands (Hartmannbund, e.V.).

Scheur, W. 1967. Einrichtungen und Massnahmen der sozialen Sicherheit in der Zeit des Nationalsozialismus. Ph.D. Diss., University of Cologne.

Schumann, H. 1958. Nationalsozialismus und Gewerkschaftsbewegung. Die Vernichtung der deutschen Gewerkschaften und der Aufbau der Deutschen Arbeitsfront. Hannover: Norddeutsche Verlagsanstalt.

Silbergleit, H. 1930. Die Bevölkerungs- und Berufsverhältnisse der Juden im Deutschen Reich. Auf Grund von amtlichen Materialen bearbeitet. Volume 1. Freistaat Preussen. Berlin: Akademie Verlag.

Staehle, E. 1940. Geschichte des NSD-Ärztebundes e. V. Gau Württemberg-Hohenzollern (zum 10-jährigen Gründungstag 30.11.1940). Stuttgart: Fink.

Standfest, E., ed. 1977. Sozialpoltik und Selbstverwaltung. Zur Demokratisierung des Sozialstaats. Cologne: Bund.

Stargardt, W., et. al. 1976. "Albert Kohn—ein Freund der Kranken." Die Ortskrankenkasse 58(23–24):810–816.

Statistik des Deutschen Reiches. 1934. Die Krankenversicherung 1932 mit vorläufigen Ergebnissen für das Jahr 1933, Statistisches Reichsamt. Berlin: Reimar Hobbing. Volume 443.

Stone, D. A. 1980. The Limits of Professional Power: National Health Care in the Federal Republic of Germany. University of Chicago Press.

Tennstedt, F. 1976. "Sozialgeschichte der Sozialversicherung." In M. Blohmke et al., eds., Handbuch der Sozialmedizin, volume 3. Stuttgart: Enke.

Tennstedt, F. 1977. Geschichte der Selbstverwaltung in der Krankenversicherung von der Mitte des 19. Jahrhunderts bis zur Gründung der Bundesrepublik Deutschland. Bonn: Verlag der Ortskrankenkassen.

Tennstedt, F. 1979. "Alfred Blaschko—Das wissenschaftliche und sozialpolitische Wirken eines menschenfreundlichen Sozialhygienikers im Deutschen Reich." Zeitschrift für Sozialreform 25(9):513–523; 25(10): 600–613; 25(11):646–667.

Tennstedt, F. 1981. "Selbstabgabe von Sehhilfen. Die Selbstabgabestellen der Krankenkassen für Brillen zwischen 1926 und 1936. Historische Anmerkungen zu einem aktuellen Rechtsstriet." Die Ortskrankenkasse 63:904–916.

Tennstedt, F. 1982. "Arbeiterbewegung und Familiengeschichte bei Eduard Bernstein und Ignaz Zadeck." IWK (Internationale Wissenschaftliche Korrespondenz zur Geschichte der deutschen Arbeiterbewegung) 18(4):451–481.

Tennstedt, F. 1983. Vom Proleten zum Industriearbeiter. Arbeiter- und Sozialpolitik von 1800–1914. Cologne: Bund.

Teppe, K. 1977. "Zur Sozialpolitik des Dritten Reiches am Beispiel der Sozialversicherung." Archiv für Sozialgeschichte 17:195–250.

Vertretung 1929. Die Vertretung der Versicherten in den reichsgesetzlichen Krankenkassen. Berlin: Verlagsgesellschaft des Allgemeinen Deutschen Gewerkschaftsbundes.

Weber, 1927. Volksgesundheit und Ortskrankenkassen. Was wird aus mehr als 1 Milliarde Jahresbeiträgen. Second edition. Berlin: Verlag für Wirtschaft und Verwaltung.

Wickham, J. 1979. "Social fascism and the division of the working class movement: Workers and political parties in the Frankfurt Area 1929–1930." Capital and Class 7:1–34.

Zimmerman, H. 1938. "25 Jahre AOK Nürnberg." Die Ortskrankenkasse 26(12):388.

# 6 Public-Health Policy in Germany, 1945–1949: Continuity and a New Beginning

## Stefan Kirchberger

*Kirchberger describes the decisions made in the postwar period and their policy implications for the two German health-care systems. He points out that the decision by the Allies to leave the health-care system alone was a positive policy decision, and that the dominant event was the reestablishment of the medical profession as a political organization pursuing two goals: the limitation of access to the profession and the prevention of any significant reorganization. This does not mean, in Kirchberger's view, that the West German system exhibits free enterprise or capitalism, but rather that West German physicians are carefully regulated in ways that benefit the medical profession. Kirchberger seems sympathetic to the efforts in East Germany to eliminate underserved areas by specialty and location, minimize profiteering in the production and distribution of drugs, break down the wall between ambulatory care and hospitals, create ambulatory-care centers that reflect the technological and specialized character of modern medicine, and establish an independent system of industrial medicine that can minimize accidents and other hazards in the workplace.*

*One of the most interesting contrasts to emerge from this and the following chapter concerns the way in which the venereal-disease epidemic was handled in East and West Germany after 1945. In the Eastern zone, the Soviets established a network of clinics to systematically treat cases and track down contacts. Penicillin (a precious drug in very short supply) was made available free through the system of government clinics, which controlled the supply. In the Western zones, the Allies tried to establish public health centers to treat VD patients, but the medical associations vigorously opposed the treatment of patients by public-health physicians. At the same time, their own members showed little interest in treating the cases of these socially repugnant diseases. Penicillin was in private hands and was sold on the black market to the highest bidders.*

"Public health care." To a careful thinker, these three words express the radical and total change in our view of the relationship of medicine and the state. This expression makes clear just how mistaken it is to think that medicine has nothing to do with politics.
Virchow, 1948

A discussion of health policy in the years 1945–1949 in Germany expresses more than simply an interest in a historical reconstruction of its development in the first years after the war. The end of the rule of National Socialism (which considered the health system as a central area of political activity), the "cold war" of the superpowers then developing, and the increasingly obvious fact that Germany was to be divided into two independent states offer, as does hardly any other historical situation, the possibility of understanding public health service in its political dimension and discussing health policy as a decision between possible alternative solutions against a background of social and political maneuvering for power.

If the following discussion is nevertheless restricted to the portrayal of the development of health policy in the narrower sense (excluding the area of social security), without relating it to the context of general political and economic events, that seems to be justified by the fact that the period 1945–1949 is as yet one of the least explored periods of recent German history.[1] Sources dealing with the development of the health system in the years after the war are extremely few. Almost all relevant analyses begin with the founding of the Federal Republic of Germany (FRG; West Germany) or the German Democratic Republic (GDR; East Germany) and devote only a few generalized comments to the preceding period. The following portrayal is based mainly on published material and is designed as a sketch of the problem.

When the German armed forces capitulated on May 8, 1945, and the Allied victors took over governmental power, the National Socialist regime had left behind a largely devastated country, hardly capable of surviving without outside help. The democratic tradition of Weimar was destroyed. Who of the Germans was capable of beginning and enforcing new developments in health policy? Democratic-minded and qualified opponents of the National Socialists were scarce in Germany, and only a few émigrés were ready to return.

The National Socialist regime in the 12 years of its existence had not changed the health system fundamentally, but it had recognized and correctly assessed the special political and social importance of physicians in their state-supporting, ideology-promoting role, as well as in their many-sided functions of social control, especially distinct with regard to the German system of social security. Conversely, the regime regarded with special distrust the institution of social security, whose orientation toward Social Democratic or union politics was well known. Therefore, immediately after National Socialist seizure of power, all administrators with decision-making authority whose political orientation was uncertain were replaced by party members, whether or not they were qualified for the positions. This change in personnel was more than a legal innovation—it was a definitive change in health policy. Not only were developments of the Weimar democracy destroyed or interrupted, but—in connection with other measures[2]—new power relationships were created and a differentiated, democratic discussion of health policy programs and their realization was abruptly ended. The health policy of the National Socialists manifested itself not only in the "race laws," the laws for the prevention of hereditary diseases, the euthanasia program, and the gruesome medical experiments on prisoners; in order to achieve political conformity it was carried through systematically according to Gleichschaltung in all areas of the health system.

Health policy not directly related to traditional structures and power relationships of the period before 1945 could therefore only be instituted by the victorious powers. The interest of the Allies in the health system as a task of governmental policy corresponded to the practice in their own countries. For American authorities, health care was mainly a matter for private initiative, at most to be stimulated by increased availability of necessary funds[3] but not to be guided by the state. The Americans and the French treated the German health system as political only insofar as it was absolutely necessary for the enforcement of epidemic hygiene measures and for the rebuilding of the most urgently needed public health-care establishments.[4] The United States also aided with extensive contributions of medication and technical equipment. In the Soviet Union, on the other hand, the health system had been an important responsibility of state politics since 1917, and Great Britain began to put the concept of the National Health Service into effect at the end of the war. It was primarily the Soviet Union, therefore, that showed a political interest in shaping the German health system. In the Allied Control Council, the concept of a new organization of the health system—developed by the Soviet occupation forces in cooperation with German specialists—roused at best the interest of the British military authorities.

While a new organization of the health system was systematically developed and implemented in the Soviet zone by a staff of Russian experts and German advisors, neither the occupation powers nor the newly constituted unions or political parties in the Western zones considered it necessary to develop initiatives that would change the structure of the health system or be more than just a reaction to the immediate emergency situation. With the argument that they should take no measures that would prejudice developments and make later unified German regulations more difficult, the Western German Land (i.e. state) governments held the view that it was an inopportune time to initiate structural changes. The new organization of the health system in the Soviet zone was consistently ignored or slandered as a break with liberal German traditions. The possibility of at least discussing the appropriateness of these measures, just for the purpose of a unified German development, was not seriously considered. With the exception of the unavoidable reestablishment of the pre-1933 legal conditions (to the extent requested by the Allies), according to the prevailing opinion in the Western zones the health system needed no further governmental initiatives. Here—and this must be understood as a political decision—the health system was left to the free play of enterprise, i.e., to the influence and political power of those interest groups who were able to articulate positions immediately after 1945. There were single attempts to bring about a discussion of necessary or desirable innovations, but the situation was primarily characterized by the efforts of individual interest groups and associations to preserve their spheres of influence. Those groups that had been suppressed for 12 years and had to reorganize themselves with great effort were necessarily at a disadvantage compared with those that had been allowed to continue their work during the Nazi period and could now defend themselves against interference.

A new organization of health care was put into effect in the Soviet zone in the years 1945–1949. The concepts of this new organization corresponded in many respects to the demands already made by the unions, the representatives of the sickness funds, and Social Democrat and Communist physicians and politicians during the period of the Weimar Republic, or they were based on structures which the Soviet Union had developed as solutions to its own problems of health care. But in the Western zones, the year 1945—with the exception of the abolition of the "race laws"—did not bring about a fundamental change. It is true that certain especially committed National Socialists were replaced; however, since 1933 there has been no break in continuity, no fundamental structural innovations, in the health system. In 1933, political decisions ended the open development of health policy. All the same, the National Socialists did not effect health-policy innovations; rather, they extensively established power relationships and thereby defined the margin for possible reform. In West Germany these conditions lasted until the 1960s.

An objective discussion between health policy experts of the two German states with regard to the advantages and disadvantages of their respective systems of health care has barely begun. More frequent is the mutual objection to health policy measures as "ideological" (that is, not objectively motivated). On both sides, ideological suspicion takes the place of readiness to talk. For instance, the point that the health system of the GDR was imposed by the Soviet occupation forces has long served in the FRG as an implicit criticism of the GDR's health-care structure—as implicit proof that it is inadequate for German conditions. According to this line of reasoning, this health system may perhaps be suited for a still largely agrarian society with a so-called lower cultural and educational level and corresponding health behavior, but transferred to Germany it could mean only enforced regression.[5] Analogous to this statement is one in an East German social hygiene textbook that characterizes the West German system briefly as "capitalistic, subordinated to the profit motives of the imperialists." This questionable invective only obstructs substantial discussion of actual health policy matters. Aside from the fact that the origin of a concept is no criterion for judging its adequacy (which must be examined independently), the health system of the GDR is not modeled after that of the Soviet Union, in spite of the influence of the occupying power. It is more closely related to the manifold German traditions of the Weimar period,[6] which it has attempted to develop further. Equally incorrect is the characterization of the West German health system as "capitalistic." Its peculiarity is to be seen precisely in the fact that it is not part of the capitalistic market economy and enjoys privileges like those of a guild.

The focus of this chapter is on the development of the health system in the four occupied zones of Germany from 1945 until the founding of the two German states. A systematic comparison between the development in the Soviet zone and the Western zones is nearly impossible because of the heterogeneity of the sources; it is also not the theme of the essay, insofar as the result of developments initiated in that period (namely the present structure and effectiveness of the health systems of the GDR and the FRG) are not being debated here. If, however, the portrayal of health policy from 1945 through 1949 is to contain more than a disorganized enumeration of arbitrary political facts whose only common denominator is their relation to the health system, then it is also necessary to discuss which deficits in health care were created, perpetuated, or removed through any particular development. Only through such a discussion is it possible to define the health policy aspect, the action aspect of a certain development as a selection from among alternative possibilities. For this reason, and for a clearer understanding of the portrayal, I will quickly sketch the institutional structure of the health-care system of the FRG under the aspect of its structurally contingent drawbacks and will relate these drawbacks to the advanced state of discussion of the Weimar period. This sketch will also show which intentions gave rise to the new organization in the Soviet zone.

Although medical services in the FRG are mostly organized on a private-enterprise basis, they have been removed from the system of market economics and are subject to their own norms and regulations which protect the medical profession in special ways. All physicians are mandatorily organized into Ärztekammern (physicians' associations) on the Land level. As Körperschaften öffentlichen Rechts (semi-public bodies), these associations have sovereign rights and the possibility to enforce their own regulations against their members through disciplinary measures. The professional associations regulate professional duties and control compliance with these regulations, and at the same time they represent the socio-political concerns of their members.

Within the framework of the professional code, the physician's work is subordinated to a number of organizational and competition-limiting regulations. The general practitioner is obliged to practice in person (Zulassungsordnung für Ärzte, May 28, 1957, paragraph 1; Bundesgesetzblatt 1, 572) and is not entitled to act as employer of other physicians.[7] The physician's practice is in principle a one-man practice.[8] Competition and mutual criticism are incompatible with the professional code. Physicians are not allowed to advertise, nor are they allowed to call in question colleagues' treatments of patients or health-care workers such as nurses. The fees for treatment are fixed, agreed upon by the Kassenärztliche Vereinigungen (associations of the physicians who receive remuneration from the sickness funds) and the sickness funds.[9]

(Since more than 90 percent of West Germans are members of the sickness funds or can request treatment on the basis of the membership of a family member, private payments play only a minor role.)

A further and more important example of limitation of competition is restricted access to the market. It is true that every approbated practitioner (after compliance with certain formal requirements) can set up a practice and also a Kassenpraxis (practice as a sickness-fund physician), but since 1962 access to the study of medicine has been subjected to increasing restrictions (concomitant with an increase in the number of students wishing to enroll in medical courses). The supply of doctors, therefore, can scarcely grow out of bounds, and this has allowed the physician to set up a practice in the community of choice, largely without consideration of existing health-care shortages and often with an income far above average.

The physicians established in private practice have a monopoly on ambulatory care. This means that they alone have the right to treat all cases of sickness that do not involve hospitalization, while the hospitals are excluded from ambulatory care.[10] Similar characteristics are found— and to an even greater extent—in public and industrial health care, which play at best a marginal role in the health system of the FRG. Since public health physicians, as well as those who are employed in industry, have no right to treat patients and also must put up with considerably smaller incomes, the shortage of physicians in these areas during the last decades is not surprising.

Because of the monopoly of physicians with private practices, the effectiveness of the individual practice becomes a selection criterion for hospitalization (Volkholz 1973, pp. 18–42). Aside from acute emergencies, the practicing physician has the sole decision-making authority for referring a patient to a hospital. His experience, his technical equipment, and the capacity of his practice are therefore important decision criteria in addition to (or, perhaps, instead of) the actual need for stationary care. On the other hand, the definition of hospital care forces the hospital to take diagnostic cases as inpatients and to define them for further treatment as bedridden or to refer them back to ambulatory care—that is, back to the practicing physician. This distinct separation of inpatient from outpatient care necessarily leads to higher costs and to treatment that cannot be interpreted as the best method for the patient's recovery.

The family-doctor model, which expected from the physician the complete knowledge of the patient's medical record, has become obsolete because of the differentiation of medical responsibilities. The increasing specialization in ambulatory care results in increased strain for the patient. Since there are no standards for the flow of information, it is quite usual that the same services are provided twice. New cooperative and organizational forms that could eliminate the current information deficit are prevented largely by the structure of ambulatory care.

The flow of information between the different areas of care is even more inadequate. At hospitalization and during outpatient followup the rigid division between the ambulatory and hospital sectors leads to an aggravating loss of information and double services at the patient's expense.[11] There is practically no cooperation between the general practitioners and the physicians working in public and industrial health care. This fact goes hand in hand with the strict division between preventive and curative medicine. Knowledge gained from industrial medicine has, in fact, no meaning for curative medicine in the ambulatory sector. (Only in 1970 was this area made an obligatory subject of medical education.) Preventive health care (not early detection), which is especially meaningful in the area of occupational and paraoccupational health risks, is found—if at all—isolated from the curative area of ambulatory care (Kirchberger 1978, pp. 222–223). Since there is no institutionalized feedback to industrial health care, the experiences gained by the practicing physician that are most useful in industrial health care remain unused.

Health care in the FRG is lacking in integration in two ways. In the first place, the responsibilities in the individual areas of the health system follow an isolated and uncoordinated course, which results not only in costly duplication of services but also in gaps in medical care.[12] Second, the health system is isolated from the work and life situations of its patients, where health problems arise. The supply of medical care in the ambulatory sector is controlled neither by the market nor by centralized authority, and within the protective zone of a guildlike organization it can remain nearly uninfluenced by industrial development and can cling to forms of production that are obsolete in economic and medical terms. This "twofold lack of integration" was already criticized during the Weimar Republic. For this reason Arthur Schlossmann, the director of the pediatric hospital in Düsseldorf and a member of the National Health Board (Reichsgesundheitsrat), stated in 1929 that there was a "crisis of confidence" in the public's perception of the medical profession. This, he said, resulted from the anachronistic insistence on the family-doctor model (rendered obsolete in reality by specialization and medical-technical developments) and from the physicians' insistence on their independent professional status (which made the desperately needed integration of medical services impossible).[13] Owing to the particular constellation of vested interests, an integration of the health-care system in Germany seemed to Schlossmann (1930) to be very difficult, realizable only by a lengthy process. As a first step toward such development, Schlossmann considered the expansion of the social security system in two directions: The entire population should be insured, and, as an important expansion of its services, preventive as well as curative medicine should become the responsibility of the health insurance system. The inclusion of prevention among the services of the health insurance system was seen by Schlossmann as a decisive means toward integrating the different areas of medical care. According to him, if prevention were to be covered by the sickness funds, then the care available through the public health system and that of charitable organizations could be combined with the ambulatory services provided by the sickness-fund physicians. The same would be true of opening the hospitals for outpatient care. Ambulatory-care clinics, established by the social security system, seemed to Schlossmann to be the suitable means for enabling all to benefit from the developments in medical equipment regardless of the individual physician's amount of capital and his willingness to invest. This would relieve the flow of information between health workers of its dependence on arbitrary communication between individual physicians. It would be meaningless, according to Schlossmann, to speak of such a development as "socialization of medicine": "By far the largest percentage . . . of the total income of German physicians . . . stems from the sickness funds. . . . If one accepts money from the sickness funds, one can well concede that one's relationship to these sources of payment is similar, in many respects, to that of the civil servant to the state." (Schlossmann 1930, pp. 45–46)

The new structure of the health system in the Soviet zone was intended to provide for integration where it was lacking in the German health system—that is, to relate health care to the life and work situations of the population through institutional regulations and to interconnect the individual areas so that they would become dependent on cooperation. The central factor in this new structure, just as Schlossmann proposed, is its orientation not mainly toward curative medicine but toward preventive medicine.

The different treatment of the problems arising in medical care from 1945 through 1949 in the Western zones and in the Soviet zone was due to the different political concepts and procedural methods of the occupation powers, the special postwar situation (especially in the Soviet zone), differences in the medical profession's ability to assert political goals, and differences in the remaking of and the recourse to political traditions.

In the Soviet zone, as far as the health system was concerned, the year 1945 was understood much more in a political sense as the chance for a new beginning—a new establishing of priorities—than in the Western zones. What was initiated there between 1945 and 1949 is in many respects valid today as a model for medical care in the industrial working world.

### Initiatives in Health Policy by the Occupation Powers

On May 8, 1945, the commanders in chief of the Allied forces assumed control of Germany. In view of the defeat of the Reich, they proclaimed in the Berlin Declaration of June 5 that they had assumed all authorities of the former German governments, administrations, and offices of the municipalities, the Länder, and the Gemeinden (rural administrative districts). The Alliierte Kontrollrat (Allied Control Council) was formed to coordinate decisions affecting Germany as a whole. However, since the decisions required unanimous support, this body did not achieve the importance the Allies had intended. Consequently, supreme power was actually in the hands of the commanders in chief of the four occupation zones. The decisions of the four military governments established the general frame for the political development of Germany until the two German states were constituted, in 1949. The following pages will characterize this framework as far as the health system is concerned.

The supreme authority of the Soviet occupation forces, the Soviet Military Administration in Germany (SMAD), was set up on July 9, 1945, in Berlin-Karlshorst. It was divided into 15 departments—one solely for the health system, which was directly subordinated to the health ministry of the USSR in professional respects. About 60 persons worked in this department, at first under General Kusnezow (a physician) and later under Colonel Sokolow. They were drawn mostly from the faculties of the largest universities of the USSR—a "highly qualified professional elite," as was appreciatively reported in a West

German governmental publication of the cold war era (Weiss 1957, p. 11). The health department of the SMAD was fully active until the proclamation of the constitution of the GDR on October 7, 1949, at which time it was transferred to the health department of the Soviet Control Commission, with reduced personnel.

After August 1945, the Land (i.e. state) and province (county) administrations that had recently been set up in all occupation zones began functioning. Corresponding to Prussian and Bavarian administrative tradition, the health departments became part of the Department of the Interior.[14] At approximately the same time that the Land governments were formed,[15] the four occupation powers established in their respective zones organizations whose authority went beyond that of the individual Länder for tasks previously administered by the Reich. Thus, the SMAD established eleven Central Administrative Boards (Zentralverwaltungen) (Soviet Military Administration Order 17, September 12, 1945), among which were the Zentralverwaltung für Gesundheitswesen (ZVGes; Central Health Administration) and the Zentralverwaltung für Arbeit und Sozialfürsorge (Central Work and Social Welfare Administration).[16] Although at first these administrative boards served the Soviet military authorities exclusively as specialized advisors and had no legislative or executive power and no supervisory or administrative authority over the Länder, they soon won independent importance—and, to a certain extent, sovereign power—through their status as experts. The ZVGes, which at times had 187 members, was conceived as a comprehensive coordinating agency by which the groundwork for the establishment of organization and administration of the health system in the Soviet zone was to be accomplished (Weiss 1957, p. 13).

In January 1946, Paul Konitzer, the first president of the ZVGes, outlined its responsibilities in a programmatic essay (Konitzer 1946). The ZVGes was the first single authority in German history responsible for the whole health system. It was established to integrate the responsibilities that had until then been divided among various ministries and agencies.[17] Konitzer listed twelve areas of responsibility, which were assigned to individual departments. In at least two respects, this catalog is an important expansion of what had until then been thought of in Germany as the responsibility of health administration. First, the ZVGes was to direct the distribution of professionals in the health system according to location and specialities, especially for underserved areas. Second, it became responsible for the planning and control of the production and distribution of medicaments. In addition, it was to manage the reorganization of medical training and assume responsibility for eliminating National Socialist traditions from medical legislation and jurisdiction. The remaining duties had also been only partially under the jurisdiction of national health administration: regulation of health education, social hygiene, industrial health care, planning and direction of the treatment of tuberculosis and venereal diseases, ordinances for food hygiene and inspection, and the collection of morbidity statistics. In general, the twelve departments of the ZVGes represent a systematic classification of the concerns of the health system. On the middle administrative levels of Länder (states) and Kreise (districts), corresponding organizations were established to assist in the task.

The ZVGes existed until the beginning of 1949, when it was integrated as an independent body into the Deutsche Wirtschaftskommission (German Economic Commission) of the Soviet zone. At the founding of the GDR, in October 1949, the health system was at first joined with the Ministry of Labor and Social Welfare. A short while later, however, it was separated from the Ministry of Labor and an independent ministry for the health system was formed.

The development of the health system in the Soviet zone in the years 1945–1949 was determined on the one hand by the SMAD (the military administration) and on the other hand by the ZVGes. The contents of this health policy will be discussed later. It should be established here that the Soviet Union obviously attached eminent political importance to the German health system and its reorganization from the first; only from this motive can the qualitative and quantitative efforts of the health department of the military administration and the rapid founding and expansion of the corresponding German central administration be explained.

In line with the Soviet appraisal of the political situation in Germany, the health system clearly offered the possibility of creating a model situation in an area of social life affecting the entire population, especially the workers, and thereby demonstrating the achievements a socialist society can realize.[18]

The occupation forces of France, Great Britain, and the United States, on the other hand, possessed no agency in their military governments that even slightly resembled the health department of the Soviet Military Administration. The health system played a minor role within the framework of their rather inconsistent notions of the political future of Germany, which became more concrete only when the East-West conflict arose. For this reason, the Western military governments limited themselves to watching out for epidemics (for the protection of their own troops as well as of the Germans) and consulted experts from case to case for more significant decisions.

Analogous to the developments in the Soviet zone, German administrative organizations were also created in the American and British zones. These organizations were supposed to discharge coordinating duties which went beyond Land policies. Thus, the Länderrat (council of the states) was founded in November 1945 as a coordinating authority in the American zone. This was a council formed of the prime ministers of Bavaria, Hessen, Württemberg-Baden, and Bremen. It had the responsibilities of "collectively solving the questions which went beyond the boundaries of the individual Länder within the framework of the political directives instituted by the occupation power," "removing difficulties in the traffic between the Länder," and "ensuring the desired standardization in the political procedures of the various occupation zones."[19] For the consideration of individual, specialized questions, the Länderrat founded committees which met to formulate recommendations as the need arose. After only a short while there existed a manifold diversity of such committees and subcommittees. Sometimes they dealt with general problems such as nutrition and agriculture, traffic, salaries, energy, and the postal and communication systems; sometimes they dealt with specialized questions (above all problems of production and distribution). Problems of health care, insofar as they were not questions of finance (traditionally handled by the social-political committee), seem at first not to have been a topic of discussion at all. The Health Committee, formed in October 1946, came into existence only because of the express desire of the American military government for uniform regulation of certain aspects of the distribution and control of medicines through German agencies in all Länder of the American zone (Hartel 1951, p. 17).

Besides formulating proposals for legislation (from which, incidentally, not one bill was enacted), the Health Committee was chiefly occupied with compiling statistical data, determining the needs for medicines and other medical supplies, making agreements about the distribution of additional foodstuffs to the sick and to members of health-hazardous professions (in cooperation with the agriculture and nutrition boards), and initiating controls on the supply of narcotics.[20] The striking heterogeneity and the almost marginal character of this committee's activities are explained by the American policy of leaving the regulation of the health system primarily to the governments of the Länder, who in turn thought that legal reorganization or essentially political decisions were not necessary. Only the coordination of individual legislative measures of the Länder for the purpose of preserving uniformity in the legal system seemed urgent.

All matters concerning the British zone as a whole were regulated at first by the British military government. German agencies were active only as advising or implementing organs assisting the British Control Commission (Klein 1949, pp. 79 ff.). In March 1946, the Zonal Advisory Council was established in Hamburg. At the order of the British Occupation Authority (HQ 06208/Sec.P.Zon/1P (46) 12, February 15, 1946, Directive 12), it was created as an advisory body without any executive or legislative responsibility.[21] It was composed of representatives of the political parties, administrative officials of the provinces and the Länder, representatives of the unions and cooperative societies, and 11 specialists, who corresponded to the departments of the military government. These 27 persons were appointed by the British military government. The specialist in public health was Rudolf Degkwitz, a Hamburg University professor of pediatrics.

In contrast to the Zonal Advisory Council, the Zentralamter (central bureaus) scattered throughout the British zone were monocratic German professional agencies that had taken over certain responsibilities previously held by the authorities of the Reich. In contrast to the American zone, uniformity was stressed in the British zone; this corresponded to the more centralized structure of Great Britain. All matters not explicitly delegated to the Land governments by ordinances remained the responsibility of the Zentralamter (order 57 of the British military government). Problems of the health system, insofar as they bordered on concerns of social security, fell under the jurisdiction of the sociopolitical department of the Zentralamt for labor in Lemgo.

In line with France's desire for a federation of German states with a weak central authority, the French military government did not establish in its zone institutions that would be effective beyond their Land borders. No political concept of the future organization of the German health system seems to have existed in the Department of Health and Social Services of the French military government. The regulation of such questions remained in the hands of the individual Land governments.

Neither the Americans, nor the British, nor the French brought a special political interest to the German health system. Insofar as this area was not affected by a general regulatory ordinance (i.e., de-Nazification)—or, rather, insofar as the political responsibility of the German agencies was not already limited by general provisions—the Western Allies left health policy to the Germans.

## The Health of the Population

The fight against hunger and epidemics was the prevailing problem of the first few postwar years in Germany, as it was in the other European countries affected by the war. Although systematic portrayals are not available, from the individual data available a rather good general view of the health situation of the German population at that time can be composed.

In 1939, at the beginning of the war, the National Socialists had begun rationing all consumer goods. The system of rationing, with strictly organized control of production and distribution, centrally organized rationing plans, and delivery supervision on the Land, Kreis (regional), and Ort (municipal) levels, had initially kept the population tolerably supplied with foodstuffs. In addition to provisions from their own country, there were also foodstuffs seized from the countries conquered. With the retreat of the German troops and the constantly increasing air raids, the food situation deteriorated from 1943 on (Schmitz 1956; Schlange-Schoningen 1955), until it collapsed entirely by the end of the war, because of the destruction of the transportation system (Grunig 1947, pp. 64 ff.). Only the distribution of the remaining reserves from the stores of the rationing agencies and the German armed forces made survival possible during the first months, especially in the large cities, until the transportation system could be set in motion again by the Allied military governments (Schlange-Schoningen 1955).

At the end of the war, the eastern regions of the Reich were occupied by Poland; as a result, 25 percent of the arable land formerly available could no longer be used (Liebe 1947, p. 83). Since the foodstuffs that were lacking could not be provided through imports, the reorganization of the rationing system brought only minimal improvements. The lack of food for the population led, beyond a poor general condition, to serious health problems, which were obvious from the great increase in malnutrition symptoms. For instance, Lower Saxony, relatively fortunate due to its large farming areas, registered 30,000 new cases of illness (in a population of 6.6 million) in the first half of 1947, due to such nutritional deficiencies as nutritional edema, protein deficiencies, and loss of more than 20 percent of normal body weight (Zonenbeirat, Deutsches Sekretariat:401.48 Supplement). A representative medical checkup of the employees at the Krupp factory in Essen showed similar conditions (Wiele 1946; *Arbeitsblatt für die britische Zone* 30, 1947, p. 40). Although the number of cases had risen only minimally (since notification of sickness caused loss of the desperately needed extra food allowance), almost a third of those examined had lost more than 20 percent of their normal weight. Visible nutritional edema was found in only a small percentage of the workers, but most suffered from serious circulatory disorders and low blood pressure as a result of poor nutrition, which also contributed to the dangerous increase in infectious disease.[22] Poor nutrition and deficient hygienic conditions in overcrowded living quarters led to an increase of suppurative dermatosis and furunculosis. The rise in accidents and bone fractures must also be seen as a result of poor nutrition. As a result of insufficient worker protection and increased fatigue and lessened concentration ability, the number of fatal injuries more than doubled in the first years after the war, according to the statistics of the public industry inspectors.[23]

In the winter of 1947–48, the food allotment in North Rhine–Westphalia hardly reached subsistence level and sank in some periods to 1,000 calories, and even 800 calories, per day (Amelunxen 1948). Although children were fed at school through the efforts of foreign relief organizations, the food scarcity among workers in the industrial centers of the Ruhr area led to strikes and hunger marches, in which political demands were articulated along with demands for an improvement in the food supply.[24] The food supply in West German industrial centers improved only slightly toward the end of 1948.

The health and nutritional situation of the population in the British zone was the subject of a conference summoned by the Zonal Advisory Council and the British occupation authorities in February 1948 (Dorendorf 1953, pp. 98–106). The motive for this conference was the doubt of the British authorities as to the reliability of the descriptions of the German respresentatives on the Zonal Advisory Council. The German council members presented detailed reports of the catastrophic food shortage, the illnesses caused by nutritional deficiencies in young people, the rise in infant mortality, and the number of tuberculosis cases. The prime ministers of the Länder presented reports in which the most important data on health conditions were compiled. The results of the study by the British Nutrition Survey Group on the nutritional situation in the population of Hamburg were less alarming. The British consultant responded to the German report: "You cannot be suggesting that this is a famine of Chinese or Indian proportions."[25] He claimed that over half the population received about 1,550 calories daily and was able to increase this ration by 300 calories through the black market. The rate of infant mortality was supposedly not higher than it was before the war.[26] In general, he suggested that the health and nutritional conditions were substantially better than had been described by the German side. "Moreover," he warned, "do not exaggerate your concerns. That always makes a bad impression on us. Cautiously present the facts to us and evaluate your data as carefully as you can."[27]

Two months later the British Control Commission again notified the Zonal Advisory Board explicitly that it did not view the food situation as especially dramatic and that the tuberculosis mortality rate should even be seen as favorable in comparison with some areas of Great Britain and other European nations. The German council members proposed a combined study of the health situation in the British zone in order to clarify this controversy, but because of later political developments that led to the founding of the Federal Republic this study was never undertaken.

Whereas the problem of food supply, despite great regional differences, caused almost the same difficulties in all four zones during the first years after the war, the danger of epidemics seems to have been especially threatening in the Soviet zone during the years 1945–1947. The danger that infectious diseases might reach the epidemic stage was greatly increased in all densely populated areas by war damage and insufficient hygiene. Although the population of the four zones had risen from 59.7 million in 1939 to 65.9 million in 1946, the war had destroyed about one-fourth of the housing space and severely damaged one-third of the apartments. The overcrowding in only partially restored buildings with defective sanitation and no heat in the winter months, the shortage of clothing, and the scarcity of cleaning and disinfecting products were the major reasons for the rapid increase in contagious diseases. Although data for comparison are not available (statistics were published in the Western zones first in the fall of 1947 and never, to my knowledge, in the Soviet zone), it is reasonable to assume that the danger of epidemics was much greater in the Soviet zone. This can be deduced not only from individual data that are available, but also from the fact that the fighting of the last months of the war had caused extensive destruction in Brandenburg and Mecklenburg and from the fact that the Soviet zone was collecting the flood of refugees and exiles from the eastern areas of Germany. Millions of people who had been traveling for weeks (sometimes months) across the countryside streamed, half-starved and often sick, across the Oder into the Soviet zone. They had to be lodged in camps, and a large portion of them had to be treated with the most necessary medication for survival before they were ready to be transported to the Western zones. Beyond this, medication was at first much less readily available in the Soviet zone than in the other zones. The most important pharmaceutical factories were in the West, and the Soviet Union, itself hard hit by the war, was in a much poorer position than the United States to supply medicine.

The danger of epidemics appears to have been less great in the Western zones. Typhoid, spotted fever, and malaria appeared only occasionally.[28] Only tuberculosis intermittently became epidemic.[29] The Public Health Service (Öffentliche Gesundheitsdienst), which had been responsible for epidemic control and hygienic measures, was reorganized in all occupation zones in the fall of 1945. The first working administrative branches were established in cities and districts. In some Länder under American or British rule,[30] and in the Soviet Zone,[31] the public health agencies were incorporated into the local administration, and the elements of state control, introduced by the National Socialists, were eliminated.[32] For their professional direction and supervision, the health departments of the intermediate administrative bodies were staffed, to the extent possible, by doctors with experience in public health care. In general, the problem of growing epidemics was indeed of great importance in the Western zones and was urgently discussed in medical journals. The conventional regulations, however, seemed adequate for dealing with the difficulties. Only the necessary coordination of individual measures between the different Länder remained a problem.[33]

Since the situation in the Soviet zone was more serious, the fight against epidemic disease there was, from the first, more strictly and radically waged. In September 1945, the Zentralverwaltung für Gesundheitswesen (Central Health Administration) ordered the systematic registration of all cases of abdominal typhoid, spotted fever, malaria, tuberculosis, and other infectious diseases, and in some cases hospitalization was made compulsory.[34] This directive integrated already existing epidemic regulations and intensified them with regard to compulsory hospitalization. The motive for this measure was first and foremost the high fluctuation of the population. Although a large proportion of the hospitals were destroyed during the war and roughly constructed barracks had to be utilized, broadened compulsory hospitalization was seen as the only way to stem the multitude of epidemics. At the same time, mandatory registration of illness was uniformly regulated and rigorously enforced. A Central Office for Hygiene (Zentralstelle für Hygien) was established in each region for every 20,000 or 30,000 inhabitants to combat epidemic diseases. Each of these centers was to be staffed by one physician and at least three disinfectors. To some extent, this was an organizational restructuring of institutions that already existed; to some extent they were new institutions, established to improve diagnostic coverage substantially. As a result of the increased production of vaccines, the whole population was to be vaccinated successively against typhoid and paratyphoid, especially persons from the very vulnerable area where the last of the fighting had taken place and those from the areas along the Oder that had been immediately affected by the refugees. In addition, ten quarantine camps for 10,000 refugees and resettlers each were erected along the border. In the middle of 1947 the Soviet zone had succeeded in containing and, for the most part, eliminating the danger of epidemic disease through the systematic registration and hospitalization of the sick and through an improved screening program (Renthe 1948).

## The Fight against Venereal Disease

The measures taken to fight venereal disease present an interesting problem, as the differences between procedures in the Soviet zone and those in the Western zones cannot be explained simply by differences in the extent of the disease. In the Soviet zone they rather provided the first step toward a new organization of the health system.

In 1945, as after World War I (Schreiber 1926, pp. 24–36), the number of cases of venereal disease had risen considerably. The decline in the number of cases in the period before World War II was mainly a result of a 1927 national law concerning VD that obliged the sick to go to a physician for treatment and required in certain cases that the physician report the case. Under certain conditions it called for mandatory treatment. Special public health institutions were entrusted with implementing control measures and counseling patients.

During World War II, the number of cases had risen, although more slowly than in the years 1914–1918. The registration and treatment of the sick was complicated considerably by the increasing fluctuation of the population and the increasing lack of physicians and medications.

After the collapse of the Third Reich and the occupation of Germany by the Allied forces, there was a wave of new infections in all four zones. The available figures show that the Soviet zone was particularly affected in this respect. With the regulation of August 7, 1945, the Soviet Military Administration ordered measures for fighting venereal disease (*Deutsches Gesundheitswesen* 1946, pp. 31–32). These measures were expanded by a number of regulations from the Central Health Administration.

With explicit reference to the continued validity of the VD law of 1927,[35] the establishment of ambulatory clinics for every 50,000 or 70,000 inhabitants was ordered. These clinics, under the direction of a specialist, were to provide counseling as well as treatment. In addition, it became a strict duty of the physicians to report each patient's name (Schafer 1947) and to initiate mandatory hospitalization in cases of syphilis in its contagious stage. The treatment of venereal disease was limited to these clinics, to specialists, and to certain general practitioners who had participated in a short course of specialized instruction.[36] An explicit directive from the ZVGes in October 1945 called for the expansion of the relevant departments of the public health offices into counseling and treatment centers, to be outfitted with all necessary equipment for diagnosis and therapy. For the general practitioner, this meant an end to his exclusive right to ambulatory treatment. Some of the physicians conscripted to work in ambulatory care in the clinics expressed their opposition to this regulation by making treatment as unpleasant as possible for the patient. In the ambulatory clinics the patient had the explicit right to the free choice of a doctor, but some of the doctors "could not be forced . . . to see that each patient would be sure of seeing his doctor." The doctors "changed their consulting hours," "found substitutes when they pleased," and often behaved "without consideration" for the patient (Jahn 1949, pp. 19–20).

When considering the measures of the ZVGes, one must take into account that in the Soviet zone during these years neither penicillin[37] nor a sufficient quantity of Salvarsan was available. Treatment was therefore dependent on traditional methods, which did not bring about a rapid cure and produced negative side effects. Nevertheless, thanks to rigorous control, the authorities in the Soviet zone succeeded in the relatively short time of 3 years in reducing the number of cases of venereal disease to a "normal level" (presumably lower than that of the Western zones).

In contrast, the authorities in the Western zones were not able to come to an agreement that would go beyond the authority of the Land governments. The VD law of 1927 was still valid, and some Land governments (e.g., that of Hessen) issued ordinances making its implementation even more rigorous. In May of 1947, however, the Allies, "concerned about the increase of venereal disease," ordered in Kontrollratsdirektive (Control Council Directive) no. 52 the reexamination of existing legal provisions, especially with regard to public instruction and information, and called for official registration and treatment. They also presented a draft for legislation (a supplement to Kontrollratsdirektive 52), worked out by the British military government, that largely corresponded to the regulations enacted in the Soviet zone. This draft encountered opposition not only among the physicians but also from a number of German authorities and associations. The passing of the bill was delayed by a great number of proposals for amendments in the not-unfounded hope that the problem would in time resolve itself.[38] When the Länderrat of the American zone, in coordination with the other health authorities of the Western zones, finally passed a bill in the spring of 1948, OMGUS (the Office of Military Government for Germany, U.S.) was no longer ready to promote its enactment; presumably the intent was to leave all legislative matters to the forthcoming new West German state (Hartel 1951, p. 1617). For this reason it was only after the creation of the FRG that a new law[39] was enacted that superseded the VD law of 1927.

That new legislation did not arise was due to many factors. Allied Control Council Directive No. 52 of May 7, 1947, called for legislation in the Western zones similar to that in the Soviet zone. In a plan included in this directive,[40] it was clearly advised that the counseling centers also be "treatment centers." This move to expand the duties of the public health offices to include therapeutic measures encountered opposition from the medical practitioners in the Western zones, who saw in this measure a threat to their existence, the first step toward "socialization of medicine."

A further problem in the Western zones was that of payment responsibility. In the Soviet zone this problem had disappeared for the doctors employed in the ambulatory clinics, and the payment schedule of the social security system was used for the private general practitioners; there also seems to have been no discussion about the amount to be charged for each service rendered. In the Western zones, on the other hand, the question of remuneration for services presented an important problem. If the patient was not a member of a sickness fund, it was often unclear who was responsible for paying. Since treatment could not be postponed, however, and the patient was generally not in a position to pay for treatment (especially for expensive penicillin), doctors were often uninterested in treating those infected with venereal disease.

Just how dubious the interest of the general practitioners in health care really was is shown clearly by an (unpublished) expert's opinion that Hans Muthesius supplied for the Deutsche Verein für öffentliche und private Fürsorge (German Association for Public and Private Welfare) on December 18, 1947. Muthesius (1947, pp. 35–36) discusses the question of payment for the treatment of venereal disease and writes:

Without energetic cooperation from the physicians, the fight against VD will be hopeless. The medical departments of the universities, the Ärztekammern [physicians' professional associations], and other professional organizations now have the special responsibility for most conscientious instruction and constant retraining of all physicians to be and those already practicing medicine. That symptoms have changed to some extent . . . seems to be established according to the reports of some specialists. It is exceedingly important to make the practicing physician thoroughly familiar with these symptom changes. If here and there the insufficient interest of the physicians can be attributed to the inadequacy of the pay arrangements, then one must, in the event that an investigation does indeed show this correlation, consider a new stipulation of payment rates, without, however, overlooking the question of professional ethics.

The practicing physicians were most definitely aware of the frequent inadequacy of therapeutic measures, but they were still not prepared to transfer the responsibility for treatment to the advisory venerologists who were employed as counselors at the public health agencies. In January 1949 the *Mitteilungsblatt der Ärztekammer Nordrhein-Westfalen* (Professional Newsletter of the Physicians' Association of North Rhine–Westphalia) stated: "If the diagnosis and treatment of venereal diseases by general practitioners—and they treat at least one-fourth of the syphilis cases—do presently not meet the highest scientific standards, the advising venerologists should point this out. It is certainly the most important and rewarding responsibility of the advising venerologist to be consulted as an expert. If this is done without the knowledge of the patient and in an appropriate manner, then each colleague should accept this gratefully and not as a reprimand." Here, evidently with no consideration of the patient, a dubious division of labor is retained. The advising venerologist, who is now supposed to counsel not only the patients but also his colleagues in his capacity as specialist, can do this only after he has recognized the inadequacy of the treatment, mostly due to a false diagnosis. Aside from the fact that the discovery of the source of infection is made more difficult, if not impossible, the delay of recovery and the damage incurred by the patient are not subject to debate, nor can the patient be informed thereof, because of professional regulations. The physician of the public health agency must be content with his advisory role.

Public-assistance and welfare associations, as well as the physicians, were interested in the bill proposed by the Kontrollrat (Control Council). Although they supported the initiatives of the occupation powers, they saw their own concerns neglected, insofar as in their view prevention and rehabilitation were not adequately considered in the draft. Above all, they objected to allocating counseling responsibilities to the health agencies, since such a regulation would have limited their own sphere of activity. According to them, the responsibility of the public health offices should be not to establish but rather to "encourage and stimulate the establishment of" counseling agencies, since the people, "according to their experiences," had much greater trust in nongovernmental agencies (Rothe 1948, pp. 2, 4).

The discussion of the Allied legislation on the problem centered mainly on the proposed extension of the obligatory registration by name and stricter regulations for mandatory treatment. The call for a more stringent administration of the obligatory registration was advisable not only because the extreme mobility of the people had caused a lack of control over a great number of potential patients, but also because the physicians did not adequately enforce the legally required not-by-name registration. Because of the physicians' lack of interest, even the vital need to document the growth of epidemics was ignored.[41]

In summary, it can be said that the ominous increase in venereal disease did not lead to an integration of public and private health care, and that such an intention of the Allies failed mostly because of the opposition of the practicing physicians, who argued against it as bringing about socialized medicine.

## The Professional Politics of Physicians in the Western Zones and the Restructuring of Medical Services in the East

The situation of health policy in the Western occupation zones is characterized by the word *reconstruction*. This does not immediately make clear, however, what was to be rebuilt and what was not (or, rather, what was to be built differently). Health policy in the sense of conceptual "ideas" did not exist on the part of political authorities. Only the problem of the restructuring of social security, articulated by the Soviets and the British as an explosive political question and discussed by all parties and interest groups, occasionally touched the area of health-care policy.

The Weimar constitution had given the Reich legislative power in the area of public health (in article 7) and in the shaping of the insurance system for the "preservation of health and work capability, and for the protection of mothers" (article 161). However, health policy in a narrower sense, as the formation of the structure of the health system and the forms of its services, remained the concern of those responsible for care—that is, the physicians, if necessary in consultation with those involved in the social security system. These discussions dominated health policy during the Weimar years and were the reason that alternative forms of health care were tested and that solutions to health-care problems were approached.

It was not because the problems had been solved in the meantime that the discussion was not reopened after 1945, but rather because the National Socialists had degraded the sickness funds to the role of financial administrators and had institutionalized by law the professional power of the physicians as a Körperschaft des öffentlichen Rechts (statutory corporation), thereby ending all discussion through a political decision.

"Reconstruction," for the physicians, meant assuring their assets. The sickness funds might have asked whether they should regain competence and responsibilities in matters of health policy or whether they should have to be content with their ascribed role as administrators of health insurance payments. That the administrators of the sickness funds did not even ask these questions but seemed content with the reduced definition forced upon them seems to be supported by the available records.

The dominating factor of health policy in the Western zones from 1945 through 1949 was the reestablishment of the professional organizations of the physicians as a political factor and their orientation toward two problems: limitation of access to the medical profession and resistance to every discussion of possibilities for a new organization of the health system (i.e., to a reform of the social security system— which will not be dealt with here—or to a new organization of occupational health services) (Tennstedt 1977, pp. 227–261). At the first Deutscher Ärztetag (German physicians' parliament) after the collapse of National Socialism, in October 1948, a resolution was passed that stated: "The development of the physicians' legal relations to the sickness funds which was consolidated in 1932 has ensured a peaceful working situation between the physicians and the sickness funds. Institutionalizing the associations of the sickness funds and the associations of sickness-fund physicians as equal partners with equal rights as a Körperschaft des öffentlichen Rechts has made it possible to coordinate a close cooperation . . . in their own responsibility and by means of a veritable self-administration, to regulate mutual relations, so that close ties have developed, which work toward the welfare of the insured." (Deutschen Ärztetag 1948, p. 28) This resolution makes clear how the physicians defined their situation. Without doubt, no conflict between the physicians and the sickness funds had occurred since 1933, but then there existed neither self-administration[42] nor partners with equal rights. The final codification in the development of the Ärztrecht (the law regarding the professional organization of physicians), which a resolution of the physicians predated to 1932 in order to avoid the stigma of National Socialist ideas,[43] was indeed a result of interim regulations in the economic and political crisis of the years 1931 and 1932. The relevant laws, however, were first enacted by the National Socialists; Kassenärztliche Vereinigungen (associations of the sickness-fund physicians) and Reichsärztekammer (national physicians' professional association) were set up in 1933 or 1935. The "peaceful working relationship between the physicians and the sickness funds" was a result of this legislation.

Through the ordinance of August 2, 1933, the Deutsche Kassenarztverband (National Association of Sickness Fund Physicians in Germany) was established to be responsible for the relationship between the sickness-fund physicians and the sickness funds (Reichsgesetzblatt 1:567). It replaced the planned regional associations of sickness fund physicians, which had been established on January 14, 1932, as the bargaining partner of the sickness funds (Reichsgestzblatt 7:19). Now the more than 6,000 sickness funds were faced with a bargaining partner that represented all the physicians and their organized power. Ambulatory care for the members of the sickness funds was legally assigned to the Deutsche Kassenarztverband. Through this regulation, the sickness funds (and thus their members, the patients) were deprived of a valuable instrument of health policy-making: the right to take part in the structuring of medical services through the employment of physicians under their own administration, as had been the case in the years 1924–1933 (especially in Berlin, where ambulatory clinics had been established by the sickness funds) (Tennstedt 1977). In 1934 the structuring of medical services was turned over completely to representatives of the medical profession when National Socialist legislation abolished equal co-management and thus removed the influence of the sickness funds on the licensing of the practices of sickness-fund physicians. Now the Deutsche Kassenarztverband was alone responsible for the management of ambulatory care. The sickness funds were purged of politically unacceptable persons in consequence of the law for the reestablishment of the permanent civil service (Gesetz zur Wiederherstellung des Berufsbeamtentums) of April 7, 1933 (Reichsgesetzblatt 1:175). About 30 percent of their employees were dismissed for political reasons (Tennstedt 1976, pp. 405–406). Self-administration was abolished, the Führer principle was introduced, and the sickness funds were restructured into associations whose sole function was the administration of members' fees (Reichsgesetzblatt 1: 577).

In December 1935, the Reichsärzteordnung; was enacted (Reichsgesetzblatt 1: 1433) and, for administrative purposes, the Reichsärztekammer (National Physicians' Professional Association) was established as the representative organ for all physicians. With the Reichsärzteordnung, the physician's profession became a special profession with semi-public functions, no longer subject to trade regulations. This law united the regional associations and incorporated them as a professional Körperschaft des öffentlichen Rechts. The associations of the sickness-fund physicians were integrated into the Reichsärztekammer as a separate body and an independent department.

This legislation of 1933 and 1935 certainly corresponded to demands that physicians (or their professional organizations) had been making for decades.[44] The demands corresponded to the social concepts and political intentions of the National Socialists, who desired to remove power from the hands of the independent, socially and politically active sickness-fund associations (or force them into political conformity).

In keeping with the Allied demand for decentralization and the elimination of the Führer principle, the Reichsärztekammer and the Kassenärztliche Vereinigung were dissolved in 1945, and trustees were appointed for the administration of their capital. Since there was never an order from either the Kontrollrat or the military governments to dissolve their regional suborganizations, these remained in existence in the Western zones, although their legal status was not defined. In any case, the representatives of the physicians' profession correctly feared losing the statutory character of their representative associations (the Ärztekammern) and strove from the first to secure it through expert legal opinions.[45] However, the appropriateness of the Kassenärztliche Verinigung as the negotiating partner of the sickness funds and as the agent distributing the fees to the individual physicians was undissipated.

Since a number of Social Democratic politicians had expressed their intentions to prevent the reestablishing of the physicians' professional associations, some of the physicians' associations on the Land level declared the abolition of the sickness-fund physicians' associations in their region. They installed offices in the Ärztekammer for the remuneration of the individual physician treating sickness-fund patients (Thieding 1947). In addition, they felt that they alone should be responsible for licensing the practices of sickness funds and that each respective payment office should be responsible for the appropriate distribution of the lump-sum payment from the sickness funds.

This attempt to ensure the continued existence of the professional associations as statutory corporations succeeded only partially. The sickness-fund associations felt that the Ärtztekammer, as the association of all physicians and not just of those who were paid by the sickness funds, was not acceptable as the negotiating partner provided for in the law. In addition, they feared (not without reason) that the Ärztekammer could use funds from the lump-sum payments of sickness funds for their political goals.[46] This would have led not only to reduced payments to the sickness-fund physicians but also to an unjustifiable "subsidizing" of the professional association with the monies of the insured. After protests from the association of sickness funds (Verband der Ortskrankenkassen) in Lower Saxony, the Central Bureau of Labor (Zentralamt für Arbeit) felt compelled to intervene. With reference to Kontrollratsgesetz 57, which reserved legislation in matters of social insurance to the Allied Control Commission, the Zentralamt für Arbeit requested the physicians' representatives to reestablish the associations of sickness-fund physicians. Since these associations were firmly rooted in the Reichsversicherungsordnung (Social Security Ordinance), they were under the jurisdiction of Allied regulations.[47] At the same time, however, this request continued the physicians' belief that the Ärztekammern still existed as statutory corporations on the Land level, and that, at least in the view of the Zentralamt für Arbeit, they should continue to exist in the British zone.

In the American occupation zone, however, the continued existence of compulsory professional associations, like the Ärztekammern, was seriously questioned. The American occupation authorities considered the professional associations as economic associations and therefore judged them according to the principles underlying American antitrust legislation. Economic associations, however, were not permitted to require obligatory membership or to exercise sovereign rights. The physicians' associations contested the economic character of their organization with the argument that this side of their activities (i.e., the licensing of sickness funds' practices and the remuneration of the sickness-fund physicians) was not administered by their association, but rather by a separate department serving only those of their members who worked for the sickness funds. Nevertheless, the Americans retained their original opinion, and for this reason they prevented the reestablishment of the physicians' professional associations in their zone until the beginning of the 1950s (Berger 1974).

The effort of the physicians to ensure their legal privileges was accompanied by a no less determined political move for the maintenance of their traditional economic position. In this respect, they were primarily concerned with controlling as stringently as possible the number of physicians, especially those licensed for sickness-fund practice. To achieve this goal, two methods were used: a request for a rigorous limiting of the number of students admitted to medical school, and an attempt to make the licensing of physicians (in particular for sickness-fund practice) more difficult by any means possible. This was especially true for refugees from the eastern regions formerly belonging to Germany.

According to a report of the *Deutsche Medizinische Wochenschrift* (German Medical Weekly), the deans of the medical schools and representatives of the physicians met in May 1947 in Frankfurt and agreed that their "most important task" was "to point out that admission to medical training should be severely limited in order to adjust the number of physicians to the demand and to prevent the creation of a medical proletariat" (March 18, 1947, p. 400). At the same time, the University of Göttingen communicated that it found itself forced to discontinue admission to medical training altogether, since "only the extremely talented . . . would in the future have prospects of succeeding in this profession" (ibid., March 14, 1947, p. 144). Although information about the number of physicians and their regional distribution was not published (and was presumably available only to the extent that individual sickness-fund associations had data on the number of their respective members), the physicians presumed from the start that there would be considerably more physicians produced than needed. What actually was "needed" was not clarified.

Certainly the situation had changed markedly from that of the war. During the war medical care for the civilian population had been increasingly limited for the sake of the military,[48] but at the end of the war the majority of the conscripted physicians returned home and attempted to establish practices. To these physicians were added the refugees, especially those from the eastern regions that had belonged to Germany and those from the Soviet-occupied zone. In 1947, among the approximately 1.8 million refugees in Bavaria, there were 1,200 physicians and 300 dentists approved by the Bavarian Parliament to establish private practices (*Deutsche Medizinische Wochenschrift*, November 21, 1947, p. 656).

The few statistics available, however, support the view that a problematic situation, which no doubt existed in certain regions, was generalized for professional and political reasons. The census of 1950, for instance, reported a total of 63,391 physicians (including those employed in hospitals and administrative positions as well as those with private practices) in a total population of 50.8 million—hardly an alarming ratio.[49] The supposition that the physicians misused statistics for their own purposes is also supported by the numbers of medical students after 1933. Although this trend says nothing about the demand for and the oversupply of care (especially since medicine and the need for care changed considerably during this period and since the demand for medical care must be seen in relation to these changes), it was quoted at the 1948 Deutscher Ärztetag as an important cause of the oversupply of physicians. Rold Schlogell (1948, p. 29), in his capacity as member of the executive board of the Bund der angestellen Ärzte (Union of Employed Doctors), stated:[50]

Since 1933, and especially since 1935 (with the reinstatement of the conscription), we have seen a constantly improving economic situation and, as a result of this, a steadily growing increase in numbers of medical students and therefore of new members of the medical profession. . . . At the beginning of and during the war, a further increase in the number of medical students became evident, since the military had eased the scholastic requirements in many respects because of its great need for medical personnel. Only the intensified war situation from 1944 on led to a more stringent restriction of accessibility to medical training.

Schlogell's statements are incorrect. The number of medical students had rapidly decreased since 1933. In the winter semester of 1932–33 there were 24,298 medical students at German universities. Though this number in fact increased to 25,264 in the summer semester of 1933, it fell rapidly to 19,974 in the summer of 1935. In the summer of 1939, there were only 17,476 students, and in the spring of 1941 there were 18,742 (Lorenz 1943, vol. 1, pp. 174 ff.). In the last years of the war, the number probably decreased even more. In the course of 6 years the number of students had decreased by one-third. This decline is also apparent in the number of final examinations taken. Whereas 3,669 medical students passed the Staatsexamen in 1935, the number decreased to 2,220 in 1940 and to 2,036 in 1941 (Lorenz 1943, vol. 2, pp. 138 ff.). Statistics for the last years of the war are not available, but it may be assumed that the numbers fell even lower. In addition, the emergency examinations given in these years were not unconditionally accepted after the war, so that a number of those who had passed were reexamined.[51]

Responsibility for these limitations in admissions to medical study lay less with the universities than with the Ministries of Education of the Länder. At the 1948 Ärztetag in Stuttgart, the president of the Bavarian Ärztekammer, Karl Weiler, spoke in detail on "the catastrophic effect of the oversupply of physicians" and on the "intolerable burden . . . the entire medical profession is forced to bear . . . because of inadequately trained physicians who, moreover, had no real calling for the medical profession." In addition to a "drastic limitation of the number of students admitted to medical study," he advocated "considerably more difficult examinations" (Deutscher Ärztetag 1948, p. 13). Corresponding to these recommendations, a resolution of the Ärztetag requested the appropriate authorities to "limit drastically the number of students for several years" (ibid., p. 32). The governmental representatives of the Health Committee (Gesundheitsausschuss) in the Länderrat in Stuttgart and the directors of the health administrations of the British and French zones agreed unanimously in November 1948 that "a temporary restriction in the number of medical students in unavoidable" (Protokoll der Sitzung des Gesundheitsausschosses beim Länderrat, November 25, 1948, p. 4).

The attitude expressed at the January 1949 conference of the Ministers of Health of the Länder was more reserved. There were differences of opinion with regard to the necessity for and the extent of the limitation of the number of medical students, and it was decided to investigate the state of affairs.[52] The delegate from Hessen, Wilheim von Drigalski, posed the question whether one could actually speak of a surplus of physicians, given the overcrowding of individual physicians' practices on the one hand and, on the other hand, the difficulty of finding suitable living and office space (due to the poor regional distribution of physicians) and the fact that adequate staffing of hospitals with physicians was by no means everywhere ensured.[53] These objections raised another problem, which was also discussed at the 1948 Ärztetag: the concentration of physicians in certain towns and districts, which for a time so jeopardized equal medical coverage for larger regions that the health officers saw themselves obliged at times to limit strictly the establishment of new practices in certain towns in order to induce physicians to move to other areas. At the 1948 Ärztetag (p. 13), Karl Weiler commented on these attempts at directive regulations: "As was to be expected and to be feared, the implementation of these measures brought no real satisfaction to anyone involved, since they ran counter to the fundamental freedom of the physician's practicing of his profession; moreover, they did not eliminate the danger to the general health of the population caused by the oversupply of physicians."

In contrast to this development in the Western zones, the establishment of the health system in the Soviet zone after 1945 was only to a minor extent the result of the arrangements of various conflicting interests. The SMAD seems to have had, at least in basic principles, a clear concept of reorganization. It implemented its policy slowly, because of the possibility for an early reunification of Germany, in conjunction with the German Central Administration of Health (Zentralverwaltung für Gesundheitswesen). The Reichsärztekammer was dissolved by order of the Kontrollrat. A new establishment of a system of professional representation on the Land level was forbidden in the Soviet zone. Only the organizations of sickness-fund physicians were permitted to continue functioning as accounting bureaus with the social security agency. The physicians were advised to join the labor union.

One of the first measures in the reorganization of the health system was the removal of the division between ambulatory and stationary care through the establishment of polyclinics and ambulatory clinics. During the first months after the war, the opening of the hospitals for ambulatory care came about spontaneously, because they had the only substantial reserves of necessary medical supplies and medical equipment. Because of the shortage of physicians in many areas—many physicians had fled to the west as the Soviet Army approached—those hospital physicians who remained were forced to take over ambulatory services to the extent their already overloaded hospital duties permitted. This development, brought about by the desperate situation, had achieved policy status by the end of 1945. At the Land level, the establishment of polyclinics was called for in official statements and decrees (Winter 1948). The SMAD supported these demands by providing buildings and supplies, which were under the control of the Soviet Army. By a ministerial decree of January 9, 1947, the hospital ambulatory clinics in Land Brandenburg, until then under the direction of Chefärzte (chiefs of medical departments), were turned into polyclinics. All diagnostic and therapeutic equipment in the hospitals was to be at the disposal of the polyclinics. All hospital physicians were employed at the same time by the polyclinics. In addition, the medical practitioners of the area were requested to assist in the polyclinics. Employment in the polyclinics was made equivalent to the work of the sickness-fund physician in ambulatory care; that is, the physicians were paid a lump sum per patient for their services and received additional payment for special services. The revenues of the polyclinics were divided as follows: The physicians received 50 percent, the auxiliary personnel received 20 percent, and the agency running the hospital received 30 percent. By the end of 1947, 31 such polyclinics had been established in Brandenburg. They were available to the entire population, regardless of the individual's type of health insurance.

This reorganization was enforced against the will of the majority of the practicing physicians, who felt their traditional privileges threatened. At a meeting attended by 850 physicians in Berlin in August 1947, the establishing of polyclinics was vehemently opposed. The tenor of the discussion ran: "It is not a question of ambulatories, but rather of the abolition of physicians." (Winter 1948, p. 39)

The danger of mass-production methods in public treatment centers, the destruction of the confidential personal relationship between physician and patient by the socialization of the medical profession, and the collapse of health care due to structure-altering interference were predicted. "We have preserved our professional idealism; confronted with this, plans to introduce ambulatories will fail. We will know how to defend ourselves." (Winter 1948, p. 39; see also Linser 1948, p. 1) In order to stem the discussion and make the new orientation easier to implement, the Zentralverwaltung Gesundheitswesens organized a series of conferences to which hospital physicians, health officers, practicing physicians, and representatives of the political parties were invited.

At these conferences the necessity of cooperation between the practicing physicians and the polyclinics was emphasized. Existing forms of cooperation were illustrated by an abundance of examples.

General conclusions about the actual situation of health care cannot be drawn from these examples; however, they make clear the enormous difficulties with which the political authorities had to struggle in the reorganization of the health system. For all intended measures, they were dependent on the cooperation of the physicians and were therefore forced to consider the situation of the physicians in the Western zones. If the individual physicians did not find it necessary to stay in the Soviet zone for ideological reasons, at least an economic incentive would have to exist that would render further professional activity in the Soviet zone comparatively rewarding from an economic point of view. This explains the continuation of the system of paying the physicians at the polyclinics and ambulatory clinics according to the number of patients. "A fixed salary would certainly be the ideal solution. This would make the physician independent of the number of sickness-fund vouchers and would assess only his work. However, till today this type of payment meets with little sympathy among the majority of physicians, which is why we have thus far refrained from implementing it in Brandenburg." (Winter 1948, p. 12) The tradition of idealizing the practicing physician as a free entrepreneur could not be abruptly eliminated in favor of the idea of the physician as an employee. Especially in those cases in which practicing physicians first had to be won over to the polyclinic system, it was necessary to take this concept into consideration. Opposition to "socialization of the medical profession" was too great a tradition to be simply ignored.

In spite of these obvious difficulties, on December 11, 1947, the SMAD ordered the Land governments to "aid by all possible means the initiative of the local German authorities in establishing polyclinics and ambulatory clinics capable of guaranteeing medical care."[54] The Zentralverwaltung Gesundheitswesen was authorized to issue binding regulations for the establishment, organization, and management of polyclinics. Contrary to the German tradition of the Weimar period, these establishments were placed not under the jurisdiction of the social security agencies but under that of the body responsible for communal self-administration. The costs were to be paid by revenues and subsidies from the social security agencies and the governments of the Länder.

The polyclinics and ambulatory clinics were responsible for offering and carrying out diagnostic, therapeutic, and preventive measures. The cooperation in preventive and social-hygiene measures was explicitly emphasized in the guiding principles of the ZVGes. Thus, not only was cooperation between ambulatory and stationary care to be ensured, but also a connection to the public health system was to be established.

The ample reports on such "achievements" (that is, the profusion of descriptions of newly founded polyclinics) can be evaluated only against the background of the extreme scarcity of medical resources and the general difficulties of reconstruction. The indirect compulsory measures emphasized time and again in the Western press—i.e., supplying the polyclinics preferentially with medication and x-ray material; occasional attempts, in view of the impossibility of buying new equipment, to obtain such equipment by confiscating it from deserted private practices (Jahn 1949, p. 26)—were probably used, even though they are not evident from the information published in the Soviet zone. However, the question whether the health-policy end justified the individual means or whether other procedures would have been more appropriate is unsuited for discussion because of the lack of information. More important is a clarification of the position taken toward the problem and the related discussion on the basis of statements made by two representative health policy-makers: Julius Hadrich and Kurt Winter.

Julius Hadrich, employed from 1925 to 1934 as financial consultant in the main offices of the Hartmannbund, wrote an article entitled "Family Doctor or Ambulatory?" (Hadrich 1948) which appeared in March 1948 in the *Tagesspiegel*, a daily newspaper of the western sectors of Berlin. The article stated: "The notion of the ambulatory clinic is based on social considerations, on the one hand, and on political intent, on the other. Those who propose it for social reasons intend a miniature model of the American Mayo Brothers Clinic. . . . There the patient who is able to pay has the opportunity to be examined profoundly according to the latest medical developments. . . . The patient pays $1,000 and more for the entire procedure. . . . It could be done for less, argue those who are proponents of the ambulatory concept for social reasons." These cost considerations seem dubious to Hadrich, and as evidence he quotes the 1929 business report of the Vienna Workers' Sickness Fund on the operation of the ambulatory clinic that had been established by the fund. This report stresses the expensiveness of the endeavor to keep technical equipment up to date with scientific developments. It also notes that one could rightly contend that the ambulatory system made getting sick easier: "The worker who gives greater attention to the condition of his health will take more notice of certain symptoms than the worker for whom the concept of sickness in inseparable from the absolute inability to work. It is quite possible that establishing ambulatory clinics results in an increase of self-observation and consequently in an increase of medically registered incidence of disease." Referring to this observation, Hadrich continues: "We will do this differently, say the politicians, and the way they want to go about it is disclosed by the magazine published by the Department of Labor and Social Welfare in the Russian occupation zone. . . . According to this plan, one authorized 'representative' for the social security agency should be elected for every 50 employees in every enterprise. These representatives . . . should visit the homes of all those workers and employees who, because of sickness or other unexplained reasons, do not appear at work." At this point Hadrich describes the new regulations for the procedure toward "work absence in the case of sickness," in the supplement to Order 234 of October 9, 1947 (*Deutsches Gesundheitswesen* 1947, pp. 686–687). According to these regulations, the sick person is subject to stringent control. With few exceptions, permission for sick leave can be written by the employee's physician only for 3–10 days, after which the patient will be subject to special examination first by a consulting physician, and then (after another 10 days) by a medical commission. A commentary in the East German periodical *Arbeit und Sozialfürsorge* stated: "These measures, which should primarily serve to improve the medical care of the seriously ill, are necessary in order to check an unjustified use of the finances of the social welfare funds and to stop irresponsible absenteeism.[55] Unfortunately, it cannot be denied that workers' discipline has suffered after 5 1/2 years of Hitler's war, which destroyed all morality. . . . The difficult economic situation— the black market and other results of the war—has doubtless contributed considerably to these lamentable circumstances." (Bohlmann 1947, pp. 490–491) E. Paul of the ZVGes wrote: "This directive assigns a greater 'controlling responsibility' to the physician than before. This cannot be dispensed within a social state. A system of sick leave conscientiously administered by all doctors, together with a physicians' counseling service . . . offers assurance to the responsible employee that his social security payments will not be squandered on those unwilling to work. . . ." (Paul 1947, p. 724)

For Hadrich, the social intention of the expansion of medical services by the establishment of ambulatory clinics was inseparably tied to the political intention of expanding bureaucratic control. But this was not his only objection. The very idea of ambulatory or polyclinic medical services seemed to him fundamentally wrong:

> The advocates believe that large institutions and technical equipment are the important elements in medical care, and that the physician plays only a secondary role. . . . But more important than all technology are certain emotional ties between physician and patient. On the patient's side it is his unconditional trust in the physician, and on the physician's side it is his will to help. . . . He must possess a strong emotional appeal, which can only be the case if he is a charismatic personality. . . . Such a personality survives only in freedom. . . . The Nuremberg physicians' trial established clearly that the responsibility of the physician is indivisible and nontransferable. The physician should not and cannot submit to the power claims of a bureaucracy. . . . That presupposes, however, that he remains free from any bureaucratic regulations, and that he is not dependent on governmental or semi-governmental institutions for his economic subsistance. The ambulatory-clinic physician is no longer a free physician. He is no longer the advocate of the sick and the weak, but rather the agent of a bureaucracy, whose interests he must primarily pursue. . . . For power politicians, the social purpose of the social security system plays a secondary role. Their main goal is the extension of their power.

This extensive quotation is justified not only because its author was an important voice in German health policy in the postwar years, but also because the essay was reprinted by the *Bayerische Ärzteblatt* (Bavarian Medical Journal). It was the only commentary on the new organization of ambulatory care in the Soviet zone published by this periodical (the professional newsletter of the Bavarian physicians) during the years 1946–1948.

Compare Hadrich's statement with a few comments from the director of the Department of Health in the Land government of Brandenburg, Kurt Winter. In his introduction to a collection of essays entitled *Zur Frage der Polikliniken* (On the Question of Polyclinics), Winter programmatically explains his position. The model of the "family doctor" is simply a questionable medical habit which hinders an objective discussion of the polyclinic model. The family doctor "was certainly a capable and qualified physician . . . who worked without time constraints and who doubtless became a true counselor and spiritual advisor of the family. . . . That should not prevent us from realizing that the idyllic situations of the nineteenth century have passed. . . . The precision of scientific knowledge has increased enormously. Because of this, medicine must now put up with a great deal of technology. In the midst of all these instruments, the physician has greater difficulty in remaining the soul of medical art. . . . The development . . . of the achievements of science . . . may be realized only if this isolated and elitist position of the intellectual is overcome, and if we can break through the old petrified form of health care and develop it further." (Winter 1948, p. 8) "The polyclinic works . . . because it integrates specialists from different fields and is equipped with the necessary technical equipment. It is indispensable for the proper medical care of the population and for a more democratic health system" (ibid., p. 12). "If medicine hopes to fulfill its mission in today's world, then it must disassociate itself from old conceptions whose central focus was therapy. Medicine today is requested to regard prevention as the center of its interest, research, and endeavors. . . . The realization of this change would presuppose the registration and social-medical care of the entire population from the cradle to the grave. Consequently, the physician must begin his concern with the healthy human being." (ibid., p. 2; Winter 1971)

These statements by Kurt Winter make clear that the establishment of polyclinics and ambulatory clinics was part of a more comprehensive reorganization program, which had two primary intentions: the "democratization" of health care and an orientation toward prevention. "Democratization" means here the intention of eradicating structurally caused disparities in medical care—that is, making high-quality care equally available to all population groups. This plan assumed that medical equipment could be installed on the basis of health-care considerations and not only with short-term profit motivations in mind. It would not depend, therefore, on the individual physician's willingness to invest. The plan would also institutionally regulate the cooperation of specialists. That such a program would not lower costs, at least for the short term, is self-evident. The long-term perspective, however, with its emphasis on preventive medicine, reveals a complementary strategy. Only a cynical interpretation of the observation from the business report of the Vienna Arbeiterkasse (Workers' Sickness Fund) quoted by Hadrich (that establishing ambulatory clinics causes workers to be more observant of symptoms and more careful to make the distinction between illness and absolute inability to work, and therefore leads to an increase in the frequency of illness) can lead to the conclusion that the clinics are not desirable for these reasons.[56] If one does not wish to perpetuate class-specific differentials in medical care as an instrument of limiting social security expenses, then the double strategy proposed in the Soviet zone seems to be an exactly adequate long-term solution. I would like to reconsider this double strategy—democratization of health care and emphasis on preventive medicine—by viewing medical services at the place of employment from the perspective of the theme of this essay, "continuity and a new beginning." It is precisely from the differing development of occupational health services (increasingly a topic for discussion; see Bohle 1977) that the adequacy of certain organizational forms of medical care may be measured with regard to the demands of industrial society.

## Occupational Health Services

In order to understand the different structures of this type of medical care in the Western and Soviet zones, we must take a look at its historical development. Although the correlation between industrial employment and health hazards had long before been recognized and discussed, industry in Germany did not until late become a sphere of activity for physicians. Medical inspection of industrial plants, introduced as a voluntary measure in Prussia in 1853 and as a mandatory measure in the Reich in 1878, was understood primarily as a technical service for accident prevention. Correspondingly, to become an industrial inspector (a member of the civil service) it was first necessary to receive technical training at a school of technology (Ausbildungsordnung der Gewerbeaufsichtsbeamten für Preussen, 1897). Only after the turn of the century did public health officers in medical administration cooperate (intermittently) in industrial inspection.[57] They were expected to determine whether a plant conformed to sanitary requirements, and whether it affected the neighboring population. They were also responsible for investigating general hygienic problems (such as water pollution). Such duties are still performed today by public-health physicians.

Only with the expansion of accident insurance to include compensation for occupational illness, in 1925, did industry become an area of medical participation.[58] Alfred Beyer, then Oberregierungsrat in the Prussian Ministry for Public Welfare (he later became vice-president of the German Central Health Administration), wrote of this development: "More numerous than industrial accidents are the cases of occupational illness. . . . The physician generally becomes aware of changes of this kind only when the employee comes to him as a full-fledged patient. . . . Clearly specific symptoms . . . form a contrast to the majority of occupational illnesses, which are difficult to diagnose. . . . Also, information from the patient that he works in this or that factory may still not help the physician to clarify the connection of individual ailments to the workplace. As a speedy, effective, and appropriate preventive measure, it is necessary that the physician orient himself in the factory with regard to the particular character of the work done there." (Beyer 1925, p. 17) Here, the physician's main responsibility was limited to observation; where necessary, he could also initiate preventive measures. The few physicians who were allowed to inspect factories were members of the civil service with the title of Gewerbeaufsichtsbeamte, and they were allowed to go into a factory at any time. In 1928 there were eight such physicians in Prussia.[59]

In addition to these individual physicians employed by the state, there were, especially in the chemical industry, a number of so-called Fabrikärzte (factory physicians). Some of them were employed on behalf of the respective Betriebskrankenkassen (company sickness funds) and were available for consultation at certain times in the larger factories. Others were employed as advisors to factory directors and were also in charge of polyclinics affiliated with the factories.[60] During the period of the Weimar Republic the question of curative medical care for industrial workers in factories appears to have been discussed only occasionally.[61]

Thus, until 1933 there were two professional areas for physicians in industry:[62] Industrial physicians (Gewerbeärzte), employed by the state, were responsible for the continued supervision of working conditions and for preventive protection measures, and Fabrikärzte, who were employed either by the Betriebskrankenkassen to be responsible for the ambulatory care of the workers or by factory management in an advisory and supportive capacity. The latter model of the factory physician was assumed and developed by the National Socialists; that of the physician employed by the Betriebskrankenkasse was discontinued by the agreements concerning the sickness-fund physicians.

In 1934, the Central Office for the People's Health (Hauptamt für Volksgesundheit) and the National Association for Industry (Reichsgruppe für Industrie) agreed to establish positions for company physicians. These physicians were supposed to aid the "Führer" of the plant in his responsibilities for the "social welfare" of his "followers" (i.e. the workers) and advise him in health matters. Employing such a physician was the responsibility of the Führer of the plant. A full-time physician was to be employed in companies with over 2,000 employees, and a part-time physician in smaller companies. The responsibilities of the company physician were established by general directives. Ambulatory care for the employees other than first aid was forbidden, since the general practitioners had a legally granted monopoly on ambulatory care.

The National Socialist authorities saw fit to revise this ruling when they began to experience, under the pressure of the war, increasing shortages of sickness-fund physicians. They realized that working hours were lost, when patients were forced to travel increased distances to reach the physician and then to wait excessively in overcrowded waiting rooms. For the duration of the war, the company physicians were allowed to treat the sick, and the sickness-fund physicians were deprived of this one monopolistic privilege. By decree of the Ministry of Labor (June 6, 1940), the Deutsche Kassenarztverband was ordered, especially in strategically important plants, to ensure that the company physician or a sickness-fund physician expressly appointed for this task would take over the ambulatory care of the employees. These physicians were also obliged to hold consultation hours in the plant at certain times.

A second meaningful change was brought about through an ordinance of the Ministry of Labor on October 16, 1941. This ordinance regulated the cooperation of the medical examiner, appointed by the Verband der Arbeiterkassen (association of employees' sickness funds), with the company physician. Mutual consultation was made mandatory. Consistent with this idea, the previous separation of functions was dissolved to the extent that the medical examiners should assist in ambulatory care for the duration of the war. This regulation was explicitly termed an exception and was limited to individual cases, which needed the permission of the Office for Health and People's Protection of the German Working Front (Amt Gesundheit und Volksschutz der Deutschen Arbeitsfront). The problem of unifying the control functions of the medical examiner with the protective functions of the company physician was taken into account by the provision that, in cases of disagreement, the decision on the exceptional permission rested with the Minister of Health (Reichsgesundheitsführer).

Against this background, one assertion made by the Munich occupational physician Franz Koelsch in 1947 (two years after the war) in the second edition of his *Lehrbuch der Arbeitshygiene* (textbook for industrial medicine) is astounding. In this book, which was accepted as a standard work on the topic, Koelsch stated that the company physician was both the advisor and the medical examiner of the Workers' Sickness Fund, that he was "the bridge between the treating physician and the sickness funds, between the worker and his place of employment" (Koelsch 1947, p. 337).

The problematic (and in the Nazi period quite obviously often misused) role of the physician employed by the firm itself was unquestioningly transformed into the role of an employee of the Workers' Sickness Fund. The double function of simultaneous employment as medical examiner (accepted only with hesitation by the Nazi authorities) is preserved, although in a limited fashion; even though the company physician is to inspect the hygienic and working conditions of the plant, and, in some cases, may introduce necessary preventive measures, he is no longer authorized to treat patients.[63] As W. Dobbernack (1947) stated, "the sickness-fund physician, who could be freely chosen, was available for all other medical treatments of the employees."

Dobbernack, in his capacity as head of one department in the Central Bureau of Labor, received a letter from the Social Insurance Branch of the British military government. This letter, dated December 22, 1947, reported discussions in the Allied Control Council with respect to the introduction of medical services at the workplace, with the idea of creating medical centers or polyclinics in all larger enterprises. It stated:

It is known that the public health organizations in Germany are not concerned, as a rule, with the medical treatment of workers and employees in enterprises. The medical treatment of workers and employees in enterprises is in the hands of private companies and of physicians engaged in private practice who are pursuing their own financial interests. . . . The majority of German enterprises have no medical centers or dispensaries; where available, such centers and dispensaries are subject to the authority of the management of the enterprise and guard the interests of the company and not the health of the workers and employees. . . . Workmen and employees are compelled to turn to a private physician who, not being in contact with the enterprise in question, is unable for the purpose of effective treatment, to take into account the specific conditions under which the patient is working; but what is more important, he is not in a position to exert any influence on the adoption by the enterprise of any measures for preventing a recurrence of the illness.

For these reasons, the Allied Control Council recommended the establishment of dispensaries, and, in larger enterprises, of polyclinics, in the course of 2–3 years. The state, or rather the social security agencies, was to undertake the construction, maintenance, and supervision of these establishments.

No information on the position of the Central Bureau of Labor on this issue is available, but its tenor probably corresponds to that of the comment of W. Dobbernack quoted above. Since the recommendation of the Allies was to be handled strictly confidentially, there was no public discussion.[64] Any sort of initiative in the direction of the Allied Control Council's proposals cannot be determined. An agreement did not ensue between the Arbeitgeberverbanden (Union of Employers), the DGB (Association of German Labor Unions), and the Werksärztliche Arbeitsgemeinschaft (Council of Company Physicians) until 1950 (Babi 1950, p. 277), but that agreement largely put the traditional situation into permanent form: The establishment of medical services in the workplace was indeed recommended but not prescribed, and therefore it remained dependent on the decision of the employer. The enterprise— and not the state or the social security agency—employed the physician, limiting his responsibilities at the same time. The physician's right to provide medical care to the members of the Workers' Sickness Fund was limited, as it was before 1940, to "urgent cases."[65]

In the Soviet zone, medical care in the workplace followed a completely different development. In 1947 there were 4 polyclinics and 681 plant medical centers in the Soviet zone. Three years later, there were 36 polyclinics, 109 ambulatory clinics, and 2,369 medical centers (*Statistisches Jahrbuch der DDR*, 1955, p. 77). The company physicians were employees of the Health and Social Welfare Department of the Kreis (region). This was to guarantee that the decisions of the physicians were kept independent of economic pressure or directives from the company management and made solely on the basis of medical considerations.

The starting point for this development was the Soviet Military Administration's Order 234 of October 9, 1947.[66] This extensive directive, which consisted of a number of different "measures for increasing work productivity and for the further improvement of the material conditions of workers and other employees,"[67] included under Point 11 a concise directive to establish medical centers or polyclinics, according to size, in all plants with more than 200 employees. Expenditures for space and maintenance of these establishments were to be provided by the factories; the other costs, including the salaries of the medical personnel and payments for the necessary medical-technical equipment, were to be assumed by the social security agency. In an ordinance issued simultaneously by the Verwaltung für Arbeit und Sozialfürsorge (Administration of Labor and Social Welfare) and the Central Health Administration, it was further specified that the medical centers and polyclinics were to assume the following responsibilities: implementation of preventive health measures, control of the organization of accident prevention, first aid for illness and accidents, ambulatory treatment of the sick (with special reference to safeguarding the free choice of physician), examinations for granting sick leave, and analysis of accidents and cases of sickness among the personnel.

Fritz Bohlmann of the Verwaltung für Arbeit und Sozialfürsorge based the introduction of a new form of integrated health care in the workplace on the following reasons:

The present organization of medical services is outdated and does not meet requirements. The shortage of physicians, especially in working-class neighborhoods, has led to the fact that reaching medical assistance is extremely time-consuming . . . long distances to the physician's office are an obstacle to prompt seeking of medical attention. As a result, illnesses that would be easily treated in their beginning stages suffer delay. . . . Industrial workers and employees require health care patterned after progressive principles. The achievements of science in all special branches, in particular those of medical technology, must be available to them. This will be possible to the highest degree in company polyclinics. . . . Because of his professional training and his special knowledge of the specific conditions of the working situation, the physician will be better able to correctly diagnose the symptoms and take appropriate measures to treat the disease. (Bohlmann 1947, p. 490)

It was thus acknowledged that the negative effects of the workplace in industrial society were to be regarded as central risk factors and that the emphasis in health care should be on prevention.

### Acknowledgments

I am much indebted to Wilhelm Hagen, Erwin Jahn, Ludwig von Manger-Konig, Josef Scholmerich, the Archives of the Friedrich-Ebert Stiftung, and the Archives of the Bundesverband der Arbeiterwohlfahrt (in Bonn) for permission to use unpublished materials, for discussion references, and for information.

### Notes

1. Since 1978, the Volkswagen Foundation has been preparing a new project in contemporary historical research: "Germany after 1945—The Founding and Development of the Federal Republic of Germany and the German Democratic Republic."

2. These measures, which were part of the Nazis' program of Gleichschaltung (political coordination, i.e. the process of forcing all social and political organizations into political conformity with National Socialism), included abolishing

self-administration in the sickness funds and expropriating or prohibiting politically unpopular welfare organizations.

3. For instance, the founding of the Deutsche Zentrale für Volksgesundheitspflege was due to an American initiative.

4. There were of course ordinances of the American military government that also affected the health system—for instance, the prohibition of physicians' professional associations and the much-discussed directives for ensuring freedom of trade. The first measure was seen by the U.S. authorities as an antitrust measure, since (contrary to German legal interpretation) they saw the professional associations as economic organizations. In the second case, the economic-political intent was obvious. Reasonable legal regulations such as the right of midwives to practice were repealed at the same time. Such measures did not result from the intention to force economic competition also in this area, but rather from an ignorance of German legal conditions.

5. Indirect remarks of this sort are found throughout Weiss 1957.

6. Discussions and health-policy conceptions of the Weimar period can only occasionally be referred to in this chapter. Of great interest would be a comparative study of the health-policy ideas of the Russian Communist Nikolai Semaschko, German Social Democrats (and health policy makers associated with them) such as Alfred Grotjahn and Arthur Schlossmann, and the English Liberal Sir William Beveridge. In spite of their differences (due to their respective historical and political conditions), such a comparison would demonstrate fundamental similarities in their conceptions of the structure and organization of health care. It seems that, above and beyond political party platforms, certain requirements for health care were understood as necessary and certain solutions as optimal.

7. Within the framework of the further training needed for specialization, the general practitioner may hire assistants for his practice (Praxisassistenten). This is a case, however, of temporary employment with the goal of establishing his own practice after the completion of specialized training.

8. Until 1968, partnership in a practice (Gruppenpraxis) was allowed only for family members (Ärztliche Berufsordnung, paragraph 18). Since that time teamwork seems to gain ground among younger doctors in spite of incumbent difficulties.

9. See Thiemeyer 1971 on the payment system.

10. Polyclinic treatment and hospital ambulatories are permitted only for training purposes in medical schools. (See Reichsversicherungsordnung, section 369d, paragraph 1.)

11. "An uninterrupted transition from hospital treatment . . . to treatment by a sickness fund physician is not assured. If . . . further ambulatory treatment is necessary, the hospital is not permitted to continue treatment. This must be assumed by a sickness fund physician. Normally he must wait four or more weeks for the final report of the hospital. . . . Thus a therapeutic 'gap' results,

which may cause physical complications for the patient." (Jahn et al. 1971, p. 32)

12. See the discussion (not followed up) of necessary reforms at the beginning of the 1970s, i.e., Jahn et al. 1971; Scholmer 1973.

13. Schlossmann 1930. Similar reflections are found in Roeder 1920. The actual position of the Kassenärzte was approximately that of employees.

14. In Niedersachsen and later in Rheinland-Pfalz, the health system was made part of the Sozialministerium (Ministry of Social Welfare).

15. This amounted to the refounding of Länder, which depended on economic exchange and a certain legal unity and could not survive as completely independent units.

16. See Punder 1966, p. 38. The activities of the two Central Administrations are thoroughly documented in the periodicals they published, *Das Deutsche Gesundheitswesen* (The German Health System) and *Arbeit and Sozialfürsorge* (Work and Social Welfare).

17. There were similar endeavors—even though unsuccessful—in the Western occupation zones; see the Protokoll des Generalausschusses beim Landerrat of September 3, 1948, and the petition of the Advisory Committee for Social Hygiene of the German Physicians to the Parliamentary Council on December 3, 1948. See *Hippokrates* 2(1949):57.

18. See also the Gesundheitspolitischen Richtlinien der SED (Health Policy Principles of the German Socialist Unity Party) in *Dokumente der SED* 1(1952):171.

19. Statut für den Länderrat des amerikanischen Besetzungsgebietes (Statute for the Länder Parliament of the American Occupation Zone), paragraph 2, cited in Hartel 1951 (p. 187) with respect to the construction of the constitutional and administrative institutions in the three Western occupation zones.

20. A compilation of the most important activities and resolutions of the Health Committee is found on pp. 160–162 of Hartel 1951.

21. On this see Hartel 1951, p. 51, against Weisser 1953, pp. 13 ff.

22. In July 1947, the British military government requested reliable information about the number of cases of nutritional edema that had appeared, in order to develop an idea of the nutritional situation and the aid that was needed. The Ministry of Social Welfare in North Rhine–Westphalia asked the physicians' associations to request their members to "report by name (and address) every patient treated for nutritional edema," so that the public health officers could give an accurate description of living conditions to the Regierungspräsident. (Mitteilungsblatt der Ärztekammern Nordrhein-Westfalen 1.1 (July 1947).

23. There are many (unpublished) reports and investigations of the nutritional and health situation of the population in 1946–47 by the Bureaus of Public Health (Gesundheitsamter) and private business. In addition to Wiele 1946, I wish to mention Rupprecht's (1947) study for the Gesundheitsamt in Remscheid,

the 1947 *Jahresbericht des Gesundheitsamt der Stadt Kiel*, and the reports of the routine investigations of the Labor Bureau of Lower Saxony.

24. This is documented in Klessmann and Friedemann 1977. See also *Der Spiegel* of February 8, 1947.

25. In contrast hereto, see "Report of the Results of the Combined Nutritional Committee of April 1947," *British Medical Journal*, May 17, 1947:684–685.

26. This corresponds to the German findings for Hamburg—1938: 5.1; 1945:14; 1947: 6.1.

27. Quoted from Dorendorf (1953, p. 105). A resolution of the West German physicians with regard to the German nutritional situation stated on June 15, 1947: "As a result of malnutrition the German people are becoming dull, distrustful, at the same time irritable and unpredictable, without ideals or moral firmness, unable especially to think or act democratically responsible. What we are experiencing is the extermination of the spiritual and physical substance of a great people. Anyone in the world who does not do everything in his power to alleviate this situation shares in the guilt." (*Hippokrates* 2, 1949:43)

28. In Kiel, for example, there were in 1946 an unusually high number of cases of malaria (Jahresbericht des Gesundheitsamtes Kiel [unpublished], 1947). See the report of R. Amelunxen on the health situation in North Rhein–Westphalia of February 18, 1948: "In contrast to tuberculosis and venereal disease, the number of cases of other types of infectious disease, such as diphtheria, scarlet fever, typhoid, and paratyphoid, has not increased, owing to comprehensive prevention measures and inoculations. The number as to frequency of illness and fatalities is well below that of 1939. Only in a few areas have typhoid and paratyphoid been determined in any great number. These small endemic outbreaks could be controlled, so epidemic growth was prevented."

29. Thus, the tuberculosis rate in Lower Saxony rose from 15.1 reported new cases per 1,000 inhabitants in 1938 to 39.9 in 1947 at an incidence rate of 915 per 100,000 inhabitants. According to a report for the special socio-political conference of the Zonenbeirat at the end of 1947, 3,271 adults and over 1,000 children were waiting for treatment as inpatients, which was not surprising considering the shortage of hospital beds. For information on the spread of tuberculosis in Lower Saxony, see Ickert 1948.

30. Within the framework of financial adjustments for the year 1946, Hessen ordered the communalization of the Bureaus of Public Health to take effect October 1, 1947. See also the 1947 decision of the municipal parliament entitled Zur Kommunalisierung der Gesundheits und Veterinarzamter. A corresponding decision was passed by the Land Parliament of Lower Saxony.

31. Verordnung über den Neuaufbau des öffentlichen Gesundheitswesens of September 18, 1945 (paragraph 1, in *Deutsches Gesundheitswesen*, 1946:28).

32. Gesetz über die Vereinheitlichung des Gesundheitswesens of July 3, 1934 (*Reichsgesetzblatt* 1:531).

33. See Protokoll der Sitzung des Gesundheitsausschusses beim Länderrat, April 28, 1948, p. 7, and June 2, 1948, p. 8.

34. Anweisung no. 1 on the Verordnung über den Aufbau des öffentlichen Gesundheitswesens of September 17, 1945: Bekampfung übertragbarer Krankheiten, in *Deutsches Gesundheitswesen*, 1946:28.

35. See regulation of October 29, 1945, point 8, in *Deutsches Gesundheitswesen*, 1946:32.

36. In addition, the members of a number of professions (especially in food production and the hotel industry) were subjected to regular preventive examinations.

37. Industrial production of penicillin, discovered in 1928 by A. Fleming, was taken up for the first time in 1943–44 with the support of the War Production Board. In January 1944, it amounted to 125,000 parcels of 100,000 Oxford Units each; in January 1945, to ca. 2,000,000 parcels. In other countries (including the USSR), production began after the war. Export of penicillin to the Western occupation zones increased rapidly, and according to a report of the *Deutsche Medizinische Wochenschrift* (a medical periodical) it was possible in July 1947 in almost all the regions of Lower Saxony (British zone) to treat infections of gonorrhea with penicillin. (*Deutsche Medizinische Wochenschrift*, August 1, 1947:432)

38. For instance, at the conference of specialists of the Health Committee of the German City Councils on March 12 and 13, 1948, in Gelsenkirchen.

39. The Gesetz zur Bekampfung von Geschlechtskrankheiten of July 23, 1953 (*Bundesgesetzbuch* 1:700).

40. Draft of an ordinance for regulating the establishment of counseling centers and infection departments for venereal diseases. Appendix C to Kontrollratsdirektive no. 52, article II. 1 and article V (cited in Muthesius 1947, pp. 30–31).

41. The insufficient registration of venereal diseases is also reported in the professional periodicals; see for example *Bayerisches Ärzteblatt*, March 1947:5; *Mitteilungsblatt der Ärztekammer Nordrhein-Westfalen*, April 1948. That the different interest groups nevertheless succeeded in preventing new legislation can only be explained by the fact that the Western Allies could be certain of keeping the problem under control with the help of sufficient quantities of penicillin.

42. Friedrich Langbein, the honorary president of the 51st German Physicians' Conference, stated in 1948: "At the 50th German Physicians' Conference in Cologne in 1931, the demand for a physicians' professional association within a Reichsärzteordnung was made . . . but it was implemented first by the National Socialist government. On December 13, 1935, the Reichsärzteordnung was proclaimed, and for its administration the Physicians' Professional Association was established. With this measure, important fundamental demands of the medical profession were met, but the enforcement of the National-Socialist Führer principle within the physicians' organizations inhibited the formerly lively interest of the individual physician for the task of his profession, since

criticism was forbidden and suggestions or complaints almost never obtained a hearing." (Langbein 1948, p. 4)

43. Haedenkamp (1947, p. 102) writes: "After the takeover by the National Socialists, some changes took place [in the Kassenarztrecht]; but these did not affect the meaning of the regulation arrived at in 1931–32. . . . After the collapse these National Socialist elements of the sickness fund system were immediately eliminated. . . . The cooperation of sickness funds and physicians was not interrupted by the events of the year 1945 and the postwar period. . . . The contracts are still valid." In a commentary to Haedenkamp's essay, however, Selpien (1947) states that one cannot speak of "elimination" of National Socialist elements of the Kassenarztrecht after 1945; he supports this by citing a number of regulations still in effect.

44. Thieding (1947) writes: "Removing the medical profession from the sphere of trade regulations (Gewerbeordnung) and transferring it to the Reichsärzteordnung satisfies a demand of the physicians made and advocated since the seventies of the last century."

45. For example, the expert opinion of Professor Laun for the Hamburg Ärztekammer, as well as H. Wirschinger (1947) for the Bavarian Ärztekammer.

46. This is evident from a communication of the Verband der Ortskrankenkassen Niedersachsen dated April 5, 1947.

47. See correspondence between Dobbernack and Haedenkamp of October 30, 1947, and November 3, 1947, as well as the directive of the Zentralamt für Arbeit of February 11, 1948.

48. At the beginning of the war, establishing a medical practice was made subject to authorization, and the Reichsgesundheitsführer had decreed that one physician was alloted for every 1,500 inhabitants. This number was reduced during the war.

49. For the sake of comparison, there were 99,654 physicians in the FRG in 1970: 50,731 general practitioners, 38,655 hospital physicians, and 10,268 working in administration. The population of the FRG at that time amounted to 60,650,000.

50. Stockhausen (1947) writes similarly: "As a result of the war and the propaganda adapted to war necessities and soliciting, the number of medical students rose significantly shortly before and during the beginning of the war." Stockhausen, however, emphasizes reservedly that "along with the increase in the number of medical students during the war, there was an extremely high rate of casualties among younger army physicians at the front, especially in the last years of the war, as well as a higher mortality rate among the physicians who had remained at home, due to premature exhaustion and especially heart disease."

51. The so-called ungraded medical approbations made out by the Bavarian Ministry of the Interior in 1945 were declared void as of October 1, 1947, and the holders of such degrees were obliged to pass an additional medical ex-

amination, given by a special examination committee. See *Staatsanzeiger für das Land Hessen*, March 29, 1947, p. 119 (Decree of January 27, 1947).

52. Konferenz der für das Gesundheitswesen verantwortlichen Minister, Protokoll der 1. Sitzung, January 1, 1949, p. 20.

53. Ibid., p. 19.

54. Order 272 of the Soviet Military Administration (*Deutsches Gesundheitswesen*, 1948, pp. 27–28).

55. The West German physicians were also occupied with similar problems. See Dobler, in *Deutschen Ärztetag* 1948, p. 22.

56. The connection assumed by Hadrich between the establishment of polyclinics and ambulatories on the one hand and the intensifying of control over the patients on the other hand is by no means clearly established. Rather, we must look at the extensive command no. 234, which combined a number of measures for the improvement of living and working conditions of the population with control measures—first and foremost as an economic measure for increasing productivity, which had fallen 50% from its prewar level. (See Staritz 1976, pp. 108 ff.)

57. The cooperation of the Kreisärzte (district medical officers) was stipulated with regard to permissions to erect industrial facilities (Dienstanweisung für Kreisärzte in Preussen, paragraphs 91, 93).

58. Ordinance of the Reichsministerium of Labor, May 11, 1925, with regard to the extension of accident insurance to diseases caused by industrial employment (Reichsarbeitsblatt).

59. In 1906 Baden had employed the first physician as a Gewerbeaufsichtsbeamte; Bavaria followed in 1909, Saxony in 1919. In 1921, the first five positions for Gewerbeärzte (company physicians) were created in Prussia.

60. In 1914 the Leuna factory had founded a polyclinic, whose physicians were Betriebsangestellte (company employees) or Vertrauensärzte (medical examiners) of the industrial sickness funds. Similar services were created by the Siemens Factory, Agfa-Wolfen, and Knorr Brakes.

61. See the Gorlitz SPD Party Platform (1922) and the statement of the 1925 German Sickness Funds Conference in Munich.

62. There were also physicians, active in the area of public accident insurance (a branch of the social insurance system), who played only a minor role in the question of injuries resulting from the work itself and thereby with the development of possibilities for work-oriented health care.

63. On May 17, 1947, the Executive Board of the Bavarian Physicians' Association resolved that the "system of so-called Betriebsärzte (company physicians)" that had arisen during the Nazi period should be dissolved "in the interest of maintaining the free choice of physician." Insofar as larger companies were willing to employ Werksärzte (factory physicians), these would be prohibited from giving medical treatment or advice exceeding first aid in emergency sit-

uations. "After emergency first aid treatment, the patients are to be transferred immediately to a practicing physician." The employment contract between the industry and the physician was to be presented to the Land Physicians' Association for approval before it could be signed. (See *Bayerisches Ärzteblatt*, May 1947, p. 7 and July 16, 1947, p. 415.)

64. That no substantial public discussion seems to have arisen is surprising, insofar as the measures proposed by the Control Council were introduced in the Soviet zone 2 months before the letter of the "Social Insurance Branch" to the Central Labor Bureau. In the medical and professional-political journals I examined, this development was mentioned only in passing, if at all. One could explain the professional journals' complete neglect by the intention of "letting sleeping dogs lie." Astounding—and in no way to be explained only by negative experiences with the company physicians (Betriebsärzte) of the Nazi period—is the fact that the unions have only hesitatingly taken up this topic. A bill for medical care by factory physicians (Werksärzte) was drawn up by the Bayrischer Gewerkschaftler in 1947; unfortunately, this was not available to me.

65. On the development of services provided by the Werksarzt (factory physician) in the FRG, see Kaiser 1973.

66. *Arbeit und Sozialfürsorge* 20 (1947):452.

67. For the other measures and their political context see Staritz 1976, p. 102–120.

## References

Amelunxen, R. 1948. Gesundheitliche Lage in Nordrhein-Westfalen am Ende des Jahres 1947: Bericht des Spezialreferenten des Landes Nordrhein-Westfalen vom 18.2.1948. Unpublished manuscript.

Babi, 1950. Bayrischer Gewerkschaftler.

Berger, M. 1974. "Sozialversicherungs reform und Kassenarztrecht: Zur Verhinderung der Reform des Kassenarztrechtes in den Westzonen nach 1945." Das Argument, special volume 4, pp. 73–93.

Beyer, A. 1925. "Gewerbehygiene." Der Sozialistische Arzt 1:16–18.

Bohle, F. 1977. "Humanisierung der Arbeit und Sozialpolitik." Kölner Zeitschrift für Soziologie und Sozialpsychologie 19: 290–423.

Bohlmann, F. 1947. "Gesundheitlicher Schutz der Arbeitskraft." Arbeit und Sozialfürsorge, pp. 489–491.

Deutscher Ärztetag am 16 und 17 Oktober 1948: Referate, Entschliessungen, und Beschlusse. Bad Neuheim.

Dobbernack, W. 1947. "Braucht unser Betrieh einen Betriebsarzt?" Der Bund.

Dorendorf, A. 1953. Der Zonenbeirat der Britischen Zone. Göttingen.

Grunig, F. 1947. "Die Wirtschaftstatigkeit nach dem Zusammenbruch im Vergleich zur Vorkriegszeit (Statistischer Bericht)." In Die Deutsche Wirtschaft zwei Jahre nach dem Zusammenbruch, Tatsachen und Probleme. Berlin: Deutsches Institut für Wirtschaftsforschung.

Hadrich, J. 1948. "Hausarzt oder Ambulatorium?" Bayerisches Ärzteblatt 34–36.

Haedenkamp, K. 1947. "Ärzt und Krankenversicherung." Arbeitsblatt für die Britische Zone, pp. 100–103.

Hartel, L. 1951. Der Länderrat des amerikanischen Besetzungsgebiets. Stuttgart and Cologne.

Ickert, F. 1948. Die Tuberkulose in der Britischen Zone. Hannover.

Jahn, E. 1949. Die Medizinal politik in der russischen Besetzungszone Deutschlands. Unpublished manuscript.

Jahn, E., et al. 1971. Die Gesundheitssicherung in der Bundesrepublik Deutschland. Cologne.

Kaiser, S. 1973. Betriebsarztliche Versorgung in der BRD und in anderen E-G Staaten. Berlin.

Kirchberger, S. 1978. "Prävention als Aufgabe der Gesundheitspolitik: Überlegungen zur Umgestaltung der Arbeitgeberbeitrage in der gesetzlichen krankenversicherung." Politische Vierteljahrschrift, special issue 9, pp. 220–235.

Klein, F. 1949. Neues Deutsches Verfassungsrecht. Frankfurt.

Klessmann, C., and P. Friedemann. 1977. Streiks und Hungermarsche im Ruhrgebiet, 1946–1948. Frankfurt.

Koelsch, F. 1947. Lehrbuch der Arbeitshygiene, vol. 1. Munich.

Konitzer, P. 1946. "Die Aufgaben der Deutschen Zentralverwaltung für das Gesundheitswesen in der Sowjetischen Besetzungszone." Das Deutsche Gesundheitswesen 1.1:4–6.

Langbein, F. 1948. In 51. Deutschen Arztetag. Bad Neuheim: Arbeitsgemeinschaft der westdeutschen Ärztekammern.

Linser, K. 1948. "Zum Befehl Nr. 272 vom 11. 12. 1947 über die Errichtung von Ambulanzen und Polikliniken." Das Deutsche Gesundheitswesen 3 (7):1–2.

Liebe, H. 1947. In Die Deutsche Wirtschaft zwei Jahre nach dem Zusammenbruch, Tatsachen und Probleme. Berlin: Deutsches Institut für Wirtschaftsforschung.

Lorenz, C. Zehnjahres-Statistik des Hochschulbesuchs und der Abschlussprüfungen, vol. 1, Hochschulbesuch; vol. 2, Abschlussprüfugen (Berlin, 1943); Supplement: Die Entwicklung des Fachstudiums wahrend des Krieges (Berlin, 1944).

Muthesius, H. 1947. Voraussetzungen für eine wirksame Bekampfung der epidemisch auftretenden Geschlechtskrankheiten: Gutachten. Unpublished document, Deutscher Verein für öffentliche und private Fürsorge, December 18.

Paul, E. 1947. "Grundsatzliches zum Befehl 234." Das Deutsche Gesundheitswesen, pp. 723–724.

Punder, T. 1966. Das Bizonale Interregnum: Die Geschichte des Vereinigten
Wirtschaftsgebietes 1946–1949. Waiblingen.

Renthe, B. V. 1948. "Die Erfolge der Seuchenbekampfung in der sowjetischen
Besetzungszone." In Kongressbericht über die Epidemiologen-Tagung in Berlin
vom 23.–25.3.1948. Berlin.

Roeder, R. 1920. Die Sozialisierung der ärztlichen Heiltätigkeit im Berbande
der Gesundheitsversicherung. Berlin.

Rothe. Stellungnahme des Landesfürsorgeverbandes Nordrhein betrefflich. Den
Entwurf eines Gesetzes zur Bekampfung der Geschlechtskrankheiten, aufgestellt
von der Fachkonferenz des Gesundheitsausschusses des Deutschen Stadtetages
am 12. und 13. März 1948 zu Gelsenkirchen. Unpublished manuscript.

Rupprecht. 1947. Die Auswirkungen des Nahrungsmangels bei den kindern
und Jugendlichen Remscheids. Unpublished document, Remscheid.

Schafer, E. 1947. "Namentliche Anzeigepflicht und arztliche Schweigepflicht:
Gegensatze bei der Bekampfung der Geschlechtskrankheiten." Das Deutsche
Gesundheitswesen, p. 259.

Schlange-Schoningen, H. 1955. Im Schatten des Hungers: Dokumentarisches
zur Ernahrungspolitik und Ernahrungswirtschaft in den Jahren 1945–1949.
Hamburg and Berlin.

Schlogell, R. 1948. Pflichten und Rechte des Krankenhausarztes. In Deutscher
Ärztetag 1948.

Schlossmann, A. 1930. Die Krise des Arztestandes und die Sozialhygiene. Paper
presented at the request of the chairman of the Deutschen Sozialhygienischen
Gesellschaft on September 2, 1929.

Schmitz, H. 1956. Die Bewirtschaftung der Nahrungsmittel und Verbrauchsguter
1939–1950, dargestellt am Beispiel der Stadt Essen. Essen.

Scholmer, J. 1973. Patient und Profitmedizin: Das Gesundheitswesen in der
Bundesrepublik zwischen Krise und Reform. Opladen.

Schreiber, G. 1926. Deutsches Reich und Deutsche Medizin. Leipzig.

Selpien, L. 1947. "Arzt und Krankenversicherung: Bemerkung zum gleich-
namigen Aufsatz von K. Haedenkamp." Arbeitsblatt für die Britische Zone,
pp. 220–221.

Staritz, D. 1976. Sozialismus in einem halben Land: Zur Programmatik und
Politik der KPD/SED in der Phase der antifaschistisch-demokratischen
Umwalzung in der DDR. Berlin.

Stockhausen, J. 1947. "Jungärzte in Gefahr!" Mitteilungsblatt der Ärztekammern
Nordrhein-Westfalen 1.4.

Tennstedt, F. 1977. Soziale Selbstverwaltung: Geschichte der Selbstverwaltung in der Krankenversicherung von der Mitte des 19. Jahrhunderts bis zur Grundung der Bundesrepublik Deutschland. Bonn: Verlag der Ortskrankenkassen.

Thieding, F. 1947. "Die kassenärztliche Vereinigung und die Staatsaufsicht." Mitteilungsblatt der Ärztekammern Nordrhein-Westfalen 1.5.

Thiemeyer, T. 1971. "Das ärztliche Honorar als Preis im System der gesetzlichen Krankenversicherung." Soziale Sicherheit 20:131.

Volkholz, V. 1973. Krankenschwestern, Krankenhaus, Gesundheitssystem: Eine Kritik. Stuttgart.

Weiss, W. 1957. Das Gesundheitswesen in der Sowjetischen Besetzungszone, vols. 1 and 2. Bonn: Bonner Berichte aus Mittel- und Ostdeutschland.

Weisser, G. 1953. Introduction to A. Dorendorf, Der Zonenbeirat der Britisch Besetzenzone. Göttingen.

Wiele, G. 1946. Ärztlicher Bericht über den Gesundheitszustand von 1059 Arbeitern und Angestellten im Juli 1946. Unpublished manuscript.

Winter, K. 1948. "Demokratisierung des Gesundheitswesens und Errichtung von Polikliniken." In Zur Frage der Polikliniken: Ein Diskussionsbeitrag. Probleme der Gesundheitspolitik, vol. 1. Potsdam.

Winter, K. 1971. "Aufgaben, Stellung, und Rolle der Polikliniken im system der ambulaten Betreuung." Zeitschrift für ärztliche Fortbildung, Beiheft 2.

Wirschinger, H. 1947. "Rechtsgrundlage der Bayrischen Ärztekammer." Bayrisches Ärzteblatt, pp. 1–3.

Zonenbeirat, Deutsches Sekretariat, ed. 1948. Material für die Sondertagung des Sozialpolitischen Ausschusses am 23.2.1948. Unpublished document.

## Legal References

Anlage zur Kontrollratsdirektive 52.

Anweisung Nr. 1 zur Verordnung über den Neubau des öffentlichen Gesundheitswesens, September 17, 1945. In Das Deutsche Gesundheitswesen: Zeitschrift für Medizin.

Arbeitsblatt für die Britische Zone, 1947.

Ärztliche Berufsordnung.

Ausbildungsordnung der Gewerbeaufsichtsbeamten für Preussen, 1897.

Bekampfung der Geschlechtskrankheiten, Verordnung, October 29, 1945.

Bekampfung übertragbarer Krankheiten, Verordnung, September 17, 1945.

Britische Besetzungsmacht, Anweisung Nr. 12, February 15, 1946 (HQ 062081 Sec. P. Zon 1P; (46)12).

Das Deutsche Gesundheitswesen: Zeitschrift für Medizin 1946.

Dienstanweisung für Kreisärzte in Preussen (Erlass des Reichsarbeitsministerium), June 6, 1940 (Amtliche Nachrichten II).

Gesetz über die Vereinheitlichung des Gesundheitswesens, July 3, 1934 (Reichsgesetzblatt I, p. 531).

Gesetz zum Aufbau der Sozialversicherung, July 5, 1934, Reichsgesetzblatt I.

Gesetz zur Bekampfung von Geschlechtskrankeiten, July 23, 1953 (Bundesgesetzblatt I.)

Gesetz zur Wiederherstellung des Berufsbeamtentums, April 7, 1933 (Reichsgesetzblatt I).

Kontrollratsdirektive Nr. 52, May 7, 1947.

Reichsärzteordnung, Reichsgesetzblatt I.

Reichsgesetzblatt I (note 86).

Anon., February 18, 1927, in Reichsgesetzblatt I, p. 61.

Reichsversicherungsordnung.

Sowjetische Militäradministration Deutschlands (SMAD), Befehl Nr. 17, September 9, 1947: Arbeit und Sozialfürsorge 20.

SMAD, Befehl Nr. 234, October 9, 1947, Appendix I, "Arbeitsbefreiung in Krankheitsfall," Das Deutsche Gesundheitswesen: Zeitschrift für Medizin.

SMAD, Befehl Nr. 272, Das Deutsche Gesundheitswesen: Zeitschrift für Medizin, 1948.

Verordnung, August 2, 1933, Reichsgesetzblatt I.

Verordnung des Reichsarbeitsministeriums über die Ausdehnung der Unfallversicherung auf die gewerblicher Berufskrankheiten, May 11, 1925, Reichsarbeitsblatt.

Verordnung Nr. 57 der britischen Militarregierung.

Verordnung über den Neuaufbau des öffentlichen Gesundheitswesens, September 18, 1945, Das Deutsche Gesundheitswesen: Zeitschrift für Medizin, 1946.

Verordnung vom October 29, 1945, Point 8, Das Deutsche Gesundheitswesen: Zeitschrift für Medizin.

I. Verordnung zur Bekämpfung der Geschlechtskrankheiten, April 11, 1946, Gesetz- und Verordnungsblatt für Grosshessen, May 10, 1946.

Zulassungsordnung für Ärzte, May 28, 1957, Bundesgesetzblatt I.

# 7 Out of the Rubble: Political Values and Reconstruction

Renata Baum

*From her unique perspective, Renata Baum briefly reviews a number of issues concerning the formation of the two German health-care systems after World War II. One of the most interesting concerns two principles of a social health-care system: that the state is responsible for the protection of people's health and that citizens are legally responsible to maintain good health as an obligation to society and their fellow citizens. To the extent that the state (or any other paternalistic organization) takes charge of health care and health education, it weakens the sense of initiative and self-responsibility one wishes to instill in employees and citizens concerning their health. On the other hand, the West German experience indicates that, left to their own devices, most people do not bother with preventive measures and health maintenance. Throughout the chapter, Baum manifests a certain ambivalence between her commitment to personal freedom and her preference for well-organized, efficient health-care services, an ambivalence increasingly manifest in American health-care institutions.*

The situation in which occupied Germany found itself after World War II can be described only as chaotic. Three and a half million soldiers had not returned from the war, countless civilians had also died, and many people had lost their homes and possessions. The economic system had utterly collapsed, and providing the population with the basic necessities was possible, if at all, only with great difficulty. The situation of the health system reflected these problems: hunger, epidemics, and poor availability of medical supplies led to even more deaths after the war. During the period in which Germany was being divided into four occupied zones, the Soviet-administered zone—the present German Democratic Republic (GDR)—was the scene of the most extreme want. Typhoid, tuberculosis, and venereal diseases could not be even partially stemmed, as in the Western zones, because the Soviets lacked access to medications that were readily available to the Americans.

## Background

Until "zero hour" on May 8, 1945, there had been a unified medical system in Germany. At the founding of the German Empire in 1871, national laws were enacted also in the health sector. In the period after World War I, efforts to legislate health and social welfare policies were increased, especially by the Social Democratic Party (SPD). At its 1891 party convention in Erfurt, the SPD for the first time developed a health policy program. Proposed were free medical services, medications, and funerals; introduction of the 8-hour workday; the abolition of child labor; the abolition of night work, with the exception of industries in which night work was unavoidable for technical reasons or those of public welfare; a 36-hour work break per week; supervision of industrial shops; control of working conditions by a federal department; hygienic working conditions; and nationalization of insurance, with worker participation in its administration.

While the KPD (the German Communist Party) consistently adhered to the idea of implementing a socialistic health system (among other things by the 1921 founding of the Proletarian Health Services, an organization which served mainly to provide information and propaganda), the SPD demanded nationalization of the health system for the last time at its 1922 party convention in Gorlitz. In 1925 at the party convention in Heidelberg, the Social Democrats dropped this idea from their platform. This did not prevent them, however, from advocating improvements in health safeguards and a greater degree of social security for all citizens. In the years from 1920 to 1930 of the Weimar Republic, various important health regulations were introduced, which would not have been possible without the constant influence of the Social Democrats. Among these are the Reichsjugendwohl-fahrtsgesetz (National Youth Welfare Law) of 1922, the Prussian Tuberculosis Law of 1923, the Reichs-Fürsorgepflichtverordnung (National Welfare Law) of 1924, and the Reichslebensmittelgesetz (National Grocery Law) and Reichsgesetz zur Bekampfung der Geschlechtskrankheiten (National Ordinance for the Eradication of Venereal Disease), both of 1927. Besides these, family insurance and workers' insurance were introduced within the framework of social insurance. The physician and Social Democrat Alfred Grotjahn, a member of the parliament from 1921 to 1924, designed a comprehensive health program. In the GDR today, Grotjahn, although a bourgeois, is considered to be a forerunner in the field of social and health policies. This is logical, since certain correspondences are apparent between Grotjahn's program and the Soviet socialistic health system of the 1920s and 1930s (which reappeared in modified form after World War II in the GDR).

During Hitler's dictatorship, the unification of the health system that took place served to eliminate democratic forces and facilitate enforcement of new legislation. Among the new laws were the race regulations, the marriage health law, and the euthanasia law.

### Initial Differences

After the division of Germany into occupied zones in 1945, it first seemed likely that the Eastern and Western zones would develop along similar lines. This impression came about because the Soviet Union at this time cleverly veiled its true political maneuverings and goals for the future development of East Germany. In order to lull the three Western powers into complacency and acceptance, the communists engaged in certain democratic trends east of the Elbe. Several parties were allowed, and prominent politicians from the Weimar Republic were asked to take a part in the reconstruction effort. At the same time, however, old comrades and newly won "party-line faithfuls" were given the greatest possible executive power. Since it had been clear from the beginning that East Germany would receive a social order patterned on that of the Soviet Union, the communist forces constituted the underlying support for the conditions which were to be created.

In the zones administered by the Western powers—today's Federal Republic of Germany (FRG)—public health welfare policy was more or less a reinstatement of prewar conditions. Legislation that had proved viable was retained or modified. Eugenics and euthanasia legislation were abolished. The pluralism of West German society set the character for the present organization of the health-care system. Besides municipal institutions, which are a part of the public service sector and therefore practically part of the state, there are cooperative and private institutions. This plurality is especially apparent in the realm of stationary services; hospitals may be administered communally and staffed by salaried doctors, classed as civil servants, or they may be run by specific religious denominations and be supported by associations (e.g. the Red Cross) or private individuals. Principally, in the FRG, one proceeds from the assumption that the hospital will operate as profitably as possible. Since this is almost never entirely possible, clinics are more or less subsidized by the public sector. Besides hospital doctors, who to some extent have the right to receive outpatients within the hospital, the FRG possesses general practitioners and specialists with private practices who are paid privately or through the sickness funds.

The conditions in the GDR were quite different. On June 9, 1945, the Soviet Military Administration in Germany (SMAD) was established in the Soviet-occupied zone. In the same year, the SMAD carried out extensive reappropriation measures with the motto "Reform" or "Reorganization." Step by step, the health system was nationalized, all the more easily since absolutely no functioning health service existed after the war. Epidemics and infectious diseases (syphilis, spotted fever, dysentery, typhoid abdominalis), nutrition problems, untenable living conditions due to the devastation, and the lack of hospital beds and medications encouraged a "central regulation from above," since it was argued that the speedy, decisive action that was necessary was possible only through a central administration.

With SMAD Regulation No. 30, for the eradication of venereal disease, war was openly declared on private practice. Treatment of venereal disease was forbidden to doctors in private practice and transferred to ambulatory clinics established for this purpose. The prohibition was absolutely effective, since the distribution of Salvarsan and penicillin was controlled and independent general practitioners had no access to them. After 1947, on the basis of SMAD Decrees 234 and 272, outpatient clinics, factory clinics, and first-aid stations were set up on a large scale. By this point at the very latest, the undisguised adoption of the social and political conditions of the Soviet Union had begun.

On March 31, 1947, the SED (Sozialistische Einheitspartei Deutschland, the Communist Party in the GDR) marked out the party line with respect to health policy. Separation from the "capitalistic social order" was declared, and a program for the future organization of the health system was developed. The health system was included in the first installation of an economic plan for the year 1948–49. By the beginning of the 1950s, the GDR had established a health policy closely following the Soviet model. The attempt was made to transfer the socialist form of organization as rigorously as possible into the German context. Still, there are today in the GDR a few (although a very few) private medical practices, whereas these disappeared decades ago in the Soviet Union.

In the USSR there is only the "medical worker," who is an employee of the state and whose salary is even more modest than those of other professionals.

At this point I should include a few comments on the Soviet health system, since its fundamental concepts are valid also for the GDR. Catastrophic conditions, not unlike those in Germany after World War II, were prevalent in Russia after World War I, the October Revolution, and the Civil War. Famine, sickness, and total disorganization on every level made immediate and purposeful action imperative, especially in the public health sector. The Moscow social hygienist and first People's Commissar for Public Health, N. I. Semaschko, had a decisive influence on the organization of the Soviet public health system. He embraced I. P. Pavlov's ideas of social pathology and made them the central principles of his program. Pavlov had taken the view that sickness is not caused by an immutable fate but is rather a disturbance in human life, created by empirical (societal) factors, and therefore curable and even preventable. On the basis of this idea, prevention has always held preeminence in socialistic health policies.

## The Socialistic Health-Care System

The socialistic health-care system is based on the following principles:

1. The state is directly responsible for protection of the people's health.

The basis for this principle is that social injustice can be avoided only when every aspect of medical care is taken from private control. But as praxis shows—a vehement discussion of this topic has occupied the *Literaturnaja Gazeta* for months—even nationalized health care cannot fully stamp out unequal treatment; by special payments, a patient even today can acquire special individual treatment.

2. Health care is "free" and generally available.

Because of health insurance (the sickness funds), medical care is generally available in the FRG as well.[1] The word *free*, which is used in the GDR as well as in the USSR, should be replaced by the phrase *without direct payment*, for the socialistic health system is by no means free; on the contrary, workers in the GDR and especially the Soviet Union must give up a part of their incomes to enjoy them. The per capita income in the GDR—even with allowances for differences in buying power—is considerably lower than that in the FRG. In addition, the GDR spends a smaller percentage of its total budget than the FRG for social needs.

3. The citizen is held legally responsible for the maintenance, restoration, and betterment of his health.

In West Germany, treatment is mandatory only for persons who are carriers of an epidemic or suffer from a disease that endangers their lives and those of people around them. In the socialist state, however, there are more far-reaching means of forcing a person to submit to treatment. Since the individual is responsible to society for his health, he must maintain his health. Because it is the basis for his economic productivity, he can be held accountable for irresponsible or willful injury to his health, and for this he can be deprived of professional and social advantages (such as promotions, premiums, vacation coupons at a reduced rate, and opportunities for better housing). In this context, health education plays a different role than it does in the FRG. It is an inherent part of the general education and indoctrination programs.

4. Within the system of medical care, prevention plays a primary role.

The health system in socialism aims primarily at retaining the worker's and thus the state's productive capacity. It is important, therefore, not so much to heal already existing illness as to prevent the development of disease. The clearest difference between East and West German health systems, then, is in the area of prevention. In contrast to the FRG, the GDR has developed (or is seeking to develop) strict organizational structures for prevention praxis.

## The Dispensaire

One distinctive organizational structure adopted in the GDR was the dispensaire. Ostensibly imported from the Soviet Union, the dispensaire system began in Germany during the 1920s and the early 1930s. Some sickness funds created dispensaire centers as an alternative to physicians' offices. In them, preventive medicine had a stronger emphasis, and a number of specialities were integrated. Ironically, the Soviet Union adopted the dispensaire system and then exported it after World War II in altered form back to East Germany. The East Germans retained elements of the original model, such as pulmonary and pediatric services, so the present form in the GDR resembles neither the West German social health system nor the thoroughly organized form of the Soviet dispensaire system.

In the USSR there is now dispensaire supervision in almost all medical areas. Apart from specialized and spatially autonomous institutions specifically called dispensaires, it is possible to utilize the dispensaire method in every medical institution involving ambulatory care (general outpatient clinics, factory clinics, etc.). This is not yet the case in the GDR. For the most part, the dispensaire system has been limited to factory clinics in the GDR, as it also was in the beginning in the USSR. Obstetrics and pediatrics have, from the very beginning, however, been permanently included in the dispensaire model. The GDR is behind the Soviet Union in including other medical areas in the dispensaire system, but since the 1960s it has gradually been spreading to include the general outpatient clinics.

The dispensaire method unifies prevention, diagnosis, and therapy. With the idea of increasing the rationality of the system, certain societal groups are classed together for treatment, i.e. people of the same age or profession. The goals of optimal care are to keep healthy persons under continuous monitoring; to supervise risk groups; to identify at an earlier stage, treat, and rehabilitate the sick; and to constantly control, treat, and rehabilitate the permanently injured or handicapped. The GDR is still far from attaining these goals, not only because of organizational difficulties but also because of the lack of fiscal resources and manpower.

At this time, the GDR has organized its dispensaire system in three ways:

1. General dispensaire care. This is employed in the ambulatory clinics and aims at reducing the incidence of sickness, maintaining worker productivity, and avoiding health risks. The sick are classified and treated according to numerous aspects (nosological forms, etiology, general fitness, high risk groups, and so on). This form of care has the serious disadvantage that compiling and comparing statistics is impossible because of the splintered character of these various groups.

2. Specialized dispensaire care with vertical coordination throughout. The target groups in this system are organized according to their morbidity. The organization of the treatment is continuous through all levels, reaching from the smallest ambulatory clinic to the university institute. This organizational model is much more effective than the first, since the systematic organization according to disease facilitates a rational use of personnel and medical technology. The results of treatment can be analyzed and compared and give clearer information about the success or failure of a particular treatment.

3. Specialized dispensaire care without vertical coordination. This form often arose spontaneously—for example, from state regulations, special demographic or epidemiological conditions, or scientific interests. This form of organization seems to be just as ill-suited to statistical analysis as the first, since in many cases epidemiological studies are not being done and state coordination is lacking. Each treatment center is responsible only to itself, cares for small groups, and has almost no association with other centers and their therapeutic practices.

None of the three dispensaire systems has yet proved itself thoroughly successful. To be sure, the GDR has worked with this model only since the late 1950s, whereas the first dispensaires in the Soviet Union were created in the 1920s. The advantage of a three-decade head start should not be underestimated.

That in the final analysis the second form of organization will prevail is shown by the experiences of the cardiological dispensaire in metropolitan Cottbus, which was conceived as a model institution. Since 1975 this dispensaire has serviced an area with 90,000–95,000 inhabitants, under the direction of a cardiologist. Except for life-and-death cases, patients are admitted for first visits only by referral from a factory clinic, an ambulatory clinic, or a general practitioner. In general, all necessary tests and examinations take place on one day, about a week after the patient first requested an appointment. The physician in charge of the case receives the report and treats the patient accordingly. Thereafter, one regular checkup per year in the cardiological dispensaire has proved necessary and adequate. In difficult cases, the cardiologist will treat the patient in the dispensaire until the patient's primary physician can resume ambulatory treatment. Treatment by the cardiologist may last up to 2 years in cases of serious illness (angiopathy, certain cases of hypertension, infarction of the heart). All rehabilitation measures after a heart attack—special nursing care, physical therapy, and psychological help—are taken care of by the dispensaire.

In 1975, 67 percent of the 40–44-year-old inhabitants of the area were diagnosed. Blood-pressure tests, electrocardiograms, and x-rays were part of the control. It soon became apparent that a regular control of this age group, let alone an expansion to include those between the ages of 31 and 60, was impossible given the capacity of the Cottbus dispensaire. If the supervision is to be expanded in the future to include screenings at 2-year intervals, the system must be modified in several points: The relevant examinations must be performed for employees by the doctor at the place of employment and for other groups by health workers of the dispensaire. The dispensaire's cardiologist must then be charged with all coordinating and consulting duties; that is, he must advise and support the primary physician with diagnosis and treatment of cardiovascular patients.

Although the dispensaire system in the GDR displays shortcomings that will not be easily overcome in the near future, it seems basically correct and successful, at least in a country whose health system has the maintenance of health (and, with it, manpower) as its main goal. This can be ensured only through systematic control of all population groups (from infancy on) and will be achieved all the more quickly as greater numbers of healthy persons become included in regular prevention.

In the FRG, where different ideologies prevail, such a system could hardly be implemented; it would conflict with the constitution. According to legal practice in the FRG, mandatory regular checkups and the consequences thereof (i.e. mandatory treatment if needed) would attack an individual's basic rights. Thus, the discovery of disease depends to a certain degree on coincidence; that is, a patient requests an examination only after he has developed symptoms. In the case of a sickness that must be reported,[2] such as tuberculosis or venereal disease, the appropriate part of the medical-welfare system intervenes, discovers contact persons, and urges treatment. These methods are not comparable with the dispensaire method.

## Preventive Checkups: Differences and Controversies

The overall medical programs of the GDR and the FRG differ because of different ideological beliefs. Concerning heart disease, for example, the FRG, not the least for economic considerations, prefers health education to institutionalized prevention. Conversely, in the GDR the "cardiovascular registry" recommended by the World Health Organization, has been provisionally introduced into some areas of East Berlin and other regional districts. The long-range goals are supervised full physical examinations according to registration and the treatment and rehabilitation of afflicted groups. The "people's serial x-ray examinations" are used for this purpose, since certain cardiovascular illnesses are diagnosable from a thorax x-ray. This procedure is indeed reasonable, since the population has been accustomed to mandatory x-ray examinations for years. The time and personnel expenditures are kept to a minimum, since the analysis as well as the actual examination has been largely automated.

Were one to analyze this system according to its effectiveness, its practicality would no longer be completely obvious. According to certain statistics, only 3–20 percent of all susceptible and ailing persons obtain immediate treatment and are continuously supervised. It is doubtful, however, that a maximum 20 percent rate of detection justifies the rather significant expenditure. In recognition of this fact, Cobet et al. (1977), of East Berlin, recently recommended a new focus and different tactics with regard to cardiovascular screening. They write: "Decisive for the success of such studies are a clear and limited interest, the restriction of the diagnostic spectrum to practical and standardized methods which supply essential information, and close work with medical establishments in the region. Cooperation from data processing specialists in the planning stages is recommended." Such modified proposals for general cardiovascular screening are more easily defended.

In some Länder (states) of the FRG, attitudes toward tuberculosis prevention are not so different from those of the GDR. A rule has existed in the GDR since 1955 (this became law in 1963) that every citizen over 15 years of age must undergo an x-ray examination every year. The appropriate dispensaire takes over the social and medical care of persons in need of treatment. In the same way, Schleswig-Holstein (since 1947), Baden-Württemburg (since 1948), Lower Saxony (since 1958), and Bavaria (since 1953) legally require an x-ray examination every 5 years. However, citizens who refuse to undergo this examination are no longer penalized, and in the other Länder participation in such an examination is voluntary. The discussion of mandatory examinations has never been satisfactorily concluded in the FRG, in spite of the fact that the basic debate of several years ago on this question was settled in favor of the Epidemic Law, somewhat at the expense of basic rights.

There is still much disagreement on the possible side effects of x-rays, and the purpose of these mandatory examinations is often contested. The appropriate Bavarian Public Health officer, B. Kranig, gives the rate of newly diagnosed cases as 40 per 100,000 examinations. W. Faass of the regional x-ray office in Schleswig-Holstein reports on a targeted examination of the 12–18-year-olds, which revealed 23 actual cases in 100,000 examinations. Such rates draw criticism, and a better utilization of the health system is being sought.

In 1976, a scant 30 per 100,000 new cases of lung tuberculosis were reported in the GDR. In the same year, 53.3 cases per 100,000 were reported in the FRG. Before one becomes an advocate of the mandatory x-ray examination on the basis of the lower tuberculosis statistics of the GDR, one should consider the fact that by the end of 1975 in the FRG one-tenth of all workers were foreign, and a percentage of these were from medically undersupplied countries. As experience shows, this group tends to influence the health statistics considerably. It is true that the GDR also employs foreigners, but almost all of these come from neighboring communist countries with socialist health systems similar to that of the USSR. Therefore the entire population, at least with regard to epidemic disease, is officially registered and controlled.

In order to make the examinations more effective in the future, the following plans are now under discussion in the Federal Republic:

• X-ray technology could be used more intensely for the early detection of cancer and cardiovascular diseases, as is currently the case in the GDR.

• The serial examination should not be used for the detection of tuberculosis if fewer than 4 cases per 10,000 examinations are found; rather, specific age and professional groups and specific regions in which this number is exceeded should be targeted for examinations.

• A centralized organization for tuberculosis care should even out the distribution of resources and manpower and better coordinate the work of individual health establishments.

The expenditures for early detection of cancer in the two German states are nearly equal. Since 1952 in the GDR, malignant tumors must be reported; examinations for early detection are carried out if the patient wishes. There is indeed encouragement through health propaganda for all women over 30 and all men over 45 to have yearly checkups and for women to examine themselves for breast cancer. This goal is far from being reached. Since the East German citizen must undergo several mandatory examinations anyway and is burdened otherwise by his profession and his expected participation in political organizations, he does not sufficiently make use of the voluntary health control. For those who do not take advantage of the early detection examination, it will be only through coincidence that the cancer is caught in its early stages. Painful symptoms or noticeable changes will first bring the patient to the doctor for an examination. The exception to this is lung cancer, which can be discovered through the obligatory yearly x-ray.

Since January 1, 1971, every man over 45 and every woman over 30 in the FRG has the right to one early-detection examination per year. For women, this includes gynecological, rectal, kidney, urinary tract, and skin examinations; after the age of 45, a colon examination may also be included. Normally, however, women make use only of the gynecological and rectal control, through either a gynecologist or their general practitioner. For men, the examination includes the outer genitalia, the prostate gland, and the rectum. Less often, it includes the colon, the kidneys, the urinary tract, and the skin. The costs of the preventive measures are carried by the sickness funds. Currently, about 20 percent of the women and less than 10 percent of the men of high-risk age make use of this offer. To be sure, the available medical staffs and technology could never accommodate a participation of 100 percent.

The opinion that the preventive control is useless and expensive has been gaining adherents. On the one hand, the rate of early diagnoses remains relatively small, and on the other, there have been a number of cases in which an already present case of cancer has not been diagnosed. There are now three cancer registries in the FRG: in Hamburg (since 1929), in the Saarland (since 1966), and in Baden-Württemberg. The statistics available there involve the reports of public and private infirmaries and clinics, pathological and radiation institutes, and general practitioners. The general practitioners, however, are not required to report their patients, because it is assumed that all cancer patients will at some point appear in the reports of a clinic or an institute. It is hoped that, by adequately detailed specifications, double registrations will be avoided. There are no centrally controlled statistics for the FRG, so a comparison of the frequency of illness with that of other countries is impossible. If one quotes statistics from Hamburg, one must take into account that this is a large metropolis, with a harbor, much industry, and almost no agriculture, while a region such as the Saarland includes agriculture as well as a great deal of industry. In spite of the difficulty of comparison, there are a few figures available which give an approximate idea of the cancer morbidity in the GDR and FRG. In 1974, the cancer registry in Hamburg reported 420.3 illnesses and deaths per 100,000 men and 421.6 per 100,000 women. In the same year, the registry in the Saarland reported 372.3 illnesses and deaths per 100,000 men and 363.7 per 100,000 women. The difference may be explained in demographic and geographical terms (Hamburg is a city-state, whereas the Saarland encompasses a larger region), or by differences in assembling statistics of a disease which need not be reported.

The GDR showed figures in 1974 of 350.2 per 100,000 men and 358.4 per 100,000 women. These are figures, however, only for newly reported illness. The mortality rate was not given until 1975: 237.9 per 100,000 men and 215.8 per 100,000 women (220.7 per 100,000 in general). It must be mentioned again that these are not statistically comparable figures; they must be seen only as rough approximations.

## Health Education

The topic of "health education" has always been a ticklish one in both the GDR and the FRG. The GDR is more intensely engaged in public information and education (this is also easier for a state-controlled health system); its success, however, leaves much to be desired. This is especially true of citizens' behavior patterns with regard to the consumption of the "poisons of prosperity," such as tobacco, alcohol, pills, and drugs, which have pathogenetic effects. Through the propaganda of the media and the medical system the public is indeed well informed of the dangers of this poisonous consumption, but it continues to consume. This means, in short, that public health education as now practiced is not effective.[3] Andrzejak and Kunzendorff (1977) of the Institute for Social Hygiene in Erfurt describe the situation as follows: "It is perhaps not true to report no change whatsoever; for a certain percentage (of smokers for example, under 10 percent) is influenced. However, this number includes only those who already lead healthy lives "with a vengeance"—in other words, "those who are nervous worriers and tend to hypochondria, who utilize every opportunity to extend their extravagant health regimentations (including ritualization, sectarianism, and mysticism, especially with regard to diet) just one step more." Like West German authors, Andrzejak and Kunzendorff point out that it cannot be the goal of public health education to further frighten those who are already nervous, to awaken twinges of bad conscience wherever possible, or, on the other hand, to strengthen the complacency of the careless, who are, after all, the ones the program is trying to reach. To turn away from this form of education, however, means that the real purpose of health education must lie in a change of consciousness in the individual. In other words, it is not enough that the individual become aware of the danger of his own conduct; he must also understand that he must change his behavior out of responsibility to himself and his society.

This seems to contain certain difficulties even—or perhaps especially—for a state such as the GDR, in which so much seems to be based on rules and regulations. And this may be precisely why internal self-regulation is weaker. Beyond the effect of a regulated society, these habits are rather a sign of something else. A number of both East and West German authors have pointed out that the careless trafficking in noxious substances of our industrialized age can be traced to the manifold aspects of environmental stress. It makes little difference, then, that health education sessions are conducted during work breaks (as they are in the GDR) if the workplace does not have a friendly atmosphere. The increasing technology of work and environment, and even of the entire process of medical care, tends to increase the feeling of helplessness and anonymity in the individual, which in turn causes stress. Personal and social problems are also stress factors which lead to unhealthy patterns of behavior (alcoholism, excessive smoking, overeating). One must of course keep in mind that, as Affemann (1977, pp. 95–98) points out, "The main cause of the increase in stress [is] to be seen more in the inner susceptibility of the individual to stress than in outside stress-causing factors. His ego-strength decreases. Thus even average burdens become over-taxing." Affemann speaks in this context of the "risk personality," for whom health education is senseless before personality stabilization.

Most authors agree that a personality-stabilizing influence must be present from childhood on, for which the family climate (i.e. an intact parent-child emotional relationship) is of great importance. As a result of this finding, the GDR begins health education indirectly right after birth, through specific instruction for the mother, and directly in kindergarten. In the maternity home the mother not only learns how to care for and feed the infant, she also receives advice for its upbringing. Health propaganda will then appear in the kindergarten, in school, and finally at work—and also in the cinema, on T.V., on the radio, and on posters. There are also "health corners" modeled on the Soviet pattern: stands at work and in public buildings from which informational material is distributed and where one can receive answers to practical questions. Lectures with discussion periods are given by the responsible health departments. During a house call, the doctor or welfare worker is obligated to influence patients, young mothers, and other members of the household through health education.

In the FRG, the attempts at health education are considerably less systematic and more coincidental. Certainly the school doctor will give children various rules, the general practitioner or the specialist will warn his patient of this or that health risk, and seriously warning or jokingly horrifying posters hang in the waiting rooms of doctors and other health and social welfare officials. From time to time campaigns (e.g., against smoking) with flyers, brochures, and posters are carried out; the same methods are used to encourage more physical activity. Certain points are chosen by the media for emphasis—the "slim down" campaign has already achieved attitudinal changes, polio vaccination is advertised in T.V. spots, the results of a head-first dive into unknown water are shown, and so on. These activities lack the tightly organized character of those in the GDR. If one compares health education methods by their success, however, the measures in the GDR are hardly more effective. In this area, influences on individual attitudes seem to depend to a much lesser degree on the state's prevailing ideology than on environmental and living conditions, which are common to all modern industrial nations.

## Conclusion

Comparison shows that in the FRG there is greater plurality in the area of medical care. The general practitioner is relatively free in his decisionmaking, and the chief physician in charge of a hospital can organize many areas according to his own ideas. The patient also enjoys a greater degree of freedom. Aside from the mandatory quarantine of those being treated for tuberculosis and venereal diseases, no citizen of the FRG can be forced to undergo treatment. He has a free choice of physicians and may even break off treatment and seek a new one. An ironic consequence is that the West German medical system costs more and is afflicted with too much bureaucracy and too little effectiveness. On the other hand, the nationalized East German system, in which all physicians are state employees, leaves little freedom for creative initiative. The FRG seems to have an advantage over the GDR only because its free-market economy enables it to afford superficial services. Therefore, the fact remains that in both systems the cost-effectiveness relation is negative. Why the results of neither system can justify the expenditures cannot be more closely investigated at this time but requires new research. The author of this article tends to give preference to a health system that offers both the physician and the patient the greatest amount of personal freedom.

## Notes

1. In the FRG health insurance is required for all workers and employees with gross monthly earnings up to DM3,000.00 (status on January 1, 1979). The contribution is calculated proportionately from the gross salary, whereby family status is also taken into account. All medical services, as well as hospitalization costs, are covered by the contribution.

2. This is legally anchored in the Federal Plague Law, which is limited by the Grundgesetz.

3. One notes with interest that in a society where health is the responsibility of the state, smoking and drinking alcohol (as well as industrial pollution) are permitted. In fact, the state owns and enforces a monopoly over the production and sale of alcohol and the sale of tobacco. This ideological lapse has profound implications for the limits of state socialism.

## References

Affemann, R. 1977. "Gesundheitserziehung." Ärzteblatt Baden-Württemberg 32:95–98.

Andrzejak, K., and E. Kunzendorff. 1977. "Zu einigen Problemen der Gesundheitserziehung." Zeitschrift für die gesamte Hygiene 23:178–181.

Cobet, H., et al. 1977. "Automatische Röntgenschirm—Bildauswertung als Herskreislauf-screening." Das deutsche Gesundheitswesen 32:2041–2043.

# III

**Structural Aspects of Health Care in the Two Germanies**

# 8          Social Security and Health-Care Systems

Peter Rosenberg and
Maria Elizabeth Ruban

*In another look at the postwar development of the two health-care systems, Rosenberg and Ruban seem more critical of the West German system than the one built on earlier German and Soviet ideas in East Germany. They describe the continuing maldistribution of physicians in West Germany; the oligarchical growth of pharmaceutical firms, which flood the market with drugs of marginal significance; the underfunding of public health and industrial medicine, which results in the inability of those fields to attract physicians; and the unfortunate segregation of hospital care from ambulatory care. These and other characteristics are attributed to the postwar dominance of the medical profession and its policies of fee for service, minimal government intervention, and curative medicine. In East Germany, the authors see a system that has organized ambulatory care around multi-specialty clinics and that structurally recognizes the technological and specialized nature of modern medicine. They speak favorably of the integration of hospital care with ambulatory services.*

In Germany there developed during the first half of this century a system of social security that acquired great social and economic significance because of its breadth of performance and the size of its insured clientele. Before World War II, for example, approximately two-thirds of the German population had statutory medical insurance. Government insurance thus became the major financial support for the health-care system. In addition, relations between the two domains resulted in a number of mutual accommodations affecting both the form of services and the institutional arrangements. The following is a description of the social security and health-care systems in the Federal Republic of Germany (FRG; West Germany) and the German Democratic Republic (GDR; East Germany) as they have developed since the end of World War II. We shall also consider the extent to which historical factors have influenced and still influence common developments in the two countries, and discuss recent influences that have produced diverging trends.

## Health-Care Systems in the Two Countries

"Health-care system" refers here to all institutions and procedures that directly provide a population with those goods and services that are necessary for the maintenance and recovery of health, as well as for the alleviation of illness and its aftereffects.

The Health-Care System in the FRG

*Recent Historic Developments*
The health-care system of the FRG after World War II continued essentially along the same lines as in the Third Reich, at least as regards institutional, professional, and financial structures. Apart from the racist goals of the Third Reich, which were eliminated, the previous program seems to have been continued.

First priority in this type of health care is given to somatically oriented treatment by the physician, who alone is considered the expert in matters of health and disease. Characteristic features of the system, which have changed little since the end of the war, are a general neglect of the psychic and social aspects relevant to diagnosis and treatment and a lack of preventive concepts. Evidence for this is the virtual absence of research, training, and practice in industrial and social medicine.

Until the 1960s, the physicians were the sole authority in matters of health and occupational policy, almost without criticism; even essential tasks of political control were subject to professional self-regulation. This position of power, together with a notable absence of control through the state, enabled physicians and their professional associations to formulate a professional role similar to that of private entrepreneurs. The dominant goal of a physician is still the solo practice or a leading position in a hospital; in contrast, various forms of group practice or salaried employment are rejected, though with somewhat diminishing emphasis.[1]

*Institutional Structure*
The institutional structure of the health-care system in the FRG has been, and still is, decisively influenced by the providers of the various

**Table 1**
Physicians by mode of practice and specialty in FRG.

|  | 1960 | | 1978 | |
| --- | --- | --- | --- | --- |
|  | Number | Percent | Number | Percent |
| Free practice |  |  |  |  |
| General practice | 30,025 | 37.8 | 27,568 | 21.2 |
| Specialists | 19,200 | 24.2 | 31,468 | 24.2 |
| ophthalmology | 1,800 | 9.4 | 2,799 | 8.9 |
| gynecology and obstetrics | 2,311 | 12.0 | 5,568 | 14.2 |
| medicine | 4,119 | 21.5 | 8,812 | 28.0 |
| pediatrics | 1,780 | 9.3 | 2,924 | 9.3 |
| neurology and psychology | 948 | 4.9 | 1,665 | 5.3 |
| orthopedics | 802 | 4.2 | 1,929 | 6.1 |
| radiology | 693 | 3.6 | 1,128 | 3.6 |
| urology | 364 | 1.9 | 1,130 | 3.6 |
| Full-time hospital physicians | 22,646 | 28.5 | 59,183 | 45.5 |
| Administration and research | 7,479 | 9.4 | 11,814 | 9.1 |
| Total | 79,350 |  | 130,033 |  |

Source: *Daten des Gesundheitswesens* (Stuttgart: Bundesminister für Jugend, Familie und Gesundheit, 1980), vol. 198, p. 213.

services, i.e., outpatient care by physicians; inpatient care (until 1970) by community, public, and private supports; pharmaceutical care by industry and commerce; and occupational health services by employers.

Governmental health policy, which is mostly delegated to the regional states, had previously been limited exclusively to laws affecting public health and a few preventive measures. Only since the beginning of the 1970s have the federal government and the states developed methods and regulations that allow for control over several types of services, among them hospital care, occupational health services, and panel services.

1. Outpatient care. Almost all general and specialist outpatient care in the FRG is delivered by solo practitioners. The number of general practitioners has declined in the last 15 years, both in absolute terms and relative to the population, while the number of specialists has increased. In 1976, approximately equal numbers of general practitioners and specialists were engaged in outpatient care (table 1). This restructuring of the supply of medical personnel is generally perceived as unsatisfactory, especially since it is accompanied by regional shifts. Thus, many of the thinly populated areas are inadequately served, while there is an oversupply in large population centers.

The existing social security legislation has produced a sharp separation between outpatient and inpatient care. Physicians employed by hospitals are allowed to participate in the care of panel patients[2] on a strictly limited basis. Only in the area of psychiatric treatment has it become legally possible in recent years for hospitals to extend services to outpatients.

2. Inpatient care. Inpatient care of the acutely ill is delivered in army hospitals, which are owned by the federal government; by the states in university hospitals; or by local communities, churches, and private persons. In addition, there are a large number of inpatient or semi-inpatient centers, such as baths and sanatoriums, which provide preventive or rehabilitative care.

The number of hospital beds in the FRG was already high in 1950 (108 per 10,000 inhabitants); since then it has increased still further. Only since 1975 has the number of beds begun to decrease slightly. In 1978, 117 beds per 10,000 inhabitants were available, 79 of these in general hospitals. In comparison with international figures, and in view of the recent decline in population, this indicates an oversupply. A set of regulations that will permit the federal government and the states to influence the inventory of hospital beds as well as the regional and professional structure of the hospital system has been in force only since the early 1970s. Previously, this initiative was exercised solely by those in charge of the various hospitals, a state of affairs that led to regional and professional shortcomings. Although the number of hospital personnel has grown more than proportionately to the number of hospital beds, the present situation is still unsatisfactory in some respects. Psychiatric care, especially, suffers from shortages of specialists and nurses. The problem is that the incomes of resident specialists, except in top positions, are significantly lower than those of their self-employed colleagues. Therefore, specialist residency is frequently seen as merely a way station on the road to a private practice.

3. Pharmaceutical services. The pharmaceutical industry in the FRG recovered very rapidly after the end of World War II and developed into a strong, export-oriented business. It also floods the domestic market with vast quantities of different or apparently different drugs, confusing both physicians and consumers. Currently there are approximately 26,000 medical products on the market. If one counts different forms of administration (injections, pills, etc.) and packaging, the total amounts to something like 80,000 different articles. Greiser's (1981) investigation of drugs for coronary diseases (coronary insufficiency, arrhythmia)

demonstrates the nontransparency of the market nicely. He examined 567 preparations: 231 single-purpose and 336 multipurpose drugs. One-fourth of the former and nearly all of the latter were judged to be inadequate.

Structurally, the industry consists of a few very large corporations and a greater number of smaller enterprises. A fair number of medications and disease-related families of drugs are subject to monopolistic or oligopolistic market controls. Distribution of medical supplies is either direct to hospitals, if they have their own dispensary, or through wholesalers to individual pharmacies. Retail sales of drugs are largely confined to pharmacies, which are managed and privately owned by certified pharmacists. Sickness funds and similar institutions may not maintain dispensaries. Although the number of pharmacies has increased dramatically since the 1950s, this has again not led to a better regional distribution. For 1975 the total consumption of medicines and drugs in the FRG was estimated at 14.6 billion DM, which was 1.7 percent of the national income (Commission of the European Community 1978, pp. 12, 14).

4. The public health service. The "Public Health Service" in the FRG includes all those medical services which are carried out by government and community clinics. The number of these clinics, their functions, and their numbers of medical personnel have declined steadily in the last few years (table 2). Neither the salaries (which are lower than the incomes of self-employed physicians) nor the type and the conditions of work attract physicians into the public health service. The functional scope of the public health service is under dispute. In general, it is thought that the public health service should supervise public hygiene and provide general medical education and expert medical opinion. What is under debate is the extent to which it should provide preventive services to individuals. It has been found that the greatest financial retrenchments have taken place—mostly to the advantage of private physicians—in school medicine, dental prophylaxis, and screening services for larger populations.

In summary: It appears that the public health service in the FRG has a poorly defined functional sphere and is inadequately coordinated with other medical services. It also has gradually been circumscribed to the point where it performs mostly those services which are essential for the public well-being but are considered unattractive by other institutions.

**Table 2**
Public health services and personnel in FRG.

|                        | 1960  | 1975  | 1978    |
|------------------------|-------|-------|---------|
| Public health agencies | 502   | 341   | 337     |
| Physicians             | 4,335 | 2,473 | 4,135[a] |
| Dentists               | 2,305 | 1,358 | 1,763[a] |
| Social workers         | 4,347 | 2,660 | 2,454   |

a. Including part-time physicians and dentists.

5. Occupational health services. Occupational medical care for employees in the FRG also is in a marginal position. While large enterprises generally maintain well-equipped facilities, medical care in medium-size firms is being developed only gradually, in response to a law passed in 1973. In 1975, the FRG had only 650 full-time industrial physicians; the number of part-time physicians is estimated at double that.

Industrial physicians are responsible for occupational health care, which focuses on the physical well-being of employees and on their working conditions. Industrial physicians may not provide treatment other than emergency first aid. There is also no direct link between industrial medical services and other sections of the health-care system. No empirical research is available on the functions and performance of occupational health services, but it may be assumed that their task is confined chiefly to medical checkups, which are either prescribed by law or agreed on in negotiations between employers and unions. Systematic examination of working conditions and intervention for their improvement are probably the exception rather than the rule.

*Financial Structure*

Financial policy in the FRG has significantly affected both the services and the institutional structure of the health-care system. In the absence of administrative control, increasing impetus toward control arose from the measures and agreements that were adopted to regulate payment for services.

1. Outpatient medical services. Private physicians receive 80–85 percent of their incomes from panel care; they are paid directly by the official sickness funds. The remainder of their income is derived from private practice and is paid directly by the patient, who is usually insured with a private sickness fund.

Fees for panel services are determined according to an extremely detailed service schedule, determined jointly by the official sickness funds and the association of panel physicians.[3] Although the rate structure has been amended several times in the past few years, it still favors surgical treatment and auxiliary services at the expense of such time-consuming activities as consultation and house calls. This system of remuneration has led to a considerable increase in the incomes of physicians since the war, chiefly in three ways: by general increases in fees per service; through a marked increase in the number of services performed by each physician; and through a shift from labor-intensive to rationalized, technical services which can be delegated to auxiliary personnel. So far, sickness funds have been unable to deal effectively with the deficiencies that have developed from changes in the supply and professional structures and from increasing discrepancies in the income structure for all physicians.

2. Hospital care. A nationwide legal basis for the financing of hospitals was established for the first time in 1972–73. Thereafter investments were financed from the general revenues of the regional bodies; running expenses, in contrast, are covered by charges to patients or sickness funds. Overhead financing with tax monies served at the same time as an occasion to introduce planning methods into the hospital system. Up to the time of this regulation, hospital managers had been able to decide on investments entirely autonomously, without regard to the regional distribution or the need for beds and equipment; the nursing charges were used to finance not only running expenses but general depreciation as well. Moreover, there was frequently no agreement on the amount of nursing charges that would cover costs, so that either renovation and maintenance were neglected or else the hospital owners—especially public ones—had to raise additional funds. The basic result of this system of financing, i.e. fixed hospital charges in combination with a prohibition on providing outpatient services, was a high rate of hospitalization and a lengthy average hospital stay.

The present combination of hospital planning and financing is intended to yield a hospital system that covers costs, meets existing needs, and is efficient. However, so far there are no concrete criteria for need, cost effectiveness, and efficiency, and these objectives have not been realized.

Physicians in hospitals are usually employees and receive a fixed salary. Physicians in charge of clinics and department heads are, in addition to their salaries, permitted to charge private patients for their services. Moreover, they are usually allowed to maintain a private practice or participate, within certain limits, in panel care. With the help of these "part-time activities" they often make several times their salaries.

3. Pharmaceutical services. The pharmacies receive their income from the sale of medicines and a limited variety of other commodities, such as infant formulas and hygiene preparations. Medicines prescribed by any of the panel services are paid for directly by the sickness funds, minus a 5 percent rebate and minus a further deduction of 1.50 DM per medicine (which is paid by the patient). The profit margins of pharmacies and pharmaceutical wholesalers are legally prescribed, but there are no restrictions on the factory prices laid down by manufacturers. By fixing the factory prices, the manufacturer thus automatically also determines the retail prices of his medicines. Consumers and sickness funds have no direct influence on the pricing mechanism; instead it is assumed that free competition will determine prices. As the market is insufficiently transparent to scrutiny, however, this is seldom or never the case.

4. Public health. The public health service is financed with federal revenues. The personnel and income structures typically employed by the civil service are generally not very attractive to physicians. In order to avoid a total depletion of personnel, physicians may, as in hospitals, engage in well-paid work (such as medical consultation) on the side.

5. Occupational medical services. Occupational medical services are equipped and financed directly by the employer, or several employers may (perhaps with the help of their employers' association) establish joint occupational health centers. Some industrial physicians are salaried employees, but the majority work for a fee on an hourly basis and have a full-time private practice of their own. Even the relatively high salaries offered by industry have apparently not attracted a sufficient number of full-time industrial physicians.

## The Health-Care System in the GDR

### Historical Roots

The health-care system of the GDR shows, even today, characteristic features of the two systems from which it evolved: that of the German Reich and that of the Soviet Union. Elements of the German system are in evidence in the principles of individual participation, personal responsibility, and self-determination, which are firmly established within the framework of nationalized health care. For example, the principle of free choice of physician (unknown in the Soviet system) was taken over from the old state insurance system and incorporated in the social security system founded in 1947; it still is in force today. Indeed, it was explicitly confirmed in the program of the Ninth Party Congress, in May 1976. Also retained was the system of member contributions toward the cost of health care; this and the system of old-age pensions are the two main supports of the social security system. In the GDR (as in Germany earlier and in the FRG), the insurance premiums are shared in equal parts by employees (in the form of wage deductions) and their employers. With the introduction of a "voluntary surcharge" in 1968 (extended further in 1971 and 1977), the GDR went even further on the road to self-determination. Members with monthly incomes of more than 600 marks can now voluntarily purchase higher coverage for temporary disability and increase their old-age pensions by increasing their premiums; employers will then match their premiums by the same amount.

While the German tradition is most evident in the system of cost sharing and in the emphasis on individual rights and obligations, the Soviet example appears to have had a decisive influence on the distribution system, i.e. on the choice of priorities and objectives. The centralized administration and hierarchical structure of the health-care system, too, are largely modeled on the Soviet example.

The health-care system of the GDR thus shares many of the features that characterize the systems of the USSR and other Eastern-bloc countries. The basic premise is that health care is societal in character. Health and disease are not considered to be private concerns of the individual, but are social concerns in which the state has a legitimate interest—according to Lenin, "health is a valuable property of the state." In concrete terms this implies

providing a network of health-care facilities which are free and accessible to all,

an emphasis on preventive medicine which is, however, not confined to the control of epidemics but is also directed at early diagnosis and prevention of an ever-growing list of diseases by means of mass immunizations and regular screening examinations,

a gradual conversion of outpatient facilities from solo practices to polyclinics and outpatient departments, construction and extension of an occupational health service with functions that far exceed those of industrial physicians in the FRG, and

inclusion of the population in the fight for better national health.

Intensive health education and information about a healthy life are designed to teach people that health is "the result of a learning process" (Findeisen 1974, p. 18).

*Institutional Structure*

The highest authority in the East German health-care system is the Ministry for Health. It is affiliated with the Department of Health Policy in the Central Committee of the SED (Social Unity Party) and coordinates all management and control functions. Under the ministry are several departments for Health Care and Social Welfare and Medical Facilities for the various local districts. The main functions of these regional administrative centers are the supervision of public health, the provision of medical supplies, the regulation of pharmaceutical services, and (above all) the "medical care of the population." The latter comprises two sections: inpatient and outpatient facilities.

1. Inpatient facilities. The number of hospitals has decreased steadily since 1950, and the number of hospital beds since 1962. The decrease in hospitals was the result of deliberate concentration on larger, more efficient units, while the reduction in hospital beds was the result of diminishing demands. The latter is due to the decline in population, the lower incidence of infectious diseases, e.g. tuberculosis, and a shortening of the average hospital stay.

At the end of 1980, there were 549 hospitals with a total of 171,895 beds, i.e. 103 beds per 10,000 inhabitants (*Statistisches Jahrbuch*, 1981, p. 330). The hospital sector in the GDR is hierarchically structured on three levels: tertiary (university and state hospitals with high technology and research orientation), secondary (community and city hospitals), and primary (local hospitals). All three levels of hospitals are affiliated with polyclinics and ambulatory services, whose function is the selection and referral of patients. There are considerable qualitative differences among the three levels. Equipment and medical supplies of the tertiary hospitals are intended to conform to the most modern medical standards. These hospitals set medical standards, train physicians, and advise the staffs of smaller, subordinate hospitals. Performance levels of the hospitals generally decrease with diminishing numbers of beds and increasing distances from larger cities. This applies to hospital accommodations as well as to technical equipment. There are still a few privately owned hospitals, which are now under government supervision. In 1980, 80 nongovernment hospitals with approximately 12,000 beds were still in operation; most of these were church-affiliated (*Statistisches Jahrbuch*, 1981, p. 330).

2. Outpatient services. The most important contribution to outpatient care is made by polyclinics and outpatient clinics, which developed in all urban and rural areas from 1947 on. Since then their number and capacity has steadily increased. These state-run facilities have the advantage that they concentrate a variety of specialists under the same roof, so that patients are spared the inconvenience and waste of time attached to the referral process. According to regulations, a polyclinic should have at least five specialty departments, a dental clinic, a dispensary, a laboratory, and facilities for physical therapy.

Outpatient clinics are smaller units which are supposed to have at least two specialties and a dental department. A polyclinic or an outpatient clinic may function as an autonomous economic unit, but may also be affiliated with a hospital or a manufacturing plant.[4] The form and the capacity of an industrial medical facility depend very much on the size of the firm. Large firms with more than 4,000 employees have fully equipped industrial polyclinics. Industrial clinics are planned for firms with 2,000–4,000 employees. Smaller firms maintain first aid stations headed by a physician (1,000–2,000 employees) or a trained nurse (200–1,000 employees). Very small enterprises (50–200 employees) have one-room facilities staffed by members of the Red Cross on a part-time basis. The tasks of industrial physicians in the GDR are more varied and broader than those of industrial physicians in the FRG, since they not only perform occupational medical and hygienic functions but also provide treatment for sick employees and their families and participate in the programs for prevention and early diagnosis. Ambulatory and community health centers perform auxiliary services similar to those provided by the first aid stations. All these services are generally coordinated with polyclinics or outpatient clinics, carrying out preventive and nursing care according to their instructions. Polyclinics and outpatient clinics also often maintain special facilities which are run along the same lines as the Soviet "dispensaires." Such "dispensaires" provide care for persons with special needs, e.g. pregnant women and infants, as well as those suffering from certain chronic diseases such as tuberculosis or diabetes. A typical feature of "dispensaires" is that they combine medical treatment with preventive care and social work.

A special type of outpatient care was introduced in the GDR in 1956 with state-run general and dental practices. These are found predominantly in rural areas and are generally staffed by older physicians whose private practices were nationalized. This means that the formerly independent private physician becomes an employee of the national health service and continues to work in his own consulting rooms for a fixed salary. The costs are paid by the government. The increase in such state-run practices has been accompanied by a gradual decrease in the number of private general and dental practices, which will probably disappear altogether.

3. Medical personnel. In 1976, an average of just under 430,000 persons were employed by the national health and social welfare service, corresponding to 5.3 percent of the total work force. Approximately two-thirds of the health-service personnel had completed higher education or professional training (Muller-Dietz 1978, pp. 49 ff.).[5]

The severe shortage of physicians in the GDR (in 1950 the number of physicians relative to the population was about half that in the FRG) was gradually alleviated during the 1960s. With 32,000 physicians, or 19 per 10,000 inhabitants, the GDR is now on a par with the FRG. The regional distribution of physicians in the GDR is admittedly still uneven. Berlin, with 36.5 physicians per 10,000 inhabitants, has the highest ratio; worst off is the rural district of Neubrandenburg, with a ratio of 14.8.

In the effort to increase the number of physicians, the training of dentists was apparently neglected for a long time. As a result, the number of dentists actually decreased after 1961 and only exceeded the level of 1955 in 1970. Dental care is still a problem area in the East German health-care system. In 1976, nearly 17,000 physicians, i.e. more than half, were engaged in outpatient care, 81 percent of them in polyclinics and outpatient clinics and the rest in state-run or private solo practices.

4. Pharmaceutical services. The pharmaceutical industry in the GDR has in recent years undergone a process of concentration in the number of manufacturing firms and in the variety of drugs. Of the 230 pharmaceutical firms that existed in 1959, only 18 were still in operation in 1975, employing 12,000 workers (Pritzel 1976). Although the quantity of drugs was dramatically increased, the number of different brands decreased from around 5,000 in 1947 to around 1,500 in 1974 (Zerbst

1975). Distribution of drugs takes place through 1,398 pharmacies, of which only 36 were privately owned in 1976 (*Gesundheitswesen der DDR* 12, 1977:259).

A pharmacy supplies approximately 12,300 inhabitants, whereas in the FRG there is one pharmacy to every 5,000 inhabitants. There are, however, in addition some 566 medicine "depots" which help to relieve the work of the pharmacies. Current supplies of standard drugs seem to be relatively secure. However, an unexpectedly high demand, for instance in an influenza epidemic, might cause problems. According to official statements, the GDR produced 93–94 percent of its pharmaceutical supplies domestically (*Pharmazeutische Zeitung* 14, 1970). All medically insured persons (practically the entire population) are entitled to have their prescriptions filled free of charge.

Drugs in the GDR are considerably cheaper than in the FRG. The GDR spends little on research, one of the main factors in the high price of drugs in the FRG. The GDR, moreover, supports the price of drugs, although the amount is not exactly known.

## The Social Security Systems

### Social Security for Illness and Its Effects in the FRG

After the war, the social security system in the FRG continued along much the same lines as during the Third Reich as regards membership, types of services, and institutional structure, with two reservations. In the first place, allowance had to be made for injuries that were directly or indirectly caused by the war, e.g. services for veterans, compensations for refugees, and reparations. Second, the principle of self-determination by the employers and the insured members—which had been introduced under Bismarck and eliminated under Hitler—was restored, though it was modified to the disadvantage of employees.

### *Service Organizations and Services*

In the FRG several service organizations may be responsible for dealing with a physiological and/or physical disability, either to cover costs for treatment and alleviation or to provide compensation for loss of income. The basic features of this extremely complex system include three social security organizations financed with members' contributions, and three public service organizations financed with government revenues.

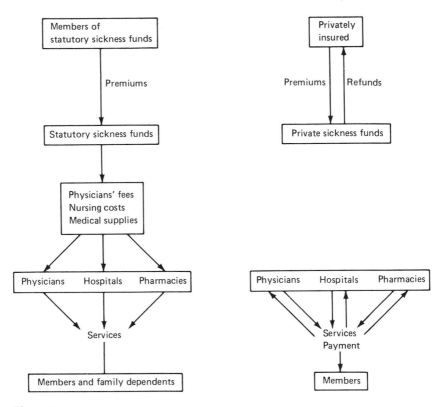

**Figure 1**
Medical insurance in the FRG.

The statutory medical insurance system is the most encompassing (figure 1). Its members are entitled to certain specified examinations for early diagnosis; preventive treatment at health spas; medical treatment for illness and pregnancy, including all outpatient, hospital, and pharmaceutical services; dental services, including treatment and prostheses; and compensation for loss of income through disability, once payments by employers are discontinued,[6] for a maximum of 76 weeks within 3 years for the same disability.

The compulsory accident insurance pays for medical treatment and loss of income if the disability has been incurred either at work or on the way to work, or if it is a recognized occupational health hazard. In the case of permanent disability affecting earning capacity, a pension is paid, the amount of which is determined by the degree of disability. The compulsory pension fund also pays pensions when the ability to engage in gainful employment is severely restricted (disability pension) or when regular gainful employment becomes impossible (total disability pension). In addition, members are entitled to therapeutic services (treatments, rehabilitation) if their earning capacity is affected or threatened. The social welfare service pays for medical treatment when an individual is not covered by any of the other agencies and has no means or income of his own to pay for physicians, hospitals, or medicines. The social welfare service thus represents a safety net which prevents any citizen from going without medical care solely for financial reasons.

The veterans' service is responsible for disabilities caused by the war, especially rehabilitative care and pensions.

Civil servants are covered against illness and disability by a special system. In their case, the employer (the government) pays 50 percent or more (depending on family status) of the medical costs. The rest is generally met by private sickness funds which members join individually. Only the private sickness funds require that patients initially pay medical costs themselves and then be reimbursed. In the other systems, the agency itself performs the service or pays the providers of various services (physicians, hospitals, pharmacies, etc.) directly. Except for civil servants, who are only partially reimbursed, members of compulsory sickness funds must contribute to the costs of treatment, although only to a very limited extent: 1.50 DM per medicine, and for dental prostheses 40 percent of materials and laboratory costs (but not of the dentist's fees).

*Range of Persons Covered*

Statutory medical insurance covers approximately 90 percent of the population in the FRG. For workers, for pensioners, and for salaried employees below a certain income, medical insurance is compulsory. Almost all other population groups have the option of joining voluntarily. Family members without incomes of their own are included in the coverage without extra charge.

Compulsory accident insurance, taken out by employers, covers all employees except civil servants. In addition, school and university students and children in nursery schools are protected against accidents at school and on the way there and back.

The statutory pension fund carries, on a compulsory basis, all workers and salaried employees, as well as certain categories of self-employed persons. Others may join on a voluntary basis. Voluntarily insured members do not have to contribute regularly, but they are eligible only for limited therapeutic benefits.

While eligibility for the above services depends on direct and indirect contributions by members, eligibility for services from other organizations is part of the government's responsibility for the public welfare in general (social welfare), for civil servants, and for victims of the war.

*Financing for the Social Security System*

The statutory medical insurance is financed entirely from funds that are, as a rule, contributed in equal parts by employers and employees (table 3). Partial payments for retired employees are made by their pension fund. Insurance rates for workers and salaried employees vary with their earned income up to a ceiling which is determined annually from general income levels. The rates are determined by the various sickness funds according to their financial needs, and thus they vary, currently between 7 and 14 percent (shares for employers and employees). Since the 1,300 sickness funds are subdivided according to vastly different criteria—there are regional funds, industrial funds, funds for artisans, farmers, and mining workers, and a number of independent funds (Ersatzkassen)—a number of different factors determine the incomes and expenditures of the sickness funds and consequently the membership premiums. Certain regions or industrial branches have, for example, different mean income levels. There are variations in age and sex structures, in the distribution of medical facilities (a choice of only one expensive university hospital), different occupational risks (e.g. administration vs. mining), and different quotas for family dependents. Sickness funds have only limited influence over the risk structure of their members. However, industrial and artisans' sickness funds may close down if their premiums become too high. In such a case, "bad risks" automatically become the responsibility of the regional sickness funds.

Statutory accident insurance (excluding students' accident insurance) has since its introduction always been perceived as the responsibility of employers and is still paid by them alone. Accident insurance is carried by the labor unions, which are subdivided by industries and in some cases by regions as well. Insurance rates differ not only between unions, but frequently also within them, according to certain risk categories. The disproportionately high rates for employers with high-risk working environments are intended to motivate them to greater efforts in accident prevention.

The statutory pension fund is financed from membership dues and government subsidies. The present nationwide rate for employers and employees (each pays half) is 18 percent of the earned income. Government subsidies are generally increased annually, following rising national incomes; they are, however, revised retroactively, so that it has been necessary in the past to raise the member rates several times. General government revenues are used to finance the service organizations for veterans, the social welfare service and subsidies and pensions for civil servants.

*Organizational Structure and Administration of the Social Security System*

Statutory medical insurance in the FRG is administered by about 1,400 sickness funds, which are grouped according to different criteria (regions, companies, occupational groups, wage workers, salaried employees). The individual sickness funds are financially relatively autonomous; negotiations with suppliers about the cost and type of services are conducted either by the individual funds or by their regional or federal associations.

This fragmentation is the reason that sickness funds do not pursue uniform health policies. This applies, for example, to the recognition of new medical techniques or treatments, to the exclusion of medicines of doubtful value, and to efforts at controlling hospital and medical costs. They also differ frequently in their positions when negotiating prices and fees. Independent sickness funds, for example, pay out approximately 15 percent more for comparable outpatient services than regional funds. Until recently there were some differences among regional funds, but these have gradually diminished. This convergence is due largely to the fact that the negotiations between medical associations and sickness funds are increasingly conducted at the state or the federal level.

The internal structure of the sickness funds is based largely on the principle of autonomy, as is the social security system in general. The idea at the foundation of the social security system was essentially that it should not become a government bureaucracy, but that insured members should be represented on the administrative level. Employers too participated in administration, although they had only one-third of the vote, with two-thirds given to employees.[7] During the Third Reich, this self-government was replaced with a powerless advisory council with equal representation. After the war, the right to self-government

**Table 3**
Health expenditures (millions of marks) in FRG, by type of service and funding agency, for 1978.

| | Total | Public budgets | Statutory sickness funds | Pension funds | Compulsory accident insurance | Private sickness funds | Employers | Private households |
|---|---|---|---|---|---|---|---|---|
| Preventive and nursing care | 10,200 | 5,923 | 2,147 | 232 | 296 | 2 | 1,600 | — |
| Health services | 3,546 | 1,490 | 224 | 232 | — | — | 1,600 | — |
| Prevention and early diagnosis | 1,252 | 113 | 843 | — | 296 | — | — | — |
| Nursing care | 5,402 | 4,320 | 1,080 | — | — | 2 | — | — |
| pre- and postnatal care | 1,119 | 37 | 1,080 | — | — | 2 | — | — |
| maternity services | 4,283 | 4,283 | — | — | — | — | — | — |
| Treatment | 96,093 | 7,204 | 61,869 | 2,810 | 1,269 | 4,655 | 4,507 | 13,779 |
| Outpatient treatment | 27,319 | 1,184 | 18,372 | 1 | 466 | 1,355 | 1,397 | 4,544 |
| Hospital treatment | 33,793 | 5,774 | 22,924 | — | 768 | 2,162 | 1,683 | 482 |
| Sanatorium treatment | 5,224 | 72 | 219 | 2,750 | 20 | — | 383 | 1,780 |
| Medical supplies | 21,382 | 174 | 14,599 | — | — | 763 | 710 | 5,136 |
| Dental prostheses | 8,375 | — | 5,755 | 59 | 15 | 375 | 334 | 1,837 |
| Aftercare services | 50,027 | 6,641 | 6,150 | 9,722 | 2,723 | 1,033 | 23,758 | — |
| Occupational rehabilitation | 3,256 | 2,488 | — | 662 | 106 | — | — | — |
| Social rehabilitation | 504 | 504 | — | — | — | — | — | — |
| Financial support in event of illness or disability | 46,082 | 3,618 | 6,069 | 9,001 | 2,612 | 1,033 | 23,749 | — |
| compensation | 20,600 | — | — | — | — | — | 20,600 | — |
| other financial support | 9,333 | 645 | 6,069 | 552 | 508 | 1,033 | 526 | — |
| disability pensions | 16,149 | 2,973 | — | 8,449 | 2,104 | — | 2,623 | — |

| | | | | | | | | |
|---|---|---|---|---|---|---|---|---|
| Other aftercare services | 185 | 31 | 81 | 59 | 5 | — | 9 | — |
| Training and research | 2,309 | 2,309 | — | — | — | — | — | — |
| Training of medical personnel, medical research at universities | 1,962 | 1,962 | — | — | — | — | — | — |
| Research outside universities | 347 | 347 | — | — | — | — | — | — |
| Miscellaneous | 6,553 | — | 3,386 | 446 | 1,062 | 1,659 | — | — |
| Total | 165,182 | 22,077 | 73,552 | 13,210 | 5,350 | 7,349 | 29,865 | 13,779 |

was restored, but the principle of equal representation was also retained. The powers of these self-governing boards—originally very extensive—have since been gradually undermined by government regulations concerning the extent of coverage. The idea that member participation would create and strengthen their solidarity with the insurance institutions has thus lost much of its meaning.

The statutory pension fund, too, is not a unified system, but consists of a number of organizations, e.g. one for salaried employees, 18 regional bodies, a miners' pension fund, and numerous other occupational funds. However, the pension funds for workers and salaried employees are uniform in their benefits and are financed in practice from the same "pail," since the several agencies are closely affiliated.

It has already been mentioned that statutory accident insurance also includes several industrial and public organizations. Although these employers' insurance associations are financially supported solely by employers, they do have equal representation of employees on their administrative boards.

## The Social Security System in the GDR

The development of the present social security system—which incorporates elements of both the old German system and the Soviet system—has progressed in stages and is probably not yet complete. The situation in the first postwar years demanded emergency measures, which were frequently improvised and therefore not oriented toward a comprehensive system. However, the rudiments of later developments were evident early. In February 1946, at the congress for the founding of the Free German Trade Union Association (FDGB), it was decided to establish social security organizations for the separate regions in the Soviet occupation zone, with the aim to ultimately create a unified system. Thereby, the essential feature of the present system was laid down: the principle of a unified insurance system under the administration of the official trade-union association, the FDGB. The system of unified insurance diverged from the former German social security system in two important aspects: the aggregation of all types of insurance (medical, accident, old age, and disability) into a single insurance, and the introduction of a uniform social security rate, irrespective of individual risk factors.

The elimination of insurance ceilings and the inclusion of additional groups (civil servants, businessmen with no more than five employees, veterans) extended insurance coverage significantly. Today, practically the whole population, with a few exceptions such as church ministers, is covered by social security. In the FRG, as well, almost the entire population is covered by the mandatory health insurance system— more than 99 percent either on their own as part of the work force, as retired, or as dependents. The insurance system is constituted by a multitude of both private and mandatory sickness funds (Mitzscherling 1971, p. 30).

Despite its unitary character, the social security system is, in fact, organized into two distinct parts. The majority of the insured population, i.e. workers, salaried employees, and several similar groups, is subsumed under the FDGB's administration. Businessmen with more than five employees, professionals, farmers, and artisans (whether members of trade unions or not) are covered by the Government Insurance of the GDR, formerly the German Insurance Society.

*Types of Service*

Indications for social assistance in the GDR, as in the FRG, are primarily the loss of earning capacity through age, illness, disability, or pregnancy, and also involuntary unemployment and loss of the breadwinner. There are, however, distinct differences in the range of service offered and in the conditions that qualify for assistance. These differences are system-related and are more evident in financial assistance than in nonmonetary services.

1. Monetary services. Approximately two-thirds of the total expenditure for social security goes toward pensions and sick pay, including home nursing benefits. In addition, social security intervenes with regular or lump-sum payments in a number of other cases, e.g. nursing allowances for a sick child, pregnancy or maternity assistance, subsidies or home care for the blind, and funeral assistance. Monetary assistance is also given outside of the social security system and paid from government and industry funds. These include maternity benefits and/or government-paid child allowances, honorary pensions and supplementary pensions for certain privileged groups, and sick-pay subsidies by industry. The structure of financial assistance (and of the whole social service) is markedly influenced by the overwhelming volume of expenditures for pensions. Policies affecting pensions are thus of central importance for social policies in general and for the whole economy.

A characteristic feature of the pension scheme in the GDR is that pensions for permanent incapacitation through age or disability are very low in comparison with earned incomes. In 1980, when the average income was 1,030 marks per month, the average disability pension was 340 marks, the average old-age pension 321 marks and the average old-age-plus-disability pension 302 marks (*Statistisches Jahrbuch der DDR*, 1981, pp. 109 and 341). Retirement thus forces most workers and salaried employees to reduce their standard of living noticeably. There are no systematic adjustments of pensions to rising wage levels, but only sporadic raises in the minimum and average pensions, so that the pensioners' share in the general economic progress is limited and very delayed. All the same, the occasional nominal raise in the pensions corresponds to an increase in buying power, since the GDR has so far been able to keep its retail prices constant—at least as far as goods and services for the basic needs are concerned. Also, various conditions attached to receiving pensions narrow down the range of eligibility in the GDR. For example, to qualify for disability pension requires a higher degree of incapacitation than in the FRG. A widow receives a pension only if she is unfit for work or has one child under the age of 3 years or two children under the age of 8 years. A few privileged groups are entitled to special services in addition to their compulsory social security benefits. These include leaders of industry (the technical intelligentsia), scientists, teachers and artists, victims of political persecution in the Third Reich, and men and women who have rendered special services to the state. These extra benefits, which have been granted ever since 1950, can now, with the introduction of the voluntary supplementary pension, be purchased by all employees with a monthly income of 600 marks or more.

After 25 years of full-time work, employees buying supplementary insurance are entitled to a pension that is 65 percent of their last gross salary (Presseamt beim Vorsitzenden des Ministerrats der DDR 1977, p. 3)—more than double the average pension. Similar provisions exist for the determination of disability and widows' and orphans' pensions. Benefits for temporary disability (e.g. sick pay and home nursing pay) are also higher for persons with supplementary insurance, but here the differences are not so large, because these payments are more generous. In contrast with old-age and disability pensions, these benefits are adjusted to earned incomes and not to a subsistence minimum. The same applies to pregnancy and maternity benefits, which have been upgraded considerably in the last few years. Maternity leave was increased from 18 to 26 weeks in 1976, and a woman now receives financial assistance equal to her last average income. Since July 1, 1976, a woman also receives 1,000 marks from the government at the birth of each child. Payment of this allowance is contingent on proof of regular attendance at a pre- and postnatal clinic.

2. Non-monetary services. A central achievement of the health-care and social-welfare systems in the GDR is the construction and maintenance of a national health service that is available to all insured persons free of charge. This includes medical and dental outpatient care; hospital treatment; preventive and rehabilitative treatment in sanatoriums, health clinics, and convalescent homes; medicines; prostheses; and ambulance services.

The demand for these services has increased strongly, as is shown by the example of outpatient care. In 1976 the average number of consultations (including house calls) per inhabitant was 9; in 1965 it was 4.6 (*Gesundheitswesen der DDR*, 1977, pp. 181 and 245).

Since further increases are expected in the demand for medical and dental services, it is planned to substantially expand outpatient facilities. However, services for single and indigent old people are still inadequate. Although the number of retirement and nursing homes has steadily increased, the present supply of 33 places per 1,000 senior citizens (1976) seems insufficient for the large population of old people who live on their own. The expansion of facilities for infants and preschool children has proceeded at a much more rapid pace. The extremely high labor-force participation of women (87 percent of all women of working age) makes the social organization of child care a matter of extraordinary economic and demographic importance. While birth rates were declining between 1964 and 1974, the number of places in day-care centers and nursery schools was increased, so that supply and demand gradually converged. The sudden resurgence of birth rates since 1975, which was an unexpected response to the improvements in mother and child care, has led to a new shortage of infant and day-care facilities. However, the supply of places for preschool children had increased sufficiently by 1976 that 57 percent of children under 3 years and 87 percent of children between 3 and 6 years were cared for in day-care centers and children's homes (*Statistisches Jahrbuch der DDR*, 1977, pp. 320 and 378).

*Financial Structure*

The funds for the health-care and social-welfare systems come from three sources: government, industry, and insured members.

Social insurance is part and parcel of the national budget in the GDR, with separate funds allotted to the two main insurance bodies. Revenues accrued from insurance premiums are earmarked for social expenditures only.

At the founding of the social security system in 1947, insurance rates for the majority of insured persons were set at 20 percent of earned incomes below 600 marks. Half of this was to be paid by the employer, the other half by the member. Special arrangements were made for some occupational groups, such as miners. In the first few years the revenues obtained from insurance premiums were sufficient to cover the costs of all services to which the social security system had committed itself. However, somewhat later expenditures began to exceed revenues. The ever-larger deficit that developed over the years had to be paid for out of public funds. Even the introduction of the voluntary supplementary pension (which now makes up 11 percent of the revenues from premiums) could only slow this trend.

In 1976 the government subsidized social security to the amount of 47 percent of its total expenditure, as compared with 2.5 percent in 1955. The government's financial participation is not limited to these subsidies. Various nonmonetary and monetary services which go beyond the scope of the social security system are totally paid from public revenues. Among them are financial investments in health care and the payment of child allowances. Social welfare, too, is financed from public revenues; the government is fully responsible for needy citizens who for various reasons are not entitled to social security benefits.

## Interactions between Social Security and Health-Care Systems

### Effects of the Social Security System on the Supply of Health Services in the FRG

The official policy in the FRG was, until the mid 1960s, remarkably restrained with regard to imposing direct regulations on the health-care system. It was then hoped by the government that the "self-regulating forces of the market" would work in the area of health care, controlling supply and demand optimally. That this hope was not fulfilled is explained by the fact that the health-care sector lacks some of the essential ingredients of the free market. Ultimately, of course, it was also not feasible from a socio-political point of view to defend the consequences of a free-market process which could control demand through prices.

In the absence of government regulations, one might have expected that the social security agencies, especially the sickness funds, would fill the power vacuum and try to exercise control over suppliers. This was not the case. Indeed sickness funds are still unable to formulate uniform health policies, to organize scientific counseling preparatory to negotiations, or to enforce their legitimate rights of supervision and control. In this political climate it was easy for physicians, hospitals, and the pharmaceutical industry to pursue their own interests without opposition, and this has led to malfunctions detrimental to consumers.

The social welfare laws, with their effect on the institutional and financial structure of the social security system, still encourage systematic deficiencies in the provision of care. However, since the early 1970s, government intervention in the area of health and welfare policies has increased considerably. The aim here is either to influence service structures directly or to legally empower the social insurances to do so.

*Influences of Social Welfare Laws on the Health Services*
The traditional conception of social security aimed to provide a lowering of living standards after citizens had been exposed to certain risks. Most health-care measures still correspond to this policy; they are designed to come into effect after an illness or accident has occurred. As a result, preventive aspects of health care were neglected and the main emphasis came to be placed on curative services. However, even the latter were unbalanced and neglected in at least two areas. First, the judicial system, the law, and the social security system had a tendency to define "illness" as narrowly as possible by limiting it entirely to its somatic aspects. This has had an extremely negative effect on psychiatric and psychotherapeutic care in the FRG. Second, the separation of service institutions, each with its own functions, resulted in deficiencies in the area of rehabilitation. Thus, sickness funds provided, until recently, very little rehabilitative care; in contrast, pension funds and accident insurance provided primarily rehabilitative care in order to restore earning capacity. Only in the last few years has there been an attempt to coordinate services and institutions and to expand the aims to include restoration of general health and capability. However, institutional boundaries still have negative effects. Conspicuously lacking is coordination with industrial facilities, which is so important in the area of rehabilitation.

*Socio-Legal Influences on the Supply Structure*

The structure of health services is to a large extent influenced by health insurance laws. The strict division between outpatient care (provided by private physicians) and inpatient care (performed by hospitals) is entirely a consequence of the law protecting panel physicians. Similar restrictions exist for industrial medical services, which may not include therapeutic measures. Because sickness funds pay for services performed by ancillary medical professionals (such as psychologists) only when these have been ordered by a physician, private practitioners have in fact a monopoly over the care of 90 percent of the population.

Another problem arises from the legal distinction between "treatment" and "nursing care." Sickness funds pay for the first but not for the second, despite the fact that they may overlap. The social welfare service is the only agency that pays for nursing costs in cases of financial need. Since it is particularly older people who are in need of nursing care without necessarily requiring hospitalization, and since their pensions are usually too small to cover the cost of a nursing home, approximately two-thirds of patients in nursing homes receive social welfare support. As the decision to exclude certain services or to give them only partial recognition (e.g. permanent nursing care) determines at the same time the financial means that will be available for such services, it is inevitable that the supply will be affected. In the FRG, this has led to a quantitative and qualitative lack in purely nursing facilities for both outpatient and inpatient care. Patients in need of nursing care are thus kept in hospitals as long as possible because sickness funds cover general hospital costs. The scope of outpatient services has in recent years been increased, a development which has shortened or eliminated hospitalization and helped patients who are only moderately incapacitated to lead independent lives. For severe cases of disability these services do not, however, offer a solution. In particular, this means that geriatric care in the FRG is largely inadequate.

*Effects of Financing on the Structure of Health Care*

In a system that is administratively controlled only to a limited extent, the only goods that will be supplied are generally those which the supplier can sell at a good profit or those for which there is a strong demand. Such economic effects can be observed in the health care of the FRG. In addition, it is, of course, always possible for the supplier to influence—within limits—the structure of the demand.

Since in health care decisions about the price and quantity of goods are made not only by the consumers (patients) but also by the various financing bodies (states, communities, social security, employers), and are furthermore influenced by the suppliers, the result is a situation in which suppliers can choose from several possibilities those with the most favorable cost-price relationships. Even a surplus can at least partly be sold, while on the other hand there remain needs that are unmet. If price differentials are not then reduced rapidly, quantitative and qualitative imbalances develop between sectors (e.g. between private practice and public health services), between specialties (e.g. internal medicine and psychiatry), and in the structure of services (e.g. between technical, rationalized procedures and labor-intensive consultations). The fact that "technical" services (e.g. laboratory work and mechanical means of diagnosis and treatment) command higher fees than the labor-intensive services performed by the physician (consultations, house visits, eliciting case histories) has inevitably led physicians to expand "technical" services at the expense of medical care as such. Since the different specialties vary considerably in opportunities for such substitutions (e.g., internal medicine offers many, psychiatry very few), this process has resulted in substantial income discrepancies among the different specialties.

In general, private practitioners earn considerably more than physicians in salaried positions. This makes it very difficult to recruit the necessary number of physicians for the public health service and for industrial medicine.

The present dualistic method of financing hospital care also generates problems for the distribution and quantity of the hospital bed supply. Investments are financed from public funds with little regard for the consequent upkeep costs. The latter are paid by consumers in the form of per diem rates. This system discourages productivity and cost efficiency, and provides little incentive for reducing oversupplies.

Consumers and the financial agencies have in the past seldom attended to the economic effects of their individual decisions, and have hardly attempted to use them consciously as controls. In view of the resulting disparities, which allow short-term corrections with economic incentives only to a limited extent, control through administrative measures (such as hospital planning and regulations covering industrial services) has in recent years been increased.

*Effects of the Social Security System on Health and Health Care in the GDR*

The health and social policies of the GDR, like those of other socialist countries with planned economies, are subordinated to the general economic and social policies. They become part of governmental economic planning. The comprehensive unified form of organization and hierarchical arrangement of the social security system is an appropriate form of administration, because it can be directed and coordinated more easily than a plurality of insurance companies with differing and often overlapping tasks and principles.

With regard to financial support, the GDR has decided to continue to cover costs partially from compulsory wage deductions. Beyond its fiscal importance, this type of self-support is seen to be of psychological and pedagogical value. It is supposed to strengthen consciousness of participation and to protect the social security system from abuse. Voluntary supplementary insurance has, of course, increased the share of the budget contributed by members themselves. A direct link between socio-political and economic policies, especially with regard to goals for production and growth, can be seen in the clear differentiation in performance levels for different categories of recipients. In general, persons temporarily incapacitated by illness, accident or pregnancy are given priority over those permanently incapacitated by age or disability. Other privileged categories are workers in leadership positions or with high performance records and workers and salaried employees with higher incomes—in short, qualified workers employed in growth industries. This preferential treatment for certain groups is fully consonant with the declared aim of socialist economic policy, namely the increase of prosperity for all. This aim can only be achieved with high and steady growth rates. Preferential treatment of those workers who are in growth industries or who contribute in special ways to economic growth stimulates economic progress for the ultimate benefit of all.

The direct effects of the health-care system on the general health of the population can, of course, hardly be demonstrated, because a concept like national health cannot be quantified and because health is also affected by other factors, such as standard of living, working conditions, and the environment. There are, however, partial aspects of the health and disease complex which can be directly linked to socio-political measures. For example, the decrease in infectious diseases (particularly tuberculosis), which is proceeding more rapidly in the GDR than in the FRG, can probably be attributed to the screening programs for prevention and early detection. Similarly, the complete disappearance of poliomyelitis is the result of regular vaccination programs for age groups at risk.

The remarkable success which was achieved in lowering infant mortality rates would probably have been impossible without the mobilization of, and care for, almost all pregnant women and their infants. This was achieved mainly through linking child allowances to regular pre- and postnatal examinations.

These positive results brought about by the preventive orientation of the health-care system are counterbalanced by some negative developments in morbidity and mortality rates. Morbidity and mortality rates for diabetes, carcinoma, and heart and circulatory diseases are on the increase; indeed, the mortality rates for some of these so-called "diseases of affluence" are higher than those in the FRG. Admittedly, many of these diseases are difficult to treat, given the present state of medical knowledge, and are therefore unaffected by the system of health care.

## Summary

### Health Policies

A health-political concept which incorporates health care in the economic and social order of the nation is far more developed in the GDR than in the FRG.

The present health-care system in the FRG evolved, essentially without a break, from the system that had existed before 1945. The basic institutional structures, forms of services, and financing methods could be taken over almost unchanged. Only where specifically National Socialist policies had to be eliminated was it necessary to revert to regulations in force before 1933.

The GDR, on the other hand, had to construct a completely new economic and social order under the influence of the Soviet Union. This penetrated every area of public life and resulted in the formulation of a health-care policy which followed the general national and social developments.

### Structural Development of Health Care

The decisive differences in health care for the populations of the two German states lie in the construction and functioning of the outpatient sectors, their openness to other branches of medical care, and the emphasis placed on preventive medicine. In the FRG, outpatient care occurs almost exclusively in private practices, which are strictly separated from community facilities, especially hospitals. Polyclinics in the FRG are restricted to university-clinics and serve training purposes. In contrast, in the GDR the system of polyclinics and outpatient clinics (each with several specialists and diagnostic-therapeutic facilities under one roof) has been established as the definitive form of outpatient care. Private practices have more of a supplementary function. Coordination of outpatient and inpatient care is clearly easier in the GDR than in the FRG, and not only where polyclinics are already attached to a hospital. Cooperation also exists between industrial medical facilities (more numerous and with a larger range of functions than in the FRG) and the general outpatient services; industrial clinics in the GDR provide treatment for relatives of employees, and sometimes also for residents within the vicinity. Preventive medicine has from the beginning been a special concern of medical care in the GDR, and is combined with intensive health education of the population in order to develop awareness of the necessity of the government-sponsored preventive programs. The administrative integration between hospital and polyclinic has not had the intended effect, however; the average hospital stay in the GDR has been only marginally reduced and is hardly lower than in the FRG.

Social Security Systems

The systems of the FRG and the GDR evolved from the same root: the social security system of prewar Germany. Some features of the former system have been retained in both states, particularly the sources of financial support: government, industry, and insured members. In addition, the list of conditions covered is nearly identical in both states. But the systems differ clearly in their organizational structure. The unified system in the GDR, which includes all types of insurance and is not subdivided according to risk, can be contrasted with the pluralistic system of the FRG, where a variety of insurances and insurance carriers exist side by side. Criteria for eligibility also differ correspondingly. In the GDR, with few exceptions, the entire population is completely covered; the FRG offers a more sharply differentiated insurance system, which is in fact harder to understand and to deal with, and is probably also costlier, but which has more variety and flexibility and can thus be better adapted to the individual needs of the insured person.

## Notes

1. Schicke (1978, p. 122) estimates the number of group practices to be 3 percent of all medical practices. All of them are specialty practices, and most consist either of a married couple or a parent and child.

2. Panel care refers to outpatient treatment of patients who are insured with legally approved sickness funds.

3. Associations of panel physicians are legally recognized public bodies which represent the interests of physicians licensed to provide panel services. They also settle the accounts between physicians and sickness funds.

4. In 1976, one out of five polyclinics was an industrial one, as were one-third of all outpatient clinics (*Statistisches Jahrbuch der DDR*, 1977, p. 374).

5. Muller-Dietz treated only professionals with completed higher education (e.g. physicians, dentists, and pharmacists) as separate categories; all others were listed either as technical personnel (with technical, craft, or other skilled qualifications) or as semiskilled or unskilled workers.

6. The first 6 weeks of disability compensation are generally paid for by the employer in the form of net wages.

7. Exceptions are "auxiliary insurances" or the current "health insurance societies" in which self-management is confined to employees only.

## References

Commission of the European Community. 1978. Der Verband von Arzneimitteln. Brussels.

Findeisen, DGR. 1974. Ist der merzinfarkt leiterschicksal. Die Wirtschaft: Zeitung für Politik, Wirtschaft, und Technik 29.7.

Greiser, E. 1981. Arzneimittel-Indes, 1. Wiesbaden.

Mitzscherling, P. 1971. Sozial Politik im geteilten Deutschland. Buckeberg.

Muller-Dietz, W. 1978. "Das Gesundheitswesen in der DDR 1976–1977." Medizin in Osteuropa, 10.4 and 5.

Presseamt beim Vorsitzenden des Ministerrats der DDR, ed. 1977. "Verbesserung der freiwilligen Zusatzrenten-versicherung." Presse-Informationen 1.

Pritzel, K. 1976. "Gesundheitswesen und gesundheitspolitik in der DDR." Deutschland-Archiv 9.3.

Schicke, R. 1978. Soziale Sicherung und Gesundheitswesen. Stuttgart.

Zerbst, M. 1975. "Das gesundheitswesen der DDR." Die Pharmazeutische Industrie 37.2:3–11.

# 9 Political Values and the Regulation of Hospital Care

## Helmuth Jung

*Piece by piece, Helmuth Jung builds a complex argument to conclude that "although the political and ideological positions would lead one to expect numerous and fundamental differences, actual comparison showed that many normative and financial controls in the two German states were remarkably similar, if not identical." Although planning, administration, and financing differ considerably between the two countries, Jung maintains that the actual consequences differ little. Ironically, he concludes that the similarities arise in part from a lack of clear goals or a valid measure of output. His comments on the decision by both German states not to use market price as a means of control should particularly interest American readers. From an American point of view, one wonders if the two German health-care systems could not benefit from the ideas of American conservative economists about using market forces to solve the problems of a protected health-care market.*

Rising health-care costs in most post-industrial societies have led to increased interest in the scientific analysis of this problem. In the United States, the inflation of health-care costs is attributed to two causes: a "demand push," which was the main factor up to the early 1970s, and a "cost push" (Feldstein 1977; McMahon and Drake 1978). An additional factor—and one which affects the other two—comes from the provision of public funds (McMahon and Drake 1978; Bauer 1978). This has led to a sudden increase in expenditures, at least in the Federal Republic of Germany (FRG; West Germany).

The German Democratic Republic (GDR; East Germany) gives a somewhat less analytical and more political explanation for the rise in costs: Health-care costs are disproportionately high because the rate of increase in public funds will always be higher than that in earned income (Busch and Grotjahn 1977, p. 188). According to the 1976 Program of the Socialist Unity Party (SED), "Where real income rises, the public funds acquire increasing importance. They grow at a faster rate than wages and premiums and can thus be utilized to improve health care and social services, general education, cultural and sports facilities." (Program der SED, 1976, p. 24)

Both explanations, however different in principle, could also be seen as admissions that all strategies to contain health-care costs employed up to now have failed. It should be noted that both the FRG and the GDR have tried for some time to gain control over health-care costs and especially hospital costs, with little success (mainly because their attempts were not far-reaching enough). Their strategies were generally directed at a limited goal or area, e.g. at price control or changes in the hospital structure, often without anticipation of the possible effects on other areas. The effect is a control of the system which is contrary to its purposes (Blum 1977), so the results deviate considerably from the intended outcome. This phenomenon has been noted and discussed not only in the FRG but also in the GDR. Mann (1978, p. 23) offers an explanation which is amply supported by the relevant literature, namely that "price controls must be applied to specific products or goods; otherwise it is always possible that they will affect the wrong products and produce a false price structure, despite the fact that the right methods may have been used." In the GDR, an investigation into the method of financing hospitals on the basis of performance found that considerable differences in cost prices can be determined. When performance is measured in terms of number of beds and average utilization days, discrepancies with regard to equipment must inevitably result in similar hospitals (Richau 1967, p. 23).

In order to avoid misallocation, alternative strategies are now being tried. They are generally focused on the hospital sector, because here government intervention is already somewhat established and there is thus less resistance to it. In view of the very different economic systems in the FRG and the GDR, the range of strategies for cost containment is quite considerable, extending from nationalization and centralization to attempts at price control. The centralism of the GDR makes it impossible to apply limited price controls, but such a method is perfectly feasible in the FRG, because it is compatible with a socialist market economy.

In the following analysis I shall show how the hospital systems in the two German states are regulated. Various means can be applied at different levels. There are, on the one hand, measures which affect a hospital directly, e.g. by changing the accounting system or the organization of scientific work. One can also intervene in training and management programs, as has been done in the United States as well as the two German states. On the macro level, there are, in addition, a number of means which the government can employ and which might be characterized as normative and financial levers. These are the subject of the discussion below, and it will be shown how they affect the allocation of resources in the two German economic systems.

## Method and Problems of Comparison

Apart from the differences due to social vs. private ownership, it appears that the degree of participation that is institutionally permitted to the producers plays an important role in the disposition of public property, planning, and management (Kohlmey 1963, p. 93; Harsdorf and Friedrich 1975, pp. 68–101; Staritz 1978). Problems of control and participation are thus of crucial significance in the comparison between the two German states, not only because they have been the central theme of discussion in the GDR for a long time but also because in many Western countries it has been assumed that the causes of cost inflation are beyond the control of managers (McMahon and Drake 1978, p. 77).

A comparison of different economic systems inevitably generates a number of methodological problems, which are aggravated by partial analysis. As a result there is always a danger of distortions and premature conclusions (about, for example, the convergence of the two systems), especially when one deals with such complex phenomena as healthcare systems. I shall confine this discussion to the analysis of the hospital sector, and touch neither on the interaction between inpatient and outpatient institutions nor on the issue of utilization (*Literatur zur Inanspruchnahme* 1967).

The questions arise, of course, whether the hospital sector can be sufficiently isolated from the outpatient sector and whether control systems are specific to the hospital sector. For the FRG, these questions are relatively easily resolved since a separation between the two is prescribed by law and is evident on the concrete level. The problem is more acute in the GDR, where deliberate attempts are being made to create an integrated system by means of centralized planning, management, and control (Jannasch 1970). However, the task is made easier by the fact that the health-care system of the GDR too is built on the foundations of the social insurance system which existed in the German Reich prior to 1945, when the separation between inpatient and outpatient care was laid down by law. A further problem in socialist countries is lack of information; the literature on the subject of hospital organization and structure is relatively scanty and dries up altogether as one gets to problems of planning and control (Keck 1979, p. 436; Keck and Peuker 1978).

## Political and Ideological Aspects of Health Care

This will not be a general discussion about the relative merits of a welfare state vs. socialism or a review of the social and health policies of the past decades. Instead, I will describe the political and ideological positions which justify governmental intervention in the GDR and the FRG.

In the GDR, Marxism-Leninism provides the ideological principles on which total health care for the whole population is posited (Winter 1974, pp. 18 ff.). The practical consequences of this are that society assumes responsibility for the health of its workers and that one central authority exercises control over health care. These conditions could, however, only be realized by the nationalization of health care and the institution of democratic centralism.

In the GDR, economic laws are consciously employed in the interests of human health, but only under the conditions listed above (*Wörterbuch der Ökonomie*, 1973, p. 657; Keck and Peuker 1978). Since the health-care system is, however, not part of the productive sphere and does not contribute to national income, this application of economic laws to health care has received little theoretical attention. This gap became apparent when observers realized that Marxist economic theory focused on production but not on the processes of reproduction by which social institutions and society as a whole reproduces itself from generation to generation. Moreover, several economic categories do not apply to health systems, such as commodity economics, investment theory, amortization, and labor productivity as they are usually understood in manufacturing. The role of government in health care is large and is increasing, often at the expense of the individual's responsibility for his own health. For this reason health care is organized according to the welfare principle. Health is seen as an indispensable precondition for economic growth, and its maintenance should therefore no longer be left to the discretion of the individual but should become a social task for which the party and state authorities are responsible. "Health care means total societal responsibility for all governmental, communal, and industrial measures which ensure the health, performance, and joy of living of the population." (Keck and Winter 1975, p. 46)

In the FRG, in contrast, no single, overarching ideology is proposed to justify health-care measures, either in the constitution, in party programs, or in the relevant literature. Certain health-policy goals can be deduced from the principles of the social market economy, e.g. the acknowledgment that total reliance on the free market for health services would put some social groups at a serious disadvantage. Since health care is organized on the insurance principle, the role of government authorities is minimized and replaced by collective decisions. The state intervenes only sporadically to correct apparent inequalities in the distribution of resources. Otherwise, provision and selection of medical goods and services are left to individual discretion.

## Forms of Ownership and Structural Characteristics

Forms of ownership influence power relations, decision-making processes, and modes of implementation. The simplest formulation of this has generally hinged on the issue of the ownership of the means of production. By this criterion, one then distinguishes between private and public ownership. This crude division may have some limited application in a centralized economy with predominantly public ownership. With regard to Western market economies, however, it is somewhat obsolete, since the state increasingly intervenes in the economic sphere, not only through sweeping controls but also by offering certain goods and services.

A hospital is rarely owned by one person, but usually by a religious, charitable, or social organization. In the FRG, some health insurance societies also own hospitals. Differences between hospitals are chiefly a matter of the economic principle according to which they are run. If a hospital is privately owned, one can assume that it will be managed for profit; otherwise the nonprofit principle obtains. State-owned hospitals are generally nonprofit organizations. Yet they may differ too, usually according to what public agency is responsible for their management. In the GDR, for example, all state-owned hospitals are public property, but they are assigned to different public authorities. State hospitals (e.g. teaching hospitals) are administered directly by the Ministry of Health, while district hospitals are under the control of district councils. Smaller county hospitals are administered by regional authorities, e.g. municipal or community councils (figure 1). In the FRG, only a minority of hospitals are operated by the federal government or the states (e.g. military hospitals, hospitals for the police, penal institutions); most are managed by communal agencies.

All these various forms of ownership now exist in both the FRG and the GDR, although in different proportions. This may seem surprising, especially with regard to the GDR, but it is, in fact, a legacy of the past. Where it was necessary to maintain adequate supplies, private ownership was retained. In the early stages of the GDR, this phenomenon was observed not only in the health-care sector but also in the skilled trades. A look at the distribution of the various forms of ownership (as indicated by the number of hospitals and beds) in 1950 and 1976 shows the following patterns (table 1).

1. Private hospitals have almost disappeared in the GDR. While there were still 201 with 6,000 beds in 1950, their number had shrunk to 8 with 450 beds by 1976. The opposite trend can be observed in the FRG: In 1950, there were 600 private hospitals with 25,000 beds; by 1976, their number had increased to more than 1,000 with about 87,000 beds. They thus account for about one-third of the total number of hospitals; however, in terms of bed capacity their share is only 12 percent of the total.

2. Church-affiliated hospitals in the GDR maintained their 7 percent share of the total number of beds from 1950 to 1976; indeed, the percent of church-affiliated hospitals has actually increased, although this is in fact due to a significant decrease in the total number of hospitals. In the FRG, the number of church-affiliated hospitals has decreased slightly, but their bed capacity has increased considerably. In 1915, 188,000 beds were distributed over about 1,200 hospitals; in 1976, 1,159 hospitals offered 256,000 beds.

3. Public hospitals in the FRG showed a similar trend: The number of hospitals decreased slightly (from 1,400 in 1950 to 1,300 in 1976), but bed capacity rose by about 100,000. The trend toward concentration is even more marked in the GDR: In 1950, there were 764 hospitals with 168,000 beds. Almost the same number of beds were distributed over only 482 public hospitals in 1976.

This description of the hospital sectors in the FRG and the GDR demonstrates clearly how superficial a comparison along the lines of

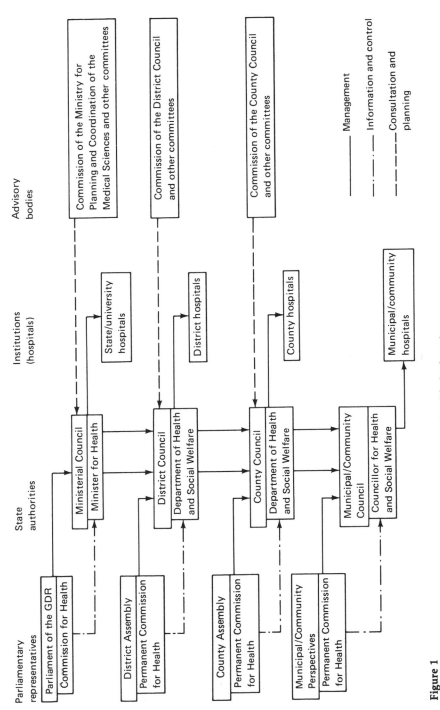

**Figure 1**
The health-care and social-welfare system of the GDR (a simplified schema).

**Table 1**
Market shares of hospitals by forms of ownership, 1950 and 1976.

| | Number of hospitals | | Number of beds | | Market share in hospitals (percent) | | Beds | |
|---|---|---|---|---|---|---|---|---|
| | 1950 | 1976 | 1950 | 1976 | 1950 | 1976 | 1950 | 1976 |
| **GDR** | | | | | | | | |
| Private | 201 | 8 | 6,141 | 456 | 18.9 | 1.4 | 3.3 | 0.2 |
| Church-affiliated | 98 | 81 | 13,288 | 12,541 | 9.2 | 14.2 | 7.1 | 7.0 |
| State | 764 | 482 | 167,790 | 167,469 | 71.9 | 84.4 | 89.6 | 92.8 |
| Total | 1,063 | 571 | 187,219 | 180,466 | 100 | 100 | 100 | 100 |
| **FRG** | | | | | | | | |
| Private (not church-affiliated) | 612 | 1,006 | 25,301 | 86,801 | 18.6 | 29.3 | 5.1 | 12.0 |
| Church-affiliated (free access) | 1,233 | 1,159 | 188,054 | 256,371 | 37.5 | 33.7 | 37.4 | 35.2 |
| Public | 1,443 | 1,271 | 289,192 | 383,674 | 43.9 | 37.0 | 57.5 | 52.8 |
| Total | 3,288 | 3,436 | 502,547 | 726,846 | 100 | 100 | 100 | 100 |

Sources: *Statistisches Jahrbuch der Deutschen Demokratischen Republik*, 1977, p. 370; BMJFG, *Daten des Gesundheitswesens*, 1977, p. 239; *Statistisches Jahrbuch 1978 für die Bundesrepublik Deutschland*, p. 381.

hospital ownership is. On the one hand, there is the problem of multiple forms of ownership in both states. On the other, even though some shifts in market shares can be observed, they cannot be explained by referring to market structures. Since there is no competition in the real sense of the word between hospitals, and since the owners do not form a coherent group but are in fact quite dissimilar, it makes no sense to describe the market as either oligopolistic or monopolistic.

Forms of ownership do, of course, signify certain legal rights and decision-making powers. When one talks in a general way about a charitable organization or a central state agency (e.g. the Ministry of Health), one leaves open questions such as who actually makes decisions, what kinds of authority relations exist, and how decisions are implemented. To answer them, one needs to look at the legal structure, the financial and normative controls, and the organization and planning in hospitals, all of which determine the allocation process.

## Hospital Legislation in the FRG and the GDR

In 1972, the West German parliament approved the Hospital Financing Act (KHG).[1] It contains regulations concerning hospital planning as well as the financing of investments and operating costs.[2] In addition, it specifies the domains of responsibility assigned to the federal government, the states, and various committees. As a result of competing legislation (Grundgesetz, article 24), planning remains essentially in the hands of the various states and is regulated by them.[3] State legislation thus covers hospital planning and execution as well as the internal administration of hospitals. Coordination between the federal government and the states is assigned to a "Committee for Hospital Financing" (KHG, paragraph 7), which consists of the relevant federal agencies (Ministry of Labor and Social Welfare, Ministry for Youth, Family, and Health) and top-level state authorities. Also included are various institutions affected by hospital planning, e.g. the German Hospitals' Association, labor unions, health insurance societies, and professional associations. The committee has a purely advisory function and concerns itself mainly with issues of hospital services (KHG, paragraph 1), building programs, and the distribution of financial resources. The committee is assisted by a subcommittee of experts in various areas of hospital management. These experts are appointed by health insurance societies, social welfare agencies, employee and employer organizations, and the medical association. The subcommittee's function is somewhat obscure, but is supposed to act in an advisory capacity to a superordinate committee which itself has a merely advisory role.

In the GDR, legislation for health care is considerably more differentiated. It covers essentially three areas:[4] laws regulating the organizational structure, responsibilities, and compentencies of the central[5] and regional authorities;[6] laws and regulations relevant to the processes of planning and implementation;[7] and laws regulating the responsibilities, organizational structure, and management within hospitals.[8] In addition to these laws, resolutions made at party congresses play an important part, especially in areas which involve the implementation of programs and employee participation. The predominance of government control in the health-care system is ensured by two items of legislation: the law on the Ministerial Council, of October 16, 1972,[9] and the law on the functions of regional parliaments and their agencies, of July 12, 1973.[10] Both laws clearly demonstrate the principle of democratic centralism; the allocation of responsibilities and competencies reflect a strictly hierarchical structure. The central government has sole decision-making powers. The task of the Ministry of Health is to "plan for the health-care needs of the population. This includes the administration of the funds for personnel, equipment, and other financial costs."[11] The regional parliaments must implement the health and social policies as formulated by the SED and as specified and supervised by the Ministry of Health. A special set of indices for the health system, the course of planning, and the areas of responsibility for central and local organs is stipulated in the Ordinance for Planning the Economy. The Hospital Framework Ordinance lays down the division of tasks and the internal hospital structure. Each hospital must submit a plan for its management which reflects a uniform organization chart.[12]

## Hospital Planning

To some extent, the process of planning in the two German states can already be deduced from the above discussion on legislation. However, further examination of the role of central authorities may be illuminating. According to the Hospital Financing Act (paragraph 6), the various states of the FRG are responsible for the maintenance and development of hospital services and for investments in the hospital sector. The law stipulates that each state must draw up a projection of its hospital-bed requirements. At this time, however, it does not specify how this is to be done. There are thus no uniform, binding standards—

a sign that planning is still in its early stages. There are also other problems. First, the individual states have very different specifications. The Bavarian law, for example, contains no specifications, while in Berlin and North Rhine–Westphalia projections must contain the number and regional distribution of hospitals, the number of existing beds, specialties, wards, and so forth.[13] Second, the projection of bed requirements is made according to a formula which is methodologically unsatisfactory, mainly because it relies on a few, very crude indicators. Finally, no time periods are specified. Regulations covering the preparation of projections are a little more precise; the relevant state agencies make a draft after they have consulted the hospital associations and the heads of insurance societies. None of these organizations have, however, the right to participate in the actual decisions. The projections form the basis for both the long-term and the annual building programs. The former is financed by the federal government, and plans must therefore include a financial estimate. The same applies to the annual building program, except that funds are requisitioned through the state authorities. The state authorities have complete autonomy with regard to planning. They must, however, obtain federal approval. This coordination takes place in the Committee for Hospital Financing. Local community authorities and other interest groups are consulted but have no decision-making powers. Hospital planning in the FRG is limited to financing and investment projections. This planning takes place in the appropriate state agencies, and communal or interest groups are not consulted until after a plan has been completed.

In contrast to the FRG, planning in the GDR is clearly conceived as a social process. Planning proceeds along the lines of democratic centralism, which means ". . . a combination of central government planning . . . with autonomous planning by industry, local authorities, and individual initiatives for the implementation of plans" (Kinze, Knop, and Seifert 1974, p. 33). The organizational principle implied in this description is strictly hierarchical; planning and decisions over all fundamental issues are in the hands of the central government, and all initiatives of the subordinate authorities (regional parliaments) are subject to government control. The "autonomous planning by local authorities" appears to leave some room for regional decision making. However, when one looks at the planning structure, it becomes obvious that autonomy may be officially institutionalized but is in reality nonexistent.

Before discussing the actual planning process, it is necessary to explain briefly the various "term" plans which are used for all economic planning in the GDR. They are designed to make planning more flexible and more realizable. One of these is the "Long-Term Plan," which covers a period of 15 years and is chiefly a means for general economic orientation. "With the adoption of a long-term plan, decisions about the utilization of economic resources are being made at the same time. These decisions are then realized concretely in the 'Five-Year' and 'One-Year' plans." (Kinze, Knop, and Seifert 1974, p. 100) The five-year plan is a medium-range plan which aims at "a complete synthesis of all economic factors, comprehensive financing, and a binding international agreement" (Kinze et al. 1974, p. 103). It provides the basic outlines (chief indicators and guiding values) for programs at the lower levels. The one-year plans provide the actual planning instrument; they are adapted to the prevailing state of economic development and other changing environmental conditions, which makes them relatively flexible. They are also characterized by accountability and controllability (Bär 1975, p. 57). Apart from quantitative information, they also contain verbal instructions.

In contrast to national economic planning, which is essentially formulated on the basis of societal aims and needs, operational planning is designed to fulfill immediate economic goals. "By introducing a limited time frame, one creates the conditions for accountable and controllable management in the social and medical services." (Bär 1975, p. 60) In addition, one-year plans contain, of course, most of the important economic information, e.g. hospital capacity, personnel inventory, funds for investment, receipts, and expenditures.

Besides government authorities, party officials too play an important role in the planning process of the GDR. All authorities are hierarchically organized into central and regional agencies, and the latter have little or no influence on the formulation of goals (Kiera 1975, p. 20). The central authority is composed of the Ministerial Council of the GDR and its planning agency, the Public Planning Commission, and the Ministry of Health. The ideological position on the "primacy of health care in a socialist society" is not supported altogether by the reality of health-care planning, especially if one compares health care with other productive and nonproductive sectors of the society (Mecklinger, Kriewald, and Lammel 1974, p. 51). The Ministry of Health is responsible for all planning and control in the health-care system. Its task is "to plan all measures for the medical care of the population, including the administration of the material, financial, and personnel resources, on the basis of health-policy directives and qualitative indicators issued by the government."[14] Indicators and guidelines are then relayed to the regional authorities. This vertical method of planning demands that activities at every level be standardized and coordinated. "It is essential that the fundamental political goals, the social and health policies deriving from them, and the concrete tasks which have been formulated by the party and government leadership are explained to, and discussed with, regional authorities and employees." (Mecklinger et al. 1974, p. 68)

A simplified, schematic description may clarify this process. In the first stage, provisional plans are drawn up at the lowest level of the hierarchy according to certain guidelines; hospitals submit requisitions based on their experiences of the previous year. The plans of individual hospitals are aggregated at the county level. The county translates them into indicators for the one-year plan. This plan, together with information about the capacities and performances of all hospitals (state, church-affiliated, and private), is submitted to the district. In the second stage, the aggregated plans are submitted to the State Planning Commission, the Ministry of Health, and the Ministry for Finances. At this level, determinations with regard to monetary and nonmonetary allocations are made. The third stage involves planning at the central government level. The State Planning Commission draws up long-range plans, which, once approved, also authorize the utilization and the allocation of economic resources. After this follows the stage of implementation; the completed plans are passed on to the next lower level for execution.

A comparison of planning processes in the GDR and the FRG shows both similarities and differences. Both countries have in common a system of government planning which operates at the highest level. This means that other organizations, institutions, or individuals do not actively participate in planning, although their participation is deemed necessary and desirable. The difference lies in the degree of centralization of the bureaucracy. Furthermore, planning in the GDR is far more comprehensive, and it includes hospital administrative structures, capacities, investments, and operating costs. The FRG confines planning to the organizational structures and to investments.

## Financing of Health Care

Richau (1975, p. 117) points out that although medical services in the GDR may be free of charge (because they are financed by the government), the financial transaction involved is by no means without significance.[15] On the contrary: "By controlling the flow of capital in the economy, the socialist state is able to influence the material aspects of the reproductive process." (Richau 1975; p. 117) Financial transactions are thus of considerable importance to the implementation of health-care programs (Schwarz 1963, pp. 32 ff.).

A similar argument was made by the federal government in the FRG, when the KHG (Hospital Financing Act) was passed. In order to guarantee an adequate supply of hospitals, it was considered necessary not only to engage in long-term planning but also to provide a comprehensive and reliable financial basis for this task. "Financial security for hospitals is not an end in itself . . . instead the construction of a modern and effective hospital system should be seen as the responsibility of the law." (Harsdorf and Friedrich 1975, p. 72) As in the GDR, the unity of planning and financing is regarded as a guarantee that the objective will be achieved.

After 1945, the Soviet Military Administration (SMAD) restructured the whole economic and socio-political system of the GDR. In this development, two military decrees were of particular significance: SMAD orders 234 and 28 (Schmunk et al., pp. 48 ff.). They created the foundations for centralized economic planning and for a unified social security system. In 1947, the SED called for the nationalization of the health-care system along guidelines of "communal policy" (*Dokumente der SED*, 1948, p. 69). In the financial sector, nationalization of health care became effective only after the budget reform of 1951. Until then, hospitals had their own budgets and dealt with the health insurance societies directly. Operating costs were charged to patients in the form of a per diem rate.[16] The account was paid either by the health insurance society or by the patient (if he was not insured). In addition to the receipts from patients and insurance societies, hospitals had other financial resources in the form of credits or interest on fixed property; deficits were covered by subsidies from local authorities (Schwarz 1963, p. 48).

In 1951, social security was incorporated in the state budget.[17] The budget reform fundamentally changed the mode of financing. Hospitals no longer charge the insurance societies directly; accounts are now settled by the Ministry of Finance by means of a statistical procedure (Schwarz 1963, p. 46). Expenditures are paid out of the state budget, because health insurance is now a state institution (Gurtz and Heiden 1977, p. 29). Not all expenditures are covered by social security; investments amounting to more than 500 marks are financed from the general budget.[18] To this extent, fulfilling social priorities does not depend on receipts. "Political and economic programs require complete financing if they are deemed socially necessary, with full regard for frugality but not according to the principle of economic accountability" (Richau 1967, p. 86). This dualistic mode of financing should present no difficulties, since ultimately the source of the funds is the same. But the apparent logic of political considerations that insist that there is and should be no circulation of funds has the consequence that, indeed, no funds exist for investment or circulation. Furthermore, although the subsidies for operating costs are receipts from the viewpoint of the hospitals, they simultaneously cover the budgets of the superordinate authorities (i.e. district, county, or town councils) (Grossmann and Richau 1962, p. 75).

Whereas the health-care system in the GDR was nationalized soon after the end of World War II, the FRG retained the old system, at least for some time. This included the method of paying for health care: All costs incurred in the hospital were paid either by the health insurance society or by the patient (if he was not insured). However, the then-existing price structure did not guarantee that hospitals were adequately recompensed for their services. Even the new Per Diem Ordinance[19] represented no significant improvement. The result was that hospitals operated at a deficit. This had a particularly detrimental effect on investments. New investments were either forgone altogether or had to be financed from state or community subsidies. The size of public subsidies depended not so much on uniform federal standards as on the financial position of individual states or communities. Decisions about investments tended to be more esoteric and random than rational. Under these conditions, an adequate supply of hospitals could, of course, by no means be guaranteed.

Despite the increasing financial involvement of states and communities, hospital deficits rose. A federally funded investigation into the financial situation of hospitals confirmed the suspicion: The hospital sector had been run at a deficit for years, and it had finally reached an estimated 800–900 million DM. As a solution to the problem the Hospital Financing Act was passed. Among other provisions, it reallocated financial responsibility for the hospital sector. All construction and maintenance of the necessary equipment and facilities is financed directly from state budgets. The money is made available from a permanent fund into which the federal government pays one-third and the various states two-thirds. The distribution of these funds takes place in the following way:[20] Large-scale projects, e.g. construction of hospitals and replacement of medium-term investments (depreciation time 15–30 years) must be requisitioned by each individual hospital; funds for the replacement of goods with a depreciation time of 3–15 years are allocated to hospitals in one gross payment (KHG, paragraph 9).[21]

Utilization costs are covered by receipts from the per diem charges, i.e. they are paid by the health insurance societies. According to the regulations, these provisions should cover all medically appropriate and adequate services. Specifically, they include personnel costs, medical and other supplies, and equipment with a depreciation rate of less than 3 years.

Subsidies and receipts together should, ideally, cover all costs. However, if additional expenses are incurred, they must be borne by either the hospital or a third party. For example, services which are neither directly nor indirectly part of hospital care must be paid by the hospital; extraordinary expenses for research and teaching must be paid out of the budgets for science and research.

Comparison between methods of financing in the FRG and the GDR thus shows that in both systems hospitals are financed from two different sources, but operating costs are covered by the various social insurance budgets whereas investments are financed directly from public/state funds. The difference between the systems lies chiefly in the degree to which hospitals are incorporated in the national budget and can dispose of their income. In the GDR hospitals are included in the budget of the next superordinate state authority; in the FRG they must, since 1978, administer their own budgets. At first glance, it seems thus that there is a tremendous discrepancy in the degree of autonomy granted to hospitals, which might well be a reflection of the economic order; the centrally administered economic system leaves hospitals no room for autonomous decisions, while the social market system allows a considerable amount of freedom. This conclusion needs to be qualified. On one hand, it only applies when one looks at the financial relations in isolation from other factors. On the other hand, it would almost certainly be wrong to equate lack of autonomy with a violation of the principle of democratic centralism. Such an argument would contradict a theoretical position which holds that planning and management oriented to objective needs obviates autonomy at the hospital level. Finally, if the financial relations are considered in conjunction with planning, it becomes clear that the freedom of action granted to hospitals in the FRG is considerably less than appears on the surface.

## Normative and Financial Regulation

In the preceding sections it has become evident that, for various political and ideological reasons, free prices as a regulating mechanism were eliminated in both systems. However, prices are only one means of coordinating economic planning. Others exist in the form of organization, legislation, use of indicators, and subsidies. The problem is that these means are not easily classified as either normative or financial controls. Especially in an economy without a free market, it is always possible to regard financial controls as a special case of normative control. If, for example, the volume of investments is determined at the highest administrative level, then the allocation of funds for investments constitutes a form of financial control. On the other hand, it is just as clearly a normative lever, because all decisions about investments must take the amount of the funds into consideration. These difficulties arise because there is no agreement as to what constitutes a norm or normative control. In this discussion, I will use the widest possible meaning, including not only laws, regulations, and guidelines but also all economic indicators which are contained in the laws and regulations. Indeed, these indicators will be the main subject of the following discussion.

In the GDR, indicators play a far more significant role than in the FRG, because they form the basis for planning and balancing the national budget. They guarantee the compatibility of planning at the institutional (hospital) level with the central economic goals. In other words, they ensure that central economic programs are implemented.[22] This definition needs to be amplified so that the essential features of economic indicators, as well as their role in planning and implementation, can be appreciated. In the first instance, it must be noted that indicators should be uniform for all sectors of the economy in order to ensure comparability. Therefore, they must be formulated on the basis of similar computation methods and measurement standards, and they must refer to similar economic concepts (Kinze et al. 1974, p. 125). Experience had shown that nonstandardized indicators which were not comparable prevented well-planned, balanced economic development. New methods were therefore introduced in which the quantitative indicators were replaced by qualitative ones,[23] and the number was reduced to 12–15 (Buck 1969, p. 304).

"In a centralized planning system, it is not possible to plan in advance every detail and part process. For this reason such a system presupposes a high degree of uniformity in judgment and action. Without a set of common and uniform norms, no real integration of the total system is possible, because regional, sectional, institutional, and individual interests will tend to diverge." (Kruppa 1976, p. 77) Indicators are also meant to function as tools for planning, management, accounting, and control. They are thus to be used simultaneously as estimates for projected performance and as controls for actual performance. In both functions they must, of course, agree conceptually, although they may differ with respect to their numerical values (as they indeed usually do). Their third characteristic is that they are formulated by the central authorities and become quasi-dogmas. Only the party leadership may interpret them, so that the unity of planning and execution will be preserved (Kruppa 1976, p. 77). Thus, in the areas of health and social welfare they become "standards for the behavior of managers and employees in all state-controlled institutions and agencies which are engaged in the task of fulfilling the cultural and social needs of the socialist state" (Heiden 1977, pp. 31–33). These standards "are laid down by the central authorities, taking into account societal needs and economic feasibility" (ibid.). The East German literature often tries to give the impression that indicators used for planning are only orientations for guiding social institutions (Kinze et al. 1974, p. 481). But since "orientations" and norms are used in centrally administered economies as a check on reports from agencies and institutions to identify deviations from the plan, they become regarded as absolutely binding.

For a critical analysis of indicators, it is important to know not only what they are but also how they are generated, i.e. what analytical or political processes precede their formulation and how these are justified ideologically. In the GDR, three fairly similar procedures are used to determine indicators. All of them are based on the same ground rules, principles, or criteria (Bär 1975, pp. 49 ff.; Ökonomische Gesetze, 1975; Kinze et al. 1974, pp. 46 ff.): "objectivity," scientific methodology, and "the unity of centralism and democracy."

The simplest way to explain the origin of social indicators is that social needs and the means of satisfying them are political decisions, which stem from the logic that there exist "objective criteria for the satisfaction of societal and individual needs" that "can be deduced from the total development of a society and its established needs" (*Materielle und Kulturelle Lebensniveau*, 1975, p. 363). This statement has been justifiably attacked by Kruppa, who maintains that the "objectivity" postulated by the SED for goal determination must remain a purely ideological construct, since there is no objective order of priorities. The concept of objectivity is thus reduced to a mere claim by the party leadership that it can define the optimal welfare of society as a representative for the working class (Kruppa 1976, p. 72). The assumption that the party can determine the society's welfare is based on the premises of the unity of centralism and democracy and the primacy of central planning. Conflicts of interest do not exist, since all decisions are made in the interests of the people.

Decisions about indicators are supported by the application of scientific principles, according to Marxist-Leninist theory. This involves appraisal of the initial situation and the projected goal as well as systematic analysis of the conditions for action. Despite the emphasis on scientific principles, political considerations are decisive. This means that the processes by which indicators are generated are evident to the party leadership but not necessarily to subordinate authorities.

Another variation of this esoteric process involves reliance on the figures of past years. Leenen (1977, p. 61) maintains that the determination of socially acknowledged needs is frequently based on certain typical, minimum values which are associated with typical need situations. "Socially recognized" needs and the degree to which they have been satisfied become then basically the performance of the previous economic year. Buck points out that neither the requisite information nor the computational means exist to compile anything like an optimal performance. The GDR also lacks the time and the personnel to assemble production figures for each year. Indicators are thus generally computed on the basis of the performance of the previous year, and increases in production are ordered by the party leadership (Buck 1969, p. 287).

The third variation of the standardization process, the "scientific organization of work," has a tradition in most socialist societies. It developed out of Taylorism and the industrial engineering movement, and it now contributes to the determination of personnel requirements, job descriptions, and the size of the wage budget (Walther 1967, p. 841). These methods, first employed in industry, have increasingly been employed in the health-care system, especially where it was possible to subdivide a job into a number of repetitive tasks. Although the methodology for these analyses has become more sophisticated, most indicators are nevertheless based on the average values of previous planning periods[24] (Walther 1967).

By and large, the three methods of developing indicators differ very little from one another. They all are subject to the same conditions, serve the same aim (increases in production and efficiency), and do not remotely approach a solution of the basic problem, namely the definition of objectively determined needs.

## Normative Controls in the FRG

Although free prices also do not play a significant role in the health-care system of the FRG, the use of indicators for planning and control has never been widely accepted by the public or by hospital experts. Since economy and efficiency are desired there too, indicators were indeed developed, but with a different meaning. In part, this may have been due to the fact that indicators and planning were reminiscent of wartime practices and therefore were seen as incompatible with a social market economy. In part, it may have been also due to the scientific and methodological inadequacies of indicators.

Setting aside their economic relevance and effect for the present, I will begin by discussing indicators from a phenomenological point of view. First, there are indicators for the medical and nursing personnel, the so-called "index figures"[25] which serve for orientation at the hospital level. They are ratios composed of the number of beds and the medical and nursing staff necessary for adequate care. They are not used to compute the total health-care labor pool or wage/salary expenditures for the whole society, as in the GDR. For projections of hospital bed requirements, the states also use a "hospital bed quota"; it represents the number of planned hospital beds per 1,000 inhabitants. These quotas are computed by means of a special formula.

A number of comments and criticisms have been made in connection with these index figures. I shall mention some of them, chiefly for two reasons: to show that index figures are not really very different from the indicators used in the GDR, both in the way they are generated and in their effect, and because index figures and their future application are at present the subject of a heated debate on health policy in the FRG.

As in the GDR, separate indices exist for measuring how many doctors and nurses are required. In the FRG, physicians called for minimum standards as early as 1948. Figures, however, were not issued until 1969, when the Hospital Physicians' Association published them. They were modified in 1973 and also endorsed by the German Hospital Association (DKG). This historical account makes it clear that indices were introduced by health-care organizations and not by government agencies; that is, indices are not governmental guidelines.

For the nursing profession, experiential values were first used as indices by the German Hospital Association in 1964 and modified in 1969. A number of work-related developments, such as the introduction of the 40-hour week, changes in the conceptions of nursing care, and technological advances, necessitated another revision in 1974. For the first time, the German Hospital Association also published the principles and methods by which indices were constructed. This is remarkable insofar as all previous indices had been based on experiential values from earlier years and not on evidence from scientific work studies.

Indices were introduced and justified in the FRG with the same argument as in the GDR: increased efficiency. They are designed "in the first instance to improve hospital performance for the benefit of the patient. This includes an adequate staff of resident physicians."[26] With regard to nursing staff, the new indices of 1974 reflected new conditions: More intensive nursing care had become necessary as a result of new methods of treatment, an increase in the number of patients, and shorter average periods of hospitalization, and the shorter work week necessitated organizational measures to ensure a better utilization of time and an improvement of the objective and subjective working conditions (Arbeitsgruppe zur Planung 1975, p. 54). The DKG pointed out that the 1974 indices were not the result of representative studies and should therefore only be used as approximate guidelines. Each hospital should work out its own exact personnel requirements and should not regard these indices as federally approved prescriptions.

The indices were criticized by other organizations as being based on current practices rather than on a scientific analysis of hospital services and as being crude averages not taking into account certain differences among hospitals, such as differences in function, methods of treatment, type of administration, nursing styles, and patient mix. Thus, critics argued, target numbers for staffing hospitals must not be considered as definitive but more as an example of how such calculations are made. In addition, critics pointed out that "the uncritical application of the

DKG indices would lead at present to an exaggerated demand for nursing staff without ensuring economical and efficient management or avoiding oversupply." The DKG formula P × D × A (Intensity of care × Share of work load × Absentee quota) can therefore not be used to determine the personnel needs of individual hospitals because it ignores regional, structural, and organizational conditions; it takes no account of over- or underutilization of the stipulated bed capacity; and it encourages manipulation of the length of hospitalization in order to disguise an oversupply of beds (Arbeitsgruppe zur Planung 1975, p. ix). Apart from these methodological objections, some criticisms have been expressed by labor unions and hospital employees. They claim that the absentee quota is considerably higher than the 15 percent assumed by the DKG (Arbeitsgruppe zur Planung 1975, p. 22).

Although there is fairly general consensus about the inadequacy and the limited applicability of indices, they nevertheless play an extremely important role in the negotiations over the per diem rate. Fehler (Arbeitsgruppe zur Planung 1975, p. 22) states that "in the conflict over personnel requirements, indices are either offensive weapons for those who are demanding more positions or defensive weapons for those who want to reject such demands." In the course of this, indices become precisely what they were not intended to be: norms with universally assumed validity. Since they are, however, ranges with upper and lower limits, the negotiating parties have considerable latitude. In the negotiations between the health insurance societies and the hospitals it is then also not methods of computation and actually computed values that are under debate, but only the question whether minimum or maximum values ought to apply.

In comparison with the GDR, indices in the FRG differ in the following respects:

They are not "federal" norms regulating personnel distribution for the whole health-care sector. Instead, indices were developed by nongovernmental health-care institutions and are employed only on the hospital level.

Indices are not meant to represent prescriptive norms but should be used as examples only. (In reality, they have, however, been elevated to binding norms. As a result they now resemble the labor-force indicators employed in the GDR fairly closely.)

The second important area that is regulated by means of indices is the distribution of hospital beds on the regional level. Various normative and programmatic indices have been used over time. Their function is "to mirror the objective needs for hospital services, so that these may be fulfilled on the basis of ethical, cultural, health-policy, and economic considerations as far as social productivity and the economic wealth of the nation permit this" (Eichhorn 1975, p. 53). This formulation contains two principles that warrant examination. First, it is evident that it is not the requirements of individual hospitals that count, but the societal goal of adequate health care. Second, the emphasis is again on "objective" planning. Both principles have had considerable influence on the development of indicators for hospital-bed planning.

Up to 1973, a formula was used that incorporated the following factors: frequency of hospitalization per 1,000 inhabitants, average length of hospitalization, average utilization, and total number of inhabitants.[27] With the help of this formula, a value for bed supply was obtained. Since, however, all the factors allow for considerable room for influence, the objective requirements cannot be derived from them. As a report from the Berlin Senate observed, "The possible influence of the participants in shaping the results, which is known and can be seen in the statistics, has cast considerable doubt on the objective predictive value of [the formula]" (Senat von Berlin 1978, p. 7). This led the senate to suggest that hospital-bed rates (number of beds per 1,000 inhabitants) might be used for comparison, and that the computed bed quota should be seen as a limiting figure only.

Nevertheless, it seems that an "objective" determination of the demand for beds remains elusive, as illustrated by this example from Berlin: "If certain factors (e.g. frequency and length of hospitalization and utilization) are manipulated in systematic and not usually detectable ways, the result may be unrealistic demands. In this case it should be possible to resort to bed rates to establish how much the quotas deviate from the average values of other, comparable federal states." (Senat von Berlin 1978, pp. 8–9) This proposition assumes that comparison between federal states is a reasonable and legitimate method, and that the demand figures submitted by other states are "correct," despite the fact that they have been computed by the same method. It may be conjectured that demand figures for beds owe their existence more to political than to scientific considerations—planning requires some suppositions about the factors influencing the demand (Senat von Berlin 1978, p. 93)—and that they are presented as numerical values (ibid., p. 99). Since the aim of mutual accommodation is usually to arrive at the lowest possible figure, it may be assumed that financial considerations play a more important part than "objectively recognized needs," whatever they are.

It seems thus that the bed quota serves less as an indicator of real needs than as a guarantee that financial resources are allocated according to priorities approved by the various health-care agencies. The emphasis here is on the allocation of investment funds, but these have, of course, a considerable influence on the total financial situation of hospitals.

## Financial Levers in the GDR and the FRG

In addition to normative controls, there are also financial means of control. A clear distinction between them is problematic, as already mentioned. However, it is possible to define and accept as financial controls all factors that are expressed in monetary terms. First, there are the operating costs (per diem rates) which act at the hospital level and the individual level. Then there are the various funds; in the GDR, for example, the Social Consumption Fund contains all the monies necessary for the provision of health-care services, e.g. wages, salaries, capital goods, and investments. In the FRG there is no directly comparable fund; however, the social budget[28] and the Fund for Hospital Investments (KHG, paragraph 22) are somewhat similar, at least in effect.[29] Furthermore, all financial "incentives" can be considered instruments of coordination, such as the premium fund for workers in the GDR or the salary for the thirteenth month in the FRG. These various financial controls will be examined in detail with special reference of their usefulness as financial levers. Of these, direct costs probably assume the most important position among possible instruments of coordination. Although the limited value (in respect to business) of the concept of "direct costs" is repeatedly pointed out in both German states, the expectations for its use are unrealistically high because some very basic costs, such as investments, are not included. In hospital care, there is no clear connection between expenditures and output. Nevertheless, both Germanies use direct costs because "in the direct cost index, the various factors of hospital economics take effect in a complex and visible manner; thus its use has central meaning" (Richau 1967, p. 82).

The operating costs for one day of hospital care (in the FRG it is the per diem rate) are thus treated in much the same way as a market-determined price would be. This is particularly so in the FRG, where the per diem rates are the result of bargaining between the hospitals and the health insurance societies.[30] Seen in this way, prices could exert effects in two directions: to the outside, on the patient and his decisions, and to the inside, on hospital performance. The first of these effects is considerably attenuated by the fact that patients are largely unaware of the per diem rates and select a hospital by other criteria (proximity, reputation, recommendations by others), and by the fact that potential costs are of no consequence to them because in both systems a third party (insurance society or social security) pays the bills.

Now it is always possible that operating costs could have an effect on the performance of the hospital, i.e. that the price becomes an instrument for cost control instead of depending on the cost (Thiemeyer 1975, p. 127). It is conceivable, for example, that a fixed price would encourage efficiency, provided the hospital administration was free to dispose of the profits as it saw fit. Since all profits would, however, be revoked at the next bargaining session, there are no incentives for efficient and sensible management (Bauer 1978, p. 324).

There is general agreement in the GDR and the FRG about this point: A fixed per diem rate which is independent of real costs and remains the same for each day of hospital care leads to indifference to cost containment. The fixed rate has thus the exact opposite effect from the one intended: it forces hospitals to operate at full capacity. The more beds are, on the average, occupied by patients with minor illnesses, the greater the margin for diagnosis and treatment of the seriously ill. For example, if the average length of hospitalization is reduced—a measure which might be considered conducive to efficiency and cost control—a paradoxical situation arises: If the average utilization or the number of cases remains constant, the income of the hospital must surely decline. Since this inevitably means that there will be less money for the next financial year, the logical consequence is reductions in personnel. The hospital is punished for its own cost efficiency.

Operating costs were dealt with in some detail because they are regarded as likely prospects for cost containment, not only by official authorities but also by virtue of being determined in a process that is somewhat like bargaining. However, given that no objective criteria to justify expenditures exist, the final decision is left to the relevant authority. In the FRG, this authority is the Board of Price Control, which must approve increases in the per diem rate after considering their merit and the general financial situation of the health insurance societies. This decision is naturally not solely based on the actual financial situation of hospitals, but also involves political considerations. Increases in the per diem rate may lead to increased insurance premiums, and this may have political repercussions. Increases in health-care costs may also be interpreted as a failure of the current health and social policies, with negative consequences at the next election. It is therefore not surprising that the authorities frequently override or modify the decisions made at the bargaining table.

In the GDR these problems are not as visible, but they exist nevertheless, at least as far as can be ascertained from the literature and the press. Here, the decision over per diem rates is, of course, incorporated in the planning process, i.e. hospitals are provided with indicators which serve for their orientation. The state authorities need, however, only take available resources into account and can ignore voter opinions. However, effective supervision and control of medical services seem to present as many problems as in the FRG, and thus one finds considerable differences in the quality of hospital performances. As Richau (1967, p. 82) expresses it: "Subjective points of view, different degrees of ruthlessness, the insight (or lack of it) on the part of authorities, negligence or efficiency, the level of the economic development in the individual counties or districts—all play an important role in creating the vast difference in the performance of otherwise comparable hospitals and in the incongruity between facilities and efficiency."

Among the financial controls are various funds, such as the social consumption fund and the accumulation fund. Previous analyses of these funds have generally focused on their distribution and the resulting effects on the material and cultural niveau of the population. Their role in the health-care system has been somewhat neglected, but it is as significant. "The dynamics of progress in a socialist society demand that the theoretical as well as the practical issues of health care are given increased priority. We are dealing here with one of the most important sectors of the economy, with far-reaching consequences for the structure and dynamics of the national economy." (Keck 1979, p. 429)

A balanced and orderly development of the health-care system demands serious consideration of the growing importance of social needs and of the increasing demand for the means to finance social consumption (e.g. new hospitals) (Kinze et al. 1974, pp. 256, 263). In contrast to the FRG, where only the funds for investment are directly controlled, all health-care programs in the GDR, including investments, are financed from public funds, and expenditures are already held in check at the planning stage. Once they have been allocated by the central government, they are administered and distributed by the various state agencies. This means that individual hospitals have little influence over the cost of medical services.

At the level of the central government, the funds are generally assigned for global purposes, i.e., they are instruments for the realization of nationwide social programs (*Das materielle und kulturelle Lebensniveau*, 1975, pp. 196, 225). They become amenable to control only at the regional level, when they are actually allocated to particular hospitals. It is at this point that Richau's criticism, namely that real control ceases to exist because there are no objective criteria for allocation, becomes relevant. The principles which guide decision making at the macro level do not have a counterpart at the micro level. The funds acquire a normative character, i.e. expenditures may not exceed a stipulated ceiling, but there is no guidance as to how they are to be spent. This casts, of course, considerable doubt on the effectiveness of plans and decisions made at the highest level.

The FRG also represents its social consumption in a "Social Budget"; however, there is no attempt to use the latter as an instrument for cost control. Instead, the Social Budget is a summary survey of all social services and their financing. "It describes . . . the various aspects of the social security system . . . and relates its financial data to those of the whole economy." (Bundesminister für Arbeit und Sozialordnung 1978, p. 66) In contrast to the public fund in the GDR, which represents a norm, the Social Budget is merely intended to provide guidelines for socio-political decisions.

The situation is somewhat different with respect to the funds for hospital investments. Here the law proceeded on the assumption that the structure of the hospital sector could indeed be influenced by controlling investment funds. This was to be achieved by limiting both the funds and the criteria for eligibility, but the demand for beds and hospital buildings was also to be taken into account. A resemblance to the accumulated fund in the GDR is evident. Allocation of finances is in principle already predetermined by the size of the federal budget and decisions about its distribution. In addition, it is subject to a priority determination which is oriented to the available funds.

Finally, I should mention the role of wages, premiums, and bonuses in the efforts to contain costs, especially in view of the fact that they are regarded as one of the chief incentives for productivity in the GDR. While it is relatively easy to establish a connection between performance and remuneration in the productive sphere, attempts to do the same in the nonproductive sphere meet with considerable difficulties and limit the effectiveness of economic stimuli. "Since the health-care and social welfare institutions produce no profit, they have neither the resources to provide material incentives for their employees nor funds for improvement. This fact must, of course, be taken into account when health-care programs and salaries for employees in a socialist state are considered. The present criteria for incentive premiums are professional qualifications, degree of responsibility, work experience, and certain aggravated working conditions." (Keck 1979, p. 440) Because these premiums are fixed in advance for each employee, however, their function as incentives for performance is seriously compromised. "All state-operated institutions have a premium fund as well as a cultural and social fund; these are part of the total budget. Institutions which operated within the framework of state planning and had (up to 1972) an incentive program received a minimum of 340 marks a year in premiums and 125 marks in social and cultural benefits for each full employee. In all other institutions, the premiums amount (since 1978) to 4.1 or 3.1% of the total wages, with a minimum of 240 marks per employee unit a year." (Gurtz and Heiden 1977, p. 30)

An attempt is being made to adjust premium payments to performance by regulating the distribution of premium funds: ". . . if the planned objective is not achieved, the premium fund can be reduced to 80% of the total sum" (König et al. 1978, p. 341). This, of course, still does not make it a genuine incentive scheme; 80 percent of the premiums are guaranteed regardless of performance, and the regulation refers only to the "planned objective" and not to individual performance.

## Summary and Conclusion

This chapter has dealt with the normative and financial controls which regulate hospital services in the GDR and the FRG. In view of the fundamentally different economic systems, the question was asked whether significant differences could be said to exist in this particular area too.

As instruments or means of control I selected not only prices and economic programs, but also forms of organization in the hospital sector, as well as legal and normative prescriptions. Although the political and ideological positions would lead one to expect numerous and fundamental differences, actual comparison showed that many normative and financial controls in the two German states were remarkably similar, if not identical. In both systems, planning is by law assigned to government or state authorities. Though theoretically provisions exist for the participation of employees and patients in the decision-making processes, in practice such participation is nonexistent.

One major difference between the GDR and the FRG is the degree to which planning is centralized. In the GDR, all authority for planning rests with the central government (Ministerial Council, State Planning Commission, Ministry of Health), and planning is organized on strictly hierarchical principles. In the FRG, the federal states exercise this authority, with the federal government acting in a coordinating role.

The political decision to exclude the market price as a means of control over the health-care system has led to the development of a system of indicators which are intended to control planning and financing at the national as well as the institutional level. Planning at the national level proceeds chiefly on the basis of a number of indicators which relate the number of beds to the number of inhabitants (bed rates or quotas) and determine the regional distribution of hospitals.

At the institutional level, labor-force indices (personnel codes, etc.) have become increasingly important, particularly since the methods of ergonomic analysis have been applied to the health-care occupations. The processes by which indicators are generated vary little between the two states, the reason being that both use the single hospital bed as the elementary unit (without, however, having found satisfactory methods for evaluating the services attached to this unit).

Nevertheless, indicators play a decisive role in the allocation of funds to the hospital sector. Fundamental health-policy principles, codified in the law, result in methods of financing that are practically identical. Hospital operating costs are covered by social insurance budgets. At first glance, there seems to be some difference here. In the GDR, social insurance is part of the state budget and is financed by taxes and not membership fees. In the FRG, the registered health insurance societies have the status of "parafisci" (state-supported facilities), meaning that they collect compulsory premiums. However, since about 90 percent of the population is insured with these societies and the government covers any potential deficits by means of subsidies, the differences that remain are minimal. Also similar are the methods of financing investments. In both states such costs are paid out of the public or state budget.

The fact that normative and financial controls in the two German states are almost identical, in general as well as in detail, may at first seem surprising. However, there are several explanations for this. In the first instance, it must be remembered that the GDR and the FRG have a common past, and that their health-care and social security systems are based on the system that originated in the German Reich in 1881. Both states rebuilt their health-care services on the foundations of institutions as they existed in 1945.

A further reason for the high degree of similarity lies in the absence of valid definitions for hospital performance (system output) and in the one-sided reliance on the "hospital bed" as the unit of measurement and planning. This leaves practically no alternative methods for planning and financing. The problem is aggravated by the lack of employee participation. It seems that economy, performance, and efficiency will remain out of reach as long as goals are not defined precisely, priorities are not firmly established, and strategies for goal achievement are not planned with greater complexity and attention to detail—if that is, indeed, possible.

## Notes

1. "Gesetz zur wirtschaftlichen Sicherung der Krankenhäuser und zur Regelung der Krankenhauspflegesatze (KHG)," June 29, 1972 (Bundesgesetzbuch I:1009).

2. The Hospital Financing Act and the Federal Per Diem Ordinance (Verordnung zur Regelung der Krankenhauspflegesatze) regulate the accounting procedures between health insurance societies and hospitals. The regulations determine who participates in the negotiations over per diem rates, and what costs are to be included. (Bundespflegesatz Verordnung, April 25, 1973; Bundesgesetzbuch I:33)

3. Bayrisches Krankenhausgesetz, June 21, 1974 (Gesetz- und Verordnungsblatt I:256ff); Hessisches Krankenhausgesetz, April 4, 1973 (Gesetz- und Verordnungsblatt I:145); Niedersachsisches Gesetz zum Bundesgesetz zur wirtschaftlichen Sicherung der Krankenhäuser und zur Regelung der Krankenhauspflegesatze, July 12, 1973 (Niedersachsisches Gesetz- und Verordnungsblatt I:237); Krankenhausgesetz des Landes Nordrhein-Westfalen, February 25, 1975 (Gesetze und Verordnungen für Nordrhein-Westfalen, 1975:210); Landgesetz zur Reform des Krankenhauswesens in Rheinland Pfalz, June 29, 1973 (Gesetz- und Verordnungsblatt I:199); Landeskrankenhausgesetz Berlin, December 13, 1974 (Gesetz- und Verordnungsblatt I:2810).

4. This division is analytical, however. Fields of responsibility and competence are not only demarcated by law, but are also concretely evident in the planning process.

5. Ministerial Council of the GDR, State Planning Commission, Ministry of Health.

6. Council of Districts, Cities, and Communities.

7. Anordnung über die Ordnung der Planung der Volkswirtschaft der DDR von 1976–1980. Gesetzblatt der Deutschen Demokratischen Republik, December 15, 1974, reprint 775a.

8. Aufgaben und Organisation der Krankenhäuser des staatlichen Gesundheitswesens-Rahmenkrankenhausordnung, November 5, 1954, Gesetzblatt-Zentralblatt der DDR, reprint 1954.

9. Gesetz über den Ministerrat der DDR, October 16, 1972 (Gesetzbuch I:253).

10. Gesetz über die ortlichen Volksvertretungen und ihre Organe in der Deutschen Demokratischen Republik, July 12, 1973 (Gesetzbuch I:313).

11. Ordnung der Planung (Gesetzblatt der DDR: Sonderdruck, 1974:451).

12. Verordnung über die Aufgaben, Rechte, und Pflichten der volkseigenen Betriebe, Kombinate, und VVB, March 28, 1973 (Gesetzblatt 1.5, 1973:131).

13. Compare Bayrisches Krankenhausgesetz, Krankenhausgesetz von Nordrhein-Westfalen, and Landeskrankenhausgesetz Berlin.

14. Ordnung der Planung 2:457.

15. In a socialist society, financial is understood to refer to all monetary relations connected with the formation, distribution, and utilization of capital and organized and utilized according to a plan. (Wörterbuch der Ökonomie Sozialismus, 1973.

16. The per diem rate is the average cost of a hospital bed plus treatment for one day. Individual variations are not taken into consideration.

17. Gesetz über die Eingliederung der Sozialversicherung in den Staatshaushalt.

18. Gesetz über den Staatshaushalts plan 1978, paragraphs 1 and 2, December 21, 1977 (Gesetzbuch I:37:419).

19 Verordnung PR7/54, August 31, 1954 (Bundesanzeiger 173, 1954).

20. This is a presentation of the purely technical procedure. In reality distribution is, of course, incorporated in the planning process conducted by the authorities. Autonomous decisions by hospitals are therefore not possible.

21. The yearly depreciation rate is 8.33 percent of the standard rate per hospital bed. The standard rate depends on the number of years the hospital has been in service and its bed capacity.

22. Compare Ökonomisches Lexikon, Wörterbuch der Ökonomie Sozialismus (1973), and Empfehlungen zur Gestaltung des Planes der Einrichtungen (1972).

23. Examples of quantitative indicators are production goals (in quantitative units) and volume of investments (in monetary units). Some qualitative indicators are profitability, effectivity, and productivity measures. See also Buck 1969, p. 304.

24. A detailed analysis of the WAO methods and their application to the health-care system (in the GDR) would lead us too far astray at this stage. This has been called "human engineering," although not in reference to health care but more generally. It is thus a further stage in industrial engineering.

25. This term was coined by the German Hospital Association and is now in common usage. Index figures are general guidelines based on estimated values.

26. See the DKG's reports in Der Krankenhausarzt (1973:434).

27. Projected bed quota

$$= \frac{\text{Frequency of hospitalization} \times \text{Average length} \times \text{Population}}{\text{Average utilization} \times 365}$$

28. The social budget is a governmental review of all social services in the FRG and their finances. It also provides information about social security agencies and their connection to the total economic system.

29. Until now I have dealt with the problems of comparison only from the viewpoint of methodology and functional boundaries (von Beyme 1977, p. 27). Here we encounter a different issue, namely that of the effect of funds, and problems of comparison and demarcation recede into the background.

30. Regulations for this are laid down in paragraphs 17 and 18 of the KHG and in the Federal Per Diem Ordinance of April 25, 1975.

## References

Arbeitsgruppe zur Planung und Beratung von Einrichtungen des Gesundheits-wesens, ed. 1975. "Empfehlung der Deutschen Krankenhausgesellschaft vom 9.9 1974." In Kritische Analyse der Empfehlung der Deutschen Krankenhaus-gesellschaft vom 9. September 1974, vol. 1. Leverkusen.

Bär, A. 1975. "Zur methodischen Gestaltung der Planung des Gesundheits-wesens." In Ausgewahlte Probleme der Ökonomie und Planung des Gesund-heitswesens der DDR, ed. A. Bär et al. Zeitschrift für ärztliche Fortbildung, supplementary vol. 4.

Bauer, K. 1978. "Hospital Rate Setting—This Way to Salvation?" In Hospital Cost Containment: Selected Notes for Future Policy, ed. M. Zubkoff, I. E. Rastein, and R. S. Hanft. New York.

Blum, R. 1977. "Die Problematik systemkonformer Steuerung sozialer Systeme." Zeitschrift für die gesamte Staatswissenschaft 133:128–146.

Buck, H. 1969. Technik der Wirtschaftsplanung in Kommunistischen Staaten, vol. 1. Coburg.

Bundesminister für Arbeit und Sozialordnung. 1978. Sozialbericht. Bonn.

Busch, U., and E. Grotjahn. 1977. "Die Rolle der sozialistischen Verteilungsweise der konsumtionsmittel bei der Verwirklichung der Einheit von Wirtschafts-und Sozialpolitik." Wirtschaftswissenschaft 2.

Eichhorn, S. 1975. Krankenhausbetriebslehre. Stuttgart.

Entwurf eines Gesetzes zur wirtschaftlichen Sicherung der krankenhäuser und zur Regelung der Krankenhauspflegesätze (KHG). Bundestagsdrucksache VI/ 1874. Begründung zum Regierungsentwurf. In Krankenhausfinanzierungsgesetz, ed. Harsdorf and Friedrich, 1975, vol. 1. Cologne.

Feldstein, M. 1977. "Quality Change and the Demand for Hospital Care." Econometrica 45.7:1681–1702.

Grossmann, W., and H. Richau. 1962. Zur Ökonomik des staatlichen Gesundheitswesens in der Deutschen Demokratischen Republik. East Berlin.

Gurtz, J., and H. Heiden. 1977. "Die Finanzierung der staatlichen Einrichtungen des Kulturellsozialen Bereiches." Sozialistische Finanzwirtschaft 10.

Harsdorf, F., ed. 1975. "Regierungsentwurf." In Krankenhausfinanzierungsgesetz, vol. 1. Cologne.

Heiden, H. 1977. "Aufwandsmasstäbe in kulturellensozialen Bereich." Sozialistische Finanzwirtschaft 10.

Jannasch, G. 1970. "Die Struktur und Netzplanung des Gesundheitswesens." In Gesundheitswesen und Ökonomie, ed. W. Schwarz and A. H. Bär. East Berlin.

Keck, A. 1979. "Zur Rolle der Ökonomie des Gesundheitswesens bei der Gestaltung der entwickelten sozialistischen Gesellschaft in der DDR." Wirtschaftswissenschaften 4.

Keck, A., and P. Peuker. 1978. "Ökonomische Gesetze und Gesundheitswesen." Humanitas 9.

Keck, A., and K. Winter. 1975 "Erfordernisse, Bedurfnis und Bedarf im Gesundheitswesen." In Ausgewahlte Probleme der Ökonomie und Planung des Gesundheitswesens der DDR, ed. A. H. Bär et al. Zeitschrift für ärztliche Fortbildung, supplementary vol. 4.

Kiera, H. G. 1975. Partei und Staat im Planungssystem der DDR. Düsseldorf.

Kinze, H. H., H. Knop, and E. Seifert, eds. 1974. Volkswirtschaftsplanung. East Berlin.

Kohlmey, G. 1963. "Planen als Regeln und Steuern." In Probleme der politischen Ökonomie: Deutsche Akademe der Wissenschaften zu Berlin, Jahrbuch des Instituts für Wirtschaftswissenschaften, vol. 11. East Berlin.

König, E., et al. 1978. Das sozialistische Finanzwesen in der DDR. East Berlin.

Kruppa, A. 1976. Wirtschafts- und Bildungsplanung in der DDR. Hamburg.

Leenen, W. R. 1977. Zur Frage der Wachstumsorientierung der Marxistisch-Leninistischen Sozialpolitik in der DDR. Berlin.

Literatur zur Inanspruchnahme und Planung des Gesamtbedarfs in der DDR: Das stationäre und ambulante Gesundheitswesen, vol. 10. 1967.

Mann, H. 1978. "Das Wechselverhälthis von Wert und Gebrauchswert und seine bewusste Ausnutzung mit Hilfe der planmässigen Preisbildung." Wirtschaftswissenschaften 26.1.

Das materielle und kulturelle Lebensniveau des Volkes und seine Volkswirtschaftliche Planung. 1975. East Berlin.

McMahon, J. A., and D. F. Drake. 1978. "The American Hospital Association Perspective." In Hospital Cost Containment: Selected Notes for Future Policy, ed. M. Zubkoff, I. E. Rastein, and R. S. Hanft. New York.

Mecklinger, L., H. Kriewald, and R. Lammel. 1974. Gesundheitsschutz und soziale Betreuung der Bürger. East Berlin.

Ökonomische Gesetze in der entwickelten sozialistischen Gesellschaft. 1975. East Berlin.

Richau, H. 1967. "Die Finanzierung der staatlichen Krankenhauser in der Deutschen Demokratischen Republik auf der Grundlage von Leistungskennziffern." In Das stationäre und ambulante Gesundheitswesen, vol 9. East Berlin.

Richau, H. 1975. "Die aktive Rolle der Finanzen bei der Lösung der Aufgabe im Gesundheitswesen." In Ausgewählte Probleme der Ökonomie und Planung des Gesundheitswesens der DDR. Zeitschrift für ärztliche Fortbildung, supplementary vol. 4.

Schmunk, G., et al. Marxistisch-Leninistische Sozialpolitik. East Berlin.

Schwarz, W. 1963. Zu einigen Problemen der Haushaltswirtschaft in den Krankenhäusern der Deutschen Demokratischen Republik. Dissertation. East Berlin.

Senat von Berlin. 1978. Krankenhausbedarfsplan 1978 für das Land Berlin.

Staritz, D. 1978. "Zum Verhältnis von Planungssystem und Partizipation in der DDR." Deutschland Archiv 11:1049–1070.

Thiemeyer, T. 1975. "Krankenhausfinanzierung." In Aktuelle Probleme der Gesundheitspolitik in der BRD, ed. H. Lampert. Schriften des Vereins der Sozialpolitik.

von Beyme, K. 1977. Sozialismus oder Wohlfahrtsstaat. Munich.

Walther, J. 1967. "Arbeitsstudium als Grundlage für Arbeitskräfte—Kennziffern, dargestellt an Untersuchungen der ärztlichen Tätigkeit." Das stationäre und ambulante Gesundheitswesen 10.

Winter, K. 1974. Das Gesundheitswesen in der Deutschen Demokratischen Republik. East Berlin.

Wörterbuch der Ökonomie Sozialismus. 1973. Berlin.

## Index of Laws

"Anordnung über die Ordnung der Planung der Volkswirtschaft der DDR von 1976–1980." Gesetzblatt der Deutschen Demokratischen Republik, December 15, 1974, reprint 775a.

"Aufgaben und Organisation der Krankenhäuser des staatlichen Gesundheitswesens—Rahmenkrankenhausordnung," November 5, 1954. Gesetzblatt-Zentralblatt der DDR, reprint, 1954.

"Bayrisches Krankenhausgesetz," June 21, 1974. Gesetz- und Verordnungsblatt I.

"Empfehlung zur Gestaltung des Planes der Einrichtungen." Humanitas 8 (1972).

"Gesetz über Ministerrat der DDR," October 16, 1972. Gesetzblatt I.

"Gesetz über den Staatshaushaltsplan 1978," December 21, 1977, paragraphs 2.1 and 2. Gesetzblatt I.37.

"Gesetz über die Eingliederung der Sozialversicherung in den Staatshaushalt."

"Gesetz über die örtlichen Volksvertretungen und ihre Organe in der Deutschen Demokratischen Republik," July 12, 1973. Gesetzblatt I.

"Gesetz zur wirtschaftlichen Sicherung der Krankenhäuser und zur Regelung der Krankenhauspflegesätze (KHG)," June 29, 1972. Bundesgesetzblatt I, Grundgesetz der Bundesrepublik Deutschland.

"Hessisches Krankenhausgesetz," April 4, 1973. Gesetz- und Verordnungsblatt I.

"Krankenhausgesetz des Landes Nordrhein-Westfalen," February 25, 1975. Gesetze und Verordnungen Nordrhein-Westfalens 1975.

"Landesgesetz zur Reform des Krankenhauswesens in Rheinland-Pfalz," June 29, 1973. Gesetzblatt I.

"Landeskrankenhausgesetz Berlin," December 13, 1974. Gesetz- und Verordnungsblatt I.

"Niedersächsisches Gesetz zum Bundesgesetz zur wirtschaftlichen Sicherung der Krankenhäuser und zur Regelung der Krankenhauspflegesätze," July 12, 1973. Niedersächsisches Gesetz- und Verordnungsblatt I.

"Verordnung über die Aufgaben, Rechte, und Pflichten der volkseigenen Betriebe, Kombinate, und VVB," March 28, 1973. Gesetzblatt 1.15 (April 3, 1973).

"Verordnung PR 7154," August 31, 1954. Bundesanzeiger 173 (September 9, 1954).

"Verordnung zur Regelung der Krankenhauspflegesätze (Bundespflegesatzverordnung—BPFIV," April 25, 1973. Bundesgesetzblatt I.

# 10    Ideological Influences on the Organization of Ambulatory and Hospital Care

Paul Ridder

*One of Paul Ridder's conclusions is that both patients and physicians are pawns in the organization of medical care. He finds that physicians in both East and West Germany have increasingly lost individual power to politicians and officials of the state and to officials of professional associations. Patients seem almost peripheral to the decisions about how health care should be organized, decisions based primarily on political values and power relationships. He believes that the professional associations of physicians in the FRG are almost as oligarchical as the government bureaucracy in the GDR, and that the elaborate East German reporting system may actually be superior to the loose, self-interested way in which the West German physicians' associations monitor quality control.*

*Some of Ridder's most trenchant remarks about the West German system speak directly to major issues in American health care today. He notes the almost unnatural relationship between free competition as a basic principle upon which postwar West Germany was built and the success of the medical profession in having itself defined as a noncommercial professional guild that excludes free competition. At the same time, Ridder points out that fierce competition takes place within the medical profession and its protected market.*

*A theme running through Ridder's analysis of the East German system is the dysfunctions of large bureaucracies. Health-care decisions, he thinks, have more to do with hierarchy and status than with patient care. Physicians are put under a great deal of pressure as managers who must meet quotas and work overtime. Ridder claims that physicians are transferred periodically so as not to establish personal bonds with bureaucrats or local officials— the antithesis of the concept of a community physician. Bureaucratic forms and procedures take up a great deal of time, and Ridder believes that organizing outpatient care around polyclinics and ambulatory clinics is more inefficient than organizing it around physicians' practices. He notes that the GDR is superior to the FRG in occupational health, maternal and child care, adolescent care, and preventive medicine; however, he does not believe that this superiority comes from having a central state bureaucracy, because the Netherlands has an even more impressive record in these areas without highly centralized control. Thus, structure follows values about health, autonomy, and the distribution of power, rather than a certain structure being a prerequisite for accomplishing certain goals in health care.*

## The Influence of Ideological System Control (Systemsteuerung) on the Quality of Medical Care

What happens when a nation with one language, history, culture, economy, and political orientation toward health policy is divided into two halves of differing ideological orientation? What are the changes? What remains the same? What influence do alternative ideological stances have on the structure and therefore the effectiveness of ambulatory and hospital medical care? These are the questions that arise in a comparative study of the health systems of the Federal Republic of Germany (FRG; West Germany) and the German Democratic Republic (GDR; East Germany). From the start, a comparison of this type borders on the problem of investigating relationships of a causal nature, for the effect of ideology can be thought of neither in terms of an initial impulse nor as a continuously attendant influence, but rather as a selective paradigm for choosing solutions which coincide with the given ideology. The selection of ideologically consistent structures in the course of historical development,[1] the compatibility of the part with the whole—selectivity and not causality is the principle.

This comparison will attempt to trace from ideal types the development of the specific structures which emerged, and to identify the conditions in the larger context which gave these structures meaning and significance. Thus it will be shown that ideology, power, and organization are reciprocally and interdependently related to one another.

### Ideological Traditions and Political Struggles over Health-Care Policy

The health-care system, along with the rest of Germany, lay in shambles in 1945. Reconstruction followed different paths in the two states which succeeded the German Reich. While the later FRG was able to preserve historical continuity, the later GDR was the scene of an abrupt establishment of a socialist health-care system. This became evident in the changeover of the ruling elite.

Trained cadres returned to the GDR from the Soviet Union and enforced, with clearly political objectives, the basis of a socialist health policy. Communists from the Weimar period, recently released from concentration camps, were victorious in the SED (the Sozialistische Einheitspartei—Socialist Unity Party—the official communist party in the GDR) and took command of leading positions in the health system with their specialists. After the Länder (regional governments) had been dissolved, a clear movement toward centralization began, strengthened by the Stalinism of the cadres after 1950. In the FRG, the military administration also sought German partners; emigrants and recently released concentration-camp prisoners were readily recruited for leading positions. A radical de-Nazification process took place until 1950, with considerable resistance from the physicians' professional organizations. At this time, a Social Democratic period in health administration began. Thus, while the health system in the GDR underwent a clear break with the past, that in the FRG showed more a continuity with the Nazi period than a reconnection to Weimar, as was the case in most areas of West German society. The real bifurcation in the development of health care took place in the years 1945–1950; from this point on, the two health systems developed along different paths.

Nonetheless, some common elements remain. In both states, the same technological, ideological, and political forces underlying the modern welfare state facilitated a trend toward centralization. As a result, the physician in both states was no longer subordinate to the aristocracy or the businessmen, but rather to the politicians—either those in government or those in the professional association. This evolution of the health systems in both states had one of its roots in certain ideological traditions about the role of power, most clearly formulated by Marxism.

Marxism was quick to divest medical care of its philanthropic pretenses, and tried to show that the interests of the individual classes were reflected in health-care policies. Therefore, medical care was to serve the socialist revolution. "The essential criterion of revolutionary or reformist health policy . . . lies in the 'dictatorship of the proletariat.' The issue of power was, is, and will remain the fundamental issue of politics, which includes health policy. Therefore it is inadmissible . . . to equate the problem of political power in a society with the question of whether a health system should be privately or publicly organized and controlled (which is also possible under a bourgeois regime)."[2]

For reasons which are formally similar but different in substance, the physicians' professional organizations in the FRG focused on the question of control over political power as a precondition for any health-policy measure. For this reason, they too propagated political ideology.

Even though the "unity of economic and social policy" necessarily led to the generally totalitarian social policy of the SED in the GDR, the conversion of Marxist values into practical concerns of the health system was never completely successful. While socio-political objectives were transmitted to the lower hierarchical levels, practical necessities, moral principles in the exercise of power, and a humanistically oriented professional ethic of doctors gained increasing importance. Strictly speaking, then, the implementation of ideology must be specified for each level of the social hierarchy. Unfortunately, certain gaps in the data base for each level force me to argue in a conceptual manner primarily on the societal level.

In the FRG, an extended power struggle over the role of the physician in health-care delivery lasted for a long time. The physicians' organizations succeeded in maintaining a division between the public sector, which consists mainly of hospitals, and the private sector, which consists of physicians' private practices. The division was further deepened in 1955 by the Sicherstellungsauftrag (health guarantee mandate), through which the physicians' organizations maintained their monopoly on ambulatory care to the detriment of public, hospital, and occupational health care. Since the mid 1950s, spokesmen for the physicians' organizations have energetically opposed "state medicine" (Staatsmedizin) and have been successful in hindering even moderate reformist health policy in parliament (Manger-Koenig 1975, pp. 433–448). The public health system was deprived of political significance. By contrast, in the GDR the implementation of health policy with regard to the principle of the free choice of physician was enforced by a power struggle. After the health system was nationalized and private practices were eliminated in favor of public polyclinics, a struggle developed among the population, the physicians, and the party machine about the right to choose one's own physician. Finally, however, the establishment of a socialist health system was completed by unifying hospital and ambulatory treatment as a first step toward a centralized national bureaucracy, with the help of which the SED secured its leading role as the one state party.

The development of the health system in the two German states since 1945 has been oriented toward a medical concept of health and illness and toward societal and political traditions. While the dependence of the general practitioner in the FRG on the pharmaceutical industry, on the association of sickness-fund physicians, and on other professional organizations increased, a similar process of the "proletarization" of the physician took place in the GDR in 1945. The trend toward centralization which dominated the health systems in both states seems to have benefited the professional bureaucracy in the FRG and the state bureaucracy in the GDR. Thus, it is unclear which system actually benefits the patient more, because in both Germanies the patient is the victim of power politics.

## Norms and Principles of Control of Social Roles in the Health System

The specific power structures of the health systems were the historical products of the development of power processes (Ridder 1978), that resulted in two initially diametrically opposed systems. If we compare individual subsystems, it is not enough to ascertain that in one state the economy is controlled by the private sector and in the other by the state; that in one state we find autonomous citizens and in the other authoritatively controlled citizens. The decisive questions are: What functions do these components perform in the larger picture? What systems of achievement incentives and controls do they establish? What health and sickness behavior does the individual exhibit as a result? And one question in particular always arises: To what extent have the two states succeeded in creating overall political structures which conform to their ideological self-concepts? Numerous shortcomings of both systems indicate that the systems which have been realized diverge from the conceptualized political structures in essential points.

The Differentiation and Integration of Social Roles in Politics, Economics, and Medicine

The main evolutionary difference between the two systems is the degree of autonomy between the social subsystems of medicine and economics. While physicians and therapists in other societies can alternate between a political and a professional role depending upon political conditions, the medical profession in the GDR has lost its political role.[3] East German physicians have no choice but to conform to a prescribed political role. In addition, the personal relationship of confidence between patient and physician was undermined by the elimination of patient-physician confidentiality. Moreover, the collectivistic integration of social roles also means that health policy can be used to expand the labor force (Nottrott 1975, p. 50).[3] Just as in the FRG, although with different motivations and to a much greater degree, medical care is essentially based on the principle of getting the labor force back to work and ensuring a smooth production process (Beyme 1977, p. 40; Peterhoff 1977, p. 319).[4] The objective of health policy in the GDR is, however, not health but the revolutionary struggle (Büttner and Meyer 1975); the concern over political power in the society takes precedence over economic questions.[5] It is only within a framework of political power objectives that the health system should "increase its services and effectiveness through better quality . . . in order to improve medical care" (Franz 1976, p. 9; cf. Gurtler and Rothe, pp. 76–83).

Against the background of these presuppositions, abstract values have been transformed into concrete organizational structures. Values and norms function as mechanisms for system control to the extent that the state or the profession is oriented toward them. Thus the choice between instrumental norms (such as efficiency) and basic norms (politically motivated axioms with no regard for their consequences) has consequences for the decrease or increase of deviations from a systems equivalence, such as cost explosion. In this sense, the Principles of Health Protection (Prinzipien des Gesundheitsschützes) create a relationship between ideology and the structure of medical care: "the state character, the primacy of prevention, the active participation of the whole population in the implementation and development of health protection, and the founding of a central health administration" (Winter 1974, p. 16).

State vs. Private Medical Care

If health policy issues are to a special degree the object of class struggle, then differences due to social strata and a class-specific morbidity and mortality rate must be done away with, "profiteering from sickness" must be eliminated, and free access to treatment must be provided (Hutter 1974, pp. 1032–1037). The state character of ambulatory and hospital care in the GDR is demonstrated by the overwhelming number of institutions which are state property. Of a total of 29,275 physicians in 1973, only 5.7 percent had private practices (Ludz and Kuppe 1975, p. 380). In the FRG, on the other hand, the state is more concerned with protecting and financing the health system. The ratio of privately practicing to public physicians has nevertheless changed drastically since 1960; since 1971, physicians with private practices make up less than 50 percent of the total number of physicians.

## Curative and Preventive Medicine

Total health protection for the whole society and the primary importance of prevention, which corresponds to a collectivized health concept, have arisen from the premises of socialist health policy. The clinician proceeds from the individual case to the pertinent group and is supposed to arrive at an analysis of the social environment from the sum of individual cases. The social hygienist proceeds in the opposite direction: he analyzes the environment and is supposed to proceed from this to the group and finally to the effect on the individual. Health and sickness are interpreted as collective phenomena of public responsibility in the GDR.[6] In the FRG, on the other hand, an individualization of collective causation is postulated; medicine is oriented mainly toward an individualistic-mechanistic concept of sickness, which results in the preponderance of curative medicine.[7] Therefore, the strengths of the two systems are distributed accordingly between curative and preventive medicine.

## Individual Patient Initiative vs. Control of the Masses

Health protection in the GDR, according to the constitution, is not a private matter of the individual citizen, but rather a state and social responsibility, which includes, first and foremost, the implementation of health policy. Active and preventive health care is intended to make the patient's individual initiative superfluous—the state, and not the patient, is to decide when the patient should receive medical attention.[8] The granting of social honors, participation in commissions and mass movements, and (not least) extensive propaganda to stimulate "socialist mass initiatives," which are supposed to guarantee a broad development of worker initiatives for realizing the plans, serve as a means of mass manipulation (Gesetzblatt der DDR, 1975, pp. 673 ff.).

In the FRG, on the other hand, the health system does without mass motivation. The motivation for seeking treatment is left to the individual responsibility of the patient, after the means for his medical care have been made available to him. "In order for the health-policy goal to be attained, the affected person must himself actively cooperate, insofar as this can be demanded of him. This cooperation must be made possible and easy for each individual according to his personal situation." (Jahn et al. 1977, p. 10)

Self-Administration vs. State Administration

A direct link between monopolistic party politics and health policy exists on all levels of the state hierarchy in the GDR. There is no division of politics and administration in the Western sense. The state bureaucracy (for example, the Ministry of Health as a part of it) only implements decisions authorized by the Politburo of the SED, as the highest source of authority, according to the central plan. More important than considerations of professional knowledge and professional medical work is the ideological demand of communism. The blurring of the lines between politics and administration is clearly shown by the position of the East German Kreisarzt (District Medical Officer) in comparison with that of the West German Amtsarzt (Public Health Officer) (Brunn 1972, pp. 675–687). The Kreisarzt is the "boss" of all establishments and personnel of the health system of his Kreis (equivalent to an English country district) and must be an elected member of the Kreis council. Only as a member of the council can he become the director of the Kreis Department of Health. Four assistant district medical officers are available to him for help with his responsibilities in public health: social hygiene, administrative organization, economics, and industrial hygiene. "Thanks to the delegation of responsibilities, the Kreisarzt has plenty of time to perform the political duties of his position." (Brunn 1972, p. 678)

In the FRG, on the other hand, an autonomous and competitive process of decision-making follows the rules of parliamentary democracy. The health system is oriented toward self-administration, decentralization of organizational structure, horizontal coordination of social service institutions, and citizen mobilization through participation in socio-political decisions. The extent to which these principles have been realized is still the subject of public debate between the medical profession and the public on the efficiency and quality of the health system and the rights of the patient in it (Ferber et al. 1977).

In conclusion, from one origin have emerged different structures of ambulatory and hospital care in the two states which succeeded the German Reich. In the FRG, the activity of the state is for the most part limited to providing a legal and financial frame of reference, whereas the GDR has succeeded in establishing centralized control and planning of the health system.

## Mechanisms of Social Control over the Quality of Ambulatory and Hospital Care

Service Institutions and Distributions of Power

In both states we observe a public responsibility for the implementation of quality control to ensure compliance with quality standards of medical care. In the FRG the medical profession is charged with this responsibility; in the GDR medical care is controlled by the Communist Party. In marginal cases, the power orientation of the service institutions outweighs medical and professional considerations.

The organization of health care in the GDR is one subsection of the complete national planning, the direction of which takes place through one-year plans. Consequently, the central authority depends on optimal feedback from service institutions in the field. This feedback is supposed to be provided by organizations that are structured according to the principle of "democratic centralism," i.e. those at whom medical services are directed. The lower levels of the state hierarchy (Bezirke, Kreise, and Gemeinden—which correspond roughly to states, counties, and municipalities) are supposed to design the organization of health care by themselves within a higher framework of centrally defined conditions. Initiatives that support the central program are cultivated; independent actions that run contrary to the plan are crushed.[9] In 1973, the Gesetz über die ortlichen Volksvertretungen) (Law for Regional Representation) regulated the responsibility of the regional authorities. "Medical care in the GDR is organized according to the territorial structure of the economic administration. All medical service institutions are under the jurisdiction of the respective territorial authority. The territorial unit for primary medical care is the Kreis [county]." (Stauder 1978, p. 90) Differentiated medical care for special treatment of less common diseases, however, takes place on the Bezirk (state) level and in university clinics. It is only at this level that highly sophisticated, internationally comparable medical services are provided.

The concrete realization of health policy is expressed in the specific details of the health plan that are subject to financial and administrative control: quantified goals, refinement of health indicators, measures of the degree to which the numerical indicators have to be realized, and specifications for the individual levels of the administrative hierarchy. These directives include regulations which preserve a certain amount of freedom for decision-making by the regional authority while fulfilling the prescribed responsibilities. This gives the unwieldy system at least a certain amount of flexibility. In cases in which the formally established system does not work, corruption, which has a useful compensatory function, takes over.[10] The boundaries of this system are defined by the "double subordination" of the regional councils (Bezirk, Kreis, Gemeinde) and their specialized authorities. "The legal draft which stipulates a double subordination gives the higher-ranking professional authorities the right of enforcement and ensures a uniform implementation of state policies." (Stauder 1978, p. 78) It is supposed to make the health bureaucracy more flexible without endangering the power monopoly of the SED.

Since the Grundgesetz (constitution) of 1949, legislators in the FRG have oriented themselves toward a "model of the Social Welfare State" whose socio-political principle is not direct control but rather, at most, the exercise of influence through indirect measures such as state subsidies in order to orient private interests toward public needs (Hardwick 1973, pp. 183–201).[11] The liberality of this principle grants a multitude of interests a wide range of activity.[12] However, the characteristics of a free market are considerably altered by the emergence of professional monopolies. In view of the oligarchic power of the medical profession, even the formation of a contrary opinion is difficult.

The professional physicians' organizations succeeded in having laws passed that defined their profession as "noncommercial" and thus a professional guild. It was postulated that the physician does not simply belong to a business but, as a professional, incorporates central values of Western civilization and guards the central values of free ("capitalist") society. Thus legitimated, the professional should also be granted sovereign functions. The physicians' conception of the state is oriented toward reputedly conservative, even reactionary ideas. They poorly embody an orientation toward the liberal market system, with which they live in an asymmetrical symbiosis. There is competition and power struggle between ambulatory and hospital care and between general physicians and specialists, and there is fear of an "oversupply" of doctors. The profession justifies itself by reference to the "special achievements" of the profession and implies elitism and the right to special privileges (Lüth 1973, p. 371). The main ideas of organizing health services through a sickness fund are self-administration, legislated health insurance (Gesetzliche Krankenversicherung), the free exercise of the profession, a proposed noncommercial orientation, and the health guarantee mandate for ambulatory care (Sicherstellungsauftrag); these principles fit into the model of a market economy run by organized professional power without living up to its central economic or social idea. Free competition is a principle which otherwise serves as the foundation of social order in the FRG. Only very recently have market-economy principles begun to assert themselves through the increased competition among physicians and the obstruction of monopolies.

The health system in the FRG is decentralized, according to the principle of self-administration. "The responsibilities for health and work protection are divided in the Federal Republic; companies, free professional associations, institutions of social security, the medical profession, the governments of the Länder, and the federal government work together to ensure health." (Bundesministerium für innerdeutsche Beziehungen 1974) The system is dependent on the citizen's individual responsibility and cooperation, the self-administration of the institutions, and the conflict of interests among patients, social security agencies, and physicians for structuring health policy. Cooperation is made possible through the organizational structure of the institutions of self-administration, which, in the case of the sickness funds, have a double function: On the one hand they dispose of public power in their own right, and on the other they represent the socio-political interests of the consumer. "The sickness fund is an organization of medical laymen for the articulation of the needs of its insured members and their families. It disposes of quasi-public powers to achieve its tasks. Compared with the more professionally organized interests of the physicians, the other professions, and the institutions that deliver health care, the self-administrated sickness funds have an important mediating and balancing function for social policy." (Ferber 1977, p. 525)

The organization of the medical profession in the FRG is divided into associations of sickness-fund physicians (Kassenärztliche Verein-igungen), physicians' professional associations (Ärztekammern), and independent professional associations (freie Verbände) which serve the function of influencing public government. The associations of sickness-fund physicians are semi-public bodies (Körperschaften des öffentlichen Rechts) and are therefore themselves a part of the state public administration. From the viewpoint of the state they provide semi-public administration; from the members' point of view they function to articulate group interests. On the one hand they represent the interests of the sickness-fund physicians; on the other, they represent the interests of the sickness funds, that is, of the social system itself. A similar double function is served by the Ärztekammern; they are supposed to represent the physicians' interests and at the same time carry out supervisory functions and exercise disciplinary jurisdiction over the practicing physicians. The resulting conflict between representing members' interests and disciplining them is "solved" by specializing in interest politics. Up until now there has not been as sharp an increase in malpractice suits in the FRG as in the United States. Inasmuch as the Ärztekammern functions as an interest group, it is supported by the freie Verbande, which must actively recruit members. These independent professional associations usually remain within the general lines of the mandatory Ärztekammern. Frequently, high-ranking leaders of these professional organizations hold positions in more than one of the medical professional organizations. Their only indirect relationship to the state secures advantages for both sides in obtaining their objectives; both the state and the physicians' associations see every reason to resist energetically any incorporation of the medical profession into the state bureaucracy (Lüth 1973, p. 371).

The decision-making process within these organizations takes place within an oligarchy, a fact criticized by some members without much success. The establishment of oligarchies always leads to conflicts between organizational leaders and the base membership, and furthermore to conservatism.[13] The tendency toward inertia, inherent in an oligarchy, seems to prevent overdue reforms and in this way perpetuates poor quality (Deppe et al. 1977). Ironically, the tendency toward oligarchy within professional associations in the FRG thus leads to similar effects as the centralization of state bureaucracy in the GDR.

The principle of self-administration should make openness and flexibility in the further development of the health system possible. It can be tied to a more equal distribution of influence and initiative, if it is not blocked by a political monopoly. Because of the caste orientation of the physicians' professional organizations (especially the Sicherstellungsauftrag), the power distribution in the West German health system has perverted the liberal market-economy model. A pluralistic distribution of power exists only in a limited sense. In fact, there are considerable distortions in the structure of political competition, which functions, at best, only in the limited area of the political elite in the highest echelons of the state. The structure of medical care is mainly the result of the actions of this elite, through its ideological direction by bureaucrats in the state and the profession.

Indirect Incentives and Direct Controls in Health-Care Delivery

In the past, physicians were not only responsible for health care; by political means they also influenced health-care institutions and the quality of care. The low visibility of doctor's performance to lay evaluation and the indispensability and autonomy of the profession mean it is highly resistant to any state system of quality control.

In the GDR, one extensively used control mechanism is the value commitment (Wertbindung) involved in the ideal of the "political physician." Politicization and ideological pressure, along with the prohibition of physicians' professional organizations, are meant to help consolidate the SED's claim to power against opposition from a medical professional ethic. "The party bureaucrats exploit the Hippocratic Oath for their own socio-political objectives." "Only a good Socialist can be a good physician." "Medical students may receive their M.D. or qualify as specialists only after they have completed an intensive ideological training and have demonstrated adequate knowledge of Marxist ideology." (*Frankfurter Allgemeine Zeitung*, August 1, 1977, p. 2) In addition, it is mainly children from workers' and peasants' families who are recruited for medical school.[14]

In 1963, an attempt to supplement the social control of direct administrative regulations with indirect control through monetary incentives began in the GDR. (It was called a "system of economic leverage.") The so-called scientific organization of work in the health system (wissenschaftliche Arbeitsorganisation im Gesundheitssystem) was based on a Tayloristic description of the workplace (standardization, classification, and stimulation of the work process) (Walther, Neukirch, and Schiddel 1974; Tornar 1974). A system of premiums was supposed to motivate compliance with norms and fulfillment of the plans. The work behavior in the hospital was clearly characterized by norms and plans. Because of the limited bed capacity, physicians and nursing staff received a "performance salary" (Leistungslohn), which increased in an inverse proportion to the length of the patient's hospital stay.

In both German states, then, achievement motivation is used and activated through appropriate stimuli, such as economic incentives,[15] as well as symbolic incentives such as social prestige,[16] professional reputation, and public praise or criticism.[17] But while the control of interests in the FRG is carried out by the interest groups themselves, a system of political control by the state exists in the GDR.

Formally, quality control for medical care in the FRG is under the jurisdiction of public health authorities. In fact, however, it is under the control of the profession itself. The sickness-fund physicians' association (Kassenärztliche Vereinigung) holds the monopoly on disciplinary action, which above all neutralizes the possible influence or claim of the sickness funds; that is, the sickness funds must finance medical services without having the authority to exercise control. Thus, the physician is monitored by no neutral authority other than his professional organization, which, at the same time, represents his interests. Only recently has a quality control which systematically combines the specialties been introduced into surgery, emergency medicine, and gynecology (*Münchener Medizinische Wochenschrift*, 1977, pp. 569–600).

Control of Health Behavior

Distinct differences between the GDR and the FRG are also apparent in the mechanisms for the control of the patient's health behavior. In contrast with the authoritarian control in the GDR, there is confidence in the individual's responsibility to utilize the available services in the FRG. Illustrative is the repeated and therefore effective registration of the individual patient by overlapping institutions of the socialist health system; payment of premiums for good health behavior (for example during pregnancy) is made in installments and in each case always after an exhaustive examination. Thanks to financial incentives and considerable encroachment on individual freedom of choice, the GDR has been extremely successful in implementing medical prevention. A glance at the inoculation calendar (table 1) illustrates the differences (Brunn 1972, pp. 688 ff.).

**Table 1**
Inoculation schedule for the GDR and the FRG.

| Age | GDR[a] | FRG[b] |
|---|---|---|
| Week 1 | BCG | BCG |
| After month 2 | | |
| (1st year) | Oral polio I, II, III | |
| Month 3 | 1. DPT | 1. DPTM |
| Month 4 | 2. DPT | 2. DPTM |
| Month 5 | 3. DPT | 3. DPTM |
| Months 6–7 | | Oral polio I, II |
| Month 9 | Measles | |
| 1st year | Smallpox | Smallpox |
| | Polio booster I | Oral polio III |
| 3rd year | 4. DPT | |
| 5th year | 5. DPT | Voluntary BDG booster |
| 6th year | Possible BCG booster | DPT booster |
| 8th year | Polio booster II | |
| 9th year | Smallpox | |
| 10th year | | Polio booster I |
| 11th year | 6. DT | |
| 12th year | Possible BCG booster | Smallpox |
| 16th year | Smallpox | T booster |
| | T booster | |
| 18th year | Possible BCG booster | |

a. All inoculations are compulsory.
b. All inoculations are recommended.

## Consequences of Social Structure for Hospital Care

### General Development

Since the 1950s, state administration in the GDR and self-administration in the FRG have characterized the two systems and shaped the way they solve problems. Nevertheless, experts agree that the principal differences between the two systems are not in the hospital sector.

The [GDR's] hospital system does not differ substantially from that of the Federal Republic. At the beginning of 1974, there were 588 hospitals with ca. 185,000 beds, that is, 108 beds per 100,000 inhabitants. (Federal Republic: 108/100,000.) However, there are some differences. Only 98 hospitals, with a total of 13,130 beds, are still in the hands of churches or "other private owners." In 1950, there were 299 hospitals with 19,429 beds. Of these, seven were psychiatric institutions. (Ludz and Kuppe 1975, p. 375)

In the FRG (with 54.1 percent of all beds in 1974) the number of public and nonprofit hospitals (with 35.5 percent of all beds in 1974) is decreasing, while the number of private institutions (with 10.5 percent of all beds in 1974) is increasing continuously. (*Daten des Gesundheitswesens* 1977, p. 239)

The average number of beds in a hospital is high: 315 in the GDR compared with 195 in the Federal Republic. Barely half of all hospitals in the GDR have fewer than 200 beds (FRG: 70 percent), and almost 20 percent have more than 500 beds (FRG: 7.2 percent). A "process of concentrating" beds in the larger hospitals will be carried out systematically, according to plan. Differentiation into departments of specialization is the rule; hospital beds not organized according to specialized fields make up only 5 percent of the total (3.4 percent in the Federal Republic). The main fields of internal medicine, surgery, gynecology, and pediatrics take up 60 percent of all hospital beds (62 percent in the Federal Republic), and psychiatry, 18.2 percent (Federal Republic: 16.4 percent). In every Kreis and Bezirk, a Kreis- or Bezirk hospital is designated to fulfill duties of a "leading institution" in relation to the other hospitals of the area. In their functions for health-care delivery, however (compared with the Federal Republic), Kreis hospitals provide secondary health care, whereas the Bezirk hospital provides tertiary health care. About 10 percent of the available hospital beds in the GDR are part of medical school clinics and scientific institutes (Federal Republic: 6 percent). The level of equipment in the smaller and middle-size hospitals is only slowly approaching the standard of institutions with comparable functions in Western industrial nations. However, the Zentralversorgung-hospitals (tertiary care) are only somewhat behind the Western nations in their medical-technical equipment; and medical school clinics are almost on a par with those in the West. This is now also the case for the highly technical fields of diagnosis and therapy. (Ludz and Kuppe 1975)

The division of hospital care into city, Kreis, and Bezirk administration is correlated in the GDR with the number of departments of specialization in each type of hospital. Hierarchy, territorial subdivisions, and subdivisions according to function—whether primary care, specialized care, or highly specialized care—are coordinated with each other. As in the FRG, regional inequalities in medical care also exist in the GDR. These can be explained by state health policy. The planning bureaucracy has divided health-care resources with an emphasis on the industrial regions, so that rural areas of the GDR are relatively undersupplied (Stauder 1978, pp. 98 ff.). Specially privileged hospitals and wards exist for members of the government and party bureaucrats. The average hospital stay in the GDR in 1970 was 23.3 days (FRG: 24.3).

## Authority Structure in the Hospital

The power structure of the health system reveals itself clearly in the day-to-day situation of the hospital, in the ranking order of social values, in the styles of management, in status differentiation, in the level of information, and in psycho-social stress. Empirical studies of the authority structure in East German hospitals have become public only in brief verbal reports. They impressively demonstrate the influence of the societal power structure on the organizational structure of the hospital. In a representative study which examined the workplace characteristics of supervising personnel [Stationsarzt (ward physician), clinic director, Kreis physician], Wiesenhutter (1976) found that the type and extent of demands made on a director varied greatly according to his position within the hierarchy. A factor analysis revealed a strong emphasis on bureaucratic relations rather than a focus on patients and their care. This study supported another (by K. Schneider) which found that hospital personnel in the GDR claimed to value patient communication highly but did not act on their conviction.

Few good studies have been done in either German state on the inner structure of hospitals, but from the data available it appears that relations are hierarchical and authoritarian. Nurses in the FRG and the GDR both claim that these qualities pervade their work experience (Freyberger, Porschek, and Haan 1972; Bohm et al. 1971; Proschild 1976, pp. 37–44). Other studies have found an authoritarian managerial style and large information gaps by status. In patient care, however, the differentiation between physicians and nurses is decreasing.

## Psycho-Social Consequences

Wiesenhutter (1976, pp. 79–95), writing on the correlation between managerial function and psycho-social stress, states that psychic strains increase with hierarchical status: "The greatest consequences of psychological strain are to be found in the Kreis physician. The socialist system burdens the individual with its contradictions, which must then be resolved individually, sometimes with pathological results." In a factor analysis, Proschild (1976, p. 37) concluded: "One has to admit that supervising physicians are subject to considerable time pressure, indicated by, among other things, an increase in overtime. The causes for this are to be found in administrative structures and in the obligation to participate in state and societal activities. . . ."

In the GDR, the arbitrary transfer of personnel and an authoritarian supervisory style leads to characteristic results. "Every two or three years . . . there is a reorganization or restructuring of the health system. . . . The main reason for the periodic transfers is indeed to ensure that the physicians be kept in a state of anxiety. . . . insecurity must prevail." The physician should never "warm up" to a place, and "should never become well-acquainted with his patients." The physician "must be afraid of the authorities. . . . Friendship or a warm partnership between the physician and the directors of the polyclinic should never develop. In such a case, the arbitrary directives given daily . . . would not be carried out." (*Deutsches Ärzteblatt* 1974, p. 1577) The system leads to unconditional bureaucratic control in the interest of power politics, and to a fundamentally disturbed, anxiety-ridden relationship between patient and physician (ibid., p. 1650). Unfortunately, comparable data on the psycho-social effects of the management style in West German hospitals were not available when this chapter was written.

## The Dependence of Ambulatory Care on the Social Structure

### Development of Medical Care

There is a considerable difference between a medical system which is run by the state and one which is run by the medical profession. This difference becomes most evident in the ambulatory sector of the health system, although the increasing importance of hospital care is evident in both German states. First, a state-run system has proportionately fewer physicians. In 1960, the physician/population ratio was 1/1,181 in the GDR and 1/703 in the FRG. By 1973, the respective ratios were 1/580 and 1/482 (Bundesministerium für innerdeutsche Beziehungen 1974, p. 33). In 1975, approximately 28,500 physicians were working in the entire outpatient field, and about 1,765 physicians still had individual practices. "One must concede that these 6 percent of the physicians perform 35 percent of the outpatient services." (Bourmer 1974)

On the other hand, there were in the FRG (on the reference day of the census on January 19, 1978) a total of 144,336 physicians, a figure which emerges from statistics based on material from state medical committees. Of these, 43 percent work chiefly in hospitals, 38.1 percent work in private practice, 6.9 percent work in research, administration, and other related activities, and 12.9 percent do not practice medicine. In 1974 there was one active physician for every 482 inhabitants of the FRG. Recomputing this according to the main groupings of the physicians, however, shows that there was only one practicing physician for every 2,261 inhabitants, one practicing specialist for every 2,192 inhabitants, and one hospital physician for every 986 inhabitants (*Frankfurter Allgemeine Zeitung*, August 26, 1977). Not all of these physicians in the FRG practice only ambulatory care, because the health-care system strictly separates ambulatory practice from hospital practice. Thus, 90 percent of the West Germans are potential patients of the ambulatory private physicians. This constitutes a third difference from East Germany's effort to concentrate on ambulatory services and to "increase collective work in medical services" (Harych and Riedel 1974). Even the physicians' practices run by the state are to serve only as a transitional solution in the progress toward total care through polyclinics and ambulatory clinics. Concentrating medical institutions implies huge administrative bureaucracies. "The cost of labor is not decreased, but increased. The physician who has immediate contact with the patient is further burdened by unnecessary demands on his time as a result of meeting and reports, instead of allowing him more time for his patient: bureaucratic harassment, unnecessary intermediate structures, illegitimate dependencies, and the lack of coordination prevent improvements." (Muller-Dietz 1975, p. 126)

The organization of ambulatory care began in the GDR with the forming of a national health-care system in 1947. Polyclinics and ambulatory-care clinics were established on the municipal and Land levels. State-administered medical and dental practices were added after 1956. In addition, small rural hospitals have Ambulanzen, or outpatient clinics, which are run by the hospital physicians. Gemeinde-Schwesternstationen (visiting nurses' associations) regularly work with ambulatory clinics and state-owned medical practices; if possible, they— along with the midwives—are housed in the same building. According to present standards, a polyclinic should have at least five areas of specialization, a dental practice, facilities for physical therapy, and a pharmacy. An ambulatory clinic must have at least two areas of specialization (general medicine and pediatrics) and one dental practice. Specialists in other areas from the polyclinic regularly hold consultation hours in the ambulatory clinic. Polyclinics and ambulatory clinics are expected to work according to the "Dispensaire Principle": In each Kreis or Bezirk, one polyclinic is made into a "management center" for that territorial subsystem of ambulatory care, to which all other establishments of this sector are subordinated.

Part of the national plan was to have catchment areas in which there was no choice of physician. However, citizens resisted this idea, and in 1973 the free choice of physicians for primary care was granted except for specialty care, ambulatory clinics, polyclinics and hospitals. These have Bereichsarztgleiderung, or catchment areas with no free choice of physician, and their geographic size varies with population density. The presence of medical and dental practices taken over by the state also increases their size.

The national figures for this system as of 1974 were 296 polyclinics (not including industrial or university polyclinics), 150 of which were administratively associated with a hospital; 612 municipal and rural ambulatory clinics, 55 of them associated with hospitals; 989 Ambulanzen; 1,536 state-owned medical practices; and 859 dental practices. Assigned to these were 4,957 Gemeinde-Schwesternstationen, 223 of them still affiliated with the church. This ratio is up from 1950, when it was 2,620:944 (Ludz and Kupper 1975, p. 376). In 1975, patient consultation in the state ambulatory-clinic system of the GDR was divided as follows (*Statistiches Jahrbuch der DDR*, 1976, p. 379):

Polyclinics 16.6%

Ambulatory clinics 22.7%

State-owned medical practices 16.6%

Medical first-aid stations 4.9%

The network of ambulatory care in the FRG is diametrically opposed to this; it is based on the principle of professional freedom in the individual medical practice, which is the model of the physicians and their professional associations. Some of the physicians (4.3 percent) have joined together to form group practices (Gemeinschaftspraxen) or equipment collectives (Apparatengemeinschaften), or to share a larger building while maintaining their individual practices (Wirtzbach 1974, p. 1334). Even though the system strictly separates ambulatory care from hospital care, all the physicians (those reaching for ambulatory care included) get nearly all their training in hospitals.

Competition between Hospitals and General Practice

Competition between hospital and ambulatory care in the GDR can be described as follows. In order to lower costs, the hospital has been increasingly specialized to serve its actual function—making differential diagnoses and treating complicated illnesses. Since 1965, the number of beds has therefore been sinking by 1,500–4,000 beds yearly, and the expansion of the ambulatory sector has enjoyed absolute priority. The primary function of the specialist for general medicine is to refer patients to the clinic (Niehoff 1978, pp. 1144–1247). Redirection of effort toward prevention, which is chiefly a service of the Ambulanz, reduces the demand for and the costs of the hospitals (Stauder 1978, p. 100). Up until the beginning of the 1970s there was a tug-of-war regarding the free choice of physician between politicians and the public. "The state, the bureaucratic machinery, the leaders, the functionaries press the outpatient clinics ever again into the foreground, while the public turns again and again back to the freely chosen physician (legally or illegally), and the bureaucratic machinery must yield all over again and accept the general trend, openly or in silence." (*Deutsches Ärzteblatt*, 1974, p. 1647) At the end of this power struggle in 1973, free choice of physician to the fullest extent was restored.

Medical competition in the FRG exists under very different conditions. The so-called Sicherstellungsauftrag gives the sickness-fund physicians in ambulatory care the sole responsibility for medical care. The physicians with private practices (who comprise less than 50 percent of the total) not only hold the monopoly on care, but they try to keep the patient from medical specialists, most of whom are based in hospitals; even private contact between hospital and ambulatory physicians is rare (Paul and Stirn 1977, p. 203). The flow of information between the physician's practice and the clinic is insufficient.

## Coordination of Ambulatory and Hospital Care

It is generally accepted that the cooperation of the originally divided ambulatory and hospital sectors is essentially determined by the quality and costs of medical care. This cooperation takes place in the GDR by means of a politically motivated centralization, and in the FRG by means of a financially motivated referral system. This referral system operates in three ways: through simple referral from the ambulatory to the hospital sector; through the Belegarzt system, by which an ambulatory physician remains in charge of his treatment in the hospital; and through the Chefarzt system, by which the chief of a medical department has the right to treat private patients as though he were a privately practicing physician. Thus, the ambulatory sector has a grip on the hospital, but the hospital physician's cannot (except for medical directors) share in ambulatory care. Both the East and West German systems display noticeable shortcomings in their attempts to integrate medical services.

In the GDR in 1968, 83.8 percent of all recorded cases treated in the hospital were referred from ambulatory institutions; 57 percent of these were from outpatient departments of the hospitals (Wilken et al. 1974, p. 236). The centralized structure of the health system in the GDR is supposed to create cooperation in organization and treatment, but because of the relative autonomy of institutions the actual relationships in no way correspond to this ideal (Brauner 1974; Lengwinat 1971; Wehrmeister et al. 1974; Wilken et al. 1974; Sladzyck 1973; Pritzel 1976; Unger 1970; Bourmer 1974). Specialist care is concentrated entirely in ambulatory clinics, and cooperation between hospitals on the Kreis level and the ambulatory clinics can hardly be termed satisfactory, let alone optimal (Bourmer 1974, p. 1056; see also Kaser 1976, pp. 147 ff.).

On the other hand, the institutionally regulated division of labor in the FRG is based not on definitions of health problems but on professional specialization. It serves primarily to maintain general practice, and it accepts the malfunctionings implied in the strict division between the ambulatory and hospital sectors. The most important element unifying the two systems is the referral network.

According to empirical studies by Hummel et al. (1968), three-quarters of all specialists receive patients through referrals by colleagues. According to an analysis of referrals by general practitioners in North Württemberg by Haussler (1968), the general practitioner refers only 11 percent of his patients; he himself treats 89 percent. Of the 11 percent who are referred, 85 percent are treated by established specialists, and 15 percent are admitted to hospitals (Haerter 1972). All in all, the structure of the referral network reflects the informal status hierarchy among physicians more than it does strictly medical considerations.

A further link between the ambulatory and hospital sectors in the FRG is the Belegarzt system, described above. The hospitals have established large practices which they rent to independent specialists or general practitioners. In these "ambulatories," the Belegärzte are able to exercise their profession freely. If a hospital stay proves necessary for one of their patients, they are admitted to the hospital and receive further treatment from the same physician. This way he can use the technology of the hospital and not lose control of his patients once in the hospital.[18]

The division between the ambulatory and hospital sectors in the FRG makes possible a power monopoly of the physicians with private practices, because they control referrals. In the GDR, the cooperation between the two sectors is enforced by a centralized political party. The organization of medical care in both systems seems to use the patient as an instrument of power politics.

## Extent of Centralization and Quality of Care

### Evaluation

Implementing political ideology in health care depends on the organization of power and shapes the "output" and "input" by which services are evaluated. "Output" includes the medical care of the population and the working conditions of medical personnel. As "input," the delivery of services demands an institutional framework for service delivery (i.e. an organization); material, supplies, and equipment; the number and qualifications of personnel; and availability of scientific and medical information.

According to reports from refugees who are physicians and occasional proposals for improvement in the GDR, although the number of persons employed in health care in the GDR seems to be much higher than that in the FRG, the level of scientific and medical information available is considerably lower, and the state of material supplies and equipment receives a great deal of criticism. In the FRG, on the other hand, the fee schedule for the sickness-fund physicians has promoted technical equipment to such an extent that "apparatus medicine" is criticized from all sides. The high level of technical equipment in the FRG seems to be more effective in curative medicine, while the GDR achieves its successes primarily in preventive measures. The choice between the dominance of curative medicine and preventive medicine stems from differences in political values and in health-care models. Relevant statistics on evaluation are not available, however, so the only evaluative criterion that will be considered is that of the organizational structure.

### Underlying Principles

The results of health care can be compared qualitatively. In the areas of prevention, occupational health, and the care of mothers, children, and adolescents, the GDR is certainly superior to the FRG. If one investigates the principle of system control that could be responsible for these differences, one discovers in the last analysis that the firm control of the population's health behavior is the prerequisite for the effectiveness of prevention, which is responsible for the high health standard of the population in the GDR. But is a centralized state bureaucracy necessary for implementing this control? A third comparison with the Netherlands, which has a much higher health standard than either the GDR or the FRG, shows that a high degree of centralization does not seem to be necessary at all.

The Dutch health system is not centrally organized. Planning decisions are not publicly controlled. Hospital administration is in the hands of qualified managers, not administrative civil servants. Cooperation between the ambulatory and hospital sectors is brought about through a Belegarzt system. Because of the Belegarzt system, the patient's illness behavior is organized relatively early in his career as a patient, long before he reaches the hospital sector. The Dutch health system shows that the difference between centralization and decentralization contributes less to an explanation of variance than does the structuring of patient careers.

In an international comparison, Weissbenbock (1974) arrives at the conclusion that a decentralized system leads to greater technical and economic efficiency in hospital services than does centralized control. A clear link between the degree of centralization and the health standard has not yet been empirically established, and on the basis of our knowledge of social organization it cannot be expected in the future. The preference for a centralized health system is therefore historically explicable in terms of ideology and the political power motives associated with it.

## Conclusions

The centralized structure of the health system in the GDR did not arise in order to facilitate cooperation between the ambulatory and hospital sectors, but as a result of power politics. In the FRG, the deficient cooperation between the ambulatory and hospital sectors can be explained by the struggle between medical professional associations, the state bureaucracy, and the monopoly of ambulatory care.

Curative and preventive medicine do not seem optimal in either state. In the FRG, support of prevention to the detriment of curative medicine would increase the efficiency of the health system. In any case, definitive statements about the efficacy of additional preventive measures are not possible with current data.

The quality of medical care alone cannot prove the superiority of one or the other social system. A debunking of the myths that surround discussions of health policy is of the highest priority.

## Notes

1. For this evolutionary perspective, see Ridder 1972.

2. Büttner and Meyer 1975, p. 7. A striking example of power politics can also be found in Pritzel 1976, pp. 27 ff. In the course of demarcation against the West, discrimination against UNICEF and the IRC led to the refusal of a donation of streptomycin by UNICEF on direct orders of the Politburo of the SED. "This meant a sentence of death for a considerable number of seriously ill children. . . . The lives of these children were sacrificed for ideological reasons and political goals."

3. Health is seen as a socially relevant state, because labor power is social property.

4. Compare also the guidelines for labor unions in Jahn et al. 1977, p. 10.

5. According to socialist ideology, contradictions between the economy and ethics do not exist by definition, because economic action is humanistic action in a socialist health-care system.

6. In the GDR, collective medical treatment of social problems is ideologically acceptable, but the idea of social causation is not. Social disorders such as deviance, addictions, and anomie, which are expressions of alienation and require personalized treatment, are incongruent with the self-image of a socialist society. Social welfare, individualized support, and therapy in which psychic disorders are treated as a form of social deviance are therefore even less advanced than in the FRG.

7. The individualistic and mechanistic conception of disease leads to inadequacies in the formulation of health-care problems and to an overestimation of the effects of curative medicine. Historical evidence for this can be found in McKeown 1971.

8. The organization of health care should "not rigidify into a form which makes the patient decide when he needs medical care." (Winter 1971, p. 356) "The objective and goal of health policies is not health itself, but the revolutionary struggle for which the role of the patient is but an instrument." (Büttner and Meyer 1975, p. 7)

9. Compare with the firsthand material in Stauder 1978, pp. 59–91. See also Bär 1975.

10. The well-known weaknesses of hierarchical organizations do not have to be reiterated here.

11. The federal legislature has since 1949 proceeded according to a model of socialism which relies on the principle of indirect intervention. Private enterprise is encouraged by means of government incentives to attend to public needs.

12. Bundesvereinigung der deutschen Arbeitgeberverbände 1973, p. 12. Employers formulated their health policy in this way: "In our opinion, medical care should be as unrestricted as possible, both for health and for public reasons." A society of free persons requires an appropriate form of health care. For this reason, the right of the patient to his choice of physician and the right of the physician to free practice of his profession are simply indispensable.

13. Beyme 1975, p. 77. See the theoretical revision of this phenomenon by Ridder (1978).

14. Büttner and Meyer 1975, p. 13: "With the promotion of the children of workers and farmers, the socialistic foundations of the health care system have been laid."

15. In the GDR, additional compensations are usually paid on September 30 of each year, the "Day of Health Care."

16. In the GDR there are bronze, silver, and gold medals for loyal service.

17. In the FRG there have been strong criticisms of this for a number of years. See Pflanz 1974.

18. The chief physician system refers to the treatment of private patients by attendant physicians in public hospitals. For the chief physicians, the hospital serves not only as an inpatient but also as an outpatient institution.

### References

Bär, A. H. 1975. "Zur Gestaltung der Planung des Gesundheits- und Sozial-wesens." In Ausgewahlte Probleme der Ökonomie und Planung des Gesund-heitswesens in der DDR, ed. A. Bär et al. Zeitschrift für ärztliche Fortbildung, supplementary vol. 4.

Beyme, K. v. 1975. Ökonomie und Politik im Sozialismus. Munich: Piper.

Beyme, K. v. 1977. Sozialpolitik im Wohlfahrtsstaat. Stuttgart: Kohlhammer.

Bohm, H., et al. 1971. Die examinierte Krankenschwester: Soziologische Studie der beruflichen und ausserberuflichen Situation. Leipzig: VEB.

Bourmer, H. 1974. "Das Gesundheitswesen als integrierter Bestandteil der so-zialistischen Gesellschaftsordnung in der DDR." Deutsches Ärzteblatt 15:1053–1057.

Brauner, G. 1974. "Aufgaben des ambulanten Bereichs in der ambulant-sta-tionaren Betreuung und Kriterien zur Einschatzung der Leitung." Zeitschrift für ärztliche Fortbildung (DDR) 68.7:330–335.

Brunn, T. 1972. "Grundlagen des Gesundheitsschutzes und der Präventivmedizin in der DDR." Öffentliches Gesundheitswesen 34:675–687.

Bundesministerium für innerdeutsche Beziehungen. 1974. "Gesundheit zentral gesteuert." Der praktische Arzt, p. 2018

Bundesministerium für innerdeutsche Beziehungen. 1974. Materialen zum Bericht zur lage der Nation.

Bundesvereinigung der deutschen Arbeitgeberverbände, ed. 1973. Gesundheitssicherung in Freiheit und Verantwortung. Cologne.

Büttner, L., and B. Meyer. 1975. "Zur Herausbildung und Entwicklung der Gesundheitspolitik der SED nach 1945." Wissenschaftliche Zeitschrift der Universität Halle 24:7.

Daten des Gesundheitswesens. 1977. Bonn: Bundesministerium für Jugend, Familie, und Gesundheit.

Deppe, Volkholz, and Beyme. 1977. Deutsches Institut für Wirtschaftsforschung Weekly Report 32.

Deutsches Ärzteblatt. 1974. "Die sozialistische Poliklinik: 25 Jahre in einem sozialistischen Gesundheitswesen." 25.

Ferber, C. v. 1977. "Gesundheitsvorsorge im Systemvergleich BRD-DDR." In Handbuch der Sozialen Medizin, ed. H. Blohmke. Stuttgart: Enke.

Ferber, C. v., et al. 1977. Sozialpolitik und Selbstverwaltung: Zur Demokratisierung des Sozialstaats. Cologne: WSI-Studien, Bund-Verlag.

Franz, W. 1976. "Grundsatzliche Aspekte der Einordnung des Gesundheitswesens in der territoriale Struktur der Volkswirtschaft und einige Konsequenzen für die Leitung und Planung." Das stationäre und ambulante Gesundheitswesen 24:9.

Freyberger, H., B. Porschek, and D. Haan. 1972. "Eigenstandige Aufgabenbereiche der Schwestern-Pfleger-Gruppen in der modernen Medizin." In Krankenpflege in unserer gesellschaft, ed. M. Pinding. Stuttgart: Enke.

Gurtler, R., and J. Rothe. "Zur Bedeutung des staatlichen Charakters des Gesundheitsschützes im Socialismus." Leitung und Organisation im Gesundheitswesen 49:76–83.

Hardwick, H. H. 1973. "Strukturelement und entwicklungstendenzen des herrschenden Socialstaatsmodells (1949–1961)." In Analyse des Gesundheitssystems, ed. V. Volkholz. Frankfurt: Athenäum.

Haerter, G. 1972. "Die Zusammenarbeit zwischen Allgemeinarzt und Facharzt." Der Praktische Arzt 9:1256–1271.

Harych, W., and D. Riedel. 1974. "Untersuchung zur Verbesserung der Betriebsstruktur des Gesundheitswesens in der DDR." Zeitschrift für ärztliche Fortbildung 68:561–573.

Haussler, S. 1968. "Praktische Arzt—Facharzt—Klinik." Der Krankenhausarzt 2:41.

Hummel, H. J., et al. 1968. "Die Überweisung von Patienten als Bestandteil des ärztlichen Interaktionsystems." In Soziologische Probleme medizinischer Berufe, ed. J. H. Kaupen-Maas. Cologne-Opladen: Waldeintschen.

Hutter, H. 1974. "Zu Soziologischen Problemen des Gesundheitszustandes und Gesundheitsverhaltens." Zeitschrift für ärztliche Fortbildung 68(19):1032–1037.

Jahn, E., et al. 1971 and 1977. Die Gesundheitsicherung in der Bundesrepublik Deutschland.

Kaser, M. 1976. Health Care in the Soviet Union and Eastern Europe. London.

Lengwinat, A. 1971. "Verflechtungsbeziehungen zwischen ambulanter und stationarer Betreuung." Zeitschrift für die gesamte Hygiene und ihre Grenzgebiete 2F.

Ludz, P. C., and J. Kuppe, eds. 1975 DDR-Handbuch. Cologne: Verlag Wissenschaft und Politik.

Lüth, P. 1973. "Die Subkultur der Ärzte: Am Beispiel ihrer Körperschaften und Verbände." In Analyse des Gesundheitssystems, ed. V. Volkholz et al. Frankfurt: Athenäum.

Manger-Köning, L. v. 1975. "Das öffentliche Gesundheitswese zwischen Gestern und Morgen." Das öffentliche Gesundheitswesen 37:433–448.

McKeown, T. 1971. "A Historical Appraisal of the Medical Task." In Medical History and Medical Care, ed. G. MacLachlan and T. McKeown. New York: Oxford University Press.

Muller-Dietz, W. 1975. "Die ambulante medizinische Betreuung in der DDR." In Zur Entwicklung des Gesundheitswesens in der DDR, ed. H. Harmsen. Hamburg.

Niehoff, J. U. 1978. "Die Sprechstundentätigkeit des Facharztes für Allgemeinmedizin." Zeitschrift für ärztliche Fortbildung 70(23):1244–1247.

Nottrott, G. 1975. "Erschliessung von Reserven durch Senkung des Krankenstandes." Sozialistische Finanzwirtschaft 15:15.

Paul, H. A., and H. Stirn. 1977. "Die Fachärztliche Versorgung." In Handbuch der Sozialmedizin, ed. H. Blohmke. Stuttgart: Enke.

Peterhoff, R. 1977. "Sozialpolitik: Rahmenbedingungen und Strukturen." In BRD-DDR: Die Wirtsschaftssysteme, ed. H. Hamel. Munich: Beck.

Pflanz, M. 1974. "Prinzipien und Methoden der Beurteilung von Leistungen im Gesundheitswesen." Das öffentliche Gesundheitswesen 36:537–544.

Pritzel, K. 1976. Berliner Ärzteblatt 89(23):2000.

Proschild, L. 1976. "Leitung, 75: Studie zur Leitungstätigkeit (Summary)." In Leitungstätigkeit und Arbeitsorganisation im Gesundheitswesen. Berlin: Akademie für ärztliche Fortbildung der DDR.

Ridder, P. 1978. Prozesse sozialen Macht. Munich: Reinhardt.

Ridder, P. 1972. "Historischer Funktionalismus." Zeitschrift für Soziologie 1:333–352.

Sladzyck, C. 1973. "Ökonomie im Gesundheitswesen: Für eine bessere medizinische Betreuung." Sozialistische Finanzwirtschaft 1:45.

Stauder, H. J. 1978. Das Gesundheitswesen der DDR: Eine ökonomische Analyse aus ordnungstheoretischer Sicht. Dissertation, University of Marburg.

Tornar, R. M. 1974. "Qualität und Effectivität in der Gesundheitseinrichtungen." Third Congress, Association for Hospital Services in the GDR.

Unger, F. 1970. "Gesundheitswesen in der DDR: Eine Ärztin berichtet." Deutsches Ärzteblatt 21.

Walther, J., E. Neukirch, and J. Schiddel. 1974. Zusatzstudium für Leitungskader des Gesundheits und Sozialwesens: Grundlagen der sozialistischen Leitungwissenschaft. Berlin: Akademie für ärztiche Fortbildung der DDR.

Wehrmeister, W., et al. 1974. "Beurteilung ambulanter Betreuungsergebnisse und Profilbestimmung in stationaren Bereich." Zeitschrift für ärztiche Fortbildung (DDR) 68.7.

Weissenbock, H. 1974. Studien zur ökonomischen Effizienz von Gesundheitssystemen. Stuttgart: Hippokrates.

Wiesenhutter, P. 1976. "Arbeitsklassifizierung leitender Ärzte." In Leitungstätigkeit und Arbeitsorganisation (WAD) im Gesundheitswesen. Berlin: Akademie für ärztiche Fortbildung der DDR.

Wilken, H., et al. 1974. "Wechselbeziehungen zwischen Qualität ambulanter und stationarer Betreuung." Zeitschrift für ärztliche Fortbildung 68.7.

Winter, K. 1974. Editorial. In Das Gesundheitswesen in der DDR: Eine Bilanz zum 25. Jahrestag der Staatsgrundung. Berlin.

Winter, K. 1970. "Zum System Aspekt des Gesundheitswesens." In Arzt und Gesellschaft, ed. K. Winter. Jena: VEB.

Wirtzbach, H. J. 1974. "Gruppenpraxen im Kommen." Deutsches Ärzteblatt, p. 1334.

# 11         State Control and Drug Supply

## Dietrich Nord

*Dietrich Nord sees the supply of drugs as a mirror reflecting the economic and social orders of different societies. He describes the differences between the two German states in drug manufacturing, pharmaceutical research, patterns of marketing, and patterns of consumption. Of particular interest is his observation that socialist countries such as the GDR are more dependent on capitalist pharmaceutical industries than they would like to admit. His biases are clear. Nord criticizes the lack of research and original discoveries by the East German drug industry. Yet it may be a perfectly sensible (and certainly cost-effective) strategy to let others bear the burden of discovery, though that means a communist society dependent on the innovations of capitalist enterprises. At the same time, he clearly understands that the strengths of a private pharmaceutical industry produce weaknesses as well. Finally, Nord analyzes why East German citizens are such heavy consumers of certain families of drugs as a means for gaining insight into East German life.*

## Drug Supply as Systems Analysis

The supply of drugs in the Federal Republic of Germany (FRG; West Germany) and in the German Democratic Republic (GDR; East Germany) is largely determined by the respective countries' industries. Of all the areas in the field of public health, the varying systems of supplying drugs mirror above all the different economic and social orders of the two German states: market orientation and relative independence in the FRG, planned orientation and dependence upon planning in the GDR. Consequently, a comparison of the two drug-supply systems can indicate the efficiency of the differently organized branches of industry. Moreover, the consumption of drugs in countries such as the two German states, where they are readily available because of the service-oriented policy of the respective sickness funds, must be considered indicative not merely of the incidence of organic diseases but also of the incidence of psychosomatic diseases and of underlying social tensions. This inquiry will not examine the influence of physician-patient relationships or lay and professional needs on drug consumption; rather it will examine those conditions in the economic and political systems of the two countries which appear to be decisive for the quality and efficiency of their pharmaceutical supply systems.

This inquiry begins with the proposition that societies develop by producing complex and differing social systems which have their own momentum, so that the possibility of effectively directing them through individual decisions, planning, or through power elites is limited. In this context we will examine the way in which political values and systems of control in the two Germanies affect the supplies of pharmaceuticals and meet the health needs of individuals.

## The Industrial Complex

### An Overview of Drug Production and Consumption

Research on and production of drugs in the GDR take place in about 50 "people-owned plants" (VEB) and in two small privately owned businesses which each offer one or two insignificant drugs (Dr. H. Hoffmann: "Sulzberger Flusstinktur" and Pharma: Hollensteinstifte and "Tutus-Creme") (*Arzneimittelverzeichnis der DDR* 1977). Since 1959 the VEB plants have been combined in the Vereinigung Volkseigener Betriebe (VVB), a pharmaceutical-industry association that is directly subordinate to the Ministry for Chemistry (Zerbst 1975) and satisfies 95 percent of the domestic market of the GDR. Approximately a quarter of the total production is exported to some 50 almost exclusively socialist or Third World countries through a governmental wholesale organization called Intermed (Zerbst 1975). Export to Western countries is practically nonexistent; in the FRG, only two insignificant medications from the GDR are being marketed (Zerbst 1975).

Of more than 1,000 private firms offering pharmaceuticals in the FRG, the 556 members of the Federal Association of the Pharmaceutical Industry account for about 95 percent of the monetary value of the production. The association itself is exclusively directed by its members and not subject to any public control. The approximately 8,000 drugs produced by member firms (not counting varying strengths or, to some extent, different consumption forms) are registered in the annually published "Red List." Measured by value, about one-third (3.8 billion marks) of the entire production (11.8 billion marks) was exported in 1976. The German pharmaceutical industry provided 40 percent of world trade in medication before World War II, and since 1968 the West German drug industry has regained its position as the world's leading exporter (Bundesverband der Pharmazeutischen Industrie 1977, p. 31). Principal buying countries are—in the order of their import volume—Italy, Japan, France, Belgium-Luxemburg, Austria, the Netherlands, the United States, Switzerland, Great Britain and Sweden—all, except Austria, countries in which the West German products could successfully compete with domestic ones of high quality.

In the FRG, as in the GDR, the pharmaceutical industry is definitely growing. From 1960 until 1973, pharmaceutical production in the GDR rose from 471.4 million to 1,800 million GDR marks, up 290 percent (*Statistische Jahrbücher der DDR*, 1961–1968). In the FRG during the same period it rose from 2.4 billion to 8.7 billion marks, up 262 percent (Bundesverband der Pharmazeutischen Industrie 1977, p. 31).

The sales of specific drug families in proportion to the entire market differ considerably in the two states, as illustrated in table 1. No more than six drug families together make up 74 percent of all medication sales in the GDR, while the same families in the FRG represent only 38 percent of the market. The implications of this disparity for the quality of drugs will be discussed later.

Drug Distribution: Global Data

In the GDR the supply of drugs is currently effected through 1,379 pharmacies, of which 1,297 are state-operated and 42 are privately operated, 40 are hospital dispensaries, and 567 are state-run dispensaries (Institut für Sozialhygiene und Organisation des Gesundheitsschützes 1976, p. 304). In the FRG, this supply is handled by 13,900 privately owned pharmacies and 329 hospital pharmacies (Bundesverband der Pharmazeutischen Industrie 1977, p. 31). Each public pharmacy in the GDR (including dispensaries) serves almost 9,000 inhabitants, as compared to half that number for each pharmacy in the FRG. "The number of pharmacies in the Federal Republic has been mounting steadily, not only absolutely, but also in relation to the population. In the GDR, it has been dropping both relatively and in absolute numbers, thereby

**Table 1**
Market volume and sales shares of the strongest drug families or groups in the FRG and the GDR for the year 1973 at factory prices.

| | FRG | | GDR | |
| --- | --- | --- | --- | --- |
| | Sales (million DM) | Market share (%) | Sales (million M) | Market share (%) |
| Anti-rheumatics | 261 | 5.3 | n.a.[a] | — |
| Antibiotics | 268 | 5.5 | 396 | 22 |
| Cardiovascular drugs | 920 | 18.9 | 378 | 21 |
| Psychopharmacological drugs | 194 | 4.0 | 126 | 7 |
| Analgetics | 188 | 3.9 | 108 | 6 |
| Anti-diabetic agents | 183 | 3.7 | n.a. | — |
| Vitamins | 165 | 3.0 | 54 | 3 |
| Hormonal contraceptives | 137 | 2.8 | 270 | 15 |

a. Not available.
Sources: Bundesverband der Pharmazeutischen Industrie, 1977, p. 54. Nelde, 1975, p. 93.

widening even further the relation between pharmacies and inhabitants." (Rolf 1975, p. 189)

However, because of the falling profit rate for any individual pharmacy brought about by the boom in pharmacies in the FRG, the growth rate for new establishments has dropped off sharply (ABDA 1970–1977). Thus the different principles of control and regulation in the FRG and the GDR become also evident in their respective systems of distribution of drugs. While in the GDR allocations are fixed by central planning and according to normative definitions of demand, in the FRG merely structural restraints such as pharmacy profit margins influence allocation. Within this framework the West German distribution system can develop and control itself with relative independence. Dysfunctional developments, such as excessive increases in the number of pharmacies, are on the whole self-corrected by this system by means of market adjustments.

Pharmaceutical Research

The supply of drugs offered in advanced producer countries mirrors for the most part the great progress that pharmaceutical research has been able to achieve in the last 100 years. The extent of these research achievements was and remains decisive for the success of the pharmaceutical industries on the world market. The export success of West German medications and drugs should also be viewed in this context.

Worldwide between 1961 and 1973, a total of 1,017 drugs were newly developed and introduced into therapy (Reis-Arndt 1975). In this regard the FRG ranks third with 133 new drug products, behind the United States (with 247) and France (with 213) and ahead of Japan (with 98), Switzerland (with 80), and Italy (with 66), and thus furnishes 13 percent of all pharmacological innovations in the world. During that same period, all socialist countries together developed a total of 46 new drug products, 4.5 percent of all innovations. How this breaks down by individual states is not known, but presumably it is the People's Republic of Hungary that is responsible for developing most of these 46 new drug products, as it had a productive pharmaceutical industry before World War II and today offers comparatively liberal conditions for developing a pharmaceutical industry.

Of these 1,017 new drug products, 86 became worldwide successes, gaining entry into more than 50 countries all over the world thanks to their superior or novel effect. Thirty of these worldwide products originated in the United States, 24 in Switzerland, 18 in the FRG, 7 in Great Britain, 3 in Scandinavian countries, 2 in Italy, one in France, and one in Austria. No significant internationally recognized drug product originated in the laboratories of the pharmaceutical industry or the university research institutes of the socialist countries, including the GDR. Even though in the FRG only a small segment of the pharmaceutical industry actually performs research, this West German industry represents—contrary to its East German counterpart—a strongly research-oriented and efficient economic sector.

## Conditions for Development of the Pharmaceutical Industry in the FRG and the GDR

The political values and economic structures of the FRG and the GDR are reflected more distinctly in their drug-delivery systems than in other areas of public health. Private decisions in the FRG correspond to the centralized power of the state in the GDR. This is already clear in the number of firms offering pharmaceutical products. The decision to market a drug depends in the FRG solely upon the producer's judgment of his product's chances in the market. As a result of the dynamism

of this market, its trend toward innovations, and strong impulses from
the service orientation of the obligatory Health Insurance System (GKV),
there arose in the German Reich, and subsequently in the FRG, a
strongly diversified range of pharmaceutical firms, whose individual
research and production overlap considerably in some areas. As a result,
many drugs of identical composition, produced by various firms, compete for the approval of the prescribing physician or the patient buying
directly over the counter. The age structure of the West German pharmaceutical industry corresponds to this development: 12.4 percent of
the firms started production before 1900, 19.3 percent between 1900
and 1919, 21.3 percent between 1920 and 1934, 20.1 percent between
1935 and 1949, 17.2 percent between 1950 and 1960, and 9.7 percent
after 1960 (Bundesverband der Pharmazeutischen Industrie 1977,
p. 16). This historic and market-oriented growth is in line with the
number of products available in the FRG. Because the suppliers of new
or already known drugs do not have to prove a need for their products,
and because the effectiveness of new products has had to be proved
only since the second medication law (AMG) of January 1, 1978, more
drugs are available in the FRG than in the GDR. Accordingly, numerous
obsolete or possibly ineffective drugs are kept on the market as long
as there remains even a small demand for them.

A frequent criticism in the FRG is that the huge number of different
products available has made it difficult—above all for the physician—
to maintain an overview, and has brought about a worse system for
providing drugs than that in the GDR (Rolf 1975, p. 190). In this
context, demands are heard to limit the market administratively by
requiring proof of existing need for drugs and by more restrictive admission criteria (Friedrich 1977). Such views tend to overlook that the
West German market for drug products contains various control mechanisms which keep the number of products in demand on a level barely
above the state-decreed number of drugs in the GDR. "Five hundred
of the best-selling drugs make up 68 percent of total sales; the following
500 account for 15 percent, and the remaining 1,000 for only 11 percent."
(Bundesverband der Pharmazeutischen Industrie 1977, p. 36) Thus,
almost 95 percent of all drug sales in the FRG are concentrated in 2,000
products. The special drugs contained in the remaining 5 percent are,
however, hardly superfluous. Many can be kept on the market only
through manufacturers' balancing their business calculations, since there
is usually little demand for them and in numerous instances they fail
to meet their costs. This applies to almost all drugs against tropical

diseases (which must be available in the FRG if they are to be administered appropriately) and to drugs against very rare diseases and organic disorders (such as the drug "Androcur," which treats sexual deviations and hypersexuality). It also applies to vaccines stockpiled in case of epidemics.

The drug supply in the FRG must be considered sufficient in quality and in quantity. The FRG's high quality standard of drugs is also documented by its rising exports, especially to countries which impose essentially stricter admission criteria regarding safety and effectiveness than those prevailing domestically. Between 1971 and 1976, the FRG's drug exports to the United States more than doubled, while the export volume to Great Britain trebled (Bundesverband der Pharmazeutischen Industrie 1977, p. 33).

In the GDR, after years of difficulty, the supply of standard drugs now seems ensured. Still, as in the past, the GDR remains unable to provide the drugs required in cases of sudden demand, such as during influenza epidemics or for rare diseases (Unger 1970, p. 1142). Such drugs—especially high-grade, newly developed products—have to be imported from the West (Korthaus 1970, p. 41). East German authors blame insufficient organization, lack of raw materials, and delays in auxiliary industries ("DDR Arzneimittelengpass," *Deutsches Ärzteblatt* 68.36, 1971: 2415).

The quality, the quantity, and the distribution of drugs in the GDR must be viewed in the context of the structure of the pharmaceutical industry. After World War II, there existed in the territory of what is today the GDR practically no pharmaceutical industry of any significance with its own tradition of research and production (Nelde 1975). Rather, such industries were established exclusively in the western part of the former German Reich.

The drug supply offered by the gradually emerging VEB factories was determined by a centrally planned demand and in accord with the prevailing new social and economic order. Thus, the areas of special emphasis in both research and production were defined and allocated to individual plants. Consequently, there are no competing identical drugs produced by different manufacturers in the GDR. Contrary to West German industry, in which decisions to start a research project or to expand production are determined solely by profit criteria, the VEB plants receive a precisely stipulated plan. This plan governs investments and is tied to established demands, not to any profit considerations. Thus the quantity of drugs supplied is not controlled by the political system alone but by the industrial system as well. As a result, there are characteristics vital to any system which are missing in the technological-pharmaceutical "system" of the GDR: partial self-control, internal dynamism, and feedback to the political system.

Probst (1977, p. 76) has arrived at a basic conclusion: "In socialist countries, it is not easy to obtain research funds sufficient for the development of numerous new drugs. It is not easy for us because in socialist countries we cannot operate according to the profit principle. . ." Despite this confession of a research lag in the GDR, Probst goes on to claim that "under socialist production conditions, it is the needs of the people on which the planning of production and of various goods including drugs is based." The GDR's lack of pharmaceutical innovations and partial dependence upon the West for quality products are involuntarily supported by this quote.

Need or Demand Orientation and Market Supply

It has often been pointed out that only in very early phases of social development is a social system controlled by the efforts to satisfy specific needs (Hondrich 1975). In pluralistic and highly complex societies, however, where each individual is a member of several different social systems that satisfy different needs, this type of control is no longer appropriate. Through the impact of differing social systems upon the individual, numerous needs have become independent of their original objects, so that controlling needs through central planning has become largely impossible (Hondrich 1977, p. 217). In this stage of social development, needs are "merely factors in the adjustment of various social systems; they indicate the mechanisms with the help of which social systems develop and become integrated" (Hondrich 1975, p. 83). If, as in the GDR, human needs are used as "the starting point for the planned production of various goods," insurmountable difficulties arise, as the following example illustrates.

*Control of the Technological-Pharmaceutical System*
If it were ascertained that the needs of the population consisted to an overwhelming degree of vacationing on the moon, the provision of spacecraft could in theory be considered. The relevant technologies as well as the operational strategies are essentially well known. The decision to put such a scheme into practice depends, therefore, exclusively upon economic and political considerations. The need for drugs, on

the other hand, has a different character, because it refers either to known drugs or to therapies not yet developed, such as effective cancer medication, causative anti-rheumatics, or "the pill" for men. Meeting these needs, however, cannot just be planned, because "chance and coincidence play a decisive role in drug research. However, here even chance does not occur quite by chance. As a rule, chance occurs only during the course of systematic research" (Lynen 1973, p. 18). Consequently, the outcome of systematic molecular variation by no means always improves a drug. Instead, it may produce a molecular variation that serves as a departure point for an entirely different set of uses. According to Gordon (1962, p. 461), "more than half of the important pharmaceutic preparations . . . are the result of so-called 'molecule-manipulations.' "

This peculiarity of pharmacological research is supplemented by the critical role of side effects in the application of a new drug. The best-known example for this is the sulfa drugs. These were initially administered as antibacteriological substances, but clinical testing revealed their effectiveness in lowering blood sugar. This discovery marked the starting point for the development of the first oral anti-diabetics, which represented a significant research achievement on the part of the West German pharmaceutical industry. This by no means isolated instance illustrates that even the control of systems such as the technological-pharmaceutical system can no longer be influenced by individuals but develops through unanticipated results and an inner logic of its own. After a certain stage, research results are no longer achieved by focusing upon the research problem itself but increasingly by organizing the conditions of research.

Two main reasons for the dynamism of the pharmaceutical industry in the FRG and other Western countries are its profit orientation and its right to decide freely on how to invest its earnings. In order to maintain this system's efficiency, a large commitment of capital is required. In 1976 alone, the 25 leading West German manufacturers of drugs spent more than 1,000 million marks on research (Bundesverband der Pharmazeutischen Industrie 1977, p. 23). Even though worldwide the number of new discoveries recedes and research expenditures by the Western producer countries rise, the disposition of these funds remains necessary in order to preserve the preconditions for innovation.

Through the innovative process within the technological-pharmaceutical system, other systems are stimulated, such as the political system, which in part controls and directs the flow of goods. The political system, in turn, is able to influence the available volume of research funds by controlling prices for drugs and by limiting their growth rates through regulation. Controls of this kind endanger the stability of the technological-pharmaceutical system if and when they impede the system's inherent dynamism by hindering research activity. It seems that productivity and performance are inseparably linked to the system of production.

## The GDR's Drug-Supply System as a Subsystem

The pharmacological industry of the GDR has never even had the opportunity to develop as it has in the FRG. Organizational shortcomings, lack of raw materials, and problems with auxiliary industries, which East German authors blame on the partial supply shortfall and on lagging research, are themselves the result of the centralized control of the technological-pharmaceutical "system." It is not surprising that, except for some internationally insignificant products, the GDR's drug register contains almost exclusively items from the former German Reich or the laboratories of the modern Western pharmaceutical industries.

To guarantee an up-to-date inventory of drugs, the GDR resorts largely to imitations, mostly disregarding patent laws. The best-known examples are the oral anti-diabetic "Maninil 5 mg," a glibenclamide that was first introduced by Boehringer/Mannheim and Hoechst under the brand name "Euglucon 5," and the tranquilizer "Faustan," a diazepam product discovered by Hoffmann-La Roche and marketed by them as "Valium." The extent to which even East German scientists cover up this practice is evident from publications in which "Faustan" is described as a success to which East German pharmaceutical research had contributed (Winter 1974, p. 148). "That for 25 years serious drug incidents could be prevented in the GDR" and that there had "neither been children crippled by thalidomide nor damage by appetite suppressants, psychostimulants, or overdoses of Hexachlorophene" (Winter 1974, p. 143) are, when viewed in context, not explained by any stricter drug supervision in the GDR than in Sweden or Great Britain, where Thalidomide, for example, was permitted. Lacking innovations of its own, the GDR must depend on copies of Western drugs, at least as far as high-grade products are concerned, because its chronic lack of foreign currency bars direct importation (Zerbst 1975). The GDR thus enjoys the advantage of being able to monitor the widespread usage of and reactions to drugs. Drugs producing undesirable side effects in other countries are not added to the GDR's inventory. Every successful research activity also implies the risk of failure, which frequently appears only after widespread use. Without innovations, however, there are no risks. This means on the other hand that products reaching the public in the GDR have for many years been standard prescriptions in the FRG or other Western producer countries. From the perspective of Marxist theory, the ironic result is that the GDR's drug supply not only benefits significantly from the superior output of the Western pharmaceutical industry but, because of its own lack of dynamism, has become an inherent part of it. Its drug supply and its very political system are therefore subject to indirect yet significant control by the Western pharmaceutical industry.

In order to avoid emotional tensions arising from frustrated needs, the GDR's political system is bound to provide the expected goods in order to maintain its own stability. As specific demands tend to orient themselves to comparatively superior goods of the kind mostly supplied by Western systems—everyday life in the GDR illustrates this clearly— the GDR's drug system has to adapt itself accordingly. In this way Western technological-pharmaceutical systems, with their superior efficiency, exert a considerable pull and an integrative effect which stop neither at national boundaries nor at different economic or social orders. This process, which accelerates as complexity increases, also indicates why international comparisons of the efficiency of health delivery systems remain inadequate where they compare national cost-benefit analyses as if they were self-contained systems.

In the West German technological-pharmaceutical system, research and production are not centrally planned but steer in coordination with other social systems. The "nonproductive side effects" that necessarily arise, however, either in parallel research or in the manufacture of numerous superfluous or ineffective products, are balanced to a large extent by the self-correcting capabilities of the medical system discussed above. Despite its "undesirable side effects," this system is so superior that others are unable to withstand its impact. The remark by Jung (1969, p. 110) that the FRG does not have a drug market but rather a drug "raffle" is justified only if one takes a superficial view of the drug supply offered in both countries. It misunderstands completely, however, the conditions giving rise to a lastingly superior drug market from which the GDR may profit and select.

*Comparison of Prices and Efficiency*

For that reason, Rolf (1975, p. 202) also errs by concluding that "greater efficiency must be attributed to the GDR pharmaceutic sector." Rolf argues this point (among others) by claiming that, in comparison with the GDR, the FRG's drug supply "must most probably be purchased at too high a price" (p. 197). It is true that medications are cheaper in the GDR than in the FRG. For example, 20 Faustan pills cost 2.30 marks in the GDR, while 20 Valium pills of equal strength cost 5.50 DM in the FRG. In the GDR 60 Maninil pills sell for 9.45 marks, while 30 Euglucon-5 pills cost as much as 19.05 DM in the FRG. Ten Acesal tablets are offered in the GDR for 0.35 marks, compared with 20 Aspirins for 2 DM in the FRG. It is difficult, however, to accept the GDR's low prices for drugs as proof of its superiority as a delivery system. The exact opposite appears more plausible. In contrast to the GDR, prices for drugs in the FRG reflect the prevailing market situation and are thus not artificially held to a certain level. Price fluctuations reflect the system's sensitivity to changes in other systems and its partial independence. Yet this independence can only be maintained by continuous stimulation of its own dynamism through research. The volume of finances committed to this end has already been mentioned. On the average, pharmaceutical enterprises engaged in research spend up to 15 percent of their gross sales on research. Drugs developed under these circumstances must necessarily be more expensive than those produced by enterprises which merely copy them. The GDR's low price level thus reflects its dependence upon the research achievements of Western manufacturers.

A further aspect of comparing price levels is that fluctuations of exchange rates distort any evaluation of comparative efficiency. Price comparisons with countries such as the GDR, whose currency is not freely convertible, are quite impossible. In such countries, consumer monetary parities (Bingemer and Dinkel 1976) are a more adequate measure. Since the average worker's income in the FRG is three times that in the GDR, the financial burden of drugs on citizens in the two countries hardly differs.

## Consumption and Costs

The actual burden on citizens through payments of health insurance dues to the GKV (Gesetzliche Krankenversicherung) in the FRG or the SV (Sozialversicherung) in the GDR also involves pharmaceutical costs

**Table 2**
Per capita expenditures on drugs.

|      | FRG (DM) | GDR (M) |
|------|----------|---------|
| 1960 | 45       | 38      |
| 1965 | 72       | 55      |
| 1970 | 117      | 88      |
| 1971 | 130      | 94      |
| 1972 | 165      | 105     |
| 1973 | 180      | 115     |
| 1974 | 195      | 126     |
| 1975 | ca. 210  | 142     |

Sources: Nord 1976, p. 22; Institut für Sozialhygiene 1976.

as a function of price and volume and of the quantitative structure of demand (Nord 1976b, p. 28). In order to decide whether in the two German states citizens are in fact saddled with different burdens in the form of drug costs, one must analyze the structure and volume of their respective drug consumption.

Unfortunately, differences between the cost structures of the GKV and the SV make comparison difficult. In the GKV, membership dues and mandatory insurance limits are tied to the cost-of-living index; expenditures are financed exclusively out of membership dues and therefore are transparent down to every single account. By contrast, the dues in the SV have never changed since its founding; any deficits are covered by state subsidies of unknown amounts (Rolf 1975, p. 44). Consequently, East German citizens do not know with which of their payments drug costs have been paid. As a consequence, the SV lacks the characteristics of a productive system. Moreover, the SV is exclusively directed and controlled by a centralized political system so that political control by the public is not possible.

An indication of the expenditures for specific drug consumption is provided by the sales revenues of pharmacies per inhabitant (table 2).

For the evaluation of per capita costs, it is immaterial that the figures for the FRG contain prevailing price rises while the state-fixed prices for pharmaceuticals in the GDR show hardly any fluctuations. Another aspect, however, is significant: In the FRG roughly one-third of all drug sales are for private self-medication and are directly purchased at the pharmacy, whereas in the GDR this portion amounts to only 10 percent. Because the monetary volume of self-medication is contained in table

**Table 3**
Per capita consumption of analgetic pills.

|  | GDR | FRG |
|---|---|---|
| 1955 | 26.6 | n.o.[a] |
| 1960 | 40.8 | n.o. |
| 1965 | n.o. | 32 |
| 1966 | 48.6 | 45 |
| 1970 | 60.0 | 34 |
| 1971 | n.o. | 34 |

a. Not observed.
Source: Linke 1971.

2, one has to reduce the amounts listed there by one-third or by 10 percent, respectively, in order to obtain the expenditures of the GKV and the SV for prescription drugs. This includes subsidies paid out of taxes in the GDR. For the GKV the result must be taken to be lower still, since the figures for total drug consumption in the FRG also include the drug costs expended by the roughly 8 percent who have private health insurance.

On the basis of the "consumers' monetary parities," it becomes evident that in fact the average citizen incurs considerably higher drug costs in the GDR than in the FRG, and that in the end he must pay for them in the form of SV dues as well as in taxes. This is aside from the fact that these payments are largely raised by means of tax policies devised by uncontrollable bureaucratic elites.

Structure of Consumption

The level of per capita drug consumption in the GDR as compared to that in the FRG must be explained by the larger quantity as well as the different distribution of drugs consumed. On the basis of the very scant data available in either state, the complex situation of the consumer can only be sketched. One of the few available reports on the average number of pills consumed is that of Linke (1971) on the analgetics drug family shown in table 3.

That the GDR's per capita consumption of analgetics is twice that of the FRG can also be noted by their share of gross sales—as shown in table 1—which comes to 6 percent as compared to 4 percent in the FRG. The fact that these figures correspond only approximately is due to different price structures. A similar pattern exists for cardiovascular drugs, tranquilizers, and, above all, antibiotics where the share of gross sales in the GDR is 22 percent and in the FRG is 5.5 percent.

Aside from the fact that the East Germans use certain families of drugs to a much larger degree, it is clear that their heavier cost burden for drug consumption is also due to a substitution process within the supply side of the market (Prufer et al. 1977, p. 123). This process is characterized by the increasing tendency of prescribing physicians to favor more modern, more effective, but also more expensive drugs. This tendency also makes itself felt in the FRG, though to a lesser extent. It has been quantified for five important and to some extent new drug families with a growth rate of 2 percent in the drug costs of the GKV for the years 1968 to 1974 (Nord 1976b, p. 57). Yet to conclude on the basis of the dynamics of this substitution process that the GDR enjoys a qualitatively better drug-delivery system appears to be quite unwarranted. Despite the comparatively modest sales of antibiotics in the FRG, there is mounting criticism of their exaggerated use, particularly against diseases against which they are ineffective (*Bild der Wissenschaft* 12.8, 1975: 39; *Deutsche Gesundheits-Korrespondenz* 2, 1976). There are also reports from the United States and Japan—countries with essentially smaller shares of sales than the GDR—about increasing but ineffective use of antibiotics against viral infections. The use of these products in such cases is not merely ineffectual but also dangerous, since patients risk building up resistance to them. Since there are only insignificant differences in the morbidity of infectious disease between the FRG and the GDR, the fact that the sales of antibiotics in the GDR is five times higher raises less the possibility of a deficient supply system in the FRG than that of questionable drug safety in the GDR.

The GDR's obvious overmedication compared to the FRG is also discussed within the GDR. Müller and Ackerman (1974) have pointed out in no uncertain terms the extent of the abuse of analgetics containing phenacetin and the ensuing kidney damage; they have demanded that the products "Acetophen" and "Fibrex," which contain phenacetin and are widely sold, be made available by prescription only. Nevertheless, these products continue to be sold freely over the counter (*Arznei-mittelverzeichnis der DDR*, 1977).

Regarding psychopharmaceuticals, Linke (1971) even speaks of an "alarmingly mounting increase in consumption. . . . The application and prescription of psychotropic drugs threatens to degenerate into routine." In the district of Schwerin, for example, the respective consumption rose from 5.7 million pills in 1961 to 8.2 million in 1965

(Bretschneider 1968, p. 308), an increase of 44.3 percent. The same author qualifies the impact of the substitution process on the quality of the drug supply: "I respect . . . a fellow physician who prefers to treat an unstable working woman who complains of insomnia by prescribing successfully 'Plantiva,' 'Melical,' or 'Valocordin' instead of driving her into the arms of 'modern' tranquilizers, or persuades another patient suffering from a post-thrombotic syndrome to stop a continuous abuse of Saluretics against a persisting leg edema by prescribing compression types of dressing." (Linke 1971)

Ideology and Arguments for Drug Consumption

Explanations of the high drug consumption in the GDR do not usually differ from those in the FRG. For example, Miehlke (1971, p. 151) writes that the "increase in the purchase of analgetics is predominately attributed to hygienic, physiological, and psychosocial factors related to work." Other authors also give intensification of the work process as a reason for a marked increase in drug consumption. "Environmental stimuli, such as television, radio, and driving, have considerably reduced the time available for physical or mental relaxation. This additional stress, partly justified and partly irresponsibly incurred by people, has as its distinct fallout the consumption of psychosedatives." (Bretschneider 1968, p. 308) The "reality of industrial society as a pathogenetic agent" (Baier 1972) is also discussed in the GDR as a main cause for the increasing drug consumption. Yet this does not explain why per capita drug consumption in the GDR is substantially higher than in the FRG. Nor is it explained by the common observation that the supply of drugs seems to rise with the developmental level of societies, because in highly complex systems the reality of industrial society as a pathogenic agent leads to an increase in psychosomatic disturbances and thus more consumption of psychopharmaceuticals and analgetics.

When comparing two industrialized societies, it seems inappropriate to interpret "drug use as a symptom of a sick society" (Pflanz et al. 1977, p. 194), a view which draws on earlier developmental phases of social systems in order to assess current drug consumption. However, comparing divergent psychosomatic morbidity underlying the use of tranquilizers between countries of comparable complexity may reveal greater insights into the higher consumption of drugs in the GDR.

Balter et al. (1974) found that psychopharmaceuticals are used in the FRG by 14.2 percent of the population, in Belgium by 16.8 percent, in Denmark by 15.1 percent, in France by 16.7 percent, in Sweden by 15.8 percent, and in Great Britain by 14.2 percent ($n = 2,000$). Roughly two-thirds of the users were women, a result more recently reconfirmed for the FRG (Pflanz et al. 1977). On the other hand, the GDR surpasses the FRG in the consumption of psychopharmaceuticals and analgetics by a factor of 2. If it is correct that an industrial society is generally an important pathogenetic agent, the question arises why life in the GDR evidently poses comparatively greater dangers for the well-being of its citizens.

One of the important conditions for the harmonious development of individuals is their adaption to the different social spheres into which they are partially integrated. Such adaptation, however, appears to be successful only where the individual is able to distinguish between these different social spheres. Interaction among them helps the individual play different roles and reduce social and psychic pressure by participating in several spheres rather than one. The resulting control and autonomy is unknown in the GDR. The tight formation of its society into numerous functional units without the chance for self-regulation hampers the adaptation so vital on the personal level. Moreover, the central planning and control of all functional units prevent individuals from identifying with them, because the consequences of individual choices cannot be identified. Even if, for example, a factory were able to reward its workers for good performance with a raise in wages, thereby giving employees visible feedback for their efforts, such a decision—if made at all—would be taken centrally and independent of specific performance. The direct and immediate powers of the planning and managing authorities, whose decisions are mostly neither transparent nor intelligible to the individual, subject him—even where his working conditions are the same as those of his Western colleague—to comparatively more stress and less influence. "The abolition of private ownership of the means of production," remarks Fetscher (1972, p. 35), "has a liberating impact on the concrete situation of the workers only if it is accompanied by an effective democratization on all levels of political and social life. That is not the case where a small group of bureaucrats in fact controls the entire production and reduces the population's democratic rights to details within the framework of predetermined plans." Conflicts between individuals and the social system result. They are the main reason for the incidence of psychosomatic disturbances which are reflected in the GDR in a high degree of drug use and in significantly higher rates of divorce and suicide (*Statistisches Jahrbuch der DDR*, 1977, pp. 538–539).

In this context, numerous statements—some of them semi-official—in GDR publications sound rather strange. Winter et al. (1974, p. 75) declare: "In capitalist society, the value of the human commodity is assessed without regard for its physical state but only according to its capacity to perform and is dropped when it no longer produces profit. In socialist societies, on the other, the ability to perform and to enjoy during one's entire life is considered a preeminent objective." The preamble to the guidelines for public health policy decided upon in 1947 by the SED and still valid today states: "A truly democratic state . . . puts man at the center of its policy. And for man health is priceless. Consequently, the health policy of the Socialist Unity Party of Germany (SED) charges the state above all to care for the health of the population." (Winter 1974, p. 17) Hüttner (1977, p. 45) cites the "extraordinarily rapid rise in the exploitation of the working class"—caused by the "monopoly bourgeoisie"—as an explanation for the allegedly poorer state of health and the inferior medical care in the FRG. It is even claimed that "the capitalist social order and its ideology reduce man to his biological dimension because the ruling class has no interest in letting the social causes of diseases be known." Thus, it would have to be expected that, with approximately the same somatic morbidity, drug use in the GDR would lie far below that in the FRG. The tortured attempt to discover in the use of drugs the "basic contradiction between exploiter and victim" (Hüttner 1977, p. 40) turns out—despite its simplistic nature—to explain instead the reality of the GDR.

Assertions such as those just cited, in which "statements about reality are confounded with claims on how reality should be" (Hondrich 1977, p. 51), constitute ideologies that serve specific purposes in the GDR. Topitsch (1961, p. 24) has shown that in societies with mounting complexity and growing prosperity the "demand for historical and social doctrines of redemption" decline. The extremely high demand for ideology on the part of the power elite of the GDR must, therefore, be explained by their lag in the race against Western societies and their efforts to catch up. To accomplish this, the GDR increased the managerial leverage of the technical and economic intelligentsia. In 1963 it introduced the New Economic System (NOS) in the hope that added responsibility on the lower level as well as support for initiatives in some sectors would yield productive gains. The GDR's role as the leading economic power within the Comecon is certainly also due to NOS, which decreased traditional rigidity and timidly applied Western principles of systems and management. However, the transition from linear to feedback systems ran into the same difficulties encountered in the early 1950s of accepting and legitimating the concepts of cybernetics, because they do not follow the dialectic of the offical ideology (Dahm 1963). The political history of Marxism-Leninism has shown that the need of those in power for ideology rises in proportion to the degree that the true facts are being falsified (Popper 1958; Festinger et al. 1956).

## Conclusion

A systems-analytical comparison of the drug-supply system in the FRG and the GDR has shown that any evaluation based upon the collection of isolated data remains unsatisfactory since it fails to explain anything and actually tends to obscure matters. This is above all true for the question of efficiency, because the GDR's drug-supply system cannot be explained independently but only as a derivation of Western technological-pharmaceutical systems. Their superiority and integration is due to their particular combination of partial independence, with internal and external control mechanisms.

On the other hand, the lagging research of the GDR's pharmaceutical industry and its dependence upon Western systems for innovations ironically deprives the GDR of the efficiency and the dynamism so characteristic of self-regulating systems. The resulting dependence upon foreign systems is noticeable not only in the GDR's drug supply but also in most other sectors of the economy. Their inappropriate management not only produces deficits in various sectors; it is also responsible for psychic tensions, as reflected in the specific morbidity and high drug use. In addition, it puts a financial burden on the citizen, and it impairs labor productivity.

## References

ABDA (Arbeitsgemeinschaft der Berufsvertretungen Deutscher Apotheker). Berichte 1970–1977.

Arzneimittelverzeichnis der DDR, 1977, part 2. East Berlin: Volk und Gesundheit.

Baier, H. 1972. "Die Wirklichkeit der Industriegesellschaft als Krankheitsfaktor." In Der Kranke in der modernen Gesellschaft, ed. A. Mitscherlich et al. Cologne: Kiepenhever und Witsch.

Balter, M. B. 1974. "Cross National Study of the Extent of Anti-anxiety/Sedative Drug Use." New England Journal of Medicine 769–774.

Bingemer, F., and R. Dinkel. 1976. Internationale Markt- und Preisvergleiche im Pharmabereich. Basel: Prognos.

Bretschneider, K. 1968. "Analyse über der Arzneimittelverbrauch in den Jahren 1961, 1963, and 1965." Die Pharmazie 12 (supplement).

Bundesverband der pharmazeutischen Industrie, ed. 1977. Pharma-Daten 77.

Dahm, H. 1963. Die Dialektik im Wandel der Sowjetphilosophie. Cologne: Wissenschaft und Politik.

Festinger, L., et al. 1956. When Prophecy Fails—A Social and Psychological Study of a Modern Group that Predicted the Destruction of the World. New York: Harper.

Fetscher, I. 1972. Von Marx zur Sowjetideologie. Frankfurt: Diesterweg.

Friedrich, V. 1977. Neunmal teurer als Gold—die Arzneimittelversorgung in der Bundesrepublik. Hamburg: Rowohlt.

Gordon, M. 1962. "Die pharmazeutische Industrie und die pharmazeutische Forschung." Pharmazeutische Industrie 24.10.

Hondrich, K. 1975. Menschliche Bedurfnisse und soziale Steverung. Hamburg: Rowohlt.

Hondrich, K. 1977. "Soziologische Theorieansatze und ihre Relevanz für die Sozialpolitik—Der bedurfnis—theoretische Ansatz." Kölner Zeitschrift für Soziologie und Sozialpsychologie, special issue 19.

Hüttner, H. 1977. Zur Soziologie des Gesundheitsverhaltens. East Berlin: Volk und Gesundheit.

Institut für Sozialhygiene und Organisation des Gesundheitsschützes. 1976. Das Gesundheitswesen der DDR. East Berlin.

Jung, F. 1969. "Arzneimittelversorgung der Bevolkerung." In Deine Gesundheit–Unser Staat, ed. K. Winter. East Berlin: Volk und Gesundheit.

Korthaus, R. 1970. "Anforderungen des Gesundheitswesens an die chemische Industrie." In Gesundheit und Ökonomie, ed. W. Schwartz and A. H. Bär. East Berlin.

Linke, H. 1971. Therapiestandards und ärztliche Entscheidung. Lecture, Annual Session of Deutsche Akademie der Natur-Forscher, Leopoldina.

Lynen, F. 1973. "Der Einfluss der Forschung auf den Fortschritt der Arzneitherapie." Pharma-Dialog 21.

Miehlke, G. 1971. "Unkontrollierte Pharmakaeinnahme und Gesundheitsverhalten." In Arzneimittel und Gesellschaft, ed. F. Jung et al. East Berlin.

Müller, U., and E. Ackerman. 1974. "Der Analgetika-Abusus phenazetinhaltiger Medikamente—ein Problem des Gesundheitsschutzes der Werktatigen der DDR." Deutscher Gesundheitswesen 29:2113–2120.

Nelde, H. 1975. "Zur Entwicklung der pharmazeutischen Industrie in der DDR." Die Pharmazie, supplement 4.

Nord, D. 1976a. Arzneimittelkonsum in der Bundesrepublik Deutschland: Eine Verhaltensanalyse von Pharma-Industrie, Arzt, und Verbraucher. Stuttgart: Enke.

Nord, D. 1976b. Kosten des medikamentosen Fortschritts. Frankfurt: MPS.

Pflanz, M., et al. 1977. "Use of tranquilizing drugs by a middle-aged population in a West German city." Journal of Health and Social Behavior 18.

Popper, K. 1958. Die öffene Gesellschaft und ihre Feinde, vol. 2. Bern: Francke.

Probst, H. 1977. "Arzneimittel im Kapitalismus und im Sozialismus." Die Pharmazie, supplement 4.

Prufer, H., et al. 1977. "Zur Entwicklung des sozialistischen Apothekenwesens im Spiegel der betriebswirtschaftlichen Analyse." Die Pharmazie, supplement 6.

Reis-Arndt. 1975. "Neue pharmazeutische Wirkstoffe 1961–1973." Die Pharmazeutische Industrie 37.4:233–240.

Rolf, H. 1975. Sozialversicherung oder Staatlicher Gesundheitsdienst? Berlin.

Statistisches Jahrbuch der Bundesrepublik Deutschland. Stuttgart-Mainz: Kohlhammer.

Topitsch, E. 1961. Sozialphilosophie zwischen Ideologie und Wissenschaft. Neuwied: Luchterhand.

Unger, F. 1970. "Das Gesundheitswesen der DDR." Deutschland Archiv 3.11:1142.

Winter, K. 1974. Das Gesundheitswesen in der Deutschen Demokratischen Republik. East Berlin: Volk und Gesundheit.

Winter, K. 1975. Soziologie für Mediziner. East Berlin: Volk und Gesundheit.

Zerbst, H. 1975. "Das Gesundheitswesen in der DDR." Die pharmazeutische Industrie 37.2:78–87.

# 12

# The Comparative Organization of Tuberculosis Prevention: A Case Study

## Timothy Empkie

*This case study, done under the guidance of the late Manfred Pflanz and Ray Elling, examines in some detail the organization and activities around one historically important disease. Stemming from a common historical model, the organization of TB prevention is a mixture of continuities with the past and differences resulting from current political values. As with other prevention programs, the GDR achieves higher participation rates through various measures, including one of relevance to the United States: the active participation of company managers.*

The focus of this study is on the differences in the ways preventive health services are merged with other health services, particularly at the primary-care level, in the two German health systems. The problem of incorporating preventive medical care takes on added importance as developing and developed nations alike seek to maximize the impact of their available medical resources in the face of rising costs and demands for medical services. It is certain that there are important effects of socio-economic and political structure on health and health services organization which are not well understood. The Executive Board of the World Health Organization has indicated that the collection of knowledge relating to the effects of these factors on the organization of health services should be an important goal (World Health Organization 1973, p. 110). It is the aim of this study to improve the understanding of these effects.

A comparison of health services in the Federal Republic of Germany (FRG; West Germany) and the German Democratic Republic (GDR; East Germany) provides an excellent opportunity to make such an investigation. Since 1949 the FRG and the GDR have developed as separate countries despite a common cultural and historical background.

**Table 1**
Incidence of tuberculosis per 100,000 population.

|         | FRG       |           | GDR       |           |
|---------|-----------|-----------|-----------|-----------|
|         | All forms | Pulmonary | All forms | Pulmonary |
| 1965    | 93.2      | 78.8      | 94        | 79        |
| 1975    | 55.1      | 46.4      | 36.6      | 28.5      |
| 1979    | 45.4      | 39.0      | 25.0      | 19.6      |
| 1980    | 42.1      | 36.1      | 24        | 18        |

Sources: Staatliche Zentralverwaltung für Statistik 1981, p. 373; Statistisches Bundesamt 1967, p. 69; 1978, p. 372; 1981, pp. 375, 597; 1982, p. 378.

**Table 2**
Tuberculosis death rates per 100,000 population.

|         | FRG       |           | GDR       |           |
|---------|-----------|-----------|-----------|-----------|
|         | All forms | Pulmonary | All forms | Pulmonary |
| 1960    | 16.5      | 15.3      | 18        | 17        |
| 1970    | 8.3       | 6.9       | 11        | 8         |
| 1975    | 5.5       | 4.2       | 6         | 4         |
| 1979    | 3.5       | 2.5       | 4         | 3         |

Sources: Staatliche Zentralverwaltung für Statistik 1981, p. 375; Statistisches Bundesamt 1977, p. 357; 1978, p. 375; 1982, p. 378.

Although they share the same health system historically, during the past 25 years political and economic factors have combined to produce two quite different systems of health-care delivery and apparently marked differences in available medical manpower. The health services in the FRG are primarily the responsibility of the eleven states (including West Berlin), while the GDR has a centrally directed but regionalized system of health-care delivery. The hypothesis of this study is that a comparison of the two countries, using tuberculosis as a model, will show a greater emphasis on preventive services in the GDR and perhaps a greater integration of preventive and therapeutic services to account in part for this difference in performance. Statistically, the GDR has been more successful in reducing the incidence of tuberculosis (table 1) and has achieved comparably low tuberculosis death rates (table 2).

## Methods

The choice of a case study contrasting the FRG and the GDR was based on their common socio-economic, cultural, and historical background prior to the sharp split following World War II, which provides an opportunity to examine health organization as a function of political structure. This choice differs from that suggested by Elling and Kerr (1975), which involved countries with similar levels of resources and contrasting health levels.

Six weeks were spent in Hannover and other parts of the West German state of Lower Saxony, based at the Hannover Medical School Institute of Epidemiology and Social Medicine. Three weeks were later spent in the GDR in Dresden and in East Berlin, based at the Institute for Postgraduate Medical Education. Initial interviews were held with personnel involved with tuberculosis prevention, such as public health administrators and physicians, private physicians, representatives of voluntary scientific advisory groups, and medical officials of the Research Institute for Pulmonary Disease and Tuberculosis in the GDR. The field work (May–June 1975) was completed with observations of the work performed by physicians in both countries who are employed in the primary-care facilities that deal with tuberculosis patients. The data presented are believed to accurately represent the organization of preventive services for tuberculosis in the two countries, but where uncertainties exist they are noted.

## General Organization of Health Services: FRG and GDR

In the FRG (population approximately 61 million) the Federal Ministry for Youth, Family, and Health has direct responsibility for several matters, such as licensing of health professionals, drug control, and measures against infectious disease (including tuberculosis), but essentially each of the eleven states (including West Berlin) conducts its health affairs independently (Eichhorn 1973, p. 86). In each state of the FRG, matters of health are under the jurisdiction of the Health Department of the Ministry of Work and Social Welfare; the next and lowest administrative unit is the District Board of Health (Kreis Gesundheitsamt). A medical officer directs the Board of Health, which includes departments of sanitation, social services, youth health services, and youth dental services, and a department concerned with tuberculosis (Eichhorn 1973, p. 87). This Tuberculosis Department (Tuberkulosefürsorgestelle) is the center of the tuberculosis prevention effort throughout the FRG. The Board of Health also supervises all hospitals, which, with a few exceptions, provide only inpatient services. Outpatient services generally are provided by community-based private physicians (Eichhorn 1973, p. 92).

Medical care in the FRG is financed by a system of compulsory health insurance which has as its origin a national health insurance law enacted in 1883. In 1980 this system consisted of 1,319 autonomous sickness funds (Krankenkassen) (Statistisches Bundesamt 1982, p. 394) to which employees and employers contribute and from which physicians are indirectly paid (Pflanz 1971).

In the GDR (population approximately 17 million) the Ministry of Health is at the top of the general health-care system, which consists of 15 district Departments of Health and Social Services (Bezirk Abteilung für Gesundheits- und Sozialwesen) directed by District Medical Officers and 217 County Departments of Health and Social Services (Kreis Abteilung für Gesundheits- und Sozialwesen) directed by County Medical Officers. The latter have primary responsibility for all health services in the county, including inpatient and outpatient facilities (Winter 1974). The polyclinic, the largest and most important of several types of outpatient facilities, usually consists of departments of pediatrics, obstetrics and gynecology, general medicine, surgery, and dental medicine, and a department for pulmonary disease and tuberculosis referred to as PALT (Poliklinik Abteilung für Lungenkrankheiten und Tuberkulose). The PALT is the center of the tuberculosis-prevention program in the GDR. The constitution of the GDR guarantees the right of every citizen to the protection of his health and working capacity through several measures, including the provision of medical care, drugs, and other medical benefits free of charge to the individual through a social insurance system.

## General Organization of Tuberculosis Prevention: FRG and GDR

In the FRG there are two important pieces of federal legislation that deal with the problem of tuberculosis: the Federal Communicable Disease Law (Bundesseuchengesetz) and the Federal Social Assistance Law (Bundessozialhilfegesetz). The first law requires the registration, within 24 hours at the nearest Board of Health, of all known and suspected cases of tuberculosis; permits the examination and observation of such cases; details types of work in which persons with tuberculosis may not participate (e.g. the food industry); and details types of work where initial TB screening and subsequent regular examinations are required (e.g. the food industry, the schools, and generally all occupations in which one commonly comes in contact with children (Bundesseuchengesetz 1974, pp. 16–42). The Social Assistance Law guarantees

outpatient and inpatient treatment for those with tuberculosis, rehabilitation or reeducation for employment, and general social and financial assistance, with the cost covered by the federal government
and a state insurance institution, the Landesversicherungsanstalt (Bundessozialhilfegesetz 1975, pp. 50–60).

With the exception of these two federal laws, the prevention of tuberculosis is primarily the responsibility of each state, while at the local
level the Tuberculosis Department of the District Board of Health is
the center of the prevention effort throughout the FRG. In Hannover
and the state of Lower Saxony (Niedersachsen), several other administratively separate facilities and organizations are involved in specific
aspects of tuberculosis prevention in cooperation with the Tuberculosis
Department. These include hospital-based pediatricians, private pulmonary specialists, physicians in the Youth Health Services Department
of the District Board of Health who are concerned with school health,
and a private organization which is responsible for certain aspects of
prevention for the major part of Lower Saxony outside of Hannover.

Another important institution involved in the tuberculosis effort in
the FRG is a private voluntary organization based in Hamburg, the
German Central Committee to Combat Tuberculosis (Deutsches Zentralkomitee zur Bekampfung der Tuberkulose; DZK). This organization,
made up of representatives of all public and private groups involved
with tuberculosis, has two major functions: the answering of specific
questions from physicians regarding the disease and the setting of
guidelines (recommendations, not requirements) about specific preventive and therapeutic measures to be used by physicians (Lock 1975a).
This organization participates on behalf of the FRG in the International
Union Against Tuberculosis.

In the GDR, a special set of laws (Buro des Präsidiums 1961) set out
the specific steps of the tuberculosis program to be carried out uniformly
throughout the country. This program is carried out by an essentially
separate organization which has the specific task of combating tuberculosis and pulmonary disease and which parallels the bureaucratic
structure in the GDR mentioned above under General Organization.

The Ministry of Health has delegated the responsibility for tuberculosis to the Research Institute for Pulmonary Disease and Tuberculosis
in Berlin. Working under the direction of this institute are separate
Tuberculosis Officers at the district and county levels who correspond
to the Medical Officers mentioned above. The District Tuberculosis
Officer heads the District Office for Pulmonary Disease and Tuberculosis,

and the County Tuberculosis Officer heads the Polyclinic Department for Pulmonary Disease and Tuberculosis (PALT). There is close consultation between the different health officers at each bureaucratic level (district and county), but the essential difference is that the organization headed by the Research Institute concerns itself with scientific and technical matters relating to pulmonary disease while the main bureaucratic structure deals with the overall financial and organizational planning of all health matters (Mazuhr 1975). Two other important groups which support and advise the Research Institute are the Problem Commission for Pulmonary Disease and Tuberculosis and a voluntary organization made up of physicians and others interested in pulmonary disease, the Society for Pulmonary Disease and Tuberculosis. The latter represents the GDR in the International Union Against Tuberculosis.

Given the above descriptions, there appear to be several major differences between the general organization of tuberculosis prevention in the two German states. First, the central role of the Research Institute in the GDR in setting policy and not just recommending it means that the preventive program is implemented uniformly throughout the GDR, in contrast to the FRG, where the DZK in Hamburg can make recommendations but each state is free to set its own policies. Second, rather than being integrated, it appears that the tuberculosis program in the GDR is more separate at the upper bureaucratic levels from other health programs than that in the FRG. At the primary-care level, however, the tuberculosis program in the GDR appears to be concentrated under fewer administrative units while at the same time more integrated with other health services than the program in the FRG.

## Tuberculosis Prevention at the Primary-Care Level

A number of specific measures to combat tuberculosis are utilized in both the FRG and the GDR, but in different manners and to different degrees. These measures include the following:

regular examination (including sputum exam and chest x-ray) of persons known to have pulmonary tuberculosis,

special examination (including skin tests, sputum exam, and chest x-ray) of families and contacts of newly discovered cases of TB,

regular examination of persons at special risk for development of TB (or other pulmonary disease), including those with fibrotic lung lesions, chronic bronchitis, and diabetes, mass chest radiography at regular intervals of a defined population, and

BCG (Bacille-Calmette-Guerin) vaccination of newborns with subsequent skin testing and revaccination during school years.

The state of Lower Saxony will be used as a model to illustrate how these measures are applied in the FRG (although it should be kept in mind that each state's program may be very different). The center of the program throughout the state is the Tuberculosis Department (Tuberkulosefürsorgestelle) of the County Board of Health, which is identical in every county. Staffed by one or more physicians, social workers, technicians, and clerical help and equipped with devices for standard-size chest x-rays, small-format chest x-rays (7 × 7 cm), fluoroscopy, and in some cases tomography, the departments have several main duties. These include follow-up examinations (including chest x-ray and sputum exam) of known cases of tuberculosis; examination of persons known to have had contact with persons with active TB; regular examination of members of certain occupational groups (e.g. teachers) and risk groups (e.g. those with a chronic productive cough); review of chest x-rays sent from hospitals, private physicians, and other departments within the Board of Health; and generally acting as a consultant for other physicians regarding pulmonary disease. The emphasis is on diagnosis with intensive use of sputum smears and cultures. The physicians of the Tuberculosis Department do not treat the patients.

When a patient in the city of Hannover (for example) is found by the Tuberculosis Department to have active TB or a suspicious pulmonary lesion, he is referred to one of nine private pulmonary specialists in the city or to a local hospital for treatment. The Tuberculosis Department is responsible for the diagnosis and for seeing that the patient receives treatment and is followed regularly. Representatives interviewed emphasized that as a result, the department maintains a close working relationship with the pulmonary physicians (Jacobs 1975). Information on a patient's status while he is being treated is exchanged regularly. In particular, there is a weekly exchange of x-rays between the private physicians and the Tuberculosis Department. A patient may get his chest x-rays and sputum exams at the department while concurrently being treated by the private physician, or he may choose to be followed entirely by the private physician. A private pulmonary specialist in Hannover felt the two major problems with this arrangement were the occasional disagreements over interpretation of x-rays and plans for therapy and the inconvenience for the patient. He emphasized that many of the patients choose to be followed entirely by the physician, in which case the Tuberculosis Department contacts the physician periodically about the patient's status (Lutz 1975).

Another primary function of the Tuberculosis Department in the city of Hannover is conducting the mass radiography program in the city as required by state law since 1950 (Niedersächsischen Staatskanzlei 1968). Lower Saxony is one of five states that require this regular examination (Deutsches Zentralkomitee 1975, pp. 16–24). This program is carried out by a special staff at a permanent central facility in Hannover. Portable x-ray equipment which can be assembled in any location is also available for the same purpose to factories with large numbers of workers. All persons over the age of 15 who have not had a chest x-ray within 6 months are required to be examined every 3 years when they receive an appointment card. The central examining location is open during normal working hours. The physicians from the Tuberculosis Department review the small-format films within one to two days as part of their regular work, and persons with suspicious findings relating to tuberculosis or other cardio-respiratory disease are contacted directly for follow-up examination. Old chest films are reviewed for comparison.

In practice the program faces a major difficulty. Despite the state law which provides for a stiff fine for not participating, approximately 40 percent of the persons invited do not come (Jacobs 1975). That is, 60 percent of the people either come or claim they have had a chest x-ray within 6 months. For foreign workers in Hannover the participation rate is even lower, approximately 56 percent (only 46 percent until recently when the chest x-ray was required for a foreign worker's continued stay in the FRG; see Jacobs 1975). The difficulties with increasing the participation rate surely involve the understanding and motivation of the population, including the fact that the state requires each person to pay a nominal fee for his examination. In addition, however, the Tuberculosis Department does not have a sufficient staff to keep the examination center open beyond working hours, when more people might participate. The staff is also too small to check claims of recent participation and to follow up on nonparticipants. Therefore, little is really done to enforce the legal requirement of regular examination (Jacobs 1975).

In most of the remainder of the state of Lower Saxony this mass radiography program is carried out by a private voluntary organization, the Lower Saxony Union to Combat Tuberculosis (Niedersächsischer Verein zur Bekämpfung der Tuberkulose), whose administrative head- quarters is in Hannover. The Union is funded by the state of Lower Saxony and through private contributions. Its program for mass ra- diography is basically the same as that in Hannover, except that there are three permanent examination locations in the state. Four examination teams, using either specially equipped buses or portable equipment which can be assembled in a public hall, work out of each of the three centers and visit each area of the state for several months every three years. Suspicious or positive findings are registered with the appropriate Tuberculosis Department, which then contacts the person directly for follow-up examinations. Although separate organizations, the Union and the Tuberculosis Departments work in close cooperation. The par- ticipation rate is much better than that in the city of Hannover. Ap- proximately 90–94 percent of those invited either claim to have had a recent chest x-ray (approximately 15–20 percent) or come for the ex- amination. This increased success is attributed in part to the fact that the examination areas are open in the evenings and in part to the fact that most of the communities visited by the mobile teams are small and therefore the awareness of and the familiarity with the mass ra- diography program are high (Klose 1975).

The other two aspects of the tuberculosis program, BCG vaccination of newborns and skin testing and revaccination of school children at various ages, are independent of the Tuberculosis Department. In Han- nover, for example, newborns are vaccinated during the first week by hospital-based pediatricians and subsequent skin testing and revaccin- ation is performed by twelve physicians employed by the County Board of Health. BCG vaccination is not required anywhere in the FRG but is publicly recommended by the governments of seven states, including Lower Saxony (Lock 1975a). In Lower Saxony approximately 93 percent of all newborns are vaccinated with BCG, essentially because there is a physician in the District Board of Health in Hannover who started the vaccination program in 1953 and still feels strongly that it plays an important role in preventing tuberculosis in children (Maneke 1975).

In the GDR the same measures mentioned above are used at the primary care level, but with some important differences. As in the FRG, the center of the tuberculosis effort in the GDR is the institution at the county level, the Polyclinic Department for Pulmonary Disease and Tuberculosis (PALT). Both the PALT and the Tuberculosis Department of the County Board of Health in the FRG are derived from the same model, developed by Putter in Germany around 1900 (Steinbrück 1974a). That original model exists virtually intact today in the West German system, but it has been modified in the GDR. After World War II the occupying forces of the Soviet Union ordered the reconstruction of the county-level network for the eradication of tuberculosis because of the severe problem that disease posed at the time. The new county institution, while remaining separate from other health-care facilities as in the FRG today, became responsible not only for diagnosis but also for treatment and prophylaxis (Harmsen 1955). This model (called the Kreisstelle für Lungenkrankheiten und Tuberkulose) persisted until 1975, when an administrative change made the PALT one of several departments of the polyclinic, the important ambulatory facility in the GDR. Except in the newer facilities, this change is only an administrative one and the PALT is still physically separate from other polyclinic facilities. The PALT, which is usually staffed by one pulmonary specialist, several social workers, technicians, clerical help, and a specially trained immunization nurse, is the center for matters regarding the ambulatory surveillance and treatment of patients with tuberculosis and other pulmonary diseases.

Working in close cooperation with other health facilities (including hospitals, other outpatient facilities, and practicing physicians), the PALT follows patients with tuberculosis; examines yearly patients at special risk for TB (e.g. those with fibrotic lung lesions); follows patients with other pulmonary diseases, such as chronic obstructive lung disease, sarcoidosis, silicosis, and asbestosis; and examines yearly men in the 50–65 age group who have a history of smoking and are at special risk for the development of lung cancer. These last patients are being identified by the use of a questionnaire administered before the mass radiography examinations (Mazuhr 1975). In recent years, all these patients have been followed more and more by physicians outside the PALT, such as at a person's place of work or near his home when that is more convenient, although the PALT keeps in close contact with the patient's progress. This has been done for the convenience of the patient as well as because of the heavy work load of the single physician at the PALT (Eberhardt 1975). Regardless of where the patient is followed, however, since 1962 all physicians in the GDR have used a standard therapy for tuberculosis patients as outlined by the Research Institute in Berlin (Mazuhr 1975).

The last major task of the PALT, that of prophylaxis, is carried out by the immunization nurse, who goes into hospitals to vaccinate newborns with BCG, goes to schools to skin-test and revaccinate children, and vaccinates members of certain occupation groups, such as teachers and food-industry workers. The immunization of newborns was begun in 1951 and today includes over 99 percent of all newborns, as required by law since 1961 (Steinbrück 1974, p. 980).

The last major aspect of the tuberculosis-prevention program in the GDR—and the only one at the primary care level outside of the PALT— is the mass radiography program conducted by the District Office for Pulmonary Disease and Tuberculosis since 1955. Until 1973 every person 15 or older who had not had a chest x-ray in the previous 6 months was legally required to have a yearly examination. Since 1973 this exam is required only every 2 years (Steinbrück 1974b, p. 996). The participation rate of 85 percent in the cities and 95 percent in the country has been favorably affected by the active part played by personnel managers and factory directors, who are responsible for seeing that their workers take part in the mass examination (Vogtländer 1975). Several teams utilizing specially equipped buses and portable equipment travel throughout the district using the public media and personal cards to inform people of the locations of the examination teams. The small-format (7 × 7 cm) chest films are reviewed by the PALT physician, who then contacts the individual directly when there are suspicious findings. This is really the only contact the PALT has with the mass radiography process.

### Similarities and Contrasts at the Primary Care Level

At the primary care level there are several organizational similarities between the FRG and the GDR. The county-based institutions (the Tuberculosis Department and the PALT), which are based on the same original model, are the centers of the preventive effort, and they rely on close cooperation with other physicians and health facilities. Both are beginning to focus their efforts on groups at risk for tuberculosis or other pulmonary disease, although the GDR may be ahead in this regard, as is illustrated by its program to identify and screen a group of men at high risk for lung cancer. The mass radiography programs are virtually identical in basic execution and in both countries are essentially separate from other measures. Finally, both countries suffer from a shortage of the manpower that is required to carry out all measures completely.

A basic point of difference between the two systems is that the PALT in the GDR is now integrated with other ambulatory health services and concerns itself not only with the diagnosis and surveillance of tuberculosis but also with the treatment of that and other pulmonary disease. However, with the increasing emphasis on treating the tuberculosis patient in the community, patients in both countries can be followed by doctors outside the tuberculosis facilities if they so desire. In the GDR the preventive effort is concentrated in two agencies, while in Lower Saxony, for example, several agencies are involved. There appears to be a greater effort on the part of the authorities in the GDR to get people to participate directly in the preventive measures through legal requirements and to enlist the help of others, such as plant managers, in increasing participation. The last point is that the GDR appears to have had greater success in the application of preventive measures such as mass radiography and BCG vaccination. Whereas in the FRG there is a wide range in the use of BCG vaccination from state to state (Deutsches Zentralkomitee 1972), over 90 percent of all newborns in the GDR have been vaccinated since 1960 (Steinbrück 1974b, p. 982).

## Discussion

The main overall differences between the two systems appear to be that one (GDR) is a centrally planned and executed program, integrated at the periphery with other health services so that there is greater application of some preventive measures, while the other (FRG) has a central advisory body (the DZK in Hamburg) but essentially consists of eleven programs separate from other health services at the periphery. It is not clear that any specific measures have resulted in the improved tuberculosis situation in the two countries, but it is obvious that the remarkable dedication of personnel in both countries has played an important role. Certainly, the increased standard of living in both countries since World War II, with improvements in housing, nutrition, and education, has had an enormous impact. Different systems for classifying tuberculosis data (Neumann 1972; Lock 1974; Forschungsinstitut 1971) make it difficult to compare the present state of the disease, but data from the DZK in Hamburg can be used as an illustration. Although the incidence of TB in the GDR far exceeded that in the FRG in the 1950s, there has been a parallel decline in the overall incidence in both countries since about 1965 (Lock 1974), with the GDR enjoying a lower level in 1980 (Staatliche Zentralverwaltung 1981, p. 373; Statistisches Bundesamt 1982, p. 378).

This favorable situation in the two countries, however, points up interesting differences in the responsiveness of the two systems. It is believed by some that a better measure of the tuberculosis situation in developed countries is an estimation of the "infection risk" (the proportion of a population that will become infected in a given year). Styblo (1973) recommends that when this risk declines to 0.1 percent mass preventive measures (such as BCG and chest radiography) should be discontinued in favor of more emphasis on finding and treating persons with tuberculosis. Officials in both the GDR (Steinbrück 1975) and the FRG (Lock 1975a) now believe the infection risk in their countries to be 0.1 percent or less. The DZK in Hamburg has recommended that BCG vaccination be discontinued throughout the FRG (Lock 1975b; 1979). As might be expected, differing opinions mean that in some states the use of BCG will be eliminated while in others it will continue (Maneke 1975). East German officials, while acknowledging that BCG vaccination will probably have no more effect on the overall epidemiological situation, will continue it because they feel the people have accepted it and expect it and because the officials believe the vaccination program would be cheaper and more convenient than treating those who would get the disease (Steinbrück 1975; Landmann 1979; Steinbrück and Herrmann 1982; Thal and Müller 1982).

### Conclusions and Implications for Future Investigation

This study has attempted to describe the organization of tuberculosis prevention in the FRG and the GDR, especially at the primary care level, in order to identify factors which may play an important role in influencing health status. A number of prominent similarities and differences between the two systems have been identified, but exactly what effect these factors have had on the campaigns against tuberculosis is unclear. It does appear that there is a greater emphasis in the GDR on the use of preventive measures and, where possible, on the integration of such measures with other health services. The centrally directed nature of the programs in the GDR may have permitted a more uniform and intensive application of preventive measures (such as BCG vaccination and mass radiography) but at the same time may be responsible for the retention of specific programs (e.g. BCG vaccination) beyond their period of usefulness.

It is tempting to attribute the differences in programs to the overall political structures in the two countries, but certainly other factors must be considered. For example, rather than political structure, it may be the different interests of the power groups in the two countries that account for the dissimilar programs. In the GDR, where the labor pool is very small and the need for increasing industrial production very great, the economic need to protect the health of the workers is enormous. In the FRG, where full employment is not a necessity, this may not be the case. A comparison of factory or employee health services done with this in mind might provide interesting insights into the two countries.

These differences in basic interests may also have important implications for other health areas. With the increasing evidence of the role of environmental pollution in a number of disease areas, such as pulmonary disease and cancer it would be interesting to know how each country reconciles its industrial needs with the need to protect the health of its people.

## Acknowledgments

Supported in part by the Paul Dudley White Fund of the Harvard Medical School.

My special thanks to Dr. Ray Elling, University of Connecticut School of Medicine, for his support and encouragement during this study.

## References

Bundesseuchengesetz—Gesetz zur Verhutung und Bekämpfung übertragbarer Krankheiten beim Menschen. 1974. Sixth edition. Siegburg: Reckinger.

Bundessozialhilfegesetz. 1975. Fifteenth edition. Siegburg: Reckinger.

Buro des Präsidiums des Ministerrates der DDR. 1961. "Verordnung zur Verhutung und Bekämpfung der Tuberkulose." Gesetzblatt der Deutschen Demokratischen Republik, part 2, 80:509–515.

Buro des Präsidiums des Ministerrates der DDR. 1975. "Zweite Verordnung zur Verhutung und Bekämpfung der Tuberkulose." Gesetzblatt der Deutschen Demokratischen Republik, part 1, 28:521.

Deutsches Zentralkomitee zur Bekämpfung der Tuberkulose. 1972. 2. Informationsbericht.

Deutsches Zentralkomitee zur Bekämpfung der Tuberkulose. 1975. 5. Informationsbericht.

Eberhardt, A. 1975. Interview. Director, Poliklinische Abteilung für Lungenkranken und Tuberkulose, Stadt Bezirk Dresden.

Eichhorn, S. 1973. "German Federal Republic." In Health Service Prospects—An International Survey, ed. Douglas-Wilson and McLachlan. Boston: Little, Brown.

Elling, R. H., and H. Kerr. 1975. "Selection of Contrasting National Health Systems for In-depth Study." Supplement to Inquiry, 12.2:25–40.

Forschungsinstitut für Tuberkulose und Lungenkrankheiten, DDR. 1971. Richtlinien für die Registrierung und Gesundheitliche Überwachung der Tuberkulosen Betreungsfalle und der Exponierten in den Ambulaten Einrichtung der Tuberkulose-Bekämpfung. Second edition. East Berlin: Buchdruckerei Ing. H. Schroeter.

Harmsen, H. 1955. Entwicklung der Tuberkulose-Fürsorge in der UdSSR und DDR. Volume 2. Akademie für Staatsmedizin.

Jacobs, A. 1975. Interview. Tuberkulosefürsorgestelle, Stadt Hannover.

Klose, G. 1975. Interview. Director, Niedersächsischer Verein zur Bekämpfung der Tuberkulose.

Landmann, H. 1979. "Die Tuberkuloseschutzimpfung in der DDR—Rückblick und Ausblick." Zeitschrift für Erkrankungen der Atmungsorgane 153:50–79.

Lock, W. 1974. "Vergleichende Betrachtung der Tuberkulosesituation in der DDR und in der BRD." Praxis der Pneumologie 28:887–892.

Lock, W. 1975a. Interview. Director, Deutsches Zentralkomitee zur Bekämpfung der Tuberkulose, Hamburg.

Lock, W. 1975b. "Probleme der BCG-Impfung." Bundesgesundheitsblatt 18.37.

Lock, W. 1979. "Zur ungezielten BCG-Impfung der Neugeboren." Das öffentliche Gesundheitswesen 41:627–630.

Lutz, H. 1975. Interview. Private pulmonary physician. Hannover.

Maneke, M. 1975. Interview. Gesundheitsamt, Stadt Hannover.

Mazuhr, H. 1975. Interview. Forschungsinstitut für Lungenkrankheiten und Tuberkulose, Berlin-Buch, GDR.

Neumann, G. 1972. "Neuordnung der Tuberkulose Statistik." Das öffentliche Gesundheitswesen, special issue, 34.1:29–34.

Niedersächsische Staatskanzlei. 1968. "Bekanntmachung der Neufassung des Gesetzes über Röntgenreihenuntersuchung." Niedersächsisches Gesetz- und Verordnungsblatt 22.4:45–46.

Pflanz, M. 1971. "German Health Insurance: The Evolution and Current Problems of the Pioneer System." International Journal of Health Services 1.4:315–330.

Staatliche Zentralverwaltung für Statistik. 1981. Statistisches Jahrbuch der Deutschen Demokratischen Republik. East Berlin: Staatsverlag der DDR.

Statistisches Bundesamt. Statistisches Jahrbuch für die Bundesrepublik Deutschland. Stuttgart: Verlag Kohlhammer. 1967, p. 69; 1977, p. 357; 1978, pp. 372, 375; 1981, pp. 375, 597; 1982, pp. 378, 387.

Steinbrück, P. W. 1974a. "Tuberkulose Bekämpfung in der DDR von 1949–1973, Teil I." DDR Medizin Report 3.7:593.

Steinbrück, P. W. 1974b. "Tuberkulose Bekämpfung in der DDR von 1949–1973, Teil II." DDR Medizin Report 3.11:980–996.

Steinbrück, P. W. 1975. Interview. Director, Forschungsinstitut für Lungenkrankheiten und Tuberkulose, Berlin-Buch, GDR.

Steinbrück, P. W., and H. Herrmann. 1982. "Die Entwicklung der Tuberkuloseepidemiologie in der Deutschen Demokratischen Republik." Zeitschrift für Erkrankungen der Atmungsorgane 158:81–94.

Styblo, K. 1973. "The Epidemiology and Control of Tuberculosis in Developed Countries." Therapeutische Umschau 30.3:199–206.

Thal, W., and J. Müller. 1982. "Der Rückgang der Kindertuberkulose in der DDR—Fakten und Konsequenzen." Zeitschrift für Erkrankungen der Atmungsorgane 158:142–148.

Vogtländer, H. 1975. Interview. TBC-Bezirkstelle, Dresden.

Winter, Kurt. 1974. Das Gesundheitswesen in der Deutschen Demokratischen Republik. East Berlin: Akademie für Ärtzliche Fortbildung der DDR.

World Bank. 1980. World Development Report. New York: Oxford University Press.

World Health Organization. 1973. Organizational Study on Methods of Promoting the Development of Basic Health Services. Annex II to Official Records of the WHO No. 206. Geneva.

# IV

**Healers and their Patients**

# 13

## Qualification and Professionalization in the Health-Care Professions

### Barbara Bergmann-Krauss

*One of the most dynamic and unfolding aspects of modern health-care systems that deal with relatively healthy populations concerns the division of labor between physicians and other professionals. In this chapter, Barbara Bergmann-Krauss traces the rather different roads the two Germanies have taken since World War II, largely for ideological reasons. At the same time she notes ways in which forces of the welfare state exhibit themselves in both states. She also describes how some paraprofessional groups in West Germany are moving out from under the control of physicians and even competing with them. The success of these maneuvers is not unrelated to the growing irrelevance of physician training to the health needs of the population.*

This chapter aims to identify the similarities and differences in the development and the present state of the health-care professions (especially the paramedical health occupations) in the two German states with regard to the process by which occupations and professions develop. This examination of similarities and differences will be undertaken against the background of differing political ideologies, health systems, and concepts of sickness or health. In contrast to the physician, most health occupations in Germany have as yet received little theoretical or empirical attention; their roles, their socialization and professionalization processes, the educational requirements, and the conditions for advanced training have been studied only to a limited degree.

With the help of statistical data, the more formal aspects of the professional situation will be compared: regulations for professional training, possibilities for further education, and the like. Although difficult to measure or verify, differences in professional roles or identities as well as the respective responsibilities and qualification requirements of health-care professions will have to be examined in an attempt to assess the actual professional situations of these groups in the two German states.

A comparison of the training and professional situations of the health occupations in the two German states is difficult, since the situation in the German Democratic Republic (GDR; East Germany) can only be inferred from official statements in professional magazines and elsewhere. An evaluation of how these statements relate to actual practice could not be undertaken. The following portrayal is therefore based on the analysis of statistics, laws, statutes, and relevant literature from the GDR, especially the professional journals for the paramedical employees (such as *Heilberufe* and *Humanitas*).

In general, the differences in both qualification and professional situation of the health occupations in the Federal Republic of Germany (FRG; West Germany) and the GDR seem to be minimal. Because of the two states' common history, various important structural similarities typical of the German health-care system remain: a similar spectrum of health professions, similar educational structures (such as the dual apprenticeship model), the therapeutic monopoly of physicians, and the social security system (including mandatory health insurance). Thus, the similarities of training and of the professional situation of the health occupations in the two states are greater than the differences. This chapter, however, will focus on several important differences.

## The Organization of the Health-Care System

In the FRG, illness is conceived as having a somatic and individual etiology. Psychological causes are less important, and social causes are considered to play no role at all. The physician, freely chosen by the patient, determines for the patient the individual therapy. Curative measures are emphasized. The health-care system in the FRG is based on the individual doctor-patient relationship. In this relationship the sickness funds intervene as far as the costs are concerned; they define the services the physician may render within the social health insurance and the premiums the insured have to pay. The consultation of the physician then is free for the patients. Ninety-three percent of the population in the FRG are members of the social health insurance program; the other 7 percent are insured privately.

The sickness funds are self-governed; that is to say, they are conceived of as a united group of the insured. The insured elect the representatives of the sickness funds in "social elections" (Sozialwahlen). The sickness funds negotiate with the Sickness Funds Physicians' Associations (Kassenärztliche Vereinigungen) the fees for medical services.

The physicians also belong to semi-public mandatory associations (Ärztekammern, or physicians' chambers), which protect the interests of the physicians internally and externally. Their functions are to develop a homogenous concept of the profession, to consult with and support the members, to promote professional specialization and continuing education, and to protect the interests of the professional before local and state authorities, associations, and the public.

All sickness-fund physicians (Kassenärzte)—more than 90 percent of the physicians in free practice—are members of the Kassenärztliche Vereinigungen. Their function is to conclude contracts with the sickness funds, in order to obtain the funds from which their members' fees are paid. The Kassenärztliche Vereinigungen are the representatives of the interests of the Kassenärzte when negotiating with the sickness funds. The delegates and boards of directors of the Ärztekammern and the Kassenärztliche Vereinigungen are elected by the physicians every 4 years. By virtue of the element of self-government of the health insurance institutions and the physicians' associations, the system of health care in the FRG has a considerable corporate character. The intermediate level—the level between the individual physician and the state—thus has an important regulatory function within the system of health care.

Despite the fact that German doctors are private practitioners, their economic interests and their income are largely regulated by the sickness funds, of which they are almost all members. The fee schedule which the Kassenärztliche Vereinigungen negotiate with the sickness funds is passed as law by the legislature, so the specific value attributed to each service for the coming year depends on the bargaining skills of the negotiators for each side. Thus, the Vereinigungen perform a union function, though physicians would adamantly reject this view.

The state has only limited competence in the system of health care in the FRG. There is a special Ministry for Health Care, Youth, and Family on the federal level, and there are ministries in the eleven states where health care, social concerns, and labor are usually combined. However, their possibilities of influencing or shaping the health-care system are minimal; they have only an indirect effect. The state in its ministries has the legal supervision over the social health insurance, the Ärztekammern, and the Vereinigungen because they are self-governed semi-public bodies (Körperschaften öffentlichen Rechts). The state has the power to issue guidelines, and laws, and educational directives and to ratify the regulation of fees. For several years the state tried increasingly to influence and regulate materially the health-care system through laws such as the Krankenhausfinanzierunggesetz (hospital financing law) and the Kostendampfungsgesetz (cost-reduction law). Until recently these attempts at more state influence in the health-care system could be held at bay by the physicians' associations, but today there is a struggle between the state and these associations for power over the structures of medical care. The outcome is still unknown.

In sum, the health-care system in the FRG has a nongovernmental but corporate character, which is decentralized and pluralistic, with state, voluntary, and private institutions side by side. In the ambulatory-care sector the free practice is the most important institution. The health-care system in the FRG is oriented toward curative medicine based on an individual etiology of disease.

In the GDR health and disease are considered not a private but a societal matter determined by structural factors. The state thus has a legitimate interest in the health-care system (Ruban 1981). This means that the state is responsible for the organization, performance, and control of the health-care system; the individual, the societal groups, and the factories and firms are requested to contribute to the protection and maintenance of health. Prevention is especially important within the health-care system of the GDR.

The health-care system of the GDR is organized hierarchically and centrally. The Ministry of Health makes all important and basic decisions on health care with regard to target objectives for the health-care authorities in the districts, the distribution of funds and materials, and the disposition of personnel, educational, and other matters. The Ministry of Health must observe the decisions of the Central Committee of the SED (the dominant party), which has a special section for health policy.

In the fourteen regions in the Rat des Bezirken (government of the regions) there are departments of health care and social affairs, which are governed by a "district physician," who is the senior physician in the GDR. These departments decide on the locations and equipment of polyclinics and outpatient departments, but above all they realize the decisions and target objectives of the Ministry of Health.

In the "counties" (Kreisen), the administrative unit below the Bezirken, there are departments for health care and social affairs, which are controlled by the county physician (Kreisarzt). He carries out the orders of the district physician and forwards them to the local institutions; he is the controlling and central person for all the medical institutions of his county.

The medical services in the GDR are delivered in clinics and hospitals, in outpatient departments of polyclinics, in smaller ambulatory clinics (Ambulatorien), in state doctors' offices (staatliche Arztpraxes), and in dispensaries (Arztsanitätsstationen). The polyclinics, the biggest institutions in the outpatient sector, are the most frequented (by 56 percent of the population); next are the ambulatories (23 percent), then the state practices (16 percent), and the dispensaries (5 percent). There are also private physicians' and dentists' practices, but there are no data on their use. We do know, however, that their importance has been constantly decreasing. The polyclinics, the ambulatories, and the other institutions in the ambulatory sector serve a defined residential area or a factory. Today every third ambulatory and every fifth polyclinic belongs to a factory.

In sum: The health-care system in the GDR has a state character; a central, hierarchical, and uniform system; a preference for large clinics; a factory orientation in the ambulatory sector; and an emphasis on prevention.

## Spectrum of the Health Occupations

In addition to physicians, dentists, and pharmacists, which exist in both German states, there are many paramedical occupations, some of which differ between the states. In the FRG the paramedical occupations are officially defined as Heilhilfsberufe (auxiliary healing personnel). Since many find this title unsatisfactory, various other terms are used: Medizinalfachberufe (paramedical specialties), medizinische Fachkräfte (paramedical specialists), nichtärztliche Medizinalberufe (nonphysician paramedical specialties), and nichtärztliche Gesundheitsberufe (nonphysician health professions). Some of these professions are nationally recognized and therefore accepted in the entire country, while other professions are recognized and regulated only in one or several of the federal states. In the GDR, these occupations are designated as "middle-level medical personnel"; they are recognized in the entire country. Table 1 lists the occupations present in both German states. Not included are persons working in pharmacies, in veterinary medicine, and in the specialized occupations which require advanced training.

**Table 1**
Titles of auxiliary (or paramedical) health occupations.

| FRG | U.S. | GDR |
|---|---|---|
| **Occupations with same title in FRG and GDR** | | |
| Krankenschwester/pfleger | Nurse | Krankenschwester/pfleger |
| Kinderkrankenschwester | Pediatric nurse | Kinderkrankenschwester |
| Hebamme | Midwife | Hebamme |
| Medizinisch technischer Radiologieassistent | X-ray technician | Medizinisch technischer Radiologieassistent |
| Masseur | Masseur | Masseur |
| Diatassistent | Dietician | Diastassistent |
| Orthoptist | | Orthoptist |
| Desinfektor | Disinfector | Desinfektor |
| Zahntechniker | Certified dental technician | Zahntechniker |
| **Occupations with different titles but same function** | | |
| Krankenpflegehelfer | Nurse's aide | Pfacharbeiter für Krankenpflege |
| Krankengymnastin | Physical therapist | Physiotherapeut |
| Logopäde | Speech therapist | Audiologie-Phonartrie Assistent |
| Gesundheitsaufseher | Health inspector | Hygieneinspektor |
| Arzthelferin | Medical secretary | Sprechstundenschwester |
| Zahnarzthelferin | Dental assistant | Stomatologische Schwester |
| Kaufmann im Krankenhaus | Hospital administrative employee | Wirtschaftskaufmann im Gesundheits- und sozialwesen |
| **Titles existing only in FRG** | | |
| Wochenpflegerin | Visiting Obstetric Nurse | |
| Masseur und Medizinischer Bademeister | Masseur and Medical Bath Supervisor | |
| Arbeits- und Beschaftigungs-Therapeut | Work and Occupational Therapist | |
| Assistent für Exfoliatiozytologie | Assistant for exfoliation cytology | |
| Sozialmedizinischer Assistent | Assistant for social medicine | |
| Dokumentationsassistent | Document Assistant | |
| Heilpraktiker | Health Practitioner | |
| Medizintechniker | Medical Technician | |
| Bio-Ingenieur | Biological Engineer | |

| FRG | U.S. | GDR |
| --- | --- | --- |
| **Titles existing only in GDR** | | |
| | Nursery Attendant | Krippenerzieherin |
| | Occupational Health Inspector | Arbeitshygieneinspektor |
| | Assistant for Functional Diagnosis | Medizinisch Technischer Assistent für Funktionsdiagnostik |
| | Child Care Specialist | Facharbeiter für Kinderpflege |
| | Administrative Assistants | Wirtschafts- pflegerin und Wirtschaftsgehilfin |
| | Dietary Cook | Diatkoch |
| | Cosmetician | Kosmetikerin |
| | Specialist for Medical Autopsy | Facharbeiter für Medizinische Sektionstechnik |
| | Orthopedic Technician | Bandagist |

Many occupations in the health systems of the FRG and the GDR, although not always comparable in regard to educational level, correspond in definitions and responsibilities. There are traditional health occupations, such as nurse, pediatric nurse, midwife, x-ray technician, laboratory assistant, dietitian, masseur,[1] and disinfector.[2] Other professions have similar responsibilities but different names in the FRG and the GDR. This is the case for the medical and dental assistant in the FRG, who is called a Sprechstundenschwester or stomatologische Schwester in the GDR. A physical therapist is called a Krankengymnastin in the FRG and a Physiotherapeut in the GDR. A speech therapist is called a Logopäde in the FRG and an Audiologie-Phonatrie Assistent in the GDR. Other occupations exist either only in the FRG or in the GDR. This is the case especially in the medical-technical and medical-therapeutic occupations, that is, those occupations which have arisen within the last 30 years. Examples of these are (in the FRG) the Arbeits- und Beschäftigungstherapeut (work and occupational therapist), the sozialmedizinischer Assistent (social medical assistant), the Dokumentationsassistent (documentary assistant), and Medizintechniker (medical technologist), and (in the GDR) the Hygiene- und Arbeits-hygieneinspektor[3] (health and occupational health inspector) and the medizinisch-technischer Assistent für Funktionsdiagnostik (medical technical assistant for functional diagnosis). The nursery attendant (Krippenerzieherin) in the GDR is considered a middle-level medical employee because of the special organizational responsibilities for the education of small children; an equally specialized occupation is not to be found in the FRG, where the comparable occupation is part of the social-service system. Other occupations in the FRG are not so clearly assigned to either the health or the social sector, for example the Altenpfleger (geriatrics assistant) or the Heilerziehungshelfer (orthopedic assistant). Besides these, there are health occupations in the FRG which existed before the division of Germany and for which the GDR no longer offers training. This is the case especially for the Heilpraktiker (health practitioners), for whom professional regulations were established in the 1930s. The Heilpraktiker, in contrast to the other health occupations, may diagnose and treat patients on his own. He does not act under the supervision of a physician. His emphasis is on lay medical, holistic, and homeopathic procedures. The few Heilpraktiker left in the GDR were licensed before 1945. Since then no new Heilpraktiker have been licensed. The GDR rejects holistic concepts and stresses a somatic and natural-science orientation.

The spectrum of auxiliary health occupations has expanded considerably in both the FRG and the GDR since the creation of the two states. This would be even more apparent if those occupations which are based on adult education training programs were to be included in this study. There is at present a tendency toward greater differentiation in the auxiliary health occupations. New careers will appear in the years to come, especially in social medicine, medical data processing, and medical technology (Schipperges 1975). The differentiation in the health occupations also necessitates greatly increased cooperation among the members of these different professions. The integration and institutionalization of the particular activities and duties of the various occupations to form an encompassing medical service thus becomes paramount.

*Statistical Data on Employment*

The statistical data on the auxiliary health occupations in the FRG and the GDR are comparable only to a limited extent. Often only selected data are recorded and the categories for collecting and organizing the data differ.

In the GDR only the medical personnel of state institutions are included in the statistics of employment, and (in contrast to the FRG) state institutions play a prominent role. Whereas over one-fourth of all health employees in the FRG (60,000 physicians, 30,000 dentists,

100,000 doctors' assistants, and about 18,000 auxiliary health personnel such as medical technicians and nurses) are working in private practices and 62 percent of all hospitals and 46 percent of all hospital beds are maintained by voluntary or private institutions, private practices and religious or private institutions are negligible in the GDR. Only 863 physicians and 1,064 dentists had private practices in 1980 in the GDR, and this number is constantly decreasing. For example, in 1955, with fewer physicians in total, there were 5,000 private medical and dental practices (Deutsches Institut für Wirtschaftsforschung 1979, p. 281). Of the 584 hospitals with 184,214 beds available in 1974, only 96 hospitals with 13,417 beds were under private or church administration, that is, 16 percent of all hospitals and 7 percent of all hospital beds. Indeed the private and church sectors have little influence in the GDR, as these figures show; but it is difficult to judge what amount of distortion is caused by noninclusion in the statistics.

Table 2 shows the figures for employment in the health sectors of the FRG and the GDR. The year 1974 was chosen for the table because the greatest number of comparable statistics were available for that year. In any case it is not completely clear which areas or employment groups in either country have been omitted.

On the basis of the data and the officially published figures it is apparent that the FRG employs almost 3 times as many persons in the health sector as the GDR. This corresponds roughly to the population ratio of the two states (approximately 17,000,000 GDR, 60,000,000 FRG). If one compares individual professional groups, however, differences between the two states become apparent. In the GDR, for example, the number of physicians and dentists is low in comparison with the total number of employees in the health sector, and the proportion of pharmacists is even smaller. The number of pharmacists in the FRG is 8 times that of the GDR. Health practitioners, as mentioned before, hardly exist in the GDR. On the other hand, the statistics for the GDR show 4,500 additional employees with university degrees. The corresponding group does not appear in the statistics of the FRG. They are probably engineers, physicists, chemists, psychologists, economists, and sociologists. These professions are not included in the list of the health professions in the FRG. In the GDR, this figure may also include a greater number of teachers who are employed in nurseries and day-care centers (for children through the age of 3). These institutions play an important role because of the high employment rate among women in the GDR. It has already been mentioned that nurseries

**Table 2**
Employees in the health sector, 1974.

| FRG[a] | | | GDR[b] | | |
|---|---|---|---|---|---|
| Occupation | No. of employees | Percent of employees in health sector | Occupation | No. of employees | Percent of employees in health sector |
| Physician | 114,661 | 11.6 | Physician | 28,930 | 9.8 |
| Dentist | 31,538 | 3.7 | Dentist | 5,940 | 2.0 |
| Pharmacist | 24,787 | 2.9 | Pharmacist | 3,220 | 1.1 |
| Heilpraktiker | 3,362 | 0.4 | Other employees with college degree[f] | 4,500 | 1.5 |
| Nursing personnel | 262,029 | 31.0 | Middle-level medical personnel with diploma | 147,960 | 50.2 |
| Nurse | 150,344 | | Nurse | 64,050 | |
| Pediatric nurse | 21,058 | | Pediatric nurse | 13,760 | |
| Nurse's aide | 39,097 | | | | |
| Nursing personnel without degree | 49,530 | | Employees with Meister title | 1,700 | 0.6 |
| Medical technologist | 22,862 | 2.7 | Medical assistants | 46,000 | 15.3 |
| Other occupations[c] | 40,548 | 4.8 | Unskilled and semi-skilled workers[g] | 56,000 | 19.0 |
| Physician's and dentist's assistants[d] | 100,000 | 11.8 | | | |
| Administrative personnel[e] | 246,000 | 29.1 | | | |
| Total | 845,878 | 100.0 | Total | 294,850 | 100.0 |

Sources: Statistisches Bundesamt 1974, p. 26; Ruban 1981, p. 325.
a. Not including persons in training (ca. 220,000) and occupations involving handicrafts.
b. Only employees in state institutions.
c. For example, midwives, physical therapists, masseurs, medical bath directors, work and occupational therapists, dietary assistants, health inspectors, pharmaceutical assistants, speech therapists, orthopedists, cytology assistants.
d. This number is an approximation; the actual number is probably higher (Eberle and Geissler 1978, p. 512).
e. Only hospital employees (Statistisches Bundesamt 1977, p. 364).
f. The vocational diploma for middle-level medical occupations was introduced on September 1, 1974, in the GDR; this explains this low number.
g. This number, which probably also includes administrative personnel, is not reported in the statistics but was deduced from the difference between the total number of employees and the numbers for the individual occupations.

in the GDR, in contrast to the FRG, are a designated part of the health system, and this emphasizes the point that only an approximate comparison of the data in table 2 is possible.

It is also notable that the percentage of the "middle-level health employees" is higher in the GDR than in the FRG. This shows that many medical services in the GDR are performed by paramedical specialists, whereas in the FRG they are still performed by physicians. Recently, however, there have been efforts in the FRG to transfer physicians' duties to semiprofessionals, for example in health and life counseling (Schuller 1976). The middle-level health employees are not differentiated according to individual occupations in the GDR statistics, so a comparison of the individual occupations, which would certainly be interesting and could provide an indication of differing structures and areas of priorities, is not possible.

The only available data on nurses and pediatric nurses confirm that the percentage of middle-level medical personnel is higher in the GDR. Whereas the total number of health employees in the GDR amounts to 35 percent of that in the FRG, the percentage increases to 50 percent among employees of the middle level, and to 70 percent among pediatric nurses. The last figure is due to the special importance of nurseries in the GDR and to the fact that the nurseries (of which there were 5,383 with space for 224,574 children in 1974) are assigned to the health sector there. On the assumption that there should be at least one attendant for every eight infants (the minimum according to guiding directives in the FRG in 1974), there would need to be 28,000 employees in the nurseries in the GDR alone; many of these pediatric nurses are probably included in this number.

Traditionally, the auxiliary health occupations have been filled by women (Ostner and Beck-Gernsheim 1979). That is also the case in the preceding statistics for both German states. Tables 3 and 4 show the percentage of women among health employees. Even though the categories chosen for the GDR and for the FRG differ, it is still clear that the percentage of women is considerably higher in the GDR.

The health sector of the GDR is a professional field in which women dominate. Only in the organizations of hygiene and health education is the percentage of women below 80 percent. The health sector of the FRG does indeed employ many women (62 percent), but in comparison with the GDR the percentage is markedly lower. Women are employed mainly in the nursing field, and the percentages of women among physicians (20 percent) and dentists (17 percent) are considerably

**Table 3**
Percentage of women among employees in health occupations in FRG, 1975.

|  | Total no. of employees | No. of women | Percent women |
|---|---|---|---|
| Doctors | 118,726 | 23,970 | 20.2 |
| Dentists | 31,774 | 5,433 | 17.1 |
| Pharmacists | 25,597 | 12,890 | 50.3 |
| Heilpraktiker | 3,715 | 1,000 | 26.9 |
| Nursing Personnel | 223,740 | 195,016 | 87.1 |
| Other | 80,868 | 63,697 | 78.7 |
| Total | 484,420 | 302,006 | 62.3 |

Source: Statistiches Bundesamt 1977, p. 362.

**Table 4**
Percentage of women among employees in health institutions in GDR, 1975.

|  | Total no. of employees | No. of women | Percent women |
|---|---|---|---|
| Hospitals | 150,000 | 123,000 | 82.0 |
| Kur- und Badewesen | 10,300 | 8,000 | 80.6 |
| Ambulatory institutions | 123,000 | 102,400 | 83.2 |
| Hygiene and health education | 10,400 | 7,600 | 73.0 |
| Administrative bureaucracy, pharmacies | 25,700 | 22,400 | 87.2 |
| Total[a] | 319,400 | 263,700 | 82.6 |

Source: *Statistisches Jahrbuch der DDR*, 1977, p. 384.

a. The difference between the total number and the actual sum of the individual categories was not explained in the source.

**Table 5**
Students and trainees for medical occupations, 1975.

| FRG | | GDR | |
|---|---|---|---|
| **On-the-job training** | | **On-the-job training** | no data |
| Medical secretary | 31,661 | | |
| Dental assistant | 22,726 | | |
| Pharmaceutical assistant | 10,919 | | |
| **Training through health-system schools** | 88,958 | **Students in vocational schools**[a] | 27,785 |
| Nurses | 46,339 | Nursing and medical assistants | 14,220 |
| Pediatric nurses | 10,481 | Medical-technical assistants for diagnosis and therapy | 4,655 |
| Nurse's aide | 8,183 | Nursery specialists | 5,142 |
| Medical technologist | 5,396 | Pharmacists | 2,523 |
| Masseur and Medical Bademeister (in charge of aqua therapy) | 4,281 | | |

Sources: Statistisches Bundesamt 1975, 1977;
*Statistisches Jahrbuch der DDR*, 1977, pp. 334–335.
a. As of September 1, 1974, middle-level health professionals received their training at technical/vocational schools. Since then, about 14,000 new students have been admitted per year; the number had reached 40,729 by 1976.

smaller. In the GDR more women are employed as physicians (36 percent) and dentists; 60 percent of the medical students and 55 percent of the dental students in the GDR in 1978 were women (*Medizin in Osteuropa* 12, no. 5, 1980).

Statistics on students and trainees in the auxiliary health occupations in the GDR and the FRG are reproduced in table 5. The importance of on-the-job apprenticeship (for which no data are available) has decreased in the GDR, and since September 1, 1974, most of the members of the middle-level occupations received their training at Fachschulen (vocational-technical schools). The average number of vocational-technical students reached about 40,000 students in 1976. The proportional relationship between the two countries among students is similar to that among the middle-level health employees; the numbers are also in this case twice as high in the FRG as in the GDR.

Educational Situation

The education of professionals—physicians, dentists, pharmacists—
is similar in structure in the two German states. However, there are
differences in content.

In the FRG there was a reform of the curriculum for physicians with
the Approbationsordnung of 1970, which added medical sociology and
medical psychology. The structure of the education for a physician
now is as follows:

Six years of study and the completion of the state examination, the
last year being a practical year in a clinic; these six years are regulated
by federal law.

Registration (Approbation) as physician by the Ärztekammer.

At least 4–6 years of continuing education for specialization, regulated
by the Ärztekammer. There are 27 areas of specialization, and more
are under discussion.

An M.D. degree is not required for licensing. To obtain the degree one
must write a thesis, which most students do but at a rather perfunctory
level.

In the GDR the training for physicians was reformed in 1978. The
structure is now as follows:

Before beginning study, a year of practical medical care.

Five years of formal study and completion of the Staatsexamen.

One year of clinical practice, followed by registration as a certified
physician (Diplom-Mediziner).

Four years of continuing education for specialized training.

A certificate of knowledge in Marxism-Leninism is obligatory for registration. The aim of the practical year is to foster personal responsibility
in the future physician. The fulfillment of this aim of the practical year
is controlled and evaluated by the FDJ groups (the official youth organization in the GDR).

Training for the auxiliary health professions has always been very
practical. All the same, before 1945 it was not organized either as
apprenticeship or as on-the-job training, as is typical in an industry or
a trade; it possessed rather a special status as a combination of a class-
room and apprenticeship training. This system has been preserved in
the FRG. Most auxiliary health employees are educated at Schulen des

Gesundheitswesens (health-care schools). Most of these institutions are associated with hospitals or clinics, which are also legally and financially responsible for the training program. The practical training, the largest part of the training, takes place in the associated hospital. The theoretical part is taught by doctors and members of the corresponding health occupations, some of whom have received additional training and have been promoted to teach. The educational period lasts, according to the occupation, from 2 to 3 years. Health-care schools are primarily small institutions. In 1974 there were 1,797 health-care schools in the FRG, with a total of 4,551 classes and 80,995 students (Statistisches Bundesamt 1977). This means that there are on the average fewer than 50 students at each school. Their small size has had a negative effect on the quality of the teaching, since it does not allow for a differentiated teaching staff. On the other hand, the great number of schools provides a good regional distribution.

The eleven federal states are responsible for the health-care schools if the federal government is not, as laid down in the constitution under "competitive legislation" (article 74, no. 19, Grundgesetz).[4] This means that for some health occupations education is regulated on a national level, for others differently in each federal state, and for still others only in some federal states. The training for new professions is regulated on the state level only and differently in each state, whereas for the established occupations unilateral education and examination regulations have been enacted at the national level. Thus new occupational models are first tried out in a few states before being legally implemented in other states.

In addition to training in educational institutions, there is in the FRG also on-the-job training for physicians', dental, veterinary, and pharmaceutical assistants. The practical training takes place in the physician's office, and theoretical training of about 8 hours per week occurs in a vocational school. This pattern of occupational education is typical of the practically oriented German system of a 2–3-year apprenticeship after the completion of the ninth grade.

While the FRG has essentially continued the system of occupational training that existed from the Weimar Republic up to 1945, the GDR has introduced numerous changes. At first, health-occupation training in the GDR also took place at health-care schools, mostly schools of nursing. These schools were associated with government, private, and church hospitals. In 1950–51, after the founding of the GDR, these schools were taken over and transformed by the state. The training for most occupations lasted two years, with the first year emphasizing theory and the second practice (Frenz 1975).

In 1961 these state health-care schools were upgraded to Betriebsfachschulen. The training for the paramedical occupations still had a strong practical character as an in-service or apprenticeship training with some theoretical training at the Betriebsfachschule; the training then lasted 2–3 years. In 1974, a new change was introduced because of increasing demands in the socialist health system for the "auxiliary health occupations." The training for sixteen health occupations was upgraded to a "medizinische Fachschimlansbildung" or medical vocational school, and it was extended to 3 years, with the third year devoted to practical training in a medical institution. The prerequisite for admission to training at one of the 58 medical vocational schools is the completion of grade 10 of the Allgemeinbildende polytechnische Oberschule (general polytechnic high school) (Mecklinger 1974; Schönheit 1974).

In addition to the vocational school training, there is also in-service training for 13 occupations (a 3-year apprenticeship after completion of the eighth grade). For certain professions the training takes place only in the form of an Erwachsenenqualifizierung (adult education program). For specialists in child care, masseurs, or specialists in medical autopsy this training program usually lasts 1 1/2 years. Some professionals, such as nurses, pediatric nurses, physicians' assistants, and dental nurses, can also take vocational correspondence courses lasting 3 1/2 years (Finzel 1975; Friedrich 1976).

In the GDR, the training for the middle-level health occupations is centrally planned and outlined for the entire country, in both structure and content. The course of study and the apprenticeship program are designed by the Institut für die Weiterbildung mittlerer medizinischer Fachkräfte (Institute for Continued Education of the Middle-Level Health Occupations). This state institution, founded on the basis of a 1954 ministerial decree, is responsible for all education and continuing education of the middle-level health professionals (Frenz 1975).

The training period for auxiliary health occupations is somewhat shorter in the FRG than in the GDR. It is generally much less uniformly regulated, and the numerous vocational institutions have a great deal of freedom in designing their curricula within the framework of the requirements prescribed by the respective ministries of education.

*Possibilities for Advanced Training and Continuing Education*

If the initial training for the auxiliary health occupations is much less unified in the FRG than in the GDR, this is even more the case for advanced training and continuing education. The situation of advanced training in the FRG is extremely difficult to survey (Bergmann-Krauss 1979). The organizations which carry out continuing education programs are manifold and heterogeneous; in addition to government, private, and denominational hospitals, unions, municipal organizations, professional chambers (Kämmern), professional associations, Volkshochschulen,[5] public welfare organizations, and private institutions for continuing education all offer programs for advanced training. The different institutions seldom agree on or uniformly regulate the direction of further training, topics of instruction, degrees, duration of program, or terminology. Several courses of advanced training have prevailed in practice, however, and these are regulated by statutes concerning adult education and examinations. This is the case for specialized training for anaesthesia nurses, nurses for internal medicine and intensive care, surgical nurses, psychiatric nurses, and community nurses; for medical technicians in nuclear medicine, radiology, hematology, microbiology, clinical chemistry, histology, and exfoliative cytology; and for dental hygiene assistants. Furthermore there are 1–2-year programs for directors of nursing and 3–6-month courses for hospital ward directors. Moreover, nurses receive advanced training to become instructors or instructing assistants. Overspecialization and differentiation of advanced training in the health occupations are now regarded skeptically in the FRG.

In the GDR, on the other hand, continuing education is planned centrally and uniformly. There are the following possibilities for continuing education:

for specialized workers, the possibility of obtaining the "Meister" rank[6]

professional specialization in a total of 30 directions (1975) for the middle-level health professions, such as anaesthesia nurse, with further specialization planned (Institut für Weiterbildung mittlerer medizinischer Fachkräfte, 1975)

qualification for special management functions, such as ward nurse or group leader (functional specialization)

training courses which presuppose an already completed education as a middle-level health worker[7]

3–4-year training courses for some professions, which require the training of a middle-level health occupation and occupational experience.[8]

Finally, continuing education for all middle-level health employees has been required since 1965. Every employee must participate in ten in-service training sessions per year. Four sessions have fixed themes; for the other six the themes are freely chosen (Frenz 1974; Schmitt 1975).

This compilation of the different patterns for further education indicates that a wider and more differentiated spectrum of advanced training and continuing education is present in the GDR, and that this program is far more uniformly organized. It is possible therefore to assume a higher level of professionalization among the auxiliary health occupations. On the other hand, one must take into account that only a few years ago, when vocational education was much shorter, the qualification level in the GDR was quite mediocre. It is obvious that the GDR's highly organized system of training and continuing education is in keeping with the ideal of central control in a socialist state.

## The Range of Professional Duties and Functions

The data on the health occupations have as yet conveyed little about actual occupational performance. To make reliable claims in this area is difficult, because it presupposes empirical and comparable data from both German states. The range of duties and functions of the health occupations is dependent, among other things, on the concepts of health and sickness prevalent in each state. The two states differ considerably on this point. In the FRG sickness is understood as a physical, somatic disorder (although more recently, with some reluctance, psychological disturbances are also included). In either case sickness is considered and defined as an individual affliction and disturbance. As a consequence, it is the duty of physicians or health workers to treat the individual by means of medical therapy (Geissler and Thoma 1979; Schuller 1976).

The health system and its workers in the GDR have a broader range of duties to perform. Along with the responsibility for the individual's medical therapy, which is primary also in the GDR, every medical employee is also called upon to function as a health educator. Health education in the GDR, however, means above all ideological propagation of the socialistic concept of society.

The fundamentally new aspect of the socialistic health system in comparison with every other form of national health system is found in the unity of medical care, planning-organizing activity, and cultural-educational work. In its cultural-educational function, the socialist system demonstrates its superiority most clearly. The political-ideological and cultural-educational work must be a component of every medical and welfare activity. . . . Health education is therefore never simply a question of transmitting healthy behavior patterns, but always at the same time of conveying political relations in their relevance to health, which includes economic objectives as well as political strategies. (Schmieder 1974, pp. 8–10)

This quotation shows well how the concept of health is expanded in the GDR to include social and political dimensions. Such a concept includes all areas of life, especially the area of work, and thus social control and influence by medical personnel in all areas is considered advisable, justified, and necessary.

These ideologically oriented health-education duties are above all the responsibility of the middle-level health employees (Ferchland and Weyrich 1974). There are occupations whose main duty is health education: the health welfare worker, the factory nurse, the community nurse. But all other health occupations always embody this ideological policy of health education in their dealings with patients as well. The demands of the health employees are therefore high, but the actual realization and certainly the effectiveness of the measures—if one takes epidemiological studies or the frequency of sickness as indicators—are low.

The necessity of health education has been increasingly discussed of late in the FRG but without the social component. Rather, an appeal is made to values such as individual responsibility and health-conscious behavior (Baier 1978).

In general, the ideological demands of the medical.personnel in the GDR are both different from and greater than those in the FRG. Whereas in the FRG internal professional values—those of the medical community—are of primary importance, the demands on the medical personnel in the GDR are strongly oriented toward the socialist ideal of society. Not only the members of health occupations but also state or party authorities (without medical training per se) define the qualifications and the range of duties and functions in the GDR, whereas in the FRG these questions are decided solely by health-care professionals. The professional associations and self-governing professional chambers (Kämmern) play an important role in this issue, reflecting the pluralistic ideal of the FRG.

## Professionalization Processes

Occupationalization, Professionalization, Deprofessionalization

The situation of the medical professions in both German states described above must be interpreted in the context of professionalization. Therefore it is first necessary to explain how the concept of professionalization involves three processes: occupationalization (Verberuflichung), professionalization, and deprofessionalization, all of which characterize different phases in the professional organization of labor. Occupationalization is the process by which an activity (for example, the care and treatment of the sick, the education of the children) formerly carried out by the family, the community, or similar informal primary groups is taken over by specialists. The activity becomes an occupation carried out for pay (Daheim 1967; Hartmann 1972).

These processes of occupationalization of former lay functions can be observed in the transformation of societies to developed societies and also in the so-called primitive societies. Magicians, interpreters of oracles, witch doctors, wise women, medicine men, and other practitioners play an important part within the medical care in these societies. Some of these practitioners differ from laymen only by their more skillful handling of instruments, medical herbs, or spells. Others, such as witch doctors, already have a special role. With occupationalization, the medical knowledge of the body and its functions or of medical herbs is passed gradually to experts, who must acquire their special knowledge during a period of education or training. In simple societies, a master-pupil relationship is typical; at this stage the pupil is taught the secrets of the medical treatment by the master. A more systematic theoretical training in an institute especially established for this purpose is a further step in the direction of occupationalization. For example, such an occupationalization process is taking place around the care and upbringing of babies and children by trained nurses and teachers in the GDR.

Professionalization is the process by which an occupation is transformed into a profession, that is, a special type of occupation which has gained high societal approval because of special attributes. The main sociological attribute is the autonomy of control of contents and circumstances of the professional practice (Freidson 1979). From this main attribute result the following characteristics of professionals:

They have gained the legal monopoly of vocational practice.

They control the access to the profession by defining the contents of training, and they monitor professional practice.

They develop a professional code and control.

They link together in special professional organizations, which protect the interests of the profession internally and externally.

Occupationalization and professionalization are based on the division of labor and competence. In the process of professionalization, initially a number of occupations claim competence in one area, but subsequently one group becomes dominant and is in the position to establish itself as a profession, whereas the other occupations become defined as auxiliary occupations.

Medicine became officially approved as a profession when university training was established in medieval times. However, only at the end of the nineteenth century did medicine become a real profession, having created a scientific basis strong enough to demonstrate its clear superiority over amateurish and irregular practitioners. In the twentieth century, the position of medicine as a profession became stronger as the training of the average physician improved. This transition entailed medicine's differentiating itself from two groups. These two groups did not differ much from the established physicians, but their acts and measures did not gain societal approval as professions with a legal monopoly over medical practice.

One group was composed of persons who practiced medicine (with more or less competence) independent of the medical profession. They were identified as "Kurpfuscher" (quacks) by the state-licensed physicians, and they were completely excluded from licensed practice. In the literature of the late nineteenth century one finds many disputes about Kurpfuscherei (quackery). Actually, in the middle of the century there had been no homogeneous medical profession but many groups of practitioners, which can be divided into two categories: the greater part who had no academic education but were at best practically trained surgeons, barbers, dental artisans, and dental artists (Chirurgen, Wundärzte, Bader, Barbiere, Zahnartisten, Sahnkünster), and the smaller part who were learned physicians (gelehrte Ärzte) trained at the university. There was no great difference of clinical competence between these two groups, because up to the middle of the century medical knowledge was mostly symptom-oriented and speculative and hence therapeutic successes were somewhat haphazard. Finally the learned physicians gained effective scientific tools and successfully asserted themselves as a profession licensed by the state against the practically trained lay practitioners.

Besides the lay practitioners or quacks whose activity was identified as illegal, the medical profession brought a second part of the health-care system under its control: the paramedical occupations. The medical profession urged the state to delegate control of these occupations, so that the medical profession was in a position to supervise them, to limit their scope of activity, and to manage them. The paramedical occupations differ from the established medical profession—as Freidson says—by lacking autonomy (because their special knowledge is taken from physicians), responsibility (because they only support the diagnostic and therapeutic activities of the physician), authority (because they have a subordinate position, which they carry out on request or prescription of the physician), and prestige (because they have a worse public reputation than the physician).

By reason of strategies of demarcation and limitation against quacks on the one hand and paramedical occupations on the other hand, the academically trained physicians could finally establish themselves as a profession with the monopoly of professional practice and the corresponding autonomy with regard to the structure and conditions of the professional practice.

Although the physician gained full professional status only within the past 100 years, there are now some tendencies which could lead to deprofessionalization. Deprofessionalization is the process by which a profession is turned back into a normal occupation by losing those characteristics which distinguish it from a normal occupation (Bollinger and Hohl 1981, p. 443).

This deprofessionalization, which is primarily a structural process, also has consequences for professional identity. Professionals give up their full identification with the profession and develop an attitude of distance that may be described as an employee attitude or a job mentality.

Examples of deprofessionalization in the FRG include the efforts by the state to interfere with the autonomy of the physician's professional practice and to control and regulate it. Some of the legal measures to reduce the costs and some of the measures that have been proposed but have until now been prevented by the physicians' organizations tend to restrict professional autonomy. For example, the approved lists (Positivlisten) of medications advocated by the Bundesgesundheitsamt (Federal Health Office) and the diagnosis-based reimbursement recommended in the present cost-reduction law have the tendency to limit physicians' autonomy no matter how they are politically justified. In fact, it is one of the intentions of such laws to limit the physicians' omnipotence. Administrative interventions by the state into the organization of medical university education (Kapazitätsverordnung, capacity decree, Numerus Clausus), into the curriculum, and into examination regulations are further examples of deprofessionalization. The interventions of the state aim at a more uniform and efficient structure of education.

Because of the development of new health occupations requiring special knowledge that physicians do not acquire in medical education (biological engineers, psychologists, social workers), the medical profession is losing control over these occupations. A similar development can be observed with regard to the creation of special occupations in the field of prevention to take up new problems the physicians have neglected, especially the psychosocial care of the population. New professions therefore arise: social-medical assistant, assistant in the field of prevention, dental hygienist, and so on. Physicians (and dentists) lose control over formerly paramedical occupations and simultaneously over an important scope of their activity; finally they lose autonomy in their professional practice.

*Professionalization and Deprofessionalization: A Comparison*

How is the situation with regard to occupationalization, professionalization, and deprofessionalization in the two German states? Basically the degree of development in both states is similar because these occupations and professions within the health-care system had a common history up to 1945. Since then, however, there have been tendencies and trends that point to differences.

The process of transforming tasks formerly performed by the family or the primary group has been more complete in the GDR because the socialist state has taken over more of the traditional duties of the family and more completely divested the family of its ability to solve problems which affect it. The solution of these problems is relegated to professional authorities. This far-reaching process in the GDR involves not only infant and small-child care but also the responsibility for the individual's own health; all are now the responsibility of the national health system, the industrial health and welfare system, and especially the middle-level health employee. In a way, this is a process of expropriating the body.

The process by which lay functions are taken over by occupations has not progressed as far in the FRG. Nevertheless, some developments there also show a tendency toward replacing lay services by public services. The principles of the "Sozialstaat" (welfare state) increasingly determine the structure of the FRG (Baier 1978). There is a loss of individual competence in private concerns, such as family, children, and health, as these responsibilities are relegated to specialized authorities.

The higher degree of occupationalization in the GDR does not mean, however, that the health professions have more power there. Although more tasks and duties are being occupationalized, so that the health workers have more influence over the individual than in the FRG, organizationally they are under bureaucratic control. Thus, both citizens and the professions have lost autonomy and control as the state has gained power over both.

The degree of professionalization differs both within the health professions and between the two German states. The physicians in Germany were able to establish themselves as a profession at the end of the last century, and now some paramedical occupations are trying to professionalize themselves. The occupational role of the paramedical occupations has traditionally been that of physicians' assistants. This has influenced their self-image considerably. Their activities are oriented toward the physician, whose instructions must be observed by them. Naturally this orientation is extremely strong in those professions which are most closely linked to the physician—the physician's assistant and the nurse. In various paramedical professions, however, a tendency to move away from the physician can be observed. This expresses itself in longer education, where theoretical work has become increasingly important, in the founding of professional organizations, in the increased possibilities for continuing education, and in the occupation of senior administrative positions by members of the health professions other than physicians. These processes of professionalization, signifying a change in the physician-oriented system, are taking place in both German states, although with different emphases. For example, the professional organizations and scientific societies play a larger role in the FRG, resulting in more influence on the conditions of work and education and more developments toward theoretically oriented education. However, in the GDR advanced training and continuing education are state matters, so professionalization becomes a governmental and bureaucratic process.

Whereas the professionalization of physician's assistants has progressed further, there are increasing tendencies among nurses to contrast their own professional activities against those of physicians. Thus a research project on nursing was sponsored in the FRG (Pinding 1972), and an experimental model was implemented at the Free University of Berlin which organized the training of nurse-educators as a university curriculum—a trend more fully developed in the GDR. Most important, various federal states in the FRG have decreed equal representation with physicians and administrators for nursing personnel in the top administrative body of the hospital (for example, in the 1975 Hospital Law of Nordrhein-Westfalen). This constitutes a further statutory step toward the professional independence of nurses. In the GDR, one has the impression that nurses are even more subordinate to physicians than in the FRG—especially in the hospital, where the hierarchy is stronger than in the FRG (Hendrik 1975; Wowsnick 1975). How close this supposition is to the actual situation must, however, be verified.

While some of the paramedical occupations try to establish themselves as professions with more autonomy from physicians, there are some indications that physicians—the established profession—are deprofessionalizing. Using Freidsons's criteria for a profession, one can see to what degree the physicians in both German states still can be considered a profession and to what degree they are already developing back into a normal occupation.

*Control of the production and use of knowledge.* In the FRG professional control over knowledge still exists. Some restrictions upon autonomous transmission of professional knowledge have been interpreted above as a symptom of deprofessionalization (for example the interventions of the state in medical training or the regulation of standards of therapy or medications).

In the GDR, medical knowledge is brought much more into line with ideology. Courses in Marxism-Leninism are mandatory in the medical training. The regulations of training and examination are defined uniformly by central bureaucratic control. There are limitations on the freedom of treatment; for example, the ability of the physician to put people on the sick list is controlled. This means, for the production and use of knowledge as well as for the profession's control over the training of its own rising generation, that the physicians and the other medical specialists in the GDR are more controlled by state institutions. Therefore the profession's autonomy is limited as far as the production and control of medical knowledge are concerned. The control of the production and use of knowledge, however, is in both German states no longer fully realized in the medical profession. Within the paramedical occupations, of course, this fully independent knowledge never existed.

*The monopoly of treatment.* In the FRG there are already some other professions besides the physicians which act in the field of diagnosis, prevention, or therapy—for example, the Heilpraktiker (health practitioners), the psychotherapists, and most recently the counselors in preventive health. Thus the monopoly of physicians is being noticeably undercut.

In the GDR, no Heilpraktiker has received a license since 1945. Because of the hierarchical, bureaucratic setup of the health-care institutions, control over physicians and paramedical personnel is fully realized, and paramedical personnel in the GDR are strongly oriented toward physicians. Because of these conditions one can say that the monopoly of treatment by the physicians in the GDR is still intact. Paradoxically, state control has institutionalized professional dominance at the same time that it has compromised professional autonomy.

*Ethical code.* A structural comparison of the ethical codes is hardly possible, because one has to deal with internalized standards and attitudes. Physicians in both the GDR and the FRG are, of course, interested in the well-being of their patients. In the FRG the individual case is emphasized. Self-control by the self-governed professional organization exists.

*Professional organizations.* In the FRG, self-government of the profession exists in Ärztekammern and Kassenärztliche Vereinigungen. Furthermore, there are several free organizations, such as the Verband niedergelassener Ärzte, the NAV, and the Hartmannbund (organizations of physicians in free practice), and the Marburger Bund (a unionlike organization of physicians in hospitals). Paramedical personnel are also organized in many different professional organizations. Until now there were only a few interventions of the state into the professional self-government. Therefore the autonomy of the health-care professions is fully realized as far as their professional organizations are concerned.

In the GDR the professional concerns are regulated by the state. The physicians may comment if they wish, but in the final analysis decisions are taken by politicians. This means that there is no autonomy of the physicians' professional organizations.

On the basis of this comparison, the balance between the GDR and the FRG is not unequivocal as far as the degree of professionalization or deprofessionalization of the medical profession is concerned. Yet the autonomy of the medical profession is somewhat more realized in the FRG through the monopoly of knowledge and the importance of the physicians' organizations for self-government. The physician in the GDR, a state employee in a state health-care system which is organized centrally and hierarchically, is dependent in his training and his practice on state and political institutions.

Conditions of Professionalization and Deprofessionalization

On the basis of the situation of the health professions in the GDR, I support the thesis that an occupational structure rather than a professional structure has developed in the GDR. The centralized, bureaucratic health system does not allow health employees to create or direct their own training and work or to form independent and autonomous professional organizations. Therefore, important prerequisites for professionalization have not been met in the GDR. It is true that in the FRG as well there are tendencies leading to an occupational or job orientation of the physicians. In comparison with the GDR, however, physicians are still characterized by many attributes of a profession, and in some paramedical occupations too there are serious efforts to achieve professionalization.

This interpretation suggests that specific conditions are necessary for the professionalization process. Professionalization can take place only in open, democratic, and pluralistic societies. Only in such a society can the independent development from occupation to profession take place. This process cannot develop fully in a socialist state bureaucracy, or it will be revised once full professionalization has been established.

**Notes**

1. The role of the masseur is to administer the measures prescribed by the physician in the area of hydro, balneo, electro, and phototherapy as well as massages.

2. The role of the disinfector is participation in the prevention and elimination of infectious diseases, particularly in the area of hygiene and sterilization.

3. The hygiene inspector serves practical functions in the area of hygienic control within the public health-care system of the GDR; for instance, control of hygienic conditions in public buildings, the water supply system, public baths, the food industry, and restaurants. He also helps in the implementation of preventive measures aimed at infectious diseases. His activities are closely

related to those of the disinfector. The industrial hygiene inspector concentrates on the measurement of work-related hygienic conditions.

4. Competitive legislation means, according to article 72 of the constitution, that the individual federal states have the right to legislate "as long as and as far as the federal institutions do not make use of their legislative right." A need for federal legislation can arise because "the maintenance and continuity of the legal and economic unity, particularly the unity of life conditions beyond the reach of a single federal state, may demand it."

5. Volkshochschulen are institutions of adult education. They are nonvocational and state-supported, have a long tradition, and exist only in Germany and Denmark.

6. For German artisans, the training has a traditional structure: Three years of apprenticeship are followed by three years as an associate (Geselle) or skilled laborer, after which the examination for Meister (master) is taken.

7. For the public-health welfare worker, the occupational therapist, and the midwife this means they take over a new occupation.

8. Such courses of study on a high level exist for medical teachers on two levels (vocational and academic; these are teachers for practical and theoretical education in health institutions and medical vocational schools), for directors of nursing, for health and social administrators, for pharmaceutical engineers, and for engineers for hygiene and occupational hygiene.

## References

Baier, H. 1978. Medizin im Sozialstaat. Medizinsoziologische und medizin-politische Aufsatze. Stuttgart: Enke.

Bergmann-Krauss, S. 1979. Aus- und Weiterbildung im Gesundheitswesen. Ein Überblick über die Ordnungssituation in den nichtärztlichen Gesundheitsber-ufen. Berlin: Bundesinstitut für Berufsbildung.

Bollinger, H., and J. Hohl. 1981. "Auf dem Weg von der Profession zum Beruf: Zur Deprofessionalisierung des Ärztestandes." Soziale Welt 32:440–464.

Daheim, H. 1967. Der Beruf in der modernen Gesellschaft. Cologne and Berlin: Kiepenheuer & Witsch.

Deutsches Institut für Wirtschaftsforschung. 1979. "Entwicklungstendenzen im Gesundheitswesen der DDR." Wochenbericht, pp. 280–284.

Eberle, G., and U. Geissler. 1978. "Gesunheitswesen und Arbeitsmarkt." Die Ortskrankenkasse 15:510–514.

Ferchland, B., and U. Weyrich. 1974. "Sozialistische Ideologie und Gesund-heitserziehung in der Tätigkeit der mittleren medizinischen Fachkräfte." Stu-dienmaterial zur Weiterbildung mittlerer medizinischer Fachkräfte 2, Beilage zur Zeitschrift "Die Heilberufe" 2.

Finzel, S. 1975. "Zur weiteren Entwicklung der Facharbeiterausbildung im Gesundheits- und Sozialwesen." Humanitas 26.

Freidson, E. 1979. Das Ärztestand: Berufs- und wissenschaftssoziologische Durchleuchtung einer Profession. Stuttgart: Enke.

Frenz, R. 1974. "Aufgabenbezogene Weiterbildung im Bereich der ambulanten medizinischen Versorgung." Die Heilberufe 26:368–370.

Frenz, R. 1975. "Zum 20-Jahrigen Bestehen des Instituts für Weiterbildung mittlerer medizinischer Fachkräfte." Die Heilberufe 27:320–323.

Friedrich, R. 1976. "Zur Einführung des medizinischen Fachschulfernstudiums." Humanitas 16.

Geissler, B., and P. Thoma, eds. 1979. Medizinsoziologie: Eine Einführung für medizinische und soziale Berufe. Frankfurt: Campus.

Hartmann, H. 1972. "Arbeit, Beruf, Profession." In Berufssoziologie, ed. T. Luckmann and W. M. Sprondel. Cologne: Kiepenheuer & Witsch.

Hendrik, A. 1975. "Probleme und Erfahrungen in der staatlichen Leitungstätigkeit klinischer Einrichtungen des sozialistischen Gesundheitswesens in der DDR." Das Deutsche Gesundheitswesen 30:324–327.

Institut für Weiterbildung mittlerer medizinischer Fachkräfte. 1975. Beruf für Dich: Ausbildungen im Gesundheits- und Sozialwesen. Third edition. Potsdam: Ministerium für Gesundheitswesen der DDR.

Mecklinger, L. 1974. "58 Medizinische Fachschulen gegründet." Die Fachschule 22:292–295.

Ostner, I., and E. Beck-Gernsheim. 1979. Mitmenschlichkeit als Beruf: Eine Analyse des Alltags in der Krankenpflege. Frankfurt: Campus.

Pinding, M., ed. 1972. Krankenpflege in unserer Gessellschaft. Stuttgart: Enke.

Ruban, M. E. 1981. Gesundheitswesen in der DDR. Berlin: Holzapfel.

Schipperges, H. 1975. Medizinische Dienste im Wandel. Munich: Witzshock.

Schmieder, H. 1974. "Die Rolle der medizinischen Assistenten bei der Verwirklichung der Aufgaben und Schwerpunkte der Gesundheitserziehung." Die Heilberufe 26:4–11.

Schmitt, E. 1975. "Gedanken zum obligatorischen Dienstunterricht der mittleren medizinischen Fachkräfte." Die Heilberufe 27:396–397.

Schönheit, B. 1974. "Einige grundsatzliche Fragen der medizinischen Fachschulausbildung." Die Fachschule 22:265–272.

Schuller, A. 1976. "Patientenkarriere und Krankheitsbegriff." Medizin, Mensch, Gesellschaft 1:46–52.

Schuller, A. 1978. "Beratung als Politik." Medizin, Mensch, Gesellschaft 3:201–207.

Statistisches Bundesamt. 1978. Statistisches Jahrbuch der Bundesrepublik Deutschland, 1977. Stuttgart and Mainz: Kohlhammer.

Statistisches Bundesamt. 1977. Berufe des Gesundheitswesens. Fadiserie 12, Reihe 5, 1974 and 1975 editions. Stuttgart and Mainz: Kohlhammer.

Statistisches Bundesamt und Bundesminister für Bildung und Wissenschaft. 1977. Bildung im Zahlenspiegel. Stuttgart and Mainz: Kohlhammer.

Statistisches Jahrbuch der Deutschen Demokratischen Republik. 1977. Berlin: Staatsverlag der DDR.

Wowsnick, R. 1975. "Zur Stellung der leitenden Schwester im Leitungskollektiv der Gesundheitseinrichtung." Die Heilbrufe 27:14–16.

# 14 Legal Aspects of the Physician-Patient Relationship

## Ulrich Lohmann

*Ulrich Lohmann analyzes the legal statutes concerning doctor-patient relationships to unveil a portrait of fundamental values and philosophy in the two German states. He examines the ways in which the obligations of the doctor to the patient, the responsibilities of the patient, the types of contracts, and the character of damages reflect basically different concepts of how the physician, the society, and the patient relate to one another. Are the East Germans correct when they argue that laws pertaining to doctor-patient relationships cannot fall under contract law because patients cannot reasonably execute their contractual rights? To what extent do criminal acts center around the individual and to what extent around the public good? What are the consequences of conceiving informed consent around a model of biological man versus a model of self-determining man? After addressing these issues, Lohmann considers what legal model of doctor-patient relationships is best suited to the technical complexity of modern medicine and the social interdependency of modern industrial society.*

## The Legal Construction of the Physician-Patient Relationship

Formal Aspects of the Relationship

The relationship between the physician and/or the medical facility and the patient is in both German states partially but not entirely shaped by the legal structure. For instance, the courts in the Federal Republic of Germany (FRG; West Germany) occasionally refer to a "moral relationship"[1] between physician and patient in regard to service of the physician as a "charitable service" (Laufs 1971, pp. 4, 10). Similarly, some authors in the German Democratic Republic (GDR; East Germany) emphasize the moral and humanistic basis of the physician-patient relationship (Becker 1978; Franke 1976; Hansen and Vetterlein 1973). Yet these perceptions appear to be rather outdated.[2] Since the middle of the last century, Germany has increasingly regulated its medical services, in analogy to other areas of production, distribution, and consumption, by means of the law ("Decision Concerning Specialists" of the Federal Court, *Entscheidungen des Bundesverfassungsgerichts* 33:125). Several factors may have contributed to this development, such as the increasing volume and commercialization of medical services, growing specialization, and use of medical technology. As these changes made the relationship between physician and patient more impersonal, the perception of illness itself underwent changes. Modern man began to reject the idea that illness, and especially unsuccessful treatment, were determined by fate and that there would be compensation in an afterlife. Instead, he desired immediate alleviation of pain and, in case of injury, financial compensation. These two aspects, the decrease in the importance of trust and intimacy as the basis of the physician-patient relationship and the increasing emphasis upon economic interest, led to a more precise and more binding ascription of responsibilities and risks.[3] Under these conditions, only the law could effect a more precise and binding distribution of rights, duties, and risks so as to assure society of a certain measure of predictability as well as fairness and equity. For the individual person, laws ensure and provide self-determination—autonomy for the patient and professional freedom for the physician. Legal codification provides professional ethics, the structure of medical services, and the limits to professional risks. In different ways these characteristics of modernization have been incorporated in the federal code for physicians (Approbationsordnung) and in the regulation concerning the licensing of physicians (Bundesarzteordnung). They can be regarded as the centerpieces of legislation on medical services.[4] Both define the legal responsibilities of the physician and make legal certain aspects of his service which originally were outside the area of legislation.

The Place of Medicine within the Legal System[5]

The legal dimension of the physician-patient relationship can best be approached by looking at its position within the legal system. There are good theoretical and practical reasons for taking this route even though a substantial number of legal cases are indifferent to classification. Critical cases and new problems, which make up the bulk of the cases, are handled by reference to the principles of the relevant branch of law and to basic rules (person-specific or property-specific).

Medical legislation in the FRG and also in the GDR (unlike that in the Soviet Union) does not by itself form an independent branch of law with its own code. It is a more or less modified part of other legal branches. In the FRG, the physician-patient relationship falls under civil law (Zivilrecht), and especially under contract law regulating services (Dienstvertragsrecht). The interpretation of its prescriptions has been adapted by the courts to the particularities of medical service. Irrespective of this modification by interpretation, the legal form of the physician-patient relationship in the FRG derives from the basic model of the employer contracting the services of a specialist. In the GDR, this model has been deliberately rejected because of its commercial tone and because the patient, unable to evaluate medical competence, is thought to be unable to exercise contractual rights.[6] But even if the contractual model were retained in the GDR, it could not have these implications, because the "socialist" civil code, which in the GDR succeeded the imperial civil code (Zivilgesetzbuch of the GDR, June 19, 1975; Gesetzblatt der DDR I:465), does not imply a relationship between two equal contractual partners who exchange goods of equal value. Instead it postulates a material definition of civil law and a public responsibility to provide for the welfare of citizens. Although the civil code of the GDR thus provides a suitable framework, appropriate regulations referring to medicine are not in fact included.

This code might provide a proper context for medicine, but it does not suggest pertinent regulations. East German legal experts interpret this situation positively by pointing out that the physician-patient relationship constitutes a complex of constitutional law, administrative law, labor law, and welfare law. This construction, which obviously reflects an unfinished discussion,[7] can handle simple cases quite satisfactorily. The question is whether the medical relationship comes under civil law and should therefore be regarded as a commodity or whether, like education, it should be regarded as a social right which would be regulated by special laws. But in the GDR, too, certain cases are referred to "corresponding" regulations in civil law. This seems to indicate that exchange relations have not yet been fully transformed into relations of public welfare, because goods and services may still be distributed according to the principle of merit.

With regard to norms of conduct in the medical sector, the two German states also go different paths. In the FRG, any medical treatment is regarded in principle as a punishable act of bodily injury unless it has been justified through the patient's permission. In the GDR, medically indicated treatment is regarded as an expression of socialist humanism and therefore as legally irrelevant. This interpretation results from a different concept of criminal offense. It states that "punishable by law are actions which are anti-social or socially dangerous" (Strafgesetzbuch der DDR, paragraph 1, January 1, 1968, as revised April 7, 1977; Gesetzblatt der DDR I:100). In the FRG one cannot adopt such a conception of criminal offense, because there is no commonly agreed-upon social doctrine which discriminates authoritatively between collective and individual interests. Apparently the legal regulation of medical services depends on fundamentally different concepts of social order. The FRG subscribes to the principle of self-responsibility in authorized agreements; the GDR relies on the doctrine of collective responsibility.[8]

Contractual Models and Procedures

Private contracts between the physician or the hospital and the patient are an exception in both states. Most patients in both countries obtain their medical treatment as members of a legally binding medical insurance plan which is part of a comprehensive social insurance scheme. In the FRG this medical insurance plan entitles the patient to medical treatment on the basis of specific contracts with the Association of Sickness-Fund Physicians (Kassenärztliche Vereinigung), which in turn obliges its members, if necessary through disciplinary measures, to render the sought services.

In the GDR the contract deviates from classic civil law in still another way. Medical services are not rendered by independent physicians but by physicians who are employees of state, regional, or factory polyclinics and who are therefore subject to labor law. The same regulation holds for hospital physicians in both states.

This substitution of a private contract by a contract between the respective sickness fund and the association of physicians or the state (in the case of the GDR) indicates the degree to which the medical services have become a societal responsibility. In this respect the development of the GDR has gone beyond that of the FRG. This is particularly obvious in the area of ambulatory services, where nationalization has been part of the GDR's comprehensive social policy.

## The Rights and Duties of Physicians and Patients

### Information, Counsel, and Consent

On a preliminary and informal level, the physician-patient relationship begins with an exchange of information, the appropriate counsel by the physician, and acceptance and permission by the patient. Physicians in both states see this exchange primarily in a therapeutic light, but as part of a contract to obtain certain agreed-upon results it is of legal relevance. The duty to advise and inform is based in the FRG (Laufs 1971, p. 64) on the physician's accountability to the patient and in the GDR (Franke 1976, p. 107) on mutual trust. This includes informing the patient of the diagnosis, the process, and the prognosis of the disease, and the appropriate medical measures. Thus, the patient is thought to participate in and to further the therapeutic process.

In the FRG, in contrast to the GDR, the physician's duty to advise and the requirement of the patient to consent is based—particularly from the legal point of view—on the patient's personal rights and the resulting right to self-determination. This idea was unknown to classical medicine. In the Hippocratic Oath it is not recognized and is even explicitly rejected, ". . . so as not to indicate to the patient what will happen to him and threaten him; because many were driven to extreme action having been told what is threatening them" (Hinderling 1963, p. 50). Civil law outlining the duty to instruct and advise was first given in 1912 by the Reichsgericht (Imperial Court), and has since been further refined by German and West German courts (Entscheidungen des Reichsgerichts in Zivilsachen, vol. 78, p. 432). For therapeutic reasons, physicians have rejected and continue to reject this legal interpretation, because of the medical harm that might ensue. The controversy between courts and physicians rests on differences in the conception of the nature of man. If one regards man primarily from a physicial, biological point of view, then the duty to instruct is justified solely on therapeutic grounds. But if one regards man from a mental and ethical point of view and assumes a right of self-determination, then one will grant the right to full information even if it may shorten the patient's life. For example, should a physician respect the right of a mentally competent, terminally ill patient to commit suicide? Both conceptions could be integrated by a physician who refrains from volunteering in each and every case the full truth about the patient's condition but correctly answers specific questions raised by a self-responsible patient: If the patient contents himself with general optimistic statements, then he can be assumed to have exercised his rights under civil law. If, however, he regards his mental and moral "well-being" as more important than his physical recovery, then the physician does not have the right to deny him satisfaction.

Medical treatment becomes legal by the patient's consent. In neither state is the patient expected to suffer a suggested treatment without some consent. This means that the physician must accept a rejection of treatment even if he considers it medically ill-advised.

Despite this shared norm, treatment given without the patient's consent is handled differently in the two states. In the FRG, unsolicited treatment—whether medically indicated or not—is strictly illegal and punishable under civil and criminal law. In the GDR, medically indicated treatment without consent is not considered a criminal offense or subject to liability regulations. It can be dealt with only by disciplinary law. On the other hand, for elective treatment, such as plastic surgery, the law is the same in the GDR and the FRG. It is subject to criminal and liability regulations, and it requires the patient's consent. Therefore it is crucial for courts in the GDR to determine which treatment is medically indicated. However, the legal status of various treatments rests on technical issues in medicine, which hardly provide satisfactory answers to the legal questions involved.[9]

Both East and West German providers believe that to instruct the patient and to obtain his permission for suggested treatment may ease the moral burden of the physican because the patient then must bear part of the certain risk involved in all treatment. In the case of patients who are unconscious, one has to consider in both states which decision the patient would most likely have made. If there is time, one must confer with the family for clarification. In the case of minors and patients who are put under tutelage, the trustee or parent must be consulted in both states. However, should parents withhold consent without good reason, then parental consent may be substituted with a court order so as to protect the welfare of the child.[10]

Medical treatment without consent is legal in both countries only if it is designed to help maintain public order and safety. This is the case for epidemic diseases and mental disorders that endanger oneself or others and blood tests that provide legal evidence. A special case is that of transplants from cadavers. Principally, a person's right to dispose of his body beyond his death is recognized in both countries. Explicit instructions against transplants are binding in both countries. Because such explicit instruction is usually missing, legislation in the GDR has made it possible since 1975 for a team of physicians to take organs from a body that has been declared dead by another medical team.[11] There is no obligation to see if the person's will prohibits this action (Becker 1978, p. 143).

According to present law in the FRG, the right to dispose of one's body passes from the deceased who has failed to make a will to his legal heirs. This can lead to painful situations if the legal successors are close relatives and are approached with a request for organs at the same time as they are informed about the death. On the other hand, it may lead to a shortage of transplantable organs. Therefore a bill is currently being discussed that would permit the taking of organs unless expressly objected to in a formal procedure. In contrast to the regulations pertaining in the GDR, this procedure would consist of instructing citizens when their I.D. cards are issued that they may object to giving organs for future transplant. The objection would be discreetly marked on the I.D. card. After death had been declared, the physician would be legally obliged to inquire whether such a refusal existed. Otherwise the physician would take whatever organs he wished. Opponents to such a regulation argue, however, that confronting citizens with the question whether their body should remain intact after their death, and forcing the choice, would contradict the idea of human dignity. The debate on this subject is still open, and it will certainly continue in the courts, including the Constitutional Court, if the possibility to register objections to giving organs should become law.

A further question in this context of consenting to treatment concerns the behavior of the physician toward the terminally ill patient and the patient's influence on this behavior. In the GDR as well as in the FRG, direct medical measures to terminate life are unethical and illegal even if a rational and responsible patient should demand it. On the other hand, physicians in both countries are not legally obliged to prolong life and thus any unnecessary suffering in cases of unavoidable and imminent death. But while a West German physician must respect the patient's instructions, there are no precise instructions in the GDR. There are also different rules for cases where alleviation of pain may shorten life. In the GDR "every medical treatment intended to bring death nearer and to shorten life is euthanasia and punishable by law" (Hansen and Vetterlein 1973, p. 173). The West German College of Surgeons (Deutsche Gesellschaft für Chirurgie) declared such measures acceptable and therefore subject to the consent of the patient. In the

FRG there is further discussion as to whether an obligatory declaration of intent can be given, in a so-called patient's letter in case of later impaired conciousness.

## Medical Care and Patient Cooperation

The duties of the physician to provide appropriate treatment are the same in both states. Legally, the physician owes the patient the treatment which is required to restore his health or to prevent its deterioration within the limits of what the patient permits. If the patient refuses to accept a suggested therapy and opts for an alternative suitable procedure, the physician is obliged to provide it. In all cases, the physician is to proceed according to the best of his skill and medical knowledge. In reality, of course, there is some distance between these legal requirements and actual behavior. The measure of medical attention and care is based on professional standards which in case of doubt are to be explicated by medical experts.

In the GDR, the Ministry of Health issues additional instructions for therapy. First, in order to remain informed on the state of knowledge in his field, the physician must take a program of continuing education. Second, in cases of uncertainty, he consults another specialist or refers the patient to one. Third, the services of auxiliary medical staff must be supervised by the responsible physician, depending on the gravity of the case and the expertise of the staff.[12] The physician is not held responsible for the mistakes of other medical personnel, but he is responsible for the design and implementation of the treatment program. The physician must examine the patient. He may not rely on information given by others and must conduct the diagnosis personally. If the patient is immobile, the physician is expected to make a house call. Once he has accepted a case it does not suffice to give a diagnosis and advice over the telephone.[13]

The patient in turn is obliged to cooperate in the treatment. This follows from the conditions of the medical service contract and from the regulations of the Social Insurance Law. In the GDR this is also prescribed in labor law.[14] This obligation cannot be physically enforced or sanctioned, however. If the patient ignores it, he forfeits his right to obtain the normal services of the physician or the insurance benefits.[15] Enforceable, however, is the duty to pay an agreed-upon or adequate fee for treatment, or respectively the premium for the social insurance, and to make sure that it compensates the physician for medical services rendered.

## Documentation and Confidentiality

Legally, the physician-patient relationship does not end with the termination of the treatment. It continues in the keeping of records and their protection. In both states, the physician is obliged to "document sufficiently his findings and measures taken in his function as a physician" (Laufs 1971, p. 80). According to an order from the Ministry of Health of the GDR, obligatory documentation includes "history of illness; findings; diagnosis; plan of treatment; prescribed therapy (instructions such as staying in bed, diet, dispensation from work, medication, date of prescription, doses of potent drugs, duration of treatment); date of consultation; house calls, checkups, and development of the case involving changes in initial findings" (Franke 1976, p. 106). The records must be kept on file for at least 10 years unless a longer period has been determined for special cases. The primary purpose of these records is to provide the basis for further treatment. Records must therefore be transferred to the new physician if the patient requests it. In the FRG there is discussion as to whether the patient should be entitled to have access to his own records. This touches on the problems raised earlier in the context of instruction and consent. It is argued that if patients had access to their medical record, physicians might refrain from preliminary and tentative diagnoses, which they need for later recollection but would not wish to submit to their patients.

Another—increasingly important—purpose of medical records in the FRG is to provide evidence for later disputes between physicians and patients concerning possible violations of duty by the physician and resulting claims for damages. In case of litigation, the records must be submitted to the court on demand of the patient. The judge, however, may rule that certain passages need not be disclosed to the patient. As in the case of the physician's duty to inform and to obtain consent, the failure to document medical intervention may also be used as circumstantial evidence of malpractice. When documentation is incomplete, the burden of proof is reversed and the physician must prove that the damage did not result from the treatment. In civil suits, this is often decisive.

For therapeutic reasons it is essential that the patient tell the physician all relevant details, including his private fears, which, for personal and social reasons, he might prefer to conceal. In order to protect privacy (and thus, indirectly, public interest in the functioning of the health system), or to ensure good faith between physician and patient, the physician has the duty to keep confidential all information obtained professionally. Violation by the physician or his staff is a criminal offense. Paragraph 203 of the penal code of the FRG determines that "violation of personal secrets" is to be punished with jail up to one year or with a fine. Paragraph 136 of the penal code of the GDR determines that the "violation of professional discretion" is to be punished with a sentence of probation, a fine, or a public reproach. Secrecy is mandatory and includes relatives, but not minors. However, a mature youth may have a legitimate reason for concealing certain aspects of his life from his parents. Secrecy is binding, furthermore, in dealings with hospital administrations and colleagues who are not involved in the particular case. Data for medical records may be submitted for statistical or scientific reasons only if they do not reveal the identity of the patient. In order to ensure secrecy, the physician and medical staff have the right to refuse testimony and are therefore exempt from the general duty to testify before a court. Thus, in order to guarantee the smooth functioning of the health system, the state renounces certain means of investigation.

Secrecy may be waived by the patient either for the clarification of specific questions or before proper agencies. But it may also be waived in both states when it becomes necessary to weigh the implications in the investigation of a capital crime or to contain certain infectious diseases (Laufs 1971, p. 79; Franke 1976, p. 208).

## Liability of the Physician in Criminal Law and Civil Law

Responsibility as Determined by Criminal Law

The West German courts regard improper medical treatment as a case of bodily injury. It is not punishable under the law if the patient has consented to the treatment and thus eliminated its illegal quality. If such consent is missing, even medically indicated treatment is regarded as bodily injury. This legal construction is rejected by the medical profession unanimously and adamantly. It results logically from the liberal conception of law according to which the state and the court cannot establish binding values and goals on how to live but only formal procedures by which citizens are put into a position to make their own choices. Since neither the legislature nor the court wants to determine what should be done in the medical sphere, consent becomes a constitutive element in the medical contract. Such consent is either explicitly or implicitly given and may be supposed in cases where the patient is unconscious. If the physician, however, omits asking for consent or even acts against the explicit or implicit will of the patient, he commits bodily injury which even with the best of intentions may be punished with up to 5 years of jail unless there are overriding reasons for excluding guilt. In order to get away from this construction, physicians and some lawyers have suggested that since physicians do not intend to injure the body, the law should protect the freedom of choice regarding the patient's self-conduct rather than the integrity of his body. It would be the freedom to dispose one's body which would be subject to injury and not the body itself. Even if the same penalty were retained, physicians would then be free from the totally coun-terintentional charge of committing bodily harm. Theoretically, this suggestion suffers from the difficulty that the state would have to decide on the medical indication of the given treatment. The courts have therefore not shown any interest in changing their present jurisdiction.

In the GDR, medically indicated treatment does not constitute bodily injury. Proudly emphasized, this ruling derives from a socialist concept of "material offense" which regards certain actions as punishable, not for formal reasons but because they harm or endanger society materially (Strafrecht der DDR, 1976). Therefore the state, as the legislative and executive organ of the people mobilized by the Communist Party, must determine the material good of society and punish opposition to it. Consequently, patient consent is relevant only for therapeutic purposes. In order to avoid such possible disregard for the principle of self-determination characteristic of all civilized societies, legislation in the GDR retains the legal requirement of consent but prosecutes its violation only by disciplinary law rather than by civil law. What is protected, then, is not the patient's autonomy but the effectiveness of the health service. As a result, it becomes easier to ignore the patient's will, because disciplinary prosecution involves lesser charges, shorter investigations, and lighter penalties. And since investigation and sanction are performed within the same institution, there is a great risk of inward solidarity among physicians.[16] Only with regard to elective operations, such as plastic surgery, does East German law make an exception. Although the intention of the physician to help does not differ from that in other cases, plastic surgery is considered potentially as a matter of bodily injury.

## Damages

Both states make legal allowances for financial compensation in case of bodily injury, although in very different fashion. In the GDR, the state is liable if the damage occurred as the result of medical treatment provided on the basis of a contract with a state service. The patient, however, must prove that the law has been transgressed, that he has received an injury, and that both were causally connected. Contrary to normal procedure in civil law, the patient does not have to prove the physician's responsibility. If the state wishes to avoid compensation, it must prove its innocence. Because this is generally not feasible, one may speak in this case of a reversal in the burden of proof. The payment of damages becomes relatively independent of the question of guilt but not of institutional responsibility. If, however, a suit should be filed against an independent physician (not typical in the GDR), the burden of proof rests on the injured patient, as is normal in civil law.

According to Section 1 of Paragraph 337 of the Civil Code of the GDR, compensation has to restore the patient to his previous state. Over and above compensation for costs (charges for therapy, equipment, and loss of salary), the injured party may be compensated for damage to his well-being. Of course, the amounts granted in the GDR are far below those granted in the FRG (Hacks 1978).

In the GDR, medical institutions are insured through the state. Settlements of damages are usually reached out of court on the basis of expert evidence. The state may charge claims against the particular physician or medical staff, not according to criteria of adequate restitution but on the basis of "material responsibility" as derived from pedagogic principles (Lohmann 1978, pp. 356 ff.). It limits damages in the case of negligence to one month's salary. As part of the extension of social services undertaken after the Eighth Party Congress of the SED (Sozialistische Einheitspartei), the government in 1974 issued an additional decree concerning the "material support of the citizen in case of harm due to medical intervention" (Gesetzblatt der DDR I, 1975, p. 59). It makes compensation available even for the cases in which the physician had provided competent treatment. The sole prerequisite for compensation is the causal connection between the treatment and the injury. There need not be any proof of guilt or, contrary to liability claims, any proof of illegality. This means that the East German citizen can now receive compensation for any harm incurred as the result of medical treatment. Because of this decree, liability cases lose their sometimes dramatic significance. The resulting equitable redistribution of life risks among the people as a whole may be interpreted as a sign of a policy that aims at material equality and distribution according to need.

In case of illegal and personally caused injury, the patient in the FRG may file a claim against the independent physician, the privately contracted physician in a hospital, and/or the hospital. Everyone is liable only for his own mistakes. The hospital therefore is not liable for its employed physicians unless it has demonstrably acted illegally in the organization, the choice, and the supervision of its physicians. Because this is normally not the case, the hospital may, according to Paragraph 831 of the Civil Code, exculpate itself and avoid liability. In this case the patient may make a claim only against the employed physician. The patient may make a similar claim against the physician besides the contractual claim to liability. According to labor law, the hospital as the employer may have to assume liability for the contracted physician, depending on the degree of negligence and the regulations on "high-risk work." The claim presupposes that harm was caused by medical treatment. The amount of compensation includes all measures for repair and, in the case of criminal liability, payment of damages. The Civil Code prescribes that damages should provide "adequate compensation for nonmonetary injuries" and should "recognize the principle that the injurer owes satisfaction to the injured" (Entscheidungen des Bundesgerichtshofes in Zivilsachen, 18:149).

It follows from this legal construction of medical intervention that not only is malpractice illegal and subject to liability but so are medically indicated and correctly performed measures if the physician cannot prove they were performed after informed consent. Therefore, an increasing number of damage awards are granted not on the assumption of technical errors but on one of the other circumstantial grounds for liability. In case of litigation between a patient and a physician (or his insurer), there exists not only a court suit but also the possibility of referring the case to other boards which have recently been installed at the level of the Landesärztekammer (state physicians' association) in order to obtain an amicable settlement.

## Conclusion

A comparison of medical legislation in the FRG and the GDR shows that in both German states the physician-patient relationship is legally structured and that the legal structure incorporates other codes of conduct such as medical ethics. This fundamental similarity appears to result from a universal and structural demand in complex industrial societies rather than from a common national tradition.

On a second level, the differences in the legal aspects of the physician-patient relationship, the distribution of rights, duties, and risks, and the settlement of liability cases reflect systemic differences: the existence or nonexistence of a common societal goal and the priority of the individual or collectivity in social and economic matters. Even the conceptualization of "medically indicated intervention" as a probable cause of bodily injury reflects the existence of a fundamental societal goal. Unlike the socialist state, the liberal state cannot prescribe to the individual adult citizen (except where potential harm to others is involved) how to look after his health.

The leading role of the party in the socialist state is reflected in the more dominant position of the physician with respect to the patient. This is evident from the generally weaker requirement of consent to treatment, the lesser degree to which patients can influence the physicians' conduct during the course of death, and the lower volume of transplants. On the other hand, the physician, working in the service of the hierarchically structured socialist state, is subject to the political directives and medical planning of the party.

In Western capitalist countries, the idea of personal risks to the patient and personal liability of the physician is consistent with the individualism of the social order. In the GDR, damages from injuries incurred because of treatment are borne collectively, and, in keeping with the collective realization of surplus value and assumption of risk, they are the responsibility of the community as a whole.

Beyond the question of comparison and contrast, which of the two systems more adequately structures the physician-patient relationship and which of the two is more suitable for a modern industrial society? In this respect the GDR treats individual health as a universal value and therefore regards medically indicated treatment as legal if properly executed. This seems preferable to the position prevailing in the FRG. One need not, however, go so far as to regard health or the biological and corporeal aspect of human life as the only relevant criterion for a proper organization of the health system. Instead one could adopt and follow those provisions in the West German legal system which acknowledge the value of individual choice not only in the physical but also in the mental, moral, and social aspects of life. Then, instead of having to play a patriarchal and paternal role, the physician could function more as a specially trained competent partner.

In addition to the role of professional competence and authority in the physician-patient relationship, the distribution of risks and liabilities should also be reconsidered. On the one hand, particularly on the basis of professional self-image as well as the protection which the insurance system grants the physician against the charge of malpractice, the physician's legal liability does not seem to influence the quality of medical services. On the other hand, it could be argued that a modest degree of collective liability is in all cases of unavoidable medical mishaps preferable to individual liability. All material damages caused by medical intervention should be compensated by an all-encompassing insurance system. Such a solution would, moreover, render obsolete all discussions concerning the assignment of individual responsibility and guilt, which only tend to be costly and are frequently settled unsatisfactorily by means of rules that define and distribute the respective burden of proof. Such a model of the physician-patient relationship would be congenial to the present degree of social integration. It would not ignore the autonomy of the individual but would recognize its value by making the health of one the concern for all.

## Notes

1. According to the decision of the Federal Court in the appeal of E. Schmidt and K. Jaspers; see Entscheidungen des Bundesgerichtschofes in Zivilsachen, 29:46.

2. By this I do not mean to convey that the current perception is better.

3. This forms the basis for system-theoretical legal theories (Luhmann 1972).

4. Federal Physicians' Regulation, October 2, 1961, as revised October 14, 1977, Bundesgesetzblatt I:1885; Approbation Regulation for Physicians, October 28, 1970, as revised April 3, 1979, Bundesgesetzblatt I:425; Ruling on Approbation as Physician—Approbation Regulation for Physicians, January 13, 1977, Gesetzblatt der DDR I:301.

5. The terminology differs in the FRG and the GDR (Rechtsgebiet and Rechtszweigszuordnung, respectively).

6. This opinion ignores the deliberate self-control exercised by the state and civil law. The fact that the physician's contract is legally recognized as a service

contract regulating financial rights does not imply that there are not other dimensions to the doctor-patient relationship; however, civil law does not regulate the others.

7. It is in the final analysis a question of whether the medical-care relation should belong to civil law (and thus, incidentally, be conceived as a—socialist—commodity-money relationship) or whether the health system, much like the educational system, should be understood as a task for society as a whole and therewith legally as a particular branch of law or as a part of the specific administrative law.

8. For further exposition, see chapter 1 in this volume.

9. This problem also undermines the suggestion that, instead of physical injury, violations of the exercise of free will should be prosecuted.

10. For the GDR, Familiengesetzbuch, paragraph 50; for the FRG, Bürgerliches Gesetzbuch, paragraph 1666.

11. Ruling on performing organ transplants, July 4, 1975, Gesetzblatt der DDR I:597.

12. For the GDR, see Becker 1978, p. 55.

13. Decision of the Federal Court, last given on March 26, 1979, Docket Number 6ZR481178; for the GDR, see Hansen and Vetterlein 1973, p. 59.

14. Arbeitsgesetzbuch der DDR, paragraph 289, June 16, 1977, Gesetzblatt der DDR I:185.

15. For the FRG, Sozialgesetzbuch, paragraph 66; for the GDR, Sozialversicherungsordnung, paragraph 82.

16. This problem is even more visible in government liability insurance, which works according to the same principle, and it is decided within the administration whether there has been an administrative failure.

## References

Becker, G. 1978. Arzt und Patient in sozialistischen Recht. Berlin: VEB Volk und Gesundheit.

Franke, V. 1976. Das Recht in Alltag des Haus- und Betriebsarztes. East Berlin: Tribune.

Hacks, S. 1978. Schmerzensgeld Beitrage. Munich: ADAC.

Hansen, G., and H. Vetterlein. 1973. Ärztliches Handeln—Rechtliche Pflichten. Leipzig: Georg Thieme.

Hinderling, A. 1963. "Die ärztliche Aufklarungs-pflicht." In Baseler Studien zur Rechtswissenschaft, vol. 66. Basel: Universität.

Laufs, A. 1971. Arztrecht. Munich: C. H. Beck.

Lohmann, U. 1978. "Das neue Arbeitsgesetsbuch der DDR." In Das Recht der Arbeit. Munich: C. H. Beck.

Luhmann, N. 1972. Rechtssoziologie. Reinbek: Rowohlt.

# 15 The Question of Induced Abortion

## Gudrun Keiner

*A particularly interesting facet of socio-political values in health is the question of induced abortion. Keiner uses induced abortion as a vehicle for examining concepts of birth, death, the images and rights of women, and the societal need for population growth. Tracing these relationships back to Bismarck's law of 1871, Keiner describes the various positions and factions that arose and how they changed under National Socialism and after World War II. She concludes with the irony that West German women, living in a society emphasizing individual freedom, are forced to bargain with an appointed counselor about their pregnancy, whereas East German women, living in a society emphasizing social responsibility, are granted individual freedom in the decision to abort.*

Abortion is a worldwide phenomenon which affects the special relationship between the unborn life and that of the mother, a relationship for which there is no parallel. According to ethnological research, abortion is such a universal social phenomenon that it is impossible to imagine a social system in which no woman would ever want to have an abortion. It is not possible to deal with the various ethical, religious, medical, legal, demographic, and economic issues of abortion in a single essay.[1] However, we can look at how the Federal Republic of Germany (FRG; West Germany) and the German Democratic Republic (GDR; East Germany) have treated the question of induced abortion and try a comparison. Both, for example, have passed laws the purpose of which is in part to assist women seeking abortion in physical, psychological, and social ways. Yet out of a common law before 1945 the two Germanies have developed strikingly different regulations. The comparison will focus on three topics: the emancipation or equality of women, taboos and restrictions on sexuality, and demographic developments.

## Laws on Abortion in the Two Germanies

*Abortus arteficialis* is defined as abortion deliberately and artificially caused. The practice of induced abortion depends on medical factors[2] as well as on legal regulations and social sanctions. In the FRG, abortion formally retains its prewar character as a criminal offense, even after the reform laws of the early 1970s. The purpose of the law is to protect unborn life, and it is found in the penal code (Strafgesetzbuch) under "criminal offenses against life." The reformed article (section 218) of 1976 begins: "Whoever interrupts pregnancy will be sentenced to up to 3 years of imprisonment or will be fined."

Legal abortion is possible in the FRG only if a woman follows a specific legally prescribed procedure. First she must have the pregnancy verified. Then she must visit an officially recognized maternity center and explain to a medical or psychological counselor why she wants an abortion, the purpose being to encourage the woman to carry the baby to term. Among other things, the woman is informed about the various social measures available to mothers. If she still opts for an abortion, she must see another doctor, who decides if she may have one for any one of four reasons provided for in the law. If she receives this medical "indication," a physician or a clinic will perform the abortion.

The first of the four bases for certifying a legal abortion is the assertion that pregnancy entails a risk for the woman's mental or physical health. The second is the assertion that not only the woman's health but also that of the fetus is an issue. The physician attempts to determine whether genetic or other influences have caused irreversible physical, intellectual, or mental injuries to the fetus. An abortion can then be recommended to spare the woman the burden of raising a child with a hereditary disease.[3] The focus is not eugenic but social. The third basis for legal abortion is rape. Finally, the law allows abortion if the social situation of the woman and her family is such that bearing the child might lead to grave conflicts or burdens. In all cases, the indication of an abortion and the abortion itself must always be performed by a physician, who then reports it to the Federal Office of Statistics, which produces summaries like that in table 1.[4]

A legal abortion presupposes five conditions: the consent of the pregnant woman, social consultation at least 3 days before the intervention, medical consultation, a medical diagnosis, and the consent of the physician. Abortion in the FRG takes place in the context of complicated

**Table 1**
Abortions in FRG, 1977.

| | Number | Per 1,000 births[a] | Per 1,000 fertile women[b] | Reason | | | | |
|---|---|---|---|---|---|---|---|---|
| | | | | Medical-social | Eugenic | Criminal | General emergency | Unknown |
| Schleswig-Holstein | 3,123 | 150.0 | 5.8 | 50.4% | 4.8% | 0.2% | 43.8% | 0.8% |
| Hamburg | 4,224 | 258.0 | 11.7 | 40.0 | 3.9 | 0.1 | 55.3 | 0.8 |
| Niedersachsen | 7,581 | 113.0 | 5.0 | 45.1 | 4.0 | 0.1 | 48.3 | 2.4 |
| Bremen | 900 | 103.8 | 5.9 | 32.7 | 5.8 | 0.2 | 59.9 | 1.4 |
| Nordrhein-Westfalen | 10,017 | 61.9 | 2.7 | 30.0 | 4.3 | 0.2 | 64.7 | 0.8 |
| Hessen | 8,559 | 169.8 | 7.2 | 30.6 | 2.9 | 0.1 | 65.7 | 0.8 |
| Rheinland-Pfalz | 587 | 16.6 | 0.7 | 52.1 | 10.1 | 0.2 | 37.5 | 0.2 |
| Baden-Württemberg | 8,517 | 92.0 | 4.3 | 37.6 | 4.8 | 0.2 | 56.5 | 0.9 |
| Bayern | 5,889 | 55.3 | 2.5 | 42.7 | 7.4 | 0.2 | 48.4 | 1.2 |
| Saarland | 401 | 39.5 | 1.7 | 50.2 | 12.7 | — | 37.2 | — |
| Berlin (W.) | 4,511 | 267.3 | 11.3 | 24.5 | 0.8 | 0.0 | 73.7 | 1.0 |
| **National** | | | | | | | | |
| 1977 | 54,309 | 92.6 | 4.1 | 36.8% | 4.3% | 0.1% | 57.7% | 1.1% |
| 1978 | 73,548 | 127.0 | 5.6 | 28.0 | 3.7 | 0.1 | 67.0 | 1.2 |
| 1979 | 82,788 | 142.3 | 6.3 | 24.2 | 3.8 | 0.1 | 70.6 | 1.3 |

a. Live and dead births, according to place of registration.
b. Women aged 15–45 years on December 31, 1976.
Source: Federal Office of Statistics

legal provisions. Still, the fact that the rather unspecific "social indications" for abortion have from the very beginning provided the basis for more than half the abortions and now provide the basis for almost three-quarters of the abortions (see table 1) means that abortion in the FRG is in fact available to every woman who wants it. Medical, sociological, and ethical criticism against this practice have increased sharply.[5]

In the GDR, women have, since the law of March 9, 1972, had the right to abort within the first 12 weeks of pregnancy. The abortion must be performed in the obstetrical unit of a hospital. In case of medical counterindications or an interruption of pregnancy within the previous 6 months, the law prohibits an abortion. While the pregnant woman is not required to consult anyone, the physician who performs the abortion has to inform the woman about the medical aspects of the operation and about contraceptive methods, and encourage her to keep her baby. The physician must also report any premature interruption of pregnancy to the local district office for medical statistics.

Besides deciding on an abortion on her own within 3 months after conception, a woman may apply for an abortion at any time during the entire pregnancy before a commission of specialists in the local district. The application is granted if the commission believes that the pregnancy will endanger the woman's life, or if there are other grave circumstances. Thus, medico-social criteria apply during the entire pregnancy.

The law on abortion is not subsumed under criminal law in the GDR and therefore carries no penalty. Self-performed abortions are also not punishable. However, there is a law that applies chiefly to untrained quacks: "Anybody who interrupts the pregnancy of a woman against the legal regulations will be sentenced to up to 3 years of imprisonment or receive a suspended sentence." (Gesetz über der unterbrechung der Schwangerschaft, section 1531)

In the same period that women's rights to abortion were increased in the GDR, a declining birth rate prompted a strong pro-natalist campaign. Pregnancy leaves and other benefits were increased. These policies seem to have taken effect as indicated by table 2. Legal abortions declined significantly, and births rose substantially. At the same time, the more liberal abortion policies of the GDR meant that its abortion rate remained much higher than that of the FRG (see table 1).

The contrasting laws concerning abortion in the two Germanies invite comparison. A law is the compulsory standard for individual conduct

**Table 2**
Relationship between abortion and birth in GDR, 1972–1978.

|  | Number of abortions | Per 1,000 inhabitants | Per 1,000 fertile women | Per 1,000 births | Number of live births | Birth rate |
|---|---|---|---|---|---|---|
| 1972 | 114,000 | 6.7 | 31.1 | 568.7 | 200,443 | 11.8 |
| 1973 | 110,000 | 6.5 | 32.1 | 614.5 | 180,336 | 10.6 |
| 1974 | 99,681 | 5.9 | 28.7 | 556.5 | 179,127 | 10.6 |
| 1975 | 87,750 | 5.2 | 26.0 | 482.7 | 181,798 | 10.8 |
| 1976 | 81,923 | 4.9 | 23.3 | 419.0 | 195,483 | 11.6 |
| 1977 | 80,145 | 4.8 | 22.9 | 359.0 | 223,152 | 13.3 |
| 1978 | 76,211 | 4.6 | 21.1 | 328.3 | 232,151 | 13.9 |

Sources: table from Harmsen 1979, p. 77; data from Wolff 1981, p. 1118.

established by the state; it also expresses the moral standards of the society. Although the two Germanies share a tradition of common legislation from before 1945, the political division since then has led to different ideological positions which have influenced the discussion and liberalization of abortion significantly.

## Historical Background

In 1871, Bismarck united Germany. One of the consequences was the standardization of the legal system, including laws concerning "crimes and offenses against life." Sections 218–220 of the newly put-together criminal code of May 15, 1871, made abortion punishable in order to protect the embryo. Historically, the ancient Greeks, Romans, and Germans did not regard the growing life of the embryo as something to be protected. It was looked upon as a part of the mother's body (*pars viscerum matres*). Canonical law seems to have been the first to define abortion as a crime. Until the thirteenth century, the Catholic Church did not regard abortion as a criminal act if done before the begetting of a soul,[6] but thereafter it was prosecuted. This position was modified by the Enlightenment and the French Revolution, which until 1810 did not punish a woman who performed an abortion on herself. For Bismarck's Germany, however, the French Revolution was not a model. In 1871, abortion was no longer defined as murder but did merit punishment.

Since the public debate on abortion did not stop, the articles on abortions were liberalized during the Weimar Republic (1918–1933).

**Table 3**
Numbers of convictions for illegal abortion.

| | |
|---|---:|
| 1901 | 457 |
| 1906 | 578 |
| 1911 | 985 |
| 1916 | 1,164 |
| 1921 | 4,248 |
| 1926 | 6,268 |

Source: Hollein 1931, p. 232.

This was prompted by the impoverishment and the ensuing lack of food, clothing, and housing in Germany in the years following World War I. Unemployment and starvation were widespread, and many families wished to limit the number of children. Poverty and famine had an even stronger effect on women than the fear of being imprisoned or endangering their health. By 1925 there was "no fertile woman in Germany who [had] not made at least one legal attempt at abortion after she missed her period" (Hollein 1931, p. 233). Sex education at the time was taboo. Contraceptives were largely unknown or not available. The estimated number of criminal abortions was no less than 700,000 in 1925.[7] In the years of hunger and poverty the number of abortions and convictions increased steadily (table 3).

From 1923 to 1926, the average number of convictions for abortion numbered 5,660 a year. This amounts to 6 convictions per 1,000 abortions at best, only a minute fraction of the actual number of criminal abortions performed. Despite the fact that the number of criminal convictions rose steadily, it is therefore hard to decide if these convictions express a corresponding rise in abortions.

Despite this steep rise in the number of abortions, the government did not introduce any social policy but continued to rely on punitive measures. Individual physicians supported sex counseling. The Prussian Secretary of Welfare recommended marriage counseling, but with the restricted objective of medically examining matrimonial applicants to ensure their genetic fitness. This is a reflection of Social Darwinism, which later became dominant under Hitler's regime. The public propagation of contraception and the liberation of abortion were rejected by the Deutscher Ärtzebund and the Bund deutscher Frauenvereine on moral grounds. They warned against "further decay of morals" and the loss of the "respect for the woman." During the Weimar Republic, representatives of the churches (particularly Roman Catholicism) objected to the legalization of abortion, arguing that it constituted the killing of human life.

Legalized abortion became a major political goal of the Labor Movement. Social Democrats, Communists, the Union of Socialist Doctors (Verein Sozialistischer Ärzte), left-wing liberals, artists, and intellectuals played an active part in advocating free abortion within the first 3 months after contraception. The Social Democrat faction in the Reichstag (the German parliament before 1945) worked out a bill according to which an abortion performed by the woman herself or by a licensed physician within the first 3 months after conception was not punishable by law. The Communist Party of Germany (the KPD) was most vigorous to oppose the criminal laws against abortion and used the slogan "Your body belongs to yourself." The KPD demanded not only free abortion but also the propagation and distribution of contraceptives by the sickness funds. Women were unsuccessfully called on to accuse themselves en masse of having had abortions in order to demonstrate the failure of the articles against abortion to the public. The KPD also cited the good experiences of women in the Soviet Union, where abortion since 1920 had been freely available in public hospitals.

The Social Democrats and the Communists presented their respective bills several times but were always defeated. However, on May 17, 1926, the Reichstag passed a bill by a vote of 213 to 173 fusing sections of articles 218, 219, and 220 into one article.[8] The significant change was that abortion performed by the woman herself or with her consent was considered not a felony but a misdemeanor punishable by imprisonment. This amendment did not appease the public protest supported by the Socialists and Communists against the old law, nor did it reduce the number of abortions, which grew with the world depression of 1929.

Among the opponents of legalized abortion were those for whom demographic, nationalistic, and military arguments were important. World War I had greatly reduced the population. The conservative German National Party argued: "After the various misfortunes that the German people have suffered during the last decades, there is but one force left and that is our people. For their force our enemies still have considerable respect. They will continue to have this respect as long as we are a people of 70 or 80 million, whether inside or outside the present German borders. It is not the consequences of the last war that will determine our fate in the course of history, but our will to overcome.

The question today is whether we will actually succeed in maintaining our population of 70 to 80 million Germans in Central Europe."[9]

In 1930, the National Socialists presented a bill for the protection of the German nation to the Reichstag. Among other things, it said: "Anyone who attempts to inhibit artificially the natural fertility of the German people at the expense of the nation will be sentenced to penal servitude . . . , and in particularly grave cases sentenced to death for racial treason." This meant that even contraception was to be considered a criminal act. The increase of the German population was to be stimulated by a policy of fear, and the genetic quality of the population became a goal. During the regime of Hitler, "Aryan" life was protected as never before, while "non-Aryan" life was aborted for "reasons of the state."

In 1933, after Hitler and the National Socialist German Labor Party took over, section 218 was changed to read that a person who performed an abortion was in grave cases to be sentenced to death instead of being imprisoned. Moreover, the eugenic indication was altered in order to provide exceptions for those whose lives were not considered worth preserving, such as the mentally or physically handicapped or those who were a social liability. The National Socialist family and population policy aimed to restore the German people by selection on one hand and extermination on the other. Thus the social hygiene of the "race" became the principal determinant of health and abortion policy (Harmsen et al. 1957, p. 24). Underlying this policy were the ideas of Social Darwinism in which the social efficiency of individuals was determined by their genetic endowment.

In 1935, a law was passed requiring all men and women who wanted to get married to receive a medical certificate attesting to their qualification for marriage. According to Himmler's Ordinance of January 21, 1941, any obstruction to the capacity of procreation was penalized. Thus, family planning was not permitted. The systematic policy of selection and extermination forbade abortion and contraception for women who could give birth to children of high genetic quality, while women who might give birth to genetically "undesirable" children were sterilized, forced to abort, or killed. Thus the ideology of motherhood propagated by the National Socialist Party camouflaged the obligation to bear children. This racial ideology gave rise to a great deal of fear. Politically, the National Socialists' population and family policy stabilized Hitler's power through the social techniques of selection and extermination and the systematic expansion of fear.

The end of World War II and the destruction of the German Reich meant liberation from fear and terror for the majority of the German people. During the occupation, the Allies revoked all additional penalties that had been introduced by the National Socialists after January 30, 1933. Thus the death sentence or penal servitude for those performing abortions was no longer valid, and the penal code of 1871 as amended in 1926 became valid once again. Abortion was again a minor punishable offense. The only exception to abortion as a criminal offense was a restricted clause concerning medical dangers to the mother. In all other respects paragraph 218 was enforced in the American, British, French, and Soviet occupation zones equally.

Discussion of abortion resumed, however, and in 1946 the socialist doctors of Hamburg demanded that social as well as medical problems should be an indication for legal abortion. The City Council of Hamburg presented a bill proposing that abortion be permitted by an appointed commission if it was found that social circumstances would endanger the health or education of the infant to be born. It also demanded that contraceptives be promoted and distributed.

Soon after the end of the war, fundamental political differences between the Soviets and the Allies flared up and led to the division of Germany without the consent of the Germans. In the former British, American, and French zones the autonomy of the federal states and the principle of plurality were maintained, but the Soviet zone came under central communist rule. The problems of public health care and facilities were equally great in the GDR and the FRG. Both had to deal with the problems of refugees, housing shortages, inadequate food supplies, and thousands of disabled war veterans. However, as a result of different political ideologies, the question of abortion was treated differently in the two new German states.

## The Liberalization of Abortion in the FRG

Because of the generally democratic and pluralistic political organizations of the FRG, the corporate structure of medicine has been preserved to this day. Health-policy decisions are negotiated between physicians or their representatives, the sickness funds, communal or private hospital owners, and the political parties. Basically, health care is based on the principle of Subsidiarität, which means that the state steps in only after the community has reached its limits. The community in turn steps in only after the family has reached its limits. However, a lively political debate arose over the question of admitting reasons other than the restricted medical criteria for legal abortion. In the end, however, the idea of protecting growing life except in medical emergencies gained support, and the governmental bills of 1959, 1960, and 1962 provided strict penalties for illegal abortions.

Social behavior differed increasingly from the legal norms. The number of illegal abortions rose to more than a million per year (Konig 1980, pp. 69 ff.). In public discussion, it was generally agreed that the protection of unborn life through law was no longer possible (Konig 1980, pp. 70 ff.; Paczensky 1980, pp. 81 ff.; Politische Fraueninitiativ Heidelberg 1975, pp. 10 ff.). Moreover, the law put women in a difficult position if they wanted to break it. They had to either go abroad (mostly to England or Holland) or turn to an illegal abortionist and thus put their health at a considerable risk.

At the end of the 1960s, some women's differing experiences, the conflicting views in the population, and the various positions of social groups and parties led to different suggestions of what to do about section 218. The spectrum of debate, which was reflected in parliamentary discussion, ranged from abolishing section 218 altogether to tightening the existing laws. Although the need for reform was urgent, no fundamental change was made, and on June 25, 1969, the first penal reform merely redefined abortion as an infringement of the law.

However, the discussion did not stop with this reform. In 1970, the national Conference of Women and the Association of Young Social Democrats jointly demanded the cancellation of section 218. Various women's groups, especially feminists, started a public campaign against section 218. In 1971 there were nationwide coordinated activities against section 218, which began with public confessions presented to the Secretary of Justice in July 1971.[10] Thousands of women demonstrated with slogans such as "My belly belongs to me" and "Whether we want children or not is our decision."[11] Tens of thousands of signatures were collected, leaflets were distributed, and information booths were set up. Through these widespread activities, women became a major factor in public discourse. Progressive social groups and parties supported the women and their demands for the abolition of section 218.

The Catholic Church steadfastly supported the encyclicals *Casti connubi* (1930) and *Humanae vitae* (1968). *Casti connubi* opposes any form of "destruction of unborn life." It acknowledges the conflict of a woman being made involuntarily pregnant but opposes abortion. As for medical justifications, *Humanae vitae* reflects the same conflict. In a 1971 statement, German bishops argued that there should be no prosecution where an abortion has averted the danger of death or an unacceptably grave and lasting damage to the pregnant woman's body and health. Even in such a case, however, abortion was still to be regarded as morally unjustified.

In 1972 the federal government of the FRG presented a penal-reform bill to the parliament which brought in the indications for legal abortion mentioned at the beginning of this chapter. At the same time, 51 members of the SDP (the Social Democratic Party) and the FDP (the Free Democratic Party) presented their own bill to alter section 218 so that abortion would be allowed during the first months of pregnancy when performed and supervised by a physician. A variety of other, more conservative bills were presented, including some that allowed legal abortions only in the case of severe medical problems (Kommission zur Auswertung 1980, pp. 14–15). The debate in parliament ranged from the complete release of abortion from legal restrictions to almost total prohibition and prosecution. In April 1974 the position of the SPD and the FDP that abortion be freely allowed in the first months of pregnancy was passed 247 to 233, with 9 abstentions, by the lower house of parliament (the Bundestag). Members of the upper house (the Bundesrat) entered a protest and appealed to the Committee for Mediation. This protest was rejected by the Bundestag.[12]

After the law had been passed, the Christian Democrats succeeded in getting it suppressed by an interim order of the Federal Constitutional Court, and they then appealed to the court to overrule the law.[13] The court took almost a year to deliberate on the case, and on February 25, 1975, it declared unconstitutional, by a vote of 5–3, the law permitting abortion on demand during the first 3 months. It did open the way, however, for a law stipulating certain medical and social indications.

The parliamentary groups of the Bundestag presented new bills.[14] Both sides assumed that unrestricted legal abortion in the early months of pregnancy was no longer under discussion and outlined various medical, social, genetic, ethical, and social criteria for allowing a legal abortion. On February 12, 1976, the government had their bill accepted by 234 to 181 votes. Again, the parliamentary groups of the Christian Democratic and Christian Socialist parties called in the Mediation Committee. From their point of view, the law passed by the Bundestag did not sufficiently consider the decision of the Federal Constitutional Court but left the indications for legal abortion vague (Kommission zur Auswertung 1980, p. 17). This objection was overruled, and on March 21, 1976, the joint bill of the SPD and the FDP became federal law. On June 21, 1976, it went into operation.

The view of what might be appropriate criteria for legal abortion is influenced by the Zeitgeist of society. Values and public debates influence the criteria used. Table 4 shows among other things that the public discussion begun in 1971 had a liberalizing effect on the interpretation of criteria for abortion by consultants. The axiom of a pluralistic society states that everyone may pursue happiness in his own way as long as he does not infringe upon his fellow man's liberty and does not violate the legal order. The liberal pluralism and tolerance manifested by this position are achievements of enlightenment and are increasingly reflected in questions of abortion. However, the complexity of the issue is reflected in the guiding principles given by the judges of the Federal Constitutional Court:[15] that life in the womb is autonomous and protected by the constitution (article 2, paragraph 1, Basic Constitutional Laws); that the state is obliged to protect growing life, even against the mother; that the protection of the life of the fetus during the entire pregnancy takes precedence over the right of self-determination by the pregnant woman; that a legislator is not obliged to sanction abortion by means of criminal law but can do so; and that it is acknowledged that a pregnancy can be extremely burdensome for the pregnant woman, and as soon as the distress caused by this can be regarded as unacceptable an abortion can be legally executed.

Two of the three dissenting judges have since published their objections. According to them, the state forfeits the right to appropriate assistance and protects the fetus only from ineffectual and potentially harmful legislation. They pointed out that abortion cannot really be compared to other crimes against human life; that, unlike proscriptions against murder, the law against abortion demands not only that the pregnant woman abstain from performing the criminal act but also that she "submit to radical changes in her health and well-being as well as her future life and accept the responsibility for the child after its birth." They also drew attention to the fact that state and society had so far neglected to provide institutions which would enable women to combine motherhood and family life with personal development, especially in the professional area. They concluded with the opinion that "the legislature was fully entitled to compensate for the failure of state and society in protecting life by permitting free abortion within the first 3 months of pregnancy."

**Table 4**
Abortions granted in FRG.

|      | Number | Per 10,000 inhabitants |
|------|--------|------------------------|
| 1968 | 2,826  | 0.47  |
| 1969 | 3,408  | 0.56  |
| 1970 | 4,886  | 0.80  |
| 1971 | 6,859  | 1.12  |
| 1972 | 8,644  | 1.40  |
| 1973 | 13,021 | 2.23  |
| 1974 | 17,184 | 2.82  |
| 1975 | 21,231 | 3.79  |
| 1976 | 21,371 | 3.80  |
| 1977 | 54,309 | 8.00  |
| 1978 | 73,548 | 12.00 |
| 1979 | 82,788 | 13.50 |

Sources of data: for 1968–1976, Harmsen 1979, p. 86; for 1977–1979, *Statistiches Jahrbuch für die Bundesrepublick Deutschland* (Stuttgart: Kohlhammer).

The discussion about abortion has still not abated. The political parties do not, however, participate in the debate any longer with programmatic statements (Kommission zur Auswertung 1980, pp. 12 ff., 168 ff., 215 ff.). Only the Committee of Social Democratic Women has again called for free abortion. The Free Democratic Party announced during a party convention in 1978 that "the FDP still adheres to free abortion as the better, juster, and more humane solution for women who find themselves in a situation of conflict" (Kommission zur Auswertung 1980, pp. 168). The Women's Committee of the Christian Democratic Party, on the other hand, has stated that "the revised Paragraph 218 has not proved effective in protecting unborn life" (ibid.). As proof they cite the great increase in legal abortions since the introduction of the new law. They view it as an indication of the "failure of our social and constitutional order in its political, legal, and social aspects" (ibid.). They are demanding financial subsidies for pregnant women and young mothers, a range of material assistance for families, and greater societal appreciation and acceptance of children and families. The Christian Socialist Union largely shares these views (ibid.). The labor unions support the minority vote of the Federal Court and continue to ask for free abortion (ibid.).

The Federal Association of Physicians believes that particularly the criterion of social need is being abused. At present the demand for abortions exceeds the willingness of physicians to perform them. The physicians think, however, that this resistance will finally succumb to public pressure. The Federal Association of Physicians has condemned this development, pointing out that "the physician's task is not to resolve social conflicts through abortions, but to protect the unborn life" (Kommission zur Auswertung 1980, p. 170).

The most vehement opposition comes from the Catholic Church. For the Church, life begins at conception and is inviolate from then on. The mother has no rights over the unborn life, for the child is not regarded as part of the mother but as an independent being. The right to life for the unborn, its dignity, and the need for protection are the fundamental principles of all ethical and theological considerations in Catholic dogma about abortion. The Church sees in the present law no guarantee of adequate protection of the unborn life, and is not likely to ever support the law. It will continue to insist on effective legal prosecution in addition to counseling and other social and political measures (Kommission zur Auswertung 1980, pp. 170–171).

The Evangelical Church of Germany (EKD) does not take a clear position. It acknowledges that the new Paragraph 218 is an attempt to protect existing as well as unborn life. It holds that the law allows for principled individual decisions that are divinely inspired. It also accepts that, in certain situations, different but ethically equal demands may produce a conflict which defies a fully satisfactory solution. The EKD demands the adoption of socio-political measures which will make it easier for women to carry unwanted pregnancies to term (Kommission zur Auswertung 1980, pp. 171–172).

Social scientists have turned their attention to abortion only since it has been partially legalized. Next to the psycho-social and economic aspects, they have considered the role of counseling in abortion. Since counseling is designed to facilitate individual decision making and can by definition not solve social conflicts, some researchers have called for the abolition of obligatory counseling (Amendt 1979; Knieper 1981; Koschorke and Sandberger 1978).

The struggle for the repeal of Paragraph 218 seems now to have developed into a struggle for the abolition of obligatory counseling. Public interest has shifted away from the question of abortion. Only a few feminist writers still pursue the objective of free abortion. The majority of women seem to have adjusted to the law as it stands.

## Liberalization of Abortion in the GDR

The Soviet-occupied zone, like the Western zones, ignored and repressed the Hitler experience and tried to continue in the tradition of the Weimar Republic. Since it found itself under Soviet-Communist domination, it developed according to the Soviet model, which excluded pluralism in any form. The Soviet Military Administration ordered in July 1945 that the centralized government to be established in East Germany was to incorporate a centrally administered health service. A systematic reorganization of the health service took place and was pursued by the Ministry of Health when the GDR government took over from the Soviet Military Administration in October 1949.

At the time, the Socialist Unity Party (SED) had enough power to impose its Marxist-Leninist concept of a socialist society on a largely unwilling population. In accordance with the socialist principle of equality, Walter Ulbricht, the SED chairman, supported equality for women: "If one speaks of equality for all, it is nothing short of monstrous to exclude one-half of humanity. A woman has the same right as a man to develop and utilize her potential; she is a human being like the man and she should have the freedom to decide her own fate."

In a formal sense, the equality of women was thus written into the first constitution in 1949 (as it was in the FRG). In Marxism the individual is always a social being, inseparable from the social context. A certain stereotype in which the human group, the social class, is more important than the human individual is often accentuated. It often postulates an identity between the interests of the individual and those of society. Since the individual as a conscious and striving being does not cease to exist, however, revisionist Marxist thinkers have come to maintain that Marxist theory too starts with the individual, "who is a living being, made of flesh and blood, a specimen of a biological species, a part of nature. This is the first and most elementary part of the Marxist conception of the individual in his/her material manifestation." (Schaff 1969, p. 75) To view the human being as a socio-biological unit means to acknowledge his biological determinants as well as his socially constituted nature. For Marxists, the driving force of human life is "labor, especially labor that unites humans as social beings" (Schafarewitsch 1980, p. 281).

With emancipation to full membership in a Marxist society, women are said to acquire a new consciousness of themselves, because with paid labor they too contribute to the productive process. Marxist ideology also maintains that criminal law—but only in capitalism—is an instrument by which the ruling classes suppress and persecute the revolutionary forces for democracy among the masses. For this reason, the German Penal Code of 1871 is considered reactionary. In a socialist society, in contrast, criminal law is claimed to serve "objective" social justice and to embody the will and the interests of the people.

The German legal system established in the Civil Code of 1871 was replaced soon after World War II by a separate legal code for the GDR (Scholz 1977, p. 51), and in 1976 the transformation to a socialist legal order was completed. Throughout this process the question of abortion was discussed, but generally without reference to the Soviet example. Instead, the SED resumed the debate at the point where the Communist Party in the Weimar Republic had left off. In 1946, all police ordinances regarding procedures, means, and instruments for preventing or interrupting pregnancies which had been issued by Himmler were revoked. Interference with the capacity to conceive and give birth has not been a punishable offense since 1945. Between 1947 and 1948, laws regulating abortion were relaxed in a number of provinces—despite the fact that abortion was prohibited in the Soviet Union. Liberalization continued for three more years until legislation for the "protection of mother and child and the rights of women" considerably curtailed opportunities for legal abortions. The reasons for these restrictions were primarily demographic. The birth rate was to be increased, and only abortions for medical and eugenic reasons were permitted. In the Soviet Union, meanwhile, criminal prosecution for abortion was abolished in 1954, and a year later abortion was legalized. Although all other Eastern European countries followed the example of the Soviet Union, the GDR waited until 1965 before it again began to liberalize abortion laws. From 1965 on, a woman under 16 years, over 40 years, or with more than four children could apply for and have a legal abortion in a hospital. Full legalization of abortion followed in 1972.

These legal decisions were taken without reference to any of the many fundamental ideological arguments for or against abortion. Only the church made an attempt to protest in the newspaper *Neues Deutschland* in 1972. The present official literature merely refers to a step toward the emancipation of women, who now have the right to make their own decisions. With the right to legal abortion, the GDR thus transfers an important social responsibility to individual women. However, the law met with considerable resistance; it is, in fact, the only law in the GDR that was not passed unanimously. Of the 500 members of parliament, 14 abstained and 8 voted against.

In the GDR, abortion is viewed from two perspectives: as a contribution to the equality of women and as a population policy measure. The aim is "responsible motherhood." It is thought that family planning will gradually reduce the need for abortions and finally phase them out altogether. In order to realize this goal, a number of social and economic measures were introduced together with the law permitting abortion.

Since about 1963 the birth rate in the GDR had been falling, and the legalization of abortion in 1972 further reduced it until it reached its lowest level (10.6 percent) in 1974. Since then the birth rate has risen steadily. Table 2 shows that the number of legal abortions is decreasing and that live births have been increasing since 1975. This trend continues, chiefly as a result of comprehensive social policies. Though illegal abortions initially diminished by a third, they began to rise again in 1974 and by 1976 had again become considerable in number.[16] It seems that "free" abortion in the GDR is not quite as free as it appears on paper and that the process women have to go through to attain it is a process of heavy social and political control. To avoid the political control exerted over them, women therefore prefer clandestine abortions, which they appear to perceive as being "really" free.

The absence of any debate in the GDR over free abortion within the first 3 months raises some questions, particularly about the time of the decision. Some political developments may be relevant. Since the fall of party chief Walter Ulbricht, his theory that the GDR was in the process of becoming a classless society has been somewhat modified—all the more since it constituted an attempt to claim, via a covert and somewhat obscure ideological argument, a special (i.e. more independent) role in the Soviet bloc. The more recent self-conception of the GDR is that of a worker and peasant state in which the working-class women play the leading role. The percentage of economically active women has risen steadily over the years, and in 1979 they constituted 50.6 percent of the total labor force (Staatliche Zentralverwaltung für Statistik 1979). This high a percentage of women in the labor force is probably due only partly to the drive for equality. Economic conditions play an important part as well. First there is the fact that the population of the GDR is overaged, so that the proportion of those in the productive age groups is relatively small. Second, salaries are so low that the income of a single person is barely sufficient for a family. Thus women are forced to seek paid employment.

This double role of women in the GDR is explicitly recognized: Women have responsibilities in both the productive and the reproductive sphere. In order to be equal by Marxist standards, women must be able to exercise control over their biological nature. Responsible and conscious motherhood is said to demand that a woman be able to decide whether she wants to have a child within the first 3 months of pregnancy. At the same time, motherhood is encouraged by an extensive set of services and institutions that provide social and economic support during pregnancy and child rearing.

The question is whether the liberalization of abortion was the consequence of these social, political, and economic measures or whether there were also external influences, possibly coming from the FRG. There is little doubt that considerable rivalry exists between the two German states, especially with regard to social measures. In 1971, extraparliamentary opposition and activism against abortion legislation became a significant force in the FRG. Is it possible that the government in the GDR was influenced by the political events in the FRG and therefore adopted social measures by liberalizing abortion laws and making oral contraceptives available? Unfortunately, the data are sparse and it is not possible to answer these questions.

## Demography and Family Planning in the FRG and the GDR

In the FRG, as in the GDR, abortion is invariably discussed in the context of family planning and population policies. Both are, of course, connected. The current birth rate has far-reaching implications for the standard of living, and deliberate population policies depend for their success on the prevailing level of social and economic development in a society. Although there is no evidence that legalizing abortion affects the growth of a population, demographic and political considerations are raised every time abortion is discussed, usually by comparing the number of abortions with the number of live births.

The GDR has established a network of social assistance for pregnant women and mothers. There are a variety of financial aids; however, these must also be seen as attempts to control demographic developments. In the FRG, the policies relating to abortion are not as obvious, but the same tendency toward comparing live births and abortions can be observed and it is clear that abortions are seen as a method of population control. This assumed demographic effect is often cited as an argument against liberalizing abortion laws. However, the reproductive behavior of a population is subject to a number of complex factors, not all of which are related to population policies. A direct causal connection between birth rates and the legalizing of abortion does not exist, chiefly because abortion is only one of a number of possible options in reproductive behavior. Even the sudden increase in abortions after legalization is not easy to interpret, since the official figures probably constitute only a fraction of the real figures.

Also, the birth rate is not dramatically affected by legislation. In both German states the birth rates had been dropping since 1963. Legalizing abortion hardly accelerated this downward trend. On the contrary, about 3 years after legalization the birth rates started rising again. One of the factors affecting the fertility of a population is its contraceptive behavior, which in turn is influenced by the degree to which sexuality is subject to taboos. Societal taboos on sexuality inhibit the ability to deal responsibly with one's own sexuality. Although most other human activities are improved by education, sex education frequently meets with public resistance. In both German states, the schools offer sex education, which covers the biology and physiology of sex and reproduction and the social values and norms regarding sexual behavior. However, public sex education can only be regarded as supplementary. Basic attitudes toward emotions and intimate relations are formed in the family. The school can only provide information on the techniques of contraception and family planning.

In regard to abortion, knowledge about and practice of contraception may be seen as having preventive effects. The limits of prevention are defined by the reliability of contraception. It is known, for example, that persons with low incomes and little education tend to use unreliable methods of contraception (Oeter and Wilken 1979, pp. 191 ff.; Kommission zur Auswertung 1980, pp. 121 ff.). This means that unwanted pregnancies will occur despite the availability of contraceptives, and abortion is a last option.

To prevent recidivism, it is necessary that legal abortions be accompanied by determined efforts to promote contraception. Apart from the health problems connected with abortion there is the cost factor. Effective prevention through the distribution of birth-control information and contraception devices is much less of a financial drain on the national economy than abortion. It should be noted that in the GDR birth-control pills are considered a health-care matter and are distributed free of charge, while in the FRG all forms of birth control are a matter of individual choice and therefore are paid for by the sickness funds.

A sociological investigation of 2,588 patients in the GDR on the consequences of abortion showed that 63 percent of the respondents viewed abortion as a means of family planning and only one-third thought of it as a measure to promote women's rights (Wilken 1977, pp. 1106 ff.). Most working-class women used abortion as a form of birth control; indeed, they constituted 70 percent of the patients. These figures show clearly that in the GDR abortion is one instrument of family planning among others. In the FRG, in contrast, abortion is mainly a therapeutic measure to compensate for contraceptive failure. However, an investigation of 288 patients in West Berlin showed results similar to those in the GDR: 77.2 percent of the patients were working-class women (Goebel 1980). It is apparent that knowledge about the processes of conception significantly affects contraceptive behavior, and that political and ideological factors have little or no influence.

## Values and Norms

It must be understood that as far as abortions are concerned, women in the FRG and in the GDR find themselves in very different situations. The FRG is a democratic and pluralistic society which is founded on the values of individual responsibility and freedom, yet its law regulating abortions institutionalizes a social process in which the pregnant woman bargains with an appointed counselor whether and why she might want an abortion. The socialist GDR, on the other hand, emphasizes societal responsibility for the individual, yet places the sole authority over childbearing to individual women and gives them therein total freedom. In a sense, each of these societies is dealing with the issue of abortion in terms of assumptions that stand in direct contrast to its own basic values and rather resemble those of the other society.

During the public discussion about reform of the abortion laws, women in the FRG formed the "New Women's Movement." This started a process of consciousness raising and emancipation for women. In the GDR, the government introduced legal abortion and justified this with reference to the equality of women.[17] There is no women's movement in the GDR, and the cause of female equality is taken in charge by the communist government. The aim of the emancipation of women in the GDR is, expressed simply, their full integration into the existing society and their full contribution to economic productivity. The women's movement in the FRG demands, beyond full and equal integration, a specific and self-determined role in the transformation of society, in shaping its norms and values.

Autonomy and self-determination enable the individual to decide his or her own fate and overcome biological determinants. The changed consciousness of women not only alters the relations between the sexes but introduces new tensions into the whole of society. Women are consolidating their newly won freedom by making their partners participate in family and domestic tasks and by demanding social and political measures that will relieve them of their traditional work. Political action is aimed at implementing these demands. However, thus far women have not been successful in obtaining complete and sole control over childbearing. They now have the choice between going through an institutionalized bargaining process (which usually leads to abortion) and having the abortion performed illegally outside the German borders. This option obviously exists only for women who have the financial means.

The emancipation of women is a long social process, and it is inextricably linked to the issue of human autonomy. In the GDR, there is no mention of emancipation, only of equality. Equality for women is chiefly a matter of their being part of the work force. The position of women in the process of production is obviously of prime importance. Here their talents and abilities are systematically integrated and used in all economic, social, scientific, and cultural fields. Many women in the GDR are employed in male-typed occupations, and women are also more prominent in public life. Yet they do not actually shape their society. Instead they basically follow the male example, engaging in compulsive productivity within a rigidly organized system and surrendering their essential femininity. Some have argued that life in industrial societies would benefit from a stronger influence of women. This could soften the alienating impact of technology by introducing an emotional dimension, and by supplementing the glorification of power and competition with communication and cooperation. The women's movement in the FRG, however, does not have this or other clearly defined political goals and remains thus chiefly a forum for free discussion of feminist issues.

Social change and social innovation by constitutional means proceed along different lines in the two German states because of their different conceptions of the state, society, and democracy. Both states guarantee basic human rights in their constitutions. Since there are, however, limits to individual rights, the constitution specifies the means for conflict resolution. In the FRG, these rights end where they threaten the freedom of other individuals and the democratic order. Democracy in the FRG is based on free public debate and the principle of pluralism. In the GDR, the constitution guarantees the development of a communist order and assigns to the SED the official authority to realize this goal. Exercising basic rights thus means agreement with current SED policy.[18] In the FRG, that "everyone has the right to physical inviolability" (Grundegesetz, Article 2, Paragraph 2) is the fundamental constitutional right to which the Supreme Court referred when it rejected free abortion as unconstitutional. This judgment is based on a conception of man that emphasizes the elemental freedom of the individual. According to Christian tradition (particularly that of the Catholic Church), the inviolability of the individual is grounded in his being God's creation. The Catholic Church views the present West German law permitting abortion in cases of social emergency as a violation of human rights and stated after the new Paragraph 218 was passed that "this law undermines the fundamentals of our Rechtsstaat [government of law]. . . . It destroys ethical consciousness and dehumanizes society."[19] However, basic constitutional rights also protect the freedom of the individual, and consequently "the state must remain neutral. It may not identify with certain religions, nor with religiously determined convictions or beliefs."[20] Ethical norms evolve in part from the experience of living and are created by individuals and groups. The basic value of "freedom," which is endorsed by all parliamentary parties, implies many different political and religious positions and perspectives, as is to be expected in a pluralistic society (Grundgesetz, Article 4). The FRG thus only appears to be acting counter to its values, since it in fact took into account the changed position of women and amended the law regulating abortion. However, the opposition parties argued that "freedom" was neither a collective nor an individual attribute, but referred to "the dignity of the individual, to the right to live life according to his or her own design."[21]

In the GDR, societal consensus and political action are based on values and norms which refer to concrete human beings in concrete social situations and not to abstract "humanitarian" ideas (Straass 1981, p. 391). Dialectic historical materialism is based on a concrete social-historical conception of man in which human nature is shaped and altered by the process of labor. In this process, human interests and needs also change, as do ethical values. Moral and ethical values derive solely from labor and the social relations arising from it.[22] The position of women in society has changed, and the equality of women in the educational and professional sphere, in marriage, and in the family justifies their exclusive right to decide over pregnancy in deciding its termination. Some recent investigations have shown that women in the GDR are using the option to abort.[23] The number of abortions is diminishing, but it is still quite high, and one gynecologist has called for further efforts to reduce their number.[24]

Thus, the GDR too is only apparently acting in contradiction to its own values. Social labor, supported by communist education, permits the development of value patterns which enable men and women to assume responsibility in the context of this political system. If a person acts according to the principles of the SED, he is granted the right to "freedom"[25] and "freedom of conscience,"[26] since he is then acting in congruence with Marxist principles for the benefit of society.

## Notes

1. From the multiplicity of ethical problems connected with abortion I am here selecting only a few central ones which have historically recurred in the discussion on abortion and have been subjected to certain ideological influences.

2. Physicians can apply several methods to interrupt pregnancy, e.g. currettage, aspiration, medical abortion. In this chapter the methods of terminating a pregnancy will not be discussed since they have no bearing on the basic issue of abortion.

3. The future suffering of a child who sustains serious medical damage as a result of genetic or environmental prenatal influences may appear worthless from the point of view of a healthy person, but may nevertheless have meaning for the afflicted person. Legislators took into account the fact that the pregnant woman may find herself in a grave conflict.

4. This is meant to prevent "backstreet abortions." It is felt that the interests of the pregnant woman should be safeguarded by ensuring that the diagnosis is accurate and that the medical intervention is as safe as possible.

5. This is particularly true for the "social emergency" indication. The fact that every year more women make use of this reason shows that these women are no longer forced to have illegal abortions or go outside the German borders (Koschorke and Sandberger 1978, pp. 131 ff.).

6. According to the view current then, the embryo had no soul and no independent life. The soul entered the male embryo 40 days after conception and the female embryo 80 days after conception.

7. Hollein (1931, pp. 217 ff.) cites a number of physicians. Also see Harmsen et al. 1957, p. 2.

8. Voting en bloc against the new proposal were "the parties of the center, the German Nationals, and the Clerical Bavarians" (Hollein 1931, p. 236).

9. Stenographische Berichte über die Verhandlungen des Reichstages (Minutes of the Parliamentary Debates), fifth election period, 1930, volume 445, p. 178, cited by von Soden in Paczensky 1980, p. 43.

10. Self-accusations had been advocated by socialists and communists in the Weimar Republic but never carried out.

11. The slogan in the Weimar Republic was "Your body belongs to you." This change in terminology indicates in my opinion a simultaneous change in women's self-consciousness; they now represent themselves and their own convictions.

12. Federal laws which have been passed by parliament must, under certain circumstances, be approved by the Senate. In 1974 the CDU and CSU had the majority in the Senate, so the opposition parties could have defeated the new abortion bill (Kommission zur Auswertung 1980, p. 15). "The Senate considered that this law requires approval, but refused to give it even after having been called on to do so by the arbitration committee. Instead it registered a protest, according to Article 77, Paragraph 33 of the constitution. This protest was rejected with a majority of 260 to 218 and 4 abstentions by the federal parliament. The fifth draft for the reform of the penal code was ready on June 18, 1974. It was published in the Bundesgesetzblatt on June 21, 1974 and was to come into force on the next day."

13. A temporary injunction was issued on June 21, 1974, at the request of the government of Baden-Württemberg, with the order that "paragraph 218 of the Penal Code, which suspended culpability for abortion during the first twelve weeks of pregnancy, will not be in force at present. However, termination of pregnancy will not be a punishable offense if it is performed for medical, eugenic, or ethical reasons" (Kommission zur Auswertung 1980, p. 15). "193 members of the CDU/CSU representation in parliament as well as the governments of Baden-Württemberg, Bavaria, Rheinland-Pfalz, Saarland, and Schleswig-Holstein issued a request to the federal court to consider the constitutionality of Paragraph 218 as formulated in the fifth draft of the Reform Bill" (ibid.). The CDU/CSU declared abortion on demand during the first 3 months unconstitutional "because termination of pregnancy 12 weeks after conception violates Article 2, Paragraph 2, Section 1, together with Article 1, Paragraph 1 as well as Article 3 and Paragraphs 1, 2 and 4 of the Federal Constitution. It also is an infringement of the principles of a Rechtsstaat. The state governments which had proposed the motion also were of the opinion that the fifth draft of the reform bill required the approval of the Senate." (ibid.)

14. The SPD and FDP presented "the draft for the fifteenth amendment to the Penal Code on October 8, 1975; the CDU/CSU [presented] its draft for a change in the fifth draft to amend the Penal Code on October 23, 1975" (Deutscher Bundestag).

15. Five of the eight federal judges of the Supreme Court agreed with this judgment. Two judges publicly defended their minority position. See Kommission zur Auswertung 1980, p. 16.

16. Brunn estimates the number of illegal abortions in the GDR in 1976 to have been around 2,000 (1978, p. 93).

17. As written in the introduction to the Gesetz über die Unterbrechung der Schwangerschaft (1972): "Equality of women in education and occupation, marriage, and the family demands that women be able to decide for themselves whether to carry a pregnancy to term. The realization of this right is closely linked to the increasing responsibility that the socialist state and its citizens assume for the improvement of health protection for women, the benefit of the family, and greater love for children."

18. Article 29 of the Constitution of the GDR, in Lohmann 1977.

19. From the address by German bishops on the reform of Paragraph 218, May 7, 1976. See Gorschenek 1977, p. 15.

20. Chancellor Helmut Schmidt, May 23, 1976. See Gorschenek 1977, p. 19.

21. Helmut Kohl, June 13, 1976. See Gorschenek 1977, p. 61.

22. "This morality reflects the societal need (interest) for the subordination of the individual to common material conditions of a concrete historical stage in development. It consequently does not reflect individual interests nor even an aggregate of individual interests, but the fundamental need of society to maintain, further, and improve the basic conditions for its survival." (Boeck 1977, p. 156)

23. According to Informationsburo West, as stated in the *Tagesspiegel*, June 28, 1981.

24. Helmut Kraatz, according to Informationsburo West; see *Frankfurter Rundschau*, June 3, 1981.

25. Article 30 of the Constitution of the GDR; see Lohmann 1977.

26. Article 20, Paragraph 1, Constitution of the GDR. See Lohman 1977.

## References

Amendt, G. 1979. "Paragraph 218: Schafft die Zwangsberatung ab!" Psychologie heute 66:36–39.

Boeck, M. 1977. Ethics and Morality. Berlin.

Brunn. 1978. In Aktuelle Bevölkerungsfragen in Ost und West, in der DDR und der Bundesrepublik, ed. H. Harmsen. Hamburg.

Goebel, P. 1980. "Motivation zum Schwangerschaftsabbruch." 6. Internationaler Kongress für psychosomatische Geburtshilfe und Gynakologie. Abstract 9. Berlin.

Gorschenek, G., ed. 1977. Grundwerte in Staat und Gesellschaft. Munich: C. H. Beck.

Harmsen, H., ed. 1957. Zur sozialhygienischen Problematik der Gesetzgebung betreffend Schwangerschaftsunterbrechung und Abtreibung in Mitteldeutschland. Series: Zur Entwicklung und Organisation des Gesundheitswesens in Sowjet-Russland, in osteuropaischen Volksdemokratien und in Mitteldeutschland, vol. 8. Hamburg.

Harmsen, H., ed. 1979. Demographisch relevante Faktoren in der DDR–Bundesrepublik–CCSR–UdSSR. Hamburg.

Hollein, E. 1931. Gebarzwang und kein Ende. Berlin: Neuer Deutscher Verlag.

Knieper, B. 1981. "Auf der Suche nach der weiblichen Schuld." Psychologie heute 8(4):66–75.

Kommission zur Auswertung der Erfahrungen mit dem reformierten paragraph 218 des Strafgesetzbuches. 1980. Deutscher Bundestag, 8 Wahlperiode. Publication 813630. Bonn: Heger.

Konig, U. 1980. Gewalt über Frauen. Hamburg: Stern.

Koschorke, M., and J. Sandberger. 1978. Schwangerschafts—Konflikt—Beratung: Ein Handbuch. Göttingen: Vandenhoek & Ruprecht.

Lohmann, U., ed. 1977. Verfassung und Program in der DDR. Berlin: Walter de Gruyter.

Mehlan, K. H. 1961. Internationale Abortsituation, Abortbekampfung, Antikonzeption. Leipzig: VEB Georg Thieme Verlag.

Oeter, K., and M. Wilken, eds. 1979. Frau und Medizin. Stuttgart: Hippokrates.

Paczensky, V., ed. 1980. Wir sind keine Morderinnen! Reinbeck bei Hamburg: Rowohlt TB-Verlag.

Politische Fraueninitiative Heidelberg. 1975. "Recht und Menschenwurde: Zweihundertachtzehn." Psychologie heute 2(4):10–14.

Schafarewitsch, I. R. 1980. Der Todestrieb in der Geschichte. Frankfurt: Ullstein.

Schaff, A. 1969. Marxismus und das menschliche Individuum. Vienna: Europa.

Scholz, 1977. In Gesundheitspolitisch relevante Probleme der neuen Gesetzgebung in der DDR wie auch in Ungarn und auch in der UdSSR, ed. H. Harmsen. Hamburg.

Staatliche Zentralverwaltung für Statistik. 1979. Statistisches Jahrbuch 1979 der Deutschen Demokratischen Republik, vol. 24. East Berlin: Staatsverlag.

Straass, G. 1981. "Menschenbild, Wertproblematik und Abruptio-Diskussion." Zeitschrift für ärztliche Fortbildung 75:391–396.

Wilken, H. 1977. "Medizinische und soziale Probleme der menschlichen Reproduktion." DDR-Med.-Rep. 6(12):1075–1117.

Wolff, U. 1981. "Schwangerschaftsabbruch: abhangig von wechselnden politischen Bedingungen." Deutsches Ärzteblatt 21:1055–1057 and 22:1113–1119.

# Mother and Child Care

## Aloys Henning

*The extraordinary thing about mother and child care in both East and West Germany from an American point of view is the extensive, carefully thought-out services for working women and their small children. Both Germanies have concluded that this is the area of preventive health care that reaps the highest returns for a lifetime. From a comparative point of view, Henning hints at the competitive nature of West Germany's expanding provisions for expectant and young mothers to keep up with the East German system. Yet even in this subdued presentation one can sense that the East German program, out of ideological convictions, has been stronger from the start, while the West Germans have not wanted to be bested. Once again their approach has both strengths and weaknesses rooted in a less organized set of services that reach only those who seek them. Henning uses the differences in mother and child care to bring out underlying ideas and values about women and their children.*

Germany, after being defeated by the Allies in World War II, was faced with a multitude of health problems. Millions of Germans had fled from the eastern part of Germany or had been expelled. Millions had been killed, the industrial infrastructure had been destroyed, and resources were missing. What remained of Germany was divided among and administered by the four occupation powers. They and the German administration at their disposal were presented with similar problems: epidemic diseases, bombed-out cities, undernourishment. Large parts of the population were living under extremely unhygienic conditions and in poor health. Deprived of the health-care providers who had died in the war, many families had problems surviving. This meant an additional health risk for the women who, in a war-ridden economy, had had to provide for fatherless families. Obviously the health of the children was greatly endangered. Therefore, in the postwar period the medical care of women and children received the same high consideration it receives today under very different and peaceful conditions.

## The Postwar Division

Despite the ideological reshaping introduced during the Third Reich, i.e. a racial and genetically oriented medicine, and despite certain organizational structures later forbidden by the Allied Control Council, West German medicine basically took up preexisting structures. In line with the structure of the Federal Republic (FRG; West Germany) and its democratic identity, that state's health system retained its semi-public, self-governing institutions. This means that social and political struggles over possible changes or improvements are carried out between the semi-public bodies representing the physicians (those working in hospitals and those in private practice), the sickness funds, and the hospitals. Such struggles take place within the context of the "subsidiary principle," which means that the state will always keep itself subsidiary to the goals, programs, and deliberations of these self-governing bodies except when the law has defined specific supervisory tasks (such as public health) or control measures that seem best guaranteed by public health institutions (such as school health services). As a consequence, this pluralistic field of countervailing institutions is constantly subject to criticisms and controversies that contrast with the centrally controlled health-care system in the German Democratic Republic (GDR; East Germany).

In the Soviet occupation zone, the Soviet Military Administration in Germany (SMAD) instituted a Central Office of Health Services. This became the basis for a centralized, uniform health-care system which was unprecedented in Germany. The systematic reorganization of the health-care system as a response to postwar health problems was created by SMAD orders and followed up by decrees of the German Central Administration. After the founding of the GDR on October 7, 1949, the newly created Health Department took over the responsibilities of the Central Administration. These newly created health-care structures thus reflected the experiences and the ideology of the Soviet occupation power and also the health policies of the German political left that had developed in the 1920s. Under Soviet occupation and the dominance of the Sozialistische Einheitspartei Deutschlands (SED; Socialist Unity Party of Germany), these policies were to be implemented.

To correctly understand the political development in the Soviet occupation zone during the first postwar years, one must realize that the
SED imposed its political power upon the German people without
regard for their political affiliation and convictions. Opposing forces
were suppressed. The USSR of course followed a similar policy in all
the other countries under its power, installing so-called people's de-
mocracies in which the Soviet model was implemented. The uniform
Sovietization of its neighbors, which launched the Cold War, served
the Soviet Union as a power base for hegemony in Eastern Europe.

In line with this policy, the Soviet health-care system became the
model for all Soviet-controlled European countries. In these health-
care systems are manifested important postulates of the German Social
Hygiene Movement of the 1920s. These postulates had been integrated
into the Soviet system in its initial phase, and they reflected the ideas
of Grotjahn and Semaschko. The high degree of centralization is neither
particularly socialist—Marx seems to have considered voluntary
associations—nor particularly appropriate. It is simply Russian. Like
Lenin's "democratic centralism," it is derived from pre-revolutionary
organizational structures. Its absolutist semi-military administrative
structures were created by the reforms of Tsar Peter I.

### Polyclinics and Prevention in the GDR

One of the pivotal points of SMAD Order No. 272 of December 11,
1947, concerned the organization of a standardized network of outpatient departments and polyclinics. This system of complex and differentiated medical care for the whole population was intended to
successively repress the private institutions of health care.

This progressive nationalization corresponded to the Marxist-Leninist
conception of a socialist society. According to its "scientifically" justified
ideology which was actually analogous to a closed and undebatable
"doctrine of salvation," this society developed according to immutable
and necessary laws. Health, as one of the most important goods, was
a main task of social policy and was therefore necessarily subject to
the planning and control of the state, which in turn was controlled by
the SED. The health-care system, then, was supposedly freed from the
corrupting influences of special interests (commercial competition between free practitioners, pharmacological and industrial enterprises,
etc.). This centralized control system established priorities in medical
care from the very start, in line with the requirements of health and

social policy. In accordance with the Soviet model, increasing importance was attached to prophylactic measures and health-care facilities. This particular development of the East German health-care system is exemplified by its significant successes in maternal and child care.

## Maternal and Child Policies in the GDR

To elucidate the health situation of women and mothers in the GDR, some social data need to be given. Legally, equal rights for women are fully realized in the GDR. Their complete legal, economic, and political equality was already included in the first constitution of the GDR in 1949 and was expanded in the constitution of 1968 (Article 20): "Man and woman have equal rights and have the same legal status in all parts of social, national, and personal life. The promotion of women, especially in their work sphere, is a social and national task."

Among other things this reflects the specifically Marxist position that the precondition for women's rights is economic independence. This they achieve by participating in the process of production and by being completely incorporated into economic life. In 1975, 79 percent of all women of employable age were working, amounting to 47 percent of all persons employed in the East German economy. This high proportion of female workers reflects not only the emancipation of women in the GDR but also the permanent labor shortage and low productivity that characterize East German industry. Moreover, the comparatively low incomes make the employment of the wife and mother a financial requirement for the family. Aside from this, the wife and mother is exposed to rather open public pressure to be employed. As a result, the proportion of mothers who work ranges from about 75 percent of those with more affluent husbands to about 95 percent of those whose husbands earn little (*DDR Handbuch* 1975).

In line with its policy of "equal pay for equal work," the East German government tried to aid the employed mother and housewife by social measures. A catalog of social services was implemented, which increased as the gross national product increased. In the GDR this is referred to as the "unity of economic and social policy," implying the dependence of the social services on the GNP. However, certain services receive particular emphasis according to the demands of current policy or ideology.

A major portion of the social services aimed at the employed woman refer to her as mother and thus to her children as well. These services were first decreed in 1950 in the Gesetz über den Mutter- und Kindschutz und die Recht der Frau (law about mother and child care and women's rights) and then in the Gesetzbuch der Arbeit (work law) in 1961, and since then they have been frequently expanded. The current state of social measures concerning women is based on resolutions of the Ninth Party Convention of the SED in May 1976.

Under current provisions, a pregnant woman is protected against dismissal from the beginning of the third month of pregnancy until one year after delivery. She may not be subjected to any health risk during her work, and after the third month of pregnancy night shifts and overtime are forbidden. The pregnant woman has a claim to a less strenuous place of work with her full pay guaranteed. Pregnancy leave begins 6 weeks before delivery, and if the pregnancy is prolonged the woman is paid the average net income until delivery. After delivery there is a pregnancy leave of 20 weeks; in case of premature delivery it is prolonged by the time that has not been claimed before delivery. Nursing care may be provided for up to 6 months.

Employed mothers have a right to paid breaks of 90 minutes a day to nurse their babies. Beginning with the birth of the second child, the employed mother can apply for a leave of absence from her job for up to a year. During this time she receives "mother's support," the amount of which is set by sickness-fund benefits. After this has expired, a single working mother whose child cannot be offered a place in the crowded day nurseries may take a further leave of absence and receive additional financial support up to the amount of the legal sickness-fund benefits, which are never less than 250 marks per month for one child, 300 marks for two children, and 350 marks for three or more children.

As an incentive to have children, parents receive after the first child a one-time payment of 1,000 marks per child. Young couples in their first marriage can obtain until the age of 26 an interest-free loan of 5,000 marks to buy household effects, to be paid back within 8 years. In addition, all couples may receive a loan for housing space, of which 5,000 marks is offered as an interest-free loan. One thousand marks of this interest-free loan of 5,000 or 10,000 marks is canceled at the birth of the first child. At the birth of the second child another 1,500 marks is canceled, and another 2,500 marks at the birth of the third child.

In addition, parents have a claim to a child allowance for every child from the child's date of birth to his financial independence. These allowances amount to 20 marks per month for the first and the second child, 50 marks for the third, 60 for the fourth, and 70 for the fifth and every following child.

In addition to the immediate concern with mother and child care, this network of social assistance points beyond the immediate task of protecting the mother toward social and political control, especially in regard to the birth rate. This larger intent is reflected in the gradual extension of these measures parallel to the legalization of abortions in 1972. Accordingly, every woman has the right to have an abortion within the first 12 weeks as long as there is no medical counterindication. The operation has to be performed in a hospital by an obstetrics-gynecology specialist. The specialist has to inform the pregnant woman about the medical aspects of the operation and about contraceptive measures. The costs are paid by the sickness fund.

The provision of legalized abortion expresses the ideological conception of women's rights in a socialist society. At the same time, it also aims to eliminate deaths of women incurred by illegal abortions. According to East German statements (Winter 1977), the almost total elimination of such deaths since 1972 has reduced pregnancy-related mortality figures by half.

In this connection it is worth noting that, contrary to the current ideological championing of liberal abortion laws, abortions were tightly restricted until 1972 in the GDR and especially in the USSR. In the GDR these provisions were aimed at the alarming decline of the birth rate.

As expected, legalized abortion reduced the birth rate even further. But the number of legal abortions went down continuously from 119,000 in 1972 (the year of the legalization of abortion) to 83,000 in 1976 (Fleischer 1977). Meanwhile, the continuous decrease of the birth rate in the GDR from 17.2 in 1964 to a low point of 10.6 per 1,000 in 1973 and 1974 was reversed by a minor "baby boom" of 11.6 in 1976. The time lag between the initiation of the social measures mentioned above and the increase in the birth rate makes it difficult to claim a direct influence of these measures on the birth rate. Yet numerous personal statements of East German citizens indicate that the socially improved situation of the mother and her family has had a positive and stimulating effect, apart from possible attitudinal changes in regard to the "will to have a child."

In the GDR social services are intelligently linked to health-education measures. For example, the 1,000-mark birth aid is provided under conditions and in steps. One hundred marks is paid at the first visit to a maternity center if it takes place within the first 4 months of pregnancy; 25–50 marks can be subtracted if the first visit is delayed. Another 50 marks is paid on the second visit. After the birth the rest is paid—except for 100 marks. These are paid in four installments of 25 marks each at the first four monthly visits to the maternity center.

The following numbers show the weight of such measures of social control. In 1958, 271,698 pregnant women had visited the maternity centers. Seventeen percent of them first visited during the first 4 months of pregnancy, 70.7 percent between the fifth and the seventh month, and 12.0 percent in the eighth month or later. In 1974, 178,609 pregnant women were cared for in 951 maternity centers. Eighty-four percent of them had their first checkup during the first 4 months of pregnancy, 14.4 percent between the fifth and the seventh month, and 1.1 percent during the eighth month or later. The difference between the absolute numbers indicates the already mentioned high decrease in the birth rate in the GDR.

The intensive coverage of pregnant women by a centralized and much-utilized health-care system expresses the emphasis on preventive medicine in the GDR and corresponds to long-standing Soviet health policies. Home deliveries have practically ceased in the GDR because of the organization of preventive obstetric care around hospitals. In 1952, only 48.2 percent of all births took place in hospitals. Complications in pregnancies are now diagnosed early, and the woman is referred to a high-technology clinic. These measures have resulted in improved mother and child mortality figures. Infant mortality went down from 72.2 per 1,000 live births in 1950 to 14.1 and 13.1 in 1976 and 1977 respectively. Thus the GDR is clustered with France and the United States below the Scandinavian countries, the Netherlands, and Switzerland, which have an infant mortality rate of 10 or lower. One of the various measures aimed at reducing infant mortality, introduced in 1962, was the mandatory autopsy of stillborn children and those who died after birth. The results of these autopsies are documented and systematically analyzed by expert commissions on a district level. The results are used to improve the care in maternity centers and maternity hospitals.

The expert commission on maternal mortality in the GDR works in a similar pattern. The number of deaths directly related to pregnancy and delivery (according to the definition given by the GDR, this best describes maternal mortality as distinguished from indirect mortality and mortality not related to pregnancy) went down from 80 per 100,000 births in 1962 to 42 in 1970 and to 19 in 1976.

The complex maternal-care system presented above is applied to infants with the same prophylactic intent and is continued through infancy, childhood, and adolescence. There are 9,983 maternity centers on different levels, which are charged with health maintenance programs for children up to the age of 3. In 1976 these maternity centers provided for 83 percent of all infants during the first 4 weeks of life and for 98.3 percent during the first 7 weeks. In the same year 67.9 percent of the children up to the age of 12 months and 71.8 percent of those between 12 and 24 months were regularly cared for. A pediatrician carries medical responsibility for the maternity centers, while social workers and nurses offer information and suggestions aimed at creating a healthy environment for the growing baby. If necessary they also make home visits. With a total of 2,603,679 consultations in 1976, 36,430 problem children were under continuous medical and social care in the dispensaire system.

The maternity centers also advise mothers in baby care and vaccinate the children. As a rule, vaccination services are attached to the maternity centers and since parents are legally obliged to have their children vaccinated against smallpox, poliomyelitis, diphtheria, tetanus, and tuberculosis these measures enjoy a high degree of compliance. Although the legal guardians may refuse vaccination, the overwhelming majority comply and the necessary degree of immunization is achieved without difficulty.

The former practice of launching vaccination campaigns at regular intervals has been replaced by vaccinations on a fixed schedule and regulated by the Impf-Kalender (vaccination calendar). As a consequence of these efforts, poliomyelitis disappeared in the GDR in 1961 and diphtheria in 1980. Given the particular danger of infection, the strict observance of the vaccination calendar plays an important role in child care in nurseries (day and week nurseries for children up to age 3) and kindergarten (from the age of 4). The former, together with permanent homes for babies and infants, are facilities of the health-care system, whereas a "youth physician" is responsible for the medical care of the children in kindergarten. In 1973, 675,104 children were taken care of in 11,442 kindergartens. Thus 77 percent of all children between 3 and 6 years of age could receive continuous care. In the same year there were 212,650 places in day nurseries, which increased to 243,775 places in 5,745 day nurseries by 1976.

Preventive health care in preschool facilities and schools is delegated to youth information centers in which one "youth physician" and two social workers as a rule take care of 6,000–8,000 children. A medical checkup is mandatory for children entering school as well as those in grades 3, 6, 8, and 10. The examination during the sixth year of life, which is aimed at determining the child's maturity and capacity to enter school, is to be preceded by a preliminary examination at the end of the fifth year, which evaluates the need for prophylactic measures. Every child is supposed to be screened once a year. In these screenings it is decided whether the child may participate in swimming lessons, the "Produktionstag" of the polytechnical schools, and similar activities. Students in the eighth grade receive a medical checkup for purposes of vocational placement. In addition to screenings, students are examined by a "youth physician" if they are to be transferred to a school for low achievers, in case of a student's special employment such as harvesting, in case of a recreation leave or participation in military training camps, and in the case of high-performance athletes. Students of vocational schools receive medical care by company physicians.

Dental care is part of the specialized medical care offered to children and youths. It begins before school and ends at the age of 18. Annual screenings are provided under the charge of the district youth dentists. Special youth dental clinics are to be established in districts with more than 50,000 inhabitants. Since 1960, specialists in pediatric dentistry are being trained in the GDR. In 1974, 6,180,893 dental consultations were provided by 1,100 practicing pediatric dentists. Great importance is attached to educating children to brush their teeth and visit their dentist regularly.

## Maternal and Child Care in the FRG

While maternal and child care in the GDR appears to be uniformly and well organized—"all encompassing," as it is called in the GDR— it is more difficult to describe such care in the Federal Republic of Germany as a system. The differences in the political structures make for some marked differences in the health-care systems, yet both expectations and provisions in the FRG, as exemplified by the catalog of maternal and child health services, differ little from those in the GDR.

One reason is the historic development of the German Social Hygiene Movement, i.e. the scientifically founded conceptions of the need to protect the health of the individual and of certain groups of society.

As mentioned before, progressive ideas of German physicians such as Alfred Grotjahn were adopted even by Soviet social hygiene in the 1920s. Inasmuch as the health-care system of the GDR is largely oriented toward the Soviet model, continuity with German social-hygiene concepts arose in both Germanies.

Another reason for the extensive congruence of maternal and child care between both German states seems to lie in the response to health demands and thus in the development of the health-care system itself. This corresponds to the development of the health-care system in all industrial societies, which seems to support theories of convergence and has provoked criticisms against the increasing trend toward complexity and its threat to the individual's autonomy. Ivan Illich stressed this point in his book *Medical Nemesis*.

West German law outlines the social services to which employed women are entitled when they become pregnant. The original version dates back to the year 1952, but since then it has been changed and services have increased. Pregnant women and mothers of children under 4 months cannot be dismissed. The woman, however, can give notice whenever she chooses. The regulations concerning work conditions for pregnant women in regard to noxious activities, overtime, night work, and work on Sundays are largely identical to those of the GDR.

Pregnant women must be exempted from work if, according to a medical certificate, the life of the mother and the child are endangered by continued activity. Six weeks before delivery, every woman is entitled to a leave with pay. She may continue to work, however, at her own request. This regulation does not pertain to the 8-week leave after delivery, during which the mother may not work. In cases of a premature birth or multiple births, the leave extends to 12 weeks. After returning to work, a nursing mother gets two breaks of 30–45 minutes per day.

During their pregnancy and maternity leave, women receive the equivalent of their pay from the health insurance system. Women who are not employed and who are insured receive maternity allowances up to the amount of the sickness benefit. Women who are privately insured and thus do not have a claim to sickness benefits receive a payment of 150 marks after delivery. If their husbands are members of a mandatory sickness fund, they are automatically co-insured and are entitled to a payment of 35 to 150 marks from the husband's sickness fund. All expectant mothers who are members of the mandatory sickness funds are entitled to a flat sum of 50–150 marks for the expenses of the delivery.

In 1979 the maternity leave of 8 weeks was extended to 6 months. During an additional leave that may be granted, the net income will continue to be paid up to a maximum amount of 750 marks per month. The allowance for the first child remains at 50 marks per month, but the allowance for the second child was raised in 1979 from 80 to 100 marks and that for every further child from 150 to 200 marks.

Maternity payments, medical care, delivery, and care in maternity homes and hospitals are covered by the law governing the mandatory sickness funds, the Reichsversicherungsordnung. About 90 percent of all women are members themselves or through their husbands.

Medical services are regulated by the Directions of the Federal Commission of Physicians and Sickness Funds Concerning Medical Care During Pregnancy and After Delivery. According to them, the expectant mother is entitled to regular checkups (eight as a rule) by a physician of her choice. Employed women are excused from work for the checkups. Diagnostic data are recorded in a Mutterpass (mother's check-list), which serves preventive purposes and is kept by the pregnant mother. Risky pregnancies are subjected to frequent checkups, and to special examinations such as ultrasound, amniocentesis, and hormone analysis. The physician in charge must make arrangements no later than 4 weeks before the date of delivery at a maternity hospital.

These prophylactic measures are supplemented by genetic counselling in 38 genetic health centers (as of 1977), which are aimed particularly at those cases in which genetic defects seem likely. In addition, community services, maternity hospitals, voluntary associations, and public health offices maintain schools for maternal and paternal education. Gymnastics courses for pregnant mothers are also offered at these schools.

Expectant mothers and fathers receive family planning and family counseling at 61 (as of 1977) model counseling centers run by communal or voluntary organizations (welfare organizations) and funded by the Federal Department of Family, Youth, and Health. Various organizations maintain a total of 863 (as of 1977) regular counseling centers in the FRG and West Berlin. The law prescribes that one of these centers must be consulted before an abortion. The consultation serves to protect the unborn infant as well as the pregnant woman. Abortion is supposed to be performed only in extreme and exceptional cases.

The medical and social measures provided for expectant mothers, similar to those in the GDR and just as numerous, reflect the findings of modern obstetrics. In the FRG, however, every mother is free to decide to what extent she wants to make use of the health-care measures to which she is entitled. There is no attempt at social control as there is in the GDR. Most likely the use made of these preventive measures for pregnant women is less frequent and less general than in the GDR. There are, however, no conclusive data.

Although the percentage of hospital deliveries (98.3) for 1974 was practically identical with the percentage in the GDR (99), and although clinics in the FRG are probably better equipped, infant mortality rates in the FRG have for years been considerably higher than those in the GDR. Yet the initial postwar conditions in West Germany were originally better, as indicated by statistics. In 1950, the infant mortality rate was 55.3 while the GDR's was 72.2. In the FRG this index stagnated between 1965 (23.8 per 1,000) and 1973 (22.7 per 1,000) whereas in the GDR it dropped to 20.3 by 1969 and to 18.5 by 1970. It was not until 1975 that infant mortality in the FRG reached 19.7 per 1,000. In 1977 it amounted to 15.4, according to the Statistisches Bundesamt.

The differences in maternal mortality are even greater. The number of "maternal" deaths in the FRG decreased constantly from 87.1 per 100,000 deliveries in 1962 (GDR: 80 per 100,000 deliveries) to a still comparatively high 45.9 in 1973, to 34.0 in 1974, and to 39.6 in 1975 (GDR: 22 in 1975). Internationally, both German states are in the middle range.

As in the GDR, the birth rate in the FRG has dropped constantly, from 18.3 per 1,000 in 1963 to 9.7 in 1975. Compared with other nations, this places the FRG at the absolute bottom.

To provide for the health of infants and children, the Guidelines of the Federal Commission of Physicians and Sickness Funds for the primary prevention of diseases for the first four years of life have, since 1971, called for seven checkups: a first examination at birth, a general examination between the fifth and tenth days of life; one examination each between the fourth and the sixth month, between the ninth and the twelfth month, between the twenty-first and the twenty-fourth month; and one during the fourth year of life. The checkups serve to detect at an early stage those diseases which might endanger the normal physical and mental development of a child. Problems are referred to the respective specialists for diagnosis and therapy. Except for the first two examinations, to be taken at the hospital, the parents may visit a physician of their choice, a public health office, or an infant care facility for the other checkups. Checkups include counseling on educational and social problems. In addition, orthopedic exercises (gymnastics) in case of posture faults and free vaccinations according to the vaccination calendar are available. The offer of preventive checkups is not yet taken advantage of sufficiently, and as children get older the use of checkups declines still further.

Because of the epidemiological situation and the possibility of side effects, vaccination is at present not obligatory in the FRG. Yet vaccinations are recommended and utilized, especially when children (starting at the age of 5) enter into the regular care of school medical services. Infant and school medical services, school dental care, and the services of child and youth psychiatry constitute an integral unit and are called Jugendgesundheitsdienst (Youth Health Service).

The school medical services, staffed by Jugendärzte (youth physicians), evaluate preschool children for their fitness to enter school. Corresponding to the federal structure of the West German state, the types of screenings offered in the schools and the intervals vary from region to region. In West Berlin, for example, screening is done in the third and seventh grades. In accordance with the Jugendarbeitsschutzgesetz (the law for the protection of employed minors), there is a final examination in the tenth grade, which is aimed at, among other things, the evaluation of occupational fitness. The same law also requires a follow-up examination for those under the age of 18 who are employed.

School dental care includes regular checkups and annual screening. Individual dental care and orthodonture are provided by dentists and orthodontists who are not part of the school dental-care system.

Child and youth psychiatric care deals with family as well as school problems. Diagnosis and counseling provide the basis for appropriate referrals under the regulations of the federal law of public assistance (Bundessozialhilfegesetze). This aid is aimed at dyslexic children, among others.

## The Complexities of Comparison

On the surface, it seems easy to arrive at a balanced comparison of the maternal-care and child-care provisions in the two German states. The GDR has a nationalized, integrated, and uniform system, which therefore may be more efficient but which in any case is ideologically regarded as the sole guarantee for the optimal development of comprehensive, free, and generally accessible health care. The FRG, on the other hand, has a pluralistic health-care system which, because of its heterogeneous nature, may be less efficient. The advocates of this system believe it has optimal capacity for the development and adjustment of its structure as a result of the constant balance of interests.

Yet numerous difficulties arise when a comparison is attempted. Both systems are highly complex in themselves and in the way they express different social ideologies. In the GDR, collective responsibility and control by the state dominate. In the FRG it is primarily the individual who is held responsible for the preservation of his health; the state only helps according to the legally guaranteed claims of the individual upon the Solidaritätsgemeinschaft (group solidarity). It is here that the famous subsidiary principle expresses itself. This principle intends to minimize the alienation of the individual facing a centralized state such as the GDR. It is premised on the belief that a free and pluralistic society will best satisfy the individual's demand for medical care. In the GDR, however, the central control of the health-care system is regarded as an essential precondition for its functioning—just as central control is considered essential for the economy. In this context private medical practices for instance seem anachronistic.

Despite the complex mixture of ideology and social structure, one can compare health-care systems in terms of effectiveness and efficiency. While such comparisons have their difficulties, one internationally accepted measure is maternal and infant mortality. Within a few years the GDR has successfully reduced maternal and infant mortality. This seems to be due to the interdisciplinary cooperation of the specialists and to the integrated and uniform organization of medical help for pregnant women and infants. Both these factors are of primary importance, independent of the specific nature of the medical help involved. In this regard, considerable organizational deficiencies and tensions persist in the West German health-care system. These weaknesses are not primarily of a financial or technical nature. For example, to this day there are no institutions in the FRG (as there are in the GDR) that analyze every case of maternal and infant mortality. This puzzling omission affects two important indices of mortality—and the health-care system. Another issue, amidst the array of prophylactic measures focused on the perinatal period, is the health behavior of pregnant women and mothers. At present they make insufficient use of the extensive preventive program provided in the FRG, which by international standards is excellent. At first sight, the East German idea of stimulating the pregnant woman's health awareness by financial means and thus practicing health education by gentle pressure does not fit in with the conception of the individual's direct responsibility for his health. But improvement in the protection of individual health does not necessarily have to follow the East German model.

Although the GDR's maternal and infant mortality rates are lower than the FRG's, they do not match those of the leading countries: Switzerland, the Scandinavian countries, and others. Policies to improve the FRG's health-care system should be based on the policies of those countries, because they resemble the FRG in some ways more than does the GDR. Just as the GDR has health indices that are not characteristic of communist health-care systems, so the West German indices are not characteristic of structurally comparable noncommunist systems. The fact that the GDR and the FRG see themselves as representative of their respective types of systems and so frequently compare themselves is explained more by their political rivalry than by the facts.

The USSR and the other communist-bloc countries have a long tradition of propaganda based on the socialist concept of collective responsibility for the health of the individual and the community. Given the insufficient health care in Russia, China, and Cuba before their revolutions, nationalization and centralization of the health-care system led to great improvements in medical care and provided good propaganda. While health care was not insufficient in the Eastern bloc before the communist takeover, grave health problems of World War II had to be overcome, and this too has led to propoganda intending to prove the superiority not only of socialist health-care but of socialist society as a whole. The health-care system seems to serve this purpose particularly well, since it appeals to a deep need for protection against the existential threat of death. Since it is more difficult to evaluate medical achievements than other vital aspects of the social system—economy, political rights, standard of living—these claims are readily accepted, even by experts. The propagandistic intention is evident in many East German health publications which express a certain idyllic uniformity that contrasts with Western accounts in which conflicts and diversity play an important role. This uniformity attests to the Marxist emphasis on an all-encompassing, scientifically grounded, and exclusive interpretation of all social processes.

In communist publications comparing the efficiency of different health-care systems, the propagandistic intent leads to a biased use of source materials: incomplete quotations separated from their context, the comparison of incomplete data, or the comparison of incomparable dimensions. (An example is Winter 1977, p. 28.) For a socialist state, statistics are a prime weapon. The bourgeois ideal of objectivity is replaced by partisanship. Consequently, comparative studies from communist societies seem more persuasive and consistent than those from pluralistic societies. Their usefulness for comparative purposes is limited, however. For example, the indices for maternal and infant mortality in the GDR are compiled differently and are internationally not comparable.[1] They differ from those recommended by the World Health Organization, whereas the West German criteria follow them. Infant mortality figures in the FRG include all stillborn infants and all premature infants who die soon after birth. In the GDR, the same births are considered premature, as are miscarriages, and because of the stricter definitions of maturity and life they are not registered by the Bureau of Vital Statistics. For example, using the East German definition, the infant mortality rate for the FRG in 1973 (22.7) would have been reduced by about 2.5. In addition, the rate is 1.5–2.5 higher because in the FRG more older women deliver and more women have their babies spaced closer together (Müller 1977). In the GDR mothers are younger on the average, regardless of their marital status, and they give birth to 2.5 times as many illegitimate children as women in the FRG.

The age of mothers reveals differences between the two social and political settings. Authors in the GDR charge that the social conditions in the FRG are responsible for the higher average age of West German mothers. In a society that emphasizes individual choice, this kind of charge is neither easily understood nor accepted. The higher average age of women giving birth in the FRG results from a more reserved attitude toward the traditional role of the woman as mother and reflects the emphasis upon women's emancipation and feminism. In the GDR, on the other hand, it seems that people retreat into the privacy of their families to counteract the omnipresent demands of state and society. The GDR, for economic and political reasons (particularly its dependence upon the female labor force), wants to improve the social situation of the working mother and raise the birth rate. Thus individual and political interests converge in the increased East German birth rate.

The difficulties in comparing East and West German health data do not explain or justify why the West German indices of maternal and infant mortality are higher. In view of the data on maternal and infant mortality in other countries and in view of the financial resources available, there is an urgent need to improve the efficiency of the West German health-care system. Here a careful analysis of the East German health-care system and its success can only be helpful. In such an analysis, however, the high degree of centralization must be kept in mind, for it contrasts with the multitude of conflicting institutions that prevent the West German health-care system from being used for ideological purposes.

In the larger context, the efficiency of the two health-care systems is best considered in the context of national income, productivity, and the social welfare system. Between 1950 and 1975 the net national product of the FRG (with a population of 61.6 million in 1975) rose from 87.8 billion marks to 913.3 billion marks. Private income amounted to 681.4 billion marks. The social budget amounted to 263.4 billion marks, or 28.9 percent of the net national product—a rise of 9 percent in 10 years. In the FRG this is considered too high and is criticized. However, the vast social security system, which causes these expenditures, is beyond debate.

Between 1950 and 1975 the net national product in the GDR (with a population of 16.8 million in 1975) rose from 34.0 billion to 161.0 billion marks. Private income amounted to 99.8 billion marks. The public social budget amounted to 24.8 billion marks (15.4 percent) in 1975, an increase of only 0.8 percent in 10 years. Nobody in the GDR complains about the social services being "too expensive," although private incomes are comparably lower in the GDR than in the FRG. The different social budgets in the two German states indicate that more societal resources are provided for social problems in the FRG and that, because of its higher economic efficiency, the FRG can afford this. Industrial productivity is 30 percent lower in the GDR than in the FRG, which creates a permanent demand for more labor and limits the expansion of social services. This reflects the "unity of economic and social policy." By the same token, maternal and child care rank high whereas retirement benefits are low. In the FRG, on the other hand, pensions are regularly adjusted to the incomes of employees and constitute a considerable portion of the budget for social services. In this respect, the income distribution is more equitable than that in the neighboring socialist state. Thus, while the East German approach to investing less in health and social services in a more rational and effective way deserves close study, it is not without its price.

**Note**

1. General mortality figures for the GDR have been unavailable for years.

# References

Bundesministerium für innerdeutsche Beziehungen. 1975. DDR Handbuch. Cologne: Verlag Wissenschaft und Politik.

Fleischer, H. 1977. "Zur unterschiedlichen Entwicklung der Geburten in der DDR." In Zum demographischen Strukturwandel der DDR und in osteuropäischen Staaten: Seine Bedeutung für das Gesundheitswesen: Zur Entwicklung und Organisation des Gesundheitswesens in der DDR unter Mitberucksichtigung der UdSSR und Osteuropäischer Volksdemokratien, ed. H. Harmsen. Hamburg.

Müller, C. K. E. 1977. Die Säuglingssterblichkeit in der Bundesrepublik Deutschland und in der Deutschen Demokratischen Republik. Dissertation, University of Bonn.

Winter, K. 1977. Lehrbuch der Sozialhygiene. Berlin: VEB Verlag Volk und Gesundheit.

# 17 Occupational Health and the Older Worker

## Hans-Joachim von Kondratowitz

*Von Kondratowitz integrates a great deal of material to provide us with an understanding of two major topics: occupational health and treatment of the older worker. He shows the tremendous power of demography in shaping the post–World War II fate of East and West Germany and their health policies. One irony of this demography was that the prevalence of older workers in East Germany meant that they were subjected to increased hazards and stresses of intensive work, because the East Germans had no choice but to maximize productivity from them. More than any of the other authors, von Kondratowitz gives one a sense of the struggles by the East Germans to cope with the dilemmas of their own ideological approach. On one hand, centralized planning enables them to develop comprehensive manpower policies. On the other hand, this very centralization is insensitive to the needs in individual factories, so that loyal critics end up calling for decentralizing decisions on occupational health.*

*Von Kondratowitz shows the importance of bad memories of centralized governmental control from the Nazi period, which led the West Germans to shun centralized programs. The irony of this policy, of course, was that "freedom" and the emphasis on self-determination meant that those power groups that had thrived under Nazism continued to thrive afterward, while those groups that had been fatally weakened through legal policies, deportation, and extermination were not present to advocate their views. With weak representation from occupational and social medicine, factory owners and managers have done little with occupational health in West Germany. Indeed the current suggestion that companies screen out bad risks from employment in the first place indicates how occupational medicine in West Germany may be moving away from its historic mission.*

Since the end of the 1960s, increased attention has been paid in both German states to the aging process, in academic circles and above all in the context of social and health policy. Aside from arguments about various forms of old-age assistance, inquiries in both the Federal Republic of Germany (FRG; West Germany) and the German Democratic Republic (GDR; East Germany) have focused attention—though not with the same frequency—on the problems of creating and maintaining working conditions suitable for the aged. This chapter aims at elaborating the historical and the structural determinants that have shaped the general development of working conditions in the two German states for old workers and analyzing the consequent neglect of their health.

To begin with, I presuppose an understanding of the aging process as developed by the more recent gerontologists. Aging is considered here as a specific developmental phase in the human life span characterized by a broad variety of concrete outward forms, which vary from individual to individual. Class and status, however, are decisive in determining the impact of aging (see for GDR Brüschke 1974; for FRG M. Krohn 1978). The question before us is to what extent this variability of the aging process is reflected in the policies and programs for changing the work conditions for the older worker in the two German states. Realizing that the establishment of suitable working conditions for the aged cannot be separated from the state or from modifications of work conditions points up a second premise: the necessity of understanding working conditions in the context of the society and social forces that either inhibit or advance policies to change them.

This framework provides a perspective for the recent intensive debates about labor-market and social policies in capitalist and socialist states. In advanced capitalist societies, socio-political strategies cannot be separated from the demands of the labor market; they constantly influence each other (Offe and Hinrichs 1977; Sengenberger 1978; Keupp and Zaumseil 1978, especially chapter A; Rödel and Guldimann 1978). From this perspective, the latitude of governmental action gains additional significance. And, notwithstanding the apparent differences in the structure of the political and social system, quite similar questions about the relationships between power planning and the organization of labor have been asked from the experience of state-socialist countries (Maier and Tomm 1976). In state-socialist countries, it is particularly important to examine historically how governmental social policy defines the individual's ability or inability to be a full member of the labor market, for here one sees the bio-psychological aspects of aging as the basis for inclusion in one era and exclusion in another. Here, experience and skill are praised; there, one hears of "old ways" and fatigue. Thus, state policy, political values, economic conditions, and demographics interact with aging itself to shape policy.

Above all, it is simplistic to characterize the complex ideological configurations in both German states by their "official" ideologies, i.e. of Marxism-Leninism and the sort of pluralism in the FRG which has been interpreted nothing short of an "anti-ideology." It goes without saying that these are systems for legitimating health and social policies. However, within each "ideology" there are deep-seated and longitudinal ideological traditions of interest groups and occupational associations which simply cannot be subsumed simplistically under such systems. Thus, one must trace the deeper ideological structures and socio-cultural traditions that both unify and set apart the history of the two German states. Only before the backdrop of these more complex internal forces can one realistically appraise the practical implementation of measures in health and social policies designed to support aging employees.

## Policies before World War I

The significance of the development of social security institutions toward the end of the nineteenth century in Germany and the establishment of a systematic basis for social policy was certainly supreme. However, a one-sided focus upon these institutions tends to obscure the significant fact that government activities started by developing increasingly complex regulations for industrial safety. Indeed, it is this legislation that marks the actual beginning of a development of social policy in Germany.

From its beginnings in the year 1839, this legislation centered upon two crucial areas: protecting certain problem groups (such as children, juveniles, and women) in order to eliminate excessive physical deterioration of industrial workers by means of certain restrictions, and steadily institutionalizing increasingly more complex governmental control, ranging from factory inspections to state agencies for general supervision of industrial safety.

The establishment of agencies, however, does not necessarily say anything about the success of directly controlling work conditions. Frequently, scanty funds or personnel for these agencies made even halfway effective operations impossible from the start. In addition, the realistic capacity of these offices to impose sanctions was out of proportion to the social costs of jeopardizing manpower strength. And, perhaps even more important, these agencies did not have a public-health-care mission. Rather, government supervision of industrial safety was defined as a technical monitoring service. Not until the beginning of this century were physicians added to these governmental controls, and even then to a very small extent.

Another development, however, now joined this effort to protect labor safety. Since the beginning of this century, large, financially well-equipped industrial enterprises increasingly could afford in-plant physicians who either worked as straight executives or for the respective plant health insurance office. The point of such in-plant physicians was to keep costs down to a more manageable level by means of social-hygienic measures (Thiess and Flach 1970). Apart from this form of industrial hygiene, which is directly related to plant profitability, there are within the framework of governmental industrial safety only some specific public health measures which at best are occasional and apply only in individual cases to correcting special working conditions. Industrial and labor safety became activated in the form of government intervention whenever times of structural upheaveal or crisis in the capitalist economy coincided with increased jeopardy and stress for the reproduction of manpower (Renker 1957; Nahsen 1975).

It is striking that the older workers remained totally ignored by these protective safety regulations even though there would have been every reason to regard them also as a "problem group." With the development of the capitalist production methods, age had become an essential indicator for gauging the productive capacity of workers generally; this occurred just at the stage of capitalism during which its decisive method for increasing production consisted of an uninhibited exploitation of manpower. Being subjected to such excessive employment pressure, while also being exposed to dangerous and toxic substances, could only result in a rapid deterioration of the worker's health, and then—usually between 40 and 45 years—in a decline of his work performance. As a matter of paternalistic predisposition, employers would keep these workers but usually reassign them to a less skilled job at lower pay (Lande 1910; Schumann 1911; Bernays 1912; see also von Kondratowitz 1982, pp. 197–201). However, as the intensity of demands grew at the outset of the twentieth century, these workers were increasingly threatened with dismissal. In short, the worker whose health had been ruined was thrown back onto the labor market, where his chances of finding a new job were slim at best. Poverty in old age was therefore a regular consequence. Social scientists of the day coined the unintentionally cynical phrase "the vocational fate of the industrial worker," which reflects the disillusioning side of such a life (Weber 1912).

The absence of governmental action to standarize industrial safety law for old workers and employees did not mean, however, that the problem of the aging worker was ignored as a matter of general principle. Rather, the elaboration of the problem of aging was shifted to the level of actuarial discussions about insurance and encouraging an early start to life planning and preventive care. This led to the official founding of insurance schemes for old age, carried out by state authorities as of 1889. In effect this meant that social security as the last resort of economic safety went into action only when lifelong health attrition had weakened a worker to the point where he was unable to compete even minimally in the labor market. Moreover, the institutions in charge of this social security program were not to address the crucial origins of attrition.

Two control mechanisms were employed: the setting of a fixed old-age limit at which a worker has the right to receive a pension and leave employment to make way for younger replacements (this limit was set in 1889 at 70 and lowered in 1916 to 65 years for men and 60 for women), and the possibility of receiving a disability pension as a sort of premature old-age pension after a public health physician had determined the inability to earn a living.

That old age and disability are seen in this social security arrangement as a whole is really quite logical when viewed against the background of the "vocational fate" of the older worker outlined above. At least this was true as long as the actual social developments corresponded to such a whole. However, the more the influence of the various pathogenic factors in the work situation made clear that increasingly disability occurred much earlier because of such working conditions, the more problematic such a correspondence became. Equally dubious was the medical competence to define the inability to earn a living. Besides their comparatively low state of general medical knowledge, the physicians also lacked the professional knowledge of work life to be able to properly assess what specific actions might be taken to retain the capacity to perform some tasks (Tennstedt 1972b, pp. 139–141; Tennstedt 1976). Lower still was their knowledge about strain factors in actual industrial work. Thus, for some time, medicine was unable to assume its intended role of lending impartiality to legal standards, and it was not until the 1920s that occupational medicine developed as a scientific field which could provide knowledge for expert testimony (Tennstedt 1972b, pp. 141–143). These discrepancies tended to deepen the separation (already institutionalized by social security insurance) between working conditions and an analysis of the diseases causing disability. Resistance against this reciprocal process of isolation only arose among the few Socialist and Social Democrat physicians who had set out to develop an authentic insight into problems of medical care at the workplace, closely allied as they were with the workers and with trade-union movements (Tennstedt 1977a, 1977b, 1981).

These pension regulations also signal the way a society characterized by a capitalist economy deals with old age. One way is retirement from the labor market, in which the age limit is a political decision depending on the economy and the prevailing labor-market situation (for FRG: Brück 1976, p. 126). The other way is to prematurely single a person out by a disability pension, that is, by a social definition as a sick person that spares the causal social context of the disablement. This bias toward the individual is inherent in this pension process. Indirectly, these two alternatives contribute to the link between old age and loss of productive capacity as unavoidable in society's perception of the aging problem. By shifting the problem to the social security institutions, these governmental actions leave the dynamics of the labor market untouched by allowing enterprises to define old age as inadequate work capacity, and thus to define old persons as ready for unemployment.

### Policies in the Weimar Republic

One effect of the various governmental measures for industrial safety—as Böhle (1977, p. 292) correctly pointed out—was their building up "a socio-political pressure for fashioning new production methods, especially to the development and systematic introduction of Taylorist principles of work organization that aim at a more intensive use of manpower." After the confusion of the wartime economy and the inflation, "economic stabilization" prevailed in Germany. It resulted in a period of Taylorism to a degree that had been known only in the United States. It extended to the entire capitalist economy of Germany, encompassing not only economic and organizational industrial structures, but also changes in the qualification requirements for workers and salaried employees that included breaking up work tasks, increasing work speed, and altering work rhythm. This further differentiated skilled from unskilled labor and increased on-the-job training as well as re-training (Brady 1933; Preller 1949, pp. 115–169).

In this manner the actual work situation and prevailing work conditions became the center of interest, albeit for reasons of intensifying the work process. This resulted in a considerably new public health policy. Above all, the unsystematic knowledge about industrial medicine before World War I was replaced by the scientific-etiological model of illness that finally dominated industrial medicine (Borgers and Nemitz 1978; Schaefer and Blohmke, 1978, pp. 400–404). This essential step was taken in 1925 and in 1929 through the ordinance on extending industrial accident insurance to cover industrial injuries and illnesses (Preller 1949, pp. 326, 478). It had been a principal goal of the trade-union movement to have such an ordinance included in more comprehensive legislation on industrial safety. For the social perception of the aging problem, this phase had extraordinary significance: For the first time in Germany the problem of the link between work and old age was posed publicly—and by a professional group that could rightfully consider itself to have represented for a long time the rising class of the future.

One problem that emerged at the beginning of rationalization (in Weberian terms) was the job anxiety of older salaried employees (Berufsnot der älteren Angestellten). As a result of intensive discussions, this phrase soon became a standing figure of speech, and as such played an influential role in West German social-policy discussions, even up to the 1960s. The social basis of this job anxiety was clear: Rationalizing had not stopped at the threshold of the offices. Instead, through office mechanization, forms of activity had developed that demanded quick adaptability and flexibility under extreme time pressures. At the same time, intimate in-house familiarity and long, continuous work experience—which the older employees had provided—were no longer in demand. Added to this, older employees received higher salaries, so from a profit point of view they became expensive at the exact moment when they were becoming useless (Preller 1949, pp. 136–137, 421–422; Kracauer 1971, p. 45; Kocka 1974). The social consequences of this attitude signified, above all, unemployment.[1]

No matter how vehemently the associations of salaried employees protested and pressed for institutionalized remedial action, the bitter realization could no longer be denied that because of such developments, the salaried employees' ideological self-interpretation that (in comparison with workers) they were a secure and socially ascendant group was no longer reconcilable with actual trends. Instead, they were increasingly treated like laborers, not only in regard to actual working conditions but also in regard to their place in the labor market.

However, neither legislative measures nor governmental regulations on plants proved very effective, though the continued public debate raised the consciousness of a larger segment of bourgeois society. These debates legitimized the expectation of all parties concerned that the problem of old age in the workplace could be satisfactorily solved by limited, but focused, governmental intervention, leaving the bargaining position of the parties unaffected in the marketplace.

The same ideological pattern of fragmenting the old-age problem and minimizing its effects on the labor market continued in the FRG until the beginning of the 1960s. By "fragmenting" is meant the focus on one aspect of a vocational group and the attempt to repress the society-wide dimensions of the old-age problem, which along with other problems had become a permanent feature of capitalist labor markets. As for governmental control, the FRG had become if anything more reserved, digesting the National Socialist labor measures the older workers and salaried employees had used for demonstration purposes.

## Policies under National Socialism

The labor policy of the National Socialist Party is intelligible only if one understands its origins (Mason 1974; C. Krohn 1978). Rationalization had increased managerial control over work and the isolation of workers from each other through its depersonalized approach. Mass unemployment extended these trends still further as workers clung to what jobs were available. They were willing to forgo the scanty legal safeguards they did have, such as industrial safety and standard wages. That reaction helped to strengthen the entrepreneurs and weaken the trade unions.

This striking imbalance of power became legalized in the new labor constitution after the National Socialist takeover. It resulted in the Law for the Order of National Labor (AOG), promulgated on January 20, 1934. This law has for good reasons been described as the "sociopolitical basic law of the Third Reich" (Broszat 1973, p. 196), because it reorganized labor law according to the "leadership principle" (Führerprinzip). The "factory leader," that is, the owner/employer, was given almost unlimited powers. He alone could lay down plant rules, regulate working hours, and set wages and working conditions without any intervention by the work force, because the trade unions had been dissolved and banned since May 1933 (Schoenbaum 1968, pp. 125–127; Mason 1977, p. 192; Ortwein 1977, pp. 239–240; Winkler 1975, pp. 66–81).

Such a reshaping of factory structures could not leave in-plant health care untouched. This meant that the plant physician was directly attached to the "plant leader," who controlled his activities. The possibility of his position being either a full-time or a part-time job depended upon the size of the firm. It is noteworthy that the National Socialists, in the agreement about plant physicians between the Imperial Group for Industry (Reichsgruppe Industrie) and the department of public health in the Nazi headquarters, did not infringe on the free choice of physician, and therefore plant physicians could not treat factory workers beyond first aid. Only during the serious bottlenecks in medical services during World War II was this prohibition lifted (Syrup 1957, pp. 517–519).

The restructuring of in-plant organization corresponded roughly to the centralization of state policies. This can be seen in the manpower redistribution between 1933 and 1936 for the creation of an infrastructure to expand the arms industry (Syrup 1941, pp. 18–44; Syrup 1957, pp. 406–442; Petzina 1968). By means of the Ordinance on the Distribution of Manpower of August 10, 1934, the National Socialists attempted to organize a job swap of young workers and salaried employees in favor of older unemployed ones. The "plant leaders" were pledged to "check the composition by age of their employees, and replace single workers below the age of 25 with unemployed family men" above 40 (Mason 1977, p. 133). A limited financial-equalization arrangement by the government for factories willing to carry out such job swaps was also provided. To preclude new unemployment, the discharged young workers were supposed to be channeled into undermanned areas, such as agriculture or the National Labor Service (Reichsarbeitsdienst) (Syrup 1941, pp. 20–21). It was hoped that acceptance of such measures would be secured by a moral appeal to the "Emergency Community of the Nation" during the program's probationary period. This appeal failed, however, and in the end the operation met with little success. The factories were unwilling, despite prospects of material incentives, to forgo their more productive and better qualified young workers, especially since they also tended to help stabilize in-plant social control because they brought with them fewer trade union or socialist ideas (Mason 1977, p. 134). But above

all, those affected refused to make such a sacrifice for the older unemployed. Opposition was apparently stubborn (Syrup 1957, p. 420;
Mason 1975, 1977).

During the later phase of the four-year plan, the National Socialist
Party no longer relied on such comparatively appealing measures but
simply absorbed still-unemployed manpower (Petzina 1968, pp.
158–161). By 1938, some 80,000 older individuals (chiefly salaried employees) remained without work (Mason 1975). To address this problem,
the government used compulsory hiring by direct intervention according
to "the special situation of individual enterprises" (Mason 1975). This
policy succeeded, and the number of older unemployed salaried employees went down to about 12,000 by the end of 1938. Often, however,
they were placed as temporary worker's aides, which reduced them to
a last reserve in the labor force (Syrup 1941, pp. 24–25; Syrup 1957,
pp. 429–430; Schoenbaum 1968, p. 130; Mason 1977, p. 146).

The strategy of curtailing the autonomy of companies by introducing
compulsory employment, however, signaled a decline in qualification
of the workers. The strategy only worked on the premise of total dep-
rivation of the political rights of organized labor and an economic policy
that proved able to generate jobs only at the price of an expanding
central authority. This complex context—though sketched here briefly—
should be kept in mind for a historically adequate assessment of National
Socialist labor policy toward older clerical employees. Only by doing
so can one recognize the grossly oversimplified if not ideological character of the arguments that were sometimes advanced in the FRG in
the 1950s in order to reject governmental action on behalf of older
employees for fear of somehow resembling the National Socialist labor
policy. By contrast, the market's self-healing powers were made to
appear all the more glowing.

Under these historic conditions, a development that was discernible
even before the National Socialist rule in Germany intensified: the
division of factory-related health policy into two relatively separate,
unintegrated spheres. These were individual curative actions, such as
initial treatment by plant physicians, checking into specific complaints
by industrial physicians, and measures such as physical examinations
at hiring, mass check-ups, and monitoring examinations. The chances
that these measures would actually be carried out depended upon the
internal and social circumstances of the firm. Likewise, the implementation of legal standards concerning general improvements in the immediate work environment, work hygiene, and working hours were

subject to the influence of various economic and political forces, as illustrated by the period of National Socialism. An in-plant health policy for older employees actually did not exist for the entire period treated here, and the obviously marginal existence these employees eked out among plant personnel was due to their being socially stigmatized and to the threat of dismissing them as disabled or as old-age pensioners on social insurance.

## Decisions during the "New Beginning" (1945–1949)

After the complete breakdown of National Socialist rule in May 1945, the commanders-in-chief of the Allied forces took over the official reins of government in the four zones of occupation. At that time there were serious problems of public health, above all the need for rapid prevention of epidemics and malnutrition. However, these and similar measures were not applied with appropriate intensity and concentration in all of the occupation zones. Rather, the differences between the Western zones and the Soviet zone of occupation, especially in regard to the fight against venereal disease and the establishment of in-plant medical services, immediately revealed structural decisions that remained characteristic of future public health policy. Kirchberger's conclusion (chapter 6 in the present volume) that, in contrast to the Soviet zone, the Western zones—and subsequently the FRG—underwent no significant break in the continuity of public health policies with corresponding structural innovations can claim equal validity for the problem area dealt with here. Further, this result is in harmony with the tenor of discussions conducted in social science and contemporary historical research which tend to explain both the governmental organization and the development of social policy in the two German states as the product of a historic constellation of endogenous and exogenous factors (Merkl 1965; Hartwich 1970; E. Schmidt 1970; Huster et al. 1972; Ambrosius 1977; Huster 1978).

The relevance of this conclusion for old age and dependent employment can be seen in the postwar development of social security institutions. In the Soviet zone, policies moved immediately in the direction of the fundamental reform of social insurance on a universal basis.[2] This was almost the opposite of the Western occupation zones, where a bloc made up of medical associations, business interests, and various public and private insurance representatives was able not only to prevent the establishment of universal social security but even the establishment of the pre-1933 level of staffing in governmental agencies.[3]

A constellation of interrelated determinants that shaped postwar and subsequent policy in the FRG can be identified (Tennstedt 1977b, pp. 227–261; A. Schmidt 1977; Rodenstein 1978). Foremost was the ability of organized business and the professions to mount an intense and complex lobbying effort, because their organizations did not suffer during the days of National Socialism as did the trade unions. Second, the Western Allies favored the decentralization of power and the disintegration of the services structure. In a similar manner, the institutionalization of federalism in 1949 decentralized power in favor of the states (Länder) in matters of public health policy. Third, the Allies supported energetically the structure of a private economy. The resulting rationale of both exploitation and rationalization became the dominant factor of societal evolution. Nevertheless, the organization of the relation between politics and economics was newly interpreted: As a concession to historical experience and to prevailing mass unemployment, the government was given limited powers to control economic conditions. This included the possibility of political intervention in the labor market. To what extent these determinants can be identified in actual political strategies, however, will have to be established later on in an examination of those measures instituted by the FRG in order to safeguard minimal health standards for older dependent employees in the various factories and enterprises.

In the Soviet zone of occupation, this process of shaping the future social and political structure took place with much less disparity. One of the political and organizational prerequisites for the realization of socialist objectives had been created immediately after the war, namely, the coerced merger of the Social Democrat and Communist parties into a socialist mass party, the SPD. This party became less and less a mass party and took more and more to the example of a Leninist cadre party. This remained not without consequences for political and economic organization. Administrative and political organization became more designed for central competence and centralized power for long-range economic planning after 1948. Thus, there was a totally different point of departure from that prevailing in the Western zones for articulating political or private economic interests, which then were reduced to waging rear-guard battles. The dissolution of private institutions and interests became apparent in the health sector, because it conflicted with socialist convictions about public health policy. Now there was a historic opportunity to put into practice those public health principles of prevention and prophylaxis that socialist physicians and hygienists had demanded since the end of the nineteenth century (Tennstedt 1977a). The process of putting these into practical reality (specifically for older employees), and the results achieved thereby in the GDR, will now be examined more closely.

## Postwar Health Policy for Older Employees

The precedent-setting effect of fundamental structures of political and economic organization of society in the four zones, which were eventually to evolve into the two German states, had repercussions for the styles of solving those problems which were faced by both German states as a historical heritage with the same degree of urgency. The most important of those problems was the organization of the potential work force. The potential work force, in turn, was informed by strong short-term and long-term demographic imbalances after World War II.

After the war, large waves of people pressed westward from the formerly German eastern areas to the Soviet zone. As a work force, they were suitable for the desolate East German agriculture but not fit to be long-term industrial workers. This became especially evident during the energetic industrialization policy, with its steady drain on agricultural manpower, and many of these resettlers pushed on into the FRG in hopes of not losing their independence (Lungwitz 1974, pp. 67–68). This led to an absolute increase of older groups in the population, which clearly posed an urgent socio-political problem for the labor market as well as for future social services in both German states (Hoerl 1978, pp. 336–347). Moreover, the general population had been aging, as in all industrial countries. The two world wars had also depleted the ranks of working men, resulting in a preponderance of women over men and a worsening dependency ratio of working-age people to children and older people (*Bericht und Materialen* 1, chapter II, pp. 65–87; Leenen 1977a; Vortmann 1977, pp. 101–104). In table 1 one can compare this development between the two German states, including their areas in 1939.

The situation was even worse in the GDR than in the FRG, in part because throughout the 1950s a growing number of young qualified workers and their families left for the FRG. This mass flight reduced the GDR's manpower pool by an additional 2.6 million citizens until this possibility was cut off in August 1961 by the wall.

**Table 1**
Number of persons of nonworking age and retirement age per 100 persons of working age

| | Nonworking age[a] | | Retirement age[b] | |
| --- | --- | --- | --- | --- |
| | GDR | FRG | GDR | FRG |
| 1939 | 48.1 | 50.1 | 16.4 | 14.4 |
| 1946 | 60.0 | 56.2 | 20.8 | 17.6 |
| 1950 | 57.9 | 54.7 | 21.8 | 18.2 |
| 1961 | 67.2 | 56.2 | 30.0 | 21.8 |
| 1970 | 74.7 | 66.1 | 34.0 | 27.1 |

a. Men under 15 and 65 or older, women under 15 and 60 or older.
b. Men 65 or older, women 60 or older.
Source: Lungwitz 1974, p. 91.

Policies for reconstructing destroyed industries and setting up new ones needed by both German states had to make allowances for these short-range and long-range developments. The economic policy of extensive growth with an emphasis on a high degree of absorption of the available work force and a high utilization of their working time meant establishing an enlarged supply of jobs. The process of establishing this and its consequences for the social organization of manpower differed, of course, with the political economies of the two states. In the FRG the construction of production capacities could proceed smoothly thanks to governmental and foreign investment aid; the economic expansion there was further fueled by a backlog of demand for consumer and capital goods, and the expected "pull" exerted on the labor market took place until 1951–52 (with the exception of certain problem groups). As intended, the labor market remained organized along liberal principles of supply and demand, and limited government interference was tolerated only in times of economic crisis, which meant that unemployment continued as a possible fate for employees. In the GDR, the labor market was dissolved as private ownership of production was largely eliminated by 1949 through takeovers by the central government. This market was replaced in stages by a manpower policy integrated into the entire central planning. A complex system of manpower direction, however, did not develop until the late 1950s.

The consequences for the older employees (Werktätigen[4]) in the GDR were clearly evident. With the claim of building a society free from capitalist contradictions, planned unemployment was no longer compatible as a social control mechanism or as a means to discipline the work force. With a shortage of workers and a policy of extensive growth, there could be no point in retiring the older workers and employees by means of disability or old-age pensions. On the contrary, they were to be kept working for as long as possible. The different historic forms of institutionalized displacement and compensatory removal of older employees thus seemed to be finally set aside. From the viewpoint of public health this had unpleasant consequences, for it brought about a situation where older workers and employees were again subjected to stressful work conditions. These stressful working conditions would have additional adverse effects in view of the elderly's long years of health-injurious labor.

## Health Policies for Productivity among Older Workers in the GDR

Any realization of a preventive program in a socialist industrial health system (Betriebsgesundheitswesen; BGW) depends on a certain theory of society. Genuine prevention can only be realized in a society where the form of production embodies long-range health programs throughout the work life of the employee. Thus, economic requirements and health requirements should not face one another antagonistically, as under capitalism, but rather should be complementary and interrelated. In such a case, public health policy is always tied to manpower policy, and both are factors in overall social and industrial planning.

The process of realizing this theoretical perspective in the GDR was burdened with many ruptures and disproportions. One can distinguish four stages of preventive structuring of the BGW, which, of course, cannot be sharply delineated. Only the last two deal with the job-related health problems of middle-aged and old(er) employees.

1. The first stage, which lasted from 1945 until 1951, can be described as one of a general breakup of structure and of developing a situation-specific heterogeneity in the BGW.
2. The second stage coincided with the beginning of the first five-year plan and covers the period from 1951 to 1953–54. One could characterize it as a reorganization of the BGW through economizing, and in this phase there were already certain preventive strategies being tested.
3. In the third stage (1955–1958), which coincided with the beginning of the second five-year plan, the tested preventive strategies were made legally obligatory. Because of its content, one could describe this stage as one of organization of preventive structural premises. Here, for the

first time, preventive strategies were drafted and tested for middle-aged and elderly employees.

4. The fourth stage (from 1958 to 1961–62) coincided with the first attempt to reorganize the entire planning system to allow for intensive growth. It was characterized by the unification and generalization of prevention through legalization, and the dimensions of its contents are discussed below. Each state of organizing preventive strategies in the industrial health sector had a corresponding stage in the administrative mobilization of manpower.

One extraordinarily important consequence of Soviet Military Government Order No. 234 of October 9, 1947, and of the resulting restructuring of the BGW (*Deutsches Gesundheitswesen* 1947, pp. 684–687; see Winter 1947), was the separation of the in-plant physician from the immediate factory management hierarchy (for the first time in Germany) and his incorporation into the governmental public health system. The assignment of the BGW to the Health and Social Affairs Department at the county or district council level was supposed to enable the industrial in-plant physician to enjoy sufficient independence and latitude to enforce even those industrial health and safety measures that might run counter to the economic interests of the factory concerned. The BGW was further reinforced by the newly instituted option for plant personnel to receive both outpatient and inpatient treatment either from the county/district health system or from their in-plant health service. In the period of economic reconstruction, with its manifold and frequently incompatible requirements and relatively low degree of centralized planning, such a redefinition of the role of the in-plant physician resulted not merely in regional and branch disparities but also in many plant physicians' using their newly won independence to intervene against economically desirable investments in the name of prevention. Ironically, this led to demands by the party leadership, which a Health Ministry physician expressed during the second stage that followed the reorganization of the economy: "We must put a stop to this separation between factory health system and factory management. The factory health system must not be a foreign body but must instead be part and parcel of the factory. Even in their capacity as employees of the public health administration, the members of the factory health system are an integral part of the factory work crew." (Weber 1953, p. 405; see also Amon 1950)

Continuous reorganization of the BGW in order to support an extensive growth policy was instituted in 1951. Besides prohibiting employment of women and youths in work hazardous to their health, the Labor Protection Regulation of 1951 required factories to monitor continuously the health status of those workers engaged in heavy or health-endangering work (Holstein 1953; Amon 1953; Erler 1954). Starting in 1952, there was increasing emphasis on improving and supporting the BGW in the contracts of the factory collectives (Weber 1953, p. 404).[5] With this advance, which later became the rule, the BGW once again was tied immediately to a plant's performance structure. However, for reasons of legitimation, the BGW remains subordinate to the district public health system. Though there was undoubtedly the opportunity for the BGW to perform great tasks of prevention, the built-in trend toward conflict can hardly be overlooked in this dual relationship. In the social implementation of good working conditions for elderly personnel, this ambivalence certainly had a retarding effect, as shall be shown.

By the crisis of the early summer of 1953, the widespread dissatisfaction with working and living conditions in the GDR had become apparent. All the more urgent for government and party leadership was the problem of compensatory measures. The "ordinance regarding the further improvement of working and living conditions for the workers and the rights of the trade unions" (text of ordinance: *Arbeit und Sozialfürsorge* 9, no. 1, 1954: 2–3, 29–32) of December 10, 1953, tried to combine such compensatory measures (by means of housing programs, greater emphasis on consumer goods, and the like) with a more effective organization of economizing, especially in health protection. For example, inclusion of the BGW into the factory collective labor contract was made obligatory. At the same time, the funds for the protection of labor in factories were tied down (sec. 4, p. 29); this indicated that earlier funds for labor protection had been diverted under the table. Despite relatively detailed individual regulations, this ordinance was not very helpful for setting up long-range protective structures.[6] At best it furnished a compilation of measures already instituted without tackling the basic reforms of labor health protection that accorded with the general economizing. The institutionalizing of Labor Sanitary Inspections (ASANI), accomplished by this ordinance at the regional level of public health, confirms this assessment; they only monitored hygienic conditions within factories, and thus they closely followed the classical model of health inspection (sec. 12, p. 30).

The decisive step for reform was the Council of Ministers resolution of July 8, 1954, which undertook a reorganization of prevention in the

BGW (resolution in *Deutsches Gesundheitswesen* 9, no. 31, 1954: 949–964; Marcusson 1954). The most important passage in this resolution reads: "In medical care, but especially in preventive care for workers in industry, a beginning is to be made in line with the ongoing development of periodic physicals, systematic examinations, and treatment of ill patients in the industrial welfare centers and ambulatory clinics (dispensaire method)." (*Deutsches Gesundheitswesen* 1954:953) The dispensaire method, strongly recommended but not yet obligatory, was an attempt to achieve a new level of prevention within the BGW. It rested at that time on two premises: the periodic physical examination and the registration of groups of illness or diseases for prevention. The problem of these premises is that they require an objective symptomatology for early identification of pre-morbid states.

The everyday practice of periodic examinations in those years was, to judge from the abundant criticism, anything but effective. Frequently there were "complaints by workers that these examinations were often superficial and insufficient either to prevent or to diagnose illness" (Marcusson 1954, p. 965; Erler 1954, p. 671). The reorganization in June 1955 was supposed to have improved these examinations, but it received a rather skeptical evaluation as to its true adequacy and effectiveness (Brandt 1955; Winter and Neelsen 1956; Renker 1957a; Eitner 1959). The aim of this new definition was, however, clear: These serial examinations should no longer be just a periodically recurring accumulation of disparate individual cases, but should instead—as Winter and Neelsen (1956, p. 631) put it—"pose the question about the collective." This signifies the view that only an epidemiological analysis of the entire work group can identify pathogenic causes and provide the basis for organizing a preventive dispensaire program. The "systematized analysis of environmental factors"[7] thereby alluded to was to provide data for the evaluation of the physical and psychological condition in conjunction with the type of work and the labor conditions prevailing in each plant and supply data for the assessment of other conditions through an exact diagnosis by specialized physicians (Winter and Neelsen 1956, p. 663).

The far-reaching range of tasks laid down for periodic examinations implied a criticism of a too-narrow interpretation of the dispensaire method (as advocated in the Council of Ministers resolution mentioned above, with its exclusive reliance on nosological groups), because it did not assess how work conditions affected illness. Dividing up care by types of illnesses (such as ulcers, hypertension, rheumatism, and so on) could only be meaningful if working conditions and illnesses of work groups, such as welders, had been examined. Then one could form dispensaire groups with the aim of periodically observing the potentially or actually endangered groups corresponding to different types of illnesses.

The practice of dispensaires differed in many areas of the GDR. In most industrial clinics, dispensaire groupings were formed around diagnoses in the daily sick-call index cards, so any relationship of working or living conditions to disease was lost (Bittersohl 1955; Renker 1956, 1957a). The resulting fragmentation and limited effectiveness of the dispensaire soon led to the formation, in everyday in-plant medical care, of additional groupings by working conditions and degrees of endangerment (Märker et al. 1957; Eitner 1959). This informal development in the BGW then became officially sanctioned with the administrative obligation to introduce the dispensaire method generally as a structural principle of prevention. In the directive of August 4, 1956, groupings according to working conditions, age, sex, and types of illness—especially coronary and ulcer disorders—were called for, the last two groupings also to be classed according to age groupings (directive in *Deutsches Gesundheitswesen* 11, no. 46, 1956:1579–1580; Marcusson 1956). This expansion by age groups provided for the first time a compilation of working conditions for older employees. Such data were gathered indirectly, however, and were fragmented by nosological groups. Classification by age group was a rather simplified procedure for reducing dispensaire groupings, and it did not consider the specific conditions of the aging process or its possible effects upon the organization of work. The significance of aging in the course of preventive identification of working conditions was never a subject of the reporting process at that time. (For an exception see Marcusson 1956, pp. 1575, 1578.) Nevertheless, these data by age group later served as the point of departure for the setting up of the first geriatric dispensaire (Gerodispensaire) in the GDR.

By 1957, in four shops of the heavy engine construction works at Magdeburg, under the direction of Siegfried Eitner as chief of the Pavlov-Poliklinik, systematic monitoring and dispensaire care began for 50 workers over 60 years old. The objective was described as "to preserve the capability to work for as long as possible beyond the pension age" (Eitner 1959, p. 692). This goal echoes other policies at that time for enabling candidates for old-age pensions to continue working (Zetkin 1955; Lengwinat 1959). The basis for these activities was the fact that the mobilizing of manpower for extensive growth in the GDR had clearly reached its limits. In the second five-year plan, labor reserves were exhausted, and "any further increase in production could only be achieved through increased labor productivity" (Müller 1958, p. 259). Thus, the dispensaire treatment of older workers arose during the fourth stage as part of a drive for intensive growth together with the first cautiously placed reforms in the general organization of state and economy from 1958 on. Nevertheless, in the long range it led to a focus on preserving the work capacity of laborers, to the organization of geriatric health care, and to the reorganization of certain jobs so they could be performed by older employees (Eitner 1959, 1961, 1964; T. Auerbach 1961).

The dispensaire was designed to provide a combination of prophylaxis, therapy, rehabilitation, and protection against the effects of life-cycle changes. Focal points of concern were to become preventive medical measures, in turn to be subdivided into preventive "gerophylactics" and "gerohygiene" (prophylactic and hygienic measures tailored for old people). During the preventive gerophylactic measures, the problem of premature angina—which has been so controversial in the pertinent scientific literature—was supposed to be prevented (Tietze 1976; Paul 1977).

Older employees underwent two supplementary screenings. One screening was a detailed interview on the patient's entire social and mental condition and his relations to the work collective. Besides a detailed statement on the individual conditions of aging in each case, there was diagnostic screening involving a detailed inventory of health and including analyses of blood, urine, and gastric juice; control of the motor system; the gastro-intestinal tract; the respiratory system; the central and autonomic nervous systems; the coronary circulation; a thorax x-ray, a semi-axial x-ray of the cranium, and a resting stress-free EKG taken on the chest wall with six chest leads. On the basis of these examinations, Eitner developed five stages of health for older workers according to degrees of dynamism, direction, and intensity of their health development.[8] It was not for the practicality or the everyday concern of the physician in a given plant that this step-by-step approach was decisive. Much more important was that the categories for diagnosis were simultaneously designed to grade relative importance for long-range observations and cure of patients. This kind of connection is displayed in table 2.

**Table 2**
Stages of health for older workers

| Stage | Characteristics | Subsequent "dispensaire" measures |
|-------|-----------------|-----------------------------------|
| I | Practically healthy | None required; routine annual checkup as legally required. |
| II | Frequently ill (usually unable to work for short periods) or susceptible. Organic basic illness not yet established. | Periodic observation, through examination, prophylactic cures, physiotherapy, diet, periodic semi-inpatient care. |
| III | Long-time permanently (chronically) ill because of provable organic illness. | In-plant or outside nosological grouping with special consideration for the ulcer group, any postoperative states, or angina pectoris groups. Other groups: care by in-plant or outside specialists. |
| IV | Severely disabled with certificate; old-age pensioners in the work process. | Periodic observation (once a year); old-age pensioners observed twice annually. The "dispensaire" group to be observed and cared for constantly. |
| V | Incapable of work due to illness. | Outpatient or inpatient treatment required. |

Source: Eitner 1959. The distribution of the participants of the "Gerodispensaire" for the period 1957–1961 ($n=1,000$) was 10.7% for stage I, 40.8% for stage II, 31.6% for stage III, 11.2% for stage IV, and 5.7% for stage V. (See Eitner 1964, p. 1515.)

The stages, in turn, were linked to an examination of how workers' jobs fitted their health needs. This drew on the 1955 catalog of stressful job conditions that might in the long run cause geriatric problems. This catalog listed jobs by degrees of danger or physical demand, such as work in high heat, around moisture or gas, in water, mud, liquids, or moist masses, and under constant exposure to smoke, dust, arsenic, or benzene. These conditions were seen as principal causes of premature aging (Voralterung) and became the focus of study at the gerodispensaires.

Operational use of the dispositions listed in these health stages for employment at jobs with varying stresses or demands was effected by means of three phases of readiness for work: "completely fit," "conditionally fit," and "unfit." Each had its own specific set of dispensaire measures, which linked medical-therapeutic measures with the degree of stress in different jobs and rehabilitation programs (Eitner 1959, p. 694; Eitner 1964, pp. 1515–1516). With the help of job studies and work case histories, an attempt was made to arrive at a "classification of places of work or jobs while giving consideration to both worker capacity and degree of job strain." This attempt "resulted in the so-called job nomenclature" (Eitner 1964, p. 1515). This nomenclature was a listing of nominated and non-nominated jobs. Nomination meant the characterization of a job according to special medical and hygienic conditions (such as special breaks for older workers, adjustments in the job site, or special lighting and seating). Nomination precluded unrestricted employment of certain older workers. Put another way, jobs were not nominated where their "demands were in agreement with the stages of health and fitness of the persons occupying them" (Eitner 1964, p. 1516). During the further development of the gerodispensaires, this job nomenclature was refined further by phases of jobs, which were supposed to be complementary to the stages of health. There were five job phases, of which four were individually looked after by different dispensaires (Tröger 1969, p. 1330): non-nominated jobs, work relief on nominated jobs (especially nominated jobs), in-plant transfer to protected and training jobs, protected jobs for older people, and transfer to out-of-plant rehabilitation and pensioner collectives. This meshing of health stages, job phases, employment phases, and dispensaire care stages was the result of long and detailed research as well as corresponding practical testing, documented in subsequently published contributions. Table 3, which was presented by Eitner in 1971 at the Third Congress of the Society for Geriatric Research, shows what complexities have been added but also how much continuity remains.

The very possibility of such conceptual development and practical trial indicates that there were pressures to change the inefficiency and bureaucratic overkill of directly controlled planning in the GDR. Reformers advocated the increased autonomy and latitude of a given plant by way of indirect forms of leadership. They argued that only on the basis of such reform would the appropriate conceptual groundwork be laid for the process of the economy and planning. Within this frame of reference, the conceivable change of the structure of production could graduate to high standards of technique, harmonization, and automatization and their ensuing social consequences. Admittedly, such postulates were seen by the party leadership as manifestations of political opposition and met with direct reprisals. However, even East Germans who were sympathetic to official policies could no longer fail to understand that this dogmatism led to failures within the system of planning

**Table 3**
Percentage distribution of male population by pension age, health phase, job classification, and degree of work fitness ($a$ = 65–69 years; $b$ = 70–74 years).

| Phase | Health phase | Area of percent in health phase, by age | Job stage | Area of percent fit to work, by age | Degree of fitness to work (or stage of care) |
|---|---|---|---|---|---|
| 1 | Above average, able to perform work | $a$: 15–20% $b$: 10–15% | Non-nominated or noncatalogued jobs | $a$: 10–20% $b$: 5–10% | Unconditional work assignment without reservations; once-a-year physical checkup |
| 2 | Practically healthy, with slight functional or organic changes | $a$: 30–35% $b$: 15–20% | Through adjustment and arrangements for breaks, specifically nominated jobs for pensioners | $a$: 20–30% $b$: 10–20% | Limited work assignment, appropriate monitor checkups twice a year. "Dispensaire" care Stage DI. |
| 3 | Well or adequately compensated disorders without true illness | $a$: 20–30% $b$: 20–30% | Assignment to specific classified jobs with commensurately adequate conditions | $a$: 20–30% $b$: 10–20% | Limited work assignment to classified jobs. "Dispensaire" care Stage DII quarterly. |
| 4 | Considerable disorders or physical disability only marginally adjustable. Endangered persons. Prematurely aged. Severely reduced work capacity. Tied to residence | $a$: 20–30% $b$: 20–40% | Rehabilitation jobs, predominantly within area of residence (pensioner brigades, protected workshops, services for population included for pensioners requiring care) | $a$: 10–20% $b$: 5–10% | Limited work assignments under acceptable "Dispensaire" care. Limited, continuous monitoring of health. Stage DIII. Minimum of monthly checkups. |
| 5 | Requiring care, tied to home, immobile inactive, feeble, bedridden | $a$: 3–5% $b$: 5–10% | Requiring care and nursing | $a$: 20–30% $b$: 40–60% | No longer usable, but requiring special medicine and social treatment based on medical service and card index |

Source: Eitner 1972, p. 215.

as it was aiming at navigating long-term economic and societal processes of development with some degree of certainty.

At first, guarded attempts at paving the way for such reorientations were debated among those who were interested in the economy of labor in the late 1950s. For the second five-year plan there were hardly any reserves of manpower. Thus, the transition to a policy of economic growth relying on the intensifying of the work process became more and more compelling. In short, any increase of output and production hinged on a corresponding increase of the intensity of output by the manpower available (Müller 1958). This could only happen if manpower allocation was reorganized and the entire system of industrial working relations transformed. The comprehensive labor code (Gesetzbuch der Arbeit; GBA) of 1961 and the Workplace Protection Act of 1962 must be seen as the first steps in this direction. They are evidence that the protection of health and the safety of the workplace became of overriding importance. Not only was the goal to lower the rate of loss of productivity due to illness. It also was to preserve manpower, take on added diagnostic tasks, and finally improve the overall health of a given plant so as to foster productivity (Winter 1977, pp. 251–281; Bachmann et al. 1976, pp. 21–206). Health care was defined as socialist on the premise of the workers' right to co-determination.

It was not before the sweeping reform of the entire system of planning and performance in 1963, however, that the system of health planning explicitly included older working people by stating that pensioners had the right to further professional activity according to their abilities and mindful of their preferences. This provision did not yet conjure up the official and generally binding establishment of gerodispensaires, but it symbolized a breakthrough for the concept of dispensaires. It is because of this gradual success that the concept of gerodispensaires not only maintained its position as a prominent aspect of public policy during the phase of increased economic productivity in the GDR but became even more crucial.

The Politics of Appeal and Anti-Collectivist Ideology: Implications for the Lack of Understanding of Health Problems of Aging Employees in the FRG

For all their shortcomings, at least there had been experiments in the GDR to cope with the health needs of older employees. The efforts were part of the movement for dispensaires. We must not fail to acknowledge, however, that the primary motivating force had been economic calculations. The economy was so short of manpower that the only possible key to overcoming this desolate state of affairs lay in optimizing the work performance of aging pensioners. There were no similar developments in the FRG until the late 1960s. A principal reason for this dissonance was the incoherence of in-plant medical care in the FRG. It was the concerted preference of physicians' associations, employers' groups, and the state bureaucracy in charge to leave in-plant health issues alone. "Freedom" was ideologically charged in the FRG, and it became a matter of "freedom" to retain management's prerogative to decide about in-plant health care.

Thus, it comes as no surprise that, in accordance with the economic interests of specific branches of industry or specific companies, the institution and improvement of in-plant health care was deemed dispensable altogether. This was not an infrequent occurrence in small plants. This flexible definition, designed to respond with elasticity to each single case at hand, had been stipulated and declared an essential element of public policy by employers and even the trade unions and the association of in-plant physicians by 1950. The suggestion for adopting unifying legal rules for this cluster of problems was uniformly rejected as "mechanistic" or "unfeasible" (Deppe 1973; Jens 1973). The strong reaction by some parts of the trade unions shed light on the underlying set of reasons for this rejection. It demonstrated how liberal pluralism was deployed as an ideological weapon and thereby hampered any rational debate about the desirability of in-plant health-care policies. It also revealed how strongly the pressures of uniformity and discipline must have weighed on the unions. The rationale given by the unions to yield to such policies was the bad memories of the quasi-official position of in-plant physicians during the Nazi period (Deppe 1973, pp. 22–23). However, it does not seem too farfetched to assume that, instead of drawing a clear line between the FRG and the Nazi era, the driving force for such attitudes on the part of the unions was to be found in the "cold war" and the desire to be readily distinguishable from collectivist in-plant health-care schemes such as those in the GDR. It was unavoidable that in such an ideologically charged atmosphere of anticollectivist sentiments any demand for preventive systems of health care in the factory had a ring of the totalitarian social control associated with communist social ideals. This resulted in a dearth of public debates about the introduction of health care for aging employees, and, moreover, led to the general observation that not even on the level of a given plant or factory was much to be done.

But there was more to this lack of policy about and misunderstanding of health problems of older workers than some degree of societal ignorance by in-plant physicians. It seems infinitely more accurate to read this societal predisposition as a dominant ideological attitude toward the general problem of aging in an economic and political stage of development in the FRG that was marked by extensive growth of the economy. This pattern can be captured best by the concession that aging signifies an undeniable encroachment on the general well-being and outlook on life. Sad though this phenomenon may be, aging is a matter of individual responsibility. State intervention in the job market, this view holds, can at best mitigate its consequences for the individual and cannot basically alter individual life risks. On the other hand, such intervention could possibly disfigure and impair the marketplace itself.

At first glance, this line of reasoning seems to be supported by the development of the labor market during the period of economic reconstruction in the FRG. Apart from some turbulence up to the early 1950s, the economy absorbed and integrated workers of every age without limits. There was even a widespread shortage of old workers, who were sought after because of their experience and their ability to train a new body of young workers. On top of this, workers, no matter what their age or qualifications, usually found a job with the aid of labor offices (Maassen 1953, p. 391). Accordingly, age was not perceived as an individual handicap. On the contrary, experience was valued highly as an ingredient of economic reconstruction (Fiebich 1952; Balling 1952, p. 340). Borrowing from policy debates in England, some people even thought about extending the mandatory retirement age ("Verlängerung des Arbeitsalters?" *Sozialer Fortschritt* 1, no. 3, 1952:59–60); some, referring to the United States, argued that it might be worth contemplating the creation of special jobs for older workers so as to ensure the preservation of their accumulated knowledge for the overall well-being of a plant (Balling 1952, p. 340; Meyer 1957). Thus, it was only a matter of time before, at the height of this extensive growth of the economy, some political commentators declared the problem of aging employees a thing of the past (Salzmann 1958). But when, in the mid 1960s, economic growth required more intensive work in the absence of a larger pool of reserves in manpower, the demand for more work by aging pensioners and the utilization of resources theretofore untapped followed suit ("Ungenützte Arbeitskraftreserven," *Sozialer Fortschritt* 15, no. 2, 1965:29–30).

It was difficult to argue against the unrestrained postwar optimism when joblessness among older people was comparatively negligible. However, one particular group in the work force, aging white-collar employees, constantly reminded a wider public of the fact that the problematic connection between old age and unemployment was far from being settled. As early as 1949, analysts of the job market pointed out that there was a residual core group of aging employees, although not of imposing size, who could not be reintegrated into the economy by the labor offices despite rapid economic growth (Voigt 1949; Seiler 1952; Stewens 1952; Meis 1953). It did not take a long time to remember the same problem and its designation during the period of the Weimar Republic (Stewens 1952; Seiler 1952). People even thought of the frustrated attempts of National Socialism (Voigt 1949). However, surveys showed that the contemporary "aging employees" consisted mostly of on-the-job-trained or unqualified employees and were therefore quite different from older employees in the Weimer Republic (Bischoff 1954; Gaebel 1954; Dahnen 1961).

Overall, however, abstention from state intervention in the job market seemed the superior solution. In its stead, appeals to representatives of the employers seemed advisable (Balling 1952, p. 341). Indeed, Chancellor Konrad Adenauer heeded this advice in 1952 ("Ein Wort für die älteren Angestellten," *Bundesarbeitsblatt*, no. 1, 1952:28–29), and his Secretary of Labor repeated it one more time in 1958 ("Behebung der Arbeitslosigkeit älterer Arbeitnehmer," *Bundesarbeitsblatt* 9, no. 8, 1958:188). The outcome amounted to no more than slogans.

With the exception of the debate about a more progressive pension plan in 1957,[9] the controversy over the life chances of aging employees without jobs remained the only public debate on social policy about older workers during the phase of extensive growth. This was the only instance where some headway was made to counteract the ideological habit of burying the most pressing problems. There were only a few activities aimed at aging employees. In 1955 there had been a symposium on the topic of "aging people in the plant." Emphasis had been put on the problems of efficiency, memory, and speed of reaction in older workers (Kunigk 1955; Meyer 1957). Very similar emphasis was given by developmental psychologists at the University of Bonn, and pragmatic social policy could draw on a host of recommendations provided by the 1961 symposium on social care (Fürsorgetag) (which dealt with intergenerational relations) and the 1962 International Congress for Social Progress, held in Bordeaux (Wagener 1962). These recommendations were predicated on new discoveries and insights into the relevance of older people to the demographic composition of the future. These years were characterized by collection and expansion of data without much sense of direction. Only the contours of the problem surfaced. It was a far cry from specific socio-political goal setting, such as taking an inventory of the damage visited upon the health of aging workers or systematically supervising, if not preventing, deterioration of health due to work conditions. Such ambitious goals were not of central importance to this early scientific inventorying.

The incentive for such goals came about in the early 1960s, when surplus seemed possible only through a shift from extensive forms of economic growth to labor-intensive growth rates. This shift led to a reformulation of social priorities and forced the participants to seek a more differentiated mode of exploiting a stagnating reservoir of manpower. New policies were developed to phase in measures of in-plant job transfers/re-assignments, on-the-job training programs, and other strategies for adapting to the deep structural changes in manpower and the mode of production. This move was supported by ergonomics and industrial medicine (*Vorzeitige Invalidität*, 1961; Friedrichs 1964; Lehmann 1962; Holstein 1962; Wiegand 1967). It focused on the interdependence of work and the phases of the individual employee's biography. For the purpose of clarifying its specific and important effects on social and health policies, it seems wise to start with the solutions adopted to tackle this new phase in the political economy in the GDR first. This is so because the differences between the East and West German models are deep.

## Health Policies for Older Employees during Intensive Growth

Conflict of Interests in the GDR

The shortage of manpower was, and continues to be, a pressing and essential problem for the economy and society of the GDR. Analysts from Western countries have frequently claimed that this shortage is structurally "manufactured." By that they seem to allude to the possibility of ineffective organization of labor and defects in industrial leadership. Whatever the real sources of this shortage of manpower, the fact of the matter is that the interest in extending the employment span of aging pensioners became even greater during the 1960s. To clarify why, we have to review some data (Kunter and Müller 1974; Winkler 1975; Vortmann 1977).

The GDR has one of the highest percentages of pensioners in the total population of any nation—about 19 percent in 1975. However, this figure is slated to decline by the year 2000 to 14–16 percent (Vortmann 1977, pp. 101–107; Schmidt et al. 1974, pp. 123–124; Polle 1974, pp. 64–65). The current high percent applies to all regions and both sexes. Among pensioners, women outweigh men 2.2:1, which is the result of World War II and the dramatic slump in the average birth rates of the years during World War I (Eitner 1972, p. 210). Between 1955 and 1971 the share of pensioners employed beyond mandatory retirement grew steadily, with the quota of female pensioners growing more rapidly than that of males. The portion of working pensioners grew from 5.4 percent of the work force in 1955 to 8.1 percent in 1971 (Polle 1974, pp. 164–166; Eitner and Walter, 1975, p. 267). Since the 1960s, however, the share of pensioners working beyond the mandatory retirement age has remained at about 20 percent of all citizens beyond the retirement limit (Leenen 1971b, p. 14). This may be due to pension increases (Polle 1974, pp. 165–166; Leenen 1971b, p. 142, n. 156).

There are few pensioners at work in the mining industry and in chemical or electrical plants, nor are there many in the glass industry, ceramics, the construction business, mechanical engineering, or graphite firms. However, every second pensioner works for a commercial enterprise, in textile factories, in other consumer-goods branches of industry, in the service sector, in health and social institutions, or in agriculture and gardening (Eitner et al. 1971, pp. 147–148; Slawinski 1974, p. 40). These pensioners "pursue careers that, to a degree, seem no longer attractive enough to younger people, [and they] carry on in occupations still imprinted by old-fashioned modes of production that require little qualification and frequently prove to require hard physical labor . . . [and] provide unfavorable working conditions from the point of view of industrial hygiene" (Brannström and Eitner 1974, pp. 168–169). "Surveys have shown that enterprises with focal concern on economy and technology unfortunately fail to take into account the need for jobs on the part of qualified pensioners, and even skilled workers are no exception to that neglect. If we leave this development to the self-regulatory processes, as we currently do, we will soon be faced with a concentration of old people and dated jobs." (ibid., p. 169) Apologists explain this increasing marginality differently: "In the wake of step-by-step improvements of working conditions, we have to create appropriate jobs for aging citizens with added force. This is simultaneously an expression of important strides made by socialism in the utilization of scientific-technical progress. By the same token, we will be able to meet the retrograde tendencies of jobs available for pensioners effectively in the future." (Maier and Tomm 1976, p. 108; Demmler and Tietze 1976)

The first administrative moves to turn this situation around began in 1963 (von Kondratowitz 1977), when the secretary of the Governmental Planning Commission issued an ordinance requiring better working conditions for pensioners. A subsequent series of steps led in 1977 to the Arbeitsgesetzbuch (AGB) (Industrial Relations Act). This act guaranteed aging pensioners at least a part-time job. It also assured them the right to refuse the imposition of night shifts or overtime. Most important, the government extended promises to all those employees willing to carry on after reaching the retirement age. Besides dispensaire care, they were offered diverse precautionary safeguards, such as protection against sudden dismissal and the right to job transfers (von Kondratowitz 1978, pp. 89–94). Yet even this improvement of their rights could not prevent professional activity among aging people from continuing to decline (Fischer 1981a, p. 527). This requires further analysis (von Kondratowitz 1977).

As will be remembered, there were two significant purposes for going ahead with the institution of gerodispensaires. One was the expectation that such systematic care would prove beneficial for long-term preventive goals. The other was the state's desire to get more work out of pensioners. The innovation of the gerodispensaire made sense insofar as its objective, which was the prevention of illnesses by way of creating constellations favorable to health, was most attainable through such groupings. Rival strategies of prevention were doomed to failure because the elderly die from multiple problems. It would have been impossible to get a hold on the problems of aging workers if health care had been organized according to specific labor conditions. The latter would have been obsolete because of the heterogeneous exposure of old people to all sorts of jobs.

The first evaluations of experimental gerodispensaires, however, did not bring about promising results. In a study examining three factories (one in the electrical industry, one in the chemical industry, and one in refrigeration construction), "more than half of the groups of aging workers under survey were [found to be] in a general state of health that could only be described as markedly lowered," despite well-equipped, modern polyclinics or outpatient departments. The summary was not subject to doubt: "Matters are far from what is intended with care à la dispensaires." (Matthesius et al. 1974, p. 173) Other reports boiled down to a retroactive "administrative redistribution" of all illnesses. Nor was long-term preventive care restructured. For example, about 45.6 percent of the group under survey were already receiving regular treatment by a specialist.

More recent studies (Loock and Eitner 1974, 1976; Loock 1979) are particularly concerned with a central point of the entire concept of care by dispensaire: the preparation and organization of changes of jobs for older workers. It is not by accident that this policy overlaps with the simultaneous push for what is known as "scientific organization of labor" (Wissenschaftliche Arbeitsorganisation). This is a system of measures intended to improve rationalization and productivity by intensifying work, implemented in the GDR as of 1973. Indeed, dispensaires are seen as sources of valuable data (Demmler and Lohse 1976, pp. 11–124; Münzberger et al. 1976; Münzberger and Müller 1976; Fischer 1981b). Rationalization and health care are devised so as to reinforce each other.

The package of pension policies was tailored with the social goal of providing incentives for continued professional activity by pensioners. In fact, these pension policies had exactly those effects (Leenen 1977b, pp. 116–121, 130–139, 141–144, 182–188; Polle 1974, pp. 52–56). A pensioner is allowed to add the income derived from a job to the pension. In this way, working pensioners derive a de facto income more than twice that of those who no longer work.

For this reason it is not surprising that in the GDR the motives to continue working in old age apparently are exclusively economic. It is not unreasonable to believe that these incentives cause pensioners, more or less against their own volition, to keep on working. Such motives contravene and defy the alleged new quality of socialist society and its capacity to serve needs. Theoretically, what ought to happen is that the system address needs so as to weaken pensioners' economic motives and strengthen their desire for sustained work.

It is only in this context that the grimness of official political statements can be appreciated when they declare that pensioners become gradually more motivated to remain working, or prefer to resume professional life, because they increasingly like it, not because they need the money. One particular sociological study from the trade-union academy in

Bernau is referred to and made the most of over and over again. According to this study 267 workers beyond retirement age were polled about their personal motives for staying on the job. They ranked economic motives only fourth (Demmler 1974, 1976a, 1976b, 1976c). Two other studies, however, conclude that economic motives are ranked first (Loock and Eitner 1976, p. 254; Polle 1974, pp. 167–169). Insofar as the official position has now become that the declining share of pensioners in the total work force has resulted from socio-political improvements, it amounts to an implicit admission that economic motives ranked first (Fischer 1981a, p. 528).

A central problem is that companies and plants offer pensioners only those jobs that could be easily filled by any unskilled employee. Plants do not like to employ pensioners because that does not pay off economically. This reluctance, or the outright second-class treatment of older East Germans by the plant leadership, completely destroys any motivation for older workers to keep a job for reasons other than bare economic necessity. The survey by Demmler (1974, p. 36) came up with the following results, for example: "Even though there are 325 aging pensioners employed, there are only 34 workplaces provided that are suitable for people of old age. In the majority of the plants inspected, however, there are no work accommodations whatsoever that correspond specifically to the needs of employed pensioners." Plant managers decide on their assessment of the situation at hand whether, and if so how, positions suitable for aging workers are being offered at all. "Under a given set of circumstances, it may suffice to assign among all positions available those particuarly suited to accommodating aging pensioners, and, in fact, to fill these positions with aging workers." (Bressel and Marschan 1975, p. 15) This more or less symbolizes the demise of all the policy efforts under review, because this procedure justifies almost any assignment convenient to the plant leadership and its purview.

A second vital dimension of the problem is the need to balance manpower in a given plant. Plants are urged not to employ more people than are allotted to them by the respective manpower distribution plans. Rules for the wage and salary pool are also set. These constraints and regulations have prevented the plants from pursuing approaches that pay special attention to the employment of aging pensioners.

There is another angle to the problem, a structural difficulty that puts pensioners in an inescapable bind. The Party pushed for rationalization with the help of technological progress. Yet this very technical progress either eliminated positions suitable for pensioners or rendered the process of work so much more demanding that the stress made life more difficult for pensioners (Tröger 1971; Demmler and Lohse 1976, pp. 40–41). The implication is that "the creation of jobs suitable for old age has to be manufactured by putting more emphasis on working conditions in general" (Demmler 1976c, p. 426). However, improvements of working conditions are being subordinated to economic goals, so jobs suitable for pensioners become a dead issue.

## Imbalances in Occupational Health Policy in the FRG

It is standard wisdom in economics that intensifying the work process reduces unproductive time units and condenses the rate of work actually expended. This textbook truism is especially strong in times of crisis for the business cycle and of recession. Both recession and intensifying work arose during the years between 1966 and 1968 for the FRG. The social corollary was a distinct increase in unemployment. After a period of extensive saturation of the job market, this historically new confrontation with the phenomenon of joblessness, which reached far beyond small groups at the fringes of society (which it had affected in earlier times), had deep socio-political repercussions and set off unprecedented shock waves in the public mind.

The promise of the 1950s had been unlimited economic growth for the epoch to come. The content of that pledge had been that there would no longer be economic uncertainties and unemployment. Both had been deeply etched in the public consciousness ever since the collapse of the world economy and its traumatic aftermath in Germany. These promises stood naked as illusions. And it became all too obvious that they had never been anything but illusions in the first place. Even if with hindsight we tend nowadays to discount dramatic associations with that recession, because things got much worse in the period of mass unemployment in the late 1970s, there is no reason whatsoever to underestimate the deep crisis of legitimacy with which the political and economic system had been brought face to face. For it was exactly that widespread mood of crisis that lent so much thrust to reforms aligned with the postwar package of economic and social policies.

Given that the politics of maximizing jobs was a touchy issue as far as the legitimacy of the political system was concerned, it made sense to embark on a political pathway that tied the job market to future projections. The new policy was supposedly part of a much more complex and comprehensive socio-political totality. The new policy had to meet directly the demands of heterogeneous groups in the job market. This was to be done by exposing these groups to differential sets of risks in the job market. Indeed, the Law for the Creation of Jobs (Arbeitsförderungsgesetz; AFG), promulgated in 1969, took this form. Among the groups in trouble on the job market were aging employees (Kaser 1966). According to reports by the Labor Exchange Office, the share of aging employees without jobs was growing larger. The duration of unemployment was disproportionately long for them. Taking all data into account, men were more vulnerable than women, and blue-collar employees suffered more than white-collar (Schiffer 1969, p. 194).

The AFG was directed toward two key problems: that aging people out of jobs they once held found it difficult to adjust to the structure of the economy and the traditional vocations in times of recession, and that their lack of appropriate qualifications and their faltering health kept them from reentering the job market. The list of remedies encompasses the right to ask for medical and psychological help in the process of finding a new job and financial support during the process of reentry. Money allocated to support reentry is usually paid as a contribution to the wages in the new job; this is not a remedy but a way to promote additional vocational training which could help smooth the transition into the new job requirements or abet readjustment. This bundle of concrete steps worked on a tacit assumption that, as a matter of profitability, enterprises would no longer be willing to re-assign older workers to positions suitable for them internally during a time of intensification and rationalization even though they would have to pay them less and could reassign them to less demanding positions.

The policy makers assumed, furthermore, that a new strategy had been adopted by the entrepreneurs: to move older workers away from the in-plant job market and shift the "social costs" of the company to the system of social insurance. The policy makers thus reasoned that this tendency could only be counteracted by an unequivocal signal that keeping aging workers on the payroll would not necessarily have to compromise a company's profitability. At the same time, a way would have to be found to "better school" the future pensioners and the aging workers as far as additional qualifications were concerned. The underlying rationale was that the community of people participating in social insurance would voluntarily carry the burden of training programs to improve the qualifications of older employees. This would preserve the structure of employment and procure the loyalty of workers at large in the long run.

The official declarations of representatives of the employers also express interest in preserving jobs for aging employees. However, there the similarities end, and their motives could by no means be called social. They proceed from quite the opposite premise: the demand for increased exhaustion of the reservoir of labor among the elderly so as to keep constant the factor of production (called labor), decrease employment participation, maintain the rate of productivity, and keep the general amount of available manpower from shrinking (Müller-Hagen 1969, p. 31). Criticism of the marginalization of elder workers in plants was usually countered by entrepreneurs' charges that the macroeconomic perspective of the plants was not being taken into consideration. Such plants would simply neglect or underestimate the long-term burden of taxes and social costs. Thus, "those workers who had been plagued by the greatest difficulties in finding a job during the era of full employment because of diminished working capacity or other reasons were inevitably the first ones to be dismissed ( . . . in the phase of economic depression)" (Scholz 1967, p. 1984). This behavior neutralized any attempts on part of the labor-exchange branch offices to secure new positions for old people, because the agencies were challenged by "a united front of employers, workers' councils, and managers who had all consented to the dismissal of aging employees during the months of recession in order to protect the profitability of companies" ("Ein Paukenschlag aus Düsseldorf," *Sozialer Fortschritt* 18, 1969:106–107).

Even if the intention of the AFG to aid aging employees did not lead to more than negligible implementation, the experience during the recession forced all those concerned to keep their minds on health standards within the factories (Deppe 1973, pp. 44–81; Kaiser 1973, pp. 41–57). The long-term deterioration of health and the extent of harmful stresses at work became particularly manifest in the process of medical examinations for purposes of placement by the labor-exchange bureaus. The following statement by a medical examiner gives evidence of these practical experiences:

. . . all physicians in charge of social-medical examination of the efficiency of aging employees invariably reiterate how surprised and appalled they are about the unacceptability—from the vantage point of health care—of jobs and chores demanded from some of their patients, which they sometimes had to perform for years if not decades. The degree to which even so-called healthy workers—and workers are frequently declared healthy who are severely hampered in discharging their full performance—is supported by the findings of in-plant physicians. . . . one in-plant physician had written and invited plant employees who were 50 years of age and older and who had not picked up a health insurance certificate (for free treatment) in years for a free, thorough medical checkup. The diagnostic tests showed . . . that 20 percent of this group of people were so ill as to be in urgent need of treatment, the illnesses having been undetected. Among 55 percent of the patients, there were pathological changes such as—just to give an example—latent cardiac defects. Only in 25 percent of all cases were there no illnesses, if one overlooks the deficits attributable to the aging process itself. (Scholz 1967, p. 188)

The solution suggested by Scholz and by all other physicians exposed to similar experiences was to offer to all employees beyond the age of 40 a system of voluntary, systematic general and preventive examinations modified by the idiosyncrasies of each separate firm (Scholz 1967, 1972; Buckup 1974). From what unsystematic evidence we have, we may conclude that the adoption of such examinations remained the exception, when the plant physician was dedicated to prophylactic examinations and prevention (Thiess 1972, pp. 124–126; Völkner 1974). Yet the de facto rank of the plant physician within the corporate hierarchy tended to condemn these ambitions to failure, for he was the agent and confidant of the employer.

The confrontation with economic crises changed the way of thinking about procuring health care for aging employees. This shift of attitudes took place within a more general shift toward taking health policies in the workplace much more seriously. It was also based on the growing awareness of the depressing life chances of older unemployed citizens, which dawned on policy makers in the early 1970s. Such considerations usually had a rehabilitative orientation. They were connected to continued employment or reintegration of older citizens into the work process along the lines of the motives undergirding the AFG. Further, the considerable deterioration of the health not only of older unemployed persons but also of older employed citizens had become so alarming that it focused attention on another problem: the relatively high proportion of disability in the FRG in comparison with other nations (Scharf 1980, pp. 551–552). Thus, apart from unemployment of elder citizens, there was another mechanism of marginalization at hand which was brought forth by the availability of funds from the social insurance system.

In 1972, the government endorsed a reform to render the mandatory retirement regulation, unchanged since 1916, more flexible. It sought to reshape the entire procedure for separating out disabled workers from the work force. This reorganization was informed by political considerations. In the words of an advocate of this policy: "Practically, the introduction of a flexible retirement age is of great significance for the generation of workers born after 1920. That generation has suffered tremendously from unusually heavy strains, such as mass unemployment, economic exploitation under the dictatorship, war economy, warfare, economic reconstruction, and a stormy period of modernization. Many individual workers and entire subgroups of employees today can no longer cope with the speed required at work. Their efforts to carry on to the end [that is, to the mandatory retirement age] lead all too frequently to ruthless exploitation and chronic ill health. In the last 5 years alone, 6,000,000 disability pensions had to be granted." (W. Auerbach 1971, p. 292) It is a distinctive mark of the Keynesian policy of intervention in the FRG that two contradictory policies were followed, one shortly after the other: integration into the job market and elimination from the job market. The official justification was that a fixed, mandatory, retirement-age rule would not match the different degrees of abilities of aging human beings. This made desirable a regulation that would give the individual worker more latitude in deciding when to quit working.

The rules subsequently adopted supposedly relied on this line of reasoning. Accordingly, male employees could retire at the age of 63 without any loss in the rate of payment of pensions. Women had the choice to retire as early as age 60. The underlying motives leaned heavily on the prevailing schools of thought in contemporary gerontology. A typical argument was that there are differences from individual to individual in the process of aging rather than universal accumulations of ailments and physical deficits in old age (Schubert 1969). A leading distinction much favored in the discipline was that between chronological age and functional age. However, various critics took issue with this line of justification as neglecting such influences on "choice" as the general state of society and public health, the specific pressures within the respective professions, and general constraints exerted by a combination of economic and societal restrictions (Rohde, Hülsmann, and Manz, in Schiller et al. 1971, pp. 9–18, 45–52, 89–102; Tennstedt 1972a). There was more criticism to come, namely that the reform was a de facto push toward earlier elimination from the work process. Finally, critics pointed out that the quota of admissions to pension funds compensating occupational disability showed that even the new age limit for voluntary retirement came too late in life because occupational morbidity sets in earlier than that (Tennstedt 1972a).

So broad was the political appeal of this set of moves to the public that energetic support from the trade unions and comparatively little resistance on the part of managers proved instrumental for the sociopolitical implementation of this reform. The employers thought that the consequences of this reform would be beneficial to the in-plant job market. What was more important, though, was that these expectations seemed to come true; the proportion of new disability pension cases dropped considerably in the year following the introduction of flexible retirement age. This held true for both workers and white-collar employees (table 4). Hence, many employees seemed to prefer the unproblematic avenue of an early pension over the application for pension on the basis of (occupational) disability. After all, the latter would mean a tedious bureaucratic procedure and medical examinations. Before the promulgation of early retirement, workers ventured to apply for occupational disability funds only as a last resort so as to escape the pressure of work when it became intolerable.

However, this entire line of interpretation seems conceptually flawed and tends to overlook essential contributing factors. First of all, the unemployment statistics in the year immediately following the reform show conclusively a decline in the size of the group of people between ages 60 and 65, both in absolute and in relative terms. On the other hand, one must admit that the number of the "hidden unemployed," the people who "abandoned prematurely a professional career and retired, thereby managing to avert or shorten a period of unemployment" (Bäcker 1978, p. 42), increased. The change from mandatory retirement to flexible retirement thus reorganized policies addressing the distribution of jobs in society. The most notable social consequence was to ease the strain on the funds for unemployment insurance by shifting the applicants to the old-age pension funds. This was tantamount to taking the bite out of an otherwise possibly explosive sociopolitical state of crisis. Second, in table 4 one can observe the average age of retirement for total (EU) and partial (BU) disability to work. The downward movement of EU disabilities was not to last long, and the BU-type pensions were to lose much of their previous importance in the 1970s. Quite to the contrary, there was soon to come into existence another round of steady increases in the number of applicants for pensions (due to disability to perform work), which by 1979 was to reach a new all-time high. Another dramatic development was the

**Table 4**

Average age of beginning retirement because of incapacity to work (EU) and partial incapacity to work in one's profession (BU), 1970–1979.

| | Workman's Pension Fund | | | | Salaried Employees' Pension Fund | | | |
|---|---|---|---|---|---|---|---|---|
| | Men | | Women | | Men | | Women | |
| | BU | EU | BU | EU | BU | EU | BU | EU |
| 1970 | 56.2 | 57.8 | 56.6 | 60.0 | 58.4 | 59.1 | 56.9 | 56.4 |
| 1971 | 55.0 | 57.8 | 58.3 | 60.2 | 58.0 | 59.2 | 56.6 | 56.7 |
| 1972 | 54.6 | 57.9 | 58.2 | 60.4 | 58.2 | 59.4 | 56.9 | 56.9 |
| 1973 | 54.7 | 57.1 | 57.9 | 60.5 | 58.0 | 58.6 | 56.8 | 56.9 |
| 1974 | 54.7 | 56.4 | 57.4 | 60.3 | 58.8 | 58.0 | 56.1 | 56.9 |
| 1975 | 55.2 | 56.1 | 56.9 | 60.4 | 57.4 | 57.6 | 55.2 | 56.8 |
| 1976 | 56.8 | 55.3 | 55.7 | 59.4 | 57.1 | 57.3 | 54.7 | 56.4 |
| 1977 | 54.9 | 54.8 | 55.0 | 58.7 | 56.9 | 56.8 | 54.7 | 55.9 |
| 1978 | 55.2 | 54.4 | 55.4 | 58.5 | 57.5 | 56.6 | 55.7 | 56.0 |
| 1979 | 54.8 | 54.2 | 56.1 | 58.4 | 56.5 | 56.4 | 55.3 | 56.2 |
| 1970–1979 | 1.4 | 3.6 | 0.5 | 1.6 | 1.9 | 2.7 | 1.6 | 0.2 |

Source: Scharf 1980, p. 554, table 3.

lowering of the average beginning age of retirement caused by disability. Growing numbers of younger people were affected by premature disability, and the average age dropped from about 57 years for men in 1970 to about 54.5 years in 1979 (Scharf 1980, pp. 554–555). The findings of another study revealed compellingly that workers were affected not only more frequently but also earlier in life from disability than white-collar employees (Ricke et al. 1977, p. 155). The menace to health centered on the workers with the lowest social prestige: the untrained auxiliary workers (table 5). This flood of information impelled the representatives of public policy and science at the beginning of the 1970s to take the problem of rapid deterioration of health in the world of labor much more seriously than ever before, and this new consciousness was to become the platform for a much more complex package of policies to reorganize conditions at the workplace during the 1970s.

In retrospect, many of the steps taken, the recommendations formulated, and the conceptual drafts of the policy package look contradictory—especially if filtered through the lenses of the underlying rationales, which make them look either short-sighted or insufficient. Yet compared with the situation that prevailed in the 1950s, those years were a period when the connection between deterioration of health and industrial work was made a central topic on the agenda. The new consciousness was reflected in two decisive reform initiatives: on the level of legal norm-setting activities, the promulgation in 1974 of the Arbeitssicherheitsgesetz (ASiG; Act Concerning Work Safety), and, on the level of research-and-development policy, the project entitled Humanizing the Working Environment, jointly funded by the Ministry of Technology and the Ministry of Labor.

The passing of the ASiG systematized the long overdue regulation of in-plant health care performed by physicians and the technical aspects of safety in the workplace. The first evaluations of the impact of this new act focused on its compensating effects rather than on its preventive capabilities. By the end of the 1970s and the beginning of the 1980s, however, there was enough empirical data to make possible an appraisal of the 1974 act from all sorts of different angles (Konstanty 1976; Borgers and Nemitz 1978; Mertens 1978; Kühn and Hauss 1978; Borgers, in Hauss 1982, pp. 46–64; Rosenbrock 1982). According to these studies there was a rise in the number of physicians who had qualified for plant positions. However, these qualifications were acquired through a 14-day cram course. This demonstrated once again the precarious

**Table 5**
New EU admissions to retirement, 1979: occupational groups as percentages of all new admissions, by pension fund and sex.

| Male Occupational group | % | Female Occupational group | % |
|---|---|---|---|
| **Workman's pension fund** | | | |
| Temporary help, no specific indication of activity | 26.1 | Temporary help, no specific indication of activity | 31.6 |
| Full-time help, no specific indication of activity | 15.9 | Full-time help, no specific indication of activity | 20.0 |
| Occupations involving overland traffic | 8.4 | Domestic occupations | 11.7 |
| Mechanics | 5.1 | Cleaning personnel | 11.6 |
| Masons, concrete construction workers | 4.0 | Textile processing | 4.4 |
| Workers without specific occupation | 2.9 | Workers without specific occupation | 3.6 |
| Warehouse managers, transport and ware-house workers | 2.9 | Product inspectors, shippers | 1.7 |
| Service and security workers | 2.2 | Occupations involved in overland traffic | 1.2 |
| Machinists and related occupations | 2.1 | Fitters and metal workers | 1.1 |
| Construction workers | 2.1 | Warehouse managers and transport workers | 1.0 |
| All other occupations | 28.3 | All other occupations | 12.1 |
| **Salaried employees' pension fund** | | | |
| Office workers, temporary help | 29.0 | Office workers, temporary help | 40.9 |
| Commodity salesmen | 13.5 | Commodity saleswomen | 28.0 |
| Technical special workers | 5.7 | Health and related areas | 11.0 |
| Technicians | 5.5 | Accountants, data processors | 6.2 |
| Accountants, data processors | 4.8 | Social care professions | 2.0 |
| Bank and insurance personnel | 4.3 | Bank and insurance personnel | 1.8 |
| Warehouse managers, transport and ware-house workers | 4.2 | Full-time workers, no specific indication of activity | 1.6 |
| Engineers | 3.2 | Teachers | 1.5 |
| Service salesmen and related occupations | 2.2 | Technical special workers | 1.0 |
| Full-time help, no specific indication of activity | 2.0 | Journalistic occupations | .8 |
| All other occupations | 25.6 | All other occupations | 5.2 |

Source: Scharff 1980, p. 557, table 6.

and almost disreputable position of industrial medicine within the West German medical hierarchy (Andersen, in Kasiske 1976, pp. 119–120; Rutenfranz et al. 1980, p. 74). But even more salient was the increase of centers staffed by physicians specialized in industrial medicine on a trans-company level (serving employees from different firms at the same time). They were supposed to ensure regular medical attendance for small and medium-size companies. The establishment of these centers met with great resistance from the occupational associations and physicians. Ironically, these important studies and developments met a new obstacle in 1976 when the reporting requirements for each firm about in-plant medical care were abolished. Thus, today, no valid national summary statements about the extent of health care in the factories seem possible.

Abolition of the requirements to report on in-plant medical care is only one way in which owners and managers are subverting the potential and purpose of the 1974 act:

... in-plant physicians are assigned to such tasks as the selection of personnel (both in matters of employment and dismissal). . . . By this means the very purpose of the ASiG is defied and undermined: almost 80 percent of employees questioned had the opinion that personnel selection for employment in the firms that employed them was carried out on the basis of health; more than a quarter of those employees envisaged the loss of their jobs as a possible outcome of a routine in-plant medical checkup. And more than 40 percent of the members of the workers' councils are convinced that considerations for a given worker's state of health are co-determinative for dismissals. (Rosenbrock 1982, p. 175)

Such selection of personnel via medical examinations is aimed at keeping overhead costs low. It is concentrated on efficiency and effective output. Such selection contains the seeds for a division of the internal job market of a given company between an exchangeable marginal work force, which would keep fluctuation costs low (and which would consist of untrained or on-the-job-educated workers and better-qualified older workers), and a body of permanent workers on the soil of what was originally conceived as medical protection and health care in the workplace (Pohl 1976, pp. 9–23; Offe and Hinrichs 1977; Steffen and Niestrath 1977; Kühn and Hauss 1978, pp. 108–113; Sengenberger 1978; Ahner et al. 1978, pp. 140–147; Bäcker 1978, pp. 44–49).

These tendencies were joined at the end of the 1970s by the so-called Action 59. A loophole in the fabric of social insurance enables workers to benefit prematurely from the pension plan for the elderly at the age of 60 if they have been unemployed for more than a year, so it has become standard practice in certain firms to give notice of termination at the age of 59. With the consent of the workers' councils, these firms are prepared to pay the difference between the amount of social benefits for unemployment that workers were entitled to and their previous net earnings. This amount was added to the unemployment benefits so that workers could keep their standard of living until age 60. As had been the case with premature disability, the institutions of social insurance were exploited to create a "reception camp" for all those eliminated from the plant job market. Stealthily, the social insurance system has been molded into a gratuitous subsidy for rationalization (Friedmann and Weimer 1980; Dohse et al. 1982, pp. 9–61, 185–236). Even if we predict that such gratuitous subsidies for purposes of the companies' rationalization on the back of the community of the insured will be brought to an end, these later developments once again mark the de facto orientation of the companies toward the "protection" of older workers in the FRG. In such a "climate of elimination," the impact of a comprehensive health policy for aging employees has by necessity had a marginal impact.

In 1977, some physicians specializing in industrial medicine and supported by entrepreneurs spoke during a hearing conducted by the federal government to throw more light on to the problem of workers exposed to carcinogens. They advocated quite seriously the exclusive employment of workers over age 40 in those jobs, because the latency period was 26 years. "Thus, older workers would not necessarily die from cancer contracted on the job. They would, rather, die, to a great extent, because of other causes." (Konstanty 1977, p. 198; Tennstedt 1978, pp. 65–66, 74–75) This is nothing short of endorsing the abandonment of any program designed to remove carcinogens. Instead it seeks the most effective management of this occupational hazard by assigning to these dangerous jobs only such older workers who already suffer or are likely to suffer from other ailments. That carcinogens could provoke further deteriorations in the health of older workers, who often already have multiple ailments, was not even touched upon. This open perversion of any objectives proposed by industrial medicine casts the level of consciousness of this entire discipline within the FRG in its lowest form.

A larger point concerns the continued focus of medical thinking on clearly identifiable, measurable diseases rather than multicausal complexes of risk factors. Whole families of disorders will emanate from a complex and differential combination of detrimental influences at work, constitutions of the physiognomy, and everyday life styles. The following illnesses will in all likelihood develop from the sources listed:

digestive irregularities—overexposure to noise, heightened psychological strains, working night shifts, vibrations,

heart damage and circulation problems—noise (over 65 dB), increased psychological strains,

anemic heart diseases—increased psychological burdens, lack of movement, premature and pathological arteriosclerosis—heightened stress, chemically damaging substances,

gastric ulcers—heightened stress, working night shifts,

deterioration of the spinal cord and other bones, ankles, and ligaments—repeated and uniform strains and physical positions imposed by the tasks at work,

chronic bronchitis, asthma, emphysema—dust and hazardous chemical waste,

defects of liver and kidneys, polyneuropathologies—harmful chemical substances,

malignant neoplasms and tumors—harmful chemical substances (Tennstedt 1972a, p. 336; von Ferber 1972; von Ferber and von Ferber 1978; von Ferber and Slesina 1981)

Looked at from the perspective of a larger economic and societal context, the evolution of such complex spectra of illnesses is the inevitable interweaving of macroeconomic and microeconomic changes. It was Frieder Naschold who ventured to distinguish between these different levels and identify this new quality:

Problems rooted in the market economy and the economy of production, innovations in the technology of production, changes in the labor market and its requirements for qualification indicate structural changes transcending individual branches of industry . . . complex processes lead to the crystallization of a new division of labor on a worldwide scale. On the level of individual firms they bring about far-reaching changes in the structures of production and organization, thereby transforming the division of labor within a given plant. They also connote the transformation of qualification and stress-exposure on the job, of control over one's action, of latitude in making decisions, and of remuneration for workers. (Naschold 1982:22–23; *Systemanalyse des Gesundheitswesens in Oesterreich*, Vienna: Montan, 1978, vol. 1, pp. 1–73)

If we keep in mind—as projected in tables 6 and 7—the frequency of stress factors and the multiple accumulation of stress, then we can see the magnitude of the problem (Funk et al. 1974; Valentin et al. 1979; Müller-Seitz 1979; Karmaus et al. 1979; Bäcker et al. 1980, pp. 230–253; von Henninges 1981; Georg et al. 1981, 1982; Friczewski et al. 1982; Hauss 1982). It is only in this framework that the task becomes visible in its entirety: to articulate a program of health policies for the protection of those workers who will be old in the future, and for younger employees as well, that is characterized by a truly preventive orientation. Only then does it become apparent how much distance the current state of affairs has to traverse in the FRG. Although the GDR has the consciousness needed to articulate such a program, and even has carried it out to some degree, it too can succumb to narrow, short-range economic thinking.

**Table 6**
Frequency of stress factors in FRG.

| | Percentage of work-ing popula-tion affected | Number affected (millions) | Statistical range of reliability (millions) |
|---|---|---|---|
| Stress | 25.4 | 6.8 | 5.9–7.7 |
| Monotony | 22.7 | 6.1 | 5.3–6.9 |
| Noise | 22.2 | 6.0 | 5.1–6.8 |
| Shift | 21.7 | 5.8 | 5.0–6.6 |
| Heat | 17.1 | 4.6 | 3.9–5.3 |
| Outdoor work | 16.4 | 4.4 | 3.7–5.1 |
| Draft | 16.0 | 4.3 | 3.6–5.0 |
| Dust | 14.8 | 4.0 | 3.3–4.6 |
| Concentrated observation | 14.5 | 3.9 | 3.2–4.6 |
| Heavy burdens | 13.4 | 3.6 | 3.0–4.3 |
| Humidity | 10.9 | 2.9 | 2.3–3.5 |
| Night work | 8.5 | 2.3 | 1.7–2.8 |
| Constrained posture | 7.9 | 2.1 | 1.6–2.7 |
| Heavy tools | 7.6 | 2.0 | 1.5–2.5 |
| Shaking, vibration | 6.9 | 1.8 | 1.4–2.3 |
| Stench, poisonous gases | 6.5 | 1.7 | 1.3–2.2 |
| Piece work | 6.2 | 1.7 | 1.2–2.2 |
| Poor lighting | 5.5 | 1.5 | 1.0–1.9 |
| Glaring light | 4.6 | 1.2 | 0.8–1.6 |
| Cold | 3.2 | 0.9 | 0.6–1.1 |

Source: Volkholz 1977, p. 113.

**Table 7**
Distribution of stress factors according to occupational groups.

| | Number asked | Frequency of occurrence of stress factor (percentage) | | | | | | | Average frequency of stress | |
|---|---|---|---|---|---|---|---|---|---|---|
| | | None | 1 | 2 | 3 | 4 | 5 | 6 or more | All workers | Only those with 1 or more stress |
| Total employed | 1,674 | 31 | 15 | 13 | 11 | 9 | 6 | 15 | 2.52 | 3.62 |
| Independent, assistant, and freelance | 247 | 42 | 15 | 12 | 8 | 8 | 6 | 9 | 1.94 | 3.37 |
| in agriculture | 70 | 28 | 4 | 13 | 16 | 8 | 9 | 22 | 3.34 | 4.68 |
| not in agriculture | 177 | 48 | 19 | 11 | 6 | 8 | 4 | 4 | 1.38 | 2.65 |
| Workmen, total | 1,419 | 29 | 16 | 13 | 11 | 9 | 6 | 16 | 2.63 | 3.69 |
| Civil servants | 140 | 42 | 23 | 12 | 6 | 4 | 6 | 7 | 1.63 | 2.81 |
| Upper-level salaried employees | 94 | 53 | 22 | 10 | 8 | 2 | 1 | 4 | 1.14 | 2.43 |
| Other salaried employees | 442 | 46 | 18 | 15 | 8 | 4 | 4 | 5 | 1.45 | 2.70 |
| Specialists | 430 | 14 | 8 | 16 | 15 | 12 | 11 | 24 | 3.83 | 4.45 |
| Unskilled and skilled workers | 313 | 11 | 17 | 10 | 16 | 15 | 6 | 25 | 3.55 | 3.98 |
| men | 173 | 7 | 14 | 6 | 17 | 19 | 4 | 33 | 4.12 | 4.43 |
| women | 140 | 16 | 19 | 16 | 13 | 10 | 9 | 17 | 2.84 | 3.37 |

Source: Volkholz 1977, p. 113.

## Notes

1. There has been public unemployment insurance in Germany since 1928.

2. That is, all workers, employees, and self-employed persons (who, in turn, do not employ more than five people) are insured against illness, accidents, incapacity to work, and old age on the basis of a uniform but differentiated contribution fee. The uniform social insurance was an old demand of the workers' movement, particularly the trade unions.

3. Before 1933 the organs of self-government were occupied by representatives of the insured, who were the majority; after 1945 the ratio was equal between representatives of the employers and employees. Public representatives function as the third (mediating) influence in the equation.

4. "Working person" is the offical catch-all term for workers, employees, and technical intelligentsia in the GDR. This term is specifically intended to mirror the new quality of cooperation in the socialist society.

5. These agreements are stipulations among the work force (represented by the union) and the leadership of a given plant to fix beforehand the obligations toward increased productivity of labor and the plant's social commitment to the working persons.

6. Compare for example subparagraph 6, lit. c, p. 79: "Mass examinations by physicians are to be carried out regularly, focusing on those who have to work under difficult conditions detrimental to health. In accordance, the required measures are to be instituted so as to prevent illnesses."

7. This, borrowed from Pavlov, was once the frequently used term.

8. "Aging working persons" signifies in the GDR working persons five years before retirement; "old working persons" connotes old-age pensioners who have resumed a professional career or preferred to stay on the job or otherwise to continue to work (men beyond 65 and women beyond 60 years of age). "Veterans" are old pensioners no longer working.

9. "Rendering a pension progressive" means making a pension correspond to the individual's taxable income during his working life. Its amount is regularly adapted to the growing prosperity of the workers.

## References

Ahner, D., W. Thorn, and P. Huber. 1978. Zur Beschäftigungssituation älterer Arbeitsnehmer in Baden-Württemburg. Tübingen.

Ambrosius, G. 1977. Die Durchsetzung der sozialer Marktwirtschaft 1945–1949. Stuttgart: Deutsche Verlagsanstalt.

Amon. 1950. "Arbeitergesundheit und Fünfjahresplan." Deutsches Gesundheitswesen 5, no. 3:1343–1344.

Amon. 1953. "Einige sozialhygienische Aufgaben für das betriebliche Gesundheitswesen bei der weiteren Demokratisierung des Gesundheitswesens." Deutsches Gesundheitswesen 8, no. 52:1605–1607.

Auerbach, T. 1961. "Über die Bedeutung der Körperbewegung für die Dispensairebetreuung älterer Personen." Deutsches Gesundheitswesen 16, no. 1:31–39.

Auerbach, W. 1971. "Kein Verzögern der flexiblen Altersgrenze." Soziale Sicherheit 20, no. 10:291–293.

Bachmann, W., et al., eds. 1976. Handbuch für den Gesundheits- und Arbeitsschutz, vol. 1. Berlin: Verlag Tribüne.

Bäcker, G. 1978. "Beschäftigungsprobleme älterer Arbeitnehmer in der Bundesrepublik Deutschland—Ausprägungen und Ursachen." In Sozialpolitik für ältere Menschen, ed. M. Dieck and G. Nägele. Heidelberg: Quelle & Meyer.

Bäcker, G., et al., eds. 1980. Sozialpolitik—eine problemorientierte Einführung. Cologne: Bund Verlag.

Balling, H. 1952. "Alter als Arbeitsschicksal." Bundesarbeitsblatt 7:339–342.

Bericht und Materialen zur Lage Der Nation—Systemvergleich BRD-DDR 3. 1974. Bonn: Bundesverlag.

Bernays, M. 1912. "Untersuchung über die Schwankungen der Arbeitsintensität während der Arbeitswoche und während des Arbeitstages." In Untersuchungen über Auslese und Anpassung (Berufswahl und Berufsschicksal) der Arbeiter in den verschiedenen Zweigen der Grossindustrie, vol. 3, part 3. Schriften des Veriens für Sozialpolitik, vol. 135/III. Leipzig: Duncker & Humblot.

Bischoff, U. 1954. "Eine DAG-Enquete über den Altersaufbau der Angestelltenschaft in der Bundesrepublik und in Westberlin." Sozialer Fortschritt 8/9:202–204.

Bittersohl. 1955. "Über die Dispensaire-Betreuung." Arbeit und Sozialfürsorge 10, no. 19:603–604.

Böhle, F. 1977. "Humanisierung der Arbeit und Sozialpolitik." In Soziologie und Sozialpolitik, Sonderheft der KZfSS. Opladen: Westdeutscher Verlag.

Borgers, D., and B. Nemitz. 1978. "Bedingungen werksärztlicher Tätigkeit und das Arbeitssicherungsgesetz." Jahrbuch für kritische Medizin, vol. 3, pp. 116–130.

Brady, R. A. 1933. The Rationalization Movement in German Industry. Berkeley: University of California Press.

Brandt, A. 1955. "Die ärztliche Reihen untersuchung der Arbeiter—ein wesentlicher Fortschritt der gesundheitlichen Prophylaxe." Deutsches Gesundheitswesen 10:1568–1572.

Brannström, M., and S. Eitner. 1974. "Demographische Aspekte des gesellschaftlichen Arbeitsvermögens alternder und älterer Menschen." Zeitschrift für Alterforschung 29, no. 2:163–170.

Bressel, I., and P. Marschan. 1975. "Höhere Verantwortung der Betriebe gegenüber älteren Bürgern." Arbeit und Arbeitsrecht 30, no. 1:15

Broszat, M. 1973. Der Staat Hitlers. Munich: Deutscher Taschenbuchverlag.

Brück, G. 1976. Allgemeine Sozialpolitik. Cologne: Bund-Verlag.

Brüschke, G. 1974. Moderne Alternforschung. Berlin: VEB Verlag Volk und Gesundheit.

Buckup, H. 1974. "Der Stellenwart arbeitsmedizinischer Vorsorgeuntersuchungen in Abhängigkeit von ihrer Integration in den betrieblichen Gesundheitsschütz." Zentralblatt für Arbeitsmedizin 23, no. 3:67–71.

Dahnen, J. 1961. "Zur heutigen lage der älteren Angestellten." Bundesarbeitsblatt 12, no. 4:129–132.

Demmler, H. 1974. "Mehr und bessere Möglichkeiten für die Beschäftigung von Altersrentnern schaffen." Arbeit und Arbeitsrecht 29, no. 2:35–38.

Demmler, H. 1976a. "Ältere Werktätige und die Gestaltung ihrer Arbeitsbedingungen." Die Arbeit 1:53–56.

Demmler, H. 1976b. "Soziale Aspekte der Gestaltung der Arbeitsbedingungen für ältere Werktätige." Zeitschrift für Altersforschung 31, no. 2:107–114.

Demmler, H. 1976c. "Viele Bürger im Tentenalter brauchen weiterhin das Arbeitskollektiv." Arbeit und Arbeitsrecht 31, no. 14:425–428.

Demmler, H., and C. Lohse. 1976. Probleme der Arbeitsbedingungen für ältere Werktätige. Berlin: Verlag Tribüne.

Demmler, H., and G. Tietze. 1976. "Symposium zu den Arbeitsbedingungen für ältere Werktätige." Sozialistische Arbeitswissenschaft, 20, no. 2:151–154.

Deppe, H.-U. 1973. Industriearbeit und Medizin. Frankfurt: Athenaeum-Fischer.

Dohse, K. et al., eds. 1982. Ältere Arbeitnehmer zwischen Unternehmensinteressen und Sozialpolitik. Frankfurt: Campus.

Eitner, S. 1959. "Erfahrungen bei Planung und Durchführung von Dispensairemassnahmen." Deutsches Gesundheitswesen 14, no. 15:689–695.

Eitner, S. 1961. "Die Dispensairebetreuung alter Menschen." Deutsches Gesundheitswesen 16, no. 14:630–638.

Eitner, S. 1964. "Der adäquate Arbeitseinsatz des alten Arbeiters." Deutsches Gesundheitswesen 19, no. 32:1512–1517.

Eitner, S. 1968. "Zur Problematik der Beziehungen zwischen Berufsarbeit, Gesundheit und Senszenz." Arbeitsmedizin—Sozialmedizin—Arbeitshygiene 3, no. 4:89–91.

Eitner, S. 1972. "Der gegenwärtige Stand der gerohygienischen Forschungarbeit und Schlussfolgerungen für die komplexe medizinisch-soziale und kulturelle Betreuung alternder und älterer Bürger." Zentralblatt für Altersforschung 25, no. 3:209–230.

Eitner, S., A. Troeger, and E. Masius. 1971. "Schwerarbeit und Alter im mehrdimensionalen Aspekt." Zeitschrift für Altersforschung 25, no. 2:139–150.

Eitner, S., and K. Walter. 1975. "Arbeitsvermögen und Persönlichkeitsentwicklung von Menschen im höheren Lebensalter." Sozialistische Arbeitswissenschaft 19, no. 4:266–272.

Erler. 1954. "Aufgaben des Gesundheitswesens zur Verordnung über die weitere Verbesserung der Arbeits und Lebensbedingungen der Arbeiter und der Rechte der Gewerkschaften vom 10.12.1953." Deutsches Gesundheitswesen 9, no. 21:670–672.

Fiebich, K. 1952. "Verlängerung des Arbeitsalters?" Sozialer Fortschritt 1, no. 7:172–173.

Fischer, P. 1981a. "Zur Berufstätigkeit älterer und alter Menschen." Zeitschrift für Altersforschung 36, no. 6:527–532.

Fischer, P. 1981b. "Probleme und Möglichkeiten der Gruppierung von altersdispositionsgerechten Arbeitsaufgaben und Arbeitsplätzen für Werktätige im höheren Lebensalter." Wissenschaftliche Zeitschrift der Humboldt-Universität Berlin, Math. Nat. R., 30, no. 4:291–292.

Friczweski, F., et al., eds. 1982. Arbeitsbelastung und Krankheit bei Industriearbeitern. Frankfurt: Campus.

Friedmann, P., and S. Weimer. 1980. "Mit 55 zum alten Eisen? Die vorzeitige Pensionierung älterer Arbeitnehmer als betriebliche Beschäftigungsstrategie." Mitteilungen des Wirtschafts- und Sozialwissenschaftlichen Instituts des DGB 33, no. 10:563–570.

Friedrichs, H. 1964. "Der alternde Mensch im Betrieb." Arbeit und Sozialpolitik 18, no. 2:45–47.

Funk, H., et al., eds. 1974. Industriearbeit und Gesundheitsverschliess. Frankfurt: Europäische Verlagsanstalt.

Gaebel, K. 1954. "Zur Lage der älteren weiblichen Angestellten." Sozialer Fortschritt 3, no. 1:22–23.

Georg, A., R. Stuppardt, and E. Zoike. 1981. Krankheit und arbeitsbedingte Belastungen, vol. 1. Essen.

Georg, A., R. Stuppardt, and E. Zoike. Krankheit und arbeitsbedingte Belastungen, vol. 2. Essen.

Hartwich, H.-H. 1970. Sozialstaatspostulat und gesellschaftlicher Status Quo. Cologne: Westdeutscher Verlag.

Hauss, F., ed. 1982. Arbeitsmedizin und präventive Gesundheitspolitik. Frankfurt: Campus.

Holstein, E. 1953. "Der Kampf gegen die Berufskrankheiten in der DDR." Arbeit und Sozialpolitik 8, no. 15: 457–458.

Holstein, E. 1962. "Die Bedeutung des höheren Alters bei Berufskrankheiten." Ergonomics 5, no. 1:181–184.

Hoerl, J. 1978. "Strukturdaten zur gesellschaftlichen Entwicklung des Altersproblems." In Der alte Mensch in der Gesellschaft, ed. L. and H. Rosenmayr. Reinbek: Rowohlt.

Huster, E.-U. 1978. Die Politik der SPD 1945–1950. Frankfurt: Campus.

Huster, E.-U., G. Kraiker, B. Scherer, F.-K. Schlotmann, and M. Welteke. 1972. Determinanten der westdeutschen Restauration 1945–1949. Frankfurt: Suhrkamp.

Jens, H. 1973. "Werksärztliche Versorgung in der BRD." Das Argument 78, no. 5:9–51.

Kaiser, S. 1973. Betriebsärztliche Versorgung in der BRD und in anderen EG-Staaten. Gewerkschaft und Medizin, vol. 2. Berlin: VSA.

Karmaus, W., et al., eds. 1979. Stress in der Arbeitswelt. Cologne: Bund Verlag.

Kaser, P. 1966. Ältere Arbeitnehmer in der Industrie Nordrhein-Westfalens. Forschungsbericht des Landes NRW no. 1608. Cologne: Westdeutscher Verlag.

Kasiske, R., ed. 1976. Gesundheit am Arbeitsplatz. Berichte und Analysen zu Belastungen und Gefähren im Betrieb. Reinbek: Rowohlt.

Keupp, H., and M. Zaumseil. 1978. Die gesellschaftliche Organisierung psychischen Leidens. Frankfurt am Main.

Kocka, J. 1974. "Zur Problematik der deutschen Angestellten 1914–1933." In Industrielles System und politische Entwicklung in der Weimarer Republik, vol. 2, ed. H. Mommsen et al. Düsseldorf: Droste.

Konstanty, R. 1976. "Arzt im Betrieb—vom Arbeitgeber verordnet oder demokratisch bestellt?" Soziale Sicherheit 25, no. 12:358–360.

Konstanty, R. 1977. "Ältere Arbeitsnehmer an Krebsarbeitsplätze?" Soziale Sicherheit 26, no. 7:198–199.

Kracauer, S. 1929. Die Angestellten—Aus dem neuesten Deutschland. Frankfurt: Suhrkamp, 1971.

Krohn, C.-D. 1978. "Autoritärer Kapitalismus. Wirtschaftskonzeptionen im Übergang von der Weimarer Republik zum Nationalsozialismus." In Industrielle Gesellschaft und politisches System, ed. D. Stegmann et al. Berlin: Droste.

Krohn, M. 1978. "Theorien des Alterns." In Alter als Stigma, ed. J. Hohmeier and H. J. Pohl. Frankfurt: Suhrkamp.

Kühn, H., and F. Hauss. 1978. "Entwicklungstendenzen im medizinischen Arbeitsschütz—Thesen." In AS 27, Jahrbuch für kritische Medizin, vol. 3. Argument-Verlag.

Kunigk, H. 1955. "Der ältere Mensch in der Arbeit und im Betrieb." Bundesarbeitsblatt 10:378–379.

Kunter, G., and W. Müller. 1974. "Grundlagen und Problem der staatlichen Arbeitskräftepolitik." Sozialistische Arbeitswissenschaft 18, no. 1:1–9.

Lande, D. 1910. "Arbeits- und Lohnverhältnisse in der Berliner Maschinenindustrie zu Beginn des 20. Jahrhunderts." In Untersuchungen über Auslese und Anpassung (Berufswahl und Berufsschicksal) der Arbeiter in den verschiedenen Zweigen der Grossindustrie, vol. 2. Schriften des Vereins für Sozialpolitik. Leipzig.

Leenen, W.-R. 1977a. "Bevölkerungsentwicklung und Bevölkerungspolitik in beiden deutschen Staaten." Deutschland-Archiv 10, no. 6:607–625.

Leenen, W.-R. 1977b. Zur Frage der Wachstumsorientierung der marxistischleninistischen Sozialpolitik in der DDR. Berlin: Duncker & Humblot.

Lehmann, G. 1962. "Die Anpassung der Arbeit und der Arbeitsverhältnisse an den älteren Bevölkerungsteil." Ergonomics 5, no. 1:133–137.

Lengwinat, A. 1959. "Altern und Arbeit aus sozialhygienischer Sicht." Deutsches Gesundheitswesens 14, no. 47:2149–2157.

Loock, R. 1979. "Criteria of the Dispensary Attendance to Elder Workers." Zeitschrift für Altersforschung 34, no. 3:205–209.

Loock, R., and S. Eitner. 1974. "Aussagen über den Altersgang der Berufskrankheiten." Zeitschrift für Altersforschung, no. 29:175–183.

Loock, R., and S. Eitner. 1976. "Arbeitsmedizinische Dispensairebetreuung älterer Werktätiger als Mittle der Vorbereitung auf das Rentalter." Zeitschrift für Altersforschung 31, no. 3:249–260.

Lungwitz, K. 1974. "Die Bevölkerungsbewegung in der DDR und der BRD zwischen 1945 und 1970—eine komparative Untersuchung." Jahrbuch für Wirtschaftsgeschichte, I, pp. 63–95.

Maassen, P.-J. 1953. "Die Berufslage der Arbeiter und Angestellten unter Berücksichtigung der älteren Angestellten und übrigen Arbeitnehmer 1950–1952." Bundesarbeitsblatt 13:391–398.

Maier, H., and A. Tomm. 1976. "Qualitative und quantitive Aspekte der Nutzung des gesellschaftlichen Arbeitsvermögens der DDR bei der Intensivierung der Volkswirtschaft." In Arbeitskräfteresourcen und wissenschaftlich-technische Revolution. Berlin: Akademie-Verlag.

Marcusson, E. 1954. "Die Entwicklung des Gesundheitsschutzes in der DDR." Deutsches Gesundheitswesen 9, no. 31:964–968.

Marcusson, E. 1956. "Die Dispensaire-Methode in ihrer prophylaktischen und therapeutischen Aufgabenstellung bei der Bekämpfung der Koronarerkrankungen sowie der Magen- und Zwölffingerdarmgeschwüre. Deutsches Gesundheitswesen 11, no. 46:1574–1579.

Märker, K., O. Schubert, and J. Reinke. 1957. "Zur Methodik und Dokumentation der Magendispensairebetreuung." Deutsches Gesundheitswesen 12, no. 43: 1336–1340.

Mason, T. W. 1975. "Zur Entstehung des Gesetzes zur Ordnung der nationalen Arbeit vom 20. Januar 1934." In Industrielles System und politische Entwicklung in der Weimarer Republik, vol. 1, ed. H. Mommsen et al. Düsseldorf: Droste.

Mason, T. W. 1975. Arbeiterklasse und Volksgemeinschaft. Opladen: West-deutscher Verlag.

Mason, T. W. 1977. Sozialpolitik im Dritten Reich. Opladen: Westdeutscher Verlag.

Mattesius, R., et al. 1974. "Studien zum Arbeitskräfteeinsatz im Rentenalter." Zeitschrift für Alersforschung 29, no. 2:171–174.

Meis., W. 1953. "Die Vorurteile gegenüber älteren Angestellten." Sozialer Fort-schritt 2, no. 11:247–248.

Merkl, P. H. 1965. Die Entstehung der Bundesrepublik Deutschland. Stuttgart: Kohlhammer.

Mertens, A. 1978. "Zum Arbeitssicherheitsgesetz." Bundesarbeitsblatt AS, no. 1/2:3–12.

Meyer, H. 1957. "Die Einsatzmöglichkeit älterer Arbeitnehmer." In Gesund-heitsvorsorge im Betrieb. Beiheft 4 zum Zentralblatt für Arbeitsmedizin und Arbeitsschutz, ed. H. W. König.

Müller, W. 1958. "Zur regionalen Abstimmung der Arbeitskräftepläne." Arbeit und Sozialfürsorge 13, no. 9:259–264.

Müller-Hagen, D. 1969. "Auf Ältere Arbeitnehmer kann nicht verzichtet wer-den." Sozialer Fortschritt 18, no. 2:31–32.

Müller-Seitz, P. 1979. "Mehrfachbelastungen im industriellen Nachtschicht-betrieb zur arbeitswissenschaftlicher Sicht." Mitteilungen des Wirtschafts- und Sozialwissenschaftlichen Instituts des DGB 32, no. 1:45–55.

Münzberger, E., and C. Müller. 1976. "Arbeitshygienische Komplexuntersu-chungen an Arbeitsplätzen älterer Werktätiger im Fernmeldeanlagenbau." Zeit-schrift für Altersforschung 31, no. 5:429–437.

Münzberger, E., E. Springer, and C. Müller. "Untersuchungen zur masslichen Gestaltung von Arbeitsplätzen älterer Werktätiger." Zeitschrift für Altersfor-schung 31, no. 2:115–121.

Nahsen, I. 1975. "Bemerkungen zum Begriff und zur Geschichte des Arbeits-schutzes." In Arbeitssituation, Lebenslage und Konfliktpotential, ed. M. Os-terland. Frankfurt: Europäische Verlagsanstalt.

Naschold, F. 1982. "Arbeitsmedizin und präventive Gesundheitspolitik." In Arbeitsmedizin und präventive Gesundheitspolitik, ed. F. Hauss. Frankfurt: Campus.

Offe, C., and K. Hinrichs. 1977. "Sozialökonomie des Arbeitsmarktes und die Lage 'benachteiligter' Gruppen von Arbeitnehmern." In Opfer des Arbeits-marktes, ed. C. Offe. Neuwied: Luchterhand.

Ortwein, K. 1977. "Die stufenweise Liquidierung der sozialen Rechte der Lohn-abhängigen." In Die Zerstörung der Weimarer Republik, ed. R. Kühnl and G. Hardach. Cologne: Pahl-Rugenstein.

Paul, H. A. 1977. "Problembereich Voralterung." In Altern, Leistungsfähigkeit, Rehabilitation, ed. E. Jokl and E. Böhlau. Stuttgart.

Petzina, D. 1968. Autarkiepolitik im Dritten Reich—Der nationalsozialistische Vierjahresplan. Stuttgart: Deutsche Verlagsanstalt.

Pohl, H.-J. 1976. Ältere Arbeitnehmer. Ursachen und Folgen ihrer beruflichen Abwertung. Frankfurt: Campus.

Polle, H. 1974. Die Bedürfnisse der Altersrentner in der DDR und Möglichkeiten ihrer Befriedigung. Dissertation, Humboldt-Universität, Berlin.

Preller, L. 1949. Sozialpolitik in der Weimarer Republik. Stuttgart. (Kronberg: Athenaeum, 1978)

Renker, K. 1956. "Nochmals. Über die Dispensaire-Betreuung." Arbeit und Sozialfürsorge 11, no. 4:124–125.

Renker, K. 1957a. "Analyse des Krankheitsstandes und vorbeugende ärztliche Tätigkeit im Betrieb." Deutsches Gesundheitswesen 12, no. 5:158–160.

Renker, K. 1957b. "Zur Geschichte des Betriebsgesundheitsschutzes." Deutsches Gesundheitswesen 12:923–930.

Ricke, J., W. Karmaus, and R. Höh. 1977. "Frühinvalidität—Arbeiterschicksal?" In AS 17, Jahrbuch für kritische Medizin, vol. 2. Argument-Verlag.

Rodenstein, M. 1978. "Arbeiterselbsthilfe, Arbeiterselbstverwaltung und staatliche Krankenversicherungspolitik in Deutschland." In Sozialpolitik als soziale Krontrolle, Starnberger Studien 2. Frankfurt: Suhrkamp.

Rödel, U., and T. Guldimann. 1978. "Sozialpolitik als soziale Kontrolle." In Sozialpolitik als soziale Kontrolle, Starnberger Studien 2. Frankfurt: Suhrkamp.

Rosenbrock, R. 1982. Arbeitsmediziner und Sicherheitsexperten im Betrieb. Frankfurt: Campus.

Rutenfranz, J., H. Luczak, G. Lehnert, W. Rohmert, and D. Szadkowski. 1980. Denkschrift zur Lage der Arbeitmedizin und der Ergonomie in der Bundesrepublik Deutschland, verfasst im Auftrag der Senatskommsission der DFG. Boppard: Boldt.

Salzmann, W. 1958. "Gibt es noch ein Problem der älteren Arbeitnehmer?" Arbeit und Sozialpolitik 12, no. 7:225–228.

Schaefer, H., and M. Blohmke. 1978. Sozialmedizin, 2. erw. Auflage. Stuttgart: Thieme.

Scharf, B. 1980. "Frühinvalidität—Zur sozialpolitischen Bedeutung der beruflichsozialen Ausgliederung leitstungsgeminderte gesundheitlich Beeinträchtigter und Behinderter." Mitteilungen des Wirtschafts- und Sozialwissenschaftlichen Instituts des DGB 33, no. 10:550.

Schiffer, M. 1969. "Hilfen der Arbeitsämter für ältere Arbeitnehmer wenig genutzt." Arbeit und Sozialpolitik 6:194–195.

Schiller, H., et al., eds. 1971. Der alternde Mensch im Betrieb. Stuttgart: Gentner.

Schmidt, A. 1977. "Zum Entstehen der Selbstverwaltung in der Nachkriegszeit. Rückblick aus gewerkschaftlicher Sicht." In Sozialpolitik nach 1945, Geschichte und Analysen, ed. R. Bartholomaei et al. Bonn: Dietz.

Schmidt, E. 1970. Die verhinderte Neurordnung 1945–1952. Frankfurt: Europäische Verlagsanstalt.

Schmidt, U. J., et al. 1974. "Zur Situation der älteren Bürger in der DDR." Zeitschrift für Altersforschung 29, no. 2:121–144.

Schoenbaum, D. 1968. Die braune Revolution. Cologne: Kiepenheuer & Witsch.

Scholz, J. F. 1967. "Die arbeitsamtärztliche Begutachtung älterer Arbeitnehmer." In Vorzeitiger Aufbrauch im Erwerbsleben, ed. H. Valentin and R. Berensmann. ASA vol. 16. Stuttgart: Gentner.

Scholz, J. F. 1972. "Untersuchungen älterer Arbeitssuchender und Arbeitsloser." Arbeitsmedizin—Sozialmedizin—Präventivmedizin 7, no. 12:337–342.

Schubert, R., ed. 1969. Flexibilität der Ältersgrenze. Darmstadt: Steinkopff.

Schumann, F. 1911. "Die Arbeiter der Daimler-Mortorengesellschaft Stuttgart-Untertürkheim." In Untersuchungen über Auslese und Anpassung (Berufswahl und Berufsschicksal) der Arbeiter in den verschiedenen Zweigen der Grossindustrie, vol. 3, part 1. Schriften des Vereins für Sozialpolitik. Leipzig: Duncker & Humblot.

Seiler, P. 1952. "Für den älteren Angestellten." Sozialer Fortschritt l, no. 2:42–43.

Sengenberger, W. 1978. Arbeitsmarktstruktur—Ansätze zu einem Modell des segmentierten Arbeitsmarktes. Frankfurt: Campus.

Slawinski, U. 1974. "Ist Rentnerbeschäftigung erwünscht?" Arbeit und Arbeitsrecht 29, no. 2:39–41.

Steffen, M., and F.-H. Niestrath. 1977. "Die Ausgliederung älterer Arbeitnehmer aus dem Arbeitsmarkt—individuelles Versagen oder gesellschaftliche Notwendigkeit?" In Opfer des Arbeitsmarkt, ed. C. Offe. Neuwied: Luchterhand.

Stewens, H. 1952. "Die Berufsnot der älteren Angestellten." Arbeit und Sozialpolitik 6, no. 10:1–3.

Syrup, F. 1941. Staatliche Sozialpolitik, Reihe: Die Verwaltungsakademie, vol. 3, no. 65. Berlin: Spaeth & Linde.

Syrup, F. 1957. Hundert Jahre staatliche Sozialpolitik 1839–1939. Stuttgart: Kohlhammer.

Tennstedt, F. 1972a. "Berufsanforderungen und flexible Altersgrenze." Arbeitsmedizin—Sozialmedizin—Arbeitshygiene 7, no. 12:333–337.

Tennstedt, F. 1972b. Berufsunfähigkeit im Sozialrecht. Frankfurt: Europäische Verlagsanstalt.

Tennstedt, F. 1976. "Sozialgeschichte der Sozialversicherung." In Handbuch der Sozialmedizin, vol. 3. Stuttgart: Enke.

Tennstedt, F. 1977a. "Ärzte, Arbeiterbewegung und die Selbstverwaltung in der gesetzlichen Krankenversicherung." In Jahrbuch für Kritische Medizin, vol. 2. Berlin: Argument-Verlag.

Tennstedt, F. 1977b. Geschichte der Selbstverwaltung in der Krankenversicherung, Soziale Selbstverwaltung, vol. 2. Bonn: Verlag der Ortskrankenkassen.

Tennstedt, F. 1978. "Die Situation älterer Industriearbeiter—Gesundheitsverschliess im Beruf—Frühinvaliditisierung oder Prophylaxe als Ausweg?" In Sozialpolitik für ältere Menschen, ed. M. Dieck and G. Nägele. Heidelberg: Quelle & Meyer.

Tennstedt, F. 1981. Sozialgeschichte der Sozialpolitik in Deutschland. Göttingen: Vanderhoeck & Rupprecht.

Thiess, A. M. 1972. "Werksärztliche Beobachtungen bei älteren Arbeitnehmern." Aktuelle Gerontologie 2:117–127.

Thiess, A. M., and H. D. Flach. 1970. "Über die Pioniertätigkeit der ersten Werksärzte in Deutschland." Zentralblatt für Arbeitsmedizin 3:81–87.

Tietze, B. 1976. "Arbeitsorganisation und 'menschliches' Altern." In Gesundheit am Arbeitsplatz, ed. R. Kasiske. Reinbek: Rowohlt.

Tröger, A. 1969. "Indikation und Gegenindikation für den Arbeitseinsatz älterer Menschen in gerohygienischer Sicht." Deutsches Gesundheitswesen 24, no. 24:1328–1332.

Tröger, A. 1971. "Die Konfrontation des alternden Menschen mit dem Phänomen der hohen psychonervalen Beanspruchung unter den Bedingungen des Strukturwandels der Produktion." Zeitschrift für Altersforschung 25, no. 2:103–114.

Valentin, H., et al. 1979. Arbeitsmedizin. Stuttgart: Thieme.

Voight, A. 1949. "Gibt es eine Berufsnot älterer Augestellter?" Arbeit und Sozialpolitik 14:6–9.

Volkholz, V. 1977. Focal Points of Stress and the Practice of Work Safety. Bonn.

Völkner, H. 1974. "Der Anteil des Betriebsarztes an dem Bemühungen um angemessene Arbeitsplatzverhältnisse für ältere Arbeitnehmer." Aktuelle Gerontologie 4:781–785.

von Ferber, C., and L. von Ferber. 1978. Der kranke Mensch in der Gesellschaft. Reinbek: Rowohlt.

von Ferber, L. 1972. "Macht Arbeit krank?" Arbeit und Leistung 26, no. 10:257–264; 28, no. 3:57–65.

von Ferber, L., and W. Slesina. 1981. "Arbeitsbedingte Krankheiten—ihre sozialmedizinische Erfassung—Massnahmen der betrieblichen Sozialpolitik." In Sozialpolitik und Produktionsprozess, WSI-Studie zur Wirtschafts- und Sozialforschung no. 40. Cologne: Bund-Verlag.

von Henninges, H. 1981. "Arbeitsplätze mit belastenden Arbeitsanforderungen." Mitteilungen aus der Arbeitsmarkt- und Berufsforschung 14, no. 4:362–383.

von Kondratowitz, H.-J. 1977. Produktivkraft Organisation. Soziologische Aspekte von Organisation und Leitung in Wissenschaft und gesellschaftlicher Praxis der DDR. Dissertation, Technische Universität München.

von Kondratowitz, H.-J. 1978. Staatliche Sozialpolitik als Arbeitskräftelenkung— Das Problem der "Bürger im Höheren Lebensalter." DA-Sonderheft, XI. Tagung zum Stand der DDR-Forschung.

von Kondratowitz, H.-J. 1982. "Zum historischen Wandel der Altersposition in der deutschen Gesellschaft." In Altwerden in der Bundesrepublik Deutschland: Geschichte—Situationen—Perspektiven. Berlin: Deutsches Zentrum für Altersfragen.

Vortmann, H. 1977. "Beschäftigungsstruktur und Arbeitskräftpolitik in der DDR." In Arbeitsmarkt und Wirtschaftsplanung, ed. H. H. Höhmann. Frankfurt.

Vorzeitige Invalidität. 1961. Hannover: Verlag für Literatur und Zeitgeschehen.

Wagener, M. 1962. "Zur Situation der alten Menschen." Sozialer Fortschritt 11, no. 5/6:129–131; no. 8:160–163, 184–186; no. 10:232–233.

Weber, A. 1912. "Das Berufsschicksal der Industriearbeiter." Archiv für Sozialwissenschaft und Sozialpolitik 34:377–405.

Weber. 1953. "Die Bedeutung der Betriebskollektivverträge zur weiteren Verbesserung des Betriebsgesundheitswesens." Deutsches Gesundheitswesen 8, no. 13:404–406.

Wiegand, K.-H. 1967. Untersuchung über den Einsatz von Leistungsgeminderten und älteren Belagschaftsmitgliedern. Berlin: Beruth-Vertrieb.

Winkler, G. 1975. "Arbeitskräfte und Sozialpolitik." Sozialistische Arbeitswissenschaft 19, no. 7:515–521.

Winter, K. 1947. "Über die Bedeutung des Befehls 234 und Massnahmen zu seiner Durchführung." Deutsches Gesundheitswesen 2, no. 24:753–754.

Winter, K. 1977. Lehrbuch der Sozialhygiene. Berlin: VEB Verlag Volk und Gesundheit.

Winter, K., and U. Neelsen. 1956. "Analyse des Krankenstandes und vorbeugende ärztliche Tätigkeit im Betrieb." Deutsches Gesundheitswesen 11, no. 14:629–635.

Zetkin, M. 1955. Über die Beschäftigung der Rentner. Deutsches Gesundheitswesen 10, no. 33:1103–1105.

# 18

## Ideology and Psychotherapy

### Hilmar Thielen

*Psychotherapy and the care of people with mental health problems is the Achilles' heel of the generally robust and comprehensive German health-care systems. In this chapter, Hilmar Thielen focuses on psychotherapy but makes clear why mental health problems in general have been avoided in the two German states for rather different reasons. To date, psychotherapeutic services are woefully inadequate and in disarray, but Thielen foresees a period of expansion and consolidation in the near future. With consolidation, however, come ominous forms of mind control, which Thielen explores in detail. He believes that for the moment the privacy and integrity of the therapeutic relationship is better protected in the GDR than in the FRG because of professional regulations in the FRG requiring lifelong supervision (and therefore control) of psychotherapeutic work by organized and ideological schools of therapy. As a practicing therapist, Thielen concludes that only strong affirmation of therapeutic confidentiality and patients' rights can avoid this danger.*

In order to compare the impact of ideology on the psychotherapeutic process (both its availability and the psychotherapeutic process itself) in the two politically different German states, it is necessary to develop an analytical model for the definition of psychotherapy. Psychological treatment includes discussion, behavior modification, hypnosis, dream interpretation, cognitive therapy, free association, and of course many other things. The critical element of psychotherapy is its theory of mental disorders, which is particularly subject to ideology. The most important disturbances that psychotherapy deals with are psychogenic reactions, abnormal developments, and neuroses. Important forms of therapy are the various psychoanalytic procedures, client-centered therapy as introduced by Carl Rogers, and behavior therapy.

If, however, the therapeutic process is analyzed in more detail, then a more provocative definition emerges: that the deviant, inefficient, and uncomfortable cognitive models of the client are replaced by the "healthy" models of the psychotherapist (Thielen 1976, 1978). This can be shown by detailed analyses of transcribed psychotherapeutic sessions. All therapeutic methods—psychoanalysis, behavior therapy, cognitive therapy, and even client-centered therapy—result in the therapist's shaping the client's values, attitudes, and thoughts even though therapists disclaim doing so. On the one hand, the models a therapist applies are derived from the theoretical framework of the school of psychotherapy he belongs to. On the other hand, they are the more commonsensical product of his socialization and of his reference groups. Most of the therapeutic schools purport that it is their aim to help a client to his own models of behavior, but it can be shown that this is in most cases mere ideology, not scientifically supported fact. At the same time, having this ideology is of high importance for the therapist's effectiveness.

What is wrong with implanting effective models into somebody who lacks them? The problem is that through this process extraneous ideologies can influence the psychotherapeutic process. Such extraneous ideologies can be means of justifying the social or political ends of a party, a church, or a professional group.

Ideological influence can be identified at various levels of the therapeutic process: the definition of mental health and disorder, the structure of availability, the clients' and the therapists' socialization, the development of the theoretical framework in different psychotherapeutic organizations that train and license psychotherapists, and the therapeutic process itself. Applying this analysis to psychotherapy in the German Democratic Republic (GDR; East Germany) and the Federal Republic of Germany (FRG; West Germany) leads to the following conclusions:

- In both countries there are extraneous influences on psychotherapy. In the GDR the Communist Party exerts these influences in a monopolistic way, whereas in the FRG various groups exert their influence in a pluralistic and sometimes antagonistic way.

- In both countries the official societies of physicians defend their traditional power in the health system by defining in a monopolistic way what is regarded as mental illness and by demanding lifelong supervision of their members. As a consequence, only physicians are regarded as mental health professionals without supervision.

Nonmedical psychotherapists are only allowed to play a subsidiary role.

• At this moment the therapeutic process proper (the face-to-face interaction of the therapist and the client) is not influenced directly by the social groups; an indirect influence is, however, exerted by the fact that the client as well as the therapist can be assumed to have internalized the tenets of such groups.

## Ideology

The concept of ideology was introduced by Destutt De Tracy in his book *Les Elements de l'Ideologie*. His followers using the concept were then criticized by Napoleon for idealistically misrepresenting reality and ridiculed as "ideologues." Since then the concept has been negatively charged (Remmling 1967). In this sense ideology is often taken as a set of (false) ideas which serve the efforts of a particular group to achieve or maintain power. The individual can also interpret reality under ideological assumptions and thus interpret it falsely.

In contrast to this more political use of the term, Hegel, Marx, and Mannheim created a "total" concept of ideology. For Marx, the consciousness of the bourgeoisie was economically determined, ideological, and in opposition to the "true" consciousness of the proletariat. For Mannheim (1952), the consciousness of every group becomes ideological. With this generalization the concept became central to the modern debate on the relation between knowledge and interest (Habermas 1965). Today, ideology is one of the basic concepts in sociology, and it is used in the sense of the consciousness and the value system of a society or group, especially in reference to myths, cognition, and belief systems. Ideologies differ from philosophical and theoretical concepts in claiming to be definite, dogmatic truths. It is in this more general sense that the concept will be used here.

## Ideology, Society, and Psychotherapy

The cognitive theory of motivation has pointed out that people choose their cognitive models, ideologies, and world views in order to fulfill their needs. The ruling ideologies in a society are the manifestations of the objectives of the groups in power expressed in a closed cognitive framework. They influence society explicitly by laws and implicitly by norms. The justifications given for this influence are ideological in nature and differ markedly between the GDR and the FRG.

In the GDR, ideologists claim that with the victory of socialism (that is, on the basis of a dialectic materialistic epistemology and the Marxist-Leninist concept of man) the problem of value-constitution is solved because the proletariat incorporates the historical truth. In the FRG, the majority follows the international trend of thinking that the problem of normative theories remains largely unresolved (Greif 1976, p. 107). Most important for psychotherapy in socialist countries is the fact that Marxist ideology does not provide an ethical system detailed enough to govern everyday life.

The influence of ideology is shared even by the proponents of ideological systems. For instance, Thom and Weise (1973), who among others are responsible for the ideological orthodoxy of the mental health system in the GDR, state that "in fact the scientist can only liberate himself from a particular philosophy, but never from thought governed by a world view itself." Therefore this influence of ideology can be found not only in individual and social life but even in scientific model-building and experimentation. For example, Feshbach (1978, p. 452) points out the influence of economic interests on psychology: One must "recognize the influence of the economic structure and other properties of the cultural environment upon psychological research and upon psychological theory."

Returning to the main theme of this paper, I want to demonstrate in more detail the influence of ideologies upon the psychotherapeutic process in the two German countries. Put simply, there is in the GDR a state ideology which imposes itself upon the individual, reaching into his private life and incorporating him into the collective. This ideology is formulated by the party, structured throughout, and represented by various proponents and institutions of power. Historically, this ideology was developed and established by a relatively small group for purposes of political control (Remmling 1967, p. 179).

Since the party which represents the proletariat disposes the truth, one need not reflect on the basic ideological concepts. Thus, Köhler and Seidel (1974, p. 208) can in all logical consistency claim that "theoretical foundations and methods of psychotherapy in the socialist countries are determined by the socialist society, by its ideology, its norms, its requirements, and the far-reaching possibilities for the all-rounded development of man." Therefore, conflicts between the state and its citizens are in principle impossible. "Evidently, in accord with the fundamental change in the ownership of capital and of society itself, the state has lost its antagonism and gained a supportive and democratic function for the individual. In contrast to capitalistic societies, the state provides all the necessary conditions for the development of the individual in society." (Köhler and Seidel 1974, p. 208)

Such a view mandates not only a centralist planning bureaucracy but also—down to the most concrete level—its control by party functionaries. This is illustrated by a comment by the physician Hendrik (1975, p. 325) that in the administrative structures in the clinic "the leading role of the party of the working class in our socialist society and the respect for its prerogatives as laid down in the decisions of the Eighth Party Congress of the SED" must be respected. The communist ideology has concrete suggestions for the conflict between the individual and his social environment with which psychotherapy deals. "Contradictions in the development of society must be presented as part of the necessary historic process, so that the patient can contribute to his solution instead of resigning or despising society or himself." (Rösler 1977, p. 594)

The norm of a "socialist personality" which is integrated into the collective thus exerts a prejudicial influence in the GDR to deny, reinterpret, and "cure" conflicts between individuals and society. It is only a short step from this to the incarceration of dissidents in mental hospitals, as in the USSR. The state ideology is primarily an instrument of power; yet the general principles of the Marxist concept of man are hardly different from those of some Western authors. The psychotherapist Köhler establishes in an introductory text on psychotherapeutic methodology three dimensions of the Marxist concept of man which could also be accepted by non-Marxists: societal determinism; conscious, active, and creative interactions with the natural and social environment; and man as a unit of somatic and psychic processes as well as social behavior patterns. This concept demands the integration of natural science, psychology, and sociology (Köhler 1974, p. 10).

Serious differences between the political systems appear only at a more practical level where concrete decisions are taken. To trace the influence of ideology upon research and behavior is more difficult in the FRG than in the GDR. This is due on the one hand to the lack of a generally accepted and explicated ideology and on the other hand to the complex multiplicity of ideologies and their lack of reflection. In a more positive vein one could speak of a democracy of ideologies with all the advantages and disadvantages associated with a "free-market system" for ideological concepts. Thus there exist in the socio-political scene of the FRG "ideological market leaders," "ideological cartels," and "interest groups" analogous to the economic structure of society. In the marketplace of ideas, these groups are held together loosely by a vague ideology of values from the constitution and its implicit foundation in the Protestant ethic as identified by Weber's analysis of Calvinism (Kmieciak 1976).

The consequences of this state of ideology in the FRG can only be sketched: Despite freedom of thought and speech, the individual is under social and economic pressure to accept the ideology of the group upon which he is economically dependent. Thus it is common practice for an applicant to a position at a research institute to have to prove his allegiance to its academic, anthropological, and political ideology. This procedure, which protects individual groups, culminates in the FRG in the Radikalenerlass, a process of selection determined by ideology which prevents radicals from being accepted in public posts. Still, the pressure on the citizen of the FRG to accept one of the various general value systems is in no way comparable to the uniform ideological pressure in the GDR. Rather, there are the subtle pressures of group opinion and financial rewards for conformity. In the health-care system, and more particularly in psychotherapy, intense conflicts of interest are being fought with ideological arguments and financial aims.

## Psychotherapeutic Care and the Context of General Medical Care

Psychotherapy and its institutions have developed only recently, as is evidenced by the scarcity of data on psychotherapeutic care in the FRG and the GDR. Even in the large-scale study on the situation of psychiatric care initiated by the West German parliament (Bundestag) in 1975 there are no reliable data on ambulatory psychotherapeutic care (Schmidt 1978a, p. 17). The situation is even worse for the GDR, concerning which the *Psychiatrie-Enquete* (1975, p. 186) states: "Through official channels no information could be obtained on psychiatry in the GDR."

If quantitative data are to be used, a comparison of the number of persons working in psychiatric hospitals seems to be the only possibility. But since medical care and the health professions in the two German states have different emphases and involve different groups, a quantitative approach would be less revealing than the numbers it yields. Therefore the following comparison will emphasize descriptive aspects and will assume a general knowledge of the health-care systems in the two states.

Both German states started at the end of World War II from the same position. The rise of psychotherapy as a health service was inhibited by the fact that it was just beginning to become an academic discipline. Psychotherapy could attain significance only in those societies that were stable enough to be able to provide sufficient finances. It is therefore no surprise that psychotherapeutic care develops in most countries as the economy develops.

Today both German states are confronted with a similar need for psychotherapeutic care: "Epidemiological studies in industrialized societies of different political orders, including the GDR, show a rate of neurotic and functional disturbances in the population of 15–20 percent." (Hock and König 1976, p. 65)

For obvious reasons, the GDR confronts this phenomenon with ideological helplessness. "Part of the change in the development of the health-care system of the GDR includes an increasing awareness of the importance of neurotic disturbances. The increase in awareness does not necessarily, however, correspond to an epidemiological increase in neurotic disturbances. Whether neurosis has increased or—under the impact of changed social conditions—decreased is an open question to which various suggestions but no valid data have been offered. There is no doubt, however, that in the context of the changing morbidity structure a certain relative increase in neuroses has taken place. In the Prague theses on psychotherapy, this relative increase is claimed for all socialist societies." (Hock and König 1976)

The GDR would have preferred, in line with its Marxist world view, to ascribe all psychic disturbances to social determinants and thus to the capitalist social order. The fact, however, is that "a great deal of discontent among citizens about medical care derives from the insufficient medical care of functional and neurotic disturbances" (Hock and König 1976, p. 60). Thus the GDR is forced to accept neurotic disturbances as part of its own socialistic system. Neurotic disturbances are, however, given a different etiology in socialist states. "Whether in the context of the scientific technical revolution these disturbances have increased or will increase need not be discussed. It seems that these disturbances are at worst a passing effect of increasingly more complicated economic conditions. They will be corrected by new structures in the organization of work and societal life as well as the scientific control of the social psychology of work. There is no doubt, however, that as long as human society continues there will be conflicts that the individual will have to solve as part of his life endeavor." (Seidel 1976, p. 20)

In both the FRG and the GDR the problem of how the treatment of neurotic and functional disturbances is to be organized remains unresolved. It is clear, however, that the present structures are very insufficient. There are historic reasons. Important forces in both German states (Helmchen 1977; Winter, as spoken, 1976) had pleaded for practitioners to continue treating psychic disturbances and refer only the more severe cases to psychiatric hospitals. This demand has been obstructed in both Germanies by an unsatisfactory training situation, a deficiency which has ever more presented itself as a principal problem. Both the inclusion of medical psychology into the medical curriculum and an increasing range in programs of continuing education for physicians will hardly provide the highly specialized physician with a sufficiently broad knowledge of psychotherapeutic techniques and methodology. It was and is common practice for many psychotherapists to underestimate the problem and to try to acquire expertise on their own by attending courses and clinics (Hock and König 1976, p. 61). Despite the inadequate training, the physicians—in both German states equally—maintain their traditional claim on psychotherapy as a medical subspecialty (ibid., p. 67). This is expressed as follows by the West German psychiatrist Müller-Hegemann (1976, p. vii): "The phrase 'medical psychotherapy' expresses the aim of not only tying psychotherapy to medicine but integrating it into medicine." The fact that most ambulatory and institutional care is done by psychologists does not seem to vitiate this claim for medical dominance, which transcends the border between East and West. This is openly admitted. "From the very beginning clinical psychologists practiced psychotherapy. In the context of medical treatment plans, they have taken over individual and group therapy, autogenic training, special training methods, and occasionally even the organization of psychotherapeutic treatment in the hospital ward. Their activity has constantly increased, so that today in clinics and polyclinics psychotherapeutic care is also exclusively in the hands of clinical psychologists. This is the result of an inquiry we have undertaken among members of the Society for Medical Psychotherapy of the GDR during the annual congress in 1973 in Erfurt." (Rösler 1978, p. 105) But Rösler, too, supports the claim of physicians that psychotherapy and psychiatric institutions should be under them.

In view of the centralized health-care system of the GDR, this seems more reasonable there than for the mixed system in the FRG.

If we compare psychotherapeutic care in both countries, the following picture appears. In the GDR psychotherapeutic treatment is provided by about 500 specially trained clinical psychologists who work in institutions under the direction of physicians. There are also a number of more or less qualified physicians who practice psychotherapy in ambulatory clinics and state-run practices, as well as a decreasing number of private physicians (5,048 in 1950 and 1,213 in 1976) (*Mitteilungen des medizinischen Literaturdienstes* 2, 1978, p. 4). Thus only physicians can practice psychotherapy independently in the GDR. Legal provisions and the general structure of the health-care system prevent development in any other direction (Hock 1976, pp. 56–70; Helm 1974, p. 7). The situation in the FRG is less discernible. At present, various professional associations (physicians, sickness funds, psychologists) try to influence long-term legislative trends. The general historical process through which psychotherapy attained social recognition is concretely described for the case of medical psychotherapy by Winkler (1977). Only in 1965–1967 were the sickness funds prepared to pay for treatment by psychoanalytically trained physicians. Only in 1971 did the mandatory sickness funds accept psychotherapy by nonphysicians—but only under the condition that they had received accredited psychoanalytic training in a private institution recognized by the German Society for Psychotherapy, Psychosomatics, and Psychoanalysis. Even now, however, a therapist who is not a physician cannot accept patients on his own but only within a complicated procedure of delegation in which a physician or a committee of physicians is charged with evaluation and control. As a consequence, only those who can afford it have direct access to psychotherapy by a properly trained clinical psychologist. At 60–120 marks per hour, this constitutes an insurmountable barrier for most.

Nothing has been done politically to rectify this situation because persons needing therapy can hardly express and organize their common interest, and because a great many public institutions offer quasi-therapies. Educational counseling and psycho-hygienic institutions play an important role. Moreover, the majority of psychologically disturbed patients receive unspecific drug therapy from general practitioners and neurologists.

Therapeutic care in the FRG is thus in fact provided by a group of psychoanalytically trained physicians and clinical psychologists who work in clinics and counseling institutions, by a small number of independently practicing psychologists, by neurologists, and by all those practicing physicians who have an inclination for psychotherapy.

Most psychotic cases receive treatment in state hospitals, whereas roughly 600,000 neurotic disturbances receive treatment in the private practices of neurologists and psychotherapists (*Psychiatrie-Enquete* 1975, p. 91). However, only rarely are treatments registered statistically as psychotherapeutic. In the year 1973 a total of 8,453 cases for psychotherapy were accepted for insurance coverage (ibid., p. 91). A decisive problem of providing care is indicated when one compares these numbers with the needs: "Approximately every third German citizen has already gone through a mental illness in his life or is still suffering from it." (ibid., p. 7) For this demand there were 1,549 adult, adolescent, and child psychotherapists in 1973–74. Fifty percent of the medically trained psychotherapists were at the same time psychiatrists or neurologists or both. Very few were clinical psychologists. Conditions have changed little since the publication of the *Psychiatrie-Enquete*—with one exception: The number of clinical psychologists has increased greatly so that today about 2,000 psychotherapeutically trained clinical psychologists are pushing for legislation that would enable them to accept and treat patients on their own rather than under the supervision of a physician (Schmidt 1978b, p. 15). "To deprive clinical psychology of a legal mandate means inadequate and even irresponsible health care. Many patients now receive drugs even though these are neither necessary nor helpful." (Schmidt 1978b, p. 359)

These effects of professional ideology occasioned the experts to summarize the following four deficient areas in the care of the mentally ill and handicapped (*Psychiatrie-Enquete* 16, 1975, p. 4):

"The inadequate housing of mental patients and mentally handicapped in mental hospitals and the lack of alternative institutions to supplement hospital care.

"The insufficient number of institutions for children and minors, for alcoholics, drug addicts, psychologically impaired elderly, and adult mentally handicapped.

"The insufficient provisions for psychotherapeutic treatment of a great number of emotionally disturbed and emotionally sick persons.

"The insufficient coordination of the health-care services charged with the care for the mentally ill and retarded, particularly the frequently inadequate counseling services and social services."

This last conclusion refers to the heterogeneous interests that are characteristic of a pluralistic democracy: "Even in times of limited financial means, a society has to face the question of how much it is willing to sacrifice to bring relief to the mentally ill and retarded who depend on help."

The reorganization of the mental-health system faces considerable financial and ideological obstacles—among them the objections of conservative psychiatrists and psychological and psychoanalytic associations. One member of a major commission to study mental health care clearly described the difficulties which structural changes face in a pluralistic democracy because heterogeneous interests have to be counterbalanced:

The differences in power and privilege among the various professional groups offering therapy, care, and counsel turn out to be an important source of conflict. In the beginning the psychiatrists tried to keep the psychotherapists out of the Commission and to accept only those who worked in psychiatric institutions under the supervision of psychiatrists. Six months after the Commission had started to work, its chairman confessed to having forgotten the psychotherapists. Those psychotherapists who with the help of the Ministry of Health managed to enter the Commission and to present their special interests attempted to also speak for the social and counseling services. Now it was the psychiatrists' turn to object, although admittedly a great number of psychosocial cases were taken care of by counselors and social workers outside of psychiatry. The hierarchical structure of the institutions and professions of psychosocial care creates an atmosphere of competition for privileges. Practicing neurologists fight the colleagues in the clinics; the psychiatrists as a group fight the psychotherapists; the psychologists fight the physicians. Rivalries erupt when one group raises claims that infringe upon the traditional rights of another group. Examples are the attempts of clinicians to participate in ambulatory care, of psychologists to practice independently, of social workers to be accepted to social therapeutic continuing education, and of physician psychotherapists to establish their own accepted specialty. (Richter 1978a, p. 18)

Richter himself advocated the integration of the various professions into a system and speculated that "psychosocial therapy will evolve to cover the whole range of tightly and carefully coordinated cooperative measures of all those social professions that are part of the mental health care system" (Richter 1978a, p. 16). Despite many unresolved problems, including finances, competing responsibilities, and coordination, Richter's suggestions seem to combine the advantages of public and private care.

## Ideology and the Theory of Psychotherapy

The fundamental dependence of scientific theory building upon implicit or explicit ideologies is particularly evident in psychotherapy, which without self-critical reflection on its ideology-tainted values would degenerate to a mere technology (without escaping ideological limitations, of course). "Psychotherapy without anthropological (that is, ideological) implications is fictitious." (Pongratz 1973, p. 30) Thus, both theory building and its practical application are ideologically determined. In theory building, it is the ideological conception of the scholar or group of scholars that is important; in therapeutic practice it is the ideology of the individual psychotherapist.

How then does this structural dependence affect the acceptance and development of psychotherapeutic theories in both German states? In communist societies, such as the GDR, psychotherapy is always a process by which the patient is educated to become a socialist human being. To give an extreme example: In the People's Republic of China, reading and collectively interpreting key Marxist writings is a serious psychotherapeutic procedure. In the GDR, too, this approach, called bibliotherapy, has been propagated, although as a therapy for patients more generally. "Bibliotherapy in its theoretical endeavor starts from a conception of social determinants for health and sickness. The link between a socialist culture and health policy expresses itself primarily in forms of care which stress the pedagogical, the ideological, and the aesthetic influence upon the patient." (Fabian 1975, p. 1607) The primary concern is to have the patient accept Marxist ideology. All other aspects, theoretical and therapeutic, are secondary. It is not surprising, therefore, that in the dispute with Western schools of therapeutic thinking—the primary source for therapeutic techniques in the GDR—practical and technical procedures of a more methodological kind are strictly separated from their theoretical context. Western authors, too, sometimes separate theory and practice, either for scholarly reasons or because of an inadequate and unsystematic integration of method and theory in particular schools of therapeutic thinking (London 1973; Schwitzgebel and Schwitzgebel 1974). In the GDR, however, the acceptance of psychotherapeutic theory is a question of political ideology. Psychotherapy, then, is used "primarily as a methodological discipline" (Seidel 1976, p. 25), which is then placed in the context of an ideological concept of man.

The preeminence of ideology in the GDR has a high price. The necessity of psychotherapeutic care in a 30-year-old socialist system and the need to accept Western psychotherapeutic theories strain the communist ideology. At the same time, psychotherapeutic theory has to be refuted on ideological grounds while therapeutic techniques have to be accepted. Less problematic are the generally vague attempts to propose a Marxist-Leninist theory of personality (Hiebsch 1973; Mysliwtschenko 1974; Platonow 1974; Schorochowa 1976). This concept of man is supposed to provide the basis for research and therapy—a claim that severely limits psychotherapeutic research. The relationship between dialectic materialistic philosophy and the respective academic discipline is supposed to correspond—according to this ideological assumption—to the relationship between the general and the specific (Eckhardt 1973, p. 33). Supposedly, the academic discipline concerned derives its fundamental theoretical assumptions from Marxist philosophy (Klaus 1958, p. 23) and in turn contributes its empirical results to support and develop Marxist theory.

The circularity of this argument need not concern us in detail. Important, however, is that every theory adopted in the GDR is evaluated and has to comply with the "Marxist w-criterion," i.e., the Marxist world view (Herrmann 1976, p. 144). "Psychological facts which comply with the w-criterion and which the Marxist may thus accept then have to be cleared for further acceptability on the basis of the e-criterion (empirical proof). Psychological facts which do not comply with the w-criterion are either not dealt with, refuted, or transformed into Marxist vocabulary" (ibid., p. 144).

It is not surprising, therefore, that East German research has excelled primarily in those areas in which the w-criterion was easy to satisfy, such as the areas of general psychology that deal with information processes (Klix 1971). Psychotherapeutic theories of Western origin, however, always had difficulties complying with the Marxist concept of personality. The East German authors, therefore, adopt only the well-proven (that is, internationally successful) techniques that can easily be separated from the theories from which they were derived. This is particualarly true for behavior therapy, with its special emphasis upon Soviet physiology and psychology of learning, and for speech therapy with its emphasis on speech techniques without any humanism.

Psychoanalysis, however, is still completely rejected as biologistic and individualistic, despite the various Marxist attempts in the West to integrate psychoanalysis into Marxism (Köhler 1974, pp. 20 ff.). For

these reasons, psychotherapeutic practice in the GDR is methodologically pragmatic and even eclectic but is kept under control by regularly
presented Marxist interpretations.

For behavioral therapy, Franz and Thom (1978, p. 129) have proposed
that: "For the practicing clinical psychologist, philosophical reflections
on man in general and certain theories of neurosis in particular seem
to have little significance. Primarily he is concerned with concrete psychotherapeutic procedures and methods to deal with neurotic disturbances. Although he can choose among a wide range of approaches, he
has to consider what the theoretical implications of the specific techniques are." The methodological naiveté expressed in this quote, which
in Western countries has long been replaced by a differentiated view
of the relationship between theory and method and the consequences
of psychotherapeutic actions, need not concern us here (Strupp and
Hadley 1977). The methodological faith to which the quote refers is
explained by the political importance of psychotherapy as an institution
that regulates and solves social conflicts. In reference to the goals of
psychotherapy, Franz and Thom (1978, p. 132) make this quite clear:
"Under the conditions of socialism, the therapy of neurosis and other
psychic defects must not only deal with symptoms, but more important,
must stimulate as much as possible those forces of active and autonomous social behavior which both the individual and the society need.
This presupposes even in the individual therapist-patient relationship
a clear perception of the claims society has upon the individual." It is
not surprising that under these conditions there have been very few
significant developments in psychotherapeutic research. The few exceptions are restricted to therapeutic technology (Helm 1974). Original
theoretical contributions to psychotherapy have not been made.

In the FRG the situation is fundamentally different. The pluralistic
structure of society is reflected in a seemingly unlimited range of theoretical options in the field. All known psychotherapeutic positions can
be and are presented and researched. This freedom, however, has its
limits as well as its specific disadvantages. These limits of research and
theory building in the FRG are primarily economic and thus subject
to the influence of interest groups. The controversy surrounding the
question of who may legitimately have psychotherapeutic services
reimbursed by the sickness funds, for example, has consequences for
the theoretical orientation of young therapists and their professional
training. The psychoanalytic schools, for instance, retain their high
status with medical psychotherapists in part because their procedures

are oriented along medical lines of training and medical practice and thus are reimbursed by the sickness funds. Behavioral therapy and speech therapy take an intermediate position. The training program is provided primarily by private institutions, who promise their members that they too will be reimbursed by the sickness funds in the near future. All this means that the student of psychotherapy will prefer to specialize in an area and with a method that will later provide him economic safety.

These preferences, of course, have far-reaching consequences for the financial power and group politics of the respective schools of therapy. One may call this theory-transcending factor the economic implementation of a paradigm. It emphasizes economic motives as one technique in paradigms to establish dominance. These strategies are, however, not limited to the FRG. That advocates of a theory defend their concepts not only intellectually but also institutionally, politically, and of course financially is well known in pluralistic societies.

Although psychotherapeutic theory building is more independent of political and ideological influences in the FRG than in the GDR, for that very reason it is less concerned with how people can most effectively live together. While heuristically valuable, the competition among various schools of therapy is not apt to produce social discussion on the nature of coexistence. But the uncritical adherence to scientific and methodological criteria has changed fundamentally within the last few years. Indeed, the program of ideology has been raised with particular vehemence for psychotherapeutic research (Iseler and Perrez 1976). In more recent works on the impact of ideology, important cultural and value determinants of the dominant forms of therapy have been laid open, particularly the function in postindustrial societies of attitudes and values, which are generally the latent determinants of therapeutic goals (Bell 1973; North 1972).

The more recent publications seem to indicate that the traditional ideological structure, with its dominance of achievement orientation and its mixture of conformity and individual freedom (Kmieciak 1976), seems to be subject to a process of differentation and attrition. How this process will find its political expression is yet to be seen.

## Psychotherapeutic Practice and the Analysis of Microprocesses

As already indicated, psychotherapeutic practices in the two German states are very similar. It seems as if problems of interpersonal interaction, the focus of all psychotherapeutic endeavors, are more important than ideological context. Before looking at special methods in general medical and psychiatric care of the mentally ill (including numerous medication "side treatments"), it is above all necessary to examine the common-sense method of rationally reorienting the patient and attempting to alter deviant cognitions, a procedure that was already described at the turn of the century. Dubois, Rosenbach, and Neutra made important contributions to systematizing this approach (Pongratz 1973, pp. 68 ff.). This corresponds to the rather untheoretical, rational method of psychotherapy practiced in the Soviet Union (Lauterbach 1978). This procedure is supplemented in medical psychotherapy by more suggestive forms of therapy, such as hypnosis and autogenetic training.

Procedures used by psychologically trained psychotherapists are more diverse. Of these, behavioral therapy and speech therapy dominate in the GDR. In the FRG, the analytic schools of therapy—psychoanalysis and neopsychoanalysis in particular—also play an important and institutionally powerful role. Of the wide range of therapeutic approaches available, most are variations of the main schools already mentioned. However, there is an increasing willingness to attempt to integrate these various approaches (Bastine 1975; Thielen 1978).

Today the privacy of the therapeutic situation is guaranteed with all the procedures mentioned and in both the FRG and the GDR. The therapist may express what he considers appropriate in line with his long-range psychotherapeutic conception and his actual psychotherapeutic hypothesis, including his own ideological predispositions. There are, however, two tendencies opposed to this which raise the concerns expressed at the beginning of the chapter: an increasing tendency toward group psychotherapy—particularly in the GDR (Hock 1976)—and an increasing tendency toward programs in which the psychotherapist is submitted to permanent supervision. This indicates an increasing degree of social control over the therapist-patient dialogue. This tendency may also reach into training and research. Societal insight into the psychotherapeutic situation becomes social control only if the psychotherapeutic interaction can be critically analyzed for its ideological components. However, the critique of ideology itself can serve as an ideological weapon.

Recent developments, however, in the psychology of communications have produced analytic instruments that permit using interview records to precisely describe the implicit ideological goals held by both the therapist and the client. This of course does not refer to the cognitively reflected and manifestly argued values but to the almost unconsciously presented cognitive value structure.

Before considering the implications of such an analysis of the therapeutic dialogue we shall have to look at the method involved. The theoretical point of departure was the turning away from a psychoanalytic model which was onesidely directed toward unconscious processes, and from the reductionistic behavioral model in which man is reduced to a stimulus-response apparatus, and toward a theory of the epistemological subject (Groeben and Scheele 1977; Thielen and Budde 1978). In the context of this theory, models have been developed that relate emotional and cognitive patterns to behavioral patterns (that is, speech patterns) and apply methods that decipher microprocesses in human communication (Vukovich 1977) so that the latent cognitive and emotional structure of speech patterns can be discovered (Budde and Thielen 1978; Thielen and Budde 1978).

In order to demonstrate my thesis about the influence of ideology on psychotherapy, I will analyze the transcription of a therapeutic session to point out how the therapist changes statements of the client into statements more in line with his own Weltanschauung. In intensive therapy, the client has no chance to escape this modeling process. The following part of the transcription shows that even Carl Rogers himself intervenes at the very moment when the client starts to develop his own model, despite the fact that Rogers believes that it is his goal to help the client to develop his own way of living—the main goal of Rogerian therapy. I do not purport to make the trivial statement that therapists can make mistakes. Quite to the contrary; Rogers is a psychotherapeutic genius in this session too. What I want to point out is the fact that the psychotherapist cannot help but model the client.

Patient: I have a practical problem. Supposing I have the choice between two healthy situations. Shall I first tackle the easy one then work to the more difficult or shall I first deal with the more difficult? I've been wondering whether I should risk frustration but have the chance for a more satisfying solution or whether I should tackle the safer, but less satisfying problem.

Therapist: I think it is difficult to say. Obviously, you have reflected on how many frustrations you can bear.

Patient: Yes.

Therapist: And your goal is I believe to be able to accept both successes and failures without being bothered too much by either.

With this last remark the therapist offers a certain model of equanimity not strictly derived from the patient's statements and revealing the therapist's own view.

Patient: I think all depends on the mood you are in. Sometimes you feel like gambling all-or-nothing. Sometimes one says for the moment a failure in this particular case will do me more harm. A modest success will tend to help me. Therefore I choose the easier task. I think I would choose the easier. Probably that is all much more flexible. . . .

Therapist: I don't believe there is a rigid rule.

The therapist supports the model the patient expressed in his last phrase.

Patient: Perhaps a grand success can speed up getting better by a month or so. I feel that an overwhelming success even if it demands a lot of courage and determination will improve things.

This is an important point. The patient proposes a model that is in conflict with the aim of therapy: He must have a grand success to be cured. For the therapist the moment has arrived to bring the patient back to the proper path with a subtle remark: One must not become dependent upon superficial successes or failures. One must accept both with equanimity and be self-reliant. Let us observe how Rogers directs the patient to the desired ideological position without direct admonition.

Therapist: That is possible. Do you feel that you can only be cured if you have success?

The technique used by the therapist here and contained in the word *only* is called provocative verbalization. Its function is to issue a friendly threat coupled with the request of the patient to clarify the misunderstanding and reaffirm that the patient really meant to say something different than at first glance he really said. In an established therapeutic relationship the patient will react promptly to this implicit reprimand.

Patient: That depends on what you call success. If you call success the total control in every situation—no. But if you call success the ability to bear the ups and downs—then yes.

If one considers that the patient—a painter—had always dreamt of success, had in a previous sequence talked about a friend who had become a famous writer, and now talks about his own possible success, then this passage demonstrates with what little verbal effort the therapist can provide his patient with the "proper" orientation, without the therapist even having to realize what he is doing. It is the unreflected attitude of the therapist in particular that is transmitted in this subtle fashion. Let us see finally how Rogers "rewards" his patient for his return to the proper "attitude."

Therapist: That's right. I wasn't quite sure how you had meant it. Yes, I think that is the proper way.

It is tempting to analyze and compare psychotherapeutic protocols from the FRG and the GDR in order to discover their latent ideological frames of reference. Unfortunately there are no protocols from the GDR, and requests are strictly refused. Since the analytic method here referred to is generally accessible, one may speculate on the understanding it would produce of the hidden concepts of man in each of the German states. If one could demonstrate the impact of the ideological context on therapeutic dialogue, the practice of therapy itself could be revised and improved. An increasingly subtle and critical evaluation of the ideology of both therapist and client would become not only possible but inevitable. There are good therapeutic reasons for subjecting therapeutic dialogue to methodological controls. Increasingly, however, this leads to the subjugation of the individual therapist to the ideology of the group or collective supervising him. The critical reflection of the goals of therapy is therefore a crucial undertaking.

Information provided by East German psychotherapists suggests that—given the methods for the analysis of microprocesses—the GDR can and will implement its ideology down to every single therapeutic dialogue. No therapist will be able to treat "anti-ideologically." In the FRG there is a tendency of various groups to force their members to conform to their respective interests and ideologies. However, it is hoped that the realization of this process may lead to countermeasures. In this sense one has to agree with Mailloux, who during the 1978 Congress for Applied Psychology in Munich demanded that clinical psychology turn to the question of ethics both in research and in therapy. Particularly in the tension between the authoritarian power of the therapist and the postulated freedom of choice of the patient, we must reflect carefully on the conception of therapeutic goals. All said, the question arises whether—without disposing of research and ideological critique—psychotherapy cannot indeed learn from medicine that the privacy of the therapist-patient relationship has to be guaranteed or even extended to protect the individual from being manipulated. To claim the necessity of both empirical research and ideological critique is no valid counterargument.

## Summary

Ideological Influence on the Availability of Psychotherapy

In both the GDR and the FRG there is a marked discrepancy between the provision of psychotherapy and the demand for psychotherapy. Traditionally the field of psychotherapy is heavily influenced by physicians and their professional societies acting as pressure groups. It is apparent that their ideological positions toward mental health and other societal topics are cognitive manifestations of their economic interests. In consequence of this ideologically impregnated view of mental health, the qualitative and quantitative development in this field is hampered or even blocked.

Despite the power of physicians to define the field and its terms, in practice psychotherapy is done by psychologists or social workers, but under the formal control of physicians. As one might expect, the cooperation between psychologists and physicians usually does not work well. "After more than 20 years of experience in the field of psychotherapy in hospitals, there remains only the pessimistic statement that physicians and psychologists are usually rivals and do not cooperate." (Ploeger 1982, p. 69)

In both countries the relationship between professional societies of physicians and government works well, and there is no indication of any important ideological conflict. For this reason, and in order to avoid the costs of a sufficient supply of psychotherapy, the governments do not touch the physicians' monopoly which puts them in charge of psychotherapy. Nevertheless, there are tendencies which indicate that in the GDR the position of psychologists and other nonmedical professions is strengthening. This move is due not only to an improvement in the availability of provision with psychotherapy but also to the attempt to circumvent the well-protected privacy of medical treatment. The promotion of group therapy can be assumed to be motivated by the same reasons.

In the FRG there are similar developments. This can be seen in the growing importance of self-help groups for the mutual support of laypeople. At the same time, psychologists keep trying to get their share of the influence and money in the field of mental health. Even with imposed concepts of prevention, various groups are trying to get influence in this field (Herder-Dorneich and Schuller 1982; Light 1982).

The Specific Influence of Ideology on Psychotherapy

I have pointed out that psychotherapy is a modeling process. The deviant cognitive models which the client has are exchanged for the more "healthy" models the therapist provides. It is assumed that in a well-functioning therapy the client experiences a greater amount of satisfaction by following these models.

Modeling that is due to the theoretical framework of the therapist's school constitutes only a small part of the models in therapy. The greater part is due to common sense applied with little conscious reflection. These common-sense models are heavily impregnated with the social ideologies that are behind the therapist's socialization and those ideologies that are experienced in everyday life. Therefore the therapist's ideological background is implanted into the client by the subtle means of psychotherapy.

It is apparent that any group interested in exerting ideological control will come across this by-product of psychotherapy, which can work very effectively for its goals. In the GDR as well as in the FRG this adulteration of psychotherapy can be prevented only if the privacy of the relationship between therapist and client is protected.

Contrary to the usual precognitions about socialist countries, the above-mentioned privacy is less threatened in the GDR than in the FRG. One reason for the comparatively positive state of psychotherapy in the GDR is that the framework for the control of everyday life provided by the communist ideology is not tight enough to interfere with the privacy of psychotherapy. Furthermore, the influence of therapeutic professional societies on the behavior of their members is not very strong.

On the other hand, in the FRG there is a tightly woven net of professional societies and official institutions which control not only the training of health professionals but their ongoing practice as well. The individual therapist is forced to comply with the ideology of his professional reference group because only with the aid of his professional society will he be able to fulfill his economic needs satisfactorily.

*The Ominous Future of Psychotherapy*

Extrapolating from the developments that can be observed in both German countries, one may ask whether psychotherapy might degenerate into a method of mind control. In the FRG various social forces, and in the GDR the ruling Communist Party, try to gain control of the therapeutic process, with the ulterior motive of controlling people by means of psychotherapy. The tendency for more mind control in the GDR seems unavoidable.

Under what conditions is it possible to avoid this development in Western countries? The deterioration of psychotherapy into a method of control can be prevented only if the privacy of the relationship between client and therapist is protected. This privacy implies the freedom of the well-trained therapist to develop his own therapeutic models and to be independent of the professional society he belongs to or any other ideological group. For the client, this privacy is possible only if he has the right to choose a therapist he trusts. The psychotherapeutic process in principle is to be protected against any improper visibility; what is spoken in psychotherapy belongs to the intimate relationship of psychotherapy. If these proposals are not taken seriously, psychotherapy might harm mankind more than it helps.

## References

Bastine, R. 1975. "Auf dem Weg zu einer integrierten Psychotherapie." Psychologie Heute July:53–58.

Bell, D. 1973. The Coming of Post-Industrial Society: A Venture in Social Forecasting. New York: Basic Books.

Budde, H.-G., and H. Thielen. 1978. "MESO—Multimodale Erschliessung subjektiver Orientierungen." Handout for the presentation "Psychische Verabeitung erworbener körperlicher Beeintrachtigungen." 19th International Convention for Applied Psychology, Munich.

Eckhardt, G. 1973. "Zur wissenschaftstheoretischen Diskussion in der marxistisch-leninistischen Psychologie und zur Auseinandersetzung mit der kritisch-emanzipatorischen psychologie." In Aufgaben, Perspektiven und methodologische Grundlagen der marxistischen Psychologie in der DDR, ed. H. Hiebsch and L. Sprung. Berlin.

Fabian, D. 1975. "Zu theoretischen Fragen der Bibliotherapie im sozialistischen Gesundheits- und Sozialwesen." Deutsches Gesundheitswesen 30:1606–1611.

Feshbach, S. 1978. "The environment of personality." American Psychologist May:447–455.

Franz, B., and A. Thom. 1978. "Kritische anmerkungen zur Theorie und Praxis der Verhaltenstherapie aus der Sicht der marxistisch-leninistischen Philosophie." Psychiatrie, Neurologie, Medizinische Psychologie 30:129–137.

Greif, S. 1976. "Ansätze zur normativen Grundlegung der Psychologie." In Relevanz in der Psychologie, ed. A. Iseler and M. Perrez. Munich: Reinhardt.

Groeben, N., and B. Scheele. 1977. Argumente für eine Psychologie des reflexiven Subjekts. Darmstadt: Steinkopf.

Habermas, J. 1965. "Erkenntnis und Interesse." Merkur 213:1139–1153.

Helm, J., ed. 1974. Psychotherapieforschung. Berlin: VEB.

Helmchen, H. 1977. "Der sachverstandigenbericht zur Lage der Psychiatrie." DBA 3:142–145.

Hendrik, A. 1975. "Probleme und Erfahrungen in der staatlichen Leitungstatigkeit klinischer Einrichtungen des sozialistischen Gesundheitswesens in der DDR." Deutsches Gesundheitswesen 30:324–327.

Herder-Dorneich, P., and A. Schuller, eds. 1982. Vorsorge zwischen Versorgungsstaat und Selbstbestimmung. Stuttgart: Kohlhammer.

Herrmann, T. 1976. Die Psychologie und ihre Forschungsprogramme. Göttingen: Hogrefe.

Hiebsch, H. 1973. "Perspektiven und Aufgaben der Psychologie in der entwickelten sozialistischen Gesellschaft." In Aufgaben, Perspektiven und methodologischen Grundlagen der marxistischen Psychologie in der DDR, ed. H. Hiebsch and L. Sprung. Berlin.

Hock, K., ed. 1976. Gruppenpsychotherapie. Berlin: VEB.

Hock, K., and W. König. 1976. "Aufgaben und Bedeutung der Psychotherapie in der modernen Medizin." In Psychotherapie und Gesellschaft, ed. K. Hock and K. Seidel. Berlin: VEB.

Iseler, A., and M. Perrez, eds. 1976. Relevanz in der Psychologie. Munich: Reinhardt.

Klaus, G. 1958. Philosophie und Einzelwissenschaft. Berlin: VEB.

Klix, F. 1971. Information und Verhalten. Berlin: VEB.

Kmieciak, P. 1976. "Wertstrukturen und Wertwandlungen in der Bundesrepublik: Bericht über ein laufendes Forschungsprojekt." In Gesellschaftspolitische Zielsysteme, ed. W. Zapf. Frankfurt: Campus.

Köhler, C. 1974. "Grundsatzprobleme der Psychotherapieforschung." In Psychotherapieforschung, ed. J. Helm. Berlin: VEB.

Köhler, C., and K. Seidel. 1974. "Beziehungen zwischen Menschenbild und Psychotherapie." Psychother. Psychosom. 24:203–211.

Lauterbach, W. 1978. Psychotherapie in der Sowjetunion. Munich: Urban und Schwarenberg.

Light, D. 1982. "Laienmedizin und professionale Medizine: Eine internationale Übersicht." In Vorsorge zwischen Versorgungsstaat und Selbstbestimmung, ed. P. Herder-Dorneich and A. Schuller. Stuttgart: Kohlhammer.

London, P. 1973. "Das Ende der Ideologie in der Verhaltensmodifikation." Mitteilungen der Gesellschaft für Förderung der Verhaltenstherapie 5:73–86.

Mannheim, K. 1952. Ideologie und Utopie. Frankfurt.

Müller-Hegemann, D. 1976. Medizinische Psychotherapie. Stuttgart: Fischer.

Mysliwtschenko, A. G. 1974. "Die Personlichkeit in der entwickelten sozialistischen Gesellschaft." In II. Konferenz der Pädagogen sozialistischer Länder. *Arbeitsprotokoll I.* Berlin: Akademie der pädagogischen Wissenschaften der DDR.

North, M. 1972. The Secular Priests: Psychotherapists in Contemporary Society. London: Allen & Unwin.

Platonow, K. K. 1974. "Das Personlichkeitsprinzip in der Psychologie." In Methodologische und theoretische Probleme der Psychologie, ed. E. W. Schorochowa. Berlin.

Ploeger, A. 1982. "Ärzte und Psychologen in der stationaren Psychotherapie: Kompetition oder Kooperation?" Psychother. Med. Psychol. 32:69–71.

Pongratz, L. J. 1973. Lehrbuch der klinischen Psychologie. Göttingen: Hogrefe.

Psychiatrie-Enquete: Berichte über die Lage der Psychiatrie in der Bundesrepublik Deutschland. Zur psychiatrischen und psychotherapeutisch-psychosomatischen versorgung der Bevölkerung: Unterrrichtung durch die Bundesregierung. 1975. Publication 7/4200, Bonn.

Remmling, G. W. 1967. Road to Suspicion. New York: Appleton-Century-Crofts.

Richter, H.-E. 1976. "Die Psychosoziale Arbeitsgemeinschaft Giessen/Wetzlar." Sozialpsychiartische Informationen 35/36:100–113.

Richter, H.-E. 1978a. "Psychoanalyse und psychosoziale Therapie." Psychosozial. 1:7–29.

Richter, H.-E. 1978b. Engagierte Analysen: Über den Umgang des Menschen mit dem Menschen. Reinbek: Rowohlt.

Rogers, C. R. 1972. Die nicht-direktive Beratung. Munich: Kindler.

Rösler, H.-D. 1977. "Zur Begriffsbestimmung der Psychotherapie unter methodischem Gesichtspunkt." Psychiat. Neurol. Med. Psychol. 29:593–597.

Rösler, H.-D. 1978. "Klinische Psychologie im sozialistischen Gesundheitswesen." In Psychologie in der DDR: Entwicklung—Aufgaben—Perspektiven. Berlin: VEB.

Schmidt, L. R. 1978a. "Klinische Psychologie." In Lehrbuch der klinischen Psychologie, ed. L. R. Schmidt. Stuttgart: Enke.

Schmidt, L. R. 1978b. "Überblick zur Psychotherapie." In Lehrbuch der klinischen Psychologie, ed. L. R. Schmidt. Stuttgart: Enke.

Schorochowa, E. W. 1976. "Der psychologische Aspekt des Persönlichkeitsproblems." In Zur Psychologie der Persönlichkeit, ed. E. W. Schorochowa. Berlin.

Schwitzgebel, R. L., and R. K. Schwitzgebel. 1974. Psychotechnology. New York: Holt, Rinehart & Winston.

Seidel, K. 1976. "Psychotherapie und Gesellschaft aus medizinischer Sicht." In Psychotherapie und Gesellschaft, ed. K. Hock and K. Seidel. Berlin: VEB.

Strupp, H. H., and S. W. Hadley. 1977. "A Tripartite Model of Mental Health and Therapeutic Outcome." American Psychologist, March:187–197.

Thielen, H. 1976. Modellierung und Metaphorik in der Psychotherapie. Dissertation, University of Regensburg.

Thielen, H. 1978. "Der Therapeut in der Psychotherapie." MMG 3:71–78.

Thielen, H., and H.-G. Budde. 1978. "Ein Beitrag zur Erfassung der subjektiven Bedeutung einer gravierenden Veränderung der individuellen Lebenssituation." Psychologische Beitrage 20:115–128.

Thom, A., and K. Weise. 1973. Medizin und Weltanschauung. Schwerte: Freistuhler.

Vukovich, A. 1977. "Der rhetorische Forschungsansatz in der Kommunikationspsychologie." In Bericht über den 30. Kongress der Deutschen Gesellschaft für Psychologie in Regensburg 1976, vol. 1. Göttingen: Hogrefe.

Winkler, W. T. 1977. "50 Jahre AAGP—ein Rückblick." Psychother. Med. Psychol. 27.

Winter, W. 1976. "Psychotherapie aus soziologischer Sicht." In Psychotherapie und Gesellschaft, ed. K. Hock and K. Seidel. Berlin: VEB.

# Conclusion

## Values and Health in the Two Germanies

Donald W. Light

The authors of this volume have addressed six common issues: the primacy of the individual versus that of the state, concepts of illness and health care, questions of organizational integration, dimensions of social class, the distrust of democratic power, and the struggle between professional and state power. These issues reflect the models of health care presented in the introduction. Each model involves a basic concept of the individual's relationship to society and to the state. Organization is a major dimension of each model, and the degree of integration varies with how much it is valued. Social class differences are implicit, because the mutual-aid and state models value equal care while the professional model does not at the systemic level we are addressing. Distrust of democratic power is a basic tension between the mutual-aid model and those models in which health care is dominated by either the profession or the state. Likewise, the struggle between the latter is implicit in the models and plays a central role in the history of health care.

### The Individual versus the State

A primary interest among those comparing a communist with a democratic society is the relation between the individual and the state. In this study we have learned that individual rights have been emphasized above all other rights in the FRG. The state is regarded as a subsystem to be kept sufficiently distant from the rest of society to prevent the tragedies of National Socialism from repeating themselves. Political parties are charged with organizing public opinion, and elections are genuine contests involving several parties of distinctly different ideologies. This theme of limiting the state also manifests itself in the horizontal separation of institutional powers and in the relative independence of Länder (federal states). In a similar spirit, unions, professional associations, and other groups are allowed to form and to represent the interests of their members. Property is private, and in a sense so are jobs. While the West German system promotes civil equality, inequalities of success or failure are fully accepted. Likewise, moral standards are an individual matter, for better or for worse.

In contrast, our authors observe that in the GDR state and society have been fused in such a way that the state organizes and guides all societal functions. The state presumes that the interests of the individual coincide with the interests of society as a whole. Democratic Centralism thus means vertical concentration of power as well as horizontal integration, at least until the proleteriat has developed enough political consciousness to allow a more democratic form of rule. The rights of individuals, therefore, are seen in the context of the community. Property is public, and the state proscribes behaviors which it believes conflict with the interests of the community. In this context, the state draws up five-year plans and organizes work to a large degree. Likewise, health care, education, housing, and other basic social needs are organized and guaranteed by state agencies. The disadvantaged are given compensatory assistance so that equality of result (rather than equality of opportunity, as in the FRG) is more likely to be achieved.

While there is much truth to these contrasting portraits by our authors of relations between individuals and the state, they are overdrawn. The individual does have some autonomy in the GDR, and there are some constraints on individuals in the FRG. In particular, the rise of the welfare state and of modern corporations raises the question in the FRG, as in the United States and other mature capitalist countries, of what individualism means. As social and economic life have become more and more complex and intertwined, the West German government has necessarily become more active in many realms than originally was conceived after World War II. The power of corporations, not only directly in the economy but indirectly in the very concept of self, has become so pervasive, yet insidious, that many observers wonder whether the concepts and images by which individuals lead their private lives derive from corporate advertising. Thus, perhaps the contrast between the GDR and the FRG is not between the primacy of the individual and the primacy of the state but between the primacy of corporate culture and the primacy of state culture. As Lohmann points out in chapter 3, neither state has created conditions for harmonious life. The society of individualism measures its days in material trappings, while the society of dialectical materialism is full of individuals focusing on family life, their children, reading books, and protecting themselves from what the statistics portray as a grim world of lower pay, long hours, short vacations, and a good hard drink at the end of the day.

Nord (chapter 11) notes the higher consumption of drugs related to stress and its manifestations in the GDR, and he suggests that this is due to inhumane treatment and exploitation. Perhaps so. But the degree of stress in the West German corporate culture is not trivial, and the enemies of self-emancipation are more ingrained and therefore more difficult to identify. Is private and family life a sounder haven from state influence in the GDR than it is from corporate influence in the FRG?

## Concepts of Illness and Health Care

In the GDR, illness and health are conceived of epidemiologically rather than individually. As an integrated state system which plans health care for its people, the East German government is concerned about the health patterns of a community or a factory. The state considers itself responsible for the protection of its citizens' health, and, as members of a people's communist society, individuals are expected to maintain good health. This approach puts a heavy emphasis on prevention, and in the GDR health education starts at an early age (Baum, chapter 7).

The East German concept of health is also functional. The goal is to return ill people to work and to have everyone perform his functions in society. Mental disorders, depression, and the like are not acknowledged or attended to, because by definition people should be fulfilled in a worker's state. Also, medicine as a consumer service (like getting one's car repaired) or as a luxury item (like having age lines removed) is incompatible with the political and social values of the GDR. Thus, doctor shopping and other forms of discretionary consumer behavior are rare. The purpose of the health-care system is to provide competent, cost-efficient service to everyone.

The concepts of illness and health care in the FRG that emerge from these pages are profoundly different and begin with an emphasis on the individual. Thus, epidemiological planning and resource allocation are kept to a minimum, and individual choice is emphasized. While the functional concept of illness and health care—to get sick people back on their feet, working and being productive again—is certainly present in the utilitarian ethos of capitalist West Germany, one is most struck by the consumer quality of health care in its market economy. Health care is both a consumer service and a luxury item for which people will shop, inside and outside the official health-care system. This has created an extensive private market in luxury health-care services (Stone 1980, pp. 79–80). It is a highly glamorous industry, with heavy emphasis placed by the press on the latest breakthroughs and fashions. The health-care industry has a religious quality in that West German society emphasizes the miracles of modern cures. As in other modern capitalist cultures, individualism has led to a growing narcissism that glorifies self-fulfillment and abhors death as the unacceptable negation of self. Thus West Germans, like Americans, show a great interest in new protocols or procedures that promise to slow the aging process or to make them more beautiful or more "alive." Yet, oddly enough, the West German health-care system has neglected social and psychological factors in illness. This suggests that the neglect of these factors in the GDR may not be so much the product of a communist ideology that cannot admit the fallibility of a "workers' society" as it is the manifestation of a common German culture that emphasizes technology and the externalizing of one's inner problems.

These contrasts in concepts of illness are echoed in how the two systems look at health care. The West German health-care system is relatively unplanned. The principle of individualism means that ambulatory-care physicians secure a monopoly from competitors who might interfere with professional autonomy (Baum, chapter 7; Rosenberg, chapter 4). Competition is carefully regulated within the corporatist model so that special-interest groups, such as physicians, insurers, unions and employee groups, and the state, serve as countervailing forces in negotiation. The health-care system is badly coordinated, especially between ambulatory-care physicians and hospitals and between general practitioners and specialists (Ridder, chapter 10). Thus, the principle of self-administration by physicians—the free exercise of the profession in a purportedly non-commercial monopoly—carries with it the high price of costly fiefdoms that will increasingly come under pressure from the market competition that informs the rest of society.

In the GDR, health care is a state function and part of the state bureaucracy. This approach, naturally, has benefits and liabilities. On one hand the state bureaucracy has great powers for achieving the goals of integrating ambulatory and hospital care, making the distribution of resources more equitable, providing a detailed and systematic program of quality control, developing a strong program of occupational medicine, and implementing an extensive program in preventive medicine. On the other hand, the bureaucracy is insensitive at times to local circumstances (though the East German system works hard at gathering data from district officers) and becomes entrenched in petty or not-so-petty games of bureaucratic careers and power plays (Ridder, chapter 10; Baum, chapter 7). In this system, doctors serve as managers who are under pressure to meet quotas and who are not allowed to establish personal bonds with local staff or patients because they are transferred every two or three years (Ridder, chapter 10).

As is reflected in these observations, health care in the GDR does not just happen but is planned. It is a social responsibility, because market forces, left to their own devices, do not meet the health needs of the less privileged. Likewise, the patient is not an individual actor, but rather the recipient of a service vital to the well-being of the community. Thus, medically indicated procedures are considered correct by definition, and a patient's consent need be sought only for elective procedures (Lohmann, chapter 14). For this reason, crime in the GDR is a matter of acting against social interests, while crime in the FRG concerns acts against individual property, body, and mind. One system protects the effectiveness of the health-care system; the other protects the patient's autonomy.

## The Focus of Health-Care Services

Although both of the current systems stem from a national health insurance system with an early emphasis on prevention and primary care, they now differ to some degree on this dimension. In concert with its emphasis on a healthy state, the GDR focuses heavily on prevention and early treatment through a national network of primary-care dispensaires and polyclinics. In addition, the GDR has developed a sizable program in occupational health, employing government physicians to inspect working conditions and establish clinics at offices and factories to provide primary care. Nothing comparable exists in the FRG, in large part because the medical societies put through regulations after World War II which prohibited occupational physicians and physicians in the public health service from treating patients. Both occupational medicine and public health have been underfunded in the FRG. As in other countries where the values of the medical profession prevail in designing delivery systems, the FRG goal is to provide the most up-to-date, technical, specialized care for patients once they are ill.

## The Degree of Integration

Health-care services in the FRG are apparently not well integrated. Rosenberg and Ruban (chapter 8), Ridder (chapter 10), and Kirchberger (chapter 6) all report that ambulatory and hospital services are poorly coordinated. It appears that ambulatory-care physicians try to protect and enhance their income by keeping their patients away from hospitals and the specialists in them. Hospital specialists, on the other hand, do not readily share information with the primary physician about what happened to the patient in the hospital. They seem more concerned about maintaining a superior attitude than about continuity of care for patients.

In the GDR, one of the major goals of reconstruction after World War II was to integrate ambulatory and hospital care. Apparently this has succeeded, in part by driving out the independent medical profession and in part by imposing integrating strategies through central authority (chapters 7, 8, 16). Levels of care were also much more integrated into a vertical system of local, district, and regional organization.

A second dimension of integration concerns the relationship between interventive and preventive care. In the FRG, the question is somewhat moot because the medical profession made sure that the public health service was kept weak, had small budgets, and was not allowed to treat patients (chapters 4, 5, 7, 8). The emphasis on acute intervention has to date been relatively narrow, which also means that rehabilitative care is apparently not well developed or coordinated (chapter 8).

The differences between the two systems are illustrated by Empkie's comparative analysis of tuberculosis prevention (chapter 12). While both systems have regulations for preventing TB, the East Germans have far more detailed laws concerning the specific steps to be taken, and they have a separate national organization for carrying them out. Likewise, they have a research institute focused on the problem. In the FRG, the Boards of Health and the Public Health Officers diagnose cases, but they cannot treat them, so that the integration of prevention and treatment found in the GDR is not possible. Voluntary participation in TB examinations in the FRG is low, and the program is underfunded and understaffed. In contrast, the GDR has a single network of clinics which provides a full range of prevention, diagnosis, and treatment.

Throughout its entire system, the GDR monitors health problems, especially in high-risk groups, from an early stage (chapter 7), and integrates prevention, health education, diagnosis, and treatment.

A third form of integration which is gaining increased attention concerns the relationship between work and home, that is, between health risks and care at the workplace and in individuals' private lives. These relationships run in both directions. Workers who consume alcohol and drugs bring hazards to the workplace, and workers under stress or exposed to pollutants bring hazards home to their families. After World War II, the West German medical profession constrained occupational medicine programs in its effort to eliminate rivals to ambulatory private practitioners and successfully put a law in place that prohibits occupational physicians from treating employees. Since there is no federal or state program of occupational medicine independent of physicians working for private corporations, occupational medicine in the FRG is, to say the least, weak. By contrast, the East German system made occupational health a high priority and organized a cadre of occupational physicians employed under the Ministry of Health (chapters 6, 17).

A fourth dimension of integration concerns the distribution of resources and physicians by specialty and region. Maldistribution in rural areas continues to be a problem in both the FRG and the GDR (chapter 8), but the East Germans have used their centralized authority to send physicians out into underserved regions and to establish clinics (chapter 6). As for maldistribution by specialty, if one starts with American and British data, which indicate that about 10–15 percent of all persons coming to a doctor have problems of sufficient complexity that a general practitioner cannot treat them, or if one begins with Fry's (1970) analysis of how many specialists are needed for a population, then both German systems have too many specialists. The problem has been getting progressively worse in the FRG. The number and the proportion of specialists, who work principally in hospitals, have grown steadily since the 1960s, well past the number required to treat the illnesses of the population. The rest provide elaborated and expensive care. Thus, the health-care system has become a welfare state for surplus physicians.

A fifth level of integration concerns the administration and planning of services. Jung (chapter 9), concentrating on this issue in the hospital sector, finds that both the GDR and the FRG lack valid measures of output and productivity so that their goals are not clear. Hospitals, Jung claims, cannot measure efficiency. Thus, not much planning can take place, and what planning does take place is political. Efforts in both countries to integrate services so that costs will be controlled, Jung maintains, have not worked particularly well. Jung overstates his case when he says there are no overarching values or ideology which inform the West German health-care system, as we have amply documented already. But he is correct in pointing out that West German committees are advisory, with no clear method for drawing up projections, and that requirements vary greatly from state to state. The East German machinery for planning is, of course, much more centralized and co-ordinated, with systematic reports from each clinic and hospital used in the development of long-range plans. The East German administration has much more power for implementing its recommendations and, therefore, integrating services.

Finally, we come to the integration of training with care. The lack of integration is manifested by the presence of too many specialists for the epidemiological patterns of pathology in the population. Another facet of this question concerns the proportions of physicians and their helpers. As chapter 13 shows, the East Germans have proportionately more nurses and other physician helpers in the clinical areas, and a larger range of other semi-autonomous providers of special services. This distribution is also much closer to that recommended by an epidemiological analysis or a review of literature on international standards for the division of labor in medicine. It comes as no surprise that, since the West German system is dominated by the medical profession, which took pains to strongly discourage clinics and other more organized forms of ambulatory care, nonphysician providers of various services are underrepresented. For similar reasons, the training of nonphysicians is more uneven and more loosely coordinated in the FRG than in the GDR; the same is true for continuing education programs for both physicians and nonphysicians.

To summarize, the GDR sees illness as a social problem for which the state is responsible to provide coordinated, centrally organized care, with priorities on prevention and ambulatory care through a network of service facilities. Personnel are trained in a coordinated set of schools that produce proportionately more nonphysician providers and that keeps them trained through an organized system of continuing medical education. In the FRG, illness is regarded as an individual matter, and individualism is also a central thesis among physicians. Under a protected monopoly, however, individualism has rather different results for providers than it does for patients. It has resulted in a loose federation of ambulatory-care physicians, who are poorly coordinated with specialists and hospitals and who are also politically effective in passing regulations that maximize professional income. Programs in continuing medical education are spotty and relatively uncoordinated.

## Class, Status, and Health Care

Although the subject is not discussed very much in this volume, discrimination by class and status seems to be a problem in both systems. If Stone (1980, pp. 79–80) is correct in suggesting that the private health-care market is large, then the discrimination by social class is probably greater in the FRG, where the class structure of the society as a whole is also more stratified. Nevertheless, it appears that party and government officials in the GDR enjoy the use of special clinics and hospitals with the best of equipment and treatment (chapter 10). At the other end of the scale, we have no information on the health care of Gastarbeiter (imported workers) in the FRG, but presumably their care is not as good as that of their German fellow workers.

## The Distrust of Democratic Power

One of the most powerful themes of this comparative social analysis is the resistance by both the state and the profession to grass-roots organization or control of health services by patients. One might say that the history of the German health-care system is the history of the profession and the state crushing grass-roots organizations of mutual aid. No one, it seems, has been interested in helping workers' groups organize and run their own health-care systems. Bismarck began by trying to co-opt workers belonging to mutual-aid societies into a state-run system that would weaken the power of labor groups and make workers more dependent on the state (Stone 1980; Rosenberg, chapter 4). Though he failed in his effort, he did succeed in tying workers to employers. In this context, workers in mutual-aid societies dominated for the first decades and established innovative forms of ambulatory care that were cost-effective and well integrated with the health problems they faced. These programs engendered the fierce opposition of physicians who could not tolerate being hired and managed by uneducated workers, and of physicians in the private sector who increasingly felt inroads being made on their private market. The militant organization of physicians and the fierce strikes which ensued could lead one to conclude that the German medical profession became an organizational and political reality in order to oppose the democratic power of patient-run groups (Stone 1980; Rosenberg, chapter 4; Leibfried and Tennstedt, chapter 5). The conservative politics of most physicians coincided with those of National Socialists and led to the effective destruction of worker-run groups and socialist physicians (chapters 4, 5). After 1945, the medical profession in the FRG made sure that regulations were passed which would prevent the reemergence of these groups (chapters 4, 5, 6, 8).

In the GDR, it was the state that eliminated the individual autonomy of both physicians and workers. Here it was a matter of state power over professional power. As Ridder concludes in chapter 10, power is a fundamental issue of health-care policy, and it is unclear whether the patient benefits more as a victim of the state's power politics in the GDR or as a victim of the profession's power politics in the FRG. Although the FRG has a market economy and emphasizes the role of the individual actor, such is not the case in its health-care system.

## Professional Power versus State Power

The distrust of democratic power could be rephrased as "people power versus institutionalized power." Within institutionalized power, one finds the tension between the power of the medical profession and the power of the state. In the GDR there was no contest; the government eliminated the medical profession as a political force. This does not mean that physicians are not very powerful, but rather that those physicians who are powerful work for the state and the party. The state in the GDR has made a considerable effort to deprofessionalize health care and to give nonphysicians a large role in health care (Bergmann-Krauss, chapter 13). This lowers costs and provides patients with a wider range of secondary providers. Another important difference between the dominance of professional power and the dominance of state power is the degree of integration by the state. Medical professions everywhere do not seem very interested in the issues of coordination and integration, because their priorities lie elsewhere, as indicated by the professional model described in the introduction. Control over quality is, ironically, better and more systematic under a state-run system than under a profession-run system (Light 1983; Ridder, chapter 10). As Ridder also points out, productivity is also a more seriously addressed issue under a state system because of the government's wish to minimize costs.

## Medical Technology versus Political Values

A basic question underlying this study is whether there exists a professional culture and a common level of medical technology which causes national boundaries and political values to make little difference in health-care systems. One is struck by the extent to which physicians, hospitals, and medical technicians share a common international body of knowledge and values in Western countries. Moreover, there seem to be common waves of problems that go beyond new technology. For example, many Western countries experienced at about the same time the perception of a physician shortage and subsequently the perception of a physician surplus. Many of them also experienced a surplus (or perceived surplus) of hospital beds. The reaffirmation of general practice and ambulatory care was echoed in many countries. These cross-national movements suggest a common culture that goes beyond technological determinism. In the case of the countries studied here, there is also a shared cultural heritage and even the same organization and structure of health-care services before World War II.

Perhaps the best argument for the influence of medical technology and culture is that made by Jung (chapter 9) with regard to hospitals. He notes that administrative and financial controls of the hospitals in the FRG and the GDR are remarkably similar. Planning is legislated by law and assigned in an undemocratic way to specific committees or authorities. Despite the fundamental differences in the economies of the two countries, Jung notes that both systems have made the political decision not to use price as a means for controlling the hospital system. In both systems operating costs are covered by insurance budgets, though the character of those insurance budgets is different in the two nations. In both cases insurance is required, and deficits are picked up by the government. The distinction between private and nonprivate ownership, Jung argues, is superficial.

Yet one finds, even in Jung's chapter, important differences which reflect political values. In the FRG, planning is decentralized and rests with the individual states rather than being centralized in a powerful national ministry of health. Hospital planning in the FRG is advisory, while in the GDR there is tangible power for implementing recommendations. In the GDR, financing from the general state budget means that social priorities are not closely linked to premiums receipts, and this can have an important impact on decisions. Because of its centralized organization, the East German system has taken indicators of performance in the health-care system far more seriously than does the West German system. Financial incentives have been adopted to reduce the number of bed days and to achieve other health-care planning goals (chapter 10).

At the less technical levels of health care than the hospital, political values play an increasing role. One could conclude that there is an inverse relationship between the technological level of care and political influence, with the latter constantly trying to create new devices to control the former. It is in ambulatory care that the biggest differences are apparent between a state-run and a profession-run system with similar technological bases. Thus the answer to the question of which is more influential—medical technology and culture or political values—depends on the level of health care and on the level of analysis.

## Reflections

This study has been a unique opportunity to observe how two distinct health-care systems evolved through time from a common background which "controls for" cultural, organizational, economic, and political differences. It thus has allowed us to overcome the methodological problem of periodicity in which a system at one period of time is compared with a system at another period of time (such as pre- and post-revolutionary Russia, China, or Cuba). Comparisons of this kind too often assume implicitly that the old system would have stayed as it was. In West Germany we learned that the old system did not stand still but rather continued to evolve toward increased professional control. Ironically, the West German emphasis on individual free choice, combined with the dominance of the medical profession, led postwar West Germany away from the original impetus in 1883 to develop a health-care system that focused on the health needs of workers. That purpose was carried out to some degree in the democratic localism of mutual-aid societies and the subsequent local sickness funds, but it dissipated as the medical profession gained dominance. In East Germany, however, something quite different occurred. Its political regime restructured health care to embrace the much older German idea of the state taking responsibility for the health of its people. In essence, then, the West German system has come to represent a continuing departure from its foundations, while the new system in the GDR represents a radical return to it.

Today, the West German system emphasizes high-technology cures; protects the individual autonomy of ambulatory physicians as gate-keepers to the system; defends the free choice of patients; preserves the fragmenting turfs of specialists, hospital physicians, and general practitioners; and minimizes preventive and occupational medicine. The resulting system is expensive (about twice the percent of GNP of the East German system) but popular. In effect, the West German system shifted its legitimacy from one based on the health needs of society to one based on the miracles of medical science and the su-premacy of the physician as a figure of authority, expertise, and prestige. In the GDR, however, the return to the legitimacy of meeting the health needs of a society led to integrating ambulatory with hospital care, disbanding the medical profession as a political entity, installing ex-tensive programs in prevention, emphasizing a centralized state system with an emphasis on occupational medicine, and linking health with housing, the workplace, and the schools, as Johann Peter Frank first proposed so long ago.

Although the two German systems made fundamentally different choices, there are some notable similarities in the ways they have evolved. Both have snuffed out the mutual-aid, grassroots, local delivery systems that were so influential in the early decades of the national health system. In the GDR, the communist state (in the name of "work-ers' democracy") instituted a national bureaucracy to run medical serv-ices. In the FRG, the medical profession continued its prewar campaign against services run by sickness funds and for monopoly in ambulatory care.

Two organizational changes played a key role in eliminating the competition that had provided inexpensive, consumer-oriented care for workers. First was the fateful change of rules so that sickness funds could no longer provide services directly. Insurers could no longer be providers, and a gap was forged between citizens as premium payers and as patients. The second change was the replacement of direct negotiations by funds with doctors by collective contracts with phy-sicians' associations, which in turn paid their members for services rendered.

While these changes were reinforced in the FRG after World War II, so that competition there decreased still further, competition between the West German and East German systems grew. Each wanted to match the achievements of the other in certain areas, while claiming ideological superiority. This has led, for example, to the FRG's building up its mother-and-child-care program to match that of the GDR (as much as it could within a system emphasizing free choice and physician autonomy). In the GDR, competition led to granting citizens the right to choose their personal physician, within a centralized system in which physicians are assigned and transferred.

In more recent years, however, common problems of cost containment and the burden of the welfare state have been shared by the two systems despite their ideological competition. The burden of this problem, which most industrialized nations share (Wolfe 1985), falls more heavily on the FRG, because medical care consumes about twice as much of the GNP there as in the GDR. At the center of this difference is the fact that the medical profession has increasingly shaped the health-care system in the FRG. Whenever and wherever the medical profession as a political body has shaped medical services, those services have been less affordable, less accountable, and less justly distributed than they would have been if consumers or the state had set policy. Physicians are masters of clinical medicine; however, when they turn to organizing delivery systems—and it is medical societies as political institutions that do it—the quality of care in meeting social needs and the clinical quality relative to price may be lower (Light 1983).

The interests of the medical profession differ profoundly from the interests of society, but are made to seem compatible. The medical profession, like any profession, seeks to refine its skills on the most challenging cases and to enhance its power, prestige, and wealth. Thus, medical professions everywhere emphasize specialization, technical innovations, scientific breakthroughs, acute intervention, and hospital care. Much of this emphasis applies to only a small percentage of cases. The benefits are clouded by the poor prognosis in many of the cases, by complications or new disorders the treatment produces, and by the personal suffering that accompanies some treatments. Medical professions are not in the business of emphasizing public health, prevention, self-care  low-cost treatments, and primary care.

If the prominent role of the medical profession as a political institution in the FRG lies at the center of its cost crisis, it follows that one can expect its influence to decline as the FRG confronts its cost problem. Within the corporatist model described in the introduction, the balance of power is likely to shift toward employers, unions, and the government, because they pay for medical services. Whether accomplished more by the state or by those who pay premiums (as in the United States), the West German system may institute reforms that emphasize cost-effective prevention, less hospitalization, an integration of ambulatory and hospital care,[1] and health-promotion plans in factories or corporations. Rules may be changed so that less costly personnel than physicians can carry on the large amount of ordinary and chronic care that is provided in any modern society. In essence, the West German system may become more like the East German system as political values shift toward cost-effective care and health promotion. However, it may well surpass the East German system by using competition among sickness funds to organize services so that they are more diverse and responsive to the needs of different groups of citizens. A cost-effective yet flexible and sensitive system is what both nations continue to seek.

## Note

1. The separation of ambulatory from hospital care is particularly expensive. Ambulatory physicians see patients as much as they can (11.5 times a year) and delay hospitalizing them, while hospital physicians hold onto patients as long as they can (the average length of a stay exceeds 16 days; see Schulenberg 1983).

## References

Fry, J. 1970. Medicine in Three Societies. New York: American Elsevier.

Glaser, W. A. 1983. "Lessons from Germany: Some Reflections Occasioned by Schulenburg's Report." Journal of Health Politics, Policy and Law 8(2):352–365.

Light, D. W. 1983. "Is Competition Bad?" New England Journal of Medicine 301:1315–1319.

Schulenburg, J. M. G. 1983. "Report from Germany: Current Conditions and Controversies in the Health Care System." Journal of Health Politics, Policy and Law 8(2).

Stone, D. 1980. The Limits of Professional Power. University of Chicago Press.

Wolfe, Alan. 1985. "The Death of Social Democracy." New Republic (February 25):21–23.

# Appendix

# On Methods: The Paradox of Comparative Policy Research

Mindy Widman and
Donald W. Light

*Comparison is fundamental to scientific inquiry, and yet it is the bane of comparative policy researchers. Searching the literature for the "true way" to compare policies is like reading about various schools of therapy; everyone has the right answer, but no one fully agrees on what it is. The arguments are often reduced to "my magic versus your magic." Moreover, the abstract complexity of these arguments is so great that one wonders if its latent function is somnolence rather than enlightenment. We shall try to do better.*

## The Six Elements of Policy Analysis

If one culls the literature, one will find six elements, or dimensions, about which almost everyone agrees. First, one must investigate the ways in which policies are legitimized, regulated, and validated (Austin et al. 1978; Field 1976; Pye 1968; Roemer 1976). Once a policy is legislated it becomes legitimate. Regulations necessary for its implementation, including licensure of providers, are then established by those in power. However, the extent to which a policy can be successfully implemented is dependent on how "valid" the policy is believed to be by both its agents and those affected. Prohibition, for example, was legislated but could not be successfully implemented because it was never considered valid by most of the population or indeed by many of those empowered to enforce it.

Second, comparative policy research must examine financing (Austin et al. 1978; Field 1976; Fry 1970; Gilbert and Specht 1974; Leichter 1979; Maynard 1975; Morris 1979; Pye 1968; Roemer 1976, 1977). Some would say that one approaches financing by analyzing the economic character of the society, while others would say that one should focus on the specific financing of the policy in question. We shall turn to such matters shortly, but the point is that how financing is arranged, where it comes from, and what amounts are available in return for what tradeoffs are important matters to consider.

A third element important for many policies are the rules of eligibility (Altenstetter and Bjorkman 1978; Haveman 1977; Maynard 1975; Morris 1979; Pye 1968). Certainly these rules can be revealing. Who is covered for what, and under what circumstances, can tell one far more about a society and its policies than a simple reading of the law.

A rather obvious fourth element is the organization and administration of a policy as it is implemented. (See the references for financing, plus Shortell 1982.) This and the final two elements below indicate that comparative policy research often is not confined to policy per se but concerns a subsystem of the polity that manifests past policies and influences current and future policy formation. Such is the case in comparing health-care systems. Policy and institution are intertwined. The structure of the institutions, the degree of delegation and to whom, the dislocations between responsibility and authority, and the way in which recipients (or victims) of the policy are to be processed through the system constitute an important dimension of comparative policy research.

A fifth discernible element of policy research concerns the scope and kind of benefits (Austin et al. 1978; Fry 1970; Gilbert and Specht 1974; Haveman 1977). This is clearly related to the previous two elements and yet deserves separate attention in the case of policies that involve benefits. Most policies do involve benefits. They may be direct or indirect, and they usually involve more than one kind of gain. In fact, "cui bono?" is the key question for one famous approach to distinguishing between different types of organizations (Blau and Scott 1962). While *benefits* is often construed in a rather literary way to mean such things as welfare payments or health-care benefits, a more insightful analysis comes from construing it more broadly to mean the political, cultural, and economic gains to different parties by various means.

Finally, writers on comparative policy research agree that one should attend to outcomes (Altenstetter and Bjorkman 1978; Andersen 1976; Fry 1970; Härö 1976; Kohn 1976; Pflanz 1976; Tuene 1978). What were the results of different policies, or of the same policy area in different countries? Clearly, the idea behind any policy initiative is to change something and have an effect.

## History and Values: Basic Influences

Underlying and shaping these six elements of comparative policy analysis are the values and political ideology of a people. All of the references cited agree on this, and many of them also emphasize the importance of a historical perspective. As Abel-Smith (1976, p. 26) notes: "The variations in organization and financing of medical care in different countries are the product of long-established customs modified by long histories of development. But beneath these customs and histories are fundamental differences in attitudes and values." Such differences determine which policies will be promoted, who will become the policy-forming and policy-implementing elite, and therefore which specific goals will be pursued (Lockhart 1981). Yet the unfolding of policy is not a natural progression but a series of fits and starts, countervailing forces, and historical accidents against a background of basic values. Consider, for example, an administration committed to reducing the costs of medical care as well as eliminating any government restrictions on a free market. In the United States, such commitments face the countervailing power of the American Medical Association (Marmor and Christianson 1982) and the social value of government as the insurer of last resort (Axinn and Levin 1975). It is our contention that the nature of policy can best be understood as an interplay, over time, of values and power.

While most agree that contemporary policies are best understood dynamically over time, this approach is often not followed, for reasons summarized by Heisler and Peters (1978, p. 57): "It is both desirable and possible to ask for design of . . . studies to include time-series analyses that permit developmental insights. . . . In practice, researchers are not likely to have the resources—funds, time, human skills, or, for that matter, extant or available data—to undertake such a study. Minimally, what is necessary is a conscious, active concern with the cross-time, cross-level, and cross-national dimensions of policy analysis. . . ." Aside from these practical issues, however, the emphasis on values, ideology, and historical perspective is reassuring. Unfortunately, at this point complexities set in.

## Policy from Whose Point of View?

As was foreshadowed in the discussion of financing, many of these common dimensions can be approached from the viewpoints of rather different actors and thereby yield different results. Let us take, for example, the dimension of outcome. It presents special problems of design and analysis, because comparable statistics are often lacking, operationalizing variables is often difficult, and primary data do not exist (Härö 1976; Elling 1980; Kobben 1968; Pflanz 1976; Sartorius 1976; Tuene 1978). But these problems are compounded by the question of whose outcomes are relevant. Consumers? Clinicians? Health-care organizations? Moral philosophers? Consider the following list of questions concerning health care.

| Interest group | Outcome questions |
| --- | --- |
| Consumers | How healthy am I? |
| | How satisfied am I with the care I get? |
| | How much does my care cost me? |
| | How much control do I give up to get the care I need? |
| Clinicians | How useful or fulfilling is my work? |
| | Am I being paid sufficiently well? |
| | Do I have the power and autonomy I want? |
| | Do I have the status I want? |
| Health-care organizations | How solvent or profitable are we? |
| | How much control do we have over our destiny? |
| | How effective are we? |
| Government leaders | Does this system enhance our political power and popularity? |
| | How well does this system meet national priorities? |
| | How much is it costing us relative to other programs in our budget? |
| Organizational and governmental bureaucrats | Will I have a job in the future? |
| | How well does this system enhance our role and scope of power? |
| | How well are we being paid? |
| Moral philosophers | How equitable is the system? |
| | How well does it protect individual rights? |
| | How well does it manifest social justice? |
| Health policy researchers | To what extent does this system expand my knowledge and understanding? |
| | To what extent does it illuminate policy analysis? |
| | How well does it fulfill its goals? |

Thus, outcomes, like legitimation, organization, and financing, operate at many conflicting levels (Elling 1980), and some researchers get attached to one interest group and take for granted their world view.

## Focus of Analysis

Another question is whether it is best to focus on the whole social system in which a policy is embedded, on an element of that system that seems particularly central, or on the policy itself. Lowi (1978) advocates focusing on the policy itself, because it will most effectively lead one to understand the larger issues of power and the state. Roemer (1977), on the other hand, argues vaguely for focusing on the system as a whole of which the policy itself is a part. Stone's (1980) analysis of professional power manifests the belief that the greatest insight can be gained by following through the ramifications of one central element of a policy area.

## Range of Comparison

Another complication lies in whether to choose the most similar or the most different cases to compare. Advocates of most similar cases argue that when one controls background variables, as in an experiment in social psychology, similar cases produce the power of specificity. As Tuene (1978, p. 54) puts it, "the primary purpose of comparative policy research . . . is not to establish the universality of relationships. Rather it is to enhance the credibility of specific predictions about specific cases." But the price is precisely the range or universality of one's conclusions. Champions of the most-different-cases approach seek to identify the universal variables or relationships that explain why similar policy objectives are carried out in such different ways (Ashford 1978).

## Unit of Analysis

Most comparative policy research uses the nation as its unit of analysis, but is this realistic? Are nations that unified, or are their regional differences of such magnitude that one should not hitch one's analytic wagon to the nation-state? The answer will depend on both the coherence of the nation and the policy areas being investigated, but the discipline too often assumes that whole nations are a trouble-free unit of analysis.

## Resolving the Paradox in This Study

The approach of this study overcomes, to some degree, the obstacles to comparative research we have discussed. It begins with values and political ideology as central forces shaping social welfare institutions. These lie at the core of the models in chapter 1 and are addressed in many other chapters as well. The models also provide a clear framework for comparative analysis. Inherent in the dynamics of the models and in the substance of the book is a historical approach to contemporary health-care policy. Within this context, the study addresses the six elements of policy analysis: legitimation, financing, organization, eligibility, benefits, and outcomes. How these terms are defined and at what level they are examined varies from chapter to chapter. The study also examines all three levels of analysis: the whole social system, elements of the system, and policies themselves.

Most interesting are the ways in which the question of most-similar versus most-different comparisons was handled. Essentially, as a natural experiment in history, East and West Germany are both one nation-state and health-care system divided and two historically different regions returning in part to their politically distinct values. This less obvious contrast needs explanation. Although Germany shared a cultural life during its 60 years of unification (Durant 1957; Sontheimer and Bleek 1975), there were distinct differences between what are now the GDR and the FRG. Czarist Russia had a long history of ideological and political connections with Prussia, whose former territories make up the bulk of the GDR (*Historical Atlas of the World*, 1965; Kohn 1946). The Prussian monarchy, particularly since the time of Frederick the Great, admired the absolute power of the czars, and the czars, in turn, recognized the military prowess of the Prussians (Massie 1980). Exchanges of personnel between these two autocracies were common in the eighteenth and nineteenth centuries (Goldman 1974). The USSR could thus logically view this territory as being within its sphere of influence.

In the West, there was a more liberal tradition, particularly after the imposition of the Code Napoleon on the Confederation of the Rhine, most of which forms the present Federal Republic (Durant and Durant 1975; Goldman 1974; *Historical Atlas of the World*, 1965; Hobsbaum 1962). During unification in the nineteenth century, western and southern Germany resisted the imposition of strong state control and the extension of Prussian power under the emperor and Bismarck (Eyck 1958; Hobsbaum 1962).

It was no accident that the Allied forces divided Germany in 1945 the way they did. The American version—that the line of partition is where Allied forces met up with the forward push of the Soviet army—is misleading. Demarcations had been drawn up as early as 1943 at the Teheran Conference, and by the time of the Yalta Conference in 1945 the specific boundaries of partition were already set (Deutscher 1967; Hartmann 1965). The armies of the Western Allies were prevented from advancing at the end of the war so that the Russian army could occupy the agreed-upon territory (Benns and Seldon 1965). Those boundaries reasserted old regional differences in political values. Thus the comparative and historical study of the two Germanies involves both most-similar and most-different comparisons between two halves of a once-united national health-care system and two distinct cultural traditions.

In conclusion, comparative research on policies requires a historical approach that recognizes how basic values and conflicts among them become manifested in the six elements of policy. Within the constraints of this study, we have tried to resolve differences of approach in the comparative research literature by combining the best ideas of different commentators.

## References

Abel-Smith, B. 1976. Value for Money in Health Services. New York: St. Martin's.

Altenstetter, C., and J. W. Bjorkman. 1978. Federal-State Health Policies and Impacts: The Politics of Implementation. Washington, D.C.: University Press of America.

Andersen, R. 1976. "A Framework for Cross-National Comparisons of Health Services Systems." In Cross-National Sociomedical Research: Concepts, Methods, Practice, ed. M. Pflanz and E. Schach. Stuttgart: Georg Thieme.

Ashford, D. 1978. "The Structural Analysis of Policy, or Institutions Really Do Matter." In Comparing Public Policies, ed. D. E. Ashford. Beverly Hills, Calif.: Sage.

Austin, M. J., B. Segal, and M. Schwartz. 1978. "Comparing Social Welfare Systems: A Schema for Analysis." In Reaching People, ed. D. Thursz and J. L. Vigilante. Beverly Hills, Calif.: Sage.

Axinn, J., and H. Levin. 1975. Social Welfare: A History of the American Response to Need. New York: Dodd, Mead.

Benns, F. L., and M. E. Seldon. 1965. Europe: 1939 to the Present. New York: Appleton-Century-Crofts.

Blau, P. M., and W. R. Scott. 1962. Formal Organizations. San Francisco: Chandler.

Deutscher, I. 1967. Stalin. New York: Oxford University Press.

Durant, W. 1957. The Reformation. New York: Simon and Schuster.

Durant, W., and A. Durant. 1975. The Age of Napoleon. New York: Simon and Schuster.

Elling, R. H. 1980. Cross-National Study of Health Systems. New Brunswick, N.J.: Transaction Books.

Eyck, E. 1958. Bismarck and the German Empire. New York: Norton.

Field, M. G. 1976. "The Need for Cross-National Studies in Health Services." In Cross-National Sociomedical Research: Concepts, Methods, Practice, ed. M. Pflanz and E. Schach. Stuttgart: Georg Thieme.

Fry, J. 1970. Medicine in Three Societies. New York: American Elsevier.

Gilbert, N., and H. Specht. 1974. Dimensions of Social Welfare Policy. Englewood Cliffs, N.J.: Prentice-Hall.

Goldman, G. 1974. The German Political System. New York: Random House.

Härö, A. S. 1976. "Strategies for the Development of Health Related Statistics." In Cross-National Sociomedical Research: Concepts, Methods, Practice, ed. M. Pflanz and E. Schach. Stuttgart: Georg Thieme.

Hartmann, F. H. 1965. Germany Between East and West: The Reunification Problem. Englewood Cliffs, N.J.: Prentice-Hall.

Haveman, R. H., ed. 1977. A Decade of Federal Antipoverty Programs. New York: Academic.

Heisler, M. O., and B. G. Peters. 1978. "Comparing Social Policy Across Levels of Government, Countries, and Time: Belgium and Sweden Since 1870." In Comparing Public Policies, ed. D. E. Ashford. Beverly Hills, Calif.: Sage.

Historical Atlas of the World. 1965. Chicago: Rand McNally.

Hobsbaum, E. J. 1962. The Age of Revolution. New York: Mentor.

Kobben, A. J. F. 1968. "The Logic of Cross-Cultural Analysis: Why Exceptions?" In Comparative Research Across Cultures and Nations, ed. S. Rokkan. Paris: Mouton.

Kohn, H. 1946. Prophets and Peoples. New York: Collier.

Kohn, R. 1976. "Development of Cross-National Comparisons of Health Services Use." In Cross-National Sociomedical Research: Concepts, Methods, Practice, ed. M. Pflanz and E. Schach. Stuttgart: Georg Thieme.

Leichter, H. M. 1979. A Comparative Approach to Policy Analysis. Cambridge University Press.

Lockhart, C. 1981. "Values and Policy Conceptions of Health Policy Elites in the United States, the United Kingdom, and the Federal Republic of Germany." Journal of Health Politics, Policy and Law 6(1):98–119.

Lowi, T. J. 1978. "Public Policy and Bureaucracy in the United States and France." In Comparing Public Policies, ed. D. E. Ashford. Beverly Hills, Calif.: Sage.

Marmor, T. R., and J. B. Christianson. 1982. Health Care Policy. Beverly Hills, Calif.: Sage.

Massie, R. K. 1980. Peter the Great: His Life and World. New York: Knopf.

Maynard, A. 1975. Health Care in the European Community. University of Pittsburgh Press.

Morris, R. 1979. Social Policy of the American Welfare State. New York: Harper and Row.

Pflanz, M. 1976. "Problems and Methods in Cross-National Comparison of Diagnoses and Diseases." In Cross-National Sociomedical Research: Concepts, Methods, Practice, ed. M. Pflanz and E. Schach. Stuttgart: Georg Thieme.

Pye, L. W. 1968. "Political Systems and Political Development." In Comparative Research Across Cultures and Nations, ed. S. Rokkan. Paris: Mouton.

Roemer, M. I. 1976. Health Care Systems in World Perspective. Ann Arbor, Mich.: Health Administration Press.

Roemer, M. I. 1977. Comparative National Policies on Health Care. New York: Marcel Dekker.

Sartorius, N. 1976. "The Cross-National Standardization of Psychiatric Diagnoses and Classifications." In Cross-National Sociomedical Research: Concepts, Methods, Practice, ed. M. Pflanz and E. Schach. Stuttgart: Georg Thieme.

Shortell, S. M. 1982. "The Contribution and Relevance of Sociology to Health Services Research." In Social Science Approaches to Health Services Research, ed. T. Choi and J. N. Greenberg. Ann Arbor, Mich.: Health Administration Press.

Sontheimer, K., and W. Bleek. 1975. The Government and Politics of East Germany. London: Hutchinson University Library.

Stone, D. 1980. The Limits of Professional Power: National Health Care in the Federal Republic of Germany. University of Chicago Press.

Tuene, H. 1978. "A Logic of Comparative Policy Analysis." In Comparing Public Policies, ed. D. E. Ashford. Beverly Hills, Calif.: Sage.

# About the Authors

Renata Baum, Ph.D., is a senior researcher at the East Europe Institute of the Free University of Berlin, where she carries out a number of research projects in comparative health care.

Barbara Bergmann-Krauss, Diplom-Soziologie, has been the director of the Institute of General Health Policy and Adult Education of the German Dental Association since 1979 and was previously responsible for paramedical education at the Federal Research Institute of Semi-Professional Training in Berlin.

Timothy M. Empkie, M.D., M.P.H., is a physician with a special interest in how primary care is practiced in the two Germanies. Currently in the Department of Family Practice at the University of Iowa, Dr. Empkie has studied and traveled in the FRG and the GDR over the past fifteen years.

Aloys Henning, M.D., conducts research in comparative health care at the East Europe Institute of the Free University of Berlin.

Helmuth Jung received his M.A. and Ph.D. degrees in economics at the Free University of Berlin, where he also studied sociology. His research has focused on the health economy of Eastern European countries, especially the GDR, and he now serves as a consultant to hospitals, welfare institutions, and political and labor organizations. He has been a researcher at the East Europe Institute of the Free University of Berlin, where he has also taught.

Gudrun Keiner, Dr. Phil., Dipl. Päd., M.T.A., carried out her research for this volume at the Institute for Social Medicine of the Free University of Berlin. She holds three graduate degrees and has been conducting research in the health field for more than ten years, focusing on social, economic, and professional aspects of health care.

Stefan Kirchberger, Dr. Phil., holds the chair in medical sociology at Münster University. He is particularly interested in the diffusion of medical technology, its impact on professionalization, and health economics.

Erich Klinkmüller, Dipl. Volkswirt., Dr. Rer. Pol., is a professor at the Free University of Berlin. He was formerly an associate professor of economics at the University of California at Santa Barbara and at St. Louis University and a professor of economics at the University of Arizona at Tucson. He is interested in comparative economic systems and European history.

Hans-Joachim von Kondratowitz, Dipl. Pol., Dr. Phil., is affiliated with the German Center for Gerontology in Munich, where he carries out comparative studies of social policy pertaining to work, gerontology, and welfare programs in the East and the West. He studied at the Free University of Berlin, the University of Saarbrücken, and Washington University. Prior to his current position he was an assistant professor at the Technical University of Munich.

Stephan Leibfried, Dr. Phil., is a professor of social policy and welfare law in comparative and historical perspective at the University of Bremen. Since 1978 he has been working with Florian Tennstedt on a series of books and essays concerning locked alternatives in German health policy.

Donald W. Light, Ph.D., is a professor of social medicine and psychiatry at the University of Medicine and Dentistry of New Jersey–School of Osteopathic Medicine. He is also a professor in the graduate program in sociology at Rutgers University and a senior fellow at the Leonard Davis Institute of Health Economics at the University of Pennsylvania. Professor Light has a continuing interest in comparative health care and the rapid changes which health care systems are currently experiencing. He has been selected by the Twentieth Century Fund to write a book on the restructuring of the American health-care system.

Ulrich Lohmann, Dr. Jur., is a researcher at the Max Planck Institute for Foreign and International Social Law in Munich and an associate lecturer at the Free University of Berlin. He is particularly interested in East-West comparative studies of law and society.

Dietrich Nord, M.A., Dr. Phil., is the author of four books and over a hundred articles on health-care systems, the pharmaceutical industry, and drug consumption in European countries. He is an assistant professor of sociology at the University of Constance, editor of *Medizin—Mensch—Gesellschaft*, and head of the Health and Social Research Department of the Medizinisch Pharmazeutische Studiengesellschaft in Mainz.

Paul Ridder, Dr. Phil., Dipl. Soz., Dipl. Psych., carries out research in comparative health systems at the micro and macro levels and teaches at the University of Constance.

Peter Rosenberg, Dr. Rer. Pol., has been a senior economist since 1978 with the Federal Ministry of Labor and Social Affairs in Bonn. His major work has been focused on social security systems and old-age and sickness insurance. He previously held positions as a research economist at the German Institute of Economic Research and at the German Association of Trade Unions.

Maria Elizabeth Ruban, Dr. Rer. Pol., is mainly interested in the standards of living and social security of the Soviet Union and East Germany. She is author of *Gesundheitswesen in der DDR* (1981). She is a senior researcher at the German Institute for Economic Research in Berlin.

Alexander Schuller is a professor of Medical Sociology at the Free University of Berlin, where he is also a principal member of the Institute for Social Medicine. The author or co-author of books on social science curricula for medical schools, on the theory of legitimation, and on ambulatory medicine, he has written numerous articles on a broad range of topics pertaining to health care.

Florian Tennstedt, Dr. Phil., is a social historian who has written several books on German social and health policy. He is a professor at the University of Kassel and works with Stephan Leibfried.

Hilmar Thielen, Dipl. Psych., Dr. Phil., is a psychotherapist who lectures at the University of Regensburg and conducts research on the comparative dimensions of psychotherapy in the FRG and the GDR. Raised in East Berlin after World War II, he has many friends and colleagues in the GDR. He also conducts research on modeling processes in psychotherapy and cognitive psychology.

Mindy Widman, D.S.W., received her degree in social-work research from the University of Pennsylvania. She is a research social scientist at the University of Medicine and Dentistry of New Jersey–School of Osteopathic Medicine and is interested in health care for the elderly and the poor. She has worked with Donald Light on a number of research projects.

# Index